Kim Diana Connolly
Stephen M. Johnson
Douglas R. Williams

Wetlands Law and Policy

Understanding Section 404

Section of Environment, Energy, and Resources
American Bar Association

Cover design by Cathy Zaccarine.

Printed in the United States of America

09 08 07 06 05 5 4 3 2 1

Library of Congress Cataloging-in-Publication Data

Williams, Douglas R.
Wetlands law and policy : understanding section 404 / by Douglas R. Williams, Kim Diana Connolly, Stephen Johnson.
p. cm.
Includes bibliographical references and index.
ISBN 1-59031-286-4
1. Wetlands—Law and legislation—United States. 2. Environmental permits—United States. I. Connolly, Kim Diana. II. Johnson, Stephen (Stephen M.) III. American Bar Association. Section of Environment, Energy, and Resources. IV. Title.

KF5624.W55 2005
346.7304'6918—dc22

2005017030

Discounts are available for books ordered in bulk. Special consideration is given to state bars, CLE programs, and other bar-related organizations. Inquire at Book Publishing, ABA Publishing, American Bar Association, 321 North Clark Street, Chicago, Illinois 60610-4714.

www.ababooks.org

SUMMARY OF CONTENTS

CONTENTS

PREFACE

For many years, wetlands (including marshes, swamps, wet meadows, prairie potholes, vernal pools, playa lakes, Carolina bays, bogs, pocosins, and fens) were treated by the federal government as worthless areas that should be filled or otherwise developed as rapidly as possible. Now, the nation's wetlands are widely regarded as having immense value and environmental importance, to be protected against unnecessary development by rigorous regulatory measures. To this end, the federal government has assumed an important—indeed, primary—role in protecting the nation's wetlands through a variety of measures. The centerpiece of these measures is the Clean Water Act's Section 404 permitting program, which is the primary focus of this book.

How large a role the federal government should play and how strictly wetlands should be protected are topics of perennial controversy. Most agree that pre–Clean Water Act destruction of wetlands was detrimental to the environment, causing the loss of significant functions and values provided by those wetlands. Yet the costs and time-consuming nature of strict regulatory measures are viewed as too high by certain developers, farmers, and other stakeholders, generating resistance and anger regarding the federal government's role. At the same time, conservationists view lax federal protections as contrary to the best interests of the nation and its citizens, also generating resistance and anger regarding the federal government's role. These competing views are exacerbated by the lack of a clear statutory mandate and resulting reliance on regulatory and judicial interpretations to regulate wetlands. All these factors and more have combined to produce a give-and-take among competing interests and a regulatory program constantly in flux, adjusting to new (and old) challenges as our understanding of the scientific, social, and legal implications of the Section 404 program evolve.

This book has been a long time in the making, in part because of the constant evolution of the Section 404 program by the implementing agencies, courts, and executive initiatives. Just as one version of the manuscript was completed, it seemed, a major new rulemaking was announced or a new court decision changed the character and scope of the regulatory program. The contributors have patiently endured these programmatic upsets, dutifully collaborating with the editors to ensure that each chapter was as up-to-date as we could make it. Undoubtedly, further changes will be forthcoming as the book goes to press and after its release. Nevertheless, we have endeavored to make this book a comprehensive introduction to federal wetlands regulation. We hope it will serve as a valuable reference tool for attorneys with extensive experience in the area and for those who are confronted with wetlands regulatory requirements for the first time. As is true of any basic treatise, we assume readers will consult referenced sources and updated materials when considering how this area of law impacts any specific situation.

Our contributors played an essential role in many of the chapters in this book, and we know you will find their expertise enlightening. We wanted to take this opportunity to express our appreciation for the knowledge, insight, and patience of each contributor. It is our sincere hope that this book assists you in research and/or practice, and provides an interesting portrait of one of the nation's most important environmental programs.

Douglas R. Williams
St. Louis University
School of Law

Kim Diana Connolly
University of South Carolina
School of Law

Stephen M. Johnson
Mercer University
School of Law

ACKNOWLEDGMENTS

Producing a book of this sort is impossible without the efforts of many devoted and talented individuals. First, and primarily, the contributors to this volume deserve praise and thanks for their patience and perseverance. Their scholarship is truly impressive and their command of their various subject matters will be of benefit to many an attorney. A hearty thanks also to Sam Kalen, who reviewed the manuscript and made invaluable comments, and to Rick Paszkiet and the ABA publications staff for their professionalism and talent.

Douglas R. Williams
Kim Diana Connolly
Stephen M. Johnson

I would also like to thank my research assistants—particularly Tom Wilson and Pat Schwomeyer—who never complained about having to run down that elusive citation or latest guidance document. The support of my school, Saint Louis University School of Law, and its dean, Jeff Lewis, has been consistent and enthusiastic. I would be remiss if I failed to acknowledge the patience, humor and understanding of my generous and wonderful wife, Constance Wagner, and my two daughters, Erin and Victoria.

Douglas R. Williams
St. Louis, Missouri

I would like to start by thanking my enthusiastic and meticulous research assistants Laura Swingle and Courtney Kerwin, as well as University of South Carolina School of Law reference librarian Rebekah Maxwell. I would also like to thank the University of South Carolina School of Law for supporting this endeavor, particularly Dean Burnele V. Powell and Associate Dean Philip T. Lacy. Furthermore, I would like to thank F. James Cumberland Jr. and Tayte Connolly Cumberland for being patient and understanding of my time away from them while working on this project. Finally, I want to acknowledge my father, Matt Connolly, for sparking and nurturing my love of wetlands and other nature.

Kim Diana Connolly
Columbia, South Carolina

I would like to thank my wife, Anne, and my children, Lyndsey, Keith, and Caroline, for their support and inspiration on this project. Finally, I would like to dedicate my contribution to this project to my former colleagues in the Environmental Defense Section of the Justice Department's Environment and Natural Resources Division, to my former colleagues in the Office of Chief Counsel of the Pennsylvania Department of Environmental Protection, and to everyone who is working to protect our nation's wetlands.

Stephen M. Johnson
Macon, Georgia

ABOUT THE EDITORS

Kim Diana Connolly is an associate professor of law at the University of South Carolina School of Law. Professor Connolly received her undergraduate degree in chemistry from the University of North Carolina at Chapel Hill, where she was a Morehead Scholar. She received her J.D. from Georgetown University Law Center in 1993. Before joining the law faculty in 1999, Professor Connolly worked at a number of Washington, D.C., law firms specializing in environmental law. Prior to law school, Professor Connolly was the director of the North Carolina Rural Communities Assistance Project, Inc., and also served as a VISTA volunteer. Professor Connolly directs the Environmental Law Clinic and teaches a variety of other courses. She is also a member of the summer faculty at Vermont Law School, where she teaches wetlands law and policy. Her areas of academic interest include natural resources and public lands law, and her scholarly works have appeared in a number of journals and other publications. She speaks regularly at national and international conferences. Professor Connolly is also an associate faculty member of the University of South Carolina School of the Environment.

Stephen M. Johnson is the associate dean and a professor of law at the Walter F. George School of Law, Mercer University, in Macon, Georgia. Professor Johnson received his J.D. from Villanova University School of Law and an LL.M. in environmental law from the National Law Center at George Washington University. He served as an attorney for the Bureau of Regulatory Counsel in the Pennsylvania Department of Environmental Resources (now DEP) and as a trial attorney for the U.S. Department of Justice, Environment and Natural Resources Division, Environmental Defense Section, where he worked on wetlands and other environmental litigation. He joined the faculty of Mercer University's Law School in 1993 and teaches or has taught environmental law, administrative law, statutory law, torts, and dispute resolution. Professor Johnson has authored numerous law review articles on wetlands and other environmental law topics, and a book on economic approaches to environmental protection.

Douglas R. Williams is a professor of law at Saint Louis University School of Law. He is the author of several articles on various subjects in environmental law. He teaches environmental law, natural resources law, administrative law, and constitutional law, among other courses. He received his J.D. degree from Duke University School of Law with high honors in 1987. He then clerked with the Hon. Douglas H. Ginsburg of the United States Court of Appeals for the District of Columbia Circuit. After three years with the Washington, D.C., firm of Covington & Burling, he began teaching at Saint Louis University School of Law in 1991.

ABOUT THE CONTRIBUTORS

Mark A. Chertok is a graduate of Harvard Law School (J.D. 1970, cum laude) and the State University of New York at Buffalo (A.B. 1967, magna cum laude). He has been active in environmental and land use counseling, permitting, enforcement, and litigation for more than twenty-five years. His experience spans a broad spectrum of substantive areas, including environmental impact statement and processing, wetland and water quality, transportation, air quality, hazardous substances, zoning, environmental compliance, coastal zone management, and historic preservation. His clients have included state, regional, and local governmental bodies; private industrial, commercial, and financial entities; and national environmental and civic organizations. He has lectured and written extensively in the environmental and land use field and is an adjunct professor at the Benjamin N. Cardozo School of Law, where he teaches environmental litigation. He is currently a member of the Executive Committee of the New York State Bar Association, Environmental Law Section and co-chair of its Committee on Environmental Impact Assessment.

William B. Ellis is a partner with Ellis & Thorp in Richmond, Virginia. His practice throughout his career has been devoted to environmental, administrative, and land use law and litigation, with emphasis on matters arising under the Clean Water Act, the National Environmental Policy Act, and the Comprehensive Environmental Response, Compensation and Liability Act. Mr. Ellis received a degree in English from Haverford College with high honors in 1974, and his law degree from the University of Pennsylvania in 1977. He was admitted to the California Bar later that year and was an associate with the litigation section of Rutan & Tucker in Los Angeles from 1977 to 1979. In July 1979, Mr. Ellis joined the environmental section of Hunton & Williams in Richmond as an associate. After becoming Counsel in that firm in 1986, Mr. Ellis joined McSweeney, Burtch & Crump, P.C., in April 1987 as a principal, director, and vice president. Mr. Ellis has participated in a number of landmark environmental cases, including *James City County v. EPA.*

Royal C. Gardner is professor of law and director of the Institute for Biodiversity Law and Policy at Stetson University College of Law in Gulfport, Florida. From 1989 to 1993, he served in the Army General Counsel's office as the Department of the Army's principal wetlands attorney, advising the Assistant Secretary of the Army (Civil Works) on legal and policy issues related to the Corps of Engineers' administration of the Clean Water Act Section 404 program. In 1999, Professor Gardner was a member of the National Research Council's Committee on Mitigating Wetland Losses, which produced *Compensating for Wetland Losses under the Clean Water Act* (2001). In November 2002, he served as a member of the United States delegation to the Eighth Conference of the Contracting Parties to the Convention on Wetlands. He is currently the vice chair of the United States National Ramsar Committee and a vice chair of the American Bar Association's Committee on Water Quality and Wetlands.

Kate L. Geoffroy was a senior associate in the Environmental Law Department of Pierce Atwood until December 2003. Her practice encompassed a variety of environmental and land use issues, with particular emphasis on endangered species issues, wetlands permitting, and hydroelectric licensing issues. She represented a wide range of clients in both rulemaking and licensing proceedings at the state and federal level. Ms. Geoffroy earned her B.S. degree from Yale University, and was graduated cum laude from Boston College Law School. She is currently practicing elder law at the Law Office of Patricia Nelson-Reade in Portland, Maine.

H. Michael Keller is a shareholder in the Salt Lake City office of Van Cott, Bagley, Cornwall & McCarthy. He practices environmental and natural resource law, with an emphasis on environmental due diligence, compliance, permitting, and enforcement matters. He received his A.B. and A.M. degrees in earth sciences from Dartmouth College and his J.D. degree from Duke Law School.

Dennis W. Magee is a vice president at Normandeau Associates Environmental Consultants in Bedford, New Hampshire, and manages the Wetland and Terrestrial Services Group there. He has thirty-two years' experience in the environmental consulting field and has been a program manager or principal investigator on several hundred projects occurring in wetland, terrestrial, intertidal, and offshore coastal environments. Mr. Magee holds a B.S. degree in zoology and wildlife and an M.S. degree in botany and forestry, both from the University of Massachusetts. His primary areas of technical expertise are vascular plant field taxonomy, wetland science, and vegetation and wildlife investigations. He served as a member of a six-person committee established under the auspices of the U.S. Army Engineer Waterways Experiment Station to prepare a nationwide guidebook for a hydrogeomorphic procedure for assessing functional capacity of depressional wetlands, and was a member of a national working group established to prepare a similar procedure for slope wetlands. In addition to various papers published in professional journals, Mr. Magee is the author of three books: *Freshwater Wetlands: A Guide to Common Indicator Plants of the Northeast* (University of Massachusetts Press, 1981), *A Rapid Procedure for Assessing Wetland Functional Capacity* (Association of State Wetland Managers, 1998) and *Flora of the Northeast* (University of Massachusetts Press, 1999). He regularly teaches workshops on field plant identification throughout New England for various professional organizations. Mr. Magee has presented testimony and served as an expert witness in over a dozen hearings and adjudicatory proceedings related to the National Environmental Policy Act, Section 404, the FERC Exhibit E Process, and the regulations of various states.

Robert Meltz is an attorney-adviser with the nonpartisan Congressional Research Service, where he has responsibility for advising Congress on takings issues and environmental law. He gives regular CLE courses for members of Congress and has testified before congressional committees on property rights legislation. Mr. Meltz also has spoken widely at takings law conferences, authored several articles on takings law such as "Wetlands Regulation and the Law of Regulatory Takings," Environmental Law Reporter, Vol. 30, p. 10,468 (2000), and coauthored The Takings Issue: Constitutional Limits on Land Use Controls and Environmental Regulation (Island Press, 1999). He has served on the steering committees of the environment sections of both the District of Columbia Bar and Federal Bar Association. He received his B.A. (cum laude) and M.A. from the University of Pennsylvania, and his J.D. from Georgetown University Law Center.

James G. O'Connor is senior corporate counsel with Steelcase Inc. in Grand Rapids, Michigan. Among other duties, he is responsible for environmental matters involving Steelcase Inc. and its affiliates. He is a graduate of Brown University and the University of Michigan Law School.

Mark T. Pifher has been the director of the Colorado Water Control Division since December 2002. In that capacity, he is responsible for all aspects of water quality protection within Colorado under both the

Clean Water Act and the Safe Drinking Water Act. He is also a board member of the Association of State and Interstate Water Pollution Control Agencies, the umbrella organization of state water quality division directors. Prior to becoming Division Director, Mr. Pifher was a practicing attorney for over twenty-three years. He handled a variety of water quality, endangered species, and related environmental matters for municipalities, special districts, and private businesses. This included litigation, rulemaking, and legislative proceedings involving wetlands, antidegradation, whole effluent toxicity, 401 certifications, discharge permits, and water rights. He is the past chair of the National Water Resources Association Water Quality Committee, the Western Coalition of Arid States Legal Issues Committee, and the Colorado Water Congress State Affairs Committee. He is a frequent author and lecturer on environmental topics. Mr. Pifher received his J.D. (cum laude) in 1979 from the University of Wisconsin–Madison. He is admitted to the bars of Wisconsin and Colorado as well as their respective federal district and circuit courts, the D.C. Circuit Court of Appeals, and the United States Supreme Court.

Kate Sinding is an associate at Sive, Paget & Riesel, P.C., with offices in New York City and White Plains, where she specializes in environmental and land use law and litigation. Ms. Sinding is a graduate of Barnard College, New York University School of Law, and the Woodrow Wilson School, Princeton University. She has authored or coauthored a number of articles in the environmental field, and is the author of "The Transboundary Movement of Waste: A Critical Comparison of U.S. Interstate Policy and the Emerging International Regime," *New York University Law Journal,* Vol. 5, No. 3 (1996). Ms. Sinding is a member of the Environmental Law Committee of the Association of the Bar of the City of New York and the Environmental Law Section of the New York State Bar Association.

William E. Taylor is a partner in the Environmental Law Department of Pierce Atwood. Since joining Pierce Atwood's Environmental Department in 1984, Mr. Taylor has devoted his legal practice to matters related to wetland and natural resource licensing, water law, compliance counseling, rulemaking, auditing, and enforcement. He regularly represents clients before local, state, and federal administrative agencies. Mr. Taylor is experienced in the negotiation and structuring of wetland alteration licenses, preparation of alternative analyses, and wetland compensation issues. He has extensive experience working with state and federal agencies on Clean Water Act, Natural Resources Protection Act, and Section 404 wetland permitting issues. Since 1991, Mr. Taylor has served as Commissioner for the State of Maine on the New England Interstate Water Pollution Control Commission. He is a member of the Maine NPDES Advisory Group (1995–present), the Maine State Wetlands Task Force (1995–1996), and the American and Maine State Bar Associations (Natural Resources and Administrative Law Sections). During 1992–1993, he was a member of the Maine Ambient Toxics Monitoring Program Committee. Mr. Taylor is the author of "Major Land Use Laws Affecting Industrial, Commercial, and Residential Development in Maine," National Business Institute, 1990; and "Wetland Permitting in Maine," *Maine Bar Journal,* September 1997. He also coauthored "A Wetlands Primer," Natural Resources & Environment, 1992, and "The Watershed Protection Approach," Water Resources, Natural Resources & Environment, 1996. Mr. Taylor received his B.A. degree from the University of Massachusetts (cum laude, 1980) and his J.D. and master's in environmental law from the Vermont Law School (1983).

Rolf R. von Oppenfeld (e-mail rvo@testlaw.com) is an environmental attorney with the Team for Environmental Science and Technology Law (TESTLaw) Practice Group, Rolf R. von Oppenfeld, P.C., in Phoenix, AZ. Mr. von Oppenfeld received his B.S. in chemistry and biology and worked as a chemist and in the enforcement and Superfund offices at EPA headquarters. He received his J.D. (summa cum laude) in 1982 from George Washington University. He has taught the one-day legal portion of the four-day Clean Water Compliance Institute for Government Institutes/ABS four times a year since 1996 at various locations around the country. He regularly lectures in Arizona and nationally on various environmental, natural resources, and water issues, and also writes articles and books on these subjects. He was lead author on *Arizona Environmental Law Handbook* (Government Institutes, 1999) and coauthor and section editor of the *Arizona Environmental Law Manual* (State Bar of Arizona, 1995, 1999).

CHAPTER 1

Federal Wetlands Regulation: An Overview

DOUGLAS R. WILLIAMS AND KIM DIANA CONNOLLY

I. Introduction/Scope

Wetlands throughout the United States have been subject to diverse forms of regulation by local, state, and federal authorities. The federal government has taken an interest in wetlands for quite some time, but its presence as a regulator of activities in wetlands is a more recent innovation. That presence is manifested predominantly through the Clean Water Act's Section 404 program, which is the centerpiece of the federal government's wetlands regulatory programs.[1] Although the United States Army Corps of Engineers (Corps) first interpreted Section 404 narrowly to exclude most of the nation's wetlands, the agency's limited interpretation was struck down in court almost three decades ago.[2] Regulatory developments and subsequent jurisprudence now authorize the Corps and the U.S. Environmental Protection Agency (EPA) to assert federal jurisdiction over many of the nation's wetlands.[3] The federal government also has embraced a national goal of no overall net loss of the nation's wetland resources since the 1980s, and on Earth Day 2004 announced a goal of achieving a net gain in wetland resources throughout the United States.[4] In addition to the Clean Water Act Section 404 regulatory program, other federal programs encourage preservation of wetlands through direct regulation, financial incentives, outright acquisition, or other management techniques. At least thirty-six federal agencies have been involved in wetland-related activities since 1990.[5]

The expansion of federal jurisdiction over wetlands reflects increased understanding of the important ecological functions that wetlands perform as well as recognition of the significant amount of wetlands acreage that has been destroyed or degraded by human activity over the years.[6] The vital functions performed by wetlands include maintaining and enhancing water quality, preventing or minimizing damage from floods and storms, protecting shorelines against erosion, providing habitat to a variety of species of fish and wildlife (many of which are endangered or threatened), and enhancing aesthetic and recreational experiences.[7] It has been estimated that since colonial times nearly half of the wetlands in the contiguous United States, or some 117 million acres, have been lost to development or otherwise destroyed.[8] Several states have lost more than 80 percent of their wetlands. Furthermore, despite programs to restrict development in wetlands, it is estimated that between 1985 and 1995 over 58,000 acres of wetlands were lost annually in the coterminous United States.[9] Though losses have been slowed in recent years, thousands of acres of wetlands continue to be lost annually due to a combination of human activities and natural events.[10]

This chapter provides an overview of federal wetlands regulation. It opens with a brief history of federal involvement with wetlands. It then provides an overview of the Clean Water Act's Section 404 program, which is the centerpiece of federal wetlands regulation. The overview includes a checklist for use in determining whether a proposed project is subject to federal regulation, and if it is, what that regulation might entail. More details about issues discussed in the second section of this introductory chapter can be found in subsequent chapters of this book.

II. A Brief History of Federal Regulation of Wetlands

At the time of European settlement and for many years thereafter, wetlands—known then generally as swamps, marshes, and bogs—were regarded widely as places of mystery, often with connotations of lurking evil.[11] Through the nineteenth century and into the twentieth century, wetlands were blamed for flooding, disease, and a host of other social problems. Those beliefs were so widespread that in 1900, in *Leovy v. United States*,[12] the United States Supreme Court concluded

> We think that the trial court might well take judicial notice that the public health is deeply concerned in the reclamation of swamp and overflowed lands. If there is any fact which may be

> supposed to be known by everybody, and, therefore, by courts, it is that swamps and stagnant waters are the cause of malarial and malignant fevers, and that the police power is never more legitimately exercised than in removing such nuisances.[13]

Until the mid to late nineteenth century, large expanses of wetlands remained in federal ownership, owing primarily to the general unsuitability of wetlands for agricultural production, given contemporaneous technological limitations. To encourage the use of these resources, Congress initiated programs to facilitate the draining and filling of wetlands. Prominent examples of this policy are the Swamp Land Acts, which transferred from the federal government to the states "the whole of the swamp and overflowed lands, made unfit thereby for cultivation."[14] These grants were conditioned on states taking steps "to make and maintain the necessary improvements"[15]—namely, draining and filling the wetlands to promote agricultural production.

Efforts by states to drain ceded swamp lands were, at first, largely unsuccessful due to financial and technological limitations. Nonetheless, the Swamp Land Acts inevitably altered the legal status of wetlands and promoted development within and destruction of these valuable natural resources. As historian Ann Vileisis notes: "In privatizing the nation's swamps, Congress gave away its ability to oversee a systematic approach to drainage planning and also eliminated the possibility of protecting the many public values not yet understood to be provided by wetlands."[16] As a result of the Swamp Land Acts and other measures, nearly 75 percent of the nation's wetlands in the lower forty-eight states are now privately owned.[17]

Until a few decades ago, federal programs continued to encourage the drainage and destruction of wetlands. The most prominent efforts were those of the U.S. Department of Agriculture (USDA) to expand agricultural production. By 1955, through USDA assistance, 103 million acres were organized into drainage systems and $900 million had been spent to promote drainage of wetlands.[18] In addition, the Corps and the Bureau of Reclamation destroyed countless acres of wetlands as a result of dam and levee projects designed to improve navigation or control water flows.

During the early decades of the twentieth century, concern about the effects of wetlands losses, particularly on migratory waterfowl, began to brew and eventually gained national prominence. With the Migratory Bird Treaty Act of 1918,[19] the Migratory Bird Conservation Act of 1929,[20] and the Migratory Bird Hunting Stamp Act of 1934,[21] this concern evolved into a national policy somewhat at odds with other federal policies, particularly the USDA's promotion of wetlands drainage and conversion to agricultural production. The migratory bird statutes, most particularly the 1929 Act, authorized the Department of the Interior to acquire and protect important wetland resources.[22] Though modest in scope, federal acquisition and conservation programs remained the primary federal response to growing wetland losses until the passage of the Federal Water Pollution Control Act (which later became known as the Clean Water Act (CWA)) in 1972.[23]

During the period between passage of the migratory bird statutes and the CWA, the importance of wetlands to overall ecosystem functioning was steadily becoming apparent. A signal event occurred in 1956 with the Fish and Wildlife Service's publication of Samuel P. Shaw and C. Gordon Fredine's *Wetlands of the United States*.[24] This publication provided a new vocabulary—using the generic term "wetlands" in place of terms such as "swamp" or "bog"—that "conveyed positive symbolic value born from trustworthy scientific expertise."[25] Known as Circular 39, the report articulated a taxonomy of wetland types and clearly explained the value of wetlands as habitat for fish and wildlife. The authors urgently concluded that "[n]ever before in the Nation's history has it been so necessary to plan for the setting aside of land and water areas to serve the future needs of fish and wildlife."[26] In estimating wetland losses, the report provided a baseline from which future rates of losses might be estimated.

Despite the alarm call of Circular 39, federal efforts to regulate the environmental impact of private development in wetlands did not emerge until the late 1960s and early 1970s. Until this period, federal management of water resources generally was focused on protecting and facilitating commerce and navigability and, to a lesser extent, hydropower development. Protection of water quality was primarily a responsibility of state and local governments. The most important federal legislation governing water resources was the Rivers and Harbors Act of 1899 (RHA),[27] which has been administered continuously by the Corps. Under Section 10 of that statute, the Corps was given authority to issue permits for certain activities in "navigable waters."[28] Additionally, Section 13 of the RHA, popularly known as the Refuse Act, declared it unlawful

> to throw, discharge, or deposit, or cause, suffer, or procure to be thrown, discharged, or deposited either from or out of any ship, barge, or other floating craft of any kind, or from the shore, wharf, manufacturing establishment, or mill of any kind, any refuse matter of any kind or description whatever other than

> that flowing from streets and sewers and passing therefrom in a liquid state, into any navigable water of the United States, or into any tributary of any navigable water from which the same shall float or be washed into such navigable water.[29]

Despite generous judicial interpretations of the Corps's authority under the RHA,[30] the Corps's authority to deny an RHA permit on environmental grounds was not established firmly until 1970.[31] Until that time it generally was assumed that the Corps's role under the RHA was to maintain and improve navigation.

Change became evident when, with the passage of amendments to the Fish and Wildlife Coordination Act in 1965,[32] the Corps agreed to consult with the Department of the Interior's resource agencies when considering whether to authorize proposed projects under the RHA.[33] Moreover, the Corps revised its permit regulations to require a "public interest review" of proposed projects through which the agency would consider a wide variety of factors, including environmental values, when determining whether to authorize such projects.[34] The passage of the National Environmental Policy Act of 1969[35] reinforced the Corps's responsibility to consider environmental values in its administration of the RHA.

In the 1970 decision *Zabel v. Tabb*,[36] landowners had sued the Corps, seeking an injunction compelling the agency to issue them a permit to fill eleven acres of tidelands in Florida's Boca Ciega Bay. The landowners claimed that absent a finding that this activity would interfere with navigation, the Corps was compelled to issue a permit under the RHA. The U.S. Court of Appeals for the Fifth Circuit roundly rejected this argument, concluding that "there is no doubt that the [Corps] can refuse on conservation grounds to grant a permit under the Rivers and Harbors Act."[37] According to the court, "[t]he intent of the three branches has been unequivocally expressed: The Secretary must weigh the effect a dredge and fill project will have on conservation before he issues a permit lifting the Congressional ban."[38]

The protection provided to wetlands by this expanded Corps role was, however, somewhat limited. The established jurisdictional reach of the RHA extended no farther than the mean high water mark[39]—a limit that left most wetlands vulnerable to unregulated development, save for whatever programs state and local jurisdictions might have in place. Moreover, when the Corps, acting pursuant to an executive order, attempted to create a general permit program under the RHA to control water pollution, its efforts were halted by a judicial ruling that, among other things, severely restricted the jurisdictional reach of the RHA.[40] As one court observed, the limits of jurisdiction under the RHA "worked to impede efforts to forestall the degradation of the aquatic environment. Not only did small feeder streams and tributaries remain exempt from federal jurisdiction, but, more importantly, the wetland areas adjoining the waterways did also."[41] The passage of the 1972 amendments to the Clean Water Act, provided an opportunity for more extensive regulation of activities in wetlands and led to development of the programs discussed at length in the subsequent chapters of this book.

Furthermore, current wetlands regulation has been powerfully shaped by administrative policies over the years. High-level initiatives by the George H. W. Bush administration popularized a national policy of "no net loss" of wetlands in 1988.[42] The Clinton administration likewise took an interest in wetlands and, shortly after assuming office, President Clinton convened an interagency working group to address wetland issues. The result was the 1993 Interagency Wetlands Plan, entitled *Protecting America's Wetlands: A Fair, Flexible, and Effective Approach.*[43] The plan embraced five organizing principles:

1. Establish an interim goal of no overall net loss and a long-term goal of increasing the quality and quantity of the nation's wetlands.
2. Promote changes to make the regulatory program efficient, fair, flexible, and predictable, while avoiding unnecessary and minimizing unavoidable impacts upon private property and the regulated public and providing effective protection for wetlands.
3. Reduce reliance on the Section 404 regulatory program by encouraging nonregulatory programs such as advance planning; wetland restoration, inventory, and research; and public/private cooperative efforts.
4. Expand federal partnerships with state, tribal, and local governments, the private sector, and individual citizens and approach wetland protection and restoration in an ecosystem/watershed context.
5. Base federal wetland policy on the best scientific information available.[44]

To further these principles, the plan proposed a package of reforms. With respect to the Section 404 program, the plan proposed to

- Re-commit to the no-net-loss approach to wetlands regulation.
- Establish an administrative appeal process for Corps actions under Section 404.

- Establish a ninety-day deadline for Corps action on permit applications under Section 404.
- Exempt prior converted cropland from regulation.
- Designate the Department of Agriculture's Soil Conservation Service [now the Natural Resources Conservation Service] the lead federal agency responsible for identifying wetlands on agricultural lands under both the Clean Water Act and the Food Security Act.
- Close a loophole with regulations expanding the scope of regulated activities under Section 404.
- Emphasize that all wetlands are not of equal value, and issue guidance to field staff permitting less rigorous permit review for small projects with minor environmental impacts.
- Require all federal agencies to use the same procedures to identify wetlands.
- Endorse the use of mitigation banks.[45]

Some of those reforms have been put in place. In 1997, the interagency wetlands working group issued a report entitled *Four Years of Progress: Meeting Our Commitment for Wetlands Reform*.[46] The report noted several improvements, including reduced time for processing permit applications, increased flexibility and certainty in the administration of the Section 404 program, and simplified regulatory requirements for agricultural lands. A few years later, in testimony before Congress, the Corps noted that "[b]ecause of [the agency's] effectiveness in avoiding and mitigating impacts, only three-tenths of a percent of all Section 404 [permit] requests were denied."[47] However, the Corps's average time for processing individual permits has increased in recent years, as has the backlog of individual permit applications. In the Energy and Water Appropriations Act of 2001, Congress required the Corps to develop a permit processing management plan to address these increases.[48] In 2003, the Corps issued a Regulatory Statistics document showing that the Corps processes individual permits in an average of 161 days and general permits in an average of 22 days.[49]

III. The Section 404 Program Overview and Checklist

To assist readers both in navigating this book and in navigating the Section 404 program,[50] this overview provides a "checklist" to determine whether federal regulation might be triggered by proposed activities in a wetland, and if so, how that regulation might apply. Of course, situations differ significantly, and require individual analysis and competent advice.

In order to use this checklist, a few fundamentals must be understood. First, the core basis for the Section 404 program is found in the following language of the Clean Water Act: "The Secretary [of the Army] may issue permits, after notice and opportunity for public hearings for the discharge of dredged or fill material into the navigable waters at specified disposal sites."[51] This language does not clearly define federal regulatory jurisdiction, and as a consequence, it is vital to consult implementing regulations issued by the Corps and EPA, as well as judicial decisions. Even these sources will often fail to provide clear answers because, through the years, there has been considerable discord among the agencies themselves as well as between the agencies and the courts.[52]

Second, it is important to know the key regulatory players in the wetlands regulatory arena. The Corps has responsibility for issuing permits for the discharge of dredged or fill material.[53] By statute, the Corps is also responsible for enforcing "any condition or limitation set forth in a permit issued by" the Corps under Section 404.[54] The Corps performs these responsibilities primarily through delegation to district engineers in each of the Corps's thirty-eight district offices.[55] On rare occasions, the decisions of district engineers may be "elevated" for review by Corps headquarters.[56] Recently, the Corps established an administrative appeal process for certain district engineers' decisions.[57]

The Corps has promulgated regulations to implement its Section 404 program responsibilities.[58] To supplement and clarify these regulations, the Corps occasionally issues Regulatory Guidance Letters (RGLs), which may be accessed on the Internet.[59] In addition, guidance to district engineers sometimes may be provided from Corps headquarters through memoranda.[60] These informal sources of regulatory information often provide useful and important details about particular issues under the Section 404 program and should be consulted.

In addition to regulations and guidance issued by Corps headquarters, the Corps's district engineers also may issue general permits authorizing a variety of activities within particular regions or states.[61] Corps headquarters also issues general permits, typically every five years, that authorize activities on a nationwide basis.[62]

EPA also plays a significant role in the Section 404 program. In issuing permits, the CWA requires the Corps to apply guidelines promulgated by EPA in conjunction with the Corps.[63] Commonly referred to as the 404(b)(1) Guidelines, these "guidelines" are actually formal, binding regulations.[64] Additionally, EPA may "veto" any Corps decision to issue a Section 404 permit.[65] EPA also has certain enforcement responsibilities for Section 404,[66] and is granted authority to review and approve applications by states seeking to assume some of the Corps's permitting responsibilities within the respective states' geographic boundaries.[67] The statutory division of authority between EPA and the Corps has, in some circumstances, generated confusion about program responsibilities, some of which has been clarified through Memoranda of Agreement between the agencies.[68]

Given this background with respect to the regulatory players, the following checklist can be used to ascertain whether and how activities in a particular wetland might be regulated.

1. *Does the federal government have geographic jurisdiction over the project you are proposing?*
   a. May the project area properly be delineated as a wetland? (See Chapter 2.)
   b. Assuming the project area does include wetlands, are these wetlands "navigable waters," also known as "waters of the United States"? (See Chapter 3.)
2. *Does the federal government have jurisdiction to regulate the activity you are proposing to undertake?* (See Chapter 4.)
   a. Is the activity exempted by statute from federal regulation?
   b. Does the project contemplate any discharges?
   c. If discharges are contemplated, will dredged or fill material be included in the discharge?
3. *If the government has jurisdiction over the project area and the proposed activities, do you qualify for*
   a. A Section 404(e) permit (a Nationwide Permit, a State Programmatic General Permit, or a Regional General Permit) (see Chapters 5 and 10) or
   b. A Letter of Permission?
4. *If you are required to obtain an individual permit, have the following conditions been met?* (Generally, see Chapter 6.)
   a. Compliance with the Section 404(b)(1) Guidelines, including a practicable alternatives analysis (see Chapter 7) and mitigation requirements (see Chapter 8)
   b. Satisfaction of the Public Interest Review (see Chapter 6)
   c. Compliance with other applicable laws, such as the Endangered Species Act, the National Historic Preservation Act, and the National Environmental Policy Act (see Chapter 6)
   d. Certification from the appropriate state(s) that you comply with applicable state laws, including state water quality standards

(Section 401 of the Clean Water Act) and coastal zone management programs (Coastal Zone Management Act) (see Chapters 6 and 10)

5. *If the Corps district proposes to issue a permit, do EPA and other agencies concur with its analysis?* (See Chapter 9.)
6. *If you disagree with the district office decision, will you choose to bring:*
   a. An administrative appeal (see Chapter 11)
   b. A court challenge (see Chapter 12)
   c. A takings challenge (see Chapter 13)
7. *Have you undertaken something that should require a permit, or violated a permit, triggering an enforcement action?*
8. *What other activities in wetlands might be regulated or subject to other federal programs?*

1. Does the federal government have geographic jurisdiction? As discussed in detail in Chapters 2 and 3, for Section 404 to apply, the federal government must have jurisdiction over the property proposed for development. Determining whether such jurisdiction exists requires the answering of two questions. First, can the property properly be delineated as a wetland? Second, if wetlands are part of the project area, are these wetlands "navigable waters" (otherwise known as "waters of the United States")?

Wetland delineation is based on a scientific assessment of the particular property. Both EPA and the Corps have promulgated identical regulations defining wetlands as "those areas that are inundated or saturated by surface or ground water at a frequency and duration sufficient to support, and that under normal circumstances do support, a prevalence of vegetation typically adapted for life in saturated soil conditions."[69] To ascertain whether the three parameters in this definition (hydrophytic vegetation, hydric soil, and hydrology) are met, field personnel use a delineation manual.[70] Because basic knowledge of the science underlying such delineations can be helpful, Chapter 2 of this book provides a primer on wetlands ecology for the layperson.

The second question as to whether geographic jurisdiction can be claimed requires analysis of whether a delineated wetland may properly be treated as "navigable waters" as required by the statutory language in Section 404.[71] "Navigable waters" are defined in the CWA as "waters of the United States."[72] The courts have concluded that this definition signaled Congress's intent to provide a more expansive jurisdiction under Section 404 than is provided by the Corps's jurisdiction over activities in "navigable waters" under the RHA.[73] On this basis, federal regulatory jurisdiction has evolved over the years to include areas that fall well beyond traditional views of what may be treated as "navigable waters."

The evolution of the Corps's jurisdiction shifted recently with the U.S. Supreme Court's decision in *Solid Waste Agency of Northern Cook County v. U.S. Army Corps of Engineers (SWANCC)*.[74] In that case, the Court held that the statutory term "navigable waters" does not include some areas that EPA and the Corps—and many lower courts—had previously regarded as within the reach of Section 404. The decision has generated new uncertainties about the scope of federal regulatory jurisdiction under Section 404. Lower courts have read the holding in *SWANCC* differently, but most have interpreted the decision narrowly, preserving a fairly expansive view of what may constitute "waters of the United States."[75] In addition to disagreement among the courts, the Corps has been criticized for inconsistent interpretations of *SWANCC* provided by different Corps districts in the course of acting on individual permit applications.[76] Furthermore, in 2002 the Bush administration proposed changes to the regulatory definition of navigable waters,[77] then withdrew that proposal.[78] The inconsistent interpretations of the courts and district offices and the possibility that the Bush administration may revisit the proposal to amend the regulatory definition of navigable waters leave the geographic scope of the Section 404 program somewhat in flux. This subject is treated in detail in Chapter 3.

2. Does the federal government have jurisdiction to regulate the activity? As discussed in detail in Chapter 4, even if an area is delineated as a wetland and is a "navigable water," project activities in these wetlands may not be subject to regulation under Section 404. Three questions must be answered to determine whether a proposed activity is a regulated activity: Does an exemption apply? Are you engaging in a discharge? If so, are dredged or fill material being discharged?

Congress included statutory exemptions to Section 404 regulation in Section 404(f)(1).[79] The first, and most significant, Section 404(f)(1) exemption is for "normal farming, silviculture and ranching activities."[80] That exemption applies to certain continuous activities involving farming, timber harvesting, and related activities.[81] Section 404(f)(1) also includes other exemptions for maintenance (including emergency repair of recently damaged, currently serviceable structures), construction of temporary sedimentation basins, construction or maintenance of farm ponds, irrigation ditches, farm or forest roads, and temporary roads for moving mining equipment.[82] These exemptions do not apply, however, if the proposed activity has "as its purpose bringing an area of the navigable waters into a use to which it was not previously subject, where the flow or circulation of navigable waters may be impaired or the reach of such waters be reduced. . . ."[83] More information about exemptions is provided in Chapter 4.

Assuming an exemption does not apply to a particular activity, the next question is whether the proposed activity in wetlands involves a "discharge." Discharges of dredged or fill material generally are undertaken to convert wet areas into sites suitable for agriculture or for commercial, residential, or other forms of development, or to enhance the navigability of deep water areas. Section 301 of the Clean Water Act contains a general prohibition against the "discharge of any pollutant by any person" that does not comply with conditions set forth in a permit.[84] The term "discharge of a pollutant" is defined to include "any addition of any pollutant to navigable waters from any point source."[85] The term "pollutant" is defined expansively to include a variety of fill materials, such as rock and sand, as well as "dredged spoil."[86] Thus, the prohibition against the addition of pollutants from point sources includes a variety of activities that are routinely undertaken to develop wetlands for residential, commercial, or agricultural purposes.

The term "discharge" was clarified in 1998 through a challenge to the so-called Tulloch Rule,[87] a 1993 regulation effectively regulating most development activities in wetlands, including the incidental fallback of material displaced by landclearing and agricultural operations. The D.C. Circuit, in *National Mining Association v. United States Army Corps of Engineers*,[88] held this rule invalid, concluding that incidental fallback during landclearing and excavation activities cannot properly be regarded as the "addition of a pollutant."[89] Subsequent judicial and administrative interpretations have determined that many development activities are still properly regulated as discharges.[90] Chapter 4 provides further detail on the current interpretation of the scope of activities properly classified as a "discharge."

Assuming that there is no applicable exemption and that an activity can properly be characterized as involving a discharge, the last question is whether the discharge includes dredged or fill material. Dredged material is "material that is excavated or dredged from waters of the United States."[91] Fill material has been recently redefined by the Corps as including "material placed in waters of the United States where the material has the effect of: (i) Replacing any portion of a water of the United States with dry land; or (ii) Changing the bottom elevation of any portion of a water of the United States."[92] Fill material can include rock, sand, soil, clay, plastics, construction debris, wood chips, overburden from mining or other excavation activities, or certain other materials.[93] Further details on what constitutes dredged and fill material for purposes of regulation can be found in Chapter 4.

3. If the government has jurisdiction over the project area and the proposed activities, do you qualify for expedited review? As explained above, Section 404 prohibits discharges of dredged or fill material into waters of the United States unless they are authorized by a permit issued by the Corps or expressly exempted by statute.[94] The Corps considers over 80,000 permit applications per year.[95] However, the bulk of activities subject to the Corps's Section 404 jurisdiction do not require individual permits.[96] The vast majority of activities proceed under Nationwide Permits, State Programmatic General Permits, Regional General Permits, or Letters of Permission.[97]

CWA Section 404(e) authorizes the Corps to "issue general permits on a State, regional, or nationwide basis for any category of activities involving discharges of dredged or fill material" determined to be "similar in nature" and causing "only minimal adverse environmental effects," individually or cumulatively.[98] These general permits are essentially permits by rule, although many require the permittee to notify the Corps before commencing activities involving jurisdictional discharges.[99] In addition, some require compensatory mitigation for adverse environmental impacts of the permitted activity.[100] Close to 90 percent of the activities authorized by the Corps each year are authorized through Section 404(e) permits.[101] Expedited approval of proposed activity may also be obtained through Letters of Permission. These authorizations are available when a Corps district engineer determines that the "proposed work would be minor, would not have significant individual or cumulative impacts on environmental values, and should encounter no appreciable opposition."[102] General permits, including nationwide permits, are discussed in detail in Chapter 5 and state programmatic permits are discussed in detail in Chapter 10.

4. If you are required to obtain an individual permit, have you met certain required conditions? As set forth in detail in Chapters 6, 7, and 8, once it is determined that a proposed activity necessitates an individual permit pursuant to Section 404, certain regulatory requirements will be triggered. These requirements include satisfying the 404(b)(1) Guidelines (including an analysis of practicable alternatives and provision of compensatory mitigation for unavoidable impacts), satisfying the public interest review, and ensuring compliance with other applicable federal and state laws.

The procedures for submitting and processing individual permit applications are discussed in detail in Chapter 6. The Corps cannot issue permits unless the proposed activity is in compliance with EPA's Section

404(b)(1) Guidelines.[103] The Guidelines prohibit discharges of dredged or fill material (1) if a practicable alternative with less adverse impact is available;[104] (2) if such discharge would cause or contribute to violations of various related laws, including those addressing water quality standards, toxic effluent standards, or endangered or threatened species;[105] (3) if such discharge would "cause or contribute to significant degradation of the waters of the United States;"[106] or (4) "unless appropriate and practicable steps have been taken which will minimize potential adverse impacts of the discharge on the aquatic ecosystem."[107] The Guidelines are discussed in detail in Chapter 7, with a focus on the required "practicable alternatives" analysis.

As part of Section 404(b)(1) compliance, sequenced mitigation generally requires that (1) all adverse environmental impacts first be avoided to the maximum extent practicable; (2) any unavoidable impacts be minimized; and (3) compensatory mitigation be provided for any remaining adverse impacts.[108] A variety of mitigation methods may be available, including on-site mitigation, mitigation banks, and in-lieu-fee arrangements.[109] Recent controversies with respect to implementation of mitigation requirements prompted the development of a national Mitigation Action Plan.[110] Designed to improve the ecological performance and results of compensatory mitigation, this plan sets forth seventeen tasks that federal agencies with responsibilities related to wetlands are to complete by the end of 2005.[111] Requirements with respect to mitigation are discussed in detail in Chapter 8.

Even if a proposed activity complies with the Guidelines, the district engineer must also perform a "public interest" review.[112] Corps regulations provide that wetlands are "a productive and valuable public resource, the unnecessary alteration or destruction of which should be discouraged as contrary to the public interest."[113] To that end, the Corps undertakes an evaluation of probable impacts (including cumulative impacts) on the public interest of the proposed activity and its use.[114] The public interest factors considered by the Corps include conservation, economics, aesthetics, general environmental concerns, wetlands, historic properties, fish and wildlife values, floodplain values, land use, navigation, shore erosion and accretion, recreation, water supply and conservation, water quality, energy needs, safety, food and fiber production, mineral needs, considerations of property ownership, and the needs and welfare of the people.[115] A permit will be granted unless the Corps determines that granting the permit would be contrary to the public interest.[116] Chapter 6 contains a more detailed discussion of the public interest review.

A variety of other statutes, such as the Endangered Species Act,[117] the National Environmental Policy Act,[118] and the National Historic Preservation Act,[119] may result in additional requirements and conditions on a permit application.[120] Review requirements with respect to other federal laws are covered in Chapter 6.

Where applicable, certifications from state authorities also may be required. Section 401 of the CWA grants states authority to certify, condition, or deny licenses and permits issued by federal agencies, including Section 404 permits, depending on the effects that the licensed or permitted activity may have on state water resources and water quality.[121] Likewise, the Coastal Zone Management Act (CZMA) ensures that states retain authority to regulate the use of coastal wetlands by conditioning the issuance of federal permits on state determinations that the authorized activity is consistent with the state's coastal zone management programs.[122] More details about these state certifications are provided in Chapter 10.

5. If the Corps district proposes to issue a permit, do EPA and other agencies concur with its analysis? As discussed in detail in Chapter 9, EPA may play an important role throughout the permitting process, beyond enacting the Section 404(b)(1) Guidelines discussed above.[123] Pursuant to Section 404(q) mandates, the Corps has reached agreements with various federal agencies (including EPA) regarding efficient processing of permit applications.[124] Section 404(c) grants EPA the authority to "veto" Corps decisions to permit discharges of dredged or fill material in a defined area.[125] Such a veto requires a determination that the proposed discharge "will have an unacceptable adverse effect on municipal water supplies, shellfish beds and fishery areas (including spawning and breeding areas), wildlife, or recreational areas."[126] Other agencies must also be consulted as appropriate during the permitting process, and necessary review procedures should be completed in a coordinated manner.[127]

6. If you disagree with the district office, will you challenge the decision? As discussed in Chapters 11, 12, and 13, applicants who are dissatisfied with a Corps district office decision have various options to challenge the result. Applicants may bring an administrative appeal, mount a substantive or procedural challenge in federal court, or bring a challenge pursuant to the Takings Clause of the U.S. Constitution.

Pursuant to 33 C.F.R. Part 331, a Section 404 permit applicant that is dissatisfied with a Corps district decision on either a permit application or a jurisdictional determination may appeal[128] to one of eight regional Corps offices.[129] In some circumstances, such an appeal may be a necessary prerequisite to a legal challenge in federal court.[130] The appeal process is discussed in detail in Chapter 11.

A dissatisfied permit applicant also may bring a suit in federal court challenging a final decision of the Corps or EPA, provided that certain requirements are met. Final Corps decisions are defined as "the initial decision to issue or deny a permit," unless the applicant submits an accepted request for appeal under 33 C.F.R. Part 331.[131] For cases against the Corps or EPA, typical litigation requirements of standing, exhaustion of administrative remedies, ripeness, and mootness apply to such challenges.[132] The CWA does not provide a specific statute of limitations, but some courts have applied the six-year general statute of limitations for civil actions commenced against the United States.[133] Agency decisions challenged by permit applicants will be set aside only if they are found to be "arbitrary, capricious, an abuse of discretion, or otherwise not in accordance with law."[134] Court actions are discussed more fully in Chapter 12.

In certain cases, claims may be made that a Corps or EPA decision so restricts the use of private property that the agency action amounts to a "taking" in violation of the Fifth Amendment to the Constitution of the United States.[135] Because most of the nation's wetlands are in private ownership and because the Section 404 program can impose significant costs on landowners and developers, wetland protection measures often collide with the rights and economic expectations of property owners. Wetland cases have figured prominently in the development of takings jurisprudence in federal courts.[136] Takings matters are discussed in detail in Chapter 13.

7. Have you undertaken something that should require a permit, or violated a permit, triggering an enforcement action? The CWA includes an extensive array of measures to enforce the requirements of the Section 404 program. EPA, the Corps, and the Department of Justice share these enforcement responsibilities. EPA has civil and administrative enforcement power pursuant to Section 309 of the CWA.[137] The Corps's enforcement authority is provided in Section 309 and Section 404.[138] The Department of Justice, including its U.S. Attorneys, represents the government in civil proceedings and is responsible for prosecuting persons who engage in activities prohibited and made criminal by Section 309(c).[139]

The government has several enforcement options. EPA and the Corps may issue administrative orders and cease and desist letters, respectively, requiring compliance with Section 404 program requirements.[140] Both may assess administrative penalties.[141] The government is authorized to commence civil actions for injunctive relief, including restoration of damaged wetlands and civil penalties.[142] EPA and the Corps also may refer particular violations to the Department of Justice for possible criminal prosecution.[143] In addition to such enforcement by federal agencies, Section 505 of the CWA provides for citizen suits.[144] Citizen suits may be brought (1) against "any person . . . who is alleged to be in violation of . . . an effluent standard or limitation under [the CWA]";[145] and (2) against EPA or the Corps alleging that the agency has failed to perform a nondiscretionary act or duty.[146] Enforcement matters are discussed in detail in Chapter 12.

8. What other activities in wetlands might be regulated or subject to other federal programs? The Section 404 program is the basic federal regulatory program relating to wetlands, but it is not the exclusive means through which the federal government influences the use and preservation of wetlands. A variety of "nonregulatory," incentive-based programs also exist, primarily relating to agricultural use of wetlands. In addition, the government has become very active in acquiring wetland resources, through either fee title acquisitions or the purchase of conservation easements. The full range of federal activities relating to wetlands is beyond the scope of this book, but agricultural programs are briefly addressed in Chapter 14.

IV. Conclusion

This brief introduction is meant to offer an historical overview of the federal government's role in protecting and regulating the uses of wetland resources, as well as a thumbnail sketch of the modern regulatory program. The detailed chapters that follow offer a closer look at federal efforts, particularly the regulatory efforts undertaken in the Section 404 program. Despite the years of experience gained since the passage of Section 404 in 1972, the wetland program remains a work in progress. Its evolving nature will continue to be determined by Congress, the administration, and the public at large.

Notes

1. 33 U.S.C. § 1344 (2000).

2. *See* Natural Resources Defense Council v. Callaway, 392 F. Supp. 685 (D.D.C. 1975) (rejecting the Corps's position that Section 404's jurisdiction limited to waters meeting traditional tests of navigability and holding that Congress had "asserted federal jurisdiction over the nation's waters to the maximum extent permissible under the Commerce Clause of the Constitution." *Id.* at 686.).

3. *See* 33 C.F.R. § 328.3(a)(3) (2004) (defining jurisdictional waters to include wetlands the use, degradation, or destruction of which could affect interstate or foreign commerce).

4. *See, e.g.*, U.S. Army Corps of Engineers, Regulatory Guidance Letter 02-02, Guidance on Compensatory Mitigation Projects for Aquatic Resource Impacts under the Corps Regulatory Program Pursuant to Section 404 of the Clean Water Act and Section 10 of the Rivers and Harbors Act of 1899, at 1 (Dec. 24, 2002), *available at* http://www.usace.army.mil/inet/functions/cw/cecwo/reg/RGL2-02.pdf. *See also* The White House, Fact Sheet: President Announces Wetlands Initiative on Earth Day (Apr. 22, 2004), *available at* http://www.whitehouse.gov/news/releases/2004/04/20040422-1.html (setting forth information about President George W. Bush's announcement that his administration was "moving beyond a policy of 'no net loss' of wetlands to have an overall increase of wetlands in America each year.")

5. GENERAL ACCOUNTING OFFICE, WETLANDS OVERVIEW—PROBLEMS WITH ACREAGE DATA PERSIST, GAO Letter Report No. GAO/RCED-98-150, at 1 (1998), *available through* http://www.gpoaccess.gov/gaoreports/search.html.

6. *See* THOMAS DAHL, U.S. FISH AND WILDLIFE SERVICE, STATUS AND TRENDS OF WETLANDS IN THE CONTERMINOUS UNITED STATES 1986 TO 1997, Executive Summary, *available at* http://training.fws.gov/library/Pubs9/wetlands86-97_highres.pdf ("At the time of European settlement, the area that is now the conterminous United States contained an estimated 221 million acres (89.5 million ha) of wetlands. Over time, wetlands have been drained, dredged, filled, leveled, and flooded to the extent that less than half of the original wetland acreage remains (Dahl 1990)."). For an excellent history of wetlands in America, *see* ANN VILEISIS, DISCOVERING THE UNKNOWN LANDSCAPE: A HISTORY OF AMERICA'S WETLANDS (1997).

7. *See* 33 C.F.R. § 320.4(b); Environmental Protection Agency, *America's Wetlands: Our Vital Link between Land and Water, Wetlands and People, at* http://www.epa.gov/OWOW/wetlands/vital/people.html. For an excellent training module on wetland functions and values, *see* William S. Sipple, U.S. Environmental Protection Agency Office of Water, *Wetland Functions and Values, at* http://www.epa.gov/watertrain/wetlands/.

8. *See* ANN VILEISIS, *supra* note 6, at 2–4. For other estimates of wetland losses, *see* STATUS AND TRENDS OF WETLANDS IN THE CONTERMINOUS UNITED STATES 1986 TO 1997, *supra* note 6; THOMAS DAHL & CRAIG E. JOHNSTON, U.S. FISH & WILDLIFE SERVICE, STATUS AND TRENDS OF WETLANDS IN THE COTERMINOUS UNITED STATES, MID-1970S TO MID-1980S (1991); RALPH W. TINER, JR., U.S. FISH & WILDLIFE SERVICE, WETLANDS OF THE U.S.: CURRENT STATUS AND RECENT TRENDS (1984); THOMAS DAHL, U.S. FISH & WILDLIFE SERVICE, WETLAND LOSSES IN THE UNITED STATES, 1780'S TO 1980'S (1990); NATIONAL WILDLIFE FEDERATION, STATUS REPORT ON OUR NATION'S WETLANDS (1987); UNITED STATES CONGRESS, OFFICE OF TECHNOLOGY ASSESSMENT, WETLANDS: THEIR USE AND REGULATION (1984). For a discussion of problems associated with inventorying

the nation's remaining wetlands, *see* General Accounting Office, Letter Report No. GAO/RCED-98-150, *Wetlands Overview—Problems With Acreage Data Persist* (1998), *available at* http://www.gao.gov/archive/1998/rc98150.pdf.

9. Status and Trends of Wetlands in the Conterminous United States 1986 to 1997, *supra* note 6, at 9.

10. *See* Fact Sheet: President Announces Wetlands Initiative on Earth Day, *supra* note 4.

11. *See* Ann Vileisis, *supra* note 6, at 33–37.

12. 177 U.S. 621 (1900).

13. *Id.* at 636.

14. Act of Sept. 28, 1850, ch. 84, 9 Stat. 519–520 (1850); *see also* Act of March 2, 1849, ch. 87, 9 Stat. 352 (1849); Act of March 12, 1860, ch. 5, 12 Stat. 3 (1860); Act of Feb. 19, 1874, ch. 30, 18 Stat. 16 (1874).

15. *Leovy*, 177 U.S. at 623.

16. Ann Vileisis, *supra* note 6, at 90–91.

17. White House Office on Environmental Quality, *Protecting America's Wetlands: A Fair, Flexible, and Effective Approach* (Aug. 24, 1993) (hereinafter *Fair, Flexible, and Effective Approach*), *available at* http://www.wetlands.com/fed/aug93wet.htm.

18. Ann Vileisis, *supra* note 6, at 201.

19. Act of July 3, 1918, ch. 128, 40 Stat. 755.

20. Act of Feb. 18, 1929, ch. 257, 45 Stat. 1222.

21. Act of Mar. 16, 1934, ch. 71, § 9, 48 Stat. 452.

22. *See* Michael J. Bean & Melanie J. Rowland, The Evolution of National Wildlife Law 284–85 (3d ed. 1997). The federal government's acquisition authority has given rise to some bitter disputes between the federal government and a few states. *See, e.g.,* North Dakota v. United States, 460 U.S. 300 (1983).

23. 33 U.S.C. § 1251 *et seq.*

24. Samuel P. Shaw & C. Gordon Fredine, *Wetlands of the United States: Their Extent and Their Value to Waterfowl and Other Wildlife,* Fish and Wildlife Service Circular 39 (1956), *available at* http://www.npwrc.usgs.gov/resource/1998/uswetlan/uswetlan.htm.

25. Ann Vileisis, *supra* note 6, at 209.

26. Shaw & Fredine, *supra* note 24, at 9.

27. Rivers and Harbors Act of 1899, ch. 425, 30 Stat. 1121 (1899) (codified as amended at 33 U.S.C. §§ 401–418).

28. 33 U.S.C. § 403.

29. 33 U.S.C. § 407.

30. *See, e.g.,* United States v. Republic Steel Corp., 362 U.S. 482 (1960) (RHA prohibits dumping of waste that could affect navigability of waters); United States v. Standard Oil Co., 384 U.S. 224 (1966) (RHA prohibits accidental discharges of commercially valuable petroleum products); Wyandotte Transp. Co. v. United States, 389 U.S. 191 (1967) (U.S. may recover costs of removing a negligently sunken vessel). *See generally* William H. Rodgers, Jr., Environmental

LAW 387–92 (1977); Sam Kalen, *Commerce to Conservation: The Call for a National Water Policy and the Evolution of Federal Jurisdiction Over Wetlands*, 69 N. DAK. L. REV. 873, 880–82 (1989) (discussing interpretations of the RHA).

31. *See* Zabel v. Tabb, 430 F.2d 199 (5th Cir. 1970).

32. 16 U.S.C. §§ 661–666c. The legislative history of the amendments shows that Congress contemplated a changed role for the Corps. Addressing what it described as "deficiencies" in then-current Corps policies, the Senate Report on the legislation stated:

> The amendments would provide that wildlife conservation shall receive equal consideration with other features in the planning of Federal water resource development programs. This would have the effect of putting fish and wildlife on the basis of equality with flood control, irrigation, navigation, and hydroelectric power in our water resource programs, which is highly desirable and proper, and represents an objective long sought by conservationists of the Nation.

S. REP. No. 1981, 85th Cong. 2d Sess. (July 28, 1958), *reprinted in* 958 U.S.C.C. A.N. pp. 3446, 3450 (1958).

33. Memorandum of Understanding between the Secretary of the Interior and the Secretary of the Army (July 13, 1967), *reprinted in* 33 Fed. Reg. 18,672–73 (Dec. 18, 1968).

34. 33 Fed. Reg. at 18,672.

35. 42 U.S.C. § 4321 *et seq.*

36. 430 F.2d 199 (5th Cir. 1970).

37. *Id.* at 214.

38. *Id.* at 211.

39. *See* Borax Consol., Ltd. v. Los Angeles, 296 U.S. 10 (1935).

40. *Kalur v. Resor*, 335 F. Supp. 1 (D.D.C. 1971). The *Kalur* court interpreted the Corps's authority to issue permits under the RHA as limited to navigable waters; nonnavigable tributaries of navigable waters, the court concluded, were beyond the reach of the Corps's permitting authority. *Id.* at 11. The Corps responded to the decision by adopting regulations that narrowly construed its jurisdiction under the RHA. 37 Fed. Reg. 18,289, 18,290 (1972). For general discussion of the failed permit program, see Kalen, *supra* note 30, at 884–86.

41. *United States v. Holland*, 373 F. Supp. 665, 670 (M.D. Fla. 1974).

42. *See* Hope Babcock, *Federal Wetlands Regulatory Policy: Up to Its Ears in Alligators*, 8 PACE ENVTL. L. REV. 307, 308 (1991), Alyson C. Flournoy, *Section 404 at Thirty-Something: A Program in Search of a Policy*, 55 ALA. L. REV. 607, 612–13 (2004).

43. *Fair, Flexible, and Effective Approach*, *supra* note 17.

44. *Id.* at section IV.

45. *Id.* at section V.

46. U.S. ENVIRONMENTAL PROTECTION AGENCY, FOUR YEARS OF PROGRESS: MEETING OUR COMMITMENT FOR WETLANDS REFORM (1997).

47. S. Hrg. 106-911, EPA's Clean Air Budget and the Corps of Engineers' Wetlands Budget: Hearing before the Subcommittee on Clean Air, Wetlands, Pri-

vate Property and Nuclear Safety, Committee on Environment and Public Works, 106th Cong. (2000) (statement of Michael L. Davis, Deputy Assistant Secretary of the Army (Civil Works), U.S. Army Corps of Engineers).

48. Pub. L. No. 106-377, 114 Stat. 1441, 1441A63 (2001).

49. U.S. Army Corps of Engineers, U.S. Army Corps of Engineers Regulatory Program—All Permit Decisions FY 2003, available through the "News and Information: Regulatory Statistics" link at http://www.usace.army.mil/inet/functions/cw/cecwo/reg/index.htm.

50. The Corps has put together a Regulatory Program Overview on its Web site, *at* http://www.usace.army.mil/inet/functions/cw/cecwo/reg/oceover.htm.

51. 33 U.S.C. § 1344.

52. One scholar recently summarized the tensions related to Section 404 regulation as follows: "These tensions can be traced in large measure to four structural flaws in section 404's design: the lack of a clear goal, the conflicts inherent in the Corps-EPA-section 404 relationship, reliance on a water statute to protect wetlands, and the regulation of activities in wetlands under a pollution control approach." Flournoy, *supra* n. 42, at 608. *See also* Michael C. Blumm, *The Clean Water Act's Section 404 Permit Program Enters Its Adolescence: An Institutional and Programmatic Perspective*, 8 Ecology L.Q. 409 (1980); Michael C. Blumm & D. Bernard Zaleha, *Federal Wetlands Protection under the Clean Water Act: Regulatory Ambivalence, Intergovernmental Tension, and a Call for Reform*, 60 U. Colo. L. Rev. 695 (1989); Oliver A. Houck, *Hard Choices: The Analysis of Alternatives under Section 404 of the Clean Water Act and Similar Environmental Laws*, 60 U. Colo. L. Rev. 773 (1989); and Robin Kundis Craig, *Beyond SWANCC: The New Federalism And Clean Water Act Jurisdiction*, 33 Envt. L. 113 (2003).

53. 33 U.S.C. § 1344(a)–(b), (e). The Web site for the Corps regulatory program in its headquarters office can be found at http://www.usace.army.mil/inet/functions/cw/cecwo/reg/.

54. 33 U.S.C. § 1344(s).

55. *See* http://www.usace.army.mil/inet/functions/cw/cecwo/reg/district.htm.

56. Elevations are pursuant to 33 U.S.C. § 1344(q). For an example of a Memorandum of Agreement implementing this subsection, see *Clean Water Act Section 404(q) Memorandum of Agreement between the Environmental Protection Agency and the Department of the Army* (Aug. 11, 1992), *available at* http://www.usace.army.mil/inet/functions/cw/cecwo/reg/epa404q.htm.

57. 33 C.F.R. pt. 331. See Chapter 11 for an overview of the administrative appeal process.

58. 33 C.F.R. pts 320–331, *available at* http://www.usace.army.mil/inet/functions/cw/cecwo/reg/sadmin3.htm.

59. *See* http://www.usace.army.mil/inet/functions/cw/cecwo/reg/rglsindx.htm.

60. For an example of such a "memorandum to the field" *see Memorandum to the Field: Application of Best Management Practices to Mechanical Silvicultural Site*

Preparation Activities for the Establishment of Pine Plantations in the Southeast (1995), *available at* http://www.usace.army.mil/inet/functions/cw/cecwo/reg/silvicul.htm.

61. 33 U.S.C. § 1344(e).

62. *See* 33 C.F.R. pt. 330, and Nationwide Permit Information at http://www.usace.army.mil/inet/functions/cw/cecwo/reg/nationwide_permits.htm. See Chapter 5 for a detailed overview of the nationwide permit process.

63. 33 U.S.C. § 1344(b).

64. 40 C.F.R. pt. 230, *available at* http://www.usace.army.mil/inet/functions/cw/cecwo/reg/40cfr230.htm. See Chapter 7 for a detailed overview of the Section 404(b)(1) Guidelines.

65. 33 U.S.C. § 1344(c). See Chapter 9 for a detailed overview of the EPA veto process.

66. *See* 33 U.S.C. § 1319. *See also* Memorandum between the Department of the Army and the Environmental Protection Agency, *Federal Enforcement for the Section 404 Program of the Clean Water Act* (1989), *available at* http://www.epa.gov/OWOW/wetlands/guidance/.

67. Provision for and criteria governing state assumption of permitting authority are found in Section 404(g) of the Clean Water Act, 33 U.S.C. § 1344(g).

68. *See* Memorandum of Agreement concerning the Determination of the Geographic Jurisdiction of the Section 404 Program, *reprinted in* 58 Fed. Reg. 4995 (Jan.19, 1993); Memorandum of Agreement between the Environmental Protection Agency and the Department of the Army concerning the Determination of Mitigation under the Clean Water Act Section 404(b)(1) Guidelines, *reprinted in* 55 Fed. Reg. 9210 (Mar. 12, 1990); Clean Water Section 404(q) Memorandum of Agreement between the Environmental Protection Agency and the Department of the Army, *available at* http://www.epa.gov/OWOW/wetlands/regs/dispmoa.html; Memorandum of Agreement between the Department of the Army and the Environmental Protection Agency concerning Federal Enforcement for the Section 404 Program of the Clean Water Act, *available at* http://www.epa.gov/OWOW/wetlands/regs/enfmoa.html; 1986 Memorandum of Agreement between the Assistant Administrator for External Affairs and Water, U.S. Environmental Protection Agency, and the Assistant Secretary of the Army for Civil Works concerning Regulation of Discharges of Solid Waste under the Clean Water Act, *available at* http://www.epa.gov/OWOW/wetlands/guidance/solwaste.html.

Additionally, the Corps and EPA have jointly issued field guidance concerning the Section 404 program. *See* Memorandum: Individual Permit Flexibility for Small Landowners, *available at* http://www.epa.gov/OWOW/wetlands/guidance/landowne.html; Memorandum: Appropriate Level of Analysis Required for Evaluating Compliance with the Section 404(b)(1) Guidelines Alternatives Requirements, *available at* http://www.usace.army.mil/inet/functions/cw/cecwo/reg/flexible.htm.

69. 33 C.F.R. § 328.3(b) (Corps); 40 C.F.R. § 230.3(t) (EPA).

70. U.S. Army Corps of Engineers, *Wetlands Delineation Manual* (1987), *available at* http://www.saj.usace.army.mil/permit/documents/87manual.pdf.

71. 33 U.S.C. § 1344(a).

72. 33 U.S.C. § 1362(7).

73. *See, e.g.,* Natural Resources Defense Council, Inc. v. Callaway, 392 F. Supp. 685 (D.C. Cir. 1975), United States v. Riverside Bayview Homes, 474 U.S. 121 (1985).

74. 531 U.S. 159 (2001).

75. *See* National Wildlife Federation, *Summary of Post-SWANCC Court Decisions* (Oct. 2004), *available at* http://www.nwf.org/ourprograms/ by clicking to "Wetlands Conservation."

76. United States General Accounting Office, *Waters and Wetlands—Corps of Engineers Needs to Evaluate Its District Office Practices in Determining Jurisdiction* (GAO-04-297, Feb. 2004), *available at* http://www.gao.gov/new.items/d04297.pdf.

77. Advance Notice of Proposed Rulemaking on the Clean Water Act Regulatory Definition of "Waters of the United States," 68 Fed. Reg. 1991 (Jan. 15, 2003).

78. Corps and EPA, News Release: EPA and Army Corps Issue Wetlands Decision (Dec. 16, 2003), *available at* http://www.usace.army.mil/inet/functions/cw/cecwo/reg/swancc_release.htm.

79. 33 U.S.C. § 1344(f).

80. 33 U.S.C. § 1344(f)(1)(A).

81. 33 C.F.R. § 323.4.

82. 33 U.S.C. § 1344(f)(1)(B)–(E).

83. 33 U.S.C. § 1344(f)(2).

84. 33 U.S.C. § 1311(a).

85. 33 U.S.C. § 1362(12).

86. 33 U.S.C. § 1362(6).

87. 58 Fed. Reg. 45,008 (Aug. 25, 1993); 33 C.F.R. § 323.2(d) (1994).

88. 145 F.3d 1399 (D.C. Cir. 1998).

89. *National Mining,* 145 F.3d at 1405. The district court decision, which the D.C. Circuit affirmed, also relied on the statutory term "specified disposal sites" to conclude that to constitute the "discharge of dredged or fill material," the pollutants in question must originate from a site that is distinct from the site into which they are ultimately placed. American Mining Congress v. United States Army Corps of Eng'rs, 951 F. Supp. 267, 272–78 (D.D.C. 1997), *aff'd sub nom. National Mining, supra.* This aspect of the district court's decision is discussed *infra.*

90. *See, e.g.,* Borden Ranch Partnership v. U.S. Army Corps of Engineers, 537 U.S. 99 (2002); United States v. Deaton, 209 F.3d 331 (4th Cir. 2000); 66 Fed. Reg. 4550 (Jan. 17, 2001).

91. 33 C.F.R. § 323.2(c).

92. 33 C.F.R. § 232.2(e)(1).

93. 33 C.F.R. § 232.2(e)(2).

94. Statutory exemptions are found at 33 U.S.C. § 1344(f). Regulations implementing these exemptions and promulgated by the Corps and EPA may be found, respectively, at 33 C.F.R. § 323.4 and 40 C.F.R. § 232.3.

95. U.S. Army Corps of Engineers, U.S. Army Corps of Engineers Regulatory Program—All Permit Decisions FY 2003, available through the "News and

Information; Regulatory Statistics" link at http://www.usace.army.mil/inet/functions/cw/cecwo/reg/index.htm.

96. 33 U.S.C. § 1344(e).

97. U.S. Army Corps of Engineers, U.S. Army Corps of Engineers Regulatory Program—All Permit Decisions FY 2003, available through the "News and Information; Regulatory Statistics" link at http://www.usace.army.mil/inet/functions/cw/cecwo/reg/index.htm.

98. 33 U.S.C. § 1344(e).

99. *See generally* Corps, Nationwide Permit Information, *at* http://www.usace.army.mil/inet/functions/cw/cecwo/reg/nationwide_permits.htm.

100. 61 Fed. Reg. 2020, 2092 (Jan. 15, 2002).

101. *Id.*

102. 33 C.F.R. § 325.2(e)(1).

103. 40 C.F.R. pt. 230. The Corps requires full compliance with these guidelines before a permit can be issued. 33 C.F.R. § 323.6(a) ("a permit will be denied if the discharge authorized by such a permit would not comply with the 404(b)(1) guidelines").

104. 40 C.F.R. § 230.10(a).

105. 40 C.F.R. § 230.10(b).

106. 40 C.F.R. § 230.10(c).

107. 40 C.F.R. § 230.10(d).

108. *See* Memorandum of Agreement between the Environmental Protection Agency and the Department of the Army concerning the Determination of Mitigation under the Clean Water Act Section 404(b)(1) Guidelines (Feb. 6, 1990), *available at* http://www.usace.army.mil/inet/functions/cw/cecwo/reg/moafe90.htm.

109. *See generally* Regulatory Guidance Letter 02-2, Guidance on Compensatory Mitigation Projects for Aquatic Resource Impacts under the Corps Regulatory Program Pursuant to Section 404 of the Clean Water Act and Section 10 of the Rivers and Harbors Act of 1899, Dec. 2002, *available at* http://www.usace.army.mil/inet/functions/cw/cecwo/reg/RGL2-02.pdf; Federal Guidance for the Establishment, Use and Operation of Mitigation Banks, 60 Fed. Reg. 58,605 (Nov. 28, 1995), *available at* http://www.usace.army.mil/inet/functions/cw/cecwo/reg/mitbankn.htm. Federal Guidance on the Use of In-Lieu-Fee Arrangements for Compensatory Mitigation under Section 404 of the Clean Water Act and Section 10 of the Rivers and Harbors Act, 2000, *available at* http://www.epa.gov/OWOW/wetlands/pdf/inlieufee.pdf.

110. *See* National Wetlands Mitigation Action Plan, *at* http://www.mitigationactionplan.gov/ ("In response to independent critiques of the effectiveness of wetland compensatory mitigation for authorized losses of wetlands and other waters under Section 404 of the Clean Water Act, the Environmental Protection Agency, the Army Corps of Engineers, and the Departments of Agriculture, Commerce, Interior, and Transportation released the National Wetlands Mitigation Action Plan on December 26, 2002.").

111. *Id.*

112. *See* 33 C.F.R. § 320.4(a).

113. 33 C.F.R. § 320.4(b)(1).

114. 33 C.F.R. § 320.4(a)(1).

115. In every case, the Corps also considers (1) the relative extent of the public and private need for the proposed activity; (2) the practicability of using reasonable alternative locations and methods to achieve the objective of the proposed activity (if there are unresolved conflicts regarding resource use); and (3) the extent and permanence of the beneficial and/or detrimental effect that the activity is likely to have on the public and private uses to which the area is suited. *Id.* § 320.4(a)(2).

116. 33 C.F.R. § 320.4(a)(1).

117. 16 U.S.C. § 1531 *et seq.*

118. 42 U.S.C. § 4321 *et seq.*

119. 16 U.S.C. § 470.

120. *See generally* 33 C.F.R. § 320.3.

121. 33 U.S.C. § 1341. *See* 33 C.F.R. § 320.4 (d).

122. 16 U.S.C. § 1451–1464.

123. *See supra* notes 103–107 and accompanying text.

124. 33 U.S.C. § 1344(q). *See* Clean Water Act Section 404(q) Memorandum of Agreement between the Environmental Protection Agency and the Department of the Army, *available at* http://www.usace.army.mil/inet/functions/cw/cecwo/reg/epa404q.htm.

125. 33 U.S.C. § 1344(c), 40 C.F.R. pt. 231.

126. 33 U.S.C. § 1344(c).

127. 33 C.F.R. § 320.4(j)(1).

128. The regulations define "appealable action" as "an approved [jurisdictional determination], a permit denial, or a declined permit." 33 C.F.R. § 331.1.

129. 33 C.F.R. pt. 331, *available at* http://www.usace.army.mil/inet/functions/cw/cecwo/reg/33cfr331.htm.

130. 33 C.F.R. §§ 331.10. That regulation states that "[t]he final Corps decision on a permit application is the initial decision to issue or deny a permit, unless the applicant submits an RFA, and the division engineer accepts the RFA, pursuant to this Part." *Id.* If an action is appealed, the final Corps decision depends on the merit of the appeal: "(a) If the division engineer determines that the appeal is without merit, the final Corps decision is the district engineer's letter advising the applicant that the division engineer has decided that the appeal is without merit, confirming the district engineer's initial decision, and sending the permit denial or the proffered permit for signature to the appellant; or (b) If the division engineer determines that the appeal has merit, the final Corps decision is the district engineer's decision made pursuant to the division engineer's remand of the appealed action. These regulations provide that the Corps's initial decision to issue or deny a permit is the final decision on a permit application. For an appealed action, where the division engineer determines that the appeal has merit, the final Corps permit decision is the district engineer's decision pursuant to the division engineer's remand." *Id. See* Ozark Soc'y v. Melcher, 229 F. Supp. 2d 896 (E.D. Ark. 2002); Bay-Houston Towing Co. v. United States, 58 Fed. Cl. 462, 471 (2003).

131. 33 C.F.R. § 331.10.

132. WILLIAM L. WANT, THE LAW OF WETLANDS REGULATION §§ 9.3–9.8 (2004).

133. 28 U.S.C. § 2401.

134. 5 U.S.C. § 706(2). *See* Avoyelles Sportsmen's League v. Marsh, 715 F.2d 897, 904 (5th Cir. 1983).

135. U.S. CONST. amend. V: "[N]or shall private property be taken for public use, without just compensation."

136. *Loveladies Harbor,* 21 Cl. Ct. 153 (1990); *Florida Rock,* 21 Cl. Ct. 161 (1990), *See, e.g.,* Forest Properties, Inc. v. United States, 177 F.3d 1360 (Fed. Cir.), *cert. denied,* 528 U.S. 951 (1999); Heck v. United States, 134 F.3d 1468 (Fed. Cir. 1998); Bayou des Familles v. United States, 130 F.3d 1034 (Fed. Cir. 1997); City National Bank v. United States, 33 Fed. Cl. 759 (1995).

137. 33 U.S.C. § 1319. *See also* Memorandum of Agreement between the Department of the Army and the Environmental Protection Agency concerning Federal Enforcement for the Section 404 Program of the Clean Water Act (Jan. 19, 1989), *available at* http://www.usace.army.mil/inet/functions/cw/cecwo/reg/enfmoa.htm.

138. 33 U.S.C. § 1344(s).

139. 33 U.S.C. § 1319(c).

140. 33 U.S.C. § 1319(a) (EPA); 33 U.S.C. § 1344(s)(1) (Corps).

141. 33 U.S.C. § 1319(g).

142. 33 U.S.C. § 1319(b), (d) (EPA); 33 U.S.C. § 1344(s)(3)–(4) (Corps).

143. 33 U.S.C. § 1319(c).

144. 33 U.S.C. § 1365.

145. 33 U.S.C. § 1365(a)(1).

146. 33 U.S.C. § 1365(a)(2).

CHAPTER 2

A Primer on Wetland Ecology

DENNIS W. MAGEE

I. *Introduction/Scope*

This chapter provides an introduction to wetland ecology for nonscientists.[1] It covers three main topics. Section II discusses wetland definitions and the criteria used in such definitions. It also explains the characteristics and classifications of wetlands. Section III focuses on wetland functions, particularly those that yield positive public values. Differences among the classes of wetlands relative to their performance of such functions are also discussed. Section IV describes various methods used to assess wetland functions, with particular attention to the hydrogeomorphic method (HGM), which has received nationwide attention and will contribute to the future of wetland functional assessment. The chapter concludes with a discussion of the status and applications of wetland functional assessment.

II. *Wetland Definitions and Classifications*

In order to understand wetland ecology, one must understand how a wetland is defined, the landscape settings in which wetlands occur, how wetlands are classified using hydrogeomorphic methods, and how to distinguish between various common wetlands. This section will answer these questions.

A. What Is a Wetland?

A wetland is an area in which the characteristics of the soil, vegetation, and wildlife are primarily controlled by water. Although broad definitions of wetlands are based on the presence of water and/or wetland plants, specific definitions have been developed by different agencies depending on their role in the regulation of wetland resources. For purposes of conducting a nationwide inventory of these areas,[2] the U.S. Fish and Wildlife Service (FWS) defines wetlands as transitional lands that occur between upland and aquatic environments, where the water table is usually at or near the surface, or the land is covered by shallow water.[3] For purposes of the Clean Water Act's Section 404 program, the United States Army Corps of Engineers (Corps) and the U.S. Environmental Protection Agency (EPA) define wetlands as areas inundated or saturated by surface or groundwater at a frequency and duration sufficient to support, and that under normal circumstances do support, a prevalence of vegetation typically adapted for living under saturated soil conditions.[4] A detailed set of hydrologic, soils, and vegetation criteria has been developed to identify and determine the limits of jurisdictional wetlands (those under the purview of the Section 404 Program).

In addition to the definitions developed by federal agencies, many states and local communities have developed separate definitions based on hydrology, soils, vegetation, and various combinations thereof.[5] In recent years, there has been a tendency for many states to bring their definitions into consistency with the federal definition to simplify the regulatory process.[6] Many states also recognize other habitats as wetland resource areas, including, for example, such areas as deep or flowing water (rivers, streams, lakes, ponds), land under water, and vernal pools.[7] These habitats are not discussed in this chapter because they are primarily upland or aquatic environments rather than transitional in nature, with saturated soil or shallow water.

For purposes of this chapter, a wetland is an area that is saturated or inundated at a frequency and duration sufficient to give rise to soils with characteristics distinctly different from those of upland soils (hydric soils) and/or a predominance of wetland plants that are adapted to living in saturated soil or shallow water (hydrophytes).

B. The Major Landscape Settings in Which Wetlands Occur

Wetlands occur in a variety of landscape settings, such as on hillsides, in valleys, and adjacent to lakes and rivers. The location of a wetland within the surrounding landscape is known as its geomorphic setting.

Water in a wetland derives from three major sources: precipitation, flow at or near the land surface, and discharge of groundwater at or near the land surface. The water's source, flow rate, and duration in the wetland combine to form the wetland's hydrology. Geomorphic setting and hydrology are very closely linked, since a wetland's location in the landscape determines water source and flow.

Together, geomorphic setting and hydrology form the basis of a system for classifying wetlands that is currently being applied throughout the country. The system is known as the hydrogeomorphic classification, or HGM. Seven basic HGM classes of wetlands have been distinguished on the basis of surface water flow direction. These are (1) depressional wetlands, (2) slope wetlands, (3) flats, (4) lacustrine-fringe (lake edge) wetlands, (5) riverine (river edge) wetlands, (6) extensive peatlands, and (7) coastal-fringe wetlands.

1. Depressional Wetlands

Depressional wetlands occur in low-lying areas completely surrounded by higher ground. These low-lying areas are known as topographic depressions. Depressional wetlands occur in many shapes, but are often somewhat round. Surface water flows from all directions toward the depression's lowest point.

Water sources for depressional wetlands include surface water runoff, precipitation, groundwater, or any combination of these. Wetlands may vary in wetness from temporarily saturated below the soil surface to permanently flooded. Many depressional wetlands have one or more surface-water inlets and/or outlets, either perennial (year-round flow) or ephemeral (dry part of the year) (see Figure 2-1).

FIGURE 2-1. Depressional Wetland

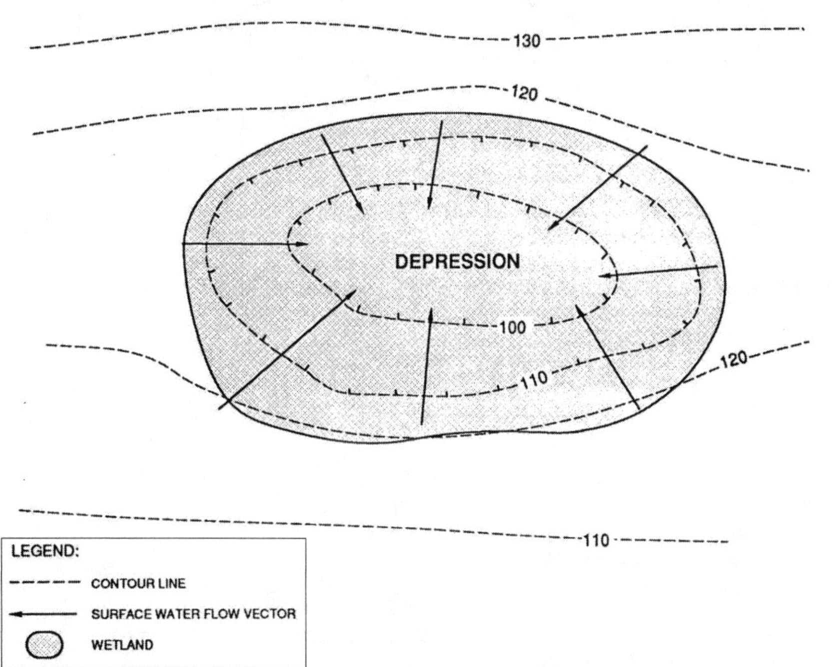

2. *Slope Wetlands*

Slope wetlands occur on hillsides with gradients ranging from very slight to steep. They may be narrow or wide, long or short. Surface water flow in slope wetlands is predominantly unidirectional, parallel to the slope and flowing in many small discontinuous channels or through the upper soil layers. Water sources for slope wetlands are predominantly groundwater and occasionally precipitation. Water that enters slope wetlands quickly flows downgradient through and out of the wetland (see Figure 2-2).

FIGURE 2-2. Slope Wetland

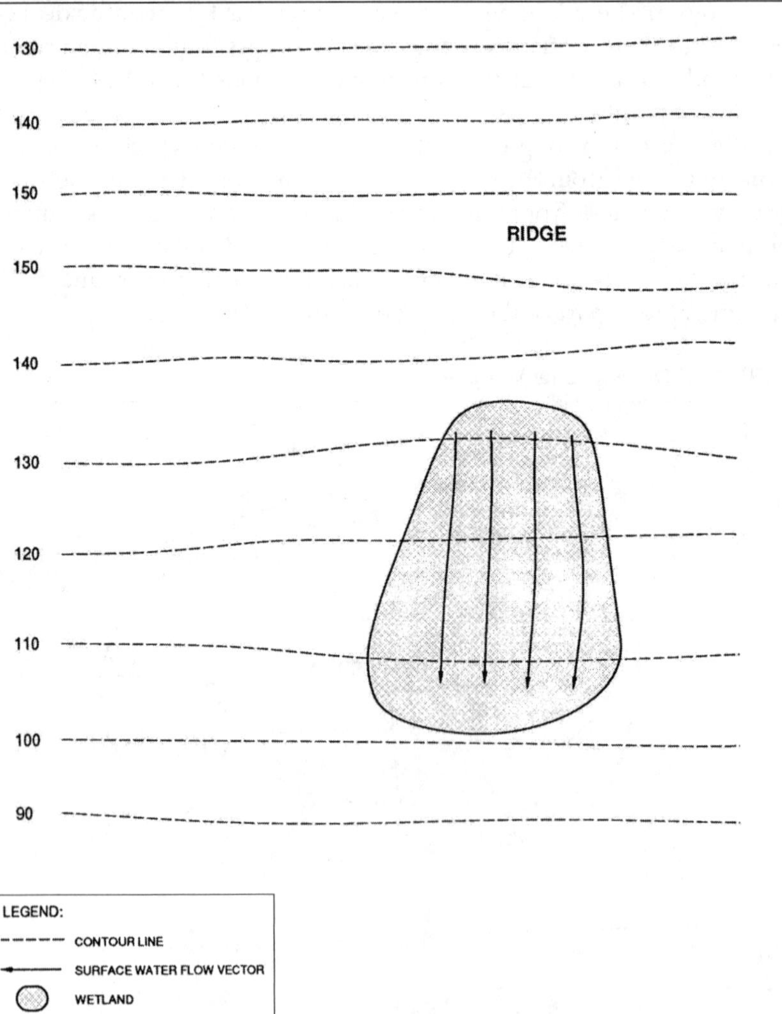

3. Flats

Flats are similar to slope wetlands, but have very slight slopes (generally less than 1 percent gradient) that are not evident to the casual observer. Flats cover extensive areas, typically occurring between two large river systems. Surface water flow is predominantly unidirectional, similar to slope wetlands. The predominant source of water for flats is precipitation. Flats occur because their very slight slope prevents water outflow from exceeding inflow. Accordingly, water moves so slowly out of such wetlands that inflowing water becomes ponded. Flats may accumulate organic sediments, which increase water storage, further reducing surface water flow-through rates. Examples of flats include central Wisconsin sand plains and the extensive pine flatwoods of the southeast.

4. Lacustrine-Fringe Wetlands

Lacustrine-fringe wetlands occur adjacent to lakes in two topographic settings: depressions and valleys. They are essentially the lake's flood plain. Water flow in lacustrine-fringe wetlands is to and from the lake and up and down as a result of lake-level fluctuation. Such water flows originate from either surface or groundwater, or both. When the water level recedes, water flows from the fringing wetland back into the lake (see Figure 2-3).

FIGURE 2-3. Lacustrine-Fringe Wetland

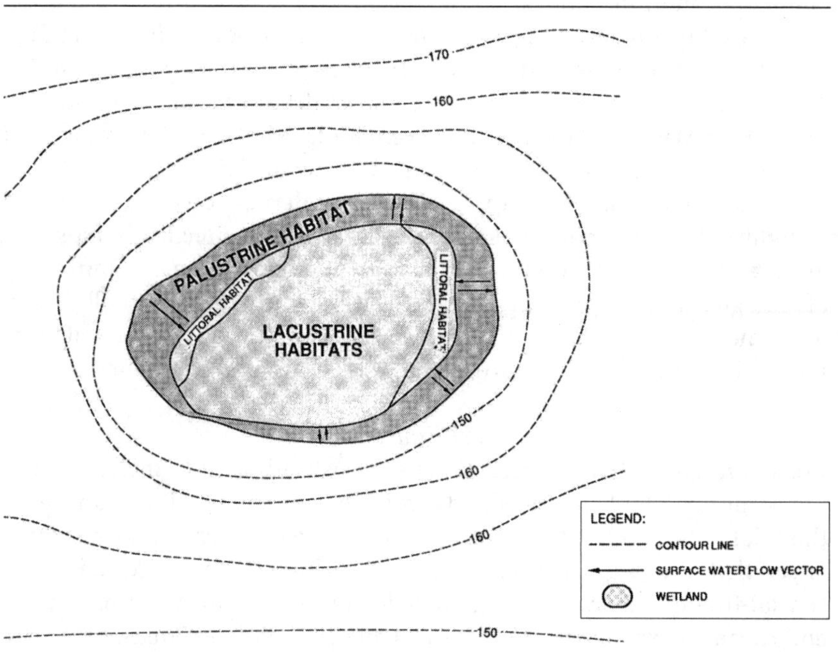

5. Riverine Wetlands

Riverine wetlands occur in valleys and in broad, flat areas where no large-scale topographic land form is evident. Such wetlands border stream channels that have floodplains. The adjacent channel may range from a very small stream with seasonal flow to a very large river channel. The predominant source of water for riverine wetlands is overbank flooding, with lesser amounts coming from groundwater flooding and overland flow from the valley sides. As flood waters recede, water drains from the riverine wetland back to the stream channel. The flooded area may be wetland or upland depending upon the frequency, duration, and predictability of flooding.

In headwater areas (locations where streams originate),[8] small streams may have little or no floodplain because the channel itself can contain most flood events. In such situations, narrow streamside wetlands may occur above the channel's banks, but these wetlands are placed in another class (commonly slope wetlands). Within such headwater channels' banks, wetland vegetation may occur in quiet-water areas. To be considered riverine wetlands, however, water sources for a wetland must be predominantly overbank flooding.

6. Extensive Peatlands

Extensive peatlands include blanket bogs, which cover large areas of landscape, and raised bogs.

Blanket bogs contain large accumulations of sphagnum moss that flow over the landscape regardless of topography and occupy large areas. They occur only in arctic and subarctic climates, including the cold, wet climates of Alaska, northern Maine, Minnesota, Michigan, Wisconsin, and southern Canada where sphagnum moss flourishes (see Figure 2-2).

Raised bogs, the topographic opposite of depressions, are located on a slight hill. Raised bogs generally began as depressional wetlands that gradually became filled with peat from the decay of large accumulations of sphagnum moss, growing upward and outward and eventually creating a mound. The primary water source for raised bogs is precipitation, where the water flows radially from the top of the hill or mound.

7. Coastal-Fringe Wetlands

Coastal-fringe wetlands occur along seacoasts adjacent to the sea. Water flows into coastal-fringe wetlands from the sea, rising and falling with the tidal cycles. Tidal salt marshes and tidal freshwater marshes include areas that are regularly inundated. The higher landward edges of coastal-fringe wetlands are inundated only during monthly high tides and during storm events. In these irregularly inundated areas, precipitation becomes more important as a water source.[9]

C. How to Distinguish HGM Wetland Classes

As discussed below in Section III, wetlands perform various functions. Because each of the seven HGM classes discussed in the previous subsection performs these various wetland functions to varying degrees, the HGM class of a wetland must be determined prior to assessing its functions. A particular wetland is placed into a particular HGM class based on the interpretation of topographic maps and determination of surface-water flow directions. Because surface water flows perpendicular to contour lines, flow directions can be predicted by the contour lines. In the field, both the visualization of contour lines and the recognition of physical evidence of surface water flow allow determination of flow direction(s).

Five basic landforms used in reading topographic maps form the basis for distinguishing inland HGM classes in the field. These are (1) hilltop, (2) depression, (3) valley, (4) ridge, and (5) saddle. These landforms are defined in any major dictionary; more thorough descriptions may be found in a basic textbook treating topographic map reading. The basic landforms are easily recognized on most topographic maps and in the field. Accordingly, when assessing HGM classes, it is generally recognized that depressional wetlands occur predominantly in depressions and occasionally in valleys; slope wetlands occur on hillsides; flats occur on very gentle regional slopes; lacustrine-fringe wetlands occur adjacent to lakes in depressions or valleys; riverine wetlands occur in valleys; and extensive peatlands occur on gentle regional slopes or as hilltops.

D. Some Common Kinds of Wetlands

There are several common kinds of wetlands that are found in the landscape settings or HGM classes described above. These wetland types are known to most people by the terms (1) marsh, (2) wet meadow, (3) swamp, (4) vernal pool, (5) floodplain forest, (6) bog, and (7) coastal wetland, often with regional modifiers such as fen, pocosin, and Carolina Bay (a depressional wetland in the Carolinas). Each of these types is discussed in turn below.

To eliminate some of the ambiguities caused by regional or local names, the FWS has developed a precise, hierarchical nationwide classification system (known also as the Cowardin system) for classifying wetlands and deep-water habitats on the basis of such criteria as vegetation structure, flooding characteristics, soils, and water chemistry.[10] To introduce the reader to some of the terminology used in the Cowardin system, the Cowardin equivalent will be given together with the familiar term in the discussion of each wetland type.

1. *Marshes*

Marshes may occur in water that is six to twelve inches deep (shallow marsh) or in water two to four feet deep (deep marsh). The equivalent designations in the Cowardin system are Palustrine Emergent wetland and Aquatic Bed, respectively.

Shallow marshes are characterized by a predominance of herbaceous emergent species (nonwoody plants growing partly in and partly out of water) such as cattail and arrowhead. In deep marshes, the predominant species are floating-leaved and submerged plants, such as water lily and pondweed. Marshes may occur in depressions, such as prairie potholes; in lacustrine-fringe and riverine settings in shallow water; or sometimes on slopes. Water levels may fluctuate widely throughout the year, from permanent inundation to seasonal inundation to seasonal drought. A fen is a type of emergent wetland characterized by saturated conditions and distinctive vegetation patterns. Some marshes, such as those in the prairie pothole region of the country, are very important waterfowl production habitats. Others, such as the Florida Everglades, are important for education and research and as habitat for rare plants and animals.

2. *Wet Meadows*

Wet meadows are similar to shallow marshes but lack surface water throughout much of the year. The Cowardin system does not distinguish between shallow marsh and wet meadow, terming both Palustrine Emergent wetland. Water levels in wet meadows may be as high as six inches for a brief period during spring, but the wetland may be saturated only at or just below the soil surface for the rest of the year. Wet meadows often occur in shallow depressions and slight slopes in grasslands. They are distinguished by the presence of characteristic plants such as certain sedges and grasses, beak rush, and ironweed.

3. *Swamps*

Swamps contain a predominance of woody plants. If the dominant growth form is arborescent (treelike), the swamp is called a forested wetland or, in the Cowardin system, a Palustrine Forested wetland. In the northeast, forested wetlands are dominated by hardwood species such as red maple, black gum, and ash, or by evergreen species such as white cedar, hemlock, and black spruce. The undergrowth in a forested wetland dominated by hardwoods may include shrubs such as wild raisin, arrow wood, highbush blueberry, sweet pepperbush, and spicebush. Herbs such as skunk cabbage, Jack-in-the-pulpit, royal fern, and cardinal flower may also be present.

Farther south, hardwood swamp forests form in swales and floodplains. They typically contain trees such as red bay persea, red gum, and water oak. They may also be characterized by an undergrowth of various holly species, blackhaw, and greenbriar. Extensive pine flatwood forests consisting of loblolly, slash, and longleaf pine occur on poorly drained soils in headwater areas. These are flats that develop on mineral soil in the coastal plain of the southeast.

In shrub swamps, the dominant growth form is shrubby. The equivalent designation in the Cowardin system is Palustrine Scrub/Shrub wetland. Plants typically found in shrub swamps include alders, dogwoods, willows, and buttonbush. One type of shrub swamp, called pocosin, is also found on the coastal plain. This is a type of flat that develops on peat derived from sedges or decayed wood. Pocosins are characterized by various species of holly, red bay persea, and pine species tolerant of saturated soils.

Hydrologic conditions in swamps range from saturated soils to standing water up to a foot deep. Swamps may be found in depressions, on slopes, and on the edges of lakes.

4. Vernal Pools

Vernal pools are shallow depressions that contain standing water for only a portion of the year, typically in spring. There is no equivalent designation for this type of wetland in the Cowardin system. When dry, vernal pools may be recognizable in the field by such signs as water-stained leaves, water marks on trees, and fingernail clam shells and caddisfly cases in the soil. They usually occur under a forest canopy, but may also be found in more open settings like shrub swamps, wet meadows, and pastures. Vernal pools provide habitat for wildlife such as certain amphibians that depend for breeding purposes on areas of seasonally present water absent fish (which eat the eggs and larvae). Vernal pools often provide habitat for unique assemblages of amphibian species and invertebrates such as fairy shrimp. They are considered significant habitats by many states and are sometimes accorded special protection.

5. Floodplain Forests

Floodplain forests, known also as bottomlands, develop on the floodplains of rivers and some larger streams. In the northern part of the country, trees such as cottonwood, silver maple, box elder, black willow, and some varieties of ash are typical components of the floodplain forest. In the extensive bottomlands of the south, the floodplain forest consists of species such as black gum, sweetgum, overcup oak, and baldcypress. Floodplain forests are associated entirely with the riverine HGM class because they are dependent upon overbank flooding. The Cowardin designation for this kind of wetland is Palustrine Forested wetland. Some of the trees found in floodplain forests are valuable for the wood they provide.

6. Bogs

Bogs develop over peat deposits formed over many years by the decomposition of plants, predominantly sphagnum moss and sedges. The peat deposits can be as much as thirty-five to forty feet thick. Because the bog surface is not in direct contact with the mineral-rich groundwater in the underlying aquifer, the bog's only source of water is direct precipitation. This results in a very nutrient-poor environment to which certain plant species are uniquely adapted. Accordingly, bogs may contain plant communities with unusual or rare species of orchids, sundews, and pitcher plants. Shrubs commonly found in bogs include leatherleaf, bog rosemary, bog laurel, and Labrador tea. The common trees are black spruce and tamarack. Bogs predominantly develop in depressions, but they are also often found in quiet coves of lakes, developing as the peat forms a floating mat over the water surface. The corresponding designation in the Cowardin system is Palustrine Scrub/Shrub wetland. Bogs are the primary source of horticultural peat and are important habitats for scientific and nature study.

7. Coastal Wetlands

Coastal wetlands are adapted to saline instead of fresh water and to the daily, monthly, and seasonal tide cycles. Several distinct habitats occur in the zone between high tide and low tide, known also as the intertidal zone. These include flat, beach, and rocky shore. More information on these habitats can be found in books or other materials on marine or coastal ecology. Coastal wetlands can be separated into two general categories: salt marshes and estuaries. In the Cowardin system the various coastal habitats are parts of the Marine and/or Estuarine systems.[11]

SALT MARSHES. The type of wetland familiar to most people as salt marsh occurs between high and low tide. That portion of the marsh known as low marsh remains submerged for most of each tidal cycle, sometimes even for the duration of low tide, and is characterized by a predominance of salt-marsh cord grass. Landward of low marsh is high marsh, an area that is inundated only during high tide. Here, the salt-marsh plant community includes salt-meadow cord grass, spike grass, blackgrass, glasswort, and sea lavenders. The highest zone of the high marsh is inundated only during the highest monthly tide, known as the spring tide or neap tide, which corresponds to the full moon. Plants such as marsh elder, switchgrass, and sweet gale characterize this zone. Salt marshes are among the most productive habitats on earth. They produce nutrients and detritus (decomposing organic matter that ultimately breaks down into tiny particles) that serve as the base of near-shore food webs and provide nursery habitat for fish as well as habitat for many other animal species.[12] Seaward of the intertidal zone is the subtidal zone, where the bottom remains submerged. There are habitats within this zone that contain aquatic beds of seagrasses such as eelgrass and turtle-grass. These beds of seagrasses are a very important resource, providing nursery habitat for various species of fish and food for marine wildlife.

Estuaries. Estuaries consist of intertidal and subtidal habitats and are typically associated with rivers, where ocean water is diluted by fresh water. In such riverine estuaries, salinities decrease upriver, and distinct assemblages of plants and animals are associated with the different salinity zones. At the uppermost end of the estuary, salinity lessens to match that of the freshwater inflow, but bordering wetlands are still affected by the daily tidal cycles. These wetlands are termed freshwater tidal wetlands.

In situations where access to the open ocean is obstructed, wetland salinities may occasionally exceed those of ocean water because of evaporation. Extreme examples of this may be found in the western United States, where very high evaporation has created salt flats vegetated by plants that typically occur in coastal environments, such as glasswort and spike grass. Salinities in the Great Salt Lake are substantially higher than those of ocean water.

III. Why Certain Activities in Wetlands Are Regulated

For centuries, wetlands were considered wastelands to be drained and used for development or for waste disposal. By the early 1970s, the important role of wetlands in our landscape had become firmly established and a new image of these environments had emerged. It is now recognized, for example, that wetlands intercept and store water during flood events, maintain a stable flow in streams throughout the year, filter pollutants, and provide habitat for wildlife, including threatened and endangered species of plants and animals. Wetlands also provide opportunities for education, research, and recreation.[13] Because of the many societal benefits resulting directly from the functions performed by wetlands, the federal government regulates many activities that directly or indirectly have the potential to compromise the functional capacity of a wetland.[14]

A. Important Functions Performed by Wetlands

Wetland functions are the normal or characteristic actions that result from soil, vegetation, and physical, chemical, and biological processes related to a particular wetland. There is considerable confusion in the literature, as well as in the language of the wetland regulations, about the distinction between wetland functions and values. As explained above, functions are those actions performed by wetlands regardless of whether such actions are perceived as benefits to society. Values, by contrast, are assigned to wetland functions by society. For example, storm damage prevention is not a wetland function because it is not a normal or characteristic action of a wetland. Storm and floodwater storage, however, is a wetland function because it prevents storm damage downstream. Although wetlands perform a wide range of functions, the focus of state and federal wetland regulation is on functions that give rise to values considered to be in the public interest.

There are three basic categories of functions performed by wetlands, yielding a range of values important to society. These categories are

- **Hydrologic**—functions that affect the quantity of water entering, stored in, and leaving the wetland
- **Water quality**—functions that affect the quality of water entering and leaving the wetland
- **Habitat**—functions that provide food and shelter for plants and animals

Federal regulations and those of various states that pertain to the policy of "no net loss of wetland functions"[15] include lists that elaborate on and further subdivide these three basic functional categories. Some of these regulatory lists include values as well as functions.

It should be recognized that some wetland functions may contribute both public benefits and public detriments. For example, at certain times of the year, some wetlands may degrade water quality by contributing tannins (substances that turn water brown) or by increasing nutrient levels. Because, on balance, most wetlands contribute benefits to rather than detract from public values, this discussion will focus on the public-benefits aspects of wetland functions.

This section discusses functions associated with subsets of each of the above three categories (hydrologic, water quality, and habitat), along with some of the resulting values. These functions are

- Modification of groundwater discharge
- Modification of groundwater recharge

- Storage of storm and flood waters
- Modification of stream flow
- Modification of water quality
- Export of detritus
- Contribution to the abundance and diversity of wetland vegetation
- Contribution to the abundance and diversity of wetland fauna

There is some controversy as to whether groundwater discharge and recharge and wetland vegetation should be considered functions performed by wetlands or characteristics of wetlands. To provide the reader with a more complete understanding of this topic, they are treated as functions in this chapter.

1. *Modification of Groundwater Discharge*

Modification of groundwater discharge is the capacity of a wetland to locally affect the amount of water moving from groundwater to surface water. Most wetlands discharge water to the surface at least for part of the year. The soils, vegetation, and surface water in a wetland affect the quantity and rate of groundwater discharge as well as the amount of water stored in the wetland. This function is important in maintaining the physical, chemical, and ecological integrity of the wetland and, when an outlet is present, the integrity of receiving waters as well. The groundwater discharge function is important for maintenance of societal values such as groundwater supply, surface water supply, and recreation. The absence of a stream flowing into the wetland coupled with the presence of a perennial stream flowing out of the wetland is the primary type of evidence that this function is being performed.

2. *Modification of Groundwater Recharge*

Modification of groundwater recharge is the capacity of a wetland to locally affect the amount of water moving from surface water to groundwater. Most wetlands that are not in a discharge condition have the ability to recharge the groundwater. Many wetlands alternate seasonally between a recharge and a discharge condition. When a wetland is in a recharge condition, accumulated surface water passes through the wetland soil to the underlying aquifer (subsurface layers of permeable rock and gravel that store water). The physical characteristics of the wetland soil play a role in controlling the rate and quantity of recharge. The shape of the wetland basin may facilitate water storage that provides for long-term recharge. The groundwater recharge function is important to societal values such as maintaining public and private water supplies. A perennial stream flowing into the wetland with no stream flowing out of the wetland is the primary type of evidence that this function is being performed.

3. *Storm and Floodwater Storage*

Storm and floodwater storage involve a wetland's ability to contain inflowing water from storm events or flooding events, resulting in detention and retention of water on the wetland surface. Wetlands perform this function because they have lower elevations and lesser slopes than the surrounding uplands. These more gentle slopes reduce flow velocity. Additionally, wetland vegetation contributes to surface roughness, which also reduces flow. A constricted stream outlet (or no outlet at all) and the mound-and-pool surface seen in many wetlands are factors that allow increased ponding and storage. A certain amount of storage also occurs in wetlands associated with river floodplains that receive overbank flooding. As with other wetland types, the duration and volume of storage on river floodplains depends upon wetland basin shape and characteristics of the vegetation and wetland surface. The storm and floodwater storage function is important to societal values such as prevention of storm damage and loss of life and property.

4. *Modification of Stream Flow*

Modification of stream flow is the capacity of a wetland to regulate the flow of water in nearby streams in ways that reduce the extremes of high flows during spring and low flows during summer. When this function is performed, stream flow is more regular and predictable throughout the year. This function occurs because water entering the wetland is modified by the wetland's characteristics and processes. Groundwater discharging up into the wetland is modified by the wetland soils, and surface water flow into the wetland is modified by factors such as wetland gradient, surface irregularity, vegetation, and outlet constriction. In essence, the wetland acts as a sponge, storing water received in high volumes and velocities during storm events, and releasing it slowly and evenly to downstream receiving waters over time. The modification of streamflow function may contribute to societal values such as public water supply, flood control, storm damage prevention, and recreational use of downstream waters.

5. *Modification of Water Quality*

Modification of water quality refers to a wetland's role in the removal of suspended and dissolved solids from surface and groundwater and the conversion of this material into other forms, e.g., plant or animal biomass or gasses. Water may enter a wetland by surface inflow, groundwater discharge, or precipitation and be discharged at a higher quality as a result of passing through the wetland. Debris and suspended solids are removed by processes such as filtration by soils and vegetation and sedimentation (settling and buildup). Nutrients, dissolved solids, and certain pollutants may be removed or broken down and degraded so that they become inactive or incorporated into biomass. This may occur through uptake by soils and vegetation and through loss to the atmosphere. The most important factors relative to performance of this function are the residence time of water in a wetland and how the water flows into that wetland. Longer residence times allow a wetland to perform this function more effectively. Diffuse rather than channelized water flows improve this function by increasing the amount of wetland soil and vegetation with which flowing water comes into contact. Residence time for water may vary considerably with HGM class. Other factors affecting this wetland function include the size of a wetland, its vegetation structure and composition, and the topography of its watershed. The modification of water quality function may contribute to societal values such as maintaining water quality for such uses as public water supplies, recreation, and aesthetics.[16]

6. Export of Detritus

Export of detritus refers to a wetland's capacity to produce and export dissolved and particulate organic carbon to receiving waters and other wetlands. This function can serve as a potential source of energy for other aquatic ecosystems and can contribute to the support of their food webs. Detritus is produced when plants die, decay, and are broken down into fine particles. Detritus is transported when the wetland is inundated by a stream flowing through it, by overbank flooding if the wetland borders a river, or by wave action if it borders a lake. The more a stream, river, or lake is in contact with a wetland—as in a meandering, highly convoluted stream, or a river or lake that floods a bordering wetland with predictable frequency—the more efficient the transport of detritus. The amount of detritus that is produced for transport depends upon the composition, structure, and density of the wetland vegetation. The export of detritus function may contribute to societal values that are related to food web support, such as nature study, education, and research, and to recreational pursuits such as fishing and hunting.

7. Contribution to the Abundance and Diversity of Wetland Vegetation

Contribution to the abundance and diversity of wetland vegetation is the capacity of a wetland to produce wetland plant species individually or as part of a group of wetlands in a local landscape. The production and support of abundant wetland vegetation is vital to maintaining fundamental processes unique to wetlands that contribute to overall ecosystem functioning at the landscape level (sometimes referred to as microclimatic effects). Furthermore, processes unique to wetlands that are in part maintained by the vegetation may also contribute to other functions. For example, because they produce plant species that cannot grow in other environments, wetlands also contribute to biodiversity at the landscape level, individually when species diversity is high and as part of a group of wetlands in a local area when diversity is low. In certain cases, a wetland's vegetation may include rare plant species adapted to conditions found only in poorly drained soil. Wetlands vary considerably in performing this function, and the individual capacity of a wetland to perform this function depends primarily upon the adequacy and reliability of its water source. The wetland vegetation function possesses various attributes that give rise to societal values such as nature study, education, research, and production of products such as timber and cranberries.

8. Contribution to the Abundance and Diversity of Wetland Fauna

Contribution to the abundance and diversity of wetland fauna is the capacity of a wetland to support large and/or diverse populations of animal species that spend all or part of their life cycle in wetlands, individually or as part of a mosaic of wetlands in a local landscape. Certain key wetland features are critical to both the kinds and numbers of animals that utilize a wetland and the wetland's short- and long-term importance for such animals. For example, the amount and distribution of surface water in the wetland controls the kinds of vegetation the wetland supports, and affects animal mobility and access to the wetland and to the food sources contained in it. Likewise, the structure and species composition of a wetland plant community are of key importance to faunal abundance and diversity. Other important factors are the spatial relationships between wetland vegetation and other plant communities and between vegetation and open water. Land use and management practices in wetlands as well as in surrounding watersheds can also greatly affect this function. A wetland with limited capacity to support large and/or diverse populations of wetland-dependent wildlife species may nonetheless contribute to the overall capacity of a local landscape to support faunal abundance and diversity.

Although these and other characteristics of wetlands and the overall landscape play a primary role in determining the importance of a wetland to wildlife, animal activity may in turn affect wetland features and ecosystem processes. The most widespread example of this throughout many parts of the country is beaver activity, creating dams and flooded landscapes. The function of wetlands' contribution to faunal abundance and diversity supports societal values such as recreation, aesthetics, education, and research.

B. Differences among HGM Classes in the Performance of Functions

The functional characteristics of a wetland vary among hydrogeomorphic method (HGM) classes. It is thus a truism that, with respect to valuable wetland functions, all wetlands are not alike. This section focuses on the relationships between the respective HGM classes of wetlands and their associated wetland functions described in the preceding section.

1. *Wetland Functions of Depressional Wetlands*

Because of their shape, depressional wetlands trap more water than some other classes of wetlands. Accordingly, the length of time that water is present in depressional wetlands is generally greater than in other HGM classes. Depressional wetlands may modify groundwater discharge or recharge, depending upon groundwater level and the nature of the soil and surface geologic deposits under the wetland. When the wetland intersects the water table it is performing the discharge function, and when the water table drops below the wetland it is recharging water downward. Depressional wetlands are more likely to have a recharge than discharge function. Depressional wetlands also modify storm and flood water storage due to maximized water retention or storage times because water leaves the wetland only through groundwater recharge or evapotranspiration (evaporation from leaf surfaces). Depressional wetlands also may present a highly effective way to modify stream flows as groundwater discharge maintains stream flow during low-flow periods and flood-water storage buffers the effect of short, intense storms. These two factors serve to even out stream flow throughout the year. Furthermore, because a wetland's ability to store surface water is strongly correlated with its capacity to modify water quality by retaining, trapping, and transforming sediment and contaminants, depressional wetlands' ability to maximize water storage makes them highly effective in modifying water quality (but they have the least capacity of any of the HGM classes for export of detritus). For these same reasons, depressional wetlands likewise provide habitat conditions required by plants and animals adapted to saturated soils. They therefore have high potential for contributing to the abundance and diversity of both wetland vegetation and wetland fauna.

2. *Wetland Functions of Slope Wetlands*

Slope wetlands, in contrast with depressional wetlands, have very short residence times for surface water. Accordingly, slope wetlands typically can perform all of the functions listed in the previous section except modification of groundwater recharge, but with less success in certain instances. Slope wetlands are formed where the water table intersects the land surface, and this provides modification of groundwater discharge. With soils generally less permeable than those of the underlying aquifer, slope wetlands generally slow the rate of discharge, which results in a longer, more constant discharge of groundwater to the wetland. Modification of groundwater recharge seldom occurs in slope wetlands because they lack the capacity for long-term water storage. On the other hand, because they are predominantly areas of groundwater discharge, slope wetlands may play a significant role in modification of stream flow for downstream receiving waters. This function is performed only by slope wetlands that are connected by stream flow to downstream waters; wetlands that have no outlet, and are therefore hydraulically isolated from downslope wetlands, do not perform this function. Slope wetlands have the least potential of any of the HGM classes to provide storm and floodwater storage. Because they occur on slopes, water moves relatively quickly through the wetland to downstream receiving waters and does not pond above the wetland's soil surface. For this reason, and the correspondingly low capacities for retaining, trapping, and transforming sediment and contaminants, slope wetlands have a very limited potential for modification of water quality compared with other HGM classes. Slope wetlands that lack an outlet do, however, have some potential for settling of sediments and particulates, transforming dissolved elements and compounds, and interacting with soils and vegetation to improve water quality. By contrast, slope wetlands can have high potential for export of detritus, particularly if they have a perennial outlet, because they have low potential for water storage and maximum water discharge. Their potential to perform this function is more restrained if the outlet is ephemeral or if the wetland is hydrologically isolated. Because retention of saturated soil conditions or standing water is low or at best unpredictable in slope wetlands, their ability to provide the conditions required by plants and animals adapted to saturated soil is also low. Therefore, slope wetlands generally have limited potential for contributing to the abundance and diversity of wetland vegetation and fauna.

3. *Wetland Functions of Flats*

Flats function similarly to depressional wetlands because of their long water residence time. For this reason, flats may modify groundwater recharge on sites where groundwater recharge aquifer conditions occur. Because their predominant source of water is precipitation, however, flats do not modify groundwater discharge. Commonly located within the floodplains of rivers and with very slight slopes, thick organic soil, and typically very dense vegetation, flats have a high potential for storing storm and flood water. Flats are also moderately effective in modifying stream flow. Their ability to store storm and flood water enables flats to buffer the effects of short, intense storms on stream flow by releasing water gradually to the stream after a storm event. Flats are less effective in maintaining stream flow over low flow periods because they have minimal groundwater discharge. These wetlands have a high potential for modification of water quality because of their very high capacity for long-term water storage. Because of their slight gradient, high degree of surface roughness, and dense vegetation, flats have very slow surface water flow rates, which allows for maximum retention, trapping, and transforming of sediment and contaminants. Flats likewise have very low potential for export of detritus owing to the very slow, unidirectional flow through them and because flow into the wetland generally exceeds flow out. A slight amount of export may occur in flats having one or more defined outlet channels, but generally speaking flats tend to accumulate detritus. Long water residence times mean hydrologic conditions in flats are highly predictable, making flats well-suited to provide the conditions required by plants and animals adapted to saturated soils. Flats' potential, therefore, for contribution to the abundance and diversity of wetland vegetation and fauna is high.

4. *Wetland Functions of Lacustrine-Fringe Wetlands*

Lacustrine-fringe wetlands are primarily groundwater discharge areas near their upland edges. They do not modify stream flow. Commonly, their soils have a lower permeability than the underlying aquifer and they slow the rate of discharge, increasing aquifer storage and the amount of water available for discharge to the adjacent lake. Groundwater stored in lacustrine-fringe wetlands can flow into the lake as lake levels drop, thereby augmenting lake water levels. Lacustrine-fringe wetlands likewise may modify groundwater recharge in the underlying aquifer when the water table drops below the wetland surface the water stored in the soils. The low-permeability soils slow the rate of recharge and even it out over time. Lacustrine-fringe wetlands are essentially the floodplain of the adjacent lake, with high potential for short-term storm and floodwater storage. Surface-water runoff flowing into the wetland from the surrounding uplands and from stream flow can also be stored for the short term and conveyed to the lake. Lacustrine-fringe wetlands have little long-term water storage potential, however, because they are predominantly groundwater discharge areas and their soils are saturated with water moving through the aquifer to the surface. Furthermore, these wetlands have high potential for modification of water quality. Periodically inundated with water from adjacent lakes or flood waters from the upland, lacustrine-fringe wetlands are mostly still-water environments where sediment and suspended solids can settle and dissolved elements and compounds can be transformed. Lacustrine-fringe wetlands also have high potential for export of detritus. Detritus accumulates in these wetlands because of their dense vegetation and settling of particulates; the periodic flooding of the wetland by the adjacent lake and subsequent draining from the wetland back into the lake creates the opportunity for detritus to be transported to the lake. The groundwater discharge areas and the periodic inundations by lake water or runoff result in continuously saturated soils and standing water, which create stable hydrologic conditions for the support of wetland-dependent flora and fauna. The potential therefore is high for contribution to the abundance and diversity of wetland vegetation and fauna.

5. *Wetland Functions of Extensive Peatlands*

Extensive peatlands, including blanket bogs and raised bogs, accumulate large amounts of water in the upper portion (active layer) of thick sphagnum peat, which is separated from the regional groundwater by underlying dense, low-permeability peat. Accordingly, this wetland type modifies groundwater discharge to a limited extent when shallow groundwater discharges from the active layer as stream flow at lower elevations along the edges of raised bogs. Overall, however, peatlands are predominantly groundwater mounds and thus are more significant for modification of groundwater recharge. The slight slopes, dense vegetation, and permeable upper peat maximize long-term water storage, creating a regional groundwater mound and inducing groundwater recharge. At depth, the peat is compacted and has lower permeability, moderating the rate of recharge and evening it out over time.

Blanket bogs have high potential for storm and floodwater storage because they occur on gentle to steep slopes over large areas. Raised bogs, on the other hand, have a very low potential for this function because they are generally regional topographic high areas where no flooding occurs and their water is derived from direct precipitation. Similarly, in raised bogs the potential to modify water quality is limited. There are no inflowing streams; hence, there is no opportunity for sediments and dissolved elements and compounds to enter the bog other than in precipitation or as wind-blown particulates and plant debris. Dissolved elements and compounds that enter a raised bog by one or more of these sources have a high potential to be removed or transformed. Furthermore, if bog ponds are present, there may be some opportunity for interaction of water with the surrounding peatland. Because of their occurrence over extensive gently sloping areas, blanket bogs can have a considerably higher potential for this function.

Raised bogs have a fairly high potential for export of detritus from their discharge streams along the edge. Large amounts of detritus are produced by the bog vegetation and are available for export by the discharge streams. In blanket bogs, because of the long water residence time, detrital export is minimal.

Peatlands have very stable hydrologic conditions because of the high water-storage capacity of peat. Physical and chemical characteristics are also very stable in these wetland types. Hydrologic, physical, and chemical characteristics typical of peatlands are unique and give rise to plants and animals found only in peatlands. Given the stable, unique conditions found in peatlands, their importance is very high for contribution to the abundance and diversity of wetland vegetation and fauna.

6. *Wetland Functions of Riverine Wetlands*

Riverine wetlands are predominantly groundwater discharge areas. Groundwater is discharged from both sides of a valley to the riverine wetlands and from those wetlands directly into the river's channel. Rates of discharge into a river may be affected by the potentially lower permeability of riverine wetland soils. In some areas of the country, such as the glaciated northeast and midwest, riverine wetlands rarely modify groundwater recharge. In other areas, such as arid regions, they do perform this function. This type of wetland should be considered to modify groundwater recharge only if groundwater studies on a specific wetland establish a recharge condition.

A riverine wetland can be important for storm and floodwater storage if its slope is nearly flat. If the floodplain is steep, however, then floodwater runs quickly off and the duration of flood storage is short. Moreover, wetlands with a high frequency of flooding perform this function to a greater degree than wetlands with low-frequency flooding. Storage time is also increased in wetlands with dense vegetation and a surface roughened by numerous small mounds and irregularities. Riverine wetlands can be important for modification of stream flow, depending upon how well they store water. The flood-storage capacity of the floodplain accomplishes much of this function, and the discharge function modifies rates and volumes of groundwater discharged to the river's flow. Both factors contribute to modification of the rate, stage, and volume of flow within the river channel.

Riverine wetlands intercept sediments and dissolved elements and compounds that enter the wetland in runoff from adjacent uplands, stream flow, and flooding from the adjacent river. During the time that the water is stored, settling and transformation occur. The wetlands thus have a high potential for modifying water quality. Riverine wetlands have a very high potential for the export of detritus. Seasonal flooding followed by periods of exposure allow for maximum decomposition rates and production of detritus. When flooding occurs, accumulated detrital matter is transported out of the wetland to the river channel.

In most riverine wetlands, flooding is a predictable seasonal event. Such flooding gives rise to stable hydrologic conditions that are essential for maintaining characteristic riverine wetland vegetation and faunal habitats. Seasonal flooding also transports seeds for colonization of other nearby areas, thereby maintaining characteristic riverine wetland vegetation. The cycles of flooding and drying result in optimal conditions for creating and sustaining a diversity of vegetation zones and habitats meaning that riverine wetlands have a high potential for contribution to the abundance and diversity of wetland vegetation and fauna.

7. Wetland Functions of Coastal-Fringe Wetlands

Some of the freshwater wetland functions described above may also be provided by coastal wetlands. For example, salt marshes have high potential to modify water quality. Research conducted over the years has found that salt marsh vegetation and sediments can retain high levels of nutrients, such as nitrogen and phosphorus, as well as heavy metals, including lead. The retention times for the heavy metals vary: metals such as cadmium and zinc are passed through the marsh quite rapidly whereas copper, mercury, and chromium are intermediate in the length of time they are retained. Other contaminants such as pesticides may also be effectively removed by salt marshes. On the other hand, the death and breakdown of salt marsh plants and animals may also result in an export of certain contaminants to coastal waters with the regular tidal cycles, particularly in marshes that have become heavily contaminated. Because salt marshes are generally highly productive, large amounts of detritus and nutrients may be produced and exported to nearshore waters in the daily and seasonal tidal cycles, thereby contributing to the support of food webs that are important to the local fishery. Salt marshes (and also estuaries) have a stable flooding regime and unique habitat conditions that support characteristic plants and provide habitat for a wide variety of invertebrate animals such as shellfish and crustaceans, in addition to fish and other vertebrates. Coastal wetlands therefore have high potential for contribution to the abundance and diversity of wetland vegetation and fauna. Likewise, storm and floodwater storage, another function performed by coastal wetlands, is extremely important in limiting storm damage in coastal communities. Numerous other functions different from those performed by freshwater wetlands have been documented for coastal wetlands.

IV. Methods Recently and Currently Used to Assess Wetland Functions

Over the years various methods have been developed for assessing wetland functions. Several of these methods were developed for nationwide application and others were developed for particular regions of the country. Some of the methods are no longer in use or are used very little; others are still in widespread use. A widely used method at this time is the U.S. Army Corps of Engineers Highway Methodology, which relies upon best professional judgment. Multiple assessment methods are briefly described in the first subsection below for historical perspective, because many of them may be cited in earlier documents and because some are still in use in certain areas of the country. The second subsection provides more detailed descriptions of the hydrogeomorphic method, or HGM. It has been receiving attention throughout the country and will contribute to the future of wetland functional assessment.[17]

A. Nationwide Methods

1. Highway Methodology

The Highway Methodology was developed by the Corps as a rapid method for assessing wetland functions. Fourteen functions are evaluated using a form with a list of questions and considerations for each function. Evaluations are based on best professional judgment and supporting rationale. Conclusions regarding functional significance are drawn from the statements on the forms.[18] Using this methodology, four to five wetlands can be assessed per day, combining the interpretation of field data with all available documentation.

2. WET 2.0 (Wetland Evaluation Technique)

The Wetland Evaluation Technique (WET) methodology assesses eleven functions plus habitat suitability for certain wetlands, wildlife, and fish. Wetlands in a given area are screened to identify those likely to be socially significant. Those considered to be potentially significant are qualitatively assessed for functional capacity and opportunity to perform the functions. For given functions, flow charts are used to rate a wetland as high, medium, or low. On average, two to three wetlands can be assessed per day using this methodology.[19]

3. HAT (Habitat Assessment Technique)

The Habitat Assessment Technique (HAT) method assesses only breeding bird habitat, and involves inventorying birds during breeding season in the wetland. A score that reflects species diversity and uniqueness is calculated based on a comparison with regional data. This approach is based on the assumption that habitats having higher uniqueness and diversity are of greater regulatory concern. Days to weeks per wetland are required to complete an assessment using this methodology.[20]

4. HEP (Habitat Evaluation Procedure)

The Habitat Evaluation Procedure (HEP) assesses the value of a habitat for selected wildlife, fish, or invertebrate species. For such an assessment, a team of biologists from federal and state agencies and the private sector is formed, and the team selects indicator species (species likely to use the habitat being evaluated). The team visits the wetland and measures habitat features known to correlate with habitat quality for each indicator species. For each species and for the wetland, a score is derived that can be compared to the scores for other wetlands, accounting for differences in wetland size. Days to weeks are required to complete an assessment for each wetland using this methodology.[21]

5. Synoptic Approach for Wetland Cumulative Effects Analysis

The Synoptic Approach for Wetland Cumulative Effects Analysis method ranks entire landscape units, such as watersheds, rather than individual wetlands. The information for the rankings is compiled from existing maps and information; site visits are not required. This method provides a landscape context for evaluating wetland-specific information and does not provide functional information on an individual wetland basis.[22]

B. Regional Methods

1. Hollands-Magee Method

The Hollands-Magee method assesses ten functions and was designed for use primarily in the glaciated northeast and midwest areas of the United States. Using a model for each function, the assessment is conducted from information available from aerial photos, maps, and a site visit to the wetland. Multiple-choice questions pertaining to the condition of functional indicators are answered for each model. Each indicator and condition has a numeric value; indicator value is multiplied by condition value and the products are summed, yielding a score for each function. The scores are then normalized to eliminate weighting of functions. On average, four to eight wetlands can be evaluated in one day using this methodology.[23]

2. *Larson-Golet Method*

The Larson-Golet method is very similar conceptually to the Hollands-Magee method and is used for assessment of wildlife habitat value, groundwater, flood storage, and visual-cultural value of wetlands in the northeast. Up to eight wetlands can be evaluated in one day using this methodology.[24]

3. *Connecticut-New Hampshire Method*

The Connecticut-New Hampshire method is also very similar conceptually to the Hollands-Magee method. It assesses fourteen functions and was designed for use in Connecticut and New Hampshire, although it can also be used elsewhere in New England. A major difference between this and Hollands-Magee is that the score for each function is multiplied by total wetland area, yielding a score for the wetland. Thus, the larger the wetland the higher its calculated value, which may or may not reflect the perceived value of its particular set of functions. Several wetlands can be evaluated in one day using this methodology.[25]

4. *Ontario Method*

The Ontario method is also very similar conceptually to the Hollands-Magee Method. It was developed for use in Ontario and assesses fifteen functions. Several wetlands can be evaluated in one day using this methodology.[26]

5. *HES (Habitat Evaluation System)*

The Habitat Evaluation System (HES) method assesses fish and wildlife habitat value of the forested wetlands of Mississippi and adjacent areas. In a field visit to the wetland, data are collected on habitat features or indicators known to correlate with habitat quality, such as number of layers of vegetation or number of dead trees. Values are assigned to these indicators and summed, resulting in a score called the Habitat Quality Index. Several wetlands can be evaluated in one day using this methodology.[27]

6. WEM (Minnesota Wetland Evaluation Methodology)

The Minnesota Wetland Evaluation Methodology (WEM) was developed for use in Minnesota and other north-central states. It assesses eleven functions. It is similar to WET 2.0, and results in a wetland rating of high, medium, or low, and alternatively, a score for each function. Several wetlands can be evaluated in one day using this methodology.[28]

C. Hydrogeomorphic Method (HGM)

1. Description of the Method

The hydrogeomorphic method (HGM) is based on the concept that wetland functions are controlled primarily by the wetland's hydrology and geomorphology, a concept that has gained wide acceptance among the scientific community in recent years. The assessment procedure is based upon the HGM classification discussed earlier in this chapter. Both the classification and assessment principles can be applied anywhere in North America and in many other regions of the world. The number of functions assessed varies with HGM class within the three broad functional categories of hydrology, water quality, and habitat.

Models that have been developed for the various functions are conceptually similar to those in several of the regional methods discussed above. The model variables, or indicators of function, take the place of quantitative, empirical data, which is generally too time-consuming and expensive to collect. Such indicators are easily measured or observable wetland characteristics that, in combination and directly or indirectly, indicate the capacity of a wetland to perform a function. The variables and their associated conditions have numerical values that are entered into a formula and yield a score, or Functional Capacity Index. The score can be multiplied by wetland acreage to yield Functional Capacity Units.

A major difference between HGM and the earlier methods is the requirement to establish reference wetlands, whereby the variable conditions are based on data collected from a reference population. In other methods, the variable conditions are values derived from the literature and/or best professional judgment. It was originally intended that HGM be implemented on a nationwide basis partly through the preparation of guidance documents, including a general procedural document and a document for each of the HGM classes. It was intended that these documents provide a template that could be adapted to the various regions of the country. At this time the only classes for which a nationwide guidance document is available are the Riverine Class and the Tidal Fringe Wetland Class.[29]

Regionally specific guidance documents have been developed in various parts of the country, as for example in Pennsylvania, for depressional wetlands in the prairie pothole region of the northern Great Plains, and for rivers in southeast Alaska. Perhaps the best example of a regional guidance document is one prepared for the extensive peatlands of interior Alaska.[30]

2. *HGM Light: A Rapid Assessment Procedure That Does Not Require Data from Reference Wetlands*

In locations where reference wetland data or the funding necessary to acquire them is not available, a procedure based upon the HGM classification but using a rapid procedure for data acquisition may provide a more convenient alternative. Such a procedure may serve as an interim measure that can be used to obtain a functional capacity index while reference data for a particular region are being developed. Such a procedure has been developed;[31] it is based on HGM classification and makes use of information available from maps, aerial photos, and a brief site reconnaissance. A very similar HGM-based procedure entitled "A Method for the Assessment of Wetland Function" was prepared for the Maryland Department of the Environment in September 1995. This procedure was designed to be used at the landscape level and is based primarily on existing data sources.

D. Status of Wetland Functional Assessment

Many of the federal and regional methods of assessing wetland function are still in use in various sections of the country. The most widely used is the Corps's Highway Methodology based on best professional judgment. The HGM procedure, or one based on HGM, has been receiving attention throughout the country and will contribute to the future of wetland functional assessment. The Corps had attempted to implement HGM in various districts and to hold training sessions for HGM for federal and state agency personnel and private individuals, but the training and full deployment is not occurring at this time. The Waterways Experiment Station of the U.S. Army Engineer Research and Development Center (ERDC)[32] prepared national guidebooks for the riverine and tidal-fringe wetlands, together with a procedural document for HGM functional assessment.[33] These guidebooks provide examples of how the HGM procedure can be modified for each region of the country. As stated above, the HGM procedure is heavily based on establishing reference wetlands, which provide data that can be used to calculate condition ranges for model variables. Reference wetlands and regional HGM models have been established for various areas.[34] Efforts to expand the reference wetland database are ongoing in various areas of the country and, over time, may make HGM more widespread and available as a procedure.

Meanwhile, a rapid procedure based on HGM that uses existing information and a short site visit in place of established reference wetlands has been developed.[35] This procedure provides a functional capacity index for each function for each freshwater HGM class. It was designed for application in the glaciated northeast and midwest, but can also serve as a template for other regions of the country. The time frame for extending this rapid procedure nationwide could be comparatively short, on the order of a few years, given a sufficient level of interest and funding.

E. Applications of Wetland Functional Assessment

Functional assessment of a wetland can be used in three ways. First, assessment can provide an evaluation of the functional capacity of a wetland in its existing, or baseline, condition. Those functions for which the functional capacity index is high are termed principal valuable functions.

Second, functional assessment can be applied to a wetland that has had impacts or for which impacts are proposed or predicted. Impacts can be human activities like dredging and filling for development, or natural threats like erosion, droughts, hurricanes, and wildlife overgrazing. In the pre-impact scenario, the variable conditions are selected based on a predicted future condition. For example, the condition for a variable called vegetation density may be high in the pre-impact scenario and low in the post-impact scenario. Each of these conditions contributes differently to the functional capacity index, and as a result of changes in other variables as well, the index in the post-impact scenario would be different from the index in the pre-impact scenario (usually lower).

The third use for functional assessment of a wetland is to set goals for mitigating impacts and compensating for unavoidable losses in a wetland's functional capacity.[36] In a manner similar to the second use, where changes in variable conditions are predicted under an impact scenario, the variable conditions can also be changed under an enhancement scenario associated with compensatory mitigation. Using the example above, an existing vegetation density condition of low could be changed to high to achieve a higher functional capacity index. Functional assessment therefore is an important tool for assessing functional capacity both under existing conditions and after impacts. It can be used to set goals and prepare performance standards for compensation. It must be remembered, however, that the attainment of functional capacity goals and performance standards ultimately depends on the limitations and opportunities of the mitigation site.

Notes

1. For further, in-depth information on this topic, see U.S. Army Corps of Engineers, Technical and Biological Information, *at* http://www.usace.army.mil/inet/functions/cw/cecwo/reg/techbio.htm; Environmental Laboratory Wetlands *at* http://el.erdc.usace.army.mil/wetlands/; and United States Geographic Services National Wetlands Research Center, Recommended Online Databases, *at* http://www.nwrc.usgs.gov/lib/recomend.htm.

2. The inventory is available from U.S. Fish and Wildlife Service, *National Wetlands Inventory, at* http://www.nwi.fws.gov.

3. *See* L. M. Cowardin *et al.*, U.S. Department of the Interior, Fish and Wildlife Service, *Classification of Wetlands and Deep-Water Habitats of the United States* (1979), *available at* http://www.npwrc.usgs.gov/resource/1998/classwet/classwet.htm.

4. 33 C.F.R. § 328.3(b) (Corps rule); 40 C.F.R. § 230.3(t) (EPA rule)

5. *See* Association of State Wetland Managers, *State Wetland Programs and Local Wetland Programs, at* http://www.aswm.org.

6. Examples include New Hampshire, Connecticut, New Jersey, Oklahoma, Mississippi. *See, e.g.,* N.H. REV. STAT. ANN. § 482-A:2, *available at* http://www.gencourt.state.nh.us/rsa/html/L/482-A/482-A-2.htm.

7. Examples include Massachusetts, Wisconsin, California, the Dakotas. *See, e.g.,* MASS CODE REGS 310 CMR 10.00.

8. *See* 33 C.F.R. § 330.2(d) ("Headwaters means non-tidal rivers, streams, and their lakes and impoundments, including adjacent wetlands, that are part of a surface tributary system to an interstate or navigable water of the United States upstream of the point on the river or stream at which the average annual flow is less than five cubic feet per second.").

9. For finer levels of resolution and further elaborations on the basic HGM classes, see M. M. Brinson, *A Hydrogeomorphic Classification for Wetlands*. Tech. Rpt. WRP-DE-4. U.S. Army Corps of Engineers, Waterways Experiment Station, Vicksburg, MS (1993).

10. *See supra* note 3.

11. For a complete discussion of the nationwide wetland classification system developed by the FWS, *see* Cowardin, *supra* note 3.

12. Mangrove swamps are forested wetlands found in the intertidal zone in parts of southern Florida.

13. For more information on wetlands functions and values, see generally William S. Sipple, *U.S. Environmental Protection Agency Watershed Academy Web, Wetlands Functions and Values, at* http://www.epa.gov/watertrain/wetlands.

14. For more information on which activities might be regulated, see Chapter 4.

15. President George W. Bush reiterated his commitment to the "no net loss of wetlands" policy on Earth Day (April 20) 2004. Fact Sheet: President Announces Wetlands Initiative on Earth Day, *available at* http://www.whitehouse.gov/news/releases/2004/04/20040422-1.html.

16. This discussion is in part adapted from the Maryland Department of the Environment's Modification of Water Quality Web page, http://www.mde.state.md.us/Programs/WaterPrograms/Wetlands_Waterways/about_wetlands/quality.asp.

17. *See* Ellis J. "Buddy" Clairain, Jr., *The Hydrogeomorphic (HGM) Approach to Wetland Assessment: Application to Corps Regulatory Needs,* 2 Aquatic Resources News 6 (2003), *available at* http://www.usace.army.mil/inet/functions/cw/cecwo/reg/vol2_4.pdf ("the HGM Approach to assessing wetland functions provides a rapid and efficient method to address many regulatory requirements. It can be used to assess existing and projected conditions of a particular wetland, compare similar wetland types, assess potential project impacts, and assess the amount and adequacy of mitigation to compensate for unavoidable wetland impacts.").

18. *See* http://www.usace.army.mil/inet/functions/cw/cecwo/reg/district.htm.

19. This method is detailed in Report #ADA 189968 from National Technical Information Service (NTIS), Springfield, VA.

20. This method is described in T. T. Cable *et al., Simplified Method for Wetland Habitat Assessment,* 13 ENV. MGMT. 213 (1989).

21. This procedure is detailed in *Habitat Evaluation Procedures (HEP) Manual* (102ESM) (1980), U.S. Fish and Wildlife Service, Washington, D.C.

22. A detailed description of this method is available from USEPA Environmental Research Laboratory, 200 S.W. 35th St., Corvallis, OR 97333.

23. This method is explained in G. G. Hollands & D. W. Magee, *A Method for Assessing the Functions of Wetlands, in* Proceedings of the National Wetland Assessment Symposium, Association of State Wetland Managers, Berne, NY, 108–18 (1985).

24. A detailed description of this method is available from the Water Resources Research Center, University of Massachusetts, Amherst, Mass.

25. A detailed description of this method is available from N.H. Dept. of Environmental Services, Water Resources Division, Wetlands Bureau, P.O. Box 2008, Concord, NH.

26. A detailed description of this method is available from Wildlife Branch, Ontario Ministry of Natural Resources, Whitney Block, Queen's Park, Toronto, Ontario, Canada.

27. A detailed description of this method is available from the Environmental Analysis Branch, Planning Division, Lower Mississippi Valley Division, U.S. Army Corps of Engineers, P.O Box 80, Vicksburg, MS.

28. A detailed description of this method is available from St. Paul District, U.S. Army Corps of Engineers, 1135 U.S. Post Office and Custom House, St. Paul, MN.

29. For information on guidance documents and the hydrogeomorphic method generally, see http://el.erdc.usace.army.mil/wetlands/hgmhp.html.

30. L. C. Lee et al., State of Alaska Department of Environmental Conservation/USA COE Waterways Experiment Station Technical Report No. WRP-DE-

1999, *Operational Draft Guidebook for Reference-Based Assessment of the Functions of Precipitation-Driven Wetlands on Discontinuous Permafrost in Interior Alaska.*

31. This method is explained in D. W. Magee, *A Rapid Procedure for Assessing Wetland Functional Capacity Based on Hydrogeomorphic (HGM) Classification*, The Association of State Wetland Managers, P.O. Box 269, Berne, NY 12023-9746.

32. As part of a reorganization in 1999, Waterways Experiment Station became part of ERDC. *See* http://www.wes.army.mil.

33. *See generally* Hydrogeomorphic Approach for Assessing Wetland Functions *at* http://www.wes.army.mil/el/wetlands/hgmhp.html.

34. For a listing of regional guidebooks, see http://el.erdc.usace.army.mil/wetlands/guidebooks.html.

35. *See supra* note 30.

36. For more information about recent mitigation efforts, including the National Wetlands Mitigation Action Plan, see http://www.mitigationactionplan.gov.

CHAPTER 3

Federal Jurisdiction over Wetlands: "Waters of the United States"

MARK A. CHERTOK AND KATE SINDING

I. Introduction/Scope

Until 1972, federal jurisdiction over wetlands was quite limited, and devolved from Section 10 of the Rivers and Harbors Appropriation Act of 1899 (Rivers and Harbors Act).[1] This legislation regulates "navigable waters of the United States" and prohibits "work" (for example, dredging or filling) or the placement of structures in or over such waters except in accordance with a permit issued by the United States Army Corps of Engineers (Corps). Jurisdiction is limited to waters affected by tidal flow or that have been used, or are susceptible to use, in interstate or foreign commerce.[2] Wetlands are often outside the mean high water mark and most frequently found in conjunction with traditionally non-navigable waters; most wetlands, as a result, generally do not fall within the ambit of the Rivers and Harbors Act.[3] Moreover, the statute is primarily intended to protect the government's interest in the navigability of waterways, and not in water quality. Consequently, wetlands received very little consideration under this legislation.

The passage of the Federal Water Pollution Control Act Amendments of 1972, popularly known as the Clean Water Act (CWA),[4] greatly expanded federal jurisdiction over wetlands through the Section 404 permitting program. The CWA reflects a far broader federal interest than the Rivers and Harbors Act. It seeks "to restore and maintain the chemical, physical, and biological integrity of the Nation's waters."[5] Although the jurisdiction of the Section 404 program, like the Rivers and Harbors Act, is limited to "navigable waters,"[6] the CWA defines this term broadly to mean "waters of the United States."[7] The courts have generally interpreted this definition to reach many nonnavigable waters, including wetlands.[8]

The potentially expansive reach of the government's Section 404 jurisdiction over wetlands has been controversial. Since the inception of the program, the agencies that administer the Section 404 program—chiefly the Corps and the U.S. Environmental Protection Agency (EPA)—have gradually expanded the program's jurisdiction.

Adding to the controversial scope of the program are the criteria that the agencies have employed to determine whether and to what extent particular sites may be characterized as wetlands. These "delineation" criteria are set forth in manuals that are used by agency personnel and other professionals. For many years, different agencies administering different wetland programs used different delineation manuals—a practice that often engendered inconsistent conclusions about whether particular sites are wetlands subject to restrictions and confusion among persons regulated under various wetland programs. Moreover, the criteria by which wetlands are delineated are themselves controversial, generating debate among legislators, agency policy makers, and wetland scientists. In recent years, there have been attempts to remove such inconsistencies and confusion through administrative reforms.

This chapter describes the jurisdiction of the Section 404 program. It analyzes statutory provisions, agency regulations, and case law pertinent to the program's jurisdiction. It also explains the delineation process, including the various manuals that have been used by agencies to delineate wetlands.

II. The Corps and EPA Authority

The Corps and EPA are jointly responsible for implementing the Section 404 program.[9] In general, the Corps performs the day-to-day administration of the program, while EPA, in conjunction with the Corps, sets guidelines and standards. The U.S. Fish and Wildlife Service (FWS) within the Department of the Interior, the National Marine Fisheries Service (NMFS) within the Department of Commerce, and the Natural Resources Conservation Service (NRCS) within the Department of Agriculture have less prominent, but important advisory and regulatory roles. The FWS and NMFS must be granted the opportunity to comment on all individual and some general Section 404 permits.[10] The NRCS administers the "Swampbuster" program, which is designed to discourage the conversion of wetlands for agricultural purposes.[11]

While the Corps and EPA are jointly responsible for implementing the Section 404 program, Congress granted the Corps the authority to issue permits for the discharge of dredged or fill material into waters governed by Section 404. The Corps grants or denies individual permit applications based on their conformity with the criteria set out in the Corps's and EPA's Section 404(b)(1) guidelines,[12] as well as Corps regulations providing for a general "public interest" review of permit applications.[13] The Corps also issues "general" permits for the conduct of similar activities with minimal environmental impacts, considered either as individual or cumulative activities.[14]

In addition, the Corps promulgates regulations pursuant to Section 404[15] and publishes nonbinding Regulatory Guidance Letters (RGLs) to aid potential and existing regulated parties. Finally, the Corps administers a "mitigation banking" program, under which landowners can offset any unavoidable wetland losses resulting from their activities with newly created or restored wetlands.[16]

EPA is also charged with implementing portions of the Section 404 program.[17] As noted, EPA, in conjunction with the Corps, developed the guidelines that must be satisfied as a prerequisite to issuance of a Section 404 permit,[18] and EPA may provide comments to the Corps on permit applications. Under CWA Section 404(c), EPA also has a "veto" power over Section 404 permits if it determines that a proposed discharge would have an "unacceptable adverse effect" on environmental resources.[19] It has exercised this authority sparingly. EPA relies on the Section 404(b)(1) guidelines in ascertaining the environmental impact of proposed permits.[20]

Because "[i]t is the Administrator [of EPA] who has general administrative responsibility under the [CWA] . . . and who has general authority to prescribe regulations," EPA has the final administrative authority to define the terms "waters of the United States" and "wetlands"—neither of which are defined in the CWA.[21] The Corps and EPA have defined these terms in the same manner.[22] The Corps, however, possesses the ultimate authority to determine whether a particular activity constitutes "a discharge of dredged or fill material," and thus requires the issuance of a permit.[23] Both the Corps and EPA have a role in the enforcement of the program.[24]

III. Statutory Provisions and Administrative Regulations

A. Statutory Provisions

Section 404(a) of the CWA authorizes the Corps to issue permits "for the discharge of dredged or fill material into the navigable waters at specified disposal sites."[25] Absent a permit, such discharges into navigable waters are unlawful and may subject offending parties to substantial civil liabilities and criminal sanctions. Accordingly, the initial determination that must be made by any person who seeks to discharge dredged or fill material is whether the discharge site is a "navigable water," as that term is defined by statute and regulation for purposes of the Section 404 program.

Section 404's use of the term "navigable waters" to describe jurisdictional waters is, at best, incomplete. The Section 404 program is clearly not limited either to waters that are navigable in fact or to those that may be navigable at some future date. In fact, the CWA specifically defines the term "navigable waters" to include all "waters of the United States," without reference to navigability.[26] Both EPA and the Corps have asserted jurisdiction over nonnavigable waters, including wetlands, in administering the Section 404 program. The next section analyzes regulations pertinent to the jurisdiction of the Section 404 program.

B. Regulations Governing the Section 404 Program's Jurisdiction

1. *Waters of the United States*

The term "waters of the United States" as employed in the CWA has been interpreted broadly. The Corps's regulations extend Section 404 jurisdiction over a range of interstate and intrastate waters, including wetlands. The Eleventh Circuit rejected a claim (in a criminal case) that Congress, in granting authority to an administrative agency to regulate "waters of the United States," had unconstitutionally delegated to the Corps its duty to set identifiable jurisdictional limits on the agency's authority.[27] The court concluded that "Congress provided sufficiently precise standards to judge the delegation in issue."[28]

The Corps's regulatory definition of waters of the United States is set forth at 33 C.F.R. § 328.3(a). It includes

> (1) All waters which are currently used, or were used in the past, or may be susceptible to use in interstate or foreign commerce;
> (2) All interstate waters including interstate wetlands;
> (3) All other waters such as intrastate lakes, rivers, streams (including intermittent streams), mudflats, sandflats, wetlands, sloughs, prairie potholes, wet meadows, playa lakes, or natural ponds, the use, degradation or destruction of which could affect interstate or foreign commerce including any such waters:
>   (i) Which are or could be used by interstate or foreign travelers for recreational or other purposes; or
>   (ii) From which fish or shellfish are or could be taken and sold in interstate or foreign commerce; or

(iii) Which are used or could be used for industrial purposes by industries in interstate commerce;

(4) All impoundments of waters otherwise defined as waters of the United States under the definition;

(5) Tributaries of waters identified in paragraphs (a) (1) through (4) of this section;

(6) The territorial seas;

(7) Wetlands adjacent to waters (other than waters that are themselves wetlands) identified in [this regulation].[29]

The regulations further provide, in a section entitled "Limits of jurisdiction," that in the case of adjacent wetlands "jurisdiction extends beyond the ordinary high water mark to the limit of the adjacent wetland"[30] and that "[w]hen the water of the United States consists only of wetlands the jurisdiction extends to the limit of the wetland."[31] Incidentally, the statutory and regulatory definitions of "waters of the United States" apply not only to the Section 404 program but also to the Section 402 permit program and throughout the Act.[32]

2. *Wetlands Generally*

As the regulatory definition of "waters of the United States" makes clear, wetlands are a significant portion of the Corps's Section 404 jurisdiction. Wetlands are, in turn, defined broadly by regulation to include

> those areas that are inundated or saturated by surface or ground water at a frequency and duration sufficient to support, and that under normal circumstances do support, a prevalence of vegetation typically adapted for life in saturated soil conditions. Wetlands generally include swamps, marshes, bogs, and similar areas.[33]

This definition delineates wetlands along three parameters: hydrophytic vegetation, hydric soil, and hydrology.

Notably, the regulations do not limit jurisdiction over wetlands according to the wetlands' size. Nor do the regulations classify wetlands by functional capabilities or ecological or social value.[34] Thus, jurisdiction over wetlands does not turn on an assessment of particular wetlands' ecological or social importance, although such an assessment may bear importantly on the Corps's decision to issue or deny a permit for discharges into wetlands. And unlike some state wetland programs, Corps and EPA regulations do not include within their jurisdiction any "buffer" or "adjacent" upland areas,[35] even though activities in such areas may have important effects on a wetlands' functions and values.

The "under normal circumstances" language in the definition of wetlands serves two functions. First, it prevents landowners from eluding jurisdiction by taking action that eliminates one or more of the three defining wetland criteria. For example, jurisdiction may be asserted, even in the absence of wetland vegetation, in "circumstances in which the vegetation in a wetland has been inadvertently or purposely removed or altered as a result of recent natural events or human activities."[36] Temporary changes or illegal activity will not exclude from the Section 404 program's jurisdiction an area that would be a wetland if "normal" conditions—those that would have existed without such activities—prevailed.[37]

Second, the "normal circumstances" language excludes from regulation areas that may be characterized by the "abnormal presence of aquatic vegetation in a nonaquatic area."[38] Similarly, former wetlands that were converted to dry land before the enactment of Section 404 are not regulated, so long as wetland characteristics have not re-emerged naturally at the site. For example, in *Golden Gate Audubon Society v. Army Corps of Engineers*,[39] the district court reviewed the Corps's decision to decline jurisdiction over wetlands that had been filled prior to the expansion of the Section 404 program in 1975.[40] In the Corps's view, under "normal circumstances," the site was not a wetland. It concluded:

> [T]hese wetlands were not jurisdictional wetlands under the "normal circumstances" principle [because] the normal circumstances of the site were that of a filled area with ongoing filling and other construction operations. . . . Only if a formerly converted area . . . is abandoned and over time regains its wetland characteristics such that it meets the definition of "wetlands," [will] the Corps' 404 jurisdiction [be] restored.[41]

In essence, the Corps concluded that ongoing filling and construction could properly be regarded as part of the "normal circumstances" affecting a site, at least for those sites that had been lawfully filled prior to the expansion of the Section 404 program and had not been "abandoned." The district court rejected this view, concluding that if the conditions of the site support wetland characteristics and those conditions are not abnormal, then the site must be considered a "water of the United States," so long as other jurisdictional elements are present.[42]

In *Leslie Salt Co. v. United States*,[43] the Ninth Circuit reached a similar result, concluding that the "normal circumstances" language refers to the presence of naturally occurring physical wetlands indicators, and does not turn on whether the landscape setting had been artificially or naturally created. Thus, the court held that the Corps could assert jurisdiction over artificially created wetlands resulting from flooding conducted by the Corps itself and third parties on land formerly put to agricultural and salt mining uses.[44] In reaching this decision, the court distinguished *United States v. City of Fort Pierre*,[45] in which the Eighth Circuit concluded that the Corps lacked jurisdiction over wetlands inadvertently created by flooding from an unrelated Corps activity. The Eighth Circuit itself had since limited *City of Fort Pierre* to its facts.[46] Notwithstanding the foregoing considerations of the "normal circumstances" criterion, the Corps has by rule excluded prior converted cropland from the Section 404 program.[47]

Once a site is properly characterized as a wetland, the Corps's regulations regard it as within the "waters of the United States" in three circumstances: (A) the wetland is an interstate wetland; (b) the wetland is adjacent to other waters of the United States; or (3) the use, degradation, or destruction of the wetland could affect interstate commerce. Interstate wetlands have received scant administrative or judicial treatment, and will not be discussed further.[48] The next sections analyze the remaining categories of jurisdictional wetlands.

3. *Adjacent Wetlands*

The Corps has construed Section 404 to encompass wetlands adjacent to waters of the United States. The Corps's regulation defines "adjacent" to mean "bordering, contiguous, or neighboring"; adjacent wetlands include "[w]etlands separated from other waters of the United States by man-made dikes or barriers, natural river berms, beach dunes and the like."[49] The Supreme Court upheld the Corps's regulation of "adjacent wetlands" in *United States v. Riverside Bayview Homes*,[50] reasoning that waters and adjacent wetlands "together form the entire aquatic system"; hence, activities in wetlands are reasonably regulated because such activity might well "affect the water quality of the other waters within that aquatic system."[51]

The regulation does not limit the term "adjacent" to a specified maximum or minimum distance between wetlands and "other waters," and no further regulatory guidance is provided. In many cases, a finding of adjacency may be unnecessary to support jurisdiction. Nonetheless, whether wetlands are characterized as adjacent to, or isolated from, waters of the United States may in many cases be significant,[52] particularly in light of the Supreme Court's recent decision in *Solid Waste Agency of Northern Cook County v. United States Army Corps of Engineers (SWANCC)*,[53] which is discussed *infra*.

As noted, the Corps's regulations classify adjacent wetlands as "waters of the United States." By contrast, jurisdiction over nonadjacent, "isolated" wetlands may be asserted only if a more searching case-by-case analysis demonstrates a nexus between activities in the wetlands and effects on interstate commerce or if the wetland meets the requirements articulated in *SWANCC.*

The term "adjacent" has been construed generously by the courts. For example, the district court in *United States v. Lee Wood Contracting, Inc.,*[54] held that the conjunction "or" in the regulation means that a wetland need not be bordering, contiguous, *and* neighboring for Section 404 jurisdiction to attach; if any of the conjoined terms are applicable, jurisdiction may be asserted. Thus, jurisdiction over the wetlands in *Lee Wood Contracting,* which were connected to a navigable river by a slough, was upheld because the wetland was found to be "neighboring" to the river, even though it was not "contiguous."[55]

Some courts have held that wetlands may be regarded as "adjacent" when groundwater aquifers provide hydrologic connections between the wetlands and other surface waters. In *United States v. Banks,*[56] for example, the necessary connection was established through groundwater, buttressed by surface waters during storm events as well as other ecological links. In *Banks,* wetlands that were separated from other waters of the United States by a human-made barrier were still considered to be "adjacent."[57]

Other courts have also found that adjacency may be demonstrated by an ecological relationship rather than a direct physical connection. Indeed, in *Riverside Bayview Homes,* the Supreme Court upheld the Corps's jurisdiction over wetlands considered to be "adjacent" by virtue of the wetlands' "function as integral parts of the aquatic environment even when the moisture creating the wetlands does not find its source in the adjacent bodies of water."[58] In such cases, noncontiguous wetlands may be considered "adjacent" if they affect the water quality and aquatic ecosystems of navigable waters. In *Conant v. United States,*[59] for instance, a wetland was found to be "adjacent" to a river because it filtered out sediment and pollutants from runoff flowing into the water body.[60]

By contrast, in *United States v. Wilson,*[61] a panel of the Fourth Circuit divided on the proper approach to an "adjacency" determination. Although a majority of the panel concluded that a criminal conviction (for "knowingly discharging fill and excavated dirt into wetlands without a permit") must be overturned because of faulty jury instructions on other matters, the court could not muster a majority on whether the district court had erred in defining "adjacent wetlands" for the jury. Judge Niemeyer concluded that the district court had erred in instructing the jury that "waters of the United States" could include adjacent wetlands "'without a direct or indirect surface connection to other waters of the

United States.'"[62] In Judge Niemeyer's view, the Supreme Court's approval of Corps jurisdiction over adjacent wetlands in *Riverside Bayview Homes* was "explicitly in the context of a wetland 'that actually abuts on a navigable waterway.'"[63] In *Wilson*, however, the extension of jurisdiction authorized by the district court's jury instruction was improper "in light of the constitutional difficulties that would arise by extending the [CWA's] coverage to waters that are connected closely to neither interstate nor navigable waters, and which do not otherwise substantially affect interstate commerce."[64]

A separate opinion by Judge Payne argued that Judge Niemeyer had improperly focused on the jury instruction's reference to a "surface connection." Judge Payne opined that the Supreme Court's holding in *Riverside Bayview Homes* was predicated on the existence of a hydrologic relationship between the wetland and a water of the United States, which might exist even without a surface connection.[65] On this view, Judge Niemeyer erred by "requir[ing] a surface connection as a condition to adjacency."[66]

Absent contiguity or an ecological relationship to other waters of the United States, a wetland is generally considered to be "isolated" rather than adjacent.[67] The next section discusses Corps regulations governing such isolated wetlands.

4. *Isolated Wetlands*

The Corps's regulations provide for jurisdiction over "other waters" of the United States, including wetlands, the "use, degradation or destruction of which could affect interstate or foreign commerce."[68] These intrastate waters do not have a hydrological or other ecological connection to "waters of the United States" and are not geographically contiguous with such waters. For this reason, they are regarded as "isolated" wetlands. As noted above, the Supreme Court in *Riverside Bayview Homes* left open the issue of whether jurisdiction could properly attach to isolated waters, stating that jurisdictional determinations over such areas would be made on a case-by-case basis.[69]

The preamble to the Corps's regulations provide for the agency to make determinations of jurisdiction over isolated wetlands based on the specific facts of each case, and articulate examples of the types of waters over which jurisdiction would typically not be asserted. These include (1) nontidal drainage and irrigation ditches excavated on dry land; (2) artificially irrigated areas that would revert to upland if the irrigation ceased; (3) artificial lakes or ponds created by excavation and that are used exclusively for stock watering, irrigation, settling ponds, or rice growing; (4) artificial reflecting ponds or swimming pools or other small ornamental bodies of water; and (5) water-filled depressions on dry land incidental to construction activity.[70]

The Corps's rules also include examples of the types of activities in isolated wetlands that "could affect" interstate commerce sufficiently for the Corps to assert Section 404 jurisdiction. Such waters include (1) those used by interstate or foreign travelers or for recreational purposes; (2) those from which fish or shellfish are taken and sold in interstate or foreign commerce; and (3) those that are or could be used for industrial purposes by industries in interstate commerce.[71]

The primary questions concerning jurisdiction over isolated wetlands, as the regulations discussed above suggest, is whether a sufficient connection exists between the activity to be regulated and interstate commerce and whether such a connection alone meets the requirements of *SWANCC*. The sufficiency of the nexus with commerce is determined in the first instance by the Corps, but set within a framework of judicial interpretations concerning the extent of regulatory power pursuant to the Commerce Clause—Article I, section 8, clause 3 of the Constitution of the United States. The *SWANCC* decision has generated much uncertainty about whether a nexus with commerce alone is sufficient to support jurisdiction. The next sections discuss the manner in which the courts have held that such a connection may be demonstrated and the Court's decision in *SWANCC*.

5. *Effects on Interstate Commerce*

a. General Considerations

Federal jurisdiction over wetlands derives from Congress's power to regulate interstate commerce.[72] The Corps's regulations recognize this derivation, generally limiting the scope of the Section 404 program to waters that affect or "could affect" interstate commerce.[73] The exercise of Section 404 jurisdiction over some wetlands, particularly isolated wetlands, depends upon a broad interpretation regarding the reach of the Commerce Clause and the statutory term "waters of the United States." For many years, the courts provided such interpretations, seeming to express a general unwillingness to limit Congress's power over interstate commerce.[74] In these circumstances, the primary limitation on the Corps's jurisdiction came from the agency itself, which has in the past declined to exercise jurisdiction over wetlands for which it believed the requisite interstate connection was lacking.

In some cases, in part because of the informal nature of these determinations and the corresponding absence of any public notice, the Corps's self-imposed jurisdictional constraints largely had gone unchallenged. In *Avoyelles Sportsmen's League, Inc. v. Marsh*,[75] however, the

Court of Appeals for the Fifth Circuit held that EPA and the Corps had erred in determining that land clearing activities resulting in an incidental redeposit of materials into an isolated wetland did not require a Section 404 permit, and required the agencies to exercise jurisdiction over the activities.[76]

In *National Wildlife Federation v. Laubscher*,[77] an environmental group challenged the Corps's policy of restricting jurisdiction where interstate commerce was allegedly lacking, arguing that the presence of migratory birds provided the needed connection to interstate commerce. The case was subsequently mooted by changes in Corps policy.[78] In fact, and as discussed in detail below, until very recently, EPA and the Corps regularly relied on the "migratory bird rule" advocated in *Laubscher* to establish jurisdiction over isolated wetlands.[79] This approach was consistent with judicial interpretations that supported an expansive view of regulatory power.

More recently, in *United States v. Lopez*,[80] however, the Supreme Court breathed new life into Commerce Clause limitations on power, holding that the regulation of firearms within certain distances of schools exceeded congressional authority under the Commerce Clause. To fall within the reach of the Commerce Clause, the Court in *Lopez* concluded, the regulated activity must fall within one or more of three broad categories:

> First, Congress may regulate the use of the channels of interstate commerce. . . . Second, Congress is empowered to regulate and protect the instrumentalities of interstate commerce, or persons or things in interstate commerce, even though the threat may come only from intrastate activities. . . . Finally, Congress' commerce authority includes the power to regulate those activities having a substantial relation to interstate commerce, . . . i.e., those activities that substantially affect interstate commerce.[81]

In a further blow to Congress's ability to legislate pursuant to the Commerce Clause, in *United States v. Morrison*,[82] the Supreme Court struck down the Violence Against Women Act.[83] The Court based its determination on the grounds that, notwithstanding the enormous amount of research and data collected by Congress to demonstrate the impacts of intrastate violence against women on interstate commerce, "[t]he regulation and punishment of intrastate violence that is not directed at the instrumentalities, channels, or goods involved in interstate commerce has always been the province of the States."[84] In an important amplification of the *Lopez* standard, the Court stated: "We . . . reject the argument that Congress may regulate non-economic, violent criminal conduct based solely on that conduct's aggregate effect on interstate commerce."[85] The Court's decisions in *Lopez* and *Morrison* focused strongly on the noneconomic character of the activities regulated by law. The *Morrison* Court distinguished the Violence Against Women Act from prior laws that the Court upheld against Commerce Clause challenges by stressing that "in those cases where we have sustained regulation of intrastate activity based upon the activity's substantial effects on interstate commerce, the activity in question has been some sort of economic endeavor."[86]

Adjacent wetlands that have surface connections to waters of the United States generally satisfy the *Lopez* test by virtue of their ecological relationship to those waters; they thus may be regarded as falling into the category of intrastate matters the regulation of which is appropriate to "protect the instrumentalities of interstate commerce." Indeed, *Riverside Bayview Homes'* emphasis on ecological relationships between wetlands and adjacent "navigable waters" directly supports this conclusion. In general, however, Corps jurisdiction over wetlands, and particularly over isolated wetlands, will depend on whether the activity to be regulated falls within the third *Lopez* category—i.e., whether the activity "substantially affects" interstate commerce.[87]

The requisite effects on interstate commerce may be established in a variety of ways. As noted above, Corps regulations consider such effects present when the site in question may be used for recreational, fishing, or industrial purposes,[88] and the courts have generally considered connections of this sort to be sufficient for constitutional purposes.[89] In addition, many of the activities that involve the discharge of dredged or fill materials in wetlands are economic activities.[90] More contentious than these recognized interstate commerce effects has been the Corps's and EPA's reliance on the presence or potential presence of migratory birds to establish the requisite effects on interstate commerce.[91]

b. The Migratory Bird Rule

In the preamble to the Corps's 1986 regulations, the Corps concluded that Section 404 jurisdiction could be established over wetlands that provide or could provide habitat for migratory birds and/or endangered species.[92] Specifically, the Corps noted:

> [W]aters of the United States at 40 CFR 328.3(a)(3) also include the following waters:
>
> a. Which are or would be used as habitat by birds protected by Migratory Bird Treaties; or

b. Which are or would be used as habitat by other migratory birds which cross state lines; or
c. Which are or would be used as habitat for endangered species; or
d. Used to irrigate crops sold in interstate commerce.[93]

Likewise, EPA concluded:

> [I]f evidence reasonably indicates that isolated waters are or would be used by migratory birds or endangered species, they are covered by EPA's regulation. Of course, the clearest evidence would be evidence showing actual use in at least a portion of the waterbody. In addition, if a particular waterbody shares the characteristics of other waterbodies whose use by and value to migratory birds as [sic] well established, and those characteristics make it likely that the waterbody in question would also be used by migratory birds, it would also seem to fall clearly within the definition (unless, of course, there is other information that indicates the particular waterbody would not in fact be so used). Endangered species are, almost by definition, rare. Therefore, in the case of endangered species, if there is no evidence of actual use of the waterbody (or similar waters in the area) by the species in question, one could actually assume that the waterbody was not susceptible to use by such species, notwithstanding the particular characteristics of the waterbody. However, in each case a specific determination of jurisdiction would have to be made, and would turn on the particular facts.[94]

In *Leslie Salt v. United States,*[95] the Court of Appeals for the Ninth Circuit upheld the "Migratory Bird Rule." The court concluded that artificial wetlands in basins and pits formerly used in salt production could be subject to Corps jurisdiction, even though they were isolated by a quarter mile from a water of the United States, so long as a sufficient connection to interstate commerce could be established. Further, neither the man-made nor the seasonal nature of the wetlands removed them from Corps jurisdiction. The wetlands provided habitat for migratory birds and the salt marsh harvest mouse, an endangered species. In sustaining the Corps's assertion of jurisdiction over the wetlands, the court stated: "The commerce clause power, and thus the Clean Water Act, is broad enough to extend the Corps's jurisdiction to local waters which may provide habitat to migratory birds and endangered species."[96]

This conclusion was promptly challenged by Justice Thomas of the Supreme Court, who dissented from the Supreme Court's denial of certiorari in *Leslie Salt*.[97] Justice Thomas noted that the "other waters" provision of the Corps's regulations defining "waters of the United States," which was asserted for jurisdictional purposes, does not require that an activity "substantially affect" interstate commerce, but only that the activity "could affect" interstate or foreign commerce. Justice Thomas found this nexus too attenuated under *Lopez*, particularly in the absence of human activity. Such an expansive view of regulatory power, concluded Justice Thomas, "likely stretches Congress' Commerce Clause powers beyond the breaking point."[98] Even the "occasional presence" of migratory birds was insufficient for constitutional purposes, as there was no linkage with commerce (such as the interstate transportation of such birds for commercial purposes).[99]

In *United States v. Wilson*,[100] a divided panel of the Fourth Circuit echoed Justice Thomas's reasoning, holding that the Corps had exceeded its statutory authority under the CWA in defining "waters of the United States" to include "other waters . . . which could affect interstate or foreign commerce."[101] The court stated, "The regulation requires neither that the regulated activity have a substantial effect on interstate commerce, nor that the covered waters have any sort of nexus with navigable, or even interstate, waters."[102] Because such an expansive interpretation of the CWA "would appear to exceed congressional authority under the Commerce Clause," the court refused to "presume . . . that Congress authorized the [Corps] to assert its jurisdiction in such a sweeping and constitutionally troubling manner."[103]

The decision in *Wilson* did not address whether the presence or potential presence of migratory birds in an isolated wetland is a sufficient predicate for the exercise of power,[104] although the logic of two of the three judges suggested that it is not. For these judges, it is necessary to establish a specific and substantial relationship more akin to that suggested by Justice Thomas.[105]

A series of decisions evaluating the Migratory Bird Rule did issue, however, from a single EPA enforcement action derived from the filling of a 0.8-acre isolated wetland.[106] The Seventh Circuit initially held in *Hoffman Homes, Inc. v. Administrator, United States EPA*[107] that jurisdiction under Section 404 is not established merely by demonstrating that the wetland in question provided, or could provide, habitat for migratory birds.[108] The court stated, "Until they are watched, photographed, shot at or otherwise impacted by people who do (or, we suppose, have the potential to) engage in interstate commerce, migratory birds do not ignite the Commerce Clause."[109]

The same panel later vacated this decision, taking the extraordinary step of ordering settlement negotiations over disputed penalties assessed by EPA for filling at the site.[110] Upon the failure of those negotiations, the court determined that EPA's regulations asserting jurisdiction over isolated, interstate wetlands were valid, in light of the potential interstate commerce connection created by the presence of migratory birds.[111] Nonetheless, the court held that EPA had improperly asserted jurisdiction over the particular isolated wetland in question because it had produced insufficient evidence to demonstrate that the wetland was used or suitable for use by migratory birds.

EPA had relied on expert testimony to provide a connection between the wetland and migratory birds, but the court regarded that testimony as "merely speculation based on the assumption that [the isolated wetland] was a wetland similar to [a nearby adjacent wetland]."[112] The court found this insufficient evidence because, unlike the nearby adjacent wetland, the isolated wetland "does not border a stream, it does not adjoin a large wetland, its only source of moisture is rainfall, it is only wet part of the year, and it covers approximately one acre instead of fifty."[113] Additionally, there was no evidence that migratory birds had ever used the isolated wetland. In these circumstances, EPA had failed to present sufficient evidence to show that the wetland provided or had the potential to provide habitat for migratory birds. The court thus concluded:

> The migratory birds are better judges of what is suitable for their welfare than are we. . . . Having avoided [the isolated wetland] the migratory birds have thus spoken and submitted their own evidence. We see no need to argue with them. No justification whatsoever is seen from the evidence to interfere with private ownership based on what appears to be no more than a well intentioned effort in these particular factual circumstances to expand government control beyond reasonable or practical limits. After April showers not every temporary wet spot necessarily becomes subject to government control.[114]

The *Hoffman Homes* court's conclusion that a potential connection to interstate commerce could be sufficient to establish jurisdiction under the Commerce Clause spawned, unsurprisingly, further litigation to clarify the extent to which the agencies may assert jurisdiction over isolated wetlands. For instance, another panel of the Seventh Circuit concluded that *Hoffman Homes* established that "nearly all wetlands fall within the jurisdiction of the CWA since one test for whether the wetland affects interstate commerce is whether migratory birds use the wetland. . . . [This best gives] full effect to Congress's intent to make the Clean Water Act as far-reaching as the Commerce Clause permits."[115]

Likewise, in *SWANCC*,[116] when the district court first heard the case it stated

> Isolated wetlands provide habitat to migratory birds whose continued existence supports billions of dollars in interstate commerce. The incremental destruction of migratory bird habitat directly and negatively impacts migratory bird populations and, thereby interstate commerce. Isolated wetlands are a crucial link in the direct chain of causation between healthy migratory bird populations and interstate commerce. It should, therefore, be irrelevant whether a migratory bird is ever observed, photographed, or hunted at the particular isolated wetland in question. Unlike in *Lopez*, the connection of isolated wetlands to interstate commerce is well-documented and does not require the court to "pile inference upon inference" in a manner that gives rise to a general police power.[117]

The district court concluded that "the commerce clause authorizes the government to regulate isolated intrastate waters that provide a habitat for migratory birds even if the particular birds on the site do not substantially affect interstate commerce."[118]

The Seventh Circuit affirmed the district court's decision in 1999, concluding that "the destruction of migratory bird habitat and the attendant decrease in the populations of these birds 'substantially affects' interstate commerce." The court also relied on the aggregate effects of the destruction of individual migratory bird habitats on interstate commerce. Thus it observed that "[t]he effect may not be observable as each isolated pond used by the birds for feeding, nesting, and breeding is filled, but the aggregate effect is clear, and that is all the Commerce Clause requires."[119] The court also distinguished the Fourth Circuit's decision in *Wilson*, concluding that "the question whether Congress may regulate waters based on their potential to affect interstate commerce is not presented, because the unchallenged facts show that the filling . . . would have an immediate effect on migratory birds that actually use the area as a habitat. Thus, we need not, and do not, reach the question of the Corps's jurisdiction over areas that are only potential habitats."[120]

In explaining the reach of the Migratory Bird Rule, the court of appeals in *SWANCC* made clear that it did not accept the view that the rule "excludes nothing" because "[v]irtually any body of water could serve as a temporary habitat for at least some of these birds." The court noted:

> [A]ny suggestion that next the Corps will be trying to regulate the filling of every puddle that forms after a rainstorm, at least if a bird is seen splashing in it, misses the point. A "habitat" is not

> simply a place where a bird might alight for a few minutes, as SWANCC suggests, but rather "the place where a plant or animal species naturally lives or grows." Webster's Third New International Dictionary 1017 (1993). Before the Corps may assert jurisdiction under the migratory bird rule, it must first make a factual determination that a particular body of water provides a habitat for migratory birds, which it has done here.[121]

On January 9, 2001, however, a 5–4 majority of the Supreme Court reversed.[122] In so doing, the Court declined to address the broad constitutional question of whether Congress has the authority under the Commerce Clause to regulate wholly intrastate, isolated bodies of water based on the presence of migratory birds. Instead, the Court limited its decision to the narrower issue of the Corps's interpretation of its own authority to regulate such waters under the CWA.

6. *Artificial Wetlands*

The preamble to the Corps's 1986 permit regulations suggests that, at least conceptually, artificial wetlands are generally considered exempt from jurisdiction. The preamble indicates, for example, that ponds created from settling basins for mining activities are generally within this exemption.[123] The preamble also notes, however, that the Corps reserves the right to exercise jurisdiction on a case-by-case basis.[124] In practice, the Corps has invariably asserted jurisdiction over artificial wetlands.

The Corps has successfully defended challenges against exercises of this authority. As discussed above, the Court of Appeals for the Ninth Circuit held in *Leslie Salt* that pits and basins formed as a result of salt-mining activities were wetlands subject to Section 404 jurisdiction.[125] In *United States v. Southern Investment Co.*,[126] the court upheld jurisdiction over an artificial, permanent pool created by the construction of a downstream dam.[127] The primary exception to broad jurisdiction over artificial wetlands has been where the Corps itself has created the wetland.[128]

IV. SWANCC

A. The Court's Ruling and Unanswered Questions

The limited holding of the Court in *Solid Waste Agency of Northern Cook County v. United States Army Corps of Engineers* (*SWANCC*) was that "33 CFR § 328.3(a)(3) (1999), as clarified and applied to petitioner's balefill site pursuant to the 'Migratory Bird Rule'. . ., exceeds the authority granted to [the Corps] under § 404(a) of the CWA."[129] While the Court's decision clearly invalidated the Migratory Bird Rule, it has generated some confusion over the scope of jurisdiction under the Clean Water Act, because the Court seemed to narrow, but did not overturn, the *Riverside Bayview Homes* decision. When the *Riverside Bayview Homes* Court upheld regulation of nonnavigable wetlands that were adjacent to other "waters of the United States," the Court stated that the term "navigable" in the CWA is of "limited import" because Congress had evidenced an intent to "regulate at least some waters that would not be deemed 'navigable' under [that term's] classical understanding."[130] However, when the *SWANCC* majority concluded that the Corps of Engineers lacked the authority to regulate the nonnavigable, isolated intrastate waters at issue in the case, it suggested that "what Congress had in mind as its authority for enacting the CWA [is] its traditional jurisdiction over waters that were or had been navigable in fact or which could reasonably be so made."[131] Those seemingly contradictory statements create some ambiguity regarding the scope of jurisdiction over nonnavigable waters under the CWA.

The *SWANCC* Court based its conclusion that the Corps did not have authority to regulate the nonnavigable isolated intrastate ponds at issue in the case on several grounds. First, the Court noted that its decision to uphold regulation of nonnavigable wetlands in *Riverside Bayview Homes* was based on the "significant nexus" between the wetlands and other navigable waters.[132] That connection was important, the Court suggested, because "Congress' concern for the protection of water quality and aquatic ecosystems indicated its intent to regulate wetlands 'inseparably bound up with the "waters" of the United States.'"[133] The Court also noted that the *Riverside Bayview Homes* Court upheld regulation of the nonnavigable wetlands at issue in that case because Congress acquiesced to, and approved of, the Corps's regulation of those wetlands.[134] The *SWANCC* Court did not conclude that Congress expressed similar concern for regulation of nonnavigable, isolated intrastate waters based on the Migratory Bird Rule.

Finally, the Court found that even if congressional intent to extend Section 404 jurisdiction to nonnavigable, isolated, intrastate waters was unclear—which it did not believe it was—the Corps's interpretation of its own jurisdiction was not entitled to deference, because the Court found that the Migratory Bird Rule raised serious constitutional problems.[135] It both "invokes the outer limits of Congress' power" under the Commerce Clause and "would result in a significant impingement on the States' traditional and primary power over land and water use."[136] Opting to interpret the statute so as to avoid these "constitutional and federalism questions," the Court struck down the Corps's exercise of jurisdiction over the SWANCC site under the Migratory Bird Rule.[137]

While clearly invalidating regulation of nonnavigable, isolated intrastate waters based on the Migratory Bird Rule, the Court's ruling in *SWANCC* does not explicitly address whether the Corps may continue to exercise jurisdiction over nonnavigable, isolated intrastate waters that have a "significant nexus" to navigable waters. Although some commentators have also suggested that *SWANCC* raises concerns about regulation of wetlands that are adjacent to a nonnavigable tributary that eventually leads to a navigable water,[138] most of the courts that have addressed the issue after *SWANCC* have concluded that such waters can be regulated, as discussed *infra*.

The Supreme Court's decision in *Riverside Bayview Homes* would seem to suggest that wetlands that are adjacent to nonnavigable tributaries that eventually lead to navigable waters are subject to Corps jurisdiction. Indeed, the Court framed the question in that case as being "whether the [CWA] . . . authorizes the Corps to require landowners to obtain permits from the Corps before discharging fill material into wetlands adjacent to navigable bodies of water *and their tributaries*."[139] Later in *Riverside Bayview Homes,* however, the Court phrased its approval of the Corps's jurisdiction over adjacent wetlands as being applicable to those wetlands adjacent to "other bodies of water over which the Corps has jurisdiction."[140] In *SWANCC,* the Court suggested that Corps jurisdiction over wetlands may depend on whether there is a "significant nexus between" the wetlands or waters and traditionally "navigable waters," for it was just such a "significant nexus" that supported Corps jurisdiction in *Riverside Bayview Homes.*[141]

The *SWANCC* Court explicitly refused to address the precise extent of the Corps's jurisdiction under Section 404. The Corps had argued that Congress's intent to reach isolated waters and wetlands could be inferred from Section 404(g). That section authorizes any state, subject to EPA approval, "to administer its own individual and general permit program for the discharge of dredged or fill material into the navigable waters (other than those waters which are presently used, or are susceptible to use in their natural condition or by reasonable improvement as a means to transport interstate or foreign commerce . . . including wetlands adjacent thereto) within its jurisdiction."[142] The Court responded:

> Section 404(g) is . . . unenlightening. In *Riverside Bayview Homes* we recognized that Congress intended the phrase "navigable waters" to include "at least some waters that would not be deemed 'navigable' under the classical understanding of that term." 474 U.S. at 133. But § 404(g) gives no intimation of what

> those waters might be; it simply refers to them as "other . . . waters." Respondents conjecture that "other . . . waters" must incorporate the Corps' 1977 regulations, but it is also plausible, as petitioner contends, that Congress simply wanted to include all waters adjacent to "navigable waters," such as nonnavigable tributaries and streams. The exact meaning of § 404(g) is not before us and we express no opinion on it, but for present purposes it is sufficient to say, as we did in Riverside Bayview Homes, that "§ 404(g)(1) does not conclusively determine the construction to be placed on the use of the term 'waters' elsewhere in the Act."[143]

The dissenting justices in *SWANCC*, led by Justice Stevens, would accept Corps jurisdiction over wetlands adjacent to nonnavigable tributaries of navigable waters. In discussing *Riverside Bayview Homes*, Justice Stevens wrote: "The Court has previously held that the Corps' broadened jurisdiction under the [Clean Water Act] properly included an 80-acre parcel of low-lying marshy land that was not itself navigable, directly adjacent to navigable water, or even hydrologically connected to navigable water, but which was part of a larger area, characterized by poor drainage, that ultimately abutted a navigable creek."[144] Most of the courts that have addressed the issue post-*SWANCC* have concluded that Corps jurisdiction over wetlands adjacent to nonnavigable tributaries of navigable waters is appropriate, as discussed *infra*.

B. Executive Interpretation of *SWANCC*

The Clinton administration adopted a narrow view of the Supreme Court's holding in *SWANCC*. In a 2001 memorandum issued jointly to field personnel by the General Counsel of EPA and the Chief Counsel of the Corps,[145] the agencies expressed their view that "the Court's holding was strictly limited to waters that are 'nonnavigable, isolated, [and] instrastate [*sic*].' With respect to any waters that fall outside of that category, field staff should continue to exercise CWA jurisdiction to the full extent of their authority under the statute and regulations and consistent with court opinions."[146]

The agencies further pointed out that the *SWANCC* Court had not overruled "the holding or rationale" of *Riverside Bayview Homes*. Thus, they maintained that "traditionally navigable waters, interstate waters, their tributaries, and wetlands adjacent to each" remain subject to regulation.[147] This list indicates the agencies' belief that wetlands adjacent to nonnavigable tributaries that ultimately lead to a navigable water body are subject to regulation.

In the agencies's view, the one subsection of the regulatory definition drawn into question by the *SWANCC* ruling is 33 C.F.R. § 328(a)(3), which, as set forth above, applies to "[a]ll other waters" such as intrastate waters "the use, degradation or destruction of which could affect interstate or foreign commerce." As to such waters, the agencies's 2001 memorandum provided the following guidance to their field personnel. Waters that fall under the subsection (a)(3) definition solely because of their use as habitat for migratory birds should no longer be considered "waters of the United States."[148] However, other "connections with interstate commerce might support the assertion of CWA jurisdiction over 'nonnavigable, isolated, intrastate waters.'"[149]

Two examples of situations in which jurisdiction might be asserted over wholly intrastate, nonnavigable waters were provided: (1) where the "use, degradation or destruction" of such waters could affect other "waters of the United States"; or (2) where the "use, degradation or destruction" of such waters could affect interstate or foreign commerce.[150] The memorandum, thus, suggests that the Corps and EPA determined that *SWANCC* did not invalidate regulation of nonnavigable, isolated, intrastate waters generally, but merely invalidated regulation of those waters based on the Migratory Bird Rule.

The Bush administration has generally adhered to the conclusions expressed in the joint memorandum issued by the Clinton administration. In a 2003 update to the Clinton administration joint memorandum, the agencies have expressed somewhat more skepticism about whether *SWANCC* permits the Corps to assert jurisdiction over nonnavigable, isolated intrastate waters and wetlands based solely on whether these waters have a significant nexus to interstate commerce.[151] Nonetheless, the memorandum directs the Corps's field staff to "seek formal project-specific Headquarters approval prior to asserting jurisdiction over such waters, including permitting and enforcement actions."[152]

The Bush memorandum focused mostly on whether *SWANCC* may be interpreted to permit the Corps to assert jurisdiction over nonnavigable tributaries (and their adjacent wetlands) to traditionally navigable waters, noting that some courts had interpreted *SWANCC* to preclude jurisdiction over such waters.[153] The memorandum concludes that, "generally speaking," the Corps will continue to assert jurisdiction over such waters.[154]

C. Judicial Interpretation of *SWANCC*

The lower courts have begun to grapple with whether the agencies' narrow reading of the *SWANCC* decision is the correct one. They have also considered whether the government may continue to assert jurisdiction over wetlands that have some ecological connection to a navigable water body, but where a direct surface water connection between the two is lacking. Most courts (including four of the five United States Circuit Courts that have addressed the question) have held that nonnavigable tributaries of navigable waters, and wetlands adjacent to nonnavigable tributaries of navigable waters, continue to be within federal jurisdiction after *SWANCC*.

In the first case to address the question of jurisdiction over wetlands that are adjacent to nonnavigable tributaries to navigable waters, the district court in *United States v. Buday*[155] held that the Corps does have jurisdiction over such wetlands. The court declined to grant the defendant's motion to withdraw his guilty plea, entered "hours before" the Supreme Court issued its decision in *SWANCC*, for discharging pollutants, including dredged and fill material, into "navigable waters," including wetlands, without a permit. The court found that the Corps retained jurisdiction over the tributary and adjacent wetlands, even though they were not navigable in fact and did not connect with a navigable-in-fact waterway for at least 235 miles. Because discharges of pollutants into those waters would eventually have an impact on waters affecting interstate commerce, the Corps could properly exercise jurisdiction.[156]

The *Buday* court's narrow interpretation of *SWANCC* was echoed by the United States Court of Appeals for the Fourth Circuit in *United States v. Interstate General Company, L.P.*[157] The court concluded that *SWANCC* affected the Corps's jurisdiction only over isolated wetlands, leaving in place Corps authority over wetlands adjacent to tributaries of traditionally navigable waters.[158]

Subsequent to *Interstate General*, the Fourth Circuit has consistently adopted a narrow reading of *SWANCC*, upholding regulation of wetlands in *United States v. Deaton*[159] and *Treacy v. Newdunn Associates, L.L.P.*[160] In *Deaton*, the defendants were sued for failing to obtain a permit from the Corps before conducting ditching and fill activities in wetlands adjacent to a roadside ditch that flowed eventually into a navigable water and the Chesapeake Bay.[161] The Fourth Circuit considered a number of important issues directed at the degree of deference owed to the Corps's interpretations of the CWA and the Corps's regulatory definition of "waters of the United States."

The court first considered whether *SWANCC* necessitated a refusal to defer to the Corps's interpretations on the grounds that asserting jurisdiction over wetlands like those filled by the Deatons involved "an administrative interpretation of a statute [that] invokes the outer limits of Congress' power."[162] The court concluded that "Congress's authority over the channels of interstate commerce is . . . broad enough to allow it to legislate, as it did in the Clean Water Act, to prevent the use of navigable waters for injurious purposes;" that Congress may appropriately consider that "the aggregate effect of all of the individual instances of discharge, [such as] the discharge by the Deatons, justifies regulating each of them;" and that "under the Corps's interpretation, the Clean Water Act does not invade an area of authority reserved to the states."[163] Accordingly, the agency's interpretation "does not present a serious constitutional question that would cause [the court] to assume that Congress did not intend to authorize the regulation" and thus "the assertion of jurisdiction over nonnavigable tributaries of navigable waters is constitutional."[164]

The court then considered whether the Corps's decision to interpret its regulations and the CWA to support jurisdiction over the Deatons' conduct was appropriate. Applying the rule articulated in *Chevron U.S.A. v. Natural Resources Defense Council,*[165] the court held that "[t]he statutory term 'waters of the United States' is sufficiently ambiguous to constitute an implied delegation of authority to the Corps; this authority permits the Corps to determine which waters are to be covered within the range suggested by *SWANCC.*"[166]

Before addressing the question of whether the Corps regulatory definition of "waters of the United States" was a reasonable interpretation of the CWA, the court first considered whether the Corps regulation could reasonably be interpreted to reach the roadside ditch and adjacent wetlands. The Deatons argued that 33 C.F.R. § 328.3(a)(5), which defines waters of the United States to include tributaries of navigable waters, could support jurisdiction only over tributaries that empty directly into a navigable waterway. The court rejected this argument, concluding that the Corps could reasonably interpret the regulatory term "tributaries" to mean "'all tributaries,' not just 'short' or 'primary' tributaries,'" and thus, under the regulation, Corps jurisdiction may extend to "any branch of a tributary system that flows into a navigable body of water."[167]

Finally, the court considered whether the Corps's regulation was based on a permissible interpretation of the CWA. The Deatons, citing *SWANCC,* argued that the Corps's 1974 regulations, which reached only navigable waters, expressed the limits of the Corps's jurisdiction under the CWA.[168] Again, the court held otherwise. The Fourth Circuit concluded that *SWANCC* should not be read "to hold that the 1974 regulations represent the only permissible interpretation of the Clean Water Act."[169] To the contrary,

> deference to [the Corps's interpretation] is appropriate. In *Riverside Bayview,* the Supreme Court concluded that the Corps regulation extending jurisdiction to adjacent wetlands was a reasonable interpretation in part because of what *SWANCC* described as

> "the significant nexus between the wetlands and 'navigable waters.'" *SWANCC*, 531 U.S. at 167. There is also a nexus between a navigable waterway and its nonnavigable tributaries. . . . [D]ischarges into nonnavigable tributaries and adjacent wetlands have a substantial effect on water quality in navigable waters. . . . This nexus, in light of the "breadth of congressional concern for protection of water quality and aquatic ecosystems," *Riverside Bayview*, 474 U.S. at 133, is sufficient to allow the Corps to determine reasonably that its jurisdiction over the whole tributary system of any navigable waterway is warranted. [170]

The Deatons' Petition for a Writ of Certiorari to the United States Supreme Court was denied on April 5, 2004.[171]

In *Treacy v. Newdunn Associates, L.L.P.*, the Fourth Circuit held that the Corps of Engineers had jurisdiction under the CWA to require a developer to obtain a permit to fill 38 acres of wetlands on its property, because, prior to the construction of an interstate highway, the wetlands had a natural hydrologic connection to Stony Run, which is a navigable-in-fact waterway.[172] After the construction of the interstate highway, the wetlands remained connected to Stony Run by "the intermittent flow of surface water through approximately 2.4 miles of natural streams and manmade ditches."[173] Relying on *Deaton*, the *Newdunn* court held that the term 'tributary' "include[s] 'the entire tributary system,' including roadside ditches."[174] The court reasoned:

> The Corps' unremarkable interpretation of the term "waters of the United States" as including wetlands adjacent to tributaries of navigable waters is permissible under the CWA because pollutants added to any of these tributaries will inevitably find their way to the very waters that Congress sought to protect.[175]

Newdunn Associates' Petition for a Writ of Certiorari to the United States Supreme Court was denied on April 5, 2004.[176]

The Sixth, Seventh, and Ninth Circuits have also adopted narrow interpretations of *SWANCC*. In *United States v. Rapanos*,[177] the United States Court of Appeals for the Sixth Circuit relied on the Fourth Circuit's *Deaton* ruling to conclude that it was appropriate for the Corps to assert jurisdiction over wetlands adjacent to a nonnavigable man-made drain that flowed almost twenty miles before emptying into a navigable water.[178] The court ruled that

> Although the *Solid Waste* opinion limits the application of the Clean Water Act, the Court did not go as far as Rapanos argues,

> restricting the Act's coverage to only wetlands directly abutting navigable water. . . . The evidence presented in this case suffices to show that the wetlands on Rapanos's land are adjacent to the Labonzinski Drain, especially in view of the hydrological connection between the two. It follows under the analysis in *Deaton,* with which we agree, that the Rapanos wetlands are covered by the Clean Water Act. Any contamination of the Rapanos wetlands could affect the Drain, which, in turn, could affect navigable-in-fact waters. Therefore, protection of the wetlands on Rapanos's land is a fair extension of the Clean Water Act. *Solid Waste* requires a "significant nexus between the wetlands and 'navigable waters'" for there to be jurisdiction under the Clean Water Act. Because the wetlands are adjacent to the Drain and there exists a hydrological connection among the wetlands, the Drain, and the Kawkawlin River, we find an ample nexus to establish jurisdiction.[179]

While the court acknowledged that *SWANCC* reduced the scope of Clean Water Act jurisdiction over nonnavigable waters, the court affirmed the need for broad protection of those waters, stating that "the Clean Water Act cannot purport to police only navigable-in-fact waters in the United States in order to keep those waters clean from pollutants. . . . Although wetlands are not traditionally navigable-in-fact, they play an important ecological role where they exist."[180] Rapanos' Petition for a Writ of Certiorari to the United States Supreme Court was denied on April 5, 2004.[181]

In *United States v. Krilich,* the United States Court of Appeals for the Seventh Circuit upheld the decision of the United States District Court for the Northern District of Illinois to deny the defendants' motion to vacate a 1992 consent decree in light of *SWANCC.*[182] In affirming the lower court's decision, the Seventh Circuit stated that the Supreme Court, in *SWANCC,* merely invalidated the Migratory Bird Rule, and that the Court's "limited holding does not represent a significant change in the law such that it would be equitable to modify or vacate the consent decree" that was entered into by the defendants.[183]

The Ninth Circuit adopted a narrow reading of *SWANCC* in *Headwaters, Inc. v. Talent Irrigation District.*[184] While the case involved a question regarding jurisdiction under Section 402 of the Clean Water Act (which regulates the issuance of permits for discharges of pollutants other than fill materials into waters of the United States), the decision is instructive, because the same definition of "waters of the United States" applies in the Section 402 context as under Section 404. In *Headwaters,* the Ninth

Circuit held that a local irrigation district violated the CWA by applying an herbicide to its canals without obtaining a National Pollutant Discharge Elimination System (NPDES) permit.[185] In so holding, the court found that the canals were not isolated waters excluded from jurisdiction under *SWANCC,* but rather were connected as tributaries to navigable waters, based on their exchange of water with "a number of natural streams and at least one lake, which no one disputes are 'waters of the United States.'"[186]

The Ninth Circuit applied similar reasoning in *Community Association for the Restoration of the Environment v. Henry Bosma Dairy,*[187] another Section 402 case, when it held that a drain that carried return flows and other waters either directly or by connecting waterways into the Yakima River (a navigable water) was within Clean Water Act jurisdiction as "waters of the United States."[188] Citing *Headwaters,* the court noted that "[a] stream which contributes its flow to a larger stream or other body of water is a tributary," and that "[e]ven tributaries that flow intermittently are 'waters of the United States.'"[189]

Although most courts have interpreted *SWANCC* narrowly, the United States Court of Appeals for the Fifth Circuit has adopted a broader reading of the decision in two cases involving the Oil Pollution Act of 1990 (OPA). In *Rice v. Harken Exploration Company,* the court held that a company could not be held liable under the OPA for discharges into "navigable waters" where the only demonstrable discharge was to groundwater.[190] Citing *SWANCC,* the court first stated:

> [R]ecently, the Supreme Court has limited the scope of the CWA. . . . Under [*SWANCC*], it appears that a body of water is subject to regulation under the CWA if the body of water is actually navigable or is adjacent to an open body of navigable water. . . . Nevertheless, under this standard the term "navigable waters" is not limited to oceans and other very large bodies of water. If the OPA and CWA have identical regulatory scope, the district court's conclusion that the OPA cannot apply to *any* inland waters was erroneous.[191]

Nonetheless, the court held that although OPA and the CWA both regulate discharges to "navigable waters," and contain "textually identical definitions" of that term, neither law has been held to regulate discharges to groundwater.[192] Further, the court held that a number of intermittent streams located on the property were not "waters of the United States" because the appellants failed to demonstrate that these streams were "sufficiently linked to an open body of navigable water."[193]

Finally, although recognizing that the CWA has been applied to discharges to wetlands adjacent to navigable waters, the court refused to conclude that "a discharge onto dry land, some of which eventually reaches groundwater and some of the latter of which still later may reach navigable waters, all by gradual, natural seepage, is the equivalent of a 'discharge' 'into or upon navigable waters.'"[194] Accordingly, the court held that "a generalized assertion that covered surface waters [in this case, the larger Canadian River] will eventually be affected by remote, gradual, natural seepage from the contaminated groundwater is insufficient to establish liability under the OPA."[195]

In basing its holding on the plaintiffs' "generalized assertions," however, the court apparently left unresolved the question of whether there would have been an actionable discharge had the plaintiffs been able to prove that oil had actually reached a covered surface water.

The Fifth Circuit provided additional guidance regarding its interpretation of *SWANCC* in dicta in *In re Needham*, another case involving the OPA.[196] The court held that the Needhams were liable for cleanup costs under the OPA caused by an oil spill into Bayou Folse, which is adjacent to Company Canal, a navigable in fact water that flows into the Gulf of Mexico.[197] In strongly worded dicta, the court expressed disapproval for the rulings of the Fourth and Sixth Circuits in *Deaton* and *Rapanos* and stated:

> The CWA and OPA are not so broad as to permit the government to impose regulations over "tributaries" that are neither themselves navigable nor truly adjacent to navigable waters. Consequently, in this circuit the United States may not simply impose regulations over puddles, sewers, roadside ditches and the like; under *SWANCC*, "a body of water is subject to regulation . . . if the body of water is actually navigable or adjacent to an open body of navigable water."[198]

The *Needham* court further stated:

> Under *Rice*, the term "adjacent" cannot include every possible source of water that eventually flows into a navigable-in-fact waterway. Rather, adjacency necessarily implicates a "significant nexus" between the water in question and the navigable-in-fact waterway.[199]

Although there is a growing consensus among the courts that *SWANCC* should be given a narrow interpretation, the varying judicial interpretations of *SWANCC* have nonetheless generated uncertainty about the jurisdictional reach of the Section 404 program. In an attempt to clarify that uncertainty, the Corps and EPA issued an advance notice of proposed rulemaking (ANPRM) to amend the regulatory definition of navigable waters.[200] The ANPRM solicited comments on what factors might support the assertion of jurisdiction over isolated, intrastate, non-navigable waters, and whether the term "isolated waters" should be defined by regulation.[201] However, after receiving more than one hundred thirty thousand comments, the Corps and EPA withdrew their proposal.[202] The Bush memorandum discussed in Section IV.B, above, thus remains the sole guidance from the Executive branch on this issue at the present time.

V. Wetland Delineation Criteria

The previous section has provided an overview of when the Corps may properly assert regulatory jurisdiction over wetlands. While these jurisdictional issues may be at times difficult and controversial, it remains to determine how the status of wetlands is bestowed upon a particular site.[203] The chief basis for making a wetlands determination is by applying the criteria in the Corps's 1987 *Wetland Delineation Manual*. This section first discusses the respective roles of EPA and the Corps in making wetlands delineations. It then discusses the criteria currently used in making such determinations.

A. Memoranda of Agreement Regarding Jurisdictional Determinations

Under the CWA, EPA possesses the ultimate authority to determine the existence of a wetland. Nonetheless, EPA and the Corps entered into a Memorandum of Agreement (MOA) in 1989 under which EPA's role is more limited. Pursuant to the MOA,[204] EPA makes jurisdictional determinations (including exemptions of discharges) only in "special cases" that involve important policy and/or technical issues.[205] Other jurisdictional determinations are made by the Corps. The MOA also provides that written, final determinations by the Corps or EPA are binding on the government and represent the government's position in any subsequent action or litigation concerning that final determination.[206] This provision lessens the chance of conflicting agency decisions on a particular property.[207]

A 1993 MOA between the agencies reiterated the basic balance of power established in the 1989 MOA.[208] While the Corps has the basic power to render jurisdictional determinations that are binding on EPA, the 1993 MOA obligates the Corps to adhere to EPA guidance on isolated waters, in addition to other guidance, interpretations, and regulations issued by EPA relating to geographic jurisdiction and exemptions. Thus, basic jurisdictional determinations continue to be made by the Corps, while EPA takes the lead in "special cases," including isolated waters.

B. Delineation Criteria

As previously mentioned, three factors have historically been used by agencies to delineate wetlands: hydrophytic vegetation, hydric soil, and hydrology.[209] These three criteria are a part of the Corps's and EPA's definition of wetlands,[210] and they have been used in the various manuals issued by agencies for the purpose of delineating wetlands. The Corps's 1987 Manual is currently used, but in the past, the Corps, EPA, the FWS, and the NRCS employed different techniques for determining whether particular areas are wetlands.

1. Vegetation

The principal criterion for ascertaining the presence of hydrophytic vegetation under normal circumstances is whether more than 50 percent of the dominant species are either obligate wetlands plants, facultative wetland plants, or facultative plants.[211] Plant species are identified by reference to the FWS publication *National List of Plant Species that Occur in Wetlands*.[212]

Courts have found that wetlands vegetation is not limited to species capable of surviving their entire lives in saturated soils.[213] Similarly, the courts have concluded that the presence of species under conditions that are transitional from wetlands to uplands do not render an area a non-wetland.[214]

2. Soil

Most wetlands determinations involve questions about vegetation and hydrology rather than soil. Hydric soils can be identified in the field by comparing soil color at pertinent depths to soil color charts. These soil charts and the corresponding gradations of color reflect the anaerobic conditions typical of water-saturated soils. Hydric soil determinations may be used in delineating wetlands boundaries. Soil is considered a less reliable criterion than plants or hydrology, however, because hydric soil may remain in an area even after other wetlands indicators are no longer present.

3. Hydrology

Sufficient hydrology exists when there is an inundation of the subject area, by either surface flow or groundwater, for a specified percentage of the growing season (approximately one week is a typical length of time).

Inundation creates the anaerobic conditions under which wetlands plants have adapted. It also produces those qualities that distinguish hydric from nonhydric soils.

The Supreme Court held in *Riverside Bayview Homes* that a groundwater source of saturation was sufficient to support wetlands jurisdiction.[215] In addition, several courts have found that groundwater need not reach the surface if wetlands plants are present or soils are sufficiently inundated to meet the regulatory jurisdictional requirements.[216] Another court has determined that rainwater may be an acceptable source of saturation for wetlands jurisdiction.[217]

C. Delineation Manuals

1. *Evolution of Criteria*

There have been various attempts by interested agencies to define wetlands in a more precise fashion, and to specify a uniform delineation methodology. Different manuals have generated considerable controversy, as divergent definitions tended to include more or fewer areas as regulated wetlands.

The Corps adopted its first formal *Wetland Delineation Manual* in 1987. In 1988, EPA adopted its own *Wetlands Identification and Delineation Manual (Interim).* In an effort to consolidate the various delineation approaches, in 1989, the Corps, EPA, the FWS, and the NRCS (then the Soil Conservation Service) coordinated to formulate the 1989 *Federal Manual for Identifying and Delineating Jurisdictional Wetlands.*[218] However, the process that the agencies used to adopt the 1989 Manual was challenged and the Manual was criticized for extending jurisdiction beyond historical limits.[219]

In response to the controversy, the Corps and EPA proposed revisions to that manual, but those revisions were criticized for significantly reducing jurisdiction over wetlands.[220] In response to the controversy over the Delineation Manuals, Congress included a rider in the 1993 Appropriations legislation for the Corps, precluding the agency from relying on the 1989 Manual or any other subsequent manual adopted without rulemaking under the Administrative Procedures Act (APA).[221] As a consequence, the Corps reverted to its 1987 Manual, and EPA and the other agencies now also rely on it.

2. *The 1987 Manual*

The 1987 Manual provides a basis for determining whether a given area constitutes a wetland for purposes of Section 404, but does not attempt to classify wetlands by type.[222] Consistent with the historical definition of wetlands, it generally requires that all three parameters discussed above—hydrology, hydrophytic vegetation, and hydric soils—be present in order to classify an area as wetlands. The Manual emphasizes plant communities, focusing on the assemblage of plant species exerting an influence on the character of the plant community rather than on indicator species, in determining whether the vegetation criterion is met in a particular area.[223] Thus, the presence of scattered individual nonwetland species in an area dominated by wetland species would not support a finding that an area was an upland. As indicated above, the presence of hydric soils is ascertained based on a list of indicators, including color and the presence of certain materials, that signify inundation of sufficient duration to effect anaerobic conditions.[224]

The Manual focuses on hydrology to a greater extent than the other two criteria. Vegetation and soils are indications that an area is a wetland, but "it is essential to establish that a wetland area is periodically inundated or has saturated soils during the growing season."[225] Generally, the Corps may not rely on hydrophytic vegetation or hydric soils alone to determine that the requisite hydrology exists.

The Manual describes several methods for making a wetland classification. In general, the methods involve (1) mapping out an area; (2) identifying its vegetative species, soil characteristics, and hydrology; and (3) comparing the findings with the Manual's wetland indicators to determine if the requisite parameters are or would normally be present during a significant portion of the growing season.[226]

Guidelines for making determinations in "atypical situations" and for attacking "problem areas" are also provided. "Atypical situations" are ones where it has been determined that "positive indicators of hydrophytic vegetation, hydric soils, and/or wetland hydrology could not be found due to effects of recent human activities or natural events."[227] Included are situations in which human activities have resulted in the alteration of an area's "normal circumstances." For example, road construction may result in an impoundment of water that affects hydrophytic vegetation and hydrology in such a way as to provide positive indicators that an area that was not previously a wetland now meets otherwise applicable wetlands criteria.

"Problem areas" are those in which "wetland indicators of one or more parameters may be periodically lacking due to *normal* seasonal or annual variations in environmental conditions that result from causes other than human activities or catastrophic natural events."[228] For instance, seasonal wetlands may exist in which all three parameters are present during a portion of the year yet hydrology and/or vegetation are lacking during the remainder of the year.

The Manual establishes a methodology for determining when such "problem areas" may be classified as wetlands. In particular, when fewer than three of the criteria are present due to seasonal or natural variations, it provides for a determination of whether all three parameters are normally present such as to support a wetlands classification.

3. *The 1989 Manual*

For the two years in which it was used, the 1989 Manual delineated a significantly larger allotment of land as wetlands. Although this Manual also specified that all three parameters must be met for a wetlands determination, it provided for a more generous determination of the presence of wetlands hydrology and vegetation. In circumstances in which hydrology is difficult to ascertain, the 1989 Manual permitted the inference of one criterion based on the presence of the others.

Following concern that its use resulted in too broad a spectrum of lands being classified as wetlands, the agencies jointly conducted an evaluation of the 1989 Manual. Although the agencies concluded that it was an improvement over prior approaches, including the 1987 Manual, they identified four areas in continued need of examination and clarification: (1) the wetland hydrology criterion; (2) the use of hydric soils for determining wetland boundaries; (3) the presumption that the presence of hydrophytic vegetation could be used to indicate hydrology; and (4) the open-ended nature of the delineation process.[229] However, as described above, EPA's attempt to revise the Manual to narrow the scope of jurisdiction met with strong opposition, resulting in the congressional command that the 1987 Manual be used until an improved guide could be adopted in compliance with the APA.[230]

4. *Recent Efforts to Update the Delineation Process*

In 1992, Congress directed the National Academy of Sciences (NAS) to conduct a wetlands study to assist in the formulation of an updated manual.[231] This study was released in 1995.[232] The report concluded that the current regulatory practice for characterizing and delineating wetlands is scientifically sound, although it stressed the need for an approach that is "more efficient, more uniform, more credible with regulated entities, and more accurate in a technical or scientific sense." This study builds on the Corps/EPA definition of a wetland, but expands it to reflect the NAS's view of wetlands as distinct ecosystems.

Specific recommendations included (1) developing more comprehensive, regionally diverse studies of wetland phenomena; (2) improving the definition and evaluation of factors assessed in the delineation of wetlands, including moving away from the three-parameter test contained in the 1987 Manual; (3) preparing a new delineation manual; (4) improving scientific understanding of especially controversial wetlands, including wetlands on agricultural lands, broader riparian zones, and permafrost, isolated, and shallow wetlands; (5) developing regional delineation practices and mapping; and (6) extending and refining analysis of wetland functions, with an emphasis on interactions between wetlands and their surroundings.[233] Thus far, the NAS recommendations have not been incorporated into a revised manual.

VI. Jurisdictional Determinations

The process for obtaining a jurisdictional determination generally involves retaining a consultant to visit a site and delineate its boundaries in accordance with the Corps's 1987 Manual. Corps district engineers are authorized to make jurisdictional determinations, but neither the Corps nor EPA is required to do so on demand. Due to limited Corps resources, obtaining an outside consultant to perform the initial determination expedites the delineation process.[234] Once the consultant has completed the delineation, a Corps staff member comes to the site and modifies the line, if necessary, also according to the Manual's criteria. A survey of the final line is then presented to the Corps. If the survey accurately reflects the field work, the agency issues a jurisdictional determination.

Sound professional judgment is required to classify an area as wetlands, based on all three delineation criteria. Because agency resources are limited, much of this judgment is exercised currently by nonagency consultants, as discussed above. The Corps has found, however, that it "routinely receives inaccurate and inconsistent wetland delineations from applicants and/or their representatives which necessitate modification(s) or redelineation(s)," resulting in delays and inefficient uses of agency resources.[235] To reduce these problems, the Corps proposed regulations establishing a Wetland Delineation Certification Program,[236] pursuant to Section 307(e) of the Water Resources Development Act of 1990.[237] The program was designed to improve the quality and consistency of wetland delineations and streamline the regulatory process.[238] The primary means of attaining this goal is giving expedited review to wetland delineations submitted by certified wetland delineators.[239] The certification program now appears to be on hold.

Jurisdictional determinations made or accepted by the Corps are valid for five years, subject to the discovery of new information.[240] The Corps has consistently, and successfully, contended that the only effect of a finding of jurisdiction is to require a permit, and thus there is no final agency action subject to judicial review until a decision on the permit has been made.[241]

VII. Conclusion

Federal jurisdiction over the identification, delineation, and regulation of wetlands remains a dynamic and contentious area. Major issues include the scope of lands that may be regulated as wetlands, the science of wetland delineation, and the allocation of authority over the Section 404 program among the various interested agencies.

Federal jurisdiction over wetlands is broad, reaching not only those "waters of the United States" that meet the traditional concept of "navigable waters," but also those that are deemed to have an effect on interstate commerce. This interstate commerce requirement has been interpreted quite permissively. Isolated, adjacent, and artificially created wetlands have all been subject to federal jurisdiction, though assertions of jurisdiction over these areas remains unsettled and controversial.

The delineation of wetlands is accomplished through utilization of three criteria—hydrophytic vegetation, hydric soils, and hydrology—and the guidance of the Corps's 1987 *Wetland Delineation Manual.* Despite calls for the changes to the wetland identification and delineation process, efforts at revising the delineation criteria and methodology, and certifying individuals as wetland delineators, are currently stalled.

Notes

1. 33 U.S.C. §§ 401 *et seq.* (2000).
2. 33 C.F.R. § 329.4 (2004).
3. *See* Borax Consolidated, Ltd. v. City of Los Angeles, 296 U.S. 10 (1935) (discussing mean high water marks).
4. 33 U.S.C. §§ 1251–1387.
5. *Id.* § 1251.
6. *Id.* § 1344(a).
7. *Id.* § 1362(7).
8. *See* Natural Resources Defense Council, Inc. v. Callaway, 392 F. Supp. 685 (D.D.C. 1975). Prior to *Callaway,* the Corps had narrowly construed Section 404's jurisdiction to be the same as the River and Harbor Act's jurisdiction.
9. State agencies also have a role in the implementation of the Section 404 program. For a detailed discussion, see Chapter 10 of this book.
10. 33 U.S.C. § 1344(m), (q); *see also* 33 C.F.R. § 323.4(c). The FWS and the NMFS are also involved in the identification and delineation of wetlands. The FWS, for example, publishes the *National List of Plant Species that Occur in Wet-*

lands, discussed *infra.* In addition, the FWS recently conducted a survey of the nation's wetlands to determine the effect of national wetlands policy during the period from 1985 to 1995. It reported that wetlands are disappearing at an average rate of 117,000 acres per year. This represents a continuation of a trend of declining net loss in wetlands over the past four decades. T. E. Dahl, R. D. Young, & M. C. Caldwell, *Status and Trends of Wetlands in the Conterminous United States* (U.S. Department of the Interior, Fish and Wildlife Service 1997).

11. The Food Security Act of 1985, Pub. L. No. 99-198, 99 Stat. 1504 (1985), 16 U.S.C. §§ 3821–3824, as amended by the Federal Agricultural Improvement and Reform Act of 1996, Pub. L. 104-127, 110 Stat. 888 (1996). A discussion of the differing definition of, and jurisdiction over, wetlands under this Act is discussed in Chapter 14 of this book.

12. 40 C.F.R. §§ 230 *et seq.*

13. 33 C.F.R. §§ 320 *et seq.*

14. 33 U.S.C. § 1344(e). *See* Chapter 5 of this book for a discussion of general permits.

15. *See generally* 33 C.F.R. §§ 320 *et seq.*

16. The five federal agencies mentioned in the text have jointly promulgated mitigation bank guidelines. Environmental Protection Agency; Department of Agriculture, Natural Resources Conservation Service; Department of the Interior, Fish and Wildlife Service; Department of Commerce, National Oceanic and Atmospheric Administration; Department of Defense, Department of the Army, United States Army Corps of Engineers; *Federal Guidance for the Establishment, Use and Operation of Mitigation Banks,* 60 Fed. Reg. 58,605 (Nov. 28, 1995). *See* Chapter 8 of this book for a discussion of mitigation requirements.

17. 33 U.S.C. § 1344(b).

18. 40 C.F.R. §§ 230 *et seq.*

19. 33 U.S.C. § 1344(c) (2000).

20. *See* Chapter 7 of this book.

21. Opinion of the Attorney General, *Administrative Authority to Construe § 404 of the Federal Water Pollution Control Act* 5–7 (Sept. 5, 1979). This opinion was extremely broad in its delegation of authority to EPA; the Attorney General, in fact, opined that EPA had final authority over all jurisdictional questions under the Clean Water Act, including Section 404. A 1989 Memorandum of Agreement between the Corps and EPA, discussed below, reversed that broad grant of authority. The Corps now may make jurisdictional determinations that are binding on EPA.

22. The term "waters of the United States" is defined by the Corps and EPA, respectively, at 33 C.F.R. § 328.3(a) and 40 C.F.R. § 230.3(s). The Corps's definition of "wetlands" is set forth at 33 C.F.R. § 328.3(b). EPA's definition is found at 40 C.F.R. § 230.3(t).

23. 33 U.S.C. § 1344(a).

24. Enforcement authorities and the division of labor between EPA and the Corps are discussed in Chapter 12 of this book.

25. 33 U.S.C. § 1344(a).

26. *Id.* § 1362(7).

27. Mills v. United States, 36 F.3d 1052, 1056 (11th Cir. 1994).

28. *Id.*

29. 33 C.F.R. § 328.3(a). The regulations contain two exclusions that are relevant to wetland jurisdiction. Not included as "waters of the United States" are "prior converted cropland" and "[w]aste treatment ponds or lagoons designed to meet the requirements of the CWA." *Id.* § 328.3(a)(8). The term "prior converted cropland" refers to land excluded from regulation under the Swampbuster program of the Food Security Act and is discussed in Chapter 14 of this book.

30. 33 C.F.R. § 328.4(c)(2).

31. *Id.* § 328.4(c)(3).

32. Op. Att'y Gen. No. 15, at 5 (Sept. 5, 1979).

33. 33 C.F.R. § 328.3(B) (Corps); 40 C.F.R. § 230.3(t) (EPA). Despite identical regulatory definitions, the Corps and EPA do not always agree on whether a particular area constitutes wetlands. This disagreement is sometimes reflected on the enforcement side, when EPA enforces a Section 404 violation where the Corps will not do so due to differences of opinion as to whether a wetlands is at issue.

34. Legislative activity has unsuccessfully sought to limit federal wetland jurisdiction, sometimes by classification schemes. *See, e.g.*, H.R. 1330, 102d Cong., 1st Sess. (1991); S. 1463, 102d Cong., 1st Sess. (1991).

35. Examples of states that regulate buffer zones are Maine, Maryland, New York, and Texas. *See* 38 ME. REV. STAT. § 480-X; MD. ENVIR. CODE ANN. § 5-901; N.Y. ENVTL. CONSERV. LAW §§ 24-0701, 25-0401; TEX. NAT. RES. CODE § 221.001. While activities in buffer zones are not within the Corps's Section 404 jurisdiction, the agency is now requiring buffer zones as mitigation in some of its recently issued nationwide general permits. *See* Chapter 5 of this book.

36. U.S. Army Corps of Engineers, *Wetlands Delineation Manual* (1987) ("1987 Manual"), p. 8; *see* RGL No. 86-9, *Clarification of "Normal Circumstances" in the Wetland Definition* (Aug. 27, 1985). The RGL explains that the phrase "is meant to respond to those situations in which an individual would attempt to eliminate the permit review requirements of Section 404 by destroying the aquatic vegetation." Although this RGL expired in 1991, this understanding of the phrase's purpose has remained unchanged, as the 1987 Manual makes clear. As discussed below, the 1987 Manual specifies particular procedures to be followed in delineating wetlands in such "atypical situations."

37. In *Riverside Bayview Homes*, the Supreme Court held that wetland vegetation supported by the presence of groundwater constituted "normal circumstances" for purposes of Section 404 jurisdiction. United States v. Riverside Bayview Homes, 474 U.S. 121, 130 n.7 (1985). The court of appeals had concluded that such vegetation, unless supported by surface waters from an adjacent navigable water or its tributaries, was "abnormal"—a conclusion the Supreme Court called "untenable in light of the explicit statements in both the [Corps's] regulation and its preamble that areas saturated by ground water can fall within the category of wetlands." *Id.* In the Court's view, "[i]t would be nonsensical for the Corps to define wetlands to include such areas and then in the

same sentence exclude them on the ground that the presence of wetland vegetation in such areas was abnormal." *Id.*

38. *Riverside Bayview Homes,* 474 U.S. at 130 n.7 (quoting 42 Fed. Reg. 37,128 (1977)).

39. 796 F. Supp. 1306 (N.D. Cal. 1992).

40. In 1975, the Corps promulgated a new definition of "waters of the United States," which enlarged the jurisdiction of the Section 404 program to include certain wetlands that, prior to 1975, the Corps viewed as outside the scope of that program. *See id.* at 1309.

41. *Id.* at 1312 (internal quotation marks and citations omitted).

42. The court stated:

> The "under normal circumstances" language allows the Corps to find that an area, which is exhibiting wetland characteristics, is nonetheless not a wetland because the area cannot under normal circumstances support that type of vegetation, etc. It does not allow the Corps to find that the presence of wetlands in an area is abnormal. On the contrary, by finding that "wetlands" are present, the Corps determines that their presence is normal.

Id. at 1313. The clear implication of the court's holding is that in referring to "normal circumstances," the Corps's definition of wetlands was making reference only to conditions brought about natural processes at the site, excluding manipulative interventions that would either prevent the re-emergence of wetland characteristics or continuously remove such characteristics as they re-emerge.

43. 896 F.2d 354, 358 (9th Cir. 1990).

44. *Id.* For a discussion of the Corps's jurisdiction over artificially created wetlands generally, see *infra* this chapter.

45. 747 F.2d 464 (8th Cir. 1984).

46. *See* United States v. Southern Inv. Co., 876 F.2d 606, 612 (8th Cir. 1989).

47. 33 C.F.R. § 328.3(a)(8). Prior converted cropland is discussed in detail in Chapter 14 of this book.

48. In United States v. Wilson, 133 F.3d 251, 256 (4th Cir. 1997), the Fourth Circuit *in dicta* expressed its view that Congressional power to regulate nonadjacent, interstate wetlands may in some cases raise troubling constitutional difficulties: "[I]t is arguable that Congress has the power to regulate the discharge of pollutants into any waters that themselves flow across state lines, or connect to waters that do so, regardless of whether such waters are navigable in fact, merely because of the interstate nature of such waters, although the existence of such a far reaching power could be drawn into question by the [Supreme] Court's recent federalism jurisprudence."

49. 33 C.F.R. § 328.3(c).

50. 474 U.S. 121 (1985).

51. *Id.* at 133–34.

52. *See, e.g.,* Carabell v. U.S. Army Corps of Engineers, 257 F. Supp. 2d 917, 932 (E.D. Mich. 2003) (because wetland was adjacent to tributary, Corps jurisdiction

proper); San Francisco Baykeeper v. Cargill Salt Div., No. C 96-2161 SI, 2003 U.S. Dist. LEXIS 8247, at 20–23 (N.D. Cal. April 30, 2003) (jurisdiction under the CWA over a pond turned on whether pond is properly considered "adjacent" to other waters.).

53. 531 U.S. 159 (2001).

54. 529 F. Supp. 119 (E.D. Mich. 1981).

55. *Id.* at 120. *See also* United States v. Tilton, 12 ENVTL. L. REP. 21,102 (M.D. Fla. 1982), *aff'd,* 705 F.2d 429 (11th Cir. 1983) (upholding a wetlands determination where separated by a 30-foot-wide river berm). *But see* United States v. Sargent County Water Resource Dist., 876 F. Supp. 1081, 1086–87 (D.N.D. 1992) (rejecting a claim of adjacency where sloughs were separated from navigable waters by more than seven miles of farmland).

56. 873 F. Supp. 650 (S.D. Fla. 1995), *aff'd* 115 F.3d 916 (11th Cir. 1997).

57. *Id.* at 658–59; *see also Carabell,* 257 F. Supp. 2d at 930–31 (suggesting that a wetland may be "adjacent" even in absence of evidence that water from wetland flowed into adjacent waterway).

58. *See Riverside Bayview Homes,* 474 U.S. at 134 (determination that wetlands are "adjacent" within the meaning of the Corps's regulations "holds true even for wetlands that are not the result of flooding or permeation by water having its source in adjacent bodies of open water.").

59. 786 F.2d 1008 (11th Cir. 1986).

60. *Id.* at 1009.

61. 133 F.3d 251 (4th Cir. 1997).

62. *Id.* at 258.

63. *Id.* at 257.

64. *Id.* at 258. The constitutional difficulties alluded to by the court are discussed in Section III.B.5. of this chapter.

65. *Id.* at 267–68.

66. *Id.* at 267.

67. In re The Hoffman Group, Inc., No. CWA 88-A0-24 (Sept. 15, 1989), *rev'd on other grounds,* DCWA Appeal No. 892 (Nov. 19, 1990), *rev'd sub nom.* Hoffman Homes, Inc. v. Administrator, 961 F.2d 1310 (7th Cir.), *vacated,* 975 F.2d 1554 (7th Cir. 1992), *administrative order for penalties vacated,* 999 F.2d 256 (7th Cir. 1993).

68. 33 C.F.R. § 328.3(a)(3).

69. *Riverside Bayview Homes,* 474 U.S. at 124 n.2, 131 n.8.

70. Army Corps of Engineers, 33 C.F.R. Parts 320, 321, 322, 323, 324, 325, 326, 327, 328, 329, and 330 Final Rule for Regulatory Programs of the Corps of Engineers, 51 Fed. Reg. 41,206, 41,217 (Nov. 13, 1986) (hereinafter *Final Rule*).

71. 33 C.F.R. § 328.3(a)(3)(i)–(iii).

72. U.S. CONST. art. I, § 8, cl. 3.

73. 33 C.F.R. § 328.3(a)(3).

74. *See, e.g.,* Heart of Atlanta Motel, Inc. v. United States, 379 U.S. 241, 252–53 (1964); Wickard v. Filburn, 317 U.S. 111 (1942). For CWA cases liberally construing the interstate commerce requirement, *see, e.g.,* Leslie Salt Co. v. United States, 55 F.3d 1388 (9th Cir. 1995) (migratory bird connection sufficient for jurisdiction); United States v. Pozsgai, 999 F.2d 719 (3d Cir. 1993) (upholding jurisdic-

tion over wetlands above headwaters and adjacent to tributaries susceptible to use in interstate commerce); United States v. Velsicol Chem. Corp., 438 F. Supp. 945, 947 (W.D. Tenn. 1976) (upholding jurisdiction over sewers that lead to the Mississippi River); Quivera Mining Co. v. United States EPA, 765 F.2d 126, 129 (10th Cir. 1985) (arroyo and creek that were not "navigable-in-fact," but where heavy rainfall at times provided a surface connection with navigable waters, subject to the Corps's jurisdiction); *United States v. Eidson*, 108 F.3d 1336, 1341–43 (11th Cir. 1997) (man-made drainage ditch that was not "navigable-in-fact"); United States v. Texas Pipe Line Co., 611 F.2d 345, 347 (10th Cir. 1979) (unnamed tributary to navigable river); State of Georgia v. City of East Ridge, 949 F. Supp. 1571, 1578 (N. D. Ga. 1996) (unnamed tributary).

75. 715 F.2d 897 (5th Cir. 1983).

76. *Id.* at 922–25. The Corps's August 1993 regulations dramatically altered its historical approach of not regulating the incidental redeposit of material. Under the so-called Tulloch Rule, the Corps asserted jurisdiction over excavation (including mechanized landclearing) that results in the redeposit or fallback of dredged or excavated material regardless of quantity. 33 C.F.R. § 323.2(d)(1)(iii) (2003); 58 Fed. Reg. 45,008, 45,035 (1993). The Tulloch Rule was successfully challenged by a coalition of trade associations on the grounds that it exceeded the authority of the Corps and EPA under the CWA. American Mining Congress v. U.S. Army Corps of Engineers, 951 F. Supp. 267 (D.D.C. 1997), *aff'd.* 145 F.3d 1399 (D.C. Cir. 1998).

77. 662 F. Supp. 548 (S.D. Tex. 1987).

78. *Id.* at 549.

79. *See* Final Rule, 51 Fed. Reg. at 41,217; Clean Water Act Section 404 Program Definitions and Permit Exemptions; Section 404 State Program Regulations, Final Rule, 53 Fed. Reg. 20,764 (June 6, 1988) (hereinafter *EPA Final Rule).*

80. 514 U.S. 549 (1995).

81. *Id.* at 558.

82. 529 U.S. 598 (2000).

83. 42 U.S.C. § 13981.

84. 529 U.S. at 617.

85. *Id.*

86. *See* United States v. Morrison, 529 U.S. 598, 610 (2000). The Court observed that "Both petitioners and Justice Souter's dissent downplay the role that the economic nature of the regulated activity plays in our Commerce Clause analysis. But a fair reading of *Lopez* shows that the noneconomic, criminal nature of the conduct at issue was central to our decision in that case." *Id.*

87. *See* United States v. Wilson, 133 F.3d 251 (4th Cir. 1997), discussed at length, *infra.*

88. *See* 33 C.F.R. § 328.3(a)(3)(i)–(iii).

89. *See, e.g.,* United States v. Byrd, 609 F.2d 1204, 1209 (7th Cir. 1979) (recreational use of wetlands by interstate travelers sufficient for Corps jurisdiction).

90. While the U.S. Army Corps of Engineers initially asserted jurisdiction over the wetlands at issue in *SWANCC* based on their potential use as habitat for migratory birds, the agency later argued that regulation was appropriate under the Commerce Clause because the activity that the petitioners planned to pursue

in the wetlands, construction of a municipal landfill, was "plainly of a commercial nature." 531 U.S. at 173.

91. *See* Final Rule, 51 Fed. Reg. at 41,217; Environmental Protection Agency, 40 C.F.R. pts. 232 and 233; EPA Final Rule, 53 Fed. Reg. at 20,765.

92. Final Rule, 51 Fed. Reg. at 41,217.

93. *Id.*

94. EPA Final Rule, 53 Fed. Reg. at 20,765.

95. 896 F.2d 354 (9th Cir. 1990), *cert. denied,* 486 U.S. 1126 (1991).

96. *Id.* at 360.

97. Cargill, Inc. v. United States, 516 U.S. 955 (1995).

98. *Id.*

99. *Id.*

100. 33 F.3d 251 (4th Cir. 1997).

101. *Id.* at 256–57.

102. *Id.* at 257.

103. *Id.*

104. *Id.* at 256. As in *Wilson,* in Tabb Lakes, Ltd. v. United States, 715 F. Supp. 726, 728–29 (E.D. Va. 1988), *aff'd n.op.,* 885 F.2d 866 (4th Cir. 1989), the district court held that the potential use of an isolated wetland by migratory birds was not enough to establish Corps jurisdiction. The court did not address the interstate commerce issue, concluding instead that the Corps's interpretation of "waters of the United States" was a rule that was not enacted in compliance with the Administrative Procedures Act (APA). Because the Migratory Bird Rule was substantive, rather than interpretive, the court held that it was invalid due to the failure of the Corps to comply with the APA's notice and comment procedures. *Id.* at 729. More recently, the Seventh Circuit rejected the holding in *Tabb Lakes,* concluding that the Corps could properly rely on the Migratory Bird Rules as an interpretation of its "other waters" regulation. *See* Solid Waste Agency of Northern Cook County v. United States Army Corps of Engineers, 191 F.3d 845 (7th Cir. 1999).

105. *Id.* at 257. Following the *Wilson* decision, the Corps and EPA issued a joint memorandum stating that because the agencies believed the case to have been decided wrongly, the ruling would be considered by the government to be binding only in the Fourth Circuit. The agencies further instructed Corps Districts and EPA Regional Offices within the Fourth Circuit to continue to assert jurisdiction where they can establish either an actual link with or a substantial effect on interstate commerce. U.S. EPA and U.S. Army Corps of Engineers, *Guidance for Corps and EPA Offices Regarding Clean Water Act Section 404 Jurisdiction Over Isolated Waters in Light of United States v. Wilson* (May 29, 1998). This guidance was subsequently withdrawn by the agencies in light of the Supreme Court's ruling in Solid Waste Agency of Northern Cook County v. United States Army Corps of Engineers, 531 U.S. 159 (2001), addressed in detail below.

106. In re The Hoffman Group, Inc., No. CWA 88-A0-24 (Sept. 15, 1989), *rev'd on other grounds,* DCWA Appeal No. 892 (Nov. 19, 1990), *rev'd sub nom.* Hoffman Homes, Inc. v. Administrator, 961 F.2d 1310 (7th Cir.), vacated, 975 F.2d

1554 (7th Cir. 1992), *administrative order for penalties vacated*, 999 F.2d 256 (7th Cir. 1993).

107. 961 F.2d 1310 (7th Cir. 1992).

108. *Id.* at 1319–21.

109. *Id.* at 1320.

110. 975 F.2d 1554 (7th Cir. 1992).

111. Hoffman Homes, Inc. v. Administrator, United States Environmental Protection Agency, 999 F.2d 256, 261 (7th Cir. 1993).

112. *Id.* at 262.

113. *Id.*

114. *Id.*

115. Reuth v. United States Environmental Protection Agency, 13 F.3d 227, 231 (7th Cir. 1993).

116. 998 F. Supp. 946 (N.D. Ill. 1998).

117. *Id.* at 952 (quoting Lori J. Warner, *The Potential Impact of United States v. Lopez on Environmental Regulations*, 7 DUKE ENVTL. L. & POL'Y F. 321, 354–55 (1997)).

118. *Id.* In contrast, the district court in United States v. Suarez read the *Hoffman Homes* decision to exclude isolated wetlands from CWA jurisdiction. 846 F. Supp. 892, 893 n.4 (D. Guam 1994).

119. Solid Waste Agency of Northern Cook County v. United States Army Corps of Engineers, 191 F.3d 845, 850 (7th Cir. 1999).

120. *Id.* at 852.

121. *Id.* at 850. In United States v. Hallmark Constr. Co., 30 F. Supp. 2d 1033, 1042 (N.D. Ill. 1998), the district court held that jurisdiction over an area was lacking because the government presented "no evidence that area was ponded over frequently or sufficiently long enough to serve as a wetland habitat" for migratory birds. In an earlier decision, the court had found that the Supreme Court's decision in *Lopez* did not, however, abrogate the Seventh Circuit's reasoning in United States v. Hallmark Constr. Co., 14 F. Supp. 2d 1069, 1074–75 (E.D. Ill. 1998).

122. Solid Waste Agency of Northern Cook County v. United States Army Corps of Engineers, 531 U.S. 159 (2001).

123. Final Rule, 51 Fed. Reg. at 41,217.

124. *Id.*

125. *Leslie Salt*, 896 F.2d at 359–60. *See also* Swanson v. United States, 789 F.2d 1368 (9th Cir. 1986) (lake high-water mark increased by construction of dam); United States v. Ciampitti, 615 F. Supp. 116 (D.N.J. 1984), *aff'd* 772 F.2d 893 (3d Cir. 1985) (man-made ditches).

126. 876 F.2d 606 (8th Cir. 1989).

127. *Id.* at 612–13.

128. *See* United States v. City of Fort Pierre, 747 F.2d 464 (8th Cir. 1984) (private land exhibiting wetland characteristics as a result of Corps's unrelated river maintenance activities).

129. 531 U.S. at 174.

130. 474 U.S. at 133.

131. 531 U.S. at 172 (citing United States v. Appalachian Elec. Power Co., 311 U.S. 377, 407–08 (1940)).

132. *Id.* at 167.

133. *Id.*

134. *Id.*

135. *Id.* at 172–74.

136. *Id.*

137. Interestingly, in late 2000, the Supreme Court denied *certiorari* in another case in which a developer sought to have the Court overturn a $1.2 million penalty assessed against him on the grounds that EPA exceeded its authority in asserting jurisdiction over isolated intrastate wetlands based solely on the actual or potential use of those waters as habitat for migratory birds. *See* Krilich v. United States, 209 F.3d 968 (7th Cir.), *cert. denied*, 531 U.S. 992 (2000). Following the Supreme Court's denial of certiorari, the defendant moved the district court to bar enforcement of the penalty in light of *SWANCC*. The court denied the motion because, *inter alia*, at the time the defendant entered into the relevant portions of the consent decree with EPA, Seventh Circuit case law held that isolated wetlands were not subject to CWA regulation, and therefore the decree was drafted in light of controlling precedent that was no less favorable to defendants than *SWANCC*. *See* United States v. Krilich, 152 F. Supp. 2d 983 (N.D. Ill. 2001).

138. *See* Virginia S. Albrecht & Stephen M. Nickelsburg, *Could SWANCC Be Right? A New Look at the Legislative History of the Clean Water Act*, 32 ENVTL. L. REP. 11,042 (2002).

139. 474 U.S. at 123.

140. *Id.* at 135.

141. *SWANCC*, 531 U.S. at 167.

142. *See id.* at 169 (quoting 33 U.S.C. § 1344(g)(1)).

143. *Id.* at 171.

144. *Id.* at 175–76.

145. Memorandum from Gary S. Guzy, General Counsel, U.S. EPA, and Robert M. Anderson, Chief Counsel, U.S. Army Corps of Engineers, re: Supreme Court Ruling concerning CWA Jurisdiction over Isolated Waters (Jan. 19, 2001).

146. *Id.* at 3.

147. *Id.*

148. *Id.* at 4.

149. *Id.*

150. *Id.* at 4–5.

151. Joint Memorandum from Robert E. Fabricant, General Counsel, U.S. EPA, and Steven J. Morello, General Counsel, Department of the Army (Jan. 15, 2003), *reproduced at* 68 Fed. Reg. 1995 (Jan. 15, 2003). The updated joint memorandum concludes that "in light of *SWANCC*, it is uncertain whether there remains any basis for jurisdiction under the other rationales of § 328.3(a)(3)(i)–(iii) over isolated, non-navigable, intrastate waters (*i.e.*, use of the water by interstate or foreign travelers for recreational or other purposes; the presence of fish or shellfish that could be taken and sold in interstate commerce; use of the water for industrial purposes by industries in interstate commerce)." 68 Fed. Reg. at 1996.

152. *Id.*
153. *Id.* at 1997.
154. *Id.*
155. 138 F. Supp. 2d 1282 (D. Mont. 2001).
156. *Id.* at 1291–92.
157. 39 Fed. Appx. 870 (4th Cir. 2002).
158. *Id.* at 874.
159. 332 F.3d 698 (4th Cir. 2003), *cert. denied,* 124 S. Ct. 1874 (2004).
160. 344 F.3d 407 (4th Cir. 2003), *cert. denied,* 124 S. Ct. 1874 (2004).
161. *Deaton,* 332 F.3d at 701–02.
162. *Id.* at 705 (quoting *SWANCC,* 485 U.S. at 172).
163. *Id.* at 707.
164. *Id.* at 708.
165. 467 U.S. 837 (1984). Under *Chevron,* the court first considers "whether Congress has directly spoken to the precise question [of statutory meaning] at issue." *Id.* at 842. If Congress has been "silent or ambiguous" on that question, the courts must defer to a reasonable agency interpretation. *Id.* at 843. As the *Deaton* court put it, congressional silence or ambiguity suggests "by implication [that Congress] delegated authority to the agency to clarify the ambiguity or fill the gap." *Deaton,* 332 F.3d at 708.
166. *Deaton,* 332 F.3d at 709–10.
167. *Id.* at 710–11.
168. In the course of rejecting the Migratory Bird Rule in *SWANCC,* the Court stated that the Corps had "put forth no persuasive evidence that the Corps mistook Congress' intent" when it promulgated the 1974 regulations. *SWANCC,* 531 U.S. at 168.
169. *Deaton,* 332 F.3d at 711.
170. *Id.* at 712. A similar conclusion was reached in Carabell v. U.S. Army Corps of Engineers, 257 F. Supp. 2d 917, 929–31 (E.D. Mich., 2003).
171. 124 S. Ct. 1874 (2004).
172. 344 F.3d 407, 409–10 (4th Cir. 2003).
173. *Id.*
174. *Id.* at 417.
175. *Id.* at 416–17.
176. 124 S. Ct. 1874 (2004).
177. 339 F.3d 447 (6th Cir. 2003), *cert. denied,* 124 S. Ct. 1875 (2004).
178. *Id.* at 449.
179. *Id.* at 453. The Sixth Circuit reiterated this reasoning in United States v. Rapanos, 376 F.3d 629 (6th Cir. 2004), a decision that resolved the civil enforcement action that the Corps brought against John Rapanos at the same time as the criminal enforcement action that was the subject of this appeal to the Sixth Circuit.
180. 339 F.3d at 451.
181. 541 U.S. 972 (2004).
182. 303 F.3d 784 (7th Cir. 2002), *cert. denied,* 123 S. Ct. 1782 (2003).
183. *Id.* at 791.
184. 243 F.3d 526 (9th Cir. 2001).

185. *Id.* at 528.

186. *Id.* at 533–34.

187. 305 F.3d 943 (9th Cir. 2002).

188. *Id.* at 954–955.

189. *Id.* at 954 (*citing Headwaters, Inc.,* 243 F.3d at 534).

190. 250 F.3d 263 (5th Cir. 2001).

191. *Id.* at 268–69 (emphasis in original).

192. *Id.* at 269–70 (citing Village of Oconomowac Lake v. Dayton Hudson Corp., 24 F.3d 962, 965 (7th Cir. 1994); Exxon Corp. v. Train, 554 F.2d 1310, 1322 (5th Cir. 1977)).

193. *Id.* at 270–71.

194. *Id.* at 271.

195. *Id.* at 272.

196. 354 F.3d 340 (5th Cir. 2003).

197. *Id.* at 347.

198. *Id.* at 345–46.

199. *Id.* at 347.

200. 68 Fed. Reg. 1991 (Jan. 15, 2003).

201. *Id.* at 1194.

202. *Effort to Define U.S. Waters Dropped, EPA, Corps to Retain 2003 Guidance,* 72 U.S.L.W. (BNA) 2361 (Dec. 23, 2003).

203. A recent General Accounting Office report concluded that the criteria used to determine which wetlands are subject to CWA jurisdiction are unevenly interpreted and applied by the Corps district offices, and that the Corps and EPA should survey all of the district offices to determine the extent of the inconsistent interpretations. *See* General Accounting Office, *Waters and Wetlands: Corps of Engineers Needs to Evaluate its District Office Practices in Determining Jurisdiction,* GAO-04-297 (2004).

204. Memorandum of Agreement between the Department of the Army and the Environmental Protection Agency concerning the Determination of the Geographic Jurisdiction of the Section 404 Program and the Application of the Exemptions under Section 404(f) of the Clean Water Act (Jan. 19, 1989).

205. *Id.* at 2. "Special cases" are defined as those "where significant issues or technical difficulties are anticipated or exist, concerning the determination of the geographic scope of waters of the United States for purposes of section 404 and where clarifying guidance is likely to be needed." *Id.*

206. *Id.* at 5.

207. Subject to a 1994 MOA, the Natural Resources Conservation Service (NRCS) is charged with delineating agricultural lands under Section 404 and the Swampbuster Program, an optional federal wetlands conservation program enacted as part of the Food Security Act of 1985 at 16 U.S.C. §§ 3821–3824. Memorandum of Agreement concerning the Delineation of Wetlands for Purposes of Section 404 of the Clean Water Act and Subtitle B of the Food Security Act. In so doing, the NRCS uses its own delineation manual.

208. Environmental Protection Agency, Memorandum of Agreement concerning the Determination of the Geographic Jurisdiction of the Section 404 Program, Notice, 58 Fed. Reg. 4995 (Jan. 19, 1993).

209. *See generally* United States v. Riverside Bayview Homes, Inc., 474 U.S. 121 (1985); Avoyelles Sportsmen's League, Inc. v. Marsh, 715 F.2d 897, 910–11 (5th Cir. 1983); United States v. Fleming Plantations, 9 ENVTL. L. REP. 20,103 (E.D. La. 1978).

210. *See* 33 C.F.R. § 328.3(b) (2003); 40 C.F.R. § 230.3(t).

211. 1987 Manual at 19–23. Obligate species are those that are found in wetlands more than 99 percent of the time. Facultative wetland species are those that occur in wetlands between 67 and 99 percent of the time. Facultative plants are species that have a similar likelihood (33 to 67 percent) of occurring in either wetlands or nonwetlands (*i.e.*, uplands).

212. *Available at* http://www.nwi.fws.gov/plants.htm.

213. Avoyelles Sportsmen's League, Inc. v. Marsh, 715 F.2d 897 (5th Cir. 1983).

214. United States v. Carter, 18 Env't. Rep. Cas. (BNA) 1705 (E.D. La. 1978).

215. 474 U.S. 121 (1985) at 130–31.

216. *See* United States v. Larkins, 852 F.2d 189, 192 (6th Cir. 1988) (vegetation); Bailey v. United States, 647 F. Supp. 44, 47–48 (D. Idaho 1986) (soils). This conclusion is supported by the Corps/EPA definition of "wetlands," which specifies that wetlands are "those areas that are inundated or saturated by surface *or* ground water." (emphasis added). *See* discussion of wetlands definition, *supra.*

217. United States v. Fleming Plantations, 9 ENVTL. L. REP. 20,103 (E.D. La. 1978).

218. Federal Interagency Committee for Wetland Delineation, *Federal Manual for Identifying and Delineating Jurisdictional Wetlands* (1989) (hereinafter "1989 Manual").

219. The United States District Court for the Eastern District of Virginia held that the 1989 Manual was an interpretive or guidance document, rather than a legislative rule, so the government was not required to use notice and comment rulemaking to adopt the Manual. *See* United States v. Hobbs, 32 Env't Rep Cas. (BNA) 2091, 2094–95 (E.D. Va. 1990), *aff'd.* 947 F.2d 941 (4th Cir. 1991), *cert. denied,* 504 U.S. 940 (1992). Two other lawsuits challenging the 1989 Manual as invalid due to the failure to comply with the APA were dismissed as unripe. Merlino v. United States, 21 ENVTL. L. REP. 21,322 (W.D. Wash. 1991); Mulberry Hills Dev. Corp. v. United States, 21 ENVTL. L. REP. 20,123 (D. Md. 1990). Opponents of the 1989 Manual included the oil and gas industry, agricultural businesses, and real estate developers, as well as representatives from Alaska and other coastal states.

220. The strongest criticism of the proposed restrictions involved a requirement that water be present at the surface for ten to twenty or more consecutive days during the growing season for there to be an affirmative wetlands determination. *See* 56 Fed. Reg. 40,446 (Aug. 14, 1991).

221. Energy and Water Development Appropriations Act of 1993, Pub. L. No. 102-337, 106 Stat. 1315 (1992).

222. The Manual leaves the classification of particular wetlands by type to the FWS, for the purpose of mapping and inventorying the nation's wetlands, as well as developing a list of plant species that occur in wetlands. 1987 Manual, p. 7.

223. *Id.* at 16.

224. *Id.* at 30–32.

225. *Id.* at 34.

226. *Id.* at 42–83.

227. *Id.* at 83.

228. *Id.* at 93.

229. *See* 1989 "Federal Manual for Identifying and Delineating Jurisdictional Wetlands"; Proposed Revisions, 56 Fed. Reg. 40,446 (Aug. 14, 1991).

230. While EPA is not bound by the 1993 Appropriations legislation, and while EPA may be legally authorized to adopt a new Delineation Manual without engaging in notice and comment rulemaking under the APA, *see* Hobbs v. U.S., 947 F.2d 941 (4th Cir. 1991), *cert. denied,* 504 U.S. 940 (1992), political forces are likely to drive the agency to engage in notice and comment rulemaking when or if it adopts a new Delineation Manual.

231. Departments of Veterans Affairs and Housing and Urban Development and Independent Agencies Appropriations Act of 1993, Pub. L. No. 102-389, 106 Stat. 1571 (1992).

232. National Academy of Sciences, National Research Council, *Wetlands: Characteristics and Boundaries* (1995).

233. *Id.*

234. 33 C.F.R. § 325.9.

235. United States Army Corps of Engineers, *Wetland Delineator Certification Program,* Proposed Rule, 60 Fed. Reg. 13,654, 13,655 (Mar. 14, 1995).

236. *Id.*

237. Pub. L. No. 101-640, 104 Stat. 4604 (1990). Under this Section, the Corps is authorized to conduct demonstration projects prior to establishing a nationwide training and certification program. The Corps is executing three such projects, in Florida, Maryland, and Washington.

238. *Wetland Delineator Certification Program, supra* note 235, at 13,654.

239. *Id.*

240. RGL 94-1, Expiration of Geographic Jurisdictional Determinations (May 23, 1994).

241. *See, e.g.,* Southern Pines Assocs. v. United States, 912 F.2d 713 (4th Cir. 1990); Hoffman Group, Inc. v. EPA, 902 F.2d 567 (7th Cir. 1990); Banks v. Page, 768 F. Supp. 809 (S.D. Fla. 1991); Route 26 Land Development Ass'n v. United States, 753 F. Supp. 532, 541 (D. Del. 1990), *aff'd n.op.,* 961 F.2d 1568 (3d Cir. 1992); Fiscella & Fiscella v. United States, 717 F. Supp. 1143 (E.D. Va. 1989).

CHAPTER 4

Regulated Activities

H. MICHAEL KELLER

I. Introduction/Scope

The Clean Water Act's Section 404 program is the federal government's primary regulatory program aimed at protecting the nation's wetlands. This emphasis is not apparent from the language of Section 404 itself or of the Clean Water Act (CWA) generally. The general regulatory provisions of the CWA protect the quality of waters[1] primarily by prohibiting discharges of pollutants without a permit.[2] Section 404 reflects this general approach. By its terms, it seeks to regulate "the discharge of dredged or fill material into the navigable waters at specified disposal sites."[3] Section 404 does not specifically mention certain activities, such as excavating or draining wetlands and clearing them of vegetation, the effects of which can be harmful to or destructive of wetland functions and values.[4] For that reason, the extent to which the Section 404 program lawfully may be used to protect wetlands by regulating these kinds of activities remains controversial. Additionally, it is important to understand that ditching, drainage, and excavation activities, even in upland areas, may be subject to stormwater regulation under Section 402 of the CWA,[5] regardless of whether the activities are also subject to regulation under Section 404.[6]

The tension between the ingredients needed for a functionally effective program for protecting wetlands, on the one hand, and the specific statutory language deployed by Congress, on the other hand, raises difficult questions concerning the scope of the Section 404 program. The passage of more than thirty years since the enactment of Section 404 has left many questions unresolved concerning the type of activities the United States Army Corps of Engineers (the Corps) may and may not regulate.

This chapter examines the scope of activities that are subject to regulation under Section 404, with particular emphasis on activities that may constitute a "discharge of dredged or fill material" within the meaning of Section 404 and pertinent regulations. Part II of this chapter examines the statutory terms and cases concerning regulated activities under Section 404. Part III discusses the Corps's regulations interpreting the scope of regulated activities under Section 404. Part IV analyzes statutory and regulatory exemptions from the Section 404 program.

II. Statutory Scope of Activities Regulated under Section 404

In evaluating whether a particular activity is regulated under Section 404, the following questions are pertinent:

- Will the activity occur in or on, or affect the quality of, "waters of the United States"?
- If so, does the activity involve "the discharge of dredged or fill material"?
- If so, is the activity exempt from Section 404 permitting requirements by statute or implementing regulations?
- If the activity is not exempt, may the activity proceed pursuant to a general permit or must an individual permit be obtained from the Corps?

As this sequence of questions shows, it is critical first to determine whether the activity will occur within or otherwise affect "waters of the United States." As discussed more fully in Chapter 3, the Corps and the Environmental Protection Agency (EPA) interpret "waters of the United States" to encompass not only navigable waters, but also wetlands adjacent to regulated waters[7] and wetlands the use, degradation, or destruction of which could affect interstate or foreign commerce.[8]

If the waters that will potentially be affected by an activity are within the Corps's jurisdiction, the inquiry directly focuses on the activity in question to determine whether it is subject to regulation under Section 404. Some activities are exempt from regulation by Section 404(f) of the CWA and implementing Corps regulations.[9] These exemptions are discussed in detail in Part IV of this chapter. The question whether a nonexempt activity may proceed under a general permit or, instead, must be approved by the Corps in an individual permit proceeding is discussed in Chapter 6 of this book. In either case, the activity must involve a "discharge of dredged or fill material at specified disposal sites,"[10] for that is the statutory predicate for the Corps's exercise of authority pursuant to Section 404. Broken into its component parts, this language establishes two elements for a regulated activity under Section 404: (1) a discharge of dredged or fill material at (2) specified disposal sites. The first element has been addressed extensively in case law, while the second element has received scant judicial attention.

A. Discharge of Dredged or Fill Material

The Clean Water Act does not provide an exhaustive list of activities that involve the "discharge of dredged or fill material."[11] The CWA does provide that "[t]he term 'discharge' when used without qualification includes a discharge of a pollutant, and a discharge of pollutants."[12] The inclusion of "dredged and fill material" in Section 404's reference to "discharge" is arguably a qualification of the term "discharge," making it questionable whether the CWA's definition of an unqualified "discharge" has any bearing on the kind of activities that may be regulated under Section 404. Nevertheless, both the Corps and the courts have concluded that to constitute a "discharge of dredged or fill material," the activity in question must also involve a "discharge" as defined in the CWA.

In concluding that Section 404 regulates only "discharges," the courts and the Corps have applied the CWA's definition of that term: "(A) any addition of any pollutant to navigable waters from any point source, (B) any addition of any pollutant to the waters of the contiguous zone or the ocean from any point source other than a vessel or other floating craft."[13] Accordingly, to fall within Section 404, a discharge must involve (1) the addition to "navigable waters" of (2) dredged or fill material that is a (3) pollutant (4) from a point source. Two of these terms—point source and pollutant—are defined by statute. The terms "dredged material" and "fill material" are defined in the Corps's regulations, which are discussed *infra*. The term "addition" is not defined by statute or by regulation.

1. Pollutant

The CWA defines "pollutant" expansively to include a variety of discharged materials, including "sewage," "waste," and such sometimes innocuous materials as "dredged spoil," "biological material," "rock," and "sand."[14] In the context of Section 404, courts have construed the definition of "pollutant" broadly to include a wide range of diverse materials, including "fill material;"[15] "dredged materials, including native soils excavated by ditching activities;"[16] "rock fill, dirt, organic debris, and biological materials;"[17] concrete rubble and cinder block;[18] bricks and sheet metal;[19] "shotcrete;"[20] "dams and riprap;"[21] and "sheared trees and vegetation and scraped soil and leaf litter."[22] One must search long and hard for any decision in which discharged material was found not to be a pollutant. That search yields the unsurprising conclusion that "pure water" is not a pollutant.[23] In the generality of cases, and given the generous interpretation of the term offered by the courts, the question of whether the discharged material is a "pollutant" is almost always resolved in favor of Section 404 jurisdiction.

Importantly, however, Section 404 regulates only pollutants that are also either "dredged material" or "fill material." As discussed more fully in Parts III.A and III.B, below, Corps regulations have defined these two terms in ways that limit the jurisdiction of the Section 404 program. Thus, while a discharge may involve a "pollutant," it may nonetheless fall outside Section 404 because it does not involve dredged or fill material.[24]

2. *Point Source*

The CWA defines a "point source" as "any discernible, confined and discrete conveyance, including but not limited to any pipe, ditch, channel, tunnel, conduit, well, discrete fissure, container, rolling stock, concentrated animal feeding operation, or vessel . . . from which pollutants are or may be discharged."[25]

The courts have consistently held that the types of equipment routinely used to develop or otherwise alter wetlands—such as bulldozers and dump trucks—constitute point sources when they are used to place or move pollutants about in jurisdictional wetlands.[26] In *Avoyelles Sportsmen's League v. Alexander,* the court expansively interpreted the statutory definition and its illustrative examples to "connote that a point source is an isolable, identifiable activity that conveys a pollutant."[27] With this broad understanding of the statutory term, the court concluded that landclearing equipment consisting of bulldozers fitted with V-blades and raking blades, tractor-pulled rakes, and excavation equipment consisting of backhoes and discing equipment were all point sources.[28] Thus, like the term "pollutant," the statute's limiting of the Section 404 program to point source discharges typically does not place significant restrictions on the Corps's jurisdiction over activities that alter wetland functions and values.

3. *Addition*

The question of whether an activity involves the "addition" of a pollutant lies at the heart of disputes about the scope of activities that may be regulated under Section 404. The lack of any statutory definition or explanation of what Congress meant in using the term "addition" leaves this question to the judgment of the agencies and the courts. There is little question that the introduction of foreign material into regulated waters constitutes a regulated "addition." Thus, in most cases involving fill material, the agencies and courts have concluded that one or more pollutants have been added to jurisdictional waters, and thus the discharge is subject to regulation under Section 404. Controversy, instead, centers on whether and the extent to which the redepositing or incidental fallback of material into the same waters from which it was dredged, excavated, cleared, or otherwise disturbed can properly be regarded as a regulated "addition" of a pollutant.

The Fifth Circuit took the lead on this issue in *Avoyelles Sportsmen's League, Inc., v. Marsh.*[29] Considering landclearing activities in regulated wetlands, the court concluded that "[t]he word 'addition,' as used in the definition of 'discharge,' may reasonably be understood to include 'redeposit,' " particularly where such "redepositing activities would significantly alter the character of the wetlands and limit the ecological functions served by the tract."[30] The court thus held that Section 404 does not require the Corps to limit its jurisdiction to pollutants "from outside sources."[31] The court noted that because " 'dredged' material is by definition material that comes from the water itself," construing the term "addition" to impose a requirement that the pollutant come from outside sources "would effectively remove the dredge-and-fill provisions from the statute."[32]

Similarly, in *United States v. M.C.C. of Florida, Inc.,* the Eleventh Circuit held that redepositing sediment and vegetation dredged by tugboat propellers onto adjacent sea grass beds was an "addition" of a pollutant.[33] Like the court in *Avoyelles Sportsmen's League,* and referencing the broad purposes of the CWA "to restore and maintain the chemical, physical, and biological integrity of the Nation's waters,"[34] the court coupled this conclusion with the observation of considerable environmental damage: "The redepositing of spoil dredged up by the tug's propellers onto the adjacent sea grass beds clearly disturbs the 'physical and biological integrity' of the subject areas. The damage done to these areas was too severe for nature to be able to restore them to their natural condition herself."[35] In *Rybachek v. EPA,*[36] the Ninth Circuit followed suit, holding that in connection with placer mining in and around a streambed, redeposition of native materials constituted a regulated "addition," "even if the material discharged originally comes from the streambed itself."[37]

More recently, in *Greenfield Mills, Inc. v. Macklin,* the Seventh Circuit held that the discharge of dredged material from a supply pond into a contiguous body of water constitutes an "addition" of dredged material.[38] The court reasoned that "soil and vegetation removed from one part of a wetland or waterway and redeposited in another could disturb the ecological balance of the affected areas" and "excluding such dredged materials from the concept of 'addition' would effectively remove the dredge-and-fill provision from the statute."[39]

The application of Section 404 to ordinary dredging operations has been more controversial. In *Weiszmann v. Dist. Eng., U.S. Army Corps of Engineers,*[40] the Fifth Circuit, without expressly analyzing the meaning of the term "addition," upheld a lower court ruling that a "discharge of a pollutant" occurred when sediment moved into an existing canal as a result of dredging operations undertaken to create a new connecting canal through dry upland. The court recognized that "it would be impossible to dredge the canal through without causing sediment to enter the preexisting canal."[41] In *Weiszmann,* however, the offending sediment was apparently derived from dredging a new canal through an unregulated upland area and not from the preexisting canal itself. Thus, there was arguably an addition of foreign material to the regulated waterway.

In *Reid v. Marsh,* the court faced a challenge to the Corps's refusal to exercise its Section 404 jurisdiction over dredging operations and squarely held that dredged spoil that falls back into the waters from which it was removed constitutes a regulated discharge.[42] Although the court agreed with the Corps that Section 404 "was not intended to cover dredging work per se," it concluded that because "the heavy equipment employed in dredging projects can result in the relocation of significant amounts of dredged material in a waterway," the activity involved a regulated "discharge."[43] Moreover, the court rejected the Corps's argument that such incidental discharges may be exempted from regulation by the agency as "de minimis" discharges. In the court's view, the CWA in general, and Section 404 in particular, provided no authority to the Corps to exempt discharges from regulation because of their *de minimis* character.[44]

United States v. Lambert, by contrast, concluded that incidental discharges—in this case fall-back from dredging operations—are not subject to regulation because no "addition" of pollutants occurs.[45] The district court held that "dredged spoil [that] simply falls back into the area from which it has just been taken . . . cannot reasonably be considered to be the addition of a pollutant."[46] The court distinguished *Weiszmann,* concluding that in that case, "the dredging of one canal . . . apparently caused sediment to enter another separate canal." By contrast, in *Lambert,* the dredging merely had the effect of "diminish[ing] the movement of a 'pollutant' from one site to another."[47]

The "addition" issue has featured prominently in decisions spawned by the Corps's efforts over the past decade to expand wetlands protection. In *National Mining Association v. U.S. Army Corps of Engineers,* the court held that Congress did not intend to regulate incidental fallback under Section 404.[48] Decisions evaluating whether various types of redepositing activities constitute regulated "addition" or unregulated "incidental fallback" ensued. In *In re Slinger Drainage Inc.*, the Environmental Appeals Board held that the use of a trenching machine that simultaneously excavated material from wetlands, laid drainage tile, and then redeposited the excavated material over the tile constituted addition of a pollutant.[49] Similarly, in *United States v. Sartori,* the court held that excavating, moving, and depositing dirt, rocks, and other indigenous materials in a wetland through the use of earth-moving machinery constituted addition, not incidental fallback.[50] In *Froebel v. Meyer,* involving a somewhat novel citizen's challenge to a state agency's faulty removal of an abandoned dam, the court held that the movement and redeposition of indigenous sediment as a result of the faulty removal of the dam was not an addition of a pollutant requiring a permit under either Section 402 or Section 404.[51]

The controversial practice of placing dredged material back into a wetland by "sidecasting" has been closely examined by the Fourth Circuit. In *United States v. Wilson,* a divided panel of the court considered, but failed to resolve, whether "sidecasting" is subject to regulation under Section 404.[52] In *U.S. v. Deaton,* another Fourth Circuit panel squarely held that sidecasting of dredged material from excavation of a drainage ditch in a regulated wetland is a regulated activity. Another activity, known as "deep ripping"—an agricultural practice in which impermeable clay soil layers that hold water in wetlands are broken up by long tines dragged through the wetland—has also generated controversy. The Ninth Circuit held in *Borden Ranch Partnership v. U.S. Army Corps of Engineers* that deep ripping constituted a jurisdictional discharge and the Supreme Court affirmed that decision.[53] These decisions have refocused the inquiry into the scope of activities regulated under Section 404. The decisions in *National Mining, Wilson, Deaton,* and *Borden Ranch* are discussed in the next sections.

4. *The* National Mining *Decision*

National Mining Association v. U.S. Army Corps of Engineers[54] involved a facial challenge to the so-called Tulloch Rule issued by the Corps in 1993. This rule is discussed more fully below. In brief, the Tulloch Rule subjected to regulation "any addition, including any redeposit, of dredged material, including excavated material, into waters of the United States which is incidental to any activity,"[55] unless it "does not have or would not have the effect of destroying or degrading an area of waters of the United States."[56] The court declared this rule invalid, concluding that incidental fallback during landclearing and excavation activities cannot properly be regarded as the "addition of a pollutant."[57]

The D.C. Circuit distinguished *Avoyelles Sportsmen's League* and other "redeposit" cases, concluding that none of those decisions specifically addressed whether incidental fallback from excavation activities constitutes a discharge.[58] On that question, the court concluded that the "term 'addition' cannot reasonably be said to encompass the situation in which material is removed from the waters of the United States and a small portion of it happens to fall back."[59] In the court's view, such a situation "represents a net withdrawal, not an addition, of material," and therefore "cannot be a discharge."[60]

The court carefully noted that its decision does not preclude the Corps from regulating "some forms of redeposit": "Since the Act sets out no bright line between incidental fallback on the one hand and redeposits subject to regulation, on the other, a reasoned attempt by the agencies to draw such a line would merit considerable deference."[61] For this reason, the court agreed with the observation in *Avoyelles Sportsmen's League* that a "requirement that all pollutants must come from outside sources would effectively remove the dredge-and-fill provision from the statute."[62] Accordingly, it limited its holding to the Corps's attempt, under the Tulloch Rule, to regulate "a wide range of activities that cannot remotely be said to 'add' anything to the waters of the United States."[63]

The decision, while invalidating the Tulloch Rule, continues to leave unsettled the scope of the Section 404 regulatory program. The court provided no clear guidance on when movement of materials during landclearing and other activities ceases to be mere "fallback" and becomes a "redeposition" subject to Corps scrutiny. That question was addressed by the Fourth Circuit in *Wilson* and *Deaton,* with respect to the practice of sidecasting.

5. *The* Wilson *Decision*

In *United States v. Wilson,*[64] the Fourth Circuit considered the Corps's authority under Section 404 to regulate "sidecasting" in jurisdictional wetlands—a practice in which material excavated during the digging of ditches in wetlands is placed alongside the ditch. Although the question has now been resolved in the Fourth Circuit by the court's subsequent decision in *Deaton,* the facts and the divergent reasoning of the divided panel in *Wilson* remain instructive.

Over a period of years, the defendants in *Wilson* attempted to drain wetlands by digging ditches and sidecasting the excavated material. They were found guilty of felonies for this conduct before the district court. On appeal the defendants contested, *inter alia,* the district court's jury instruction that "sidecasting" dredged material from the construction of drainage ditches in wetlands constituted a "discharge of dredged or fill material."

The Court of Appeals divided on this question. Judge Niemeyer concluded that sidecasting was not subject to regulation, Judge Payne concluded that it was, and Judge Luttig simply expressed no views on the matter. Judge Niemeyer acknowledged that dredged materials may constitute a "pollutant" within the meaning of the CWA, but concluded that sidecasting does not "add" anything to jurisdictional waters. He explained:

> "Addition" requires the introduction of a new material into the area, or an increase in the amount or a type of material which is already present. While soil may be definitionally transformed, through the act of excavation, from a part of the wetland into "dredged spoil," a statutory pollutant, it is not added to the site.[65]

By contrast, Judge Payne viewed *Avoyelles Sportsmen's League* as decisive of the sidecasting issue.[66] He also noted that sidecasting "added" pollutants to jurisdictional waters:

> When the extracted material is moved, its contents are released in the waters into which that material is placed . . . The contents of the excavated or dredged material then becomes a part of the receiving water to which the extracted material is added. . . .
>
> Hence, according to the usual meaning of the term "addition," the sub-surface material extracted by the excavation or dredging is added to the water and to the surface material into which the sub-surface material is deposited upon the act of sidecasting. Whether that which is thusly discharged is highly toxic kepone laying a few inches beneath the silted over bed of the James River or perhaps not so toxic fertilizer, biological material, rocks, or sand from the bottom of a wetland, a pollutant is added to the waters.[67]

6. *The* Deaton *Decision*

In *United States v. Deaton,*[68] a different panel of the Fourth Circuit, comprised of Judge Luttig—who had expressed no opinion on the subject in

Wilson—Judge Wilkinson, and Judge Michael directly addressed the issue of sidecasting and ruled that it is a regulated activity under Section 404.

James Deaton contracted to purchase a twelve-acre parcel of land in Maryland for development as a small residential subdivision. The local health department denied Deaton's application for a sewage disposal permit because of high groundwater on the parcel, and a representative of the Soil Conservation Service (now known as the Natural Resources Conservation Service) advised Deaton of the presence of regulated wetlands on the property. Without obtaining a 404 permit, Deaton hired a contractor who used a back hoe, a front-end loader, and a bulldozer to dig a 1,240-foot drainage ditch across the property and through the wetlands. The contractor piled the excavated dirt on either side of the ditch as he dug.[69] The Corps issued Deaton a stop work order. Efforts to negotiate a resolution and secure remediation of the ditch work were unsuccessful, and the government eventually filed a civil complaint against Deaton and his wife alleging they had violated Sections 301 and 304 of the CWA by sidecasting dredged material in a jurisdictional wetland.[70]

On cross motions for summary judgment, the district court denied the Deatons' motion and granted partial summary judgment to the government on the grounds that jurisdictional wetlands existed on the property and that the sidecasting of excavated material into those wetlands constituted a discharge of a pollutant under the CWA. Shortly thereafter, the Fourth Circuit issued its decision in *Wilson,* and the district court reconsidered its ruling on sidecasting. Although agreeing with Judge Payne's opinion in *Wilson* that the practice violated the CWA, the district court predicted that the appeals court would, instead, adopt the reasoning of Judge Niemeyer[71] that sidecasting did not constitute a discharge. The district court then vacated its prior ruling on sidecasting and granted summary judgment to the Deatons on that issue. The government appealed the ruling on sidecasting, while the Deatons cross-appealed the rulings on jurisdictional wetlands. The Fourth Circuit held that sidecasting was a regulated activity and remanded the case to the district court without considering the Deatons' cross appeal.[72]

Narrowly couching the sidecasting issue as whether the deposit of dredged or excavated material from a wetland back into the same wetland constitutes a discharge of a pollutant under the CWA, the court first addressed whether the redeposited material was a "pollutant."[73] Pointing to the statutory definition of "pollutant" in 33 U.S.C. § 1362(12)(A), which specifically includes "dredged spoil" that has been "discharged to water" and citing the opinions of both Judges Niemeyer and Payne in *Wilson,*[74] the court readily concluded "the piles of dirt dredged up by the Deatons' contractor were, without question, 'pollutants' within the meaning of the Act."[75]

The court then turned to the more troublesome issue of whether there had been a discharge. Focusing on the word "addition" in the statutory definition of a discharge, the Deatons argued that it meant something added that was not previously present. Sidecasting, in their view, did not involve the "addition" of a pollutant, because it resulted in no net increase in the amount of material present in the wetland.[76] They cited to Judge Niemeyer's opinion in *Wilson* and the court's statement in *National Mining:* "We fail to see how there can be an addition of dredged material when there is no addition of material."[77]

The Fourth Circuit rejected the idea that there had to be a net addition of material or new material for there to be a discharge. According to the court, the statutory definition of a discharge did not depend upon the addition of material, but, instead, on the addition of a "pollutant."[78] Effectively hoisting the Deatons on their own definition of "addition," the court found it "entirely unremarkable" that there could be an addition of a pollutant without the addition of material:

> Once removed, the excavated dirt became "dredged spoil, a statutory pollutant and a type of material that up until then was not present on the Deaton property. It is of no consequence that what is now dredged spoil was previously present on the same property in the less threatening form of dirt and vegetation in an undisturbed state. What is important is that once that material was excavated from the wetland, its redeposit in that same wetland added a pollutant where none had been before. Thus, even under the definition of "addition" (that is, "something added") offered by the Deatons, sidecasting adds a pollutant that was not present before.[79]

The court found support for its conclusion in what it viewed as the underlying rationale of Congress for defining dredged spoil as a pollutant: once excavated, even plain dirt could not be redeposited without causing harm to the environment.[80] The court explained that environmental harm could result from a release or mobilization of trapped pollutants, from an increase in suspended sediment, or from increased drainage brought about by dredging.[81] The court also stated there would be no less harm when the dredged spoil is redeposited in the same wetland from which it was excavated:

> The effects on hydrology and environment are the same. Surely congress would not have used the word "addition" (in "addition of any pollutant") to prohibit the discharge of dredged spoil in a wetland, while intending to prohibit such pollution only when the dredged material comes from outside the wetland.[82]

7. *The* Borden Ranch *Decision*

The "addition" issue has also been raised in the context of certain agricultural activities in wetlands. One of those activities is "deep ripping": "the mechanical manipulation of the soil to break up or pierce highly compacted, impermeable or slowly permeable subsurface soil layers, or other similar kinds of restrictive soil layers. These practices are typically used to break up these subsoil layers (e.g., impermeable soil layer, hardpan) as part of the initial preparation of the soil to establish an agricultural or silvicultural operation."[83] In *Borden Ranch Partnership v. U.S. Army Corps of Engineers*,[84] the Ninth Circuit held that this practice was subject to the Corps jurisdiction under Section 404. An equally divided Supreme Court affirmed, without opinion.[85]

After repeated confrontations with the Corps, Borden Ranch brought suit challenging the Corps's assertion of jurisdiction over the company's deep ripping activities. Borden Ranch was attempting to convert, into a vineyard, property that had been used primarily as rangeland for cattle. The property included vernal pools, swales, and intermittent drainage areas, all of which depended on a dense layer of "clay pan" to maintain their hydrologic features.[86] Because vineyards require a loose soil layer to permit deep rooting, Borden Ranch attempted to break up the clay pan by dragging four- to seven-foot metal prongs behind a tractor. The prongs ripped up the clay pan, permitting water to penetrate deeply below the surface and destroying the prior hydrologic conditions.

In addressing the question of whether this deep ripping involved the "addition" of a pollutant, the court of appeals closely followed the reasoning in *Deaton*. The court of appeals held that to constitute an addition within the meaning of Section 404, the discharged materials need not have come from a location different from the point of discharge. The court stated that

> activities that destroy the ecology of a wetland are not immune from the Clean Water Act merely because they do not involve the introduction of material brought in from somewhere else. In this case, the Corps alleges that [Borden Ranch] has essentially poked a hole in the bottom of protected wetlands. That is, by ripping up the bottom layer of soil, the water that was trapped can now drain out. While it is true, that in so doing, no new material has been "added," a "pollutant" has certainly been "added." Prior to the deep ripping, the protective layer of soil was intact, holding the wetland in place. Afterwards, that soil was wrenched up, moved around, and redeposited somewhere

> else. . . . We therefore conclude that deep ripping, when undertaken in the context at issue here, can constitute a discharge of a pollutant under the Clean Water Act.[87]

The *Deaton* and *Borden Ranch* decisions clearly subject a number of development and agricultural activities to regulation under Section 404, even though those activities do not involve the introduction into jurisdictional waters of materials that were not already present. To a considerable degree, these cases cannot be fully reconciled with the reasoning used in *National Mining* to conclude that incidental fallback is not an addition of a pollutant. When the Supreme Court granted certiorari in *Borden Ranch,* there was much anticipation that the Court would bring greater clarity to the scope of the Section 404 program. A divided Court has left the issue in play, and further litigation can surely be expected over this critical aspect of the program.

B. Discharge at Specified Disposal Sites

Section 404 regulates the discharge of dredged or fill material into regulated waters "at specified disposal sites."[88] The "specified disposal sites" language has received scant judicial consideration. In *American Mining Congress v. U.S. Army Corps of Engineers,*[89] which was affirmed by the D.C. Circuit in *National Mining,* the district court relied on this language to bolster its conclusion that Congress never intended to regulate incidental fallback under Section 404.[90] The court broadly concluded that this language imposes a requirement that the site at which material is discharged "must have been affirmatively selected as a disposal site by the agencies . . . and conveys Congress' understanding that 'discharges' would result in the relocation of material from one site to another."[91] Thus, the court concluded that to constitute a discharge subject to regulation under Section 404, the discharge must occur at a site that is distinct from the site from which the discharged material was excavated.

The *American Mining* court did not distinguish incidental fallback from other activities that move dredged material from one part of a jurisdictional wetland to another, somewhat removed portion of the same general wetland area. If the term "disposal site" were interpreted to mean an area of land that is geographically and hydrologically distinct or noncontiguous with the excavation site, it would appear that the Corps would lack jurisdiction to regulate the filling of a portion of a large wetland with material excavated from the same general wetland "site."

Such a result would clearly conflict with the decision in *Avoyelles Sportsmen's League* and other "redeposit" cases. Although the D.C. Circuit's opinion in *National Mining* affirmed the district court's decision, the court held that "redepositing" may be regulated in some cases. It did not squarely consider what, if any, limitations the "specified disposal site" language may place on the Corps's jurisdiction over particular activities,[92] and no other court has subsequently adopted the *American Mining* interpretation of "specified disposal sites."

III. Regulatory Interpretation of Regulated Activities

The Corps's regulations at 33 C.F.R. Part 323 govern the issuance of permits for discharges of dredged and fill material under Section 404. Originally issued in 1977,[93] the regulations draw on the statutory concept of "addition of a pollutant" and separately define the terms "discharge of fill material" and "discharge of dredged material."

A. Discharge of Fill Material

The Corps defines the discharge of fill material as "the addition of fill material into waters of the United States."[94] This portion of the definition has remained relatively unchanged since 1977. In 2002, however, the Corps amended the definition to revise a nonexclusive list of activities that will generally be considered the discharge of fill material. The list includes

> [p]lacement of fill that is necessary for the construction of any structure or infrastructure in a water of the United States; the building of any structure, infrastructure or impoundment requiring rock, sand, dirt, or other material for its construction; site-development fills for recreational, industrial, commercial, residential, or other uses; causeways or road fills; dams and dikes; artificial islands; property protection and/or reclamation devices such as riprap, groins, seawalls, breakwaters, and revetments; beach nourishment; levees; fill for structures such as sewage treatment facilities, intake and outfall pipes associated with power plants and subaqueous utility lines; placement of fill material for construction or maintenance of any liner, berm, or other infrastructure associated with solid waste landfills; placement of overburden, slurry, or tailings or similar mining-related materials; and artificial reefs. The term does not include plowing, cultivating, seeding and harvesting for the production of food, fiber, and forest products. [95]

The Corps also considers the placement of pilings in waters of the United States to constitute a discharge of fill material, and thus subject to Section 404, if the placement has or would have the "effect" of a discharge of fill material.[96] The regulation of pilings is discussed more fully below.

The primary purpose of the 2002 revisions was to clarify that discharges of fill material associated with the construction of solid waste landfills and that the placement of mining overburden in jurisdictional waters would be regulated under Section 404 rather than as "waste" subject to Section 402's National Pollutant Discharge Elimination System permitting program.[97] The revisions were part of a larger rulemaking to resolve some confusion about the appropriate division of responsibility between the Section 402 and Section 404 programs for regulating certain discharges. For many years, the Corps defined "fill material" as

> any material used for the *primary purpose* of replacing an aquatic area with dry land or of changing the bottom elevation of an [*sic*] waterbody. The term does not include any pollutant discharged into the water primarily to dispose of waste, as that activity is regulated under Section 402 of the Clean Water Act. [emphasis added][98]

Under this definition, the replacement or change in elevation must be the "primary" purpose for the use of the fill. By contrast, EPA's Section 404(b) Guidelines had defined "fill material" without reference to the purpose of the activity with which the discharge is associated. Instead, discharged material would be considered "fill material" if it had the effect of "replac[ing] portions of the 'waters of the United States' with dry land or . . . chang[ing] the bottom elevation of a water body for any purpose."[99]

The differing definitions at times generated confusion about the proper agency from which to seek a permit. Under the CWA, EPA and the states issue National Pollutant Discharge Elimination System (NPDES) permits to point sources pursuant to Section 402. These permits are primarily designed to regulate waste disposal. The Corps, of course, issues Section 404 permits. In several cases, the courts relied on the primary purpose test and the exclusion of waste discharges in the Corps's regulation to hold that the placement of mining waste or spoil in jurisdictional waters may require an NPDES permit, but not a Section 404 permit.[100] The primary purpose of the placement in these cases was disposal, not replacement of an aquatic area or changing the bottom elevation of a waterbody.[101] EPA and the Corps entered into a Memorandum of Agreement that substantially followed the results in these cases.[102]

More recent cases illustrate the confusion about whether certain discharges should be regulated under Section 402 or Section 404. In *Resource Investments, Inc. v. U.S. Army Corps of Engineers,*[103] the Ninth Circuit relied on the Corps "primary purpose" test to resolve a jurisdictional conflict between the Section 404 program and permitting authority under the Resource Conservation and Recovery Act (RCRA).[104] Under RCRA, EPA or a state-approved program is authorized to issue permits governing the siting, design, construction, operation, and closure of solid waste landfills.[105] Resource Investments, Inc., applied to the Corps for a Section 404 permit to discharge dredged and fill material in connection with its construction of a municipal solid waste landfill. The Corps denied the application. On review, Resource Investments maintained that the Corps lacked jurisdiction over its activities, primarily because the discharges were not of dredged or fill material as defined by the CWA and the Corps. The Ninth Circuit agreed, concluding that the primary purpose of neither solid waste disposal nor the placement of construction materials was to replace an aquatic area with dry land or to change the bottom elevation of a waterbody.[106] Instead, the primary purposes of these discharges are, respectively, "waste disposal" and the construction of a "leak detection and collection system."[107] The court also held that the Corps's assertion of jurisdiction over the discharges created a "regulatory overlap" with RCRA, a result inconsistent with Corps regulations that provide that "the Corps believes that state and federal regulatory programs should complement rather than duplicate one another."[108] Accordingly, the court held that "when a proposed project affecting a wetlands area is a solid waste landfill, the EPA (or the approved state program), rather than the Corps, will have permit authority under RCRA."[109]

A more complex course of litigation concerning the division of authority between the Section 402 and Section 404 programs arose out of mountaintop mining and associated valley fills. The practice is associated with surface coal mining operations in the Appalachian states of Kentucky, Tennessee, Virginia, and West Virginia. Essentially, mountaintop mining involves removal of a mountain cap to expose a coal seam. The overburden and interburden (rock above and between coal seams) cannot generally be placed back into the mining pit, so "[t]he usual method of disposing of this excess spoil is to place it in engineered earthen and rock structures known as excess spoil disposal areas or colloquially known as head-of-hollow fills, hollow fills or valley fills."[110]

In 1998, in *Bragg v. Robertson*, a variety of citizens and a conservation organization brought suit claiming, *inter alia,* that the Corps was misapplying the CWA in authorizing mountaintop mining/valley fills under a general nationwide permit.[111] More specifically, the plaintiffs argued that the disposal of coal mining overburden into jurisdictional waters should be subject to the Section 402 permitting program, and not Section 404.[112] The Corps settled this litigation, agreeing to require individual Section 404 permits for valley fills that drain a watershed of 250 acres or more.[113]

In a similar case, *Kentuckians for the Commonwealth v. Rivenburgh*, a federal district court held that "[w]hen overburden is dumped into valleys and streams to get rid of it, the disposal has the effect of creating dry land, but not the purpose. Because land creation or elevation is not a principle purpose of overburden disposal in streams, such a discharge would not meet the Corps's definition of "fill material" . . . nor be permittable under § 404."[114] The court also concluded that EPA's definition of "fill material," to the extent it would authorize the Corps to issue permits for mountaintop mining/valley fills "solely for waste disposal," was "not legal [when promulgated] and [is] not now."[115] Accordingly, the court permanently enjoined the Corps from issuing any Section 404 permits for mountaintop mining/valley fills in the Huntington District.[116] In the course of doing so, the court took the additional, and unusual, step of declaring that a proposed rule published by the Corps and EPA, amending the definition of "fill material," was "*ultra vires:* it exceeds the agencies' statutory authority granted by the CWA."[117]

The Fourth Circuit reversed. Relying on a longstanding practice of EPA and the Corps, and the ambiguous language of the Corps's "primary purpose" test, the Fourth Circuit held that the Corps's definition of "fill material" did not foreclose the Corps from assuming jurisdiction to issue permits for valley fills pursuant to Section 404.[118] Moreover, the court held that the Corps's interpretation of its regulation was permissible under the division of authority between EPA and the Corps in the CWA. Accordingly, it was appropriate for the Corps to assume jurisdiction under Section 404 over permit applications for valley fills involving discharges into jurisdictional waters.[119] Finally, the court vacated the district court's holding that the new EPA-Corps "fill material" rule was invalid, concluding that the rule's validity was not properly before the district court.[120]

The new rule was finalized on May 9, 2002. In an attempt to reduce the confusion exemplified by the *Resource Investments* and mountaintop mining/valley fill cases, the rule provides a consistent definition of "fill material" under both Corps and EPA regulations, by adopting an "effects" test similar to the one in EPA's former rule. The new rule provides that

> the term fill material means material placed in waters of the United States where the material has the effect of:
>
> (i) Replacing any portion of a water of the United States with dry land; or
>
> (ii) Changing the bottom elevation of any portion of a water of the United States.[121]

The rule goes on to provide that "[e]xamples of such fill material include, but are not limited to: rock, sand, soil, clay, plastics, construction debris, wood chips, overburden from mining or other excavation activities, and materials used to create any structure or infrastructure in the waters of the United States," but "does not include trash or garbage."[122] In the preamble to the rule, the agencies made clear that mountaintop mining/valley fills and fill used to create liners, berms, and other infrastructure associated with solid waste landfills will be subject to the Section 404 program, not the NPDES program under Section 402.[123]

B. Discharge of Dredged Material

1. 1977 Definition

Over the years, the Corps has reexamined and broadened its definition of "discharge of dredged material" and, as a result, precipitated renewed judicial scrutiny of the appropriate scope of the Corps's authority under Section 404. In 1977, the Corps defined the discharge of dredged material as "any addition of dredged material into the waters of the United States."[124] Dredged material was defined as "material that is excavated or dredged from" such waters.[125] This definition has remained unchanged, despite the Corps's enlargement of the definition of "discharge of dredged material." Combining these definitions, the initial regulatory program included any addition into waters of the United States of material excavated or dredged from such waters. Following the statutory amendments in 1977,[126] the Corps modified its regulations by issuing an interim final rule effective July 22, 1982, which left the 1977 definition of "discharge of dredged material" virtually unchanged.[127]

2. 1986 Definition

In 1986, the Corps modified the definition of "discharge of dredged material" by issuing a final rule, which became effective January 12, 1987.[128] The Corps took the traditional view that dredging was not regulated, so long as the dredged material was not redeposited within the "waters of the United States."[129] Of course, it is difficult to imagine dredging that does not involve some redeposit of material back into the waters being dredged.[130] To reconcile this potential conflict, the Corps concluded that the "discharge of dredged material" "does not include de minimis, incidental soil movement occurring during normal dredging operations."[131]

In the preamble to its 1986 rulemaking, the Corps explained that Section 404 regulates the discharge of dredged material, not the dredging itself. Accordingly, the fallback that necessarily occurs during normal dredging operations is merely incidental and considered de minimis.[132] The Corps pointed out that it had consistently provided guidance to its field offices since 1977 that such "incidental fallback" was not to be regulated under Section 404. The agency emphasized, however, that the new language applied only to incidental fallback during normal dredging operations and not to the disposal of dredged material. The latter would be regulated if disposed in waters of the United States by sidecasting or other means.[133]

3. *The 1993 "Tulloch Rule"*

The Corps's position on incidental fallback was challenged by environmental interests in *North Carolina Wildlife Federation, et al. v. Tulloch.*[134] The plaintiffs in this case sought to stop a developer's use of landclearing techniques to develop wetlands without a Section 404 permit. They took the position that landclearing activities that destroy or degrade the quality of wetlands are subject to regulation under Section 404. The EPA and the Corps entered a settlement agreement with the plaintiffs, agreeing to redefine what constitutes a discharge of dredged material. The agencies proposed regulations on June 16, 1992.[135]

In 1993, pursuant to the prior settlement, the Corps issued a final rule, commonly known as the Tulloch Rule.[136] The rule clarifies that the Corps intended to require a Section 404 permit for any incidental addition of dredged or excavated material associated with any activity that has or would have the effect of destroying or degrading an area of water of the United States.[137] The Corps redefined "discharge of dredged material" under 33 C.F.R. Part 323 to include

> any addition, including any redeposit, of dredged material within the waters of the United States. The term includes, but is not limited to, the following:
>
> (i) the addition of dredged material to a specified discharge site located in waters of the United States;
>
> (ii) the runoff or overflow from a contained land or water disposal area; and

(iii) any addition, including redeposit, of dredged material, including excavated material, into waters of the United States which is incidental to any activity, including mechanized landclearing, ditching, channelization and other excavation.[138]

Under the Corps's sweeping definition of "discharge of dredged material," virtually any addition of dredged or excavated material incidental to any activity was potentially subject to regulation. The potential reach of the definition was tempered, however, by certain exclusions,[139] including "activities that involve only cutting or removing of vegetation above the ground . . . where the activity neither substantially disturbs the root system nor involves mechanized pushing, dragging, or similar activities that redeposit excavated soil material."[140] The Corps's position on landclearing is discussed more fully below.

Additionally, and perhaps most importantly, the regulatory exclusions included "any incidental addition, including redeposit, of dredged material associated with any activity that does not have or would not have the effect of destroying or degrading an area of waters of the United States."[141] To fall within this exclusion, a party bore the burden of demonstrating to the Corps or EPA, prior to commencing the activity, that the activity would not destroy or degrade wetlands.[142] An activity would "destroy" a jurisdictional wetland "if it alters [it] in such a way that it would no longer be a water of the United States."[143] A wetland would be deemed "degraded" by an activity if the activity "has more than a *de minimis* (i.e., inconsequential) effect on the [wetland] by causing an identifiable individual or cumulative adverse effect on any aquatic function."[144]

Even prior to the settlement in *Tulloch,* the Corps acknowledged that its regulatory program had evolved from one that protected only navigation to one that "considers the full public interest by balancing the favorable impacts against the detrimental impacts."[145] Under this broad-ranging "public interest review," the Corps did not explicitly take the position that effects on water quality were decisive in determining whether an activity may be regulated under Section 404. With the Tulloch Rule, however, the Corps made this position explicit; the key factor in determining whether some activities may be regulated is the effect on water quality that those activities may have.

4. *Response to National Mining*

A challenge to the Tulloch Rule resulted in the important decision in *National Mining,* which invalidated the rule and the Corps's position on incidental fallback. In response to this decision, the Corps and EPA jointly issued amendments modifying the Tulloch Rule in two respects: First, the amended rule makes clear that not all redeposits of dredged material are "discharges" subject to regulation under Section 404. Second, the amendments exclude "incidental fallback" from the definition of "discharge of dredged materials."[146] The agencies noted, however, that the amended rule "does not alter the well-settled doctrine, recognized in *[National Mining]*, that some redeposits of dredged material in waters of the United States constitute a discharge of dredged material and therefore require a section 404 permit."[147] The agencies further concluded that they will determine whether a particular redeposit constitutes a jurisdictional "discharge" on a case-by-case basis.[148] They noted, however, that "[j]udicial decisions have established, and the D.C. Circuit recognized in *[National Mining]*, that redeposits associated with the following are subject to CWA jurisdiction: mechanized landclearing, redeposits at various distances from the point of removal (e.g., sidecasting), and removal of dirt and gravel from a streambed and its subsequent redeposit in the waterway after segregation of minerals."[149] Finally, the agencies indicated that they would attempt in a future rulemaking to further refine the Tulloch Rule to conform to the decision in *National Mining*.[150]

The agencies' actions were promptly challenged in court. In response, the same district court that invalidated the Tulloch Rule denied relief, holding that the rule was consistent with its prior decision and the decision of the court of appeals in *National Mining*.[151] The court concluded that because the rules expressly excluded "incidental fallback" from the scope of Section 404, the agencies had not run afoul of the prior decisions. Nonetheless, the court cautioned the agencies from adopting "an unduly narrow definition of the term."[152]

In January 2001, the agencies issued a new final rule defining "discharge of dredged material."[153] The new rule provides, in part

> (d)(1) Except as provided below in paragraph (d)(3), the term discharge of dredged material means any addition of dredged material into, including any redeposit of dredged material other than incidental fallback within, the waters of the United States. The term includes, but is not limited to, the following:
>
> (i) The addition of dredged material to a specified discharge site located in waters of the United States;
>
> (ii) The runoff or overflow from a contained land or water disposal area; and
>
> (iii) Any addition, including redeposit other than incidental fallback, of dredged material, including excavated

> material, into waters of the United States which is incidental to any activity, including mechanized landclearing, ditching, channelization, or other excavation.[154]

The rule also provides a definition of "incidental fallback"

> the redeposit of small volumes of dredged material that is incidental to excavation activity in waters of the United States when such material falls back to substantially the same place as the initial removal. Examples of incidental fallback include soil that is disturbed when dirt is shoveled and the back-spill that comes off a bucket when such small volume of soil or dirt falls into substantially the same place from which it was initially removed.[155]

Finally, the rule notes:

> The Corps and EPA regard the use of mechanized earth-moving equipment to conduct landclearing, ditching, channelization, in-stream mining or other earth-moving activity in waters of the United States as resulting in a discharge of dredged material unless project-specific evidence shows that the activity results in only incidental fallback.[156]

Under the rule, many of the activities sought to be captured by the Tulloch Rule will again be subject to Section 404. For that reason, many commenters objected that the agencies had not heeded the district court's warning not to adopt too narrow a view of what constitutes an excluded incidental discharge. The agencies rejected broader definitions, contending that such definitions "could potentially be read to mean that incidental fallback would include any dredged material redeposited in the same overall site where excavation occurred, as opposed to the place of initial removal."[157] According to the agencies, a broad exclusion would be inconsistent with those judicial decisions that held that Section 404 extends to redeposits placed only a short distance from the excavation or removal point,[158] and the agencies' longstanding view that mechanized landclearing will generally involve some discharges subject to Section 404. The agencies acknowledged, however, that there are situations in which a redeposit of material will involve only incidental fallback. They noted that some landclearing activities can be conducted in ways that avoid jurisdictional discharges, including the use of specialized techniques. They also noted that "discing, harrowing, and harvesting where soil is stirred, cut, or turned over to prepare for planting of crops" would not be subject to regulation as discharges of dredged material because "[t]hese practices involve only minor redistribution of soil, rock, sand, or other surface materials."[159] Given the fine line drawn between redeposits that do constitute an "addition" and incidental fallback, which does not, the rule now requires that "project-specific evidence" be gathered to show that "the use of mechanized earth-moving equipment to conduct landclearing, ditching, channelization, in-stream mining or other earth-moving activity" involves only incidental fallback.[160] Shortly after the Corps issued the new rule that defined "discharge of dredged materials," the National Association of Home Builders challenged the rule, asserting that it violates the CWA, the Administrative Procedures Act, and the Tenth Amendment of the United States Constitution.[161] However, the United States District Court for the District of Columbia dismissed the lawsuit, finding that the challenges were not ripe for review.[162]

C. Landclearing

As noted in the preceding discussion, the Corps has long considered mechanized landclearing activities in jurisdictional waters or wetlands to be subject to regulation if they result in the addition or redeposition of dredged material.[163] This position was supported by the Fifth Circuit's 1983 decision in *Avoyelles Sportsmen's League v. March,*[164] holding that landclearing activities in jurisdictional wetlands are regulated as a discharge if they involve redeposit of materials taken from the wetlands. The court considered the redeposited vegetation and soils to be a discharge of fill material, because it was done to replace an aquatic area with dry land. The court did not consider whether the vegetative material also could be regarded as dredged material.[165]

The potential reach of the decision in *Avoyelles Sportsmen's League* was limited in *Save Our Wetlands, Inc. v. Sands.*[166] There, the same court held that a utility's proposal to clear trees from a wetland for a powerline corridor was not subject to Section 404 because there was no discharge of dredged or fill material. The court found that, unlike the activity in *Avoyelles Sportsmen's League,* the landclearing did not replace an aquatic body with dry land or change the bottom elevation of a water body.[167] As noted above, Corps regulations exclude from regulation landclearing activities that do not redeposit excavated soil material.[168] At the same time, as indicated in the agencies' response to *National Mining* and the new definition of "discharge of dredged material," EPA and the Corps have concluded that redeposits associated with "mechanized landclearing" are jurisdictional "discharges."[169] In *United States v. Bay-Houston Towing Co., Inc.,*[170] the district court held that mechanized landclearing used in harvesting peat constituted a "discharge" for purposes of Section 404, notwithstanding the defendant's contention that its activities were excluded from regulation by *National Mining.* The government identified, *inter alia,* the following activities involving mechanized landclearing equipment as jurisdictional discharges: (1) sidecasting dredged peat, clay, and vegetation to excavate and maintain drainage ditches; (2) spreading excavated peat onto jurisdictional wetlands for future harvest; and (3) discing wetlands, pushing peat across the fields, and piling peat into temporary harvest windrows. Rejecting defendant's contention that these activities were merely "incidental fallback" within the meaning of *National Mining,* the court concluded that "[u]nlike incidental fallback, these activities involve purposeful relocation."[171] It also rejected the defendant's reliance on Judge Niemeyer's opinion in *Wilson* for the proposition that sidecasting does not constitute an "addition" of dredged or fill material. The court found "the reasoning of Judge Payne to be the more persuasive."[172]

Bay-Houston also argued that because its activities involved only temporary redepositing of material on jurisdictional wetlands, there were no "additions" for purposes of Section 404 jurisdiction. The court concluded, however, that "[w]hether Bay-Houston's activities may be categorized as 'discharges' when the bog material is only temporarily displaced into other areas of the bog before being removed from the bog raises a genuine issue of material fact."[173] The regulatory status of "temporary" discharges is not directly addressed in the Corps's regulations, though Section 404(f)(1) provides an exemption for discharges "for the purpose of construction or maintenance of . . . temporary roads for mining equipment," provided certain conditions are satisfied.[174]

D. Dredging

The Corps's regulations include a narrow exclusion from regulation for incidental movement of material during normal dredging operations.[175] This exclusion was not, under the invalidated Tulloch Rule, applicable to dredging activities in wetlands.[176] As indicated above, in light of *National Mining,* the agency has amended the rule to exclude "incidental fallback" from the definition of "discharge of dredged material."

E. Drainage

The Corps has long taken the position that absent an associated "discharge," Section 404 does not prohibit or regulate the drainage of wetlands. In *Save Our Community v. EPA*,[177] this position was challenged by an organization seeking to halt the expansion of a landfill into wetlands. A district court decision in the case held that a permit was required if the activity presented a threat of significant alteration or destruction of a wetland.[178] The Fifth Circuit reversed, agreeing with the Corps that a permit was not required unless the drainage involved a discharge of dredged or fill material into regulated waters.[179] An activity's effect on wetlands is not, standing alone, a sufficient basis for Section 404 jurisdiction.

Save Our Community does not affect the Corps's application of the Tulloch Rule or what may remain of it in light of *National Mining*. Because the district court relied solely on the act of draining a wetland to support Section 404 jurisdiction, the court of appeals refused to consider whether *de minimis* discharges incidental to drainage activities could provide the predicate for Section 404 jurisdiction or whether the facts of the case showed that such discharges had occurred.[180]

Persons contemplating drainage activities as a means of avoiding Section 404 scrutiny must be careful to employ techniques that do not cause the discharge of a pollutant. In light of the *Deaton* decision on sidecasting and the agencies' position against mechanized landclearing, the window provided by *National Mining* for "incidental fallback" is very narrow. Even if the drainage can be accomplished through legal means without triggering Section 404, the drained site will not likely be suitable for whatever purposes the actor may have in mind, such as residential or commercial development or expansion of agricultural land. Additional fill material or excavation may be required. One who has drained wetlands may attempt to avoid Section 404 regulation of these subsequent "discharges" of fill material, claiming that once the wetland is drained, and the requisite wetland characteristics have been eliminated, activities in or on the site cannot be regulated under Section 404 because the site is no longer within the "waters of the United States."[181] In fact, this is apparently what was intended by the defendants in *Wilson*[182] and *Deaton*.[183]

This strategic behavior was the subject of a memorandum issued by the Corps in 1990 to its districts. The Corps concluded that in such cases, draining a wetland does not eliminate Section 404 jurisdiction over subsequent filling activity.[184] The memorandum explained:

> If the Corps has reason to believe that someone intends to use, or is using, one or more pumps to remove water from a wetland, or is removing wetland vegetation, or both, for the apparent purpose of eliminating [Section] 404 jurisdiction over the area, the "under normal circumstances" concept preserves [Section] 404 jurisdiction over the area notwithstanding the drainage or

> vegetation removal. Consequently, even if the pumping or vegetation removal might conceivably be accomplished without any regulated [Section] 404 discharge, the area still cannot be filled or developed in any manner which does involve a [Section] 404 discharge unless a [Section] 404 permit is obtained.[185]

The "normal circumstances" concept to which the memorandum refers appears in the Corps's and EPA's definition of "wetland,"[186] and is discussed in detail in Chapter 3 of this book. For present purposes, it is sufficient to note that the Corps does not regard *Wilson*-type drainage activities as "normal circumstances" and, but for such activities, the site in question would exhibit the requisite wetland characteristics. As a consequence, the drained site retains its status as a part of the "waters of the United States" for purposes of Section 404, and any subsequent "discharges" are subject to regulation.

Neither *Wilson* nor *National Mining* directly addresses the issue, but in *Wilson,* the court did not disturb a jury finding that the defendant had violated Section 404 by placing additional fill material on a site that had previously been drained.[187] Thus, the effect of cases limiting the concept of "discharges" may not in many circumstances eliminate Corps jurisdiction over development projects. In such cases, the Corps's regulatory authority may turn not on the issue of whether an "addition of pollutants" has occurred, but rather on the question of how the "normal circumstances" provision in the definition of wetlands is interpreted by the courts in light of subsequent discharge activities.[188] Accordingly, those who may contemplate relying on *National Mining* to drain and then fill wetlands without Section 404 scrutiny should be advised to proceed with caution.

F. Pilings

The Corps's rules include a separate section concerning pilings. The rule specifies that the placement of pilings within jurisdictional waters does not constitute a discharge of fill material per se.[189] Instead, the placement of pilings will be subject to regulation only when a case-by-case assessment shows that "such placement would have the effect of a discharge of fill material."[190] Examples of circumstances in which the placement of pilings will be considered a jurisdictional discharge of fill material include

- Pilings placed so closely in jurisdictional waters that sedimentation rates would be increased
- The "pilings themselves effectively replace the bottom of a waterbody"

- Placement of pilings that reduces or impairs the flow or circulation of jurisdictional waters
- "The placement of pilings which would result in the adverse alteration or elimination of aquatic functions"[191]

Examples in which the placement of pilings will not generally have the effect of a discharge of fill material,[192] and thus will not be subject to regulation, include "[p]lacement of pilings for linear projects, such as bridges, elevated walkways, and powerline structures" and pilings for "piers, wharves, and an individual house on stilts."[193]

Regardless whether the placement of pilings is regarded as a "discharge of fill material," such activity will be subject to authorization under Section 10 of the Rivers and Harbors Appropriation Act of 1899 if the placement occurs in "navigable waters" within the meaning of that statute.[194]

IV. Exempt Activities

A. Statutory Exemptions

In addition to the regulatory exclusions associated with the definition of "discharge of dredged material" discussed above, Section 404(f)(1) exempts certain activities from regulation even though such activities may involve discharges otherwise subject to regulation.[195] The exemptions apply to discharges of dredged or fill material associated with the following activities:

> (A) from normal farming, silviculture and ranching activities such as plowing, seeding, cultivating, minor drainage, harvesting for the production of food, fiber, and forest products, or upland soil and water conservation projects;
>
> (B) for the purpose of maintenance, including emergency reconstruction of recently damaged parts, of currently serviceable structures such as dikes, dams, levees, groins, riprap, breakwaters, causeways, and bridge abutments or approaches, and transportation structures;
>
> (C) for the purpose of construction or maintenance of farm or stock ponds or irrigation ditches, or the maintenance of drainage ditches;
>
> (D) for the purpose of construction of temporary sedimentation basins on a construction site which does not include placement of fill material into the navigable waters;

> (E) for the purpose of construction or maintenance of farm roads or forest roads, or temporary roads for mining equipment, where such roads are constructed in accordance with best management practices, to assure that flow and circulation patterns and chemical and biological characteristics of the navigable waters is not reduced, and that any adverse effect on the aquatic environment will be otherwise minimized;
>
> (F) resulting from any activity with respect to which a State has an approved [nonpoint source management program].[196]

The exemptions are subject to various statutory and regulatory conditions and limitations [197] and they have been interpreted narrowly by the courts.[198] In addition, the breadth of these exemptions is severely restricted by Section 404(f)(2)'s "recapture" provision, which states:

> Any discharge of dredged or fill material into the navigable waters incidental to any activity having as its purpose bringing an area of the navigable waters into a use to which it was not previously subject, where the flow or circulation of navigable waters may be impaired or the reach of such waters be reduced, shall be required to have a permit under this section.[199]

These provisions establish that to be exempt from Section 404's permit requirement, the person seeking the exemption "has the burden of demonstrating that proposed activities both satisfy the requirements of Section 404(f)(1) and avoid the recapture provision of Section 404(f)(2)."[200] The Corps and the courts have interpreted these statutory provisions to exclude from Section 404 scrutiny only those discharges "that have little or no adverse effect on the waters of the United States."[201]

B. Implementing Regulations

The Corps has promulgated regulations implementing the Section 404(f)(1) exemptions and the Section 404(f)(2) recapture provision. These regulations are found at 33 C.F.R. § 323.4.

1. General Considerations Affecting Exemptions

The influence of the Section 404(f)(2) "recapture" provision is apparent in the Corps's regulations implementing the statutory exemptions. As construed by the Corps, persons may, without Section 404 scrutiny, maintain and continue established activities in regulated waters that have not caused and will not cause significant adverse effects. By contrast, activities that convert an area of regulated waters, including wetlands, to a new use will generally require a permit, so long as "there is a discharge of dredged or fill material into [regulated] waters . . . in conjunction with construction of dikes, drainage ditches or other works or structures used to effect such conversion."[202]

More generally, the regulations interpret Section 404(f)(2) to require a Section 404 permit for any activity involving discharges that convert a Section 404 wetland into a nonwetland, even if such activities otherwise fall within the Section 404(f)(1) exemptions.[203] Moreover, an activity is presumed to fall outside the statutory exemptions, and thus require a Section 404 permit, if it involves a discharge that "will result in significant discernible alterations to flow or circulation" of regulated waters, again including wetlands.[204]

2. *Particular Regulatory Exemptions*

a. Normal Farming, Silviculture, and Ranching Activities

The Section 404(f)(1) exemption for "normal farming, silviculture and ranching activities" is extensively addressed in the Corps's regulations and in regulatory guidance. While the statute includes examples of such "normal" activities—"plowing, seeding, cultivating, minor drainage, and harvesting for the production of food, fiber, and forest products, or upland soil and water conservation practices"[205]—the detailed implementing regulations provide very specific definitions for each of these illustrative terms.[206] These specific definitions qualify the reach of these terms and, accordingly, should be consulted in determining whether particular activities are exempt from the regulatory provisions of Section 404. For example, in defining "plowing," the Corps's regulation provides that the term "does not include the redistribution of soil, rock, sand, or other surficial material in a manner which changes any area of the waters of the United States to dry land."[207] Consistent with the generally narrow construction given to the Section 404(f)(1) exemptions, one court has concluded that the "normal farming" exemption applies only to "'narrowly defined activities . . . that cause little or no adverse effects either individually or cumulatively [and that do not] convert more extensive areas of water to dry land or impede circulation or reduce the reach and size of the water body.'"[208]

The regulations support this interpretation by equating "normal" farming, silviculture, or ranching activity with "established" (i.e., ongoing) operations.[209] Under the Corps's implementing regulations, "[a]ctivities which bring an area into farming, silviculture, or ranching use are not part of an established operation" and are, therefore, not exempted from regulation as "normal" activities.[210] "For example, a permit will be required for the conversion of a cypress swamp to some other use or the conversion of a wetland from silvicultural to agricultural use when there is a discharge of dredged or fill material into waters of the United States."[211]

It should be noted, however, that the Corps has amended the definition of "waters of the United States" to exclude "prior converted cropland," a term that is borrowed from the Department of Agriculture's implementation of the Food Security Act.[212] In some cases, this exclusion may permit a change in use of areas that were once wetlands without a Section 404 permit. For a discussion of the treatment of prior converted cropland, see Chapter 14 of this book.

Additionally, to be considered an "established operation" the activity must be ongoing: "An operation ceases to be established when the area on which it was conducted has been converted to another use or has lain idle so long that modifications to the hydrological regime are necessary to resume operations."[213]

The theme of regulating "new uses" of wetlands is continued in the extensive treatment given to the exemption for "minor drainage" associated with farming, silviculture, or ranching activities. Exempted drainage activities are "limited to drainage within areas that are part of an established farming or silviculture operation."[214] Accordingly, "drainage associated with the immediate or gradual conversion of a wetland to a non-wetland . . . or conversion from one wetland use to another (for example, silviculture to farming)" will require a permit if the conversion involves a discharge of dredged or fill material.[215]

b. Maintenance of Currently Serviceable Structures

The Corps's regulation implementing the statutory exemption for maintenance of currently serviceable structures tracks the language of the statute. It additionally provides that "maintenance" does not include activities that "change[] the character, scope, or size of the original fill design."[216] In the case of emergency reconstructions of recently damaged structures, the regulation requires that such reconstruction "occur within a reasonable time after the damage occurs."[217]

In *United States v. Schallom*,[218] defendant was convicted of discharging pollutants without a permit in violation of Section 309(c)(2) of the CWA. He claimed that the discharge of "shotcrete"—a sprayable combination of sand, cement, and water—during the course of bridge repairs was exempt from regulation under the "currently serviceable structures" exemption. [219]

The court rejected this argument, finding that the shotcrete was not "fill material" because it was not discharged "for the primary purpose of replacing an aquatic area with dry land or of changing the bottom elevation of a waterway."[220] While the court does not discuss the significance of this conclusion in any detail, or explain why it is material to its conclusion that the exemption was inapplicable, the facts of the case provide detail that explains the court's reasoning. The shotcrete was carelessly discharged, sometimes in large quantities, directly into surface waters. Because the defendant's discharges were not intended to change the bottom elevation of the waterway, the discharge was not subject to regulation under Section 404, but was subject to the requirements of the NPDES provisions of Section 402 of the CWA.[221] Accordingly, the Section 404(f)(1) exemptions generally, and the Section 404(f)(1)(B) maintenance exemption in particular, were not applicable to the discharges.

More recently, in *Greenfield Mills, Inc. v. Macklin*,[222] the Seventh Circuit provided guidance regarding the scope of the maintenance exemption. Riparian landowners sued employees of the Indiana Department of Environmental Management when the employees drained a hatchery supply pond into the Fawn River without obtaining a CWA permit. The trial court granted summary judgment to the defendants after determining that the draining of the supply pond fit within the Section 404(f) maintenance exemption.[223] However, the Seventh Circuit reversed, concluding that genuine issues of material fact remained to be resolved in the litigation.[224] First, the court held that "a reasonable finder of fact could conclude that the purpose of draining down the water in the supply pond was not to perform maintenance on either the pump or the drain, but rather was to dredge the supply pond without a permit."[225] In addition, the court held that "the maintenance exemption should be construed so that only dredging that is reasonably necessary to the proposed maintenance is exempt from the permit requirement"[226] and the court determined that "the plaintiffs have brought forth sufficient evidence to permit the trier of fact to conclude that the dredging of the pond was not reasonably necessary to either the maintenance of the property or the alleged inspection of the gates."[227]

In *June v. Town of Westfield*,[228] the Second Circuit held a road to be a "transportation structure" within the meaning of the maintenance exemption in Section 404(f)(1)(B). The court affirmed a lower court's grant of summary judgment in favor of a town against a citizen suit claiming the town had deposited fill to shore up the embankment along a road, thereby illegally filling the adjacent ditch. The court explained:

> An embankment supporting a road for transit by motor vehicles is a "transportation structure" [within the meaning of 33 U.S.C.S. § 1344(f)(1)]. To treat a thoroughfare like Mt. Baldy Road otherwise would be to thwart the apparent purpose of the provision: to permit routine government maintenance of transportation,

public water-supply, and similar facilities without the expense, consumption of time, and consequent danger to people and facilities that would inhere in a requirement for a prior permit.[229]

c. Construction and Maintenance of Farm or Stock Ponds, Irrigation Ditches, and Drainage Ditches

The Corps's regulatory exemption for farm or stock ponds, irrigation ditches, and drainage ditches also generally tracks the statutory language, and like the statutory exemption, is subject to the recapture provision. It also includes in the exemption "[d]ischarges associated with siphons, pumps, headgates, wingwalls, weirs, diversion structures, and such other facilities as are appurtenant and functionally related to irrigation ditches."[230] The exemption does not apply to "improvements" to existing drainage systems that alter the hydrological character of the site or make possible a new use of the site.[231]

The Corps has concluded that in applying the exemption for the construction of farm or stock ponds, it will consider "the relative size of a proposed pond in relation to the size of the farming/ranching operation."[232] Thus, to be exempt, pond construction must be limited to a "size the farmer requires to meet normal farming operations."[233] Additionally, the exemption requires that constructed ponds "must actually be used in [established] farming/ranching operations."[234]

Finally, the Corps has concluded that Section 404(f)(2)'s recapture provision applies to construction and maintenance activities only if the activity "bring[s] a water into a use to which it was not previously subject and impair[s] the flow or circulation or reduce[s] the reach of such waters."[235] Likewise, in *In re Carsten*, the court held that the construction of a farm pond would constitute a "new use" subject to the recapture provision only if such construction impairs the flow, circulation, or reach of jurisdictional waters.[236]

The scope of the exemption was also addressed in *United States v. Sargent County Water Resource District*.[237] Unlike the exemption for maintenance of currently serviceable structures, the exemption for maintenance of drainage ditches does not expressly place time limits—e.g., within a reasonable time after the need for maintenance is apparent—on when maintenance of drainage and irrigation ditches must occur to fall within the exemption.[238] In considering whether certain activities constituted "maintenance" and were, therefore, within the terms of the exemption, or "improvement," and were, therefore, subject to regulation,[239] the court in *Sargent County* held such a limitation inapplicable. It concluded that "the only relevance in inquiring into whether there has been ongoing maintenance of the drainage ditch is for the purposes of [the recapture provision's] change in use requirement."[240] Thus, so long as the purpose and effect of the activity were to return the drainage ditch to its original condition—and only to its original condition—the "maintenance" exemption was deemed applicable, regardless of the condition of the ditches at the time the activities were undertaken.[241] In *Sargent County,* the relevant benchmark for determining whether the challenged activity was permissible "maintenance," rather than "improvement" subject to regulation, was the design and character of the ditches as originally constructed and completed in the 1920s.[242]

Moreover, in determining whether a change in use had occurred such that the activities became subject to regulation under 404(f)(2)'s recapture provision, the court held that "[t]he relevant comparison is between the area after the 1980s [maintenance] work, and the area as it existed after the completion of the drain's construction in the early 1920s," not the character of the area as it existed prior to the commencement of maintenance.[243] Although the facts in *Sargent County* do not indicate precisely the extent to which farming was conducted in the area over a long period of years, the court's "baseline" comparison in considering the recapture provision contrasts to some extent with Corps regulatory guidance. The guidance provides that to avoid recapture, maintenance of drainage ditches must facilitate farming that has been conducted on a "regular but not necessarily continuous basis." Farming made possible by maintenance of drainage ditches will be considered a "new use," and thus recaptured by Section 404(f)(2) in circumstances where "there is no reasonable evidence that [areas] were ever farmed or where farming was abandoned following original ditch construction."[244]

d. Construction of Temporary Sedimentation Basins

The Corps's regulation implementing Section 404(f)(1)(D)'s exemption "for the purpose of construction of temporary sedimentation basins on a construction site which does not include placement of fill material into the navigable waters" provides a clarifying definition for the term "construction site." According to the regulation, the term includes "any site involving the erection of buildings, roads, and other discrete structures and the installation of support facilities necessary for construction and utilization of such structures."[245] The exemption also covers "any other land areas which involve land-disturbing excavation activities . . . where an increase in the runoff of sediment is controlled through the use of sedimentation basins."[246]

e. Road Construction and Best Management Practices

Section 404(f)(1)(E)'s exemption for construction or maintenance of farm roads or forest roads requires the application of best management practices (BMPs). Corps regulations provide a detailed description of applicable BMPs, which the regulation considers to be "baseline provisions."[247] In addition to these baseline provisions, road construction in any state with an approved Section 404(h) program must also comply with any "detailed BMPs described in the State's approved program description."[248]

As with other Section 404(f)(1) exemptions, the forest and farm roads exemptions require such maintenance or construction to be part of an established, ongoing farming or silvicultural operation.[249] Additionally, to be exempt, the primary purpose of the road must relate directly to farming or silviculture. For example, "if a road through a national forest would principally serve tourists visiting a recreational site in the forest, not the actual business of silviculture, it would not be a forest road" entitled to an exemption under Section 404(f)(1)(E).[250]

V. Conclusion

The scope of activities that the Corps may regulate under Section 404 has fluctuated over time. There are currently significant areas of uncertainty concerning the Corps's regulatory authority. This uncertainty results from the Corps's efforts to fashion a wetlands protection program that encompasses sufficient activities to be functionally effective and, yet, regulates only activities that may properly be regarded as involving a statutory "discharge of dredged or fill material . . . at specified disposal sites." The debate over the scope of regulated activities under Section 404 will likely continue until Congress acts to clarify Section 404's mandate or the Supreme Court provides a definitive holding on the meaning of key terms in Section 404 as it is currently written and interpreted by EPA and the Corps.

Notes

1. 33 U.S.C. § 1251(a) (2000) ("The object of this chapter is to restore and maintain the chemical, physical, and biological integrity of the Nation's waters.").
2. 33 U.S.C. § 1311.
3. 33 U.S.C. § 1344(a).
4. Excavation is an activity that is specifically regulated under the more limited jurisdictional reach of Section 10 of the Rivers and Harbors Act of 1899. 33 U.S.C. § 403.
5. 33 U.S.C. § 1342.
6. *See, e.g.,* N.C. Shellfish Growers v. Holly Ridge Assoc., 278 F. Supp. 2d 654 (E.D.N.C. 2003).
7. 33 C.F.R. § 328.3(a)(7) (2004).

8. 3 C.F.R. § 328.3.

9. The statutory exemptions are found at 33 U.S.C. § 1344(f). The Corps's exemption regulations are found at 33 C.F.R. § 323.4. EPA's regulations are found at 40 C.F.R. § 232.3.

10. 33 U.S.C. § 1344(a).

11. *Id.*

12. 33 U.S.C. § 1362(16).

13. 33 U.S.C. § 1362(12).

14. 33 U.S.C. § 1362(6).

15. United States v. Zanger, 767 F. Supp. 1030, 1034 (N.D. Cal. 1991).

16. *See, e.g.,* United States v. Wilson, 133 F.3d 251 (4th Cir. 1997).

17. United States v. Banks, 873 F. Supp. 650, 657 (S.D. Fla. 1995), citing United States v. Carter, 18 Env't Rep. Cas. (BNA) 1804, 1807 (S.D. Fla. 1982); United States v. Huebner, 752 F.2d 1235, 1242 (7th Cir.), *cert. denied,* 474 U.S. 817, 106 S. Ct. 62, 88 L. Ed. 2d 50 (1985).

18. United States v. Pozsgai, 999 F.2d 719, 725 (1993), *cert. denied,* 510 U.S. 1110.

19. Hanson v. United States, 710 F. Supp. 1105, 1107 (E.D. Tex. 1989).

20. United States v. Schallom, 998 F.2d 196, 199 (4th Cir. 1993).

21. Minnehaha Creek Watershed Dist. v. Hoffman, 597 F.2d 617, 626–27 (8th Cir. 1979).

22. Avoyelles Sportsmen's League v. Alexander, 473 F. Supp. 525, 532 (W.D. La. 1979).

23. Orleans Audubon Soc. v. Lee, 742 F.2d 901, 910 (5th Cir. 1984).

24. *See, e.g.,* Froebel v. Meyer, 13 F. Supp. 2d 843, 867–68 (E.D. Wis. 1998).

25. 33 U.S.C. § 1362(14).

26. *See, e.g.,* Borden Ranch Partnership v. U.S. Army Corps of Engineers, 261 F.3d 810, 815 (9th Cir. 2001), *aff'd by an equally divided court,* 537 U.S. 99 (2002); United States v. Pozsgai, 999 F.2d 719, 726 n.6 (3d Cir. 1993); Avoyelles Sportsmen's League v. Marsh, 715 F.2d 897, 922 (5th Cir. 1983); Matter of Alameda County Assessor's Parcel, 672 F. Supp. 1278, 1284–85 (N.D. Cal. 1987); United States v. Tull, 615 F. Supp. 610, 622 (E.D. Va. 1983), *aff'd,* 769 F.2d 182 (4th Cir. 1985), *rev'd on other grounds,* 481 U.S. 412 (1987); United States v. Weisman, 489 F. Supp. 1331, 1337 (M.D. Fla. 1980).

27. 473 F. Supp. at 532.

28. *Id.*

29. 715 F.2d 897 (5th Cir. 1983).

30. *Id.* at 923.

31. *Id.* at 924 n.43.

32. *Id.*

33. 772 F.2d 1501, 1506 (11th Cir. 1985), *vacated and remanded on other grounds,* 481 U.S. 1034 (1987), *readopted in part and remanded on other grounds,* 848 F.2d 1133 (11th Cir. 1988), *reh'g granted in other part,* 863 F.2d 802 (11th Cir. 1989).

34. 33 U.S.C. § 1251(a).

35. United States v. M.C.C. of Florida, 772 F.2d 1501, 1506 (11th Cir. 1985).

36. 942 F.2d 1276, 1285 (9th Cir. 1990).

37. *Id.* In United States v. Sinclair Oil Co., 767 F. Supp. 200, 204 (D. Mont. 1990), the court relied on these decisions to hold that rearrangement of indigenous materials in a riverbed to protect the banks and maintain the channel constituted "addition" of a pollutant.

In contrast to these cases, EPA argued in a series of cases the apparently inconsistent position that "for addition of a pollutant from a point source to occur, the point source must introduce the pollutant into navigable water from the outside world." National Wildlife Federation v. Gorsuch, 693 F.2d 156, 165 (D.C. Cir. 1982); *see* National Wildlife Federation v. Consumers Power Co., 862 F.2d 580, 584 (6th Cir. 1988); Ashcroft v. Department of Army, 672 F.2d 1297, 1304 (8th Cir. 1982). Each of these cases considered whether dam-caused pollution was subject to regulation as a "discharge of pollutants" and, thus, required a permit under Section 402 of the CWA. In *Avoyelles Sportsmen's League,* the court noted this apparent inconsistency, but concluded that the agencies' (EPA and the Corps) position that redeposit of native materials may be regarded as an "addition" "appears to have resulted from the agencies' changing view of the facts, rather than any alteration in their view of the law," and thus deference to the agencies was appropriate. *Avoyelles Sportsmen's League,* 715 F.2d at 924 n.43. In *Sinclair Oil,* the court took a different approach, concluding: "This Court specifically distinguishes these [dam] cases as inapposite. The cases . . . concerned a separate regulatory framework under Clean Water Act, and they examined the impacts of existing structures, not the construction of new ones, on the nation's waterways." *Sinclair Oil,* 767 F. Supp. at 205 n.5.

38. 361 F.3d 934, 949 (7th Cir. 2004).

39. *Id., citing Avoyelles,* 715 F.2d at 924 n.43.

40. 526 F.2d 1302 (5th Cir. 1976).

41. *Id.* at 1305.

42. 20 Env't Rep. Cas. (BNA) 1336, 1341–42 (N.D. Ohio 1984).

43. *Id.* at 1342.

44. *Id.*

45. 18 Env't Rep. Cas. (BNA) 1294, 1296 (M.D. Fla. 1981), *aff'd,* 695 F.2d 536 (11th Cir. 1983).

46. *Id.*

47. *Id.*

48. 145 F.3d 1399 (D.C. Cir. 1998).

49. Clean Water Act Appeal No. 98-10 (EPA EAB, Sept. 29, 1999).

50. 62 F. Supp. 2d 1362, 1365 (S.D. Fla. 1999).

51. 13 F. Supp. 2d at 863–69.

52. 133 F.3d 251 (4th Cir. 1997).

53. 261 F.3d 810 (9th Cir. 2001), *aff'd per curiam by an equally divided Court,* 537 U.S. 99 (2002).

54. 145 F.3d 1399 (D.C. Cir. 1998).

55. 33 C.F.R. § 323.2(d)(1)(iii) (1994).

56. 33 C.F.R. § 323.2(d)(3)(i) (1994).

57. *National Mining,* 145 F.3d at 1405. The district court decision, which the D.C. Circuit affirmed, also relied on the statutory term "specified disposal sites"

to conclude that to constitute the "discharge of dredged or fill material," the pollutants in question must originate from a site that is distinct from the site into which they are ultimately placed. American Mining Congress v. United States Army Corps of Eng'rs, 951 F. Supp. 267, 272–78 (D.D.C. 1997), *aff'd sub nom. National Mining, supra*. This aspect of the district court's decision is discussed *infra*.

58. *National Mining,* 145 F.3d at 1406.

59. *Id.* at 1404.

60. *Id.*

61. *Id.* at 1405.

62. *Id.* (quoting Avoyelles Sportsmen's League v. Marsh, 715 F.2d 897, 924 n.43 (5th Cir. 1983)).

63. *Id.*

64. 133 F.3d 251 (4th Cir. 1997).

65. *Id.* at 259.

66. *Id.* at 272.

67. *Id.* at 273.

68. 209 F.3d 331 (4th Cir. 2000).

69. *Id.* at 333.

70. *Id.*

71. *Id.* at 334.

72. *Id.*

73. *Id.*

74. 133 F.3d at 259.

75. *Deaton,* 209 F.3d at 334.

76. 133 F.3d at 259.

77. 145 F.3d at 1404.

78. *Deaton,* 209 F.3d at 335.

79. *Id.*

80. *Id; see also* United States v. Hummel, 2003 U.S. Dist. LEXIS 5656 (N.D. Ill. April 7, 2003) (following *Deaton*).

81. *Deaton,* 209 F.3d at 335–36.

82. *Id.* at 336. The court cited supporting decisions from other circuits, including *Avoyelles Sportsmen's League, M.C.C of Florida,* and *Rybachek, supra,* and acknowledged the apparently differing conclusion reached in *National Mining, i.e.,* that incidental fallback of dredged material is not an addition of a pollutant, but distinguishing between incidental fallback and sidecasting. *Id.*

83. RGL 96-2, Applicability of Exemptions under Section 404(f) to "Deep-Ripping" Activities in Wetlands, 62 Fed. Reg. 31,504 (June 9, 1997), *available at* http://www.usace.army.mil/inet/functions/cw/cecwo/reg/rgls/rgl96-02.htm.

84. 261 F.3d 810 (9th Cir. 2001).

85. Borden Ranch Partnership v. United States Army Corps of Engineers, 537 U.S. 99 (2002).

86. On appeal, the Corps abandoned its claim of jurisdiction over the vernal pools in light of the *SWANCC* decision, which is discussed in Chapter 3. *See Borden Ranch,* 261 F.3d at 816.

87. *Id.* at 814–15.

88. 33 U.S.C. § 1344(a).

89. 951 F. Supp. 267 (D.D.C. 1997), *aff'd sub nom. National Mining Association v. U.S. Army Corps of Engineers, supra.*

90. *American Mining Congress,* 951 F. Supp. at 278.

91. *Id.*

92. Judge Silberman, concurring in *National Mining,* stated, "that Congress had in mind either a temporal or geographic separation between excavation and disposal is suggested by its requirement that dredged material be discharged at 'specified disposal sites.'" 145 F.3d at 1410.

93. 42 Fed. Reg. 37,121 (July 19, 1977).

94. 33 C.F.R. § 323.2(f) (2004).

95. *Id.*

96. 33 C.F.R. § 323.3(c).

97. 67 Fed. Reg. 31,129, 31,135 (May 9, 2002).

98. 33 C.F.R.§ 323.2(e) (2001).

99. 40 C.F.R. § 232.2 (2004).

100. Bragg v. Robertson, 72 F. Supp. 2d 642, 656–57 (D.W. Va. 1999), *affirmed in part, vacated in part sub nom.* Bragg v. West Virginia Coal Ass'n., 243 F.3d 275 (4th Cir. 2001); Froebel v. Meyer, 13 F. Supp. 2d 843, 867–68 (E.D. Wis. 1998); West Virginia Coal Ass'n v. Reilly, 728 F. Supp. 1276, 1287 (S.D. W. Va. 1989); Friends of Santa Fe County v. Lac Minerals, Inc., 892 F. Supp. 1333, 1342 (D.N.M. 1995).

101. *West Virginia Coal Ass'n,* 728 F. Supp. at 1287; *Friends of Santa Fe County,* 892 F. Supp. at 1342.

102. Memorandum of Agreement between the Assistant Administrators for External Affairs and Water, U.S. Environmental Protection Agency, and the Assistant Secretary of the Army for Civil Works Concerning Regulation of Discharges of Solid Waste Under the Clean Water Act (January 17, 1986), *available at* http://www.usace.army.mil/inet/functions/cw/cecwo/reg/solwaste.htm.

103. 151 F.3d 1162 (9th Cir. 1998).

104. 42 U.S.C. §§ 6901 et seq.

105. *See Resource Investments,* 151 F.3d at 1167–68.

106. *Id.* at 1168.

107. *Id.*

108. *Id.* at 1169 (quoting 33 C.F.R. § 320.1(a)(5)).

109. *Id.*

110. U.S. Army Corps of Engineers and U.S. Environmental Protection Agency, Mid-Atlantic Mountaintop Mining/Valley Fills: Draft Environmental Impact Statement, at I-1 (2003), *available at* http://www.epa.gov/region3/mtntop/eis.htm.

111. 54 F. Supp. 2d 635 (S.D.W.Va. 1999), *affirmed in part, vacated in part sub nom.* Bragg v. West Virginia Coal Ass'n, 243 F.3d 275 (4th Cir. 2001).

112. *Id.* The plaintiffs raised a variety of additional claims, including a challenge to the use of nationwide, rather than individual, permits for mountaintop mining/valley fills; a claim that the Corps failed to prepare an appropriate environmental impact statement for its nationwide permit authorizing the activity; and claims against a state agency. Claims against the state agency were eventu-

ally held to be barred by the Eleventh Amendment. Bragg v. West Virginia Coal Ass'n, 243 F.3d 275 (4th Cir. 2001).

113. *Bragg v. Robertson,* 54 F. Supp. 2d at 639. The Corps also agreed to prepare an environmental impact statement

> on a proposal to consider developing agency policies, guidance, and coordinated agency decision-making processes to minimize, to the maximum extent practicable, the adverse environmental effects to waters of the United States and to fish and wildlife resources affected by mountaintop mining operations, and to environmental resources that could be affected by the size and location of excess spoil disposal sites in valley fills.

Id. A draft environmental impact statement was made available for public review on May 30, 2003. 68 Fed. Reg. 32,487 (May 30, 2003).

114. 204 F. Supp. 2d 927, 941 (S.D. W. Va. 2002), *rev'd,* 317 F.3d 425 (4th Cir. 2003).

115. *Id.* at 944.

116. *Id.* at 946–47, *clarified in* Kentuckians for the Commonwealth, Inc. v. Rivenburgh, 206 F. Supp. 2d 782, 808 (S.D. W. Va. 2002), *vacated,* 317 F.3d 425 (4th Cir. 2003).

117. *Id.* at 945.

118. 317 F.3d at 447.

119. *Id.* at 447–48.

120. *Id.* at 438.

121. 33 C.F.R. § 323.2(e)(1).

122. *Id.* § 323.2(e)(2)–(3).

123. 67 Fed. Reg. 31,134.

124. 42 Fed. Reg. 37,145 (July 19, 1977).

125. 33 C.F.R. § 323.2(c).

126. Pub. L. No. 95-217, 91 Stat. 76 (1977).

127. 47 Fed. Reg. 31,794 (July 22, 1982).

128. 51 Fed. Reg. 41,206 (Nov. 13, 1986).

129. *See* 33 C.F.R. § 323.2 (1989); Reid v. Marsh, 20 Env't Rep. Cas. (BNA) 1336, 1341–42 (N.D. Ohio 1984).

130. *Compare* Weiszmann v. Dist. Eng'r, 526 F.2d 1302 (5th Cir. 1976), and United States v. Lambert, 695 F.2d 536 (11th Cir. 1983). *See also* United States v. Bayshore Assoc. Inc., 934 F.2d 1391 (6th Cir. 1991).

131. 51 Fed. Reg. 41,206, 41,232 (Nov. 13, 1986); 33 C.F.R. § 323.2 (1989).

132. 51 Fed. Reg. 41,210.

133. *Id.*

134. Civil No. C90-713-CIV-5-BO (E.D. N.C. 1992).

135. 57 Fed. Reg. 26,894.

136. 58 Fed. Reg. 45,008 (Aug. 25, 1993); 33 C.F.R. § 323.2(d) (1994).

137. *Id.*

138. 33 C.F.R. § 323.2(d)(l) (1994).

139. *See* 33 C.F.R. §§ 323.2(d)(2)–(3) (1994).

140. 33 C.F.R. § 323.2(d)(2)(ii) (1994).

141. 33 C.F.R. § 323.2(d)(3)(i) (1994).

142. *Id.*

143. 33 C.F.R. § 323.2(d)(4) (1994).

144. 33 C.F.R. § 323.2(d)(5) (1994). The kind of adverse effects on wetlands that were considered by the Corps include those listed in EPA's Section 404(b) Guidelines and codified at 40 C.F.R. § 230, subpt. E.

The Corps does not require a permit for incidental movement of dredged material during normal dredging operations in navigable waters regulated under the Rivers and Harbors Act. 33 C.F.R. § 323.2(d)(3)(ii) (2004). This exception does not apply to dredging in wetlands. *Id.*

145. 33 C.F.R. § 320.1 (2004).

146. 64 Fed. Reg. 25,120, 25,121 (May 10, 1999).

147. *Id.*

148. *Id.*

149. *Id.*

150. The agencies expressed concern

> that, without further action to clarify the definition of "discharge of dredged material," large-scale destruction of wetlands could occur, resulting in increased flooding or runoff and harm to neighboring property, pollution of streams and rivers, and loss of valuable habitat. Moreover, available information indicates that such losses are already occurring. Accordingly, the Agencies will expeditiously undertake additional notice and comment rulemaking in furtherance of the CWA's objective to "restore and maintain the chemical, physical, and biological integrity of the Nation's waters." Additionally, the [*National Mining*] court recognized that the CWA "sets out no bright line between incidental fallback on the one hand and regulable redeposits on the other" and that "a reasoned attempt to draw such a line would merit considerable deference." . . . Further rulemaking thus is appropriate not only to ensure that the Nation's wetlands and other waters of the U.S. will continue to receive the protection required by section 404 of the CWA, but also to enhance clarity, certainty, and consistency in determining what activities are subject to section 404 in light of the [*National Mining*] decision.

Id.

151. American Mining Congress v. U.S. Army Corps of Engineers, 120 F. Supp. 2d 23 (D.D.C. 2000).

152. *Id.* at 30.

153. 66 Fed. Reg. 4550 (Jan. 17, 2001).

154. 33 C.F.R. § 323.3(d)(2).

155. *Id.* § 323.3(d)(2)(ii).

156. *Id.* § 323.3(d)(2)(i).

157. 66 Fed. Reg. at 4555.

158. *Id.*

159. *Id.* at 4554.

160. 33 C.F.R. § 323.3(d)(2)(i).

161. National Association of Home Builders v. U.S. Army Corps of Engineers, 311 F. Supp. 2d 91 (D.D.C. 2004).

162. *Id.* at 93.

163. *See* RGL 90-5 (July 18, 1990), *available at* http://www.usace.army.mil/inet/functions/cw/cecwo/reg/rgls/rgl90-05.htm.

164. 715 F.2d at 923.

165. *Id.* at 924–25.

166. 711 F.2d 634, 647 (5th Cir. 1983).

167. *Id.*

168. 33 C.F.R. § 323.2(d)(2)(ii).

169. *Id.; see also* 33 C.F.R. § 323.2(d)(4):

> (4) Section 404 authorization is not required for the following:
>
> (i) Any incidental addition, including redeposit, of dredged material associated with any activity that does not have or would not have the effect of destroying or degrading an area of waters of the United States as defined in paragraphs (d)(5) and (d)(6) of this section; however, this exception does not apply to any person preparing to undertake mechanized landclearing, ditching, channelization and other excavation activity in a water of the United States, which would result in a redeposit of dredged material, unless the person demonstrates to the satisfaction of the Corps, or EPA as appropriate, prior to commencing the activity involving the discharge, that the activity would not have the effect of destroying or degrading any area of waters of the United States, as defined in paragraphs (d)(5) and (d)(6) of this section. The person proposing to undertake mechanized landclearing, ditching, channelization or other excavation activity bears the burden of demonstrating that such activity would not destroy or degrade any area of waters of the United States.

170. 33 F. Supp. 2d 596 (E.D. Mich. 1999).

171. *Id.* at 605.

172. *Id.* at 606.

173. *Id.* at 607.

174. 33 U.S.C. § 1344(f)(1)(E). The conditions include the observance of "best management practices." *Id.*

175. 33 C.F.R. § 323.2(d)(3)(ii).

176. *Id.*

177. 971 F.2d 1155 (5th Cir. 1992).

178. Save Our Community v. United States EPA, 741 F. Supp. 605 (N.D. Tex. 1990).

179. *Save Our Community,* 971 F.2d at 1164.

180. *Id.* at 1167.

181. This apparently was the landfill operator's plan in *Save Our Community,* but as the court noted, "it is unclear whether [the operator] will be able to

drain the ponds completely or whether the pond sites will cease to be wetlands regardless of [the operator's] careful draining." *Save Our Community,* 971 F.2d at 1158 n.7.

182. *Id.* 133 F.3d at 254.

183. 209 F.3d at 332.

184. Memorandum from Lance Wood to All Division and District Counsels, "Evading 404 Jurisdiction by Pumping Water from Wetlands" (Apr. 10, 1990).

185. *Id.*

186. 33 C.F.R. § 328.3(b); 40 C.F.R. § 230.3(t).

187. *Wilson,* 113 F.3d at 257; *see* United States v. Brace, 41 F.3d 117, 128 (3d Cir. 1994).

188. For a discussion of how the courts have interpreted the "normal circumstances" concept, see Chapter 3 of this book.

189. 33 C.F.R. § 323.3(c)(1).

190. *Id.*

191. *Id.*

192. The qualifier "generally" reflects the Corps's unwillingness to establish a definitive rule that the placement of pilings for linear projects, piers, wharves, and individual houses on stilts "will never have the effect of fill material." 58 Fed. Reg. at 45,029.

193. 33 C.F.R. § 323.3(c)(2).

194. *See id.*

195. 33 U.S.C. § 1344(f).

196. 33 U.S.C. § 1344(f)(1)(A)–(F). These exempt activities are not prohibited by or otherwise subject to regulation under Section 404, Section 301 (governing effluent limitations), or Section 402 (governing the NPDES), but are subject to the effluent standards and prohibitions of Section 1317 governing toxic and pretreatment standards. *Id.* § 1344(f)(1).

197. 33 C.F.R. § 323.4.

198. *See, e.g.,* Greenfield Mills, Inc. v. Macklin, 361 F.3d 934, 949 (7th Cir. 2004); Borden Ranch Partnership v. U.S. Army Corps of Engineers, 261 F.3d 810, 815–16 (9th Cir. 2001), *aff'd by an equally divided court,* 537 U.S. 99 (2002); United States v. Larkins, 852 F.2d 189, 192 (6th Cir. 1988).

199. 33 U.S.C. § 1344(f)(2). The "recapture" provision includes both a "purpose" test and an "effects" test. Courts have consistently held that the recapture provision applies only when both conditions have been met. *Greenfield Mills, Inc.,* at 955, citing Borden Ranch Partnership v. U.S. Army Corps of Engineers, 261 F.3d 810, 815 (9th Cir. 2001), *aff'd by an equally divided court,* 537 U.S. 99 (2002); Avoyelles Sportsmens League Inc. v. Marsh, 715 F.2d 893, 926 (5th Cir. 1983); United States v. Sargent County Water Resource District, 876 F. Supp. 1090, 1102–1103 (N.D. 1994); In re Carsten, 211 B.R. 719, 732 (1997).

200. *Brace,* 41 F.3d at 124 (citing United States v. Akers, 785 F.2d 814, 819 (9th Cir. 1986)). *See also Greenfield Mills, Inc.,* 361 F.3d at 949.

201. *Brace,* 41 F.3d at 124 (citing Avoyelles Sportsmen's League, Inc. v. Marsh, 715 F.2d 897, 926 (5th Cir.1983)). In further support of this strict interpre-

tation of Section 404(f)(1)'s exemptions, the court quoted the following statement from Senator Muskie in the legislative history of the CWA:

> New subsection 404(f) provides that Federal permits will not be required for those narrowly defined activities that cause little or no adverse effects either individually or cumulatively. While it is understood that some of these activities may necessarily result in incidental filling and minor harm to aquatic resources, the exemptions do not apply to discharges that convert extensive areas of water into dry land or impede circulation or reduce the reach or size of the water body.

Id. (quoting 3 A LEGISLATIVE HISTORY OF THE CLEAN WATER ACT OF 1977: A CONTINUATION OF THE LEGISLATIVE HISTORY OF THE WATER POLLUTION CONTROL ACT, at 474 (1978)).

202. 33 C.F.R. § 323.4(c); *see also* RGL 96-2, Applicability of Exemptions under Section 404(f) to "Deep-Ripping" Activities in Wetlands, 62 Fed. Reg. 31,504 (June 9, 1997) ("[A]lthough Section 404 should not unnecessarily restrict farming, forestry, or ranching from continuing at a particular site, discharge activities which could destroy wetlands or other waters should be subject to regulation."), *available at* http://www.usace.army.mil/inet/functions/cw/cecwo/reg/rgls/rgl90-02.htm; Avoyelles Sportsmen's League v. Marsh, 715 F.2d at 925 ("[S]ection 404(f)(2) specifically takes away the exemption for activities that involve changing the use of the land.").

203. 33 C.F.R. § 323.4(c). This provision provides, in part:

> [A] permit will be required for the conversion of a wetland from silvicultural to agricultural use when there is a discharge of dredged or fill material into waters of the United States in conjunction with construction of dikes, drainage ditches or other works or structures used to effect such conversion. A conversion of a Section 404 wetland to a non-wetland is a change in use of an area of waters of the United States.

204. *Id.*

205. 33 U.S.C. § 1344(f)(1)(A).

206. 33 C.F.R. § 323.4(a)(1)(iii).

207. 33 C.F.R. § 323.4(a)(1)(iii)(D).

208. United States v. Huebner, 752 F.2d 1235, 1240 (7th Cir. 1985) (citations omitted).

209. 33 C.F.R. § 323.4(a)(1)(ii).

210. *Id.;* United States v. Cumberland Farms of Connecticut, Inc., 647 F. Supp. 1166, 1175 (D. Mass. 1986), *aff'd,* 826 F.2d 1151 (1st Cir. 1987) (exemption applicable only to prior established and continuing farming); Conant v. United States, 786 F.2d 1008, 1009 (11th Cir. 1986) (construction of a fish farming operation not exempt as "normal" farming activity).

211. 33 C.F.R. § 323.4(c); *see Larkins,* 852 F.2d at 192 (change from silvicultural use to agricultural use not exempt as "normal" silvicultural activities); Environmental Defense Fund v. Tidwell, 837 F. Supp. 1344, 1350 (E.D.N.C. 1992)

(converting swamp forest to pine tree farm not exempt as "normal" silvicultural activities; instead, pine tree farm was a "new use" subject to regulation). *But see Akers,* 785 F.2d at 820 (rejecting government's contention that "normal farming" exemption is unavailable to "farmers who desire merely to change from one wetland crops to another").

212. *See* 58 Fed. Reg. 45,008, 45,031–32 (Aug. 25, 1993).

213. 33 C.F.R. § 323.4(a)(1)(ii); *Brace,* 43 F.3d at 126 ("[T]he 'normal farming' exemption [is] inapplicable because modifications were required to resume farming."); *Akers,* 785 F.2d at 819–20 (farming activities requiring "substantial hydrological alteration" of site not exempt); United States v. Larkins, 657 F. Supp. 76, 85–86, n.23 (W.D. Ky. 1987), *aff'd,* 852 F.2d 189 (6th Cir. 1988) ("Activities cease to be established when the property on which they were once conducted '*has lain idle so long that modifications to the hydrological regime are necessary to resume operations.*' . . . Consequently, even if the wetland had a history of farm use, that use was no longer established at the time of defendant's activities.") (citations omitted) (emphasis by court).

214. 33 C.F.R. § 323.4(a)(1)(iii)(C)(2).

215. *Id.; see Brace,* 43 F.3d at 127 (installation of extensive drainage system not exempt as "normal farming" activity).

216. *See* 33 C.F.R. § 323.4(a)(2).

217. *Id.*

218. 998 F.2d 196 (4th Cir. 1993).

219. *Id.*

220. *Id.* at 200 (quoting 33 C.F.R. 323.2(e)).

221. For a discussion of how jurisdiction over certain pollutants is divided between the Sections 404 or 402 permit programs, see Section III.A of this chapter, *supra.*

222. 361 F.3d 934 (7th Cir. 2004).

223. *Id.* at 944–45.

224. *Id.*

225. *Id.* at 951.

226. *Id.* at 952.

227. *Id.* The plaintiffs also argued that summary judgment was improper because the defendants' actions "chang[ed] the character, scope, or size of the original fill design," in violation of the Corps's regulations. *Id.* However, the Seventh Circuit rejected that argument, concluding that "original fill design" referred to "the manmade structures that are the subject of the exemption (e.g. dikes, dams, levees) rather than a natural watercourse such as the Fawn River" and that the maintenance did not change the character, scope, or size of the dam for the supply pond. *Id.* at 953.

228. 370 F.3d 255 (2d Cir. 2004).

229. *Id.* at 255.

230. 33 C.F.R. § 323.4(a)(3).

231. *See Brace,* 43 F.3d at 128.

232. RGL 87-9, Section 404(f)(1)(C) Exemption for Construction or Maintenance of Farm or Stock Ponds, p.1 (Aug. 27, 1987), *available at* http://www.usace.army.mil/inet/functions/cw/cecwo/reg/rgls/rgl87-09.htm.

233. *Id.* The Corps expressed fear that exempting a "large pond on a small farm could in a few years become the nucleus of a residential development plan and therefore such construction may require an individual permit." *Id.*

234. *Id.* In *In re Carsten,* the Bankruptcy Court for the District of Montana concluded that the exemption applicable to construction of farm ponds is not lost because the pond was constructed, in part, for "secondary recreational use." In the court's view, "the incidental allowance of 'conoing [sic] and swimming' on a tiny landlocked water body . . . does not in any way conflict with the definition of 'farm pond' as contemplated in the farm exemption statute." 211 Bank. 719, 734 (D. Mont. 1997).

235. RGL 87-9, at 2 (alterations in original).

236. *In re Carsten,* 211 Bank. at 732–33.

237. 876 F. Supp. 1090 (D.N.D. 1994).

238. *See* RGL 87-7, Section 404(f)(1)(C) Statutory Exemption for Drainage Ditch Maintenance, p. 2 (Aug. 17, 1987): ("[T]here is no 'ongoing' requirement associated with Section 404(f)(1)(C)."), *available at* http://www.usace.army.mil/inet/functions/cw/cecwo/reg/rgls/rgl87-07.htm.

239. On the distinction between "maintenance" and "improvement" of drainage ditches, see *Brace,* 41 F.3d at 128 (concluding that excavation of site with existing drainage system coupled with "burying of several miles of plastic tubing to facilitate drainage" not properly characterized as "continuing maintenance").

240. *Sargent County,* 876 F. Supp. at 1002.

241. *Id.* at 1101–02.

242. The court alternatively rejected the contention of the government that because of the long passage of time, and the County's lack of diligence in undertaking the maintenance, a permit should be required. The court concluded "that the County neither abandoned the drain nor rested on its right to maintain it." *Id.* at 1101.

243. *Id.* at 1103.

244. RGL 87-7, at 2.

245. 33 C.F.R. § 323.4(a)(4).

246. *Id.*

247. 33 C. F. R. § 323.4(a)(6).

248. *Id.*

249. RGL 86-3, Section 404(f)(1) Exemption of Farm and Forest Roads (April 4, 1986), p. 1–2, *available at* http://www.usace.army.mil/inet/functions/cw/cecwo/reg/rgls/rgl86-03.htm.

250. *Id.* at 1.

CHAPTER 5

General and Nationwide Permits

WILLIAM E. TAYLOR AND KATE L. GEOFFROY

I. Introduction/Scope

Many activities that involve discharges of dredged or fill material into wetlands or other areas classified as "waters of the United States" may be authorized by means short of obtaining an individual permit under the United States Army Corps of Engineers (Corps) Section 404 program.[1] A variety of activities subject to Section 404 may be conducted under the authority of general permits. Additionally, in some cases, activities may be authorized through "letters of permission," which are issued through a streamlined individual permitting process. The use of available permitting options other than individual permits may save considerable time and expense. Accordingly, it is advisable to carefully review whether the proposed activity can proceed using one of these less costly, less time-consuming alternatives to the standard individual permit.

This chapter discusses these alternatives to individual permits, with particular attention devoted to the Corps's nationwide permit program.

II. Alternatives to Individual Permits under the Section 404 Program: An Overview

A. General Permits

In 1977, Congress amended Section 404 of the Clean Water Act (CWA) to authorize the Corps to issue general permits on a state, regional, or nationwide basis for activities involving discharges of dredged or fill material that are "similar in nature, will cause only minimal adverse environmental effects when performed separately, and will have only minimal cumulative adverse effect on the environment."[2] The Corps defines a general permit as

> a Department of the Army authorization that is issued on a nationwide or regional basis for a category or categories of activities when:
>
> (1) Those activities are substantially similar in nature and cause only minimal individual and cumulative environmental impacts; or
>
> (2) The general permit would result in avoiding unnecessary duplication of regulatory control exercised by another Federal, state, or local agency provided it has been determined that the environmental consequences of the action are individually and cumulatively minimal.[3]

Corps regulations governing the issuance of general permits are found in 33 C.F.R. Part 325. The Environmental Protection Agency (EPA) has also promulgated regulations governing general permits under its Section 404(b)(1) authority. These regulations are set forth in 40 C.F.R. § 230.7.

General permits have come to occupy a crucial role in the Section 404 permitting process because they offer an opportunity to avoid the more complex, time-consuming, and often burdensome individual permitting process. General permit authorization procedures usually afford a simpler, more efficient, and far less costly alternative for projects that can be designed to meet the terms of a general permit.

Statistics gathered by the Corps illustrate the substantial advantages that general permits offer to landowners. During fiscal year 2003, the Corps processed more than 85,000 Section 404 applications, including notices from persons seeking to proceed with activities under the authority of one or more general permits. Of these, 88 percent were authorized through general permits, while 4 percent were processed as individual permits.[4] The average time to evaluate projects under general permits was twenty-four days.[5] The average time needed to process applications for individual permits, on the other hand, was 187 days.[6] It is clear from these statistics that the vast majority of projects are authorized by general permits and that this option offers substantial advantages to those seeking to engage in regulated activities.

B. Types of General Permits

Section 404 authorizes the Corps to issue general permits on a state, regional, or nationwide basis.[7] The Corps has issued each of these types of general permits.

1. *State and Regional Permits*

State and regional general permits vary in different areas of the country and are issued by the various Corps district and division offices.[8] For example, the Chicago District has developed thirteen regional permits that authorize a variety of activities, including residential, commercial, and institutional developments; recreation projects; transportation projects; minor discharges and dredging; wetland/stream restoration/enhancement; completed enforcement actions; temporary construction activities; utility line projects; maintenance; bank stabilization; marine structures and activities; bridge scour protection; and cleanup of toxic and hazardous wastes.[9] Information on regional permits can be obtained from the various Corps districts.[10]

2. *Programmatic Permits*

A particular type of regional or state general permit is the programmatic permit. These permits are "founded on an existing state, local or other Federal agency program and [are] designed to avoid duplication with that program."[11] State programmatic general permits are discussed in greater detail in Chapter 10.

3. *Nationwide Permits*

Nationwide permits (NWPs) are "a type of general permit issued by the Chief of Engineers and are designed to regulate with little, if any, delay or paperwork certain activities having minimal impacts."[12] They authorize activities on a nationwide basis, unless their application is specifically limited.[13] They are issued through notice in the Federal Register and an opportunity is provided for public comment.[14]

Recently, the Corps's NWP program has undergone extensive changes. In the past, nationwide permits were printed and codified in the Code of Federal Regulations at Part 330, Appendix A of the Corps's rules. The Corps decided in 1996 that the NWPs would no longer be published in the Code of Federal Regulations but would be published in the Federal Register and announced, with regional conditions, in the public notices issued by Corps district offices and on the Internet.[15] In addition, the Corps's new NWP program relies much more on regional involvement in the development of NWPs, encouraging Corps districts to place appropriate regional conditions on NWPs to ensure that activities authorized under the NWPs will have only minimal adverse effects on the aquatic environment. Thus, it has become increasingly important to contact the local and/or regional Corps offices to determine what kinds of general permits might be available to authorize planned activities involving the discharge of dredged or fill materials. A more detailed discussion of NWPs is located in Section IV of this chapter.

C. Letters of Permission

The Corps has developed a streamlined individual permitting process for an alternative to general permits known as "letters of permission." Corps regulations define this authority as "a type of permit issued through an abbreviated processing procedure which includes coordination with Federal and state fish and wildlife agencies . . . and a public interest evaluation, but without the publishing of an individual public notice."[16] Information on the availability of this procedure can be obtained through Corps district offices. (See Web site http://www.usace.army.mil/inet/functions/cw/cecwo/reg/district.htm.)

III. Statutory Requirements Governing the Issuance of General Permits

The Corps's authority to issue general permits on a state, regional, or nationwide basis is found in Section 404(e) of the CWA. As noted above, the primary requirements of the CWA relating to general permits are that the activities authorized by such permits (1) be "similar in nature" and (2) "cause only minimal adverse environmental effects when performed separately, and will have only minimal cumulative adverse effect on the environment."[17] Section 404(e) also provides that general permits shall be based on guidelines promulgated by the Environmental Protection Agency pursuant to Section 404(b)(1)(A) and "set forth the requirements and standards which shall apply to any activity authorized by" the permits.[18] The statute also limits general permits to a period of five years.[19]

A. Activities That Are "Similar in Nature"

The Corps's general permits have rarely been challenged in court.[20] There is, accordingly, little case law interpreting the terms "similar in nature" and "minimal adverse effect on the environment." Many commenters have suggested, however, that some of the Corps's general permits are invalid because they authorize a range of activities that are not "similar in nature."

Several years ago, the Corps responded to these criticisms by phasing out the most widely used and certainly the most controversial NWP—NWP 26, which authorized a range of activities in waters above headwaters and isolated waters.[21] Nonetheless, the Corps has emphasized a pragmatic understanding of the statutory and regulatory requirement that activities authorized by NWPs be "similar in nature," noting that "it is important not to constrain this criterion to a level that makes the NWP program too complex to implement or makes a particular NWP useless because it would authorize only a small proportion of activities that result in minimal adverse effects on the aquatic environment."[22] In the Corps's view, "similar" is not equivalent to "identical"; instead, the statute embraces a "broader, and . . . more practical, definition of the word 'similar,'" that would cover descriptions of activities such as "the construction of buildings and features necessary for their operation and use."[23]

A similar approach was used by the Ninth Circuit in *Alaska Center for the Environment v. West*.[24] The court sustained a set of general permits governing construction in wetlands in Alaska. The general permits authorized fills in wetlands specified in a special area management plan developed by the city of Anchorage. One such general permit authorized construction of residential buildings. The court held

> While it may be true that the [general permits] do not specifically distinguish between such structures as "single family housing" and "two-family dwellings," we are not persuaded that the general permitting process must necessarily require such fine distinctions. In terms of permitting for commercial uses, such distinctions would appear to blur the line between specific and general permits, rendering general permits virtually unavailable for commercial development. This may be a desirable result. However, such speculation does not lead to a finding that the Corps' decision was plainly erroneous.[25]

The court also noted that the "Corps placed great weight on ensuring that the activities allowed would each have a similar minimal effect on the environment."[26] On this view, activities may be regarded as "similar in nature" by reference to the kinds of effects the activities may have on the aquatic environment, rather than the activities's purposes. The court held that the Corps could properly take account of such considerations.[27]

B. Activities Having Minimal Adverse Effects

The Corps has not developed precise standards for determining whether a particular category or categories of activities proposed to be authorized by general permits "will cause only minimal adverse environmental effects when performed separately, and will have only minimal cumulative adverse effect on the environment." By statute,[28] general permits must be based on EPA's Section 404(b)(1) Guidelines, which include a number of requirements applicable to the assessment of a general permit's effects on the environment.[29]

When the Corps amended the NWPs in 2000, the agency acknowledged that there are data gaps that impair the agency's ability to assess the impacts of activities authorized by its NWPs.[30] Because of these gaps, as well as concerns that previous NWPs may have caused adverse impacts, the Corps has developed an extensive set of general conditions to govern the use of many NWPs, including prohibitions against the use of certain NWPs in particular areas, preconstruction notification to Corps district engineers, regional conditioning of NWPs, and compensatory mitigation.[31] The Corps's general conditions are discussed in detail below.

The Ninth Circuit in *Alaska Center for the Environment* addressed the question of adverse environmental impacts, sustaining the Corps's determination that the regional general permits at issue in the case would have only minimal adverse effects on the aquatic environment.[32] The Corps had concluded that while over 2,000 acres of wetlands were potentially affected by the permits, the authorized activities would likely take place in only 360 acres of wetlands, many of which were characterized as "low value" wetlands. The court held that the Corps had acted appropriately in limiting its consideration of adverse effects to the 360 acres likely to be affected, rather than enlarging its focus to the entire 2,000 acres of potentially affected wetlands. In support, it noted that EPA regulations governing general permits provide that cumulative effects are to be predicted by evaluating "the number of . . . activities likely to be regulated under a General permit."[33]

More recently, in *Ohio Valley Environmental Coalition v. Bulen*, a federal district court held that the Corps's issuance of NWP 21, which authorizes discharges associated with surface coal mining, violates the Clean Water Act because the Corps did not determine, prior to issuing the permit, that the activities authorized by the permit would have only minimal effects on the environment.[34] NWP 21 authorizes certain discharges of dredged or fill material associated with surface mining activities but requires persons who intend to use the permit to notify the Corps before they take actions covered by the permit.[35] No person may proceed with activities covered by NWP 21 until the Corps notifies the person that the agency has determined that the activity complies with the terms and conditions of the NWP and that the adverse environmental effects are minimal both individually and cumulatively.[36] Although the Corps established a procedure, in NWP 21, to ensure that activities covered by the permit would have only minimal adverse effects on the environment, the *Bulen* court held that the procedure violates the Clean Water Act.[37] According to the court,

> The fundamental problem with the Corps approach is that NWP 21 defines a procedure instead of permitting a category of activities. Section 404(e) of the Clean Water Act directs the Corps to determine that certain activities will invariably have only minimal effects on the environment. The statute unambiguously requires determination of minimal impacts before, not after, the issuance of a nationwide permit. . . . NWP 21 provides for a post hoc, case-by-case evaluation of environmental impact. . . . By combining factors of both individual and general permitting in the NWP 21, the Corps allows an activity with the potential to have significant effects on the environment to be permitted without being subject to public notice and comment or the other procedural hurdles to authorization pursuant to Section 404(a).[38]

Accordingly, the court enjoined the Corps from issuing authorizations under NWP 21 in the Southern District of West Virginia.[39]

C. Compliance with Other Statutory Mandates

In addition to the requirements governing general permits that are set forth in Section 404(e) and implementing regulations, the Corps may, in some circumstances, be required to comply with a variety of other statutory mandates in issuing general permits. Among the more significant statutory requirements are the state certification requirements imposed by Section 401 of the CWA;[40] consistency determinations pursuant to the Coastal Zone Management Act (CZMA);[41] and the consultation requirements of the Endangered Species Act (ESA)[42] and the National Historic Preservation Act (NHPA).[43] The Corps has elected to include provisions for compliance with these statutes in its general conditions, which are discussed below.

The National Environmental Policy Act (NEPA)[44] also may apply to general permits, including the Corps's NWP program. Under NEPA, agencies are required to prepare an environmental impact statement (EIS) for any "major Federal actions significantly affecting the quality of the human environment."[45] The Corps generally prepares an environmental assessment (EA), the purpose of which is to determine whether a general permit will significantly affect the quality of the human environment and, thus, require the preparation of an EIS.[46] If the EA supports a conclusion that an EIS is not required, the Corps will make a finding of no significant impact (FONSI).[47]

The Corps has routinely made FONSIs for its general permits, supporting those conclusions with EAs. In a recent case, a federal district court enjoined the Corps's use of NWP 29, governing construction of single-family housing, concluding that the EA prepared in support of this general permit was inadequate.[48] Under NEPA regulations, an EA must include a brief discussion of an appropriate range of alternatives to the proposed action.[49] The court concluded that the Corps's EA in support of NWP 29 was inadequate because the Corps failed to consider alternatives to the acreage limits and scope of NWP 29.[50] As discussed below, the Corps has issued a modified NWP 29 to respond to the court's decision.

In March 1999, the Corps began preparation of a voluntary programmatic environmental impact statement (PEIS) for the NWP program.[51] However, the Corps maintains that a PEIS is not legally required, and that the agency can issue or amend NWPs before it completes the PEIS.[52] NEPA decision documents for all current NWPs can be found on the Corps's headquarters Web site.[53]

IV. Nationwide Permits

Because they are the most commonly used of the general permits, the remainder of this chapter will focus on the Corps's NWP program.[54] NWPs are issued by the Corps and generally apply throughout the country unless they are made specifically inapplicable in a particular state or region. The availability and terms governing the use of the NWPs are set forth in two places: (1) the Corps's general regulations on the nationwide permit program,[55] and (2) the nationwide permits themselves, along with general conditions, which are now published in the Federal Register, through the Corps's division offices, and on the Internet.[56] All relevant sources should be consulted prior to undertaking any work under any of the NWPs. Only if all of the terms and conditions, including any regional conditions, of the NWP are satisfied is the activity deemed to be authorized by the NWP.[57] The NWPs have a maximum duration of five years,[58] but most have been routinely re-issued. Note that, in some cases, a district may authorize activities to proceed under an NWP without resort to individualized proceedings even if the permit applicant has sought an individual permit.[59]

Several of the NWPs that have been issued over the last five years differ significantly from prior NWPs, both in terms of the conditions that may be applicable and the complexities associated with ensuring that they are used appropriately. Most of the complexity relates to the Corps's decision to replace NWP 26 with other, more activity-specific, NWPs.

NWP 26 had been the most frequently used and controversial of the nationwide permits. In its Environmental Assessment for the 1996 reissuance of NWP 26, the Corps estimated that NWP 26 would authorize approximately 33,800 discharges per year on a national basis. Of those discharges, the Corps concluded that approximately 7,800 discharges would have wetland impacts of approximately 8,400 acres. These impacts are roughly 75 percent of the projected total acreage impacts resulting from all activities authorized by all NWPs.[60]

What ultimately became NWP 26 started in 1977 as a nationwide permit authorizing discharges into (1) nontidal rivers and streams and adjacent wetlands above headwaters, and (2) lakes above headwaters and isolated lakes and adjacent wetlands of less than ten acres.[61] In 1982, the Corps expanded this NWP to cover all above-headwater wetlands and isolated waters regardless of size.[62] Following this expansion in the coverage of the NWP, various environmental organizations sued the Corps challenging the NWP.[63] In settlement of that lawsuit, the Corps revised NWP 26 in 1984.

The modified NWP, as issued in 1984, authorized discharges of dredged or fill material to waters above headwaters and to isolated waters, "except those which cause the loss or substantial adverse modification of ten acres or more of waters of the United States, including wetlands."[64] For discharges causing the loss or substantial adverse modification of one to ten acres of these waters, the NWP required preconstruction notice of the proposed activities to the appropriate Corps district engineer.[65] Thus, under the revised 1984 NWP 26, only projects with less than one acre of adverse impacts could proceed without Corps notification or involvement. With additional modifications, NWP 26 was reissued in 1991[66] and again in 1996.[67]

In the 1996 reissuance of NWP 26, the Corps substantially modified the NWP. Discharges were authorized only if they did not cause the loss of more than three acres of jurisdictional waters or more than 500 linear feet of a stream bed. Preconstruction notice was required for discharges causing losses in excess of one-third acre of waters. For discharges causing losses of one-third acre or less, permittees were required to submit reports within thirty days of completing the work.[68] More significantly, in 1996 the Corps signaled its intention to replace NWP 26 with "activity specific" permits,[69] and the agency issued new NWPs to replace NWP 26 on March 9, 2000.[70]

The process of replacing NWP 26 with new, activity-specific NWPs has led to a significant restructuring of the NWP program. Of particular importance, the Corps has significantly expanded the general conditions that apply to many NWPs, refocused its efforts on protecting both wetlands and open waters, and relied heavily on regional conditioning of several NWPs. In the Corps's view, the restructuring of the NWP program was necessary to ensure that activities authorized by NWPs have only minimal adverse effects on aquatic environments. The latest NWPs were issued in 2002, and are further discussed below.[71]

Responsibility for determining the applicability of NWPs is with the Corps.[72] Therefore, if there is any question about the applicability of a particular NWP, a determination from the Corps that the NWP applies to the project should be sought before initiating any project activity. In practice, it is often wise to confirm the applicability of an NWP to a proposed activity by seeking written confirmation from the Corps district office. This is particularly true when there is any question about any of the requirements of the NWP, or when opposition to a proposed project can be anticipated. Written confirmation from the Corps provides a record for the project applicant and minimizes the possibility that the activity can later be challenged as not qualifying under the NWP. It also provides written assurance that there are no particular issues about use of the NWP in the area proposed for the project.

A. Examples of NWPs

There are now forty-three NWPs. Of these, some require that the project applicant provide preconstruction notification (discussed below) to the Corps before undertaking the project and some have other significant limitations or conditions that must be met before the activity can be undertaken. Table 1 summarizes the current NWPs, identifies those

TABLE 1. Nationwide Permits

NWP No.	Title	PCN[1]	Other Significant Conditions[2]
1	Aids to Navigation	No	No
2	Structures in Artificial Canals	No	No
3	Maintenance	In some cases	Yes
4	Fish and Wildlife Harvesting, Enhancement, and Attraction Devices and Activities	No	No
5	Scientific Measuring Devices	In some cases	Yes
6	Survey Activities	No	No
7	Outfall Structures and Maintenance	Yes	Yes
8	Oil and Gas Structures	No	Yes
9	Structures in Fleeting and Anchorage Areas	No	No
10	Mooring Buoys	No	No
11	Temporary Recreational Structures	No	Must be removed within 30 days after use
12	Utility Line Activities	In some cases	Yes
13	Bank Stabilization	In some cases	Not available to place material in wetlands; other conditions may be applicable
14	Linear Transportation Crossings	In some cases	Yes
15	U.S. Coast Guard Approved Bridges	No	Does not include causeways or approach fills
16	Return Water From Upland Contained Disposal Areas	No	Quality of return water subject to 401 state certification
17	Hydropower Projects	Yes	Yes
18	Minor Discharges	If discharge exceeds 10 cubic yards or occurs in wetlands	Discharge may not exceed 25 cubic yards or cause loss of more than one-tenth acre of wetlands
19	Minor Dredging	No	May not exceed 25 cubic yards; does not authorize activities in coral reefs, submerged aquatic beds, or anadromous fish spawning areas
20	Oil Spill Cleanup	No	Must meet requirements of other applicable laws

(continued)

TABLE 1. Nationwide Permits (cont.)

NWP No.	Title	PCN[1]	Other Significant Conditions[2]
21	Surface Coal Mining	Yes	Yes
22	Removal of Vessels	If vessel listed or eligible for National Register of Historic Places	Does not authorize maintenance dredging, shoal removal, or river bank snagging
23	Approved Categorical Exclusions	No	Applies to activities determined by other federal agencies to be excluded from NEPA; certain conditions may be required on an activity-by-activity basis after notice and comment corps procedure
24	State Administered Section 404 Program (NWP for § 10 of Rivers and Harbors Act of 1899)	No	Does not authorize activities in navigable waters that require only a Section 10 permit
25	Structural Discharges (structural members for standard pile-supported structures, such as bridges, transmission line footings, and walkways or for general navigation)	No	Does not authorize building support pads
26	Expired June 7, 2000 and now noted as [Reserved] by the Corps		
27	Stream and Wetland Restoration	In some cases	Yes
28	Modifications of Existing Marinas	No	Does not authorize dredging, additional slips or dock spaces, or expansion
29	Single-Family Housing	Yes	Does not authorize activities that cause the loss of more than one-quarter acre of nontidal waters of the United States, including nontidal wetlands; other conditions apply
30	Moist Soil Management for Wildlife	No	Yes
31	Maintenance of Existing Flood Control Facilities	Yes	Yes
32	Completed Enforcement Actions	Yes[3]	Yes

(continued)

TABLE 1. Nationwide Permits (cont.)

NWP No.	Title	PCN[1]	Other Significant Conditions[2]
33	Temporary Construction, Access, and Dewatering	Yes	Yes
34	Cranberry Production	Yes	Yes
35	Maintenance Dredging of Existing Basins	No	Dredged material must be disposed of at an upland site and proper siltation controls required
36	Boat Ramps	No	Does not authorize placement of material in wetlands; other conditions apply
37	Emergency Watershed Protection and Rehabilitation	Yes	Limited to work done or funded by specific federal agencies
38	Cleanup of Hazardous and Toxic Waste	Yes	Activity must be performed, ordered, or sponsored by government agency with appropriate legal authority or pursuant to court order; other conditions apply
39	Residential, Commercial, and Institutional Developments	In some cases	Yes
40	Agricultural Activities	In some cases	Yes
41	Reshaping Existing Drainage Ditches	Yes, if more than 500 linear feet of drainage ditch is reshaped	Yes
42	Recreational Facilities	In some cases	Yes
43	Stormwater Management Facilities	In some cases	Yes
44	Mining Activities	Yes	Yes

[1] "PCN" means that preconstruction notification of the proposed activity must be made to the appropriate district engineer. Readers are advised to consult the NWP under consideration for the circumstances under which PCN is required, as well as the Corps's General Condition 13, which provides details on the form and content of PCNs.

[2] NWPs are subject to the Corps's General Conditions. Where the table indicates significant restrictions or conditions apply in addition to the General Conditions, readers should consult the terms of the specific NWP under consideration.

[3] This NWP does not require a PCN in accordance with General Condition 13, but does require a verification letter from a district engineer authorizing the activity.

Source: 67 Fed. Reg. 2020 (Jan. 15, 2002).

requiring preconstruction notification to the Corps, and highlights those NWPs which contain other significant limitations or requirements.[73]

Historically, other than NWP 26, only a few NWPs have been used on a regular and frequent basis by the regulated community. These include NWPs for maintenance and repair of authorized structures (NWP 3), outfall structures (NWP 7), utility line discharges (NWP 12), bank stabilization (NWP 13), linear transportation crossings (NWP 14), minor discharges (NWP 18), minor dredging (NWP 19), and temporary construction, access, and dewatering (NWP 33). In recent years, several new and revised NWPs have become of particular interest to the regulated community, particularly those relating to single-family housing (NWP 29); residential, commercial, and institutional developments (NWP 39); agriculture (NWP 40); and mining (NWP 44). Each of these NWPs is discussed briefly in this section. Readers are cautioned to consult the full text of the NWPs. Where there is any question about the activities authorized or conditions applicable to these NWPs, the appropriate Corps district office should be consulted.

1. *Maintenance (NWP 3)*

This NWP generally authorizes the repair, rehabilitation, or replacement of previously authorized structures and fills that do not qualify for the Section 404(f) exemption for maintenance.[74] It also authorizes the removal of accumulated sediments in the vicinity of existing structures and activities associated with restoration of uplands damaged by storms, floods, or other discrete events. Preconstruction notice to the Corps is required for these two recently added authorizations under this NWP.[75] Activities authorized by this NWP must generally commence within two years of the date on which the existing structure or fill was damaged.

2. *Outfall Structures (NWP 7)*

This NWP authorizes activities related to the construction and maintenance of outfalls authorized by or exempt from the requirements of the National Pollutant Discharge Elimination System program established pursuant to Section 402 of the CWA. It also authorizes the removal of accumulated sediments from outfall and intake structures and associated canals. The conditions applicable to this NWP include (1) preconstruction notification must be made; (2) excavated or dredged material must be the minimum amount necessary to restore the outfall to original design capacities and configurations; (3) excavated or dredged material must be deposited and retained at an upland site, unless otherwise authorized by the district engineer; and (4) reentry of sediments into waters must be minimized through proper soil erosion and sediment control measures.[76]

3. *Utility Line Activities (NWP 12)*

This NWP authorizes various activities associated with the construction, maintenance, and repair of utility lines. These activities include

- The construction and maintenance of utility lines, including outfall and intake structures and associated excavation, backfill, or bedding for utility lines, so long as the activity does not change preconstruction contours. The NWP defines "utility line" as "any pipe or pipeline for the transportation of any gaseous, liquid, liquefiable, or slurry substance, for any purpose, and any cable, line, or wire for the transmission for any purpose of electrical energy, telephone, and telegraph messages, and radio and television communication."
- The construction, maintenance, or expansion of a substation facility in nontidal waters, excluding nontidal wetlands adjacent to tidal waters, so long as the activity causes a loss of no greater than one-half acre of nontidal waters.
- The construction or maintenance of foundations for overhead utility line towers, poles, and anchors, provided the foundations are only as large as necessary and separate footings for each tower leg are used where feasible.
- The construction of access roads for construction and maintenance of utility lines, so long as the activity causes a loss of no greater than one half acre of nontidal wetlands.

Preconstruction notification is required in some circumstances, including those in which the activity involves mechanized land clearing in forested wetlands; a Section 10 permit is required; the utility line in waters exceeds 500 feet; the utility line is placed in jurisdictional waters and runs parallel to a stream bed that is within the jurisdictional area; discharges associated with utility substation construction result in a loss of greater than one-tenth acre of jurisdictional waters; permanent access roads are constructed above grade in waters for a distance of more than 500 feet; or permanent access roads are constructed in jurisdictional waters with impervious materials.[77]

4. Bank Stabilization (NWP 13)

This NWP authorizes activities necessary to prevent erosion. The activity must meet the following conditions: (1) only the minimum amount of material needed for erosion control may be placed in waters; (2) bank stabilization must be less than 500 feet in length, unless preconstruction notice is given to the district engineer and the district engineer determines that the activity otherwise complies with the terms and conditions of the NWP; (3) placement of material below the plane of the ordinary high water mark or high tide line may not exceed one cubic yard per running foot; (4) no material is placed in special aquatic sites, including wetlands; (5) placed material may not impair surface water flow into or out of any wetland area; (6) material may not be placed in a manner such that it will be eroded by normal or expected high flows; and (7) the activity is part of a single and complete project.[78]

5. Linear Transportation Crossings (NWP 14)

This NWP authorizes activities required for construction, expansion, modification, or improvement of linear transportation crossings, such as highways, railways, trails, and airport runways. The activities must meet several conditions, including acreage limitations. Discharges cannot cause the loss of greater than one-half acre for nontidal waters and one-third acre in tidal waters. Preconstruction notice is required if the activity causes losses of greater than one-tenth acre of waters or the discharge is in a special aquatic site, including wetlands. Where notification is required, it must include a mitigation proposal and, if applicable, a wetland delineation.[79]

6. Minor Discharges (NWP 18)

This NWP authorizes discharges of not more than twenty-five cubic yards, provided the discharge will not cause a loss of more than one-tenth acre of a special aquatic site, including wetlands. Preconstruction notification is required for discharges of more than ten cubic yards or those in special aquatic sites, including wetlands.[80]

7. Minor Dredging (NWP 19)

This NWP authorizes dredging of no more than twenty-five cubic yards, provided the dredging does not occur in certain kinds of aquatic sites, including wetlands.[81]

8. Single-Family Housing (NWP 29)

As issued in 1996, this NWP authorized discharges into nontidal waters, including nontidal wetlands for the construction or expansion of a single-family home. Its use was limited to activities causing a loss of no more than one-half acre of nontidal waters, including wetlands. Among other conditions, preconstruction notice was required. In *Alaska Center for the Environment v. West,* discussed above, the court remanded this NWP to the Corps, concluding that the supporting Environmental Assessment pursuant to NEPA was inadequate.[82] On remand, the Corps modified the NWP, reducing the maximum authorized loss of waters, including wetlands, to one-fourth acre.[83] The NWP may only be used once per parcel, may not be used in conjunction with NWP 14 or NWP 18, and includes several other conditions.[84]

9. Temporary Construction, Access, and Dewatering (NWP 33)

This NWP authorizes discharges associated with temporary structures and work necessary for construction activities or access fills or dewatering of construction sites. These activities must be associated with a primary activity that is either not subject to the Corps's jurisdiction or has been authorized. Preconstruction notification is required, including a "restoration plan of reasonable measures to avoid and minimize adverse effects to aquatic resources."[85]

10. Residential, Commercial, and Institutional Developments (NWP 39)

This NWP is one of the "activity based" permits adopted to replace NWP 26 and has become the most frequently used nationwide permit. This NWP authorizes discharges into nontidal waters, excluding nontidal wetlands adjacent to tidal waters, for construction or expansion of residential, commercial, and institutional building foundations and pads and "attendant features that are necessary for the use and maintenance of such structures."[86] The NWP provides examples of developments that are authorized, including multiple and single residential units, retail stores, industrial facilities, restaurants, business parks, shopping centers, schools, libraries, fire stations, government office buildings, judicial buildings, public works buildings, hospitals, and places of worship. The list of "attendant features" authorized by this NWP is quite expansive; it includes, but is not limited to, "roads, parking lots, garages, yards, utility lines, storm water management facilities, and recreation facilities such as playgrounds, playing fields, and golf courses."[87]

The NWP is subject to maximum acreage losses of nontidal waters of one-half acre. Preconstruction notice is required for discharges causing losses of greater than one-tenth acre of nontidal waters or losses of any open waters, including perennial or intermittent streams, below the ordinary high water mark. For discharges causing smaller losses, a report must be submitted to the district engineer within thirty days of the work's completion. Compensatory mitigation will ordinarily be required, and in many circumstances, wetland or upland vegetated buffers must be established and maintained.[88]

11. *Agricultural Activities (NWP 40)*

The 1996 version of this NWP authorized discharges causing losses of "farmed wetlands"—jurisdictional wetlands in agricultural production prior to December 23, 1985—of one acre or less for foundations and building pads for farm buildings.[89] With the replacement of NWP 26 with activity-specific permits, NWP 40 now authorizes discharges into nontidal waters, excluding nontidal wetlands adjacent to tidal waters, for the purpose of farm building construction and "improving agricultural production." The installation or construction of drainage tiles, ditches, and levees is authorized under this NWP, provided certain conditions are met. These conditions vary depending on whether the permittee is a participant in U.S. Department of Agriculture (USDA) programs.

Acreage limits are set at one-half acre of nontidal wetlands on a farm tract. For permittees who do not participate in USDA programs, preconstruction notification is required if the activity will cause losses in excess of one-tenth acre of nontidal wetlands. Compensatory mitigation is required.[90] While the NWP does not authorize the relocation of more than 300 linear feet of existing serviceable drainage ditches constructed in nontidal streams, the district engineer may waive that limit for drainage ditches constructed in intermittent nontidal streams on a case-by-case basis.[91]

12. *Recreational Facilities (NWP 42)*

This is another activity-specific permit designed to replace NWP 26. It authorizes discharges into nontidal waters, excluding nontidal wetlands adjacent to tidal waters, for the construction or expansion of recreational facilities that do not cause a loss of more than one-half acre of nontidal waters. The NWP does not authorize discharges that cause the loss of more than 300 linear feet of stream beds, but the district engineer may waive that limit for intermittent stream beds on a case-by-case basis. Recreational facilities authorized by NWP 42 include hiking trails, bike paths, horse paths, nature centers, and campgrounds. It does not authorize the construction or expansion of facilities that include the use of motor vehicles, buildings, or impervious surfaces. Nor does this NWP authorize the construction or expansion of football, baseball, or soccer playing fields; basketball and tennis courts; racetracks; stadiums or arenas; or new ski areas. Preconstruction notification is required if the activity causes a loss of greater than one-tenth acre of nontidal waters or if the discharge exceeds 300 linear feet of impact on intermittent stream beds.[92]

13. Mining Activities (NWP 44)

Another activity-specific permit designed to replace NWP 26, this NWP authorizes discharges

- for aggregate mining (i.e., sand, gravel, and crushed and broken stone) and associated support activities into isolated waters, streams having an annual average flow of no greater than 1 cubic foot per second, and nontidal wetlands adjacent to headwater streams;
- for aggregate mining activities (excluding associated support activities) into lower perennial streams, excluding wetlands adjacent to those streams; and
- for hard rock/mineral mining and associated support activities (extraction of metalliferous ores from subsurface locations) into isolated waters and nontidal wetlands adjacent to headwater streams.

The list of conditions for use of this NWP is extensive. It includes preconstruction notice, acreage limits, and compensatory mitigation for any wetland impacts.[93]

B. General Conditions

A project may be able to avoid individual Section 404 permitting if it comes within the terms of an NWP, but it must meet all of the applicable conditions.[94] With the recent restructuring of the NWP program, the Corps has significantly expanded the number of NWPs that are subject to conditions and has increased the number and stringency of several general conditions.[95] The following sections describe the most significant of the general conditions applicable to NWPs. Table 2 provides a listing of all general conditions, the NWPs to which each of the conditions apply, and a summary description of the conditions.[96] Readers are also reminded that several NWPs contain additional conditions that supplement the general conditions.

TABLE 2. General Conditions

No.	Title	Applicability	Summary Description
1	Navigation	All NWPs	Activity must not cause more than minimal adverse effect on navigation
2	Proper Maintenance	All NWPs	Authorized structures or fills must be properly maintained
3	Soil Erosion and Sediment Controls	All NWPs	Soil erosion and sediment controls during construction and stabilization of exposed fills and soils
4	Aquatic Life Movements	All NWPs	Activity may not substantially disrupt movement of indigenous aquatic species, unless activity's primary purpose is to impound water
5	Equipment	All NWPs	Heavy equipment in wetlands must be placed on mats or other measures must be taken to minimize soil disturbance
6	Regional and Case-By-Case Conditions	Varies	Requires compliance with conditions imposed by district or division engineers or by states through 401 certification or CZMA consistency
7	Wild and Scenic Rivers	All NWPs	Prohibits use of NWPs in specially designated waters
8	Tribal Rights	All NWPs	Activity or its operation may not impair reserved tribal rights, including reserved water rights and treaty fishing and hunting rights
9	Water Quality	NWPs requiring individual 401 certification; NWPs 12, 14, 17, 18, 32, 39, 40, 42–44 where 401 certification does not require/approve water quality plan	401 certification or waiver in certain states; for NWPs 12, 14, 17, 18, 32, 39, 40, 42–44 in states that do not require or approve water quality plan as part of 401 certification, permittee must provide for protection of aquatic resources, including stormwater management, and establish and maintain vegetated buffer zone
10	Coastal Zone Management	NWPs requiring individual CZMA consistency concurrence	Permittee must obtain consistency concurrence or waiver from state
11	Endangered Species	All NWPs	Activity may not jeopardize threatened or endangered species listed under federal Endangered Species Act; must notify district engineer if any listed species or its critical habitat might be affected by activity
12	Historic Properties	All NWPs	Activity must comply with applicable regulations (33 CFR Part 325, Appendix C) regarding historic properties listed or eligible for listing on National Register of Historic Places

(continued)

TABLE 2. General Conditions (cont.)

No.	Title	Applicability	Summary Description
13	Notification	NWPs 3, 5, 7, 12–14, 17, 18, 21, 22, 27, 29, 31–34, 37–44	Precludes commencement of activity (1) until notified in writing by district engineer that activity may proceed; (2) if notified by district engineer that an individual permit is required; or (3) until 45 days after complete notification to district engineer and no written notice from district engineer received. Extensive list of requirements for particular NWPs. Provision for agency coordination and compensatory mitigation.
14	Compliance Certification	All NWPs	Permittee must certify that work was done in accordance with authorization and that any required mitigation was completed
15	Use of Multiple Nationwide Permits	All NWPs, except for restrictions in NWPs 3, 18, 29, 39, 40	Acreage loss of waters may not exceed the acreage limit of the NWP with highest limit
16	Water Supply Intakes	All NWPs	Prohibits activities in proximity of public water supply intake, except for repairs to intakes or adjacent bank stabilization
17	Shellfish Beds	All NWPs	Except for shellfish harvesting authorized by NWP 4, activities in areas of concentrated shellfish populations are prohibited
18	Suitable Material	All NWPs	Prohibits use of unsuitable materials, such as trash, debris, car bodies, and asphalt, and prohibits use of toxic pollutants in toxic amounts
19	Mitigation	All NWPs	Activities must be minimized or avoided to the maximum extent practicable; compensatory mitigation required to ensure that authorized impacts have minimal adverse environmental effects; preference for restoration as compensatory mitigation; for projects in or near streams or other open waters, vegetated buffers may be required
20	Spawning Areas	All NWPs	Activities in spawning areas during spawning seasons must be avoided to the maximum extent practicable; physical destruction of important spawning areas is prohibited
21	Management of Water Flows	All NWPs	To the maximum extent practicable, authorized activities may not alter preconstruction downstream flow conditions, permanently restrict or impede passage of normal or expected high flows, allow excess flows from the site, increase water flows from the site, relocate water, or redirect water flow

(continued)

TABLE 2. General Conditions (cont.)

No.	Title	Applicability	Summary Description
22	Adverse Effects From Impoundments	All NWPs	If activity causes impoundment, adverse effects on aquatic system must be minimized to the maximum extent practicable
23	Waterfowl Breeding Areas	All NWPs	Prohibits, to the maximum extent practicable, activities in breeding areas for migratory waterfowl
24	Removal of Temporary Fills	All NWPs	Temporary fills must be removed in their entirety and affected areas returned to preexisting elevation
25	Designated Critical Resource Waters	NWPs 3, 7, 8, 10, 12, 13, 14, 15, 16, 17, 18, 19, 21, 22, 23, 25, 27, 28, 29, 30, 31, 33, 34, 35, 36, 37, 38, 39, 40, 42, 43, 44	For NWPs 7, 12, 14, 16, 17, 21, 29, 31, 35, 39, 40, 42, 43, and 44, activities in critical resource waters are prohibited, except in National Wild and Scenic Rivers if activity complies with General Condition 7 and except in designated critical habitat for federally listed endangered or threatened species if General Condition 11 is satisfied and appropriate resource agency has concurred in a determination of compliance with General Condition 11
26	Fills within the 100-Year Floodplain	29, 39, 40, 42, 43, 44	Permanent above-grade fills in 100-year floodplain, below headwaters, are not authorized by NWPs 39, 40, 42, 43, or 44; permanent above-grade fills in FEMA or locally mapped floodways are not authorized by NWPs 39, 40, 42, or 44
27	Construction Period	All NWPs	Limits are placed on the time period within which work must be completed under NWPs

Source: 67 Fed. Reg. 2020 (Jan. 15, 2002).

C. Regional, State, and Case-Specific Conditions and Limitations

A variety of conditions on the use of NWPs may be imposed by Corps division engineers on a regional basis, by state and tribal agencies in their Section 401 water quality certifications and Coastal Zone Management consistency concurrences of particular NWPs, and by Corps district engineers on a case-by-case basis. These conditions must be satisfied for valid use of NWPs.

1. *Section 401 Certification*

Corps regulations require, consistent with Section 401 of the Clean Water Act,[97] that a state water quality certification or a waiver of certification be obtained before an NWP becomes effective in any state.[98] Individual states may impose additional conditions on the use of a particular NWP in the certification process. It is therefore important to determine (1) whether the state has issued a water quality certification for the NWP proposed to be used, and (2) whether that certification requires the project applicant to comply with additional conditions beyond those specified in the NWP and more generally by the Corps.

In many instances, the state will not have issued a general water quality certification for a particular NWP. In such circumstances, an individual water quality certification must be obtained (or waived) in order for the project to proceed under the authority of the NWP.[99] Fortunately for project applicants, the regulations allow the project to proceed even without an individual Section 401 water quality certification if, after a reasonable period of time (usually sixty days), the state does not respond to the request for individual certification. At that point, the Corps will generally presume that the state has waived certification and will allow the activity to proceed assuming it meets the other conditions of the NWP.[100]

The Corps has specifically rejected the position that a state's denial of Section 401 certification for a particular NWP has the effect of requiring the proponent of an activity that otherwise meets the requirements of the NWP to submit to an individual permit proceeding before commencing the activity. Instead, the Corps has endorsed the issuance of provisional NWP verifications that are valid only if the permittee obtains an individual Section 401 certification for the activity from the appropriate state agency.[101]

2. *Coastal Zone Management Consistency*

Coastal zone consistency determinations are handled in a manner similar to the treatment of state water quality certifications. If the NWP authorizes activities affecting the coastal zone of a state that has an approved Coastal Zone Management Program, the Corps is required to provide a consistency determination and receive state concurrence in that determination before an NWP can be issued.[102] As in the case of water quality certifications, the Corps's rules reflect that states may impose additional conditions on the use of an NWP through the consistency determination.[103] The regulations also specify the procedures for obtaining individual coastal consistency determinations, or waivers, when a general determination has not been made with respect to a particular NWP in the state in which a proposed activity is to occur.[104]

3. Regional Conditioning of NWPs

General Condition 6 provides that activities authorized by any NWP must comply with any regional conditions added by division engineers. Division engineers may suspend, modify, or revoke NWP authority for a specific geographic region, class of activity, or class of waters upon a determination that concerns for the environment under the Section 404(b)(1) Guidelines, or "any other factor of the public interest," require such action, or upon a determination that certain activities authorized by an NWP would have more than minimal adverse environmental effects either individually or cumulatively.[105] The process for such regional conditioning involves notice and an opportunity for public comment.[106]

The Corps has emphasized the availability of the regional conditioning process for several NWPs to ensure that authorized activities will have no more than minimal adverse effects on the aquatic environment.[107] The regional conditions are developed by Corps district and division engineers and are subject to notice and an opportunity for public comment. These conditions are intended to account for regional differences in aquatic resource functions and values and, where necessary, provide greater protection for the aquatic environment. District or division offices should be consulted to determine whether and to what extent NWPs are subject to regional conditions.

4. Case-Specific Conditions

Conditions or limitations on the use of NWPs may be imposed by the Corps, acting through its division and district engineers, on a case-by-case basis. Corps regulations expressly provide that the Corps retains discretionary authority in all cases to suspend, modify, or revoke authorization under an NWP.[108] District engineers may do so for a specific activity "whenever [the district engineer] determines sufficient concerns for the environment or any other factor of the public interest so requires."[109] Whenever the district engineer determines that the authorized activity will have more than minimal adverse effects on the environment or will otherwise be contrary to the public interest, the district engineer must either modify the NWP to eliminate or reduce the adverse effects or notify the permittee that alternative authorization is necessary, such as an individual permit.[110] Such case-specific conditions are developed through an informal process involving consultations with the permittee. If agreement cannot be obtained in this manner, the district engineer may suspend a specific authorization by notifying the permittee of such action in writing, and ordering the permittee to stop any activities that may have been initiated under the NWP. Public notice is not required.[111] Although this provision has not been used frequently, it remains an option and one of which prospective applicants must remain aware, especially in instances where NWPs require preconstruction notification to the Corps prior to undertaking a project.

D. Conditions Based on Other Statutory Requirements

Like individual permits, NWPs must comply with some mandates in statutes other than Section 404 of the Clean Water Act. In addition to Section 401 state water-quality certification requirements and Coastal Zone Management Act consistency determinations discussed above, NWPs must also comply with the Endangered Species Act and the National Historic Preservation Act.

1. *Endangered Species Act Compliance*

A general issue for determining the applicability of any NWP is the presence in the project area of endangered or threatened species listed under the federal Endangered Species Act.[112] Corps regulations prohibit any activity from being authorized under an NWP if it is "likely to jeopardize the continued existence of a threatened or endangered species" listed or proposed for listing under the Endangered Species Act, or if it will destroy or adversely modify critical habitat of such species.[113]

In determining whether an activity may proceed under an NWP, the Corps must consider not only the "direct" but also any incidental or indirect effects the discharge may have on endangered species. In *Riverside Irrigation District v. Andrews,*[114] the court upheld the Corps's denial of permission for dam construction activities involving discharges of dredged and fill material to proceed under an NWP. The Corps determined that while the discharges themselves would not affect endangered species, the completed dam project would deplete stream flow and thus adversely affect downstream critical habitat of the endangered whooping crane. It therefore required the plaintiff to apply for and obtain an individual permit before commencing the proposed activities. Turning aside plaintiff's attempt to limit the Corps's authority to deny application of the NWP, the court concluded

> There is no authority for the proposition that, once it is required to consider the environmental impact of the discharge it is authorizing, the Corps is limited to consideration of the direct

> effects of the discharge. The reduction of water flows resulting from the increased consumptive use [associated with the dam] is an effect, albeit indirect, of the discharge to be authorized by the Corps. The discharge thus may "destroy or adversely modify" the critical habitat of an endangered species, and the Corps correctly found that the proposed project did not meet the requirements for a nationwide permit.[115]

The procedures required to be followed when a nonfederal applicant proposes a project under an NWP, however, are less stringent than what would be required under an individual permit. Applicants must notify the district engineer of any listed or proposed species or critical habitat that might be affected by or are in the vicinity of a project.[116] The applicant is prohibited from beginning work under the NWP until notified that the requirements of the Endangered Species Act have been satisfied and that the activity is authorized. Under this scheme, it is up to the district engineer to determine whether the activity may affect such species or habitat and, if so, to initiate consultation with the U.S. Fish and Wildlife Service (FWS) or National Marine Fisheries Service (NMFS) in accordance with the requirements of Section 7 of the Endangered Species Act.[117] The district engineer may impose additional conditions or restrictions on the activity to address species-specific issues.[118] Interestingly, the regulations "encourage" but do not require applicants to obtain information on the location of such species and critical habitats from FWS and NMFS.[119]

Although applicants are not required to determine whether the proposed activity will affect a listed or proposed species or a critical habitat, it is very important to recognize that conducting an activity pursuant to an NWP does not insulate the applicant from potential liability under the Endangered Species Act itself. As specifically set forth in the NWPs, the authorization of an activity under an NWP does not authorize "take" of a listed species, and both lethal and nonlethal "takes" of such species violate the Endangered Species Act absent a separate authorization for the take under the Endangered Species Act.[120]

2. *Historic Properties*

The application of any NWP to a particular project must also be consistent with the requirements of the National Historic Preservation Act. Similar to the requirements for endangered species, Corps regulations specify that no activity authorized under an NWP may affect properties listed or eligible for listing in the National Register of Historic Places unless and until the district engineer has complied with specific procedures for the protection of such historic properties.[121] Nonfederal permittees are required to notify the district engineer if activities may affect listed properties or properties eligible for listing on the National Register of Historic Places. In such instances, the applicant is prohibited from proceeding with the activity until notified that the requirements of the National Historic Preservation Act have been satisfied and the activity has been authorized. In some cases, the district engineer may impose additional conditions or restrictions on the activity to address potential impacts to historic properties. A permittee is required to immediately notify the district engineer if historic properties that have not been listed or determined to be eligible for listing are encountered before or during the activity authorized under the NWP.[122]

As with endangered species, Corps regulations "encourage" but do not require applicants to obtain information on the location of historic properties from the State Historic Preservation Officer and the National Register of Historic Places.[123]

E. Operational Conditions

In addition to the general requirements applicable to all NWPs under Corps regulations, there are also several operational conditions that may be applicable to particular activities otherwise authorized by NWPs.[124] As shown in Table 2, the following conditions apply to all NWPs.

1. *Navigation (General Condition 1)*

Activities conducted under authority of any NWP must not cause more than a minimal adverse effect on navigation.

2. *Proper Maintenance (General Condition 2)*

Activities conducted under authority of any NWP must be properly maintained, including measures necessary to ensure public safety.

3. *Soil Erosion and Sediment Controls (General Condition 3)*

Construction activities undertaken pursuant to an NWP must include appropriate erosion and sediment controls. Exposed soil and fills and any work below the ordinary high water mark or high tide line must be permanently stabilized.

4. *Aquatic Life Movements (General Condition 4)*

Unless the primary purpose of an activity conducted under an NWP is to impound water, the activity may not substantially disrupt the necessary life cycle movement of indigenous aquatic life.

5. Equipment (General Condition 5)

Heavy equipment used in conjunction with activities in wetlands must be placed on mats, or other measures must be employed to minimize soil disturbance.

6. Water Quality (General Condition 9)

For NWPs 12, 14, 17, 18, 32, 39, 40, 42, 43, and 44, where the state or tribal Section 401 certification does not require or approve water quality management measures, permittees are required to include measures to protect water quality, including methods for storm water management and vegetated buffers if the project occurs in the vicinity of an open water body.

7. Water Supply Intakes (General Condition 16)

Activities are generally prohibited in proximity to public water supply intakes.

8. Suitable Material (General Condition 18)

Discharges involving unsuitable materials, such as trash, car bodies, or asphalt, are prohibited, as are discharges of toxic pollutants in toxic amounts.

9. Mitigation (General Condition 19)

Permittees are generally required to conduct authorized activities in a manner that, to the maximum extent practicable, minimizes or avoids adverse impacts on aquatic resources. Compensatory mitigation may be required to offset authorized impacts, and vegetated buffers are generally required for activities in or near open waters.

10. Management of Water Flows (General Condition 21)

For projects that have the potential to affect water flows, efforts must be taken to protect preconstruction downstream flow conditions to the maximum extent practicable.

11. Adverse Effects from Impoundments (General Condition 22)

Adverse effects on aquatic resources from activities involving impoundments must be minimized to the maximum extent practicable.

12. Removal of Temporary Fills (General Condition 24)

All temporary fills must be removed in their entirety and affected areas must be returned to preexisting elevations.

13. Construction Period (General Condition 27)

Activities authorized by NWPs must be completed within specified time periods.

F. Conditions Applicable to Certain Resources or Areas

The NWPs are generally subject to conditions that prohibit or restrict activities in certain designated waters or in areas that are environmentally sensitive.

1. Wild and Scenic Rivers

Activities in a component of the National Wild and Scenic River System or in a "study river" being considered for inclusion in that system are not authorized under any NWP, "unless the appropriate Federal agency, with direct management responsibility for such river, has determined in writing that the proposed activity will not adversely affect the Wild and Scenic River designation, or study status."[125] The agencies bearing such responsibility include the National Park Service, U.S. Forest Service, the Bureau of Land Management, and the U.S. Fish and Wildlife Service.[126]

2. Tribal Rights

No activity may proceed under any NWP if it, or its operation, may impair tribal rights, including reserved water rights and hunting and fishing rights under treaty.[127]

3. Shellfish Beds

Activities are generally prohibited in areas of concentrated shellfish populations.[128]

4. Spawning Areas

Activities in spawning areas during spawning seasons must be avoided to the maximum extent practicable.[129]

5. Waterfowl Breeding Areas

Activities in breeding areas for migratory waterfowl must be avoided to the maximum extent practicable.[130]

6. Designated Critical Resource Waters

Several NWPs may not be used to authorize activities in waters, including adjacent wetlands, that have received designation as being of special value.[131] Included in such waters are marine sanctuaries designated by the National Oceanic and Atmospheric Administration, National Estuarine

Research Reserves, or National Wild and Scenic Rivers; critical habitat for federally listed threatened and endangered species; coral reefs; state natural heritage areas; and outstanding resource waters officially designated by the state in which the waters are located and identified by the district engineer after notice and opportunity for comment.[132] Additionally, district engineers may designate other waters as critical resource waters after notice and opportunity for public comment. Activities under other NWPs may proceed in critical resource waters only after notice to the appropriate district engineer and only after any other applicable conditions, such as those relating to endangered species and Wild and Scenic Rivers, have been satisfied.[133]

7. Hundred-Year Floodplain

The use of several NWPs is prohibited, and for others preconstruction notification is required, for permanent, above-grade wetland fills in the hundred-year floodplain or floodways.[134] The NWPs affected by this condition are listed in Table 2, General Condition 26.

G. Preconstruction Notification

It is usually a good idea to obtain confirmation from the Corps that a particular activity qualifies for authorization under the terms and conditions of NWP. In some instances, moreover, such advance notification is required under the terms of the particular NWP. In those instances, the applicant must submit to the district engineer a preconstruction notification (PCN) and may not begin the activity until the district engineer provides notice that the activity may proceed under the NWP (with or without special conditions) or the specified time period for Corps review has expired.[135] Table 1 notes which NWPs are subject to the PCN requirement.

In general, the notification must be in writing and must include information about the applicant and about the location and the nature of the project.[136] Some NWPs require additional information such as a wetland delineation,[137] mitigation plan, or maintenance plan.[138] Applicants may submit a mitigation plan even if not specifically required.

The Corps district engineer initially reviews the PCN to determine if it is complete. A completeness determination must be made within thirty days, and additional information may be requested from the prospective permittee only once.[139] If, however, the prospective permittee does not provide all the requested information, the district engineer may notify the permittee that the PCN is still incomplete and that the review process will not commence until all requested information has been received.[140]

Once a complete notification is received, the district engineer must determine whether the activity will result in more than minimal individual and cumulative adverse environmental effects or is otherwise contrary to the public interest. This decision must be made within forty-five days.[141] The district engineer may consider any mitigation plans submitted by the applicant in determining whether the proposed activity will have only minimal adverse effects.

For activities that require a PCN and that will cause the loss of more than one-half acre of waters, the district engineer will immediately transmit copies of the PCN to other appropriate federal and state resource agencies (e.g., the U.S. Fish and Wildlife Service, state natural resource or water quality agency, EPA, State Historic Preservation Officer, and National Marine Fisheries Service).[142] Should they desire to comment on the PCN, these agencies generally must so notify the district engineer within ten days of receiving the PCN.[143] If such notice is given, the district engineer will then wait fifteen additional days before making a decision on the PCN. The views of the resource agencies are to be fully considered by the district engineer, but, with limited exceptions, the district engineer is not required to respond to these agencies' comments.[144] To expedite the agency notification process, the Corps encourages applicants to submit multiple copies of the PCN to the district engineer.

If mitigation is included as part of the PCN, then the mitigation proposal must be approved prior to commencing work.[145] Where such mitigation is proposed, the district engineer must determine whether the net adverse effects of the project with mitigation are minimal.[146] Unless the permittee has been notified of conditions or restrictions within this forty-five-day period, the activity may commence pursuant to the terms of the NWP and any applicable general conditions.

If the proposed activity is determined to have more than minimal adverse effects, the district engineer will notify the applicant either that: (1) the activity is not authorized under the NWP and provide instructions on how to seek an individual permit; (2) the activity is authorized by the NWP subject to the submission of an acceptable mitigation plan that would reduce adverse effects; or (3) the project is authorized under the NWP with specific modifications or conditions.[147]

H. Using Multiple NWPs or NWPs with Other Authorizations

One issue that frequently arises in the context of Section 404 permitting is whether NWPs can be used in combination with one another, or whether part of a project may proceed under an NWP even if the project as a whole must obtain an individual Section 404 permit. In some circumstances, applicants may combine NWPs to obtain necessary authorization to conduct a project. To find an answer in any particular situation requires review of both Corps regulations and the specific NWPs proposed to be used.

Corps regulations provide that two or more different NWPs can be combined to authorize a "single and complete project," but the same NWP cannot be used more than once for that project.[148] The term "single and complete project" is defined to mean the total project proposed or accomplished by a single entity. The test for determining whether a proposal qualifies as a single and complete project is "whether the project has 'independent utility'—or, in other words, whether it 'would be constructed absent the construction of other projects in the project area.'"[149] The single and complete project requirement is designed to "prevent[] applicants from circumventing review of a project which would have more than minimal environmental impact by breaking it up into several smaller proposals, each of which would have sufficiently minimal impact to qualify for NWP verification."[150]

For a residential or commercial-type development, a "single and complete project" is the entire development even if it affects several different headwaters or isolated waters. For linear projects, however, a "single and complete project" means each crossing of a separate water of the United States at a particular location, unless the project crosses a single water body several times at different locations, in which case each crossing is considered a single and complete project.[151]

The question of whether a particular project can be viewed as "single and complete" can sometimes be quite complex. In *Crutchfield v. U.S. Army Corps of Engineers*, the Fourth Circuit approved Corps authorization under NWPs for the construction of a wastewater treatment system by the County of Hanover, Virginia.[152] As originally proposed, the system included a 5.6-mile pipeline for conveying wastewater to a treatment plant. The Corps concluded that the pipeline would have had more than a minimal impact on wetlands and, accordingly, treated the county's request as an application for an individual permit for this aspect of the project, while authorizing the remainder under NWPs. This procedure was successfully challenged as an improper attempt to "segment" the pipeline from the remainder of the project. A federal district court vacated the Corps's verifications for the use of the NWPs, enjoined further construction of the project, and ordered the Corps to consider the entire project as an integrated whole.[153]

On remand, the county modified its project to exclude the controversial pipeline, replacing it with one that would affect only thirty square feet of wetlands. The Corps then determined that the newly fashioned project included all reasonably related activities and proceeded to consider the proposal through an individualized permit proceeding. Eventually, however, the Corps concluded that the entire project could proceed under NWPs.[154]

This decision was also challenged. The plaintiff's principal objection to the use of NWPs was that the county's application did not include all the components necessary for the project and that the county had failed to disclose plans for all of the activities that were reasonably related to the project. In particular, plaintiffs argued that the sewage that made the treatment facilities necessary would be generated in areas not served by the replacement pipeline and that the county would eventually run pipelines to those areas. Accordingly, the plaintiffs contended that consideration of all reasonably related activities would have to include the future pipelines necessary to service the areas not served by the replacement pipeline.

A federal district court agreed with the plaintiffs' contentions and held that the proposed project was not a single and complete project. The district court held that other potential projects would have to be constructed to achieve the wastewater treatment system's purpose and that those additional projects had to be considered in the Corps's evaluation of whether to authorize the use of NWPs.[155]

The Fourth Circuit reversed. The court of appeals, while acknowledging that "other conveyance mechanisms will eventually be needed in order to take full advantage of the treatment plant's capacity," held that to constitute a "single and complete project" the county was required to include only "all of its definitely planned, concretely identifiable elements."[156] Because the exact location of additional wastewater conveyances could not be predicted with certainty, "the Clean Water Act does not require counties to set in stone their infrastructure plans for the next fifty years."[157] Moreover, the court held that "the presumptive arbiter of the point at which speculation or inchoate plans become sufficiently foreseeable to require inclusion in an NWP verification request is the Army Corps of Engineers, not an Article III court."[158]

Although Corps regulations generally allow the combination of different NWPs to authorize activities that are a part of a single and complete project (sometimes referred to as "stacking"), this authorization is limited by the general condition that the use of multiple NWPs may not cause a greater loss of waters than that authorized by the NWP with the highest specified acreage limit. Thus, the Corps provides this example: "[I]f a road crossing over tidal waters is constructed under NWP 14, with associated bank stabilization authorized by NWP 13, the maximum acreage loss of waters of the United States for the total project cannot exceed one-third acre."[159]

Additionally, a few NWPs themselves contain restrictions that prohibit certain combinations. For example, NWP 3 (maintenance) may not be used in conjunction with NWP 18 (minor discharges) or NWP 19 (minor dredging) to restore damaged upland areas.[160] Likewise, NWP 29 (single-family housing) may not be used for any parcel in conjunction with NWP 14 (linear transportation crossings) or NWP 18 (minor discharges).[161]

With respect to use of any NWP as part of a project that is also required to obtain an individual Section 404 permit, the Corps regulations allow this in only limited circumstances. Part of a project may be conducted under an NWP while an individual permit decision is pending for the larger project, but only if the portions of the project qualifying for NWP authorization would have "independent utility and are able to function or meet their purpose independent of the total project."[162] Even if an applicant could meet these criteria, it is important to bear in mind that the Corps will not allow the construction of a portion of the total project under an NWP to influence its individual permit decision on the total project.

V. Conclusion

The Corps's Section 404 program includes several means by which projects involving discharges of dredged or fill materials to waters of the United States may be authorized without the need for an individual Corps permit. By far the most commonly used authority is the nationwide permit program, which consists of forty-three permits authorizing numerous activities that the Corps has determined are similar in nature and involve minimal adverse environmental impacts. Applicants should carefully review the nationwide permits, as well as any opportunities to use regional or state permits or letters of permission, in order to take advantage of these less costly and less time-consuming alternatives to obtaining an individual Corps permit. Applicants must be careful, however, to ensure that their activities are conducted so as to fully comply with all the regulatory and permit conditions, which have become increasingly stringent in recent years.

Notes

1. Requirements associated with individual permits are discussed in Chapter 6.
2. 33 U.S.C. § 1344 (e)(1) (2000).
3. 33 C.F.R. § 323.2(h) (2004). *See also* 33 U.S.C. § 1344 (e)(1).

4. U.S. Army Corps of Engineers, Regulatory Program, *available at* http://www.usace.army.mil/inet/functions/cw/cecwo/reg/2003webcharts.pdf.

5. *Id.*

6. *Id.*

7. 33 U.S.C. § 1344(e)(1).

8. *See* 33 C.F.R. §§ 325.2(e)(2), 325.5(c).

9. *See* the Chicago District's Web site, http://www.lrc.usace.army.mil/co-r/webrpp2001.pdf.

10. In 1996, the Corps published a compilation of regional and programmatic permits and letter of permission procedures that had been established in some areas. *See* U.S. Army Corps of Engineers Regulatory Program, *General Permit Summary* (Jan. 1996). It is advisable to contact the appropriate Corps district for updated information. A list of Corps districts is available at http://www.usace.army.mil/inet/functions/cw/cecwo/reg/district.htm.

11. 33 C.F.R. § 325.5(c)(3).

12. 33 C.F.R. § 330.1(b).

13. 33 C.F.R. § 330.2(b).

14. 33 C.F.R. § 330.1(b).

15. 61 Fed. Reg. at 65,874 (Dec. 13, 1996). The Corps decision to discontinue publishing NWPs in the Code of Federal Regulations is based on the notion that the NWPs are permits, not rules.

16. 33 C.F.R. § 325. 2(e)(1). This procedure may appropriately be used under Section 404 if (1) a district engineer in consultation with federal and state resource agencies "develops a list of categories of activities proposed for authorization under [letters of permission] procedures"; (2) the proposed list is subject to public notice and comment and an opportunity for public hearing; and (3) state certification pursuant to § 401 of the CWA has been issued or waived and applicable Coastal Zone Management consistency determinations have been made and concurred in by affected states. 33 C.F.R. § 325.2(e)(1)(ii)(A)–(C).

17. 33 U.S.C. § 1344(e)(1).

18. *Id.*

19. 33 U.S.C. § 1344(e)(2).

20. While one federal district court has held that the Corps's issuance of an NWP does not constitute a final agency action that can be challenged in court, *see* National Association of Home Builders v. United States Army Corps of Engineers, 297 F. Supp. 2d 74 (D.D.C. 2003), most courts have allowed challenges to general permits to proceed. *See, e.g.*, Alaska Center for the Environment v. West, 157 F.3d 680 (9th Cir. 1998); Ohio Valley Environmental Coalition v. Bulen, 2004 U.S. Dist. LEXIS 12690 (S.D. W. Va. 2004); Utah Council, Trout Unlimited v. United States Army Corps of Engineers, 187 F. Supp. 2d 1334 (D. Utah 2002).

21. 61 Fed. Reg. 65,874 (Dec. 13, 1996).

22. 64 Fed. Reg. 39,263–64 (Jul. 21, 1999).

23. *Id.* at 39,264.

24. 157 F.3d 680 (9th Cir. 1998).

25. *Id.* at 684.

26. Id at 683.

27. *Id.*
28. 33 U.S.C. § 1344(e)(1).
29. *See* 40 C.F.R. § 230.7(b).
30. *See* 64 Fed. Reg. at 39,274.
31. 67 Fed. Reg. 2020, 2089 (Jan. 15, 2002).
32. *Alaska Center for the Environment,* 157 F.3d at 684–85.
33. *Id.* at 685 n.1. The regulation is codified at 40 C.F.R. § 230.7(b)(3).
34. 2004 U.S. Dist. LEXIS 12690 (S.D. W. Va. 2004).
35. 67 Fed. Reg. at 2081.
36. *Id.* at 2090.
37. 2004 U.S. Dist. LEXIS at 12690, *3–4.
38. *Id.* at *41–42.
39. *Id.* at *57.
40. 33 U.S.C. § 1341.
41. 16 U.S.C. §§ 1451–1464.
42. 16 U.S.C. §§ 1531 *et seq.*
43. 16 U.S.C. § 470f.
44. 42 U.S.C. §§ 4321 *et seq.*
45. 42 U.S.C. § 4332(C).
46. *See* 40 C.F.R. §§ 1501.4; 33 C.F.R. § 230.10(a). Corps regulations implementing NEPA are found at 33 C.F.R. pt. 230 and 33 C.F.R. pt. 325, app. B.
47. 33 C.F.R. § 230.11.
48. Alaska Center for the Environment v. West, 31 F. Supp. 2d 714, 722–23 (D. Alaska 1998).
49. 40 C.F.R. § 1508.9(b); 33 C.F.R. § 230.10(b); 33 C.F.R. pt. 325, Appendix B, § 7.a.
50. *Alaska Center for the Environment,* 31 F. Supp. 2d at 722–23.
51. 67 Fed. Reg. 2020, 2026 (Jan. 15, 2002). The Draft PEIS is available online at http://www.iwr.usace.army.mil/iwr/regulatory/regulintro.htm.
52. In its most recent amendment of the NWPs, the Corps stressed that "[t]he issuance of the NWPs will not preclude the ability of the Corps to modify the NWP Program or modify individual NWPs in accordance with any need for changes identified in the PEIS. The Corps is in compliance with NEPA because a FONSI for the NWP Program was issued on June 23, 1998, and the Corps issues decision documents, including EAs, for each NWP when the NWP is issued, reissued or modified." 67 Fed. Reg. at 2026.
53. U.S. Army Corps of Engineers, Current Decision Documents, http://www.usace.army.mil/inet/functions/cw/cecwo/reg/nw2002dd/index.htm.
54. Corps Headquarters has dedicated a portion of its Web site to providing information on nationwide permits at http://www.usace.army.mil/inet/functions/cw/cecwo/reg/nationwide_permits.htm.
55. 33 C.F.R. pt. 330.
56. *See supra* note 54, and specific district Web sites.
57. 33 C.F.R. § 330.1(c).
58. 33 U.S.C. § 1344(e)(2).
59. 33 C.F.R. § 330.1(f); *see* Crutchfield v. County of Hanover, 325 F.3d 211, 219–21 (4th Cir. 2003) (rejecting challenges to Corps authorization under NWPs

when permittee sought an individual permit), *cert. denied sub nom.* Crutchfield v. United States Army Corps of Engineers, 124 S. Ct. 312 (2004).

60. *See generally* 61 Fed. Reg. 65,874 (Dec. 13, 1996).

61. 42 Fed. Reg. 37,146 (July 19, 1977). Corps regulations define "headwaters" as

> non-tidal rivers, streams, and their lakes and impoundments, including adjacent wetlands, that are part of a surface tributary system to an interstate or navigable water of the United States upstream of the point on the river or stream at which the average annual flow is less than five cubic feet per second.

33 C.F.R. § 330.2(d). "Isolated" waters are

> those non-tidal waters of the United States that are:
> (1) Not part of a surface tributary system to interstate or navigable waters of the United States; and
> (2) Not adjacent to such tributary waterbodies.

33 C.F.R. § 330.2(e).

62. 47 Fed. Reg. 31,832 (July 22, 1982).

63. National Wildlife Federation v. Marsh, 14 ENVTL. L. REP. (ELI) 20,262 (D.D.C. 1984).

64. 49 Fed. Reg. 39,478 (Oct. 5, 1984).

65. *Id.*

66. 56 Fed. Reg. 59,110 (Nov. 22, 1991).

67. 61 Fed. Reg. 65,874 (Dec. 13, 1996).

68. *Id.* at 65,916.

69. *Id.* at 65,891.

70. 65 Fed. Reg. 12,885 (Mar. 9, 2000).

71. 67 Fed. Reg. at 2020.

72. Section 404 Enforcement Memorandum of Agreement (MOA): Procedures Regarding the Applicability of Previously Issued Corps Permits (Jan. 19, 1989). The MOA provides, in pertinent part, that a Corps determination that a discharge is authorized under a general permit is considered a final enforcement decision for that case.

73. The Corps has also published a helpful summary table of the 2002 NWPs, *available at* http://www.usace.army.mil/inet/functions/cw/cecwo/reg/Summary_table.pdf.

74. 67 Fed. Reg. at 2078.

75. *Id.*

76. *Id.* at 2079.

77. *Id.* at 2079–80.

78. *Id.* at 2080.

79. *Id.*

80. *Id.* at 2081.

81. *Id.*

82. 31 F. Supp. 2d 714, 722-23 (D. Alaska 1998).

83. 64 Fed. Reg. 47,175 (Aug. 30, 1999).

84. 67 Fed. Reg. at 2083.
85. *Id.* at 2084–85.
86. *Id.* at 2085–86.
87. *Id.* at 2085.
88. *Id.* at 2085–86.
89. 61 Fed. Reg. 65,919. In 1996, NWP 40 was entitled "Farm Buildings."
90. *Id.* at 2086–87.
91. *Id.* at 2087.
92. *Id.* at 2087–88.
93. *Id.* at 2088–89.
94. 33 C.F.R. § 330.1(c).
95. In the past the Corps had categorized its general conditions into those applicable to all Department of the Army permits (e.g., permits issued under either Section 404 of the CWA or Section 10 of the Rivers and Harbors Act of 1899) and "Section 404 Only" conditions. In its March 9, 2000, reissuance of NWPs, the Corps combined these two categories into one set of general conditions. 65 Fed. Reg. at 12,893–97.
96. The general conditions are set forth in a stand-alone document, U.S. Army Corps of Engineers, *Text of 2002 Nationwide Permit General Conditions, available at* http://www.usacc.army.mil/inet/functions/cw/cecwo/reg/2002nwps_cond.pdf.
97. 33 U.S.C. § 1341.
98. 33 C.F.R. § 330.4(c).
99. 33 C.F.R. § 330.4(c)(3). This limitation with respect to denial of Section 401 water quality certifications does not apply if the activity authorized under the NWP cannot reasonably be expected to result in discharges into waters of the United States. *Id.*
100. 33 C.F.R. § 330.4(c)(6).
101. *See* 64 Fed. Reg. at 39,261 (July 21, 1999).
102. 33 C.F.R. § 330.4(d)(1).
103. 33 C.F.R. § 330.4(d)(2).
104. 33 C.F.R. § 330.4(d)(6).
105. 33 C.F.R. § 330.4(e)(1).
106. 33 C.F.R. § 330.5(c),(d).
107. 65 Fed. Reg. at 12,820.
108. 33 C.F.R. § 330.4(e).
109. 33 C.F.R. § 330.4(e)(2).
110. *Id.; see* 33 C.F.R. § 330.5(d)(1).
111. 33 C.F.R. § 330.5(d)(2).
112. 16 U.S.C. §§ 1531 *et seq.*
113. 33 C.F.R. § 330.4(f); General Condition 11, 67 Fed. Reg. at 2090.
114. 758 F.2d 508 (10th Cir. 1985).
115. *Id.* at 513.
116. 33 C.F.R. § 330.4(f)(2).
117. *Id.* The consultation procedure is established pursuant to 16 U.S.C. § 1536.

118. General Condition 11, 67 Fed. Reg. at 2090.

119. 33 C.F.R. § 330.4(f)(3).

120. General Condition 11(b), 67 Fed. Reg. at 2090.

121. 33 C.F.R. § 330.4(g) (citing pt. 325 app. C—Procedures for Protection of Historic Properties); General Condition 12, 67 Fed. Reg. at 2090.

122. 33 C.F.R. § 330.4(g)(3).

123. 33 C.F.R. § 330.4(g)(4).

124. 67 Fed. Reg. at 2089–094.

125. General Condition 7, 67 Fed. Reg. at 2089.

126. A list of waters included in the Wild and Scenic River System is available at http://www.nps.gov/rivers/wildriverslist.html. A list of the management agencies can be found at http://www.nps.gov/rivers/agencies.html.

127. General Condition 8, 67 Fed. Reg. at 2089.

128. General Condition 17, 67 Fed. Reg. at 2092.

129. General Condition 20, 67 Fed. Reg. at 2093.

130. General Condition 23, 67 Fed. Reg. at 2093.

131. General Condition 25, 67 Fed. Reg. at 2093.

132. *Id.*

133. *Id.*

134. General Condition 26, 67 Fed. Reg. at 2094.

135. *See* 33 C.F.R. § 330.6(a)(1); General Condition 13(a), 67 Fed. Reg. at 2090.

136. Many districts expect a permittee to submit the standard application and notification form as part of the PCN process. *See, e.g.*, Charleston District Regulatory Program, Nationwide Permits and Regional Conditions, http://www.sac.usace.army.mil/permits/nwp.html.

137. In those cases where a wetland delineation is required to be submitted as part of a PCN, the prospective permittee may ask the Corps to delineate the site, but the forty-five-day review period will not commence until the wetland delineation has been completed and submitted to the district engineer. General Condition 13(f), 67 Fed. Reg. at 2092.

138. For a sample district office listing of additional information needs with PCN submissions, *see* Charleston District Regulatory Program, Pre-construction Notification Information Requirements, at http://www.sac.usace.army.mil/permits/nwp-notif-reqmnts.pdf.

139. General Condition 13(a), 67 Fed. Reg. at 2090.

140. *Id.*

141. *Id.*

142. General Condition 13(e), 67 Fed. Reg. at 2092.

143. *Id.*

144. *Id.* The only exception identified in the general conditions is for comments provided pursuant to Section 305(b)(4)(B) of the Magnuson-Stevens Fishery Conservation and Management Act relating to essential fish habitat. *Id.*

145. General Condition 13(d), 67 Fed. Reg. at 2092.

146. *Id.*

147. *Id.*

148. 33 C.F.R. § 330.6(c).

149. Crutchfield v. County of Hanover, 325 F.3d 211, 221 (4th Cir. 2003) (quoting 67 Fed. Reg. 2020, 2094 (Jan. 15, 2002)), *cert. denied sub nom.* Crutchfield v. United States Army Corps of Engineers, 124 S. Ct. 312 (2003).

150. *Id.*

151. 33 C.F.R. § 330.2(i); *see* 65 Fed. Reg. at 12,898.

152. *Crutchfield,* 325 F.3d at 213.

153. Crutchfield v. U.S. Army Corps of Engineers, 154 F. Supp. 2d 878 (E.D. Va. 2001); Crutchfield v. U.S. Army Corps of Engineers, 192 F. Supp. 2d 444 (E.D. Va. 2001); Crutchfield v. U.S. Army Corps of Engineers, 175 F. Supp. 2d 835 (E.D. Va. 2001).

154. *Crutchfield,* 325 F.3d at 215–16.

155. Crutchfield v. U.S. Army Corps of Engineers, 214 F. Supp. 2d 593, 651–52 (E.D. Va. 2002), *rev'd sub nom.* Crutchfield v. County of Hanover, 325 F.3d 211 (4th Cir. 2003), *cert. denied sub nom.* Crutchfield v. United States Army Corps of Engineers, 124 S. Ct. 312 (2003).

156. *Crutchfield,* 325 F.3d at 224.

157. *Id.*

158. *Id.*

159. General Condition 15, 67 Fed. Reg. at 2092.

160. 67 Fed. Reg. at 2078.

161. 67 Fed. Reg. at 2083.

162. 33 C.F.R. § 330.6(d).

CHAPTER 6

Individual Permits

STEPHEN M. JOHNSON

I. Introduction/Scope

The United States Army Corps of Engineers (Corps) administers the Clean Water Act (CWA) Section 404 permit program[1] and the Rivers and Harbors Act Section 10 permit program.[2] The procedures that are discussed in this chapter apply to permits that the Corps issues under either law.[3] States can obtain authorization to administer the Section 404 permit program for most wetlands in lieu of the Corps,[4] but only Michigan and New Jersey have assumed that authority.[5] When states assume authority to administer the Section 404 program, they must follow substantially the same procedures that the Corps would follow if it were administering the program.[6]

Although few states have assumed control of the Section 404 permit program, many have established their own state wetland protection and permitting laws.[7] Since those laws apply in addition to the federal laws, developers in those states must often obtain a federal permit and a state permit to conduct activities that alter, destroy, or adversely affect wetlands.[8] State permit application and review procedures may differ from the procedures discussed in this chapter. In many cases, though, the Corps and the state will establish a joint permit application and review process that complies with the procedures described in this chapter.[9]

Although a development activity may require a permit under Section 404 of the CWA, it will not always require an *individual* Section 404 permit. Through nationwide permits,[10] regional permits,[11] programmatic general permits,[12] and letters of permission,[13] the Corps authorizes developers who comply with streamlined procedures to undertake a variety of activities that alter or adversely impact wetlands without undergoing the individual permit application and review process described in this chapter. The Corps is usually able to review and approve qualifying activities through those streamlined procedures in a few weeks, as opposed to the several months or more that it can take to issue an individual permit.[14]

This chapter describes the process and requirements associated with obtaining an individual permit pursuant to Section 404 of the CWA.

II. Application Requirements

A. Pre-Application Consultation

The Corps encourages persons who plan to apply for a permit for a major project to contact the Corps[15] to arrange a brief pre-application consultation.[16] Although the regulations do not require permit applicants to consult with the Corps prior to filing an application, the consultation will enable the Corps to process the permit application more efficiently.[17] Several federal, state and local agencies will be involved in the permit review in addition to the Corps.[18] The Corps may invite representatives of several of those agencies and the public to the pre-application consultation.[19] During the pre-application consultation, the Corps will explain (1) the application and permit review process; (2) the factors that the agencies will consider as part of the permit review; and (3) any environmental documents or studies that the applicant must prepare as part of the permit application, including mitigation plans or documents that are required by the National Environmental Policy Act.[20] In addition, the government agencies and the potential applicant may begin to explore alternatives to the proposed activity that would have a less adverse impact on wetlands.[21]

B. Application Form and Content

The individual permit process is intended to take several months to complete, so developers should begin the application process well in advance of the time that they plan to commence the development activity. A permit applicant initiates the application process by submitting application form 4345, or a local variation of the form, to the district office of the Corps.[22] The application must include

- A complete description of the proposed activity including necessary drawings, sketches, or plans sufficient for public notice[23]
- The location, purpose, and need for the proposed activity

- Scheduling of the proposed activity
- The names and addresses of adjoining property owners
- The location and dimensions of adjacent structures
- A list of authorizations required by other federal, interstate, or local agencies for the work, including all approvals or denials already made[24]

Because Section 404 permits authorize activities that include the discharge of dredged or fill material into wetlands, the application must also include

- The purpose of the discharge
- A description of the type, composition, and quantity of the material
- The method of transportation and disposal of the material
- The location of the disposal site[25]

Applicants must submit additional information for projects that involve dredging in the navigable waters,[26] construction of a filled area or pile or float-supported platform,[27] or construction of an impoundment structure.[28]

The application should include all activities that the applicant plans to undertake that are reasonably related to the same project and for which a permit would be required.[29]

C. Signature Requirement and Fees

The application can be signed either by the applicant or by an authorized agent of the applicant.[30] Although the applicant does not have to own the site of the proposed development activity, the applicant or the agent certify, by signing the application, that the applicant possesses or will obtain whatever interest in the property is required to undertake the development activity.[31]

The fee for a permit that authorizes a noncommercial activity is $10, while the fee for commercial activities is $100.[32] The district engineer makes the final determination regarding whether an activity is commercial or noncommercial.[33] Applicants do not have to pay any fees if they withdraw their application or the Corps denies the application.[34]

III. Application Review Procedures

The Corps reviews permits applications and issues permits through informal notice and comment adjudicatory procedures, rather than formal adversarial hearing procedures.[35] The Corps can modify the procedures described below in emergency situations.[36]

A. Completeness Review

As soon as the Corps receives a permit application, it reviews the application to determine whether it is complete.[37] Within fifteen calendar days[38] after the Corps receives the application, it must either (1) determine that the application is complete, and issue a public notice,[39] or (2) determine that the application is incomplete, and notify the applicant of the missing information.[40] If the Corps notifies the applicant that the application is incomplete, the Corps will not issue a public notice regarding the permit until the applicant submits the information that is necessary to complete the application.[41]

B. Public Notice

When the Corps determines that the permit application is complete, it will issue a public notice that includes

1. The name and address of the applicant
2. The name or title, address, and phone number of the Corps contact for the permit
3. The location of the proposed activity
4. A brief description of the proposed activity, its purpose, and intended use
5. A plan and elevation drawing for the proposal
6. A list of other government authorizations obtained or requested by the applicant
7. A statement that describes the factors that the Corps will consider when it determines whether to issue the permit
8. A statement regarding the Corps's current knowledge regarding historic properties or endangered species that will be affected by the proposal
9. Information regarding the project's compliance with the National Environmental Policy Act and the Coastal Zone Management Act
10. The comment period for the application
11. A statement that any person may request, in writing, during the comment period, a public hearing on the application[42]

Through the public notice and comment process, the Corps gathers information to determine whether issuance of the permit is contrary to the public interest.[43] In addition, various federal laws authorize the U.S. Environmental Protection Agency (EPA),[44] the U.S. Fish and Wildlife Service (FWS),[45] the National Marine Fisheries Service (NMFS),[46] state wildlife, historic preservation,[47] and environmental agencies,[48] and other federal and state agencies to review and comment on the Corps's wetland permits.[49] The public notice is the tool that the Corps uses to notify those agencies that it has received a complete permit application and is soliciting their comments.[50]

The public notice for a wetland permit application must be distributed for posting in post offices or other public places in the vicinity of the site, and must be sent to the applicant, adjoining property owners, appropriate state, federal, and local agencies and officials, and several other organizations and interested parties.[51] The comment period on a proposed application must be at least fifteen days, will usually be thirty days, and can be expanded to sixty days from the date of public notice.[52] During the comment period, the Corps will consult with the federal, state, and local agencies that are reviewing the application. All of the comments are placed in the administrative record for the agency's decision.[53]

C. Review of Comments and Public Hearing

After the Corps receives the comments on the permit application, the agency must inform the applicant about substantive comments that the agency received, and must give the applicant an opportunity to provide additional information.[54] The Corps may also require the applicant to submit additional information to address specific issues raised in the public comments.[55] The applicant must respond to the Corps's request for information within thirty days, unless the applicant requests additional time to respond and the Corps grants the request.[56] If the applicant does not respond to the Corps's request for additional information, the agency will consider the application withdrawn, or will make a final decision on the application.[57]

When the Corps reviews the comments, it will also determine whether it is necessary to hold a public hearing on the permit application.[58] Corps regulations state that the agency will hold a hearing whenever any person requests a public hearing during the comment period, unless the agency determines "that the issues raised are insubstantial or there is otherwise no valid interest to be served by a hearing."[59] Nevertheless, very few permit applications involve public hearings.[60]

If the agency holds a public hearing, it must provide public notice of the hearing, through newspapers of general circulation, at least thirty days before the hearing.[61] The agency must post the notice in appropriate government buildings and must provide the notice to the person that requested the hearing, appropriate federal, state, and local agencies, and other parties having an interest in the subject matter.[62] The hearing is an informal hearing,[63] and any person can speak[64] at the hearing on his or her own behalf, or through counsel.[65] The hearing will be transcribed verbatim,[66] and the testimony, as well as any exhibits that are introduced at the hearing, become part of the administrative record for the agency's decision.[67] Written comments can be submitted for at least ten days after the hearing.[68]

D. Criteria for Permit Review

1. *404(b)(1) Guidelines*

The CWA requires the Corps to evaluate every wetland permit application under Section 404(b)(1) Guidelines, which EPA promulgated in consultation with the Corps.[69] The Guidelines prohibit the Corps from issuing a wetland permit if there is a "practicable alternative" to the proposed activity that would have a less adverse impact on the aquatic ecosystem.[70] In addition, the Guidelines create a presumption that there are practicable alternatives to discharges of dredged or fill material into wetlands when the proposed activity is not water-dependent.[71] Chapter 7 of this book discusses and analyzes practicable alternatives.

The 404(b)(1) Guidelines also prohibit the issuance of a permit when the activity authorized by the permit causes or contributes to significant degradation of waters of the United States,[72] causes or contributes to a violation of state water quality standards, violates federal toxic pollution standards, jeopardizes endangered species or destroys or adversely modifies their critical habitat, or violates federal marine sanctuary protection requirements.[73]

Further, the Guidelines prohibit the issuance of a permit unless "appropriate and practicable steps have been taken which will minimize potential adverse impacts . . . on the aquatic ecosystem."[74] These mitigation requirements are discussed in detail in other chapters of this book.

Although EPA developed the Guidelines, and EPA and other agencies can comment to the Corps regarding specific permit applications and their compliance with the Guidelines, the Corps makes the final determination regarding whether a proposed activity complies with the 404(b)(1) Guidelines.[75]

2. *Public Interest Review*

In addition to reviewing permits under the 404(b)(1) Guidelines, the Corps will decide whether to grant or deny a permit, or to grant a permit with specific conditions, based on a "public interest" review of the benefits and detriments of the proposed activity.[76] Through the public interest review, the Corps evaluates the probable impacts (including cumulative impacts) on the public interest of the proposed activity and its use.[77] The factors that the Corps weighs and balances as part of this public interest review include conservation, economics,[78] aesthetics, general environmental concerns, wetlands, historic properties, fish and wildlife values,[79] floodplain values, land use, navigation, shore erosion and accretion, recreation, water supply and conservation, water quality,[80] energy needs, safety, food and fiber production, mineral needs, considerations of property ownership,[81] and the needs and welfare of the people.[82]

The agency will grant the permit unless it determines that granting the permit would be contrary to the public interest.[83] However, when the proposed activity would alter or destroy wetlands, the Corps normally presumes that granting the permit would be contrary to the public interest.[84] In that case, the burden is on the applicant to demonstrate that the proposed activity would not be contrary to the public interest.

E. Review Requirements of Other Laws

Although the Corps issues wetland permits under Section 404 of the CWA, other federal laws require the Corps to consult with federal, state, and local agencies, and to undertake other studies during the permit review. The major laws and their requirements are discussed below.[85]

1. National Environmental Policy Act (NEPA)

The National Environmental Policy Act (NEPA) requires federal agencies to prepare an environmental impact statement (EIS) for any "major federal action significantly affecting the quality of the human environment,"[86] and to consider the environmental impacts of proposed actions and their alternatives even when an EIS is not required.[87] Both the Corps and the Council on Environmental Quality (CEQ)[88] have established regulations that set forth the procedures that the Corps must follow to comply with NEPA when it reviews a wetland permit application.[89]

When the Corps receives a permit application, it might conclude that the proposed activity is a major action that requires an EIS, or it might conclude that the activity is exempt from NEPA review.[90] In most cases, though, the agency will conduct an environmental assessment (EA) to determine whether it is necessary to prepare an EIS for the proposed activity.[91] The EA examines the environmental impacts of the proposed activity[92] and any alternatives to the proposal.[93] CEQ's regulations also require the Corps to examine mitigation measures, such as an applicant's proposal to restore or create wetlands to replace the wetlands that will be destroyed by the proposed activity, during the NEPA review.[94] Mitigation measures may reduce the impacts of a proposed activity so that an EIS is not required.[95] The Corps will solicit information for the EA from the public and other agencies through the public notice for the permit application, and will complete the EA after the end of the comment period for the application.[96]

Normally, the agency will decide, based on the EA, that the proposed activity will not have a significant impact on the human environment, and that an EIS is not necessary.[97] While other federal agencies may comment on the environmental impacts of a proposed activity, the Corps retains the ultimate authority to decide whether to prepare an EIS.[98]

In rare cases, the Corps may conclude that the likely impacts of a proposed activity are significant and that an EIS is necessary.[99] In that case, the Corps must prepare an EIS before it issues the permit.[100] The EIS process is time consuming and expensive, and the Corps often requires the permit applicant to pay for costs associated with producing an EIS.[101] Before the agency begins to prepare an EIS, it must provide notice, through the Federal Register, that it plans to prepare an EIS,[102] and it must solicit input from the public regarding the scope of issues and alternatives to be considered in the EIS.[103] After the scoping process is completed, the agency prepares a draft EIS and makes it available for public comment.[104] If the Corps will have a public hearing on the permit application, the draft EIS must be made available to the public at least fifteen days before the hearing, and the draft EIS may be discussed at that hearing.[105] The agency must respond to all of the comments that it receives on the draft EIS when it prepares the final EIS.[106] In addition, when the Corps decides to issue or deny the permit, the agency must prepare a "concise" record of decision (ROD). Among other things, the ROD details "whether all practicable means to avoid or minimize environmental harm from the alternative selected have been adopted, and if not, why they were not."[107]

2. *Endangered Species Act*

The Endangered Species Act requires federal agencies to ensure that they do not issue permits for activities that are likely to jeopardize the continued existence of an endangered or threatened species, or to destroy or adversely modify their critical habitat.[108] When the Corps receives a wetland permit application, it reviews the application to ensure that those requirements are met.[109] If the Corps concludes that the proposed activity will not affect endangered or threatened species or their critical habitat, it will include a statement to that effect in the public notice for the permit application.[110] If, on the other hand, the Corps concludes that the activity may affect an endangered or threatened species, it will begin formal consultation procedures with the Fish and Wildlife Service or the National Marine Fisheries Service[111] under the Endangered Species Act.[112] If the Corps ultimately concludes that the activity will jeopardize an endangered or threatened species or destroy or adversely affect its critical habitat, the Corps must deny the permit.[113]

3. *Clean Water Act 401 Certification*

State agencies play an important role in the Corps's review of wetland permits, as well. Section 401 of the CWA provides that federal agencies may not issue wetland permits or other water pollution permits unless the state in which the polluting activity will take place certifies that the activity will not violate various state water quality laws.[114] States can, in essence, veto permits that do not comply with state water quality standards by denying 401 certification. States can also condition their certification on the addition of conditions to the permit.[115] The state issues, denies, or conditions a 401 certification through notice and comment procedures that are established by the state.[116] Permit applicants can challenge the state's action only in state court or administrative tribunals.[117]

If the permit applicant does not submit the state's 401 certification with the application, the Corps notifies the applicant that the certification is required.[118] In such cases, the Corps will send a copy of the notice to the state environmental agency that will provide the certification, and requests certification for the proposed activity, when the Corps issues the public notice for the permit application.[119] The Corps cannot issue the permit unless the state issues the 401 certification or waives its right to issue the certification.[120] Corps regulations provide that the state will waive its right to issue a 401 certification if the state does not act on the Corps's request for certification within sixty days.[121]

4. *Coastal Zone Management Act*

The Coastal Zone Management Act authorizes states to develop management plans to protect their coastal zone, and provides grants to states to administer coastal zone management programs.[122] If a state has adopted an approved coastal zone management program,[123] the Corps cannot issue a wetland permit for an activity that affects the coastal zone unless the state certifies that the proposed activity complies with the state's program.[124]

If the activity that will be authorized by a wetland permit will affect the coastal zone of a state that has an approved coastal zone management program, the permit applicant must initially certify to the Corps that the activity complies with the state program.[125] The Corps includes that certification in the public notice for the permit application,[126] provides a copy of the notice to the state coastal zone agency, and asks the agency to concur with the applicant's certification.[127] The state agency can concur with the certification, object to the certification, or inform the Corps that the agency will review the issue further.[128] If the state agency does not concur or object to the certification within six months after the agency receives the Corps's request for concurrence, the Corps will presume that the state concurs with the certification.[129] The Corps cannot issue the wetland permit until the state agency concurs with the applicant's certification or fails to object to the certification within the six-month period.[130]

5. *National Historic Preservation Act*

The National Historic Preservation Act (NHPA) requires federal agencies that undertake or license activities that may affect properties listed on the National Register of Historic Places to consider the effect of the project on those properties and to provide the Advisory Council on Historic Preservation (ACHP) an opportunity to comment on the project.[131] The Corps has established NHPA regulations[132] that set forth additional permit review procedures that the agency must use when a permit applicant proposes to conduct an activity that would involve property listed or eligible for listing on the National Register of Historic Places (designated historic properties).[133] Compliance with those procedures may take six months or longer.[134]

When the Corps receives a complete wetland permit application, the agency's NHPA regulations require it to determine whether there are any designated historic properties or undesignated historic properties that may be affected by the proposed activity.[135] The Corps includes its determination in the public notice for the permit application, and sends a copy of the notice to the state historic preservation officer (SHPO)[136] or the tribal historic preservation officer (THPO),[137] the ACHP, the regional office of the National Park Service, and other parties for their comments.[138] The Corps may also identify properties that could be eligible for listing on the National Register during its review of the application.[139] If the Corps discovers additional historic properties that may be affected by the proposed activity after the Corps issues the public notice, it will immediately inform the applicant, the SHPO and/or THPO, the local government, and the ACHP, and allow them thirty days after that notice to provide comments.[140] The regulations establish detailed procedures that the Corps must follow, in consultation with SHPOs and/or THPOs, the ACHP, and the Keeper of the National Register, in order to evaluate historic properties that are discovered during the permitting process and to determine whether unlisted properties are eligible for inclusion in the National Register.[141]

The regulations also require the Corps to consult with the SHPO and/or THPO as well as the ACHP to determine whether the proposed activity will adversely affect designated historic properties.[142] The Corps cannot make a final decision on the permit until it consults with the SHPO, THPO (if applicable), and/or the ACHP.[143] Although the NHPA does not require the Corps to avoid or minimize the effects of a proposed activity on historic properties,[144] the Corps, through its "public interest" review, will add conditions to permits to minimize or avoid harm to historic properties if necessary to protect the public interest.[145] Finally, if the proposed activity would result in the irrevocable loss of important scientific, prehistoric, or archaeological data, the Corps must notify the National Park Service regarding the potential loss and any conditions that the Corps will place on the permit to mitigate the loss.[146]

F. Coordination of Review with Other Agencies

In order to facilitate efficient communication and coordination among federal, state, and local agencies during wetland permit reviews, the Corps has promulgated regulations and entered into Memoranda of Agreement to govern interagency review and dispute resolution.

The Corps's review of a wetland permit application generally proceeds concurrently with the review of federal, state, and local agencies described above.[147] The Corps may establish joint review procedures with those agencies on a local level.[148] The Corps must fully consider the comments of those agencies regarding compliance with NEPA, the 404(b)(1) Guidelines, the Endangered Species Act, the NHPA, and other relevant statutes, regulations, and policies.[149] The Corps must also consider the comments of those agencies when it determines whether issuance of the permit is contrary to the public interest.[150] However, the Corps retains full authority to decide whether to issue or deny the permit, or to issue the permit with specific conditions.[151] In some cases, though, EPA can veto the Corps's decision to issue a permit.[152]

If the Corps completes its review before other agencies have completed their review under other laws, the Corps can take final action on the application, unless it is required by law to wait for the approval of another agency, as in the case of Section 401 certification.[153] The Corps will not issue a permit if EPA has instituted procedures to veto the permit.[154] If the Corps issues a permit before other agencies have completed their review, the Corps will normally condition the permit on the approval of the other agencies.[155] If, on the other hand, another agency denies necessary authorizations before the Corps completes its permit review, the Corps will normally immediately deny the application without prejudice.[156] Depending on the stage of review, though, the Corps might decide to continue processing the application.[157] If it does, when it completes the review, the Corps must either (1) deny the permit as contrary to the public interest; or (2) deny the permit without prejudice and indicate that except for the local, state, or federal denial, the permit could be issued with appropriate conditions.[158]

G. Permit Issuance or Denial

The Corps's regulations require the agency to make a decision on a permit within sixty days after the agency receives a complete permit application.[159] However, the Corps can extend that deadline in many cases.[160] In addition, the regulations do not require the Corps to automatically grant the permit if it does not make a decision within the sixty-day period.

The district engineer generally makes the final decision on permit applications.[161] The district engineer will either issue the permit or deny the permit, and will support the decision with a written statement of findings (SOF).[162] If the district engineer decides to deny the permit, he must inform the applicant of that decision, and the reasons for denial, in writing.[163] If, on the other hand, the district engineer decides to issue the permit, he will include conditions in the permit that are necessary to ensure that the activity is in the public interest, and that it complies with the 404(b)(1) Guidelines, the Endangered Species Act, state water quality requirements, and all other applicable laws.[164] The engineer will sign the permit and forward it to the applicant.[165] The applicant must sign the permit to indicate that it will comply with the conditions included in the permit.[166] The issuance of the permit does not convey any property rights or exclusive privileges to the applicant.[167]

Each month, the Corps publishes a list of permits that the agency issued or denied in the previous month.[168] The list is distributed to persons who have an interest in any of the permit decisions.[169]

IV. Duration, Modification, Suspension, or Revocation of Permits

A. Permit Duration

To the extent that a Corps permit authorizes an applicant to place dredged or fill material into wetlands, the permit will normally authorize the applicant to leave the material in the wetlands indefinitely.[170] However, the permit will usually require that the permittee start and finish construction work or other work associated with the permitted activity on specific dates.[171] Corps approval for the construction work or other work associated with the activity will automatically expire on the date specified in the permit unless the permittee requests and receives an extension from the district engineer before that date.[172] A request for an extension must comply with the normal procedures for permit issuance that are described above.[173] Extensions are normally granted unless the district engineer determines that an extension would be contrary to the public interest.[174]

B. Modification, Suspension, or Revocation of Permits

The Corps may reevaluate the circumstances or conditions of any permit on its own motion or at the request of the permittee or a third party.[175] The agency may modify, suspend, or revoke the permit as necessary based on considerations of the public interest.[176] In deciding whether to modify, suspend, or revoke the permit, the Corps will consider factors such as (1) the permittee's compliance with the permit, (2) changes in circumstances relating to the permitted activity, and whether the permit conditions are adequate to address those changes; (3) significant objections to the permitted activity that were not considered earlier; (4) changes in the law; and (5) whether modification, suspension, or revocation would adversely affect the permittee's reasonable plans and investments.[177]

1. *Modification*

If the Corps determines that it is in the public interest to modify a permit, the Corps will attempt to reach a mutual agreement on modification of the permit through informal consultations with the permittee.[178] Modifications may not significantly increase the scope of the permitted activity.[179] If the parties reach a mutual agreement on permit modifications, the Corps will give the permittee written notice of the modification and the effective date of the modification.[180] If the Corps and the permittee do not reach a mutual agreement on permit modifications, the Corps can institute procedures to suspend the permit, or the Corps can unilaterally modify the permit after it informs the permittee that it intends to take that action.[181] If the Corps notifies the permittee that it intends to modify the permit, the permittee can request a meeting with the Corps or a public hearing before the Corps modifies the permit.[182]

2. *Suspension and Revocation*

If the Corps determines that it is in the public interest to suspend a permit and prepares a written determination to support that finding, the Corps can immediately suspend the permit and order the permittee to stop the activities that were authorized by the permit.[183] When the Corps suspends a permit, it must notify the permittee in writing that the permit has been suspended and it must explain the reasons for the suspension.[184] After the Corps suspends a permit, it must decide whether to reinstate, modify, or revoke the permit.[185] The permittee can request a meeting with the Corps or a public hearing to present information relating to that decision.[186] After the meeting and hearing, or within a reasonable period of time if the permittee does not request a meeting or hearing, the Corps will reinstate, modify, or revoke the permit.[187] The Corps will revoke the permit if it determines that revocation is in the public interest.[188] The agency must send written notice of the revocation decision to the permittee.[189]

V. Administrative or Judicial Review

If the Corps denies an application for an individual permit, or includes terms and conditions in an individual permit that leads an applicant to decline the permit, the applicant can appeal the Corps's action through administrative processes,[190] and the applicant must challenge the permit denial or declined permit administratively before challenging the action in a judicial proceeding.[191]

When the Corps denies an individual permit application or an applicant declines an individual permit, the Corps must notify the applicant, in writing, that the permit denial or declined permit is appealable.[192] The permit applicant must challenge the permit denial or declined permit administratively within sixty days after the Corps notifies the applicant that the action is appealable.[193] The administrative appeal process is informal, and the Corps must make a final decision on the appeal within ninety days after receiving a complete request for appeal from the permit applicant.[194] Chapter 11 of this book provides more details about the Corps's administrative appeal process.

While Corps regulations allow permit applicants to administratively appeal individual permit denials or declined permits, the regulations do not allow third parties to administratively appeal any Corps permit decisions.[195] Third parties must pursue their challenges in court.[196]

VI. Conclusion

The individual permit process can often involve a complex web of overlapping legal requirements. While years of implementation experience have clarified permit requirements and permitting procedures, applications for projects with substantial wetland impacts can be expected to take a considerable amount of time to process. Applicants should consult early with the Corps and plan development activities in light of the substantial amount of time that may be needed for the Corps to process individual permit applications. A well-prepared application, developed after informal consultation with the appropriate Corps district office, can greatly facilitate the process.

Notes

1. 33 U.S.C. § 1344 (2000). The Corps issues permits that authorize "the discharge of dredged or fill material into the navigable waters at specified disposal sites." *Id.* § 1344(a). Chapters 4 and 5 of this book identify the activities that require a permit under Section 404.

2. Section 10 of the Rivers and Harbors Act of 1899 prohibits most obstructions or alterations of navigable waters except in accordance with a permit from the Corps. 33 U.S.C. § 403. However, the Corps's jurisdiction over wetlands under the Rivers and Harbors Act is less expansive than the agency's Clean Water Act jurisdiction, because the Corps has defined "navigable waters," for purposes of the Rivers and Harbors Act, to be "those waters that are subject to the ebb and flow of the tide and/or are presently used, or have been used in the past, or may be susceptible for use to transport interstate or foreign commerce." 33 C.F.R. § 329.4 (2004).

3. Most of the Corps of Engineers general regulatory and permitting policies discussed in this chapter also apply to permits issued by the Corps pursuant to authority under Section 103 of the Marine Protection, Research and Sanctuaries Act of 1972, as amended, 33 U.S.C. § 1413. *See* 33 C.F.R. §§ 320.2(g) and 320.4; *see also* 33 C.F.R. pt. 324.

4. 33 U.S.C. § 1344(h)(2)(A); *see also* 33 C.F.R. § 323.5. States cannot obtain authority to issue permits for discharges of dredged or fill material into "waters which are presently used, or are susceptible to use in their natural condition or by reasonable improvement as a means to transport interstate or foreign commerce shoreward to their ordinary high water mark, including all waters which are subject to the ebb and flow of the tide shoreward to their mean high water mark, or mean higher high water mark on the west coast, including wetlands adjacent thereto." 33 U.S.C. § 1344(g)(1); 33 C.F.R. § 323.5.

5. *See* 59 Fed. Reg. 9933 (1994) (Final approval of New Jersey's program); 49 Fed. Reg. 38,947 (1984) (Final approval of Michigan's program).

6. *See* 40 C.F.R. §§ 233.20–233.38. State assumption of the Section 404 permit program is addressed further in Chapter 10 of this book.

7. The Clean Water Act authorizes states to establish wetland protection and permitting laws that are at least as stringent as, or more stringent than the federal program. 33 U.S.C. § 1370.

8. In certain situations there may be local laws regulating activities in wetlands with which a developer must also comply. *See, e.g.*, Maryland Department of the Environment, Maryland's Wetland Regulation Database, *available at* http://www.mde.state.md.us/Programs/WaterPrograms/Wetlands_Waterways/regulations/database.asp (providing a database for local county and city laws throughout Maryland); Wisconsin Wetlands Association, Local Level Wetland Regulations, *available at* http://www.wiscwetlands.org/local.htm (providing a discussion regarding a state-mandated, locally enforced shoreland zoning ordinance).

9. Corps regulations authorize and encourage district or division offices to establish joint permitting procedures with states and other federal agencies. 33 C.F.R. § 325.3(e)(3).

10. Nationwide permits are discussed in detail in Chapter 5 of this book.

11. Regional permits are also discussed in Chapter 5 of this book.

12. Programmatic general permits are discussed in Chapter 10 of this book.

13. Letters of permission are "a type of permit issued through an abbreviated processing procedure which includes coordination with Federal and state fish and wildlife agencies, as required by the Fish and Wildlife Coordination Act, and a public interest evaluation, but without the publishing of an individual public notice." 33 C.F.R. § 325.2(e)(1). Corps regulations identify the limited circumstances in which the agency will issue letters of permission. *Id.*

14. The Corps suggests that it normally completes the review for a routine permit in about two to four months after the agency determines that the permit application is complete. U.S. Army Corps of Engineers, Sacramento District, Regulatory Program Applicant Information (last revised Oct. 24, 1995), *at* http://www.spk.usace.army.mil/organizations/cespk-co/regulatory/instructions.html (hereinafter Applicant Information). A 1994 study conducted by a Washington, D.C., law firm suggests, though, that the Corps's permit review process for major permit applications averaged 373 days in 1992. VIRGINIA S. ALBRECHT & BERNARD N. GOODE, *Wetland Regulation in The Real World* (Feb. 1994), *cited in* Margaret N. Strand, *Recent Developments in Federal Wetlands Law: Part II*, 26 ENVTL. L. REP. 10,339, 10,342 (1996). For recent data on permitting statistics, see U.S. Army Corps of Engineers, *Regulatory Program, available at* http://www.usace.army.mil/inet/functions/cw/cecwo/reg/2003webcharts.pdf.

15. *See* http://www.usace.army.mil/inet/functions/cw/cecwo/reg/district.htm.

16. 33 C.F.R. § 325.1(b).

17. U.S. Army Corps of Engineers, Sacramento District, *The Regulatory Permit Program, A Brief Guide From the Sacramento District*, Doc. # SPK BRO 360-1-12, MAR 93 (last revised July 24, 1996), *available at* http://www.spk.usace.army.mil/organizations/cespk-co/regulatory/program.html.

18. *See infra* notes 45–49 and accompanying text.

19. 33 C.F.R. § 325.1(b); *see also* Regulatory Guidance Letter (RGL) 92-01 (May 13, 1992). The Corps may require prospective applicants to provide a summary of the project to the Corps, the United States Fish and Wildlife Service, the

United States Environmental Protection Agency, the National Marine Fisheries Service, and state wildlife agencies prior to the meeting. Applicant Information, *supra* note 14. The Corps also recommends that the applicant bring an accurate delineation of the wetlands to the meeting. *Id.*

20. 33 C.F.R. § 325.1(b). *See generally* pt. 325, app. B, NEPA Implementation.

21. *Id.*

22. 33 C.F.R. § 325.1(c). Local offices of the Corps may modify Form 4345 to facilitate coordination with other federal, state, and local agencies. *Id.* District and division engineers cannot develop additional information forms, but can request additional information from applicants on a case-by-case basis if the agency determines that the information is essential to make a public interest determination. *Id.* §§ 325.1(d)(1); 325.1(e).

23. Detailed engineering plans and specifications are not required at this stage. 33 C.F.R. § 325.1(d)(1).

24. *Id.*

25. 33 C.F.R. § 325.1(d)(4).

26. 33 C.F.R. § 325.1(d)(3).

27. 33 C.F.R. § 325.1(d)(5).

28. 33 C.F.R. § 325.1(d)(6).

29. 33 C.F.R. § 325.1(d)(2).

30. 33 C.F.R. § 325.1(d)(7). If the applicant is represented by an agent, the applicant must disclose that information on the application or in a separate written statement. *Id.*

31. *Id.* Multiple property owners can apply to conduct multiple activities under a single permit if the character of the activities is similar, the activities are in the same general area, and the owners designate a common agent to represent them and sign the application. *Id.*

32. 33 C.F.R. § 325.1(f).

33. *Id.*

34. *Id.*

35. Courts have uniformly upheld the Corps's refusal to use formal hearing procedures to issue Section 404 permits. *See, e.g.*, Buttrey v. United States, 690 F.2d 1170, 1175–76 (5th Cir. 1982); *see also* Shoreline Associates v. Marsh, 555 F. Supp. 169 (D. Md. 1983) (due process does not require the Corps to hold formal adjudicatory hearings before issuing or denying a Section 404 permit).

36. 33 C.F.R. § 325.2(e)(4). An "emergency" is "a situation which would result in an unacceptable hazard to life, a significant loss of property, or an immediate, unforeseen, and significant economic hardship if corrective action requiring a permit is not taken within a time period less than the normal time needed to process the application under standard procedures." *Id.* The division engineer must approve the emergency processing procedures, and reasonable efforts must be made to receive comments from federal, state, and local agencies and the public. *Id.*

37. 33 C.F.R. § 325.2(a). An application is complete when the Corps receives sufficient information to issue a public notice. *Id.* § 325.1(d)(9). The Corps can

request additional information after it has determined that an application is complete if it is essential to make a public interest determination. *Id.* §§ 325.1(d)(9); 325.1(e).

38. 33 C.F.R. § 325.2(d)(6). All references to time periods in this chapter are references to calendar days, unless specifically noted.

39. 33 C.F.R. § 325.2(a)(2).

40. 33 C.F.R. § 325.2(a)(1)–(2). During the initial fifteen days, the Corps must also determine whether the activity is subject to a nationwide permit, or could be subject to a nationwide permit if it is modified. *Id.* § 330.1(f). The Corps must provide that information to the applicant. *Id.*

41. 33 C.F.R. § 325.2(d)(1).

42. 33 C.F.R. § 325.3(a). This is a partial list of the information that the Corps must include in the public notice. For the complete list, *see* 33 C.F.R. §§ 325.3(a); 325(c).

43. 33 C.F.R. § 325.3(a). Accordingly, the notice must "include sufficient information to give a clear understanding of the nature and magnitude of the activity to generate meaningful comment." *Id.* In addition, the Corps must issue a supplemental, corrected, or updated public notice if it subsequently receives information that would affect the public's review of the proposal. *Id.* § 325.2(a)(2).

44. The Clean Water Act anticipates that EPA, FWS, NMFS, and other federal agencies will comment on wetland permit applications. *See* 33 U.S.C. § 1344(q). The Act also explicitly authorizes EPA to veto the Corps's issuance of a wetland permit. *Id.* § 1344(c). EPA's veto authority is discussed in detail in Chapter 9.

45. The Fish and Wildlife Coordination Act, 16 U.S.C. §§ 661–666(c), requires the Corps to consult with the FWS or the NMFS, and with the head of the appropriate state agency exercising administration over the wildlife resources of the state when the Corps reviews a wetland permit application. 33 C.F.R. §§ 320.3(e); 320.4(c). In addition, the Endangered Species Act, 16 U.S.C. § 1531, *et. seq.*, may also require the Corps to consult with the FWS and the NMFS when it issues certain permits.

46. The Magnuson-Stevens Fishery Conservation and Management Act (Magnuson-Stevens Act), 16 U.S.C. § 1855(b)(2), may require the Corps to consult with NMFS when a proposed federal activity may adversely affect identified Essential Fish Habitat (EFH). *See* 50 C.F.R. pt. 600. For general information about EFH, *see* National Oceanic and Atmospheric Administration Fisheries, Essential Fish Habitat, http://www.nmfs.noaa.gov/habitat/habitatprotection/essentialfishhabitat.htm.

47. The National Historic Preservation Act of 1966, 16 U.S.C. § 470, may require the Corps to consult with state historic preservation officers and the federal Advisory Council on Historic Preservation when it issues certain permits.

48. The Corps cannot issue a wetland permit unless the state in which the discharge will occur certifies that the discharge will not affect the quality of the water in the state in violation of any effluent limitations, water quality standards,

or water quality requirements of that state. 33 U.S.C. § 1341; 33 C.F.R. §§ 320.3(a), 325.1(d)(4), 325.2(b)(1).

49. The substantive limits that other federal laws place on the Corps when it reviews a wetland permit application are discussed in detail in Section III.E. of this chapter. The federal agencies have entered into various memoranda of agreement (MOAs) pursuant to Section 404(q) of the Clean Water Act, 33 U.S.C. § 1344(q), that govern the manner in which they will comment on proposed applications and resolve any disputes regarding applications. Copies of the MOAs may be found at http://www.usace.army.mil/inet/functions/cw/cecwo/reg/moumoas.htm.

50. 33 C.F.R. § 325.3(d)(1); *see also* RGL 92-01, Federal Agencies Roles and Responsibilities, at 3 (Aug. 19, 1992) ("[T]he Corps will ensure that public notices contain sufficient information to facilitate timely submittal of project specific comments from the federal resource agencies."), *available at* http://www.usace.army.mil/inet/functions/cw/cecwo/reg/rgls/rgl92-01.htm.

51. 33 C.F.R. § 325.3(d)(1).

52. 33 C.F.R. § 325.2(d)(2). In order to determine whether to designate a comment period longer or shorter than thirty days, the Corps will consider (1) whether the proposal is routine or noncontroversial; (2) mail time and need for comments from remote areas; (3) comments from similar proposals; and (4) the need for a site visit. *Id.*

53. 33 C.F.R. § 325.2(a)(3). The Corps presumes that persons who do not comment on a permit application do not object to the project. 33 C.F.R. § 325.3(d)(3).

54. *Id.* (The regulations specify that "[a] summary of the comments, the actual letters or portions thereof, or representative comment letters may be furnished to the applicant." *Id.*) *See also* Mall Properties, Inc. v. Marsh, 672 F. Supp. 561, 574–75 (D. Mass. 1988) (remanding a wetland permit denial to the Corps, and holding that the Corps violated its regulations when it failed to inform the permit applicant that the state governor had objected to the proposed permit), *appeal dismissed on finding that remand order was nonappealable,* 881 F.2d 440 (1st Cir. 1988).

55. 33 C.F.R. § 325.2(a)(3).

56. 33 C.F.R. § 325.2(d)(5). When an applicant requests additional time to respond to the Corps's request for information, the agency may grant the request, make a final decision on the permit, or consider the application withdrawn. *Id.*

57. *Id.*

58. 33 C.F.R. § 325.2(a)(5). It is also possible, but unlikely, that the Corps will determine that a public hearing is necessary before it issues the initial public notice regarding the permit application. *Id.* §§ 327.4(a)–(b). In that case, the Corps would announce the public hearing in the initial public notice. *Id.* § 327.4(b).

59. 33 C.F.R. § 327.4(b). The person requesting the hearing must state, with particularity, the reasons for the hearing. *Id.* Before the Corps grants a request

for a hearing, it may attempt to resolve the issues raised by the requester informally. *Id.*

60. Applicant Information, *supra* note 14. *See also* Fund for Animals, Inc. v. Rice, 85 F.3d 535, 545 (11th Cir. 1996) (upholding Corps denial of a public hearing request when the agency concluded that a hearing would not provide any new information); Friends of the Payette v. Horseshoe Bend Hydroelectric Co., 988 F.2d 989, 997 (9th Cir. 1993) (upholding Corps denial of 250 requests for a public hearing on the grounds that the hearings would not provide useful information, and would only allow proponents and opponents to express their views); Conservation Law Foundation v. Federal Highway Administration, 827 F. Supp. 871, 888–89 (D.R.I. 1993), *aff'd* 24 F.3d 1465 (1st Cir. 1994); O'Connor v. U.S. Army Corps of Engineers, 801 F. Supp. 185, 196 (N.D. Ind. 1992).

61. 33 C.F.R. § 327.11(a).

62. *Id.* The notice must identify the time, place, and nature of the hearing, the authority and jurisdiction under which it is held, and the location and availability of the draft environmental impact statement or environmental assessment for the permit. 33 C.F.R. § 327.11(b).

63. *See* 33 C.F.R. §§ 327.5 through 327.10.

64. Any person may submit oral or written statements, call witnesses to submit oral or written statements, and present recommendations for the agency's decision. 33 C.F.R. § 327.8(b). Persons may not, however, cross-examine witnesses. *Id.* § 327.8(d).

65. 33 C.F.R. § 327.7.

66. 33 C.F.R. § 327.8(e).

67. 33 C.F.R. §§ 327.5(b); 327.9.

68. 33 C.F.R. § 327.8(g).

69. 33 U.S.C. § 1344(b)(1). *See also* 33 C.F.R. §§ 320.4(a)(1) ("[A] permit will be denied if the discharge authorized by such permit would not comply with the . . . 404(b)(1) guidelines."); 33 C.F.R. § 323.6(a). Although they are referred to as guidelines, the 404(b)(1) guidelines are promulgated rules that bind the Corps and the public. The 404(b)(1) guidelines do not apply to permits that are issued solely under Section 10 of the Rivers and Harbors Act.

70. 40 C.F.R. § 230.10(a).

71. 40 C.F.R. § 230.10(a)(3).

72. 40 C.F.R. § 230.10(c). The guidelines identify effects that are deemed to be "significant," and establish tests that agencies should use to determine whether effects are "significant." *Id.* In addition, the Corps has clarified that the term "significant" under the 404(b)(1) guidelines does not have exactly the same meaning as the term "significant" under NEPA. RGL 87-02, Use of the Word "Significant" in Permit Documentation (Mar. 30, 1987). It is possible, therefore, that the agency could conclude that a proposed activity could have "significant" effects that necessitate preparation of an environmental impact statement, *see infra* notes 86–107 and accompanying text for a discussion of NEPA in the permitting process, but that the activity would not cause or contribute to "significant" degradation of waters under the 404(b)(1) guidelines. *Id.*

73. 33 C.F.R. § 230.10(b).

74. 33 C.F.R. § 230.10(d).

75. RGL 92-01, *supra* note 19.

76. The Corps conducts a "public interest" review regardless of whether the permit is issued under the Rivers and Harbors Act, the Clean Water Act, or both. 33 C.F.R. § 320.4.

77. 33 C.F.R. § 320.4(a)(1).

78. Although Corps regulations authorize it to consider economics as a factor in the public interest analysis, at least one court has suggested that the Corps may consider only economic impacts that are related to alterations of the physical environment caused by the proposed activity. *See* Mall Properties, Inc. v. Marsh, 672 F. Supp. 561, 566 (D. Mass. 1988). In the *Mall Properties* case, the court held that the Corps could not consider the impact that a proposed shopping mall would have on businesses in New Haven, Connecticut, when the agency determined whether issuance of a permit for the mall would be in the public interest. *Id.* Nevertheless, the Corps suggests that the agency will continue to consider socioeconomic impacts of a proposed activity when the impacts are proximately related to the fact that the activity will be performed in wetlands. *See* RGL 88-11, NEPA Scope of Analysis: *Mall Properties, Inc. v. Marsh* (Aug. 22, 1988), *available at* http://www.usace.army.mil/inet/functions/cw/cecwo/reg/rgls/rgl88-11.htm.

79. The comments of the Fish and Wildlife Service, NMFS, and state wildlife agencies are used by the Corps when it determines whether the permit would have an unacceptable adverse impact on wildlife, and whether permit conditions are necessary to protect wildlife. 33 C.F.R. § 320.4(c).

80. State 401 certification, *see infra* notes 114–121 and accompanying text, is usually conclusive on water quality issues. 33 C.F.R. § 320.4(d). *See also* RGL 90-04, Water Quality Considerations (Mar. 13, 1990), *available at* http://www.usace.army.mil/inet/functions/cw/cecwo/reg/rgls/rgl90-04.htm.

81. The regulations seem to establish a presumption in favor of granting a permit for activities that protect property from erosion, unless the proposed structure would cause damage to the property of others, adversely affect public health and safety, adversely impact floodplain or wetland values, or otherwise appear contrary to the public interest. 33 C.F.R. § 320.4(g)(2). The regulations also seem to establish a presumption against granting a permit that interferes with access to, or use of, navigable waters. *Id.* § 320.4(g)(3).

82. 33 C.F.R. § 320.4(a)(1). In every case, the Corps considers (1) the relative extent of the public and private need for the proposed activity; (2) the practicability of using reasonable alternative locations and methods to achieve the objective of the proposed activity (if there are unresolved conflicts regarding resource use); and (3) the extent and permanence of the beneficial and/or detrimental effect that the activity is likely to have on the public and private uses to which the area is suited. *Id.* § 320.4(a)(2).

83. 33 C.F.R. § 320.4(a)(1).

84. 33 C.F.R. § 320.4(b)(1). The regulations provide that "[m]ost wetlands constitute a productive and valuable resource, the unnecessary alteration or destruction of which should be discouraged as contrary to the public interest."

Id. The regulations specify eight types of wetlands that are considered to perform functions important to the public interest. 33 C.F.R. § 320.4(b)(2). The regulations also encourage the Corps to consider the cumulative impact of discharges into wetlands in consultation with other federal and state agencies. *Id.* § 320.4(b)(3).

85. In addition, the Submerged Lands Act, 43 U.S.C. §§ 1301 *et seq.*, may require the Corps to coordinate the permit review with the Department of Interior and the Attorney General when the proposed activity might alter the coast line or base line. 33 C.F.R. § 320.4(f). The Marine Protection, Research and Sanctuaries Act of 1972 (MPRSA) also imposes limits on the Corps. Pursuant to that act, when a proposed activity will take place in a marine sanctuary, the Corps cannot issue a permit for the activity unless the applicant provides a certification from the Secretary of Commerce that the proposed activity is consistent with Title III of the MPRSA and Department of Commerce regulations. 33 C.F.R. § 320.4(i).

86. 42 U.S.C. § 4332(2)(C).

87. 42 U.S.C. § 4332(2)(E). The Corps must consider the cumulative effects of the proposed activity, including its indirect effects. 40 C.F.R. § 1508.8.

88. The Council on Environmental Quality (CEQ) is a federal agency that was created by NEPA to administer and interpret NEPA. 42 U.S.C. § 4342. For more information on CEQ, see its Web site at http://www.whitehouse.gov/ceq, as well as NEPANet at http://ceq.eh.doe.gov/nepa/nepanet.htm.

89. *See* 33 C.F.R. pt. 230; *id.* pt. 325, app. B; 40 C.F.R. §§ 1500 *et seq.*

90. CEQ's regulations require agencies to develop regulations that identify certain types of actions that generally require an EIS and certain types of actions—categorical exclusions—that generally do not require an EIS or an EA. *See* 40 C.F.R. § 1501.4(a). If an agency proposes to take an action that does not fit within one of those two categories, the agency should prepare an EA to decide whether an EIS is necessary. *Id.* § 1501.4(b). The Corps categorically excludes small private piers, small docks, boat launching ramps, applications that qualify as letters of permission, and several other minor activities from NEPA review. 33 C.F.R. pt. 325, app. B., § 6.

91. 33 C.F.R. § 230.10; *id.* pt. 325, app. B., § 7. In lieu of preparing its own EA or EIS, the Corps sometimes relies on NEPA documents that have been prepared by other agencies for the project. *See, e.g.*, Town of Norfolk v. U.S. Army Corps of Engineers, 968 F.2d 1438, 1447–48 (1st Cir. 1992); Abenaki Nation of Mississquoi v. Hughes, 805 F. Supp. 234, 246 (D. Vt. 1992), *aff'd* 990 F.2d 729 (2d Cir. 1993); Coeur D'Alene Lake v. Kiebert, 790 F. Supp. 998 (D. Idaho 1992); *see also* 33 C.F.R. § 230.21.

92. When an activity that requires a wetland permit is part of a larger project, the Corps's NEPA regulations specify that the agency should examine the impacts of the activity that requires the permit *and* any portions of the larger project over which the Corps has sufficient "control and responsibility" to warrant review. 33 C.F.R. pt. 325, app. B, § 7(b). *See* California Trout v. Schaefer, 58 F.3d 469, 473–74 (9th Cir. 1995) (Corps appropriately examined the impacts of a

discharge of fill material into 4.18 acres of wetlands, rather than the impacts of an entire water diversion project, because the Corps had control or responsibility only over the fill activity); Winnebago Tribe of Nebraska v. Ray, 621 F.2d 269, 271 (8th Cir. 1980) (Corps appropriately examined the impacts of a 1.25 mile segment of a proposed powerline, rather than the entire 67-mile line, because the Corps did not have control over the remainder of the project); Save the Bay v. United States Army Corps of Engineers, 610 F.2d 322, 327 (5th Cir. 1980), *modified and reh'g denied en banc,* 14 Env't. Rep. Cas. (BNA) 1542.

Similarly, if a permit applicant plans to undertake several activities that would require wetland permits, and the activities are related to a single project, the applicant must include all of those activities in a single application, 33 C.F.R. § 325.1(d)(2), and the Corps should evaluate the impacts of all of the activities in a single NEPA document. 40 C.F.R. § 1502.4. The Corps cannot "'evade [its] responsibilities' under the National Environmental Policy Act by 'artificially dividing a major federal action into smaller components, each without a significant impact.'" Preserve Endangered Areas of Cobb's History, Inc. v. U.S. Army Corps of Engineers, 87 F.3d 1242, 1247 (11th Cir. 1996), citing Coalition on Sensible Transportation, Inc. v. Dole, 826 F.2d 60, 68 (D.C.Cir.1987).

93. 33 C.F.R. § 230.10; *id.* pt. 325, app. B, § 7.

94. 40 C.F.R. § 1502.14(f). The NEPA mitigation requirements are separate and distinct from the mitigation requirements of the Section 404(b)(1) guidelines.

95. *See* Friends of the Payette v. Horseshoe Bend Hydroelectric Co., 988 F.2d 989 (9th Cir. 1993) (upholding the Corps's decision to not prepare an EIS because the proposed activity, including mitigation measures, would not have a significant impact on the human environment). *See also* Preserve Endangered Areas of Cobb's History, Inc. v. U.S. Army Corps of Engineers, 87 F.3d 1242, 1248 (11th Cir. 1996); Friends of the Earth v. Hintz, 800 F.2d 822, 837–38 (9th Cir. 1986); 46 Fed. Reg. 18,026 (1981). The NEPA mitigation analysis is different from the 404(b)(1) guidelines mitigation analysis, in that the Corps may not consider proposed mitigation measures when it evaluates whether alternatives to a proposed development activity would have a less adverse impact on the environment under the guidelines. *See* Chapter 8 of this book.

96. 33 C.F.R. pt. 325, app. B, § 7.

97. When the agency concludes that it is not necessary to prepare an EIS, it issues a Finding of No Significant Impact (FONSI) for the permit application. *Id.* The agency will normally combine the EA, FONSI, Statement of Findings for the permit, *infra* note 162, and any analyses that are required to comply with the Section 404(b)(1) guidelines in a single document. *Id.*

98. *See* California Trout v. Schaefer, 58 F.3d 469 (9th Cir. 1995); Roanoke River Basin Ass'n v. Hudson, 940 F.2d 58, 64 (4th Cir. 1991).

99. The Corps processes approximately 4,000 individual permit applications each year. Corps Regulatory Statistics, *available at* http://www.usace.army.mil/inet/functions/cw/cecwo/reg/2003webcharts.pdf. *See also* William L. Want, The Law of Wetlands Regulation, § 6.59[4]. However, in 1991, the Corps prepared only seventeen draft environmental impact statements and four final

statements. *Id.* Similarly, in 1990 the agency prepared thirteen draft and nine final environmental impact statements. *Id.*

100. The EIS examines the environmental impact of the proposed action, including unavoidable adverse environmental effects, alternatives to the proposed action and their impacts, and any irretrievable commitment of resources that would be involved in the proposed action. 42 U.S.C. § 4332(2)(C).

101. *Id.; see also* RGL 87-05, EIS Costs that Can Be Paid by the Applicant (May 28, 1987), *available at* http://www.usace.army.mil/inet/functions/cw/cecwo/reg/rgls/rgl87-05.htm.

102. 33 C.F.R. § 230.12; 40 C.F.R. § 1501.7.

103. 33 C.F.R. § 230.12; 40 C.F.R. § 1508.22. At a minimum, the agency must invite "affected Federal, State, and local agencies, any affected Indian tribe, the proponent of the action, and other interested persons (including those who might not be in accord with the action on environmental grounds)" to participate in the scoping process. *Id.* § 1501.7(a)(1). To determine the scope of an EIS, agencies must consider direct, indirect, and cumulative impacts of a proposed action, and alternatives to the proposed action, including "no action," other reasonable courses of action, or mitigation measures for the proposed action. *Id.* § 1508.25. The agency must also consider (1) closely related actions that should be considered in the same EIS ("connected actions"); (2) actions that when viewed with other proposed actions have cumulatively significant impacts and should, therefore, be discussed in the same EIS ("cumulative actions"); and (3) actions that when viewed with other reasonably foreseeable or proposed agency actions have similarities that provide a basis for evaluating their consequences together, such as common timing or geography ("similar actions"). *Id.*

104. 40 C.F.R. § 1502.9(a). Agencies must circulate the draft EIS to any federal agency that has jurisdiction by law or special expertise, the applicant, if any, and any person, organization, or agency requesting the EIS. *Id.* § 1502.19. They must also provide public notice that the draft EIS is available for comment. *Id.* § 1506.6(b). CEQ's regulations require the agency to affirmatively solicit comments on the draft EIS from various persons, agencies, or organizations. *Id.* § 1503.1. EPA plays an important role in the review process because it is required by Section 309 of the Clean Air Act to "review and comment in writing on the environmental impact of any matter relating to duties or responsibilities . . . of the authority of [EPA]." 42 U.S.C. § 7609.

105. 33 C.F.R. pt. 325, app. B, § 11.

106. 33 C.F.R. pt. 325, app. B, § 13; 40 C.F.R. §§ 1502.9(b), 1503.4(a).

107. 40 C.F.R. § 1502.5(c).

108. 16 U.S.C. § 1536(a)(2). *See also* 33 C.F.R. § 320.3(i).

109. 33 C.F.R. § 325.2(b)(5). *See also* RGL 83-06, Endangered Species Act—Regulatory Program, *available at* http://www.usace.army.mil/inet/functions/cw/cecwo/reg/rgls/rgl83-06.htm.

110. *Id.*

111. The NMFS has jurisdiction over marine species under the Endangered Species Act. 50 C.F.R. § 402.01(b). For more information on NMFS activities with respect to endangered species, see http://www.nmfs.noaa.gov/pr/laws/esa.htm.

112. *Id.* The consultation procedures are codified in 50 C.F.R. pt. 402.

113. During the consultation process, the FWS or the NMFS will prepare a "biological opinion" that evaluates whether the proposed activity will jeopardize the continued existence of a threatened or endangered species. 50 C.F.R. § 402.14. The opinion may also suggest conditions that the Corps could place on the permit to ensure that the activity will not jeopardize such species. *Id.* Even if FWS or NMFS concludes that the proposed activity will jeopardize a threatened or endangered species, the Corps retains the ultimate authority to determine whether the activity will jeopardize such species. Roosevelt Campobello Int'l Park Comm'n v. U.S. Environmental Protection Agency, 684 F.2d 1041, 1049 (1st Cir. 1982); Sierra Club v. Froehlke, 534 F.2d 1289, 1303 (8th Cir. 1976).

The Corps will also consider the impacts of proposed activities on endangered or threatened species or their critical habitat as part of the agency's "public interest" review. *See* Town of Norfolk v. U.S. Army Corps of Engineers, 968 F.2d 1438, 1453 (1st Cir. 1992).

114. 33 U.S.C. § 1341(a)(1). *See also* 33 C.F.R. §§ 320.3(a); 325.1(d)(4), and Regulatory Guidance Letter 87-03, Section 401 Water Quality Certification, *available at* http://www.usace.army.mil/inet/functions/cw/cecwo/reg/rgls/rgl87-03.htm. 401 certifications may also be required from states other than the state where the polluting activity takes place. When the Corps receives a permit application, it must notify EPA that it has received the application (Section 401(a)(2) notice). 33 U.S.C. § 1341 (a)(2). If the EPA administrator determines that the activity that will be authorized by the permit may affect the water quality of any other state, the administrator notifies the other state, the Corps, and the permit applicant that the Corps has received a permit application for an activity that may affect the water quality of the state. *Id.*

115. 33 U.S.C. § 1341(a)(1).

116. *Id.*

117. Roosevelt Campobello Int'l Park Comm'n v. U.S. Environmental Protection Agency, 684 F.2d 1041, 1056 (1st Cir. 1982).

118. 33 C.F.R. § 325.2(b)(1).

119. 33 C.F.R. § 325.2(b)(1); 325.3. The public notice is also sent to EPA, and serves as the notice required by Section 401(a)(2) of the Clean Water Act. *Id.* § 325.2(b)(1)(i). If EPA determines that the proposed activity will affect the water quality of any other state, the agency will notify the other state, the Corps, and the permit applicant. *Id.* EPA must make that determination within thirty days after receipt of the Corps's notice. *Id.* If the other state determines that the proposed activity will violate any water quality requirements of that state, the state can object to the issuance of the permit within sixty days after EPA's notice. *Id.* If the objecting state requests a hearing, the Corps will hold a hearing to consider the water quality impacts of the permit on the objecting state. *Id.* Based on the comments of EPA, the objecting state, and any evidence presented at the hearing, the Corps will include conditions in the permit, if issued, that are necessary to ensure that the activity will comply with water quality requirements of the objecting state. *Id.*

120. 33 C.F.R. § 325.2(b)(1)(ii).

121. *Id.* The Corps can extend the time for the state to respond to a request for certification for as long as a year. *Id.* Normally, though, the Corps does not extend the time for the state's response.

122. 16 U.S.C. § 1455. For state-specific coastal zone information, see NOAA Ocean and Coastal Resource Management, State and Territory Coastal Management Program Summaries, *available at* http://www.ocrm.nos.noaa.gov/czm/czmsitelist.html.

123. Coastal zone management plans are reviewed and approved by the Secretary of Commerce. *Id.*

124. 16 U.S.C. § 1456(c)(3)(A). The Act places additional constraints on federal agencies when they are the permit applicant. *See* 16 U.S.C. § 1456(c); 33 C.F.R. § 325.2(b)(2)(i).

125. 33 C.F.R. § 325.2(b)(2)(ii).

126. 33 C.F.R. § 325.3(a)(16).

127. 33 C.F.R. § 325.2(ii).

128. *Id.*

129. *Id.*

130. *Id.*

131. 16 U.S.C. §§ 470, 470f. The ACHP has promulgated regulations that authorize state historic preservation officers (SHPOs) to consult with agencies and comment on projects in lieu of, or in addition to, the ACHP. 36 C.F.R. § 800.1(c)(ii).

132. 33 C.F.R. § 325, app. C.

133. 33 C.F.R. § 325.2(b)(3).

134. Want, *supra* note 99, § 6.12[5][a].

135. 33 C.F.R. pt. 325, app. C, § 3a. The regulations encourage the Corps and applicants to consider the impacts of projects at the earliest practical time. The regulations suggest that if the Corps is aware, at the time of a pre-application consultation, that a proposed project will affect a designated historic property, the Corps should inform the applicant at that time that the Corps will review the permit application pursuant to the agency's NHPA regulations. *Id.* pt. 325, app. C, § 3c. In addition, the regulations require the Corps to discuss measures or alternatives that avoid or minimize effects on historic properties at the earliest practical time. *Id.* pt. 325, app. C, § 3d.

Under the NHPA regulations, the Corps examines the impacts of the discharge of the dredged or fill material into wetlands on historic properties. However, the agency also examines the impact of activities that occur outside of the waters of the United States on historic properties if (1) the activity would not occur but for the authorization of work or structures in the waters of the United States; (2) the activity is integrally related to the work or structures authorized within the waters of the United States; and (3) the activity must be directly associated with the work or structures to be authorized. *Id.* pt. 325, app. C, § 1g(1).

136. For a list of SHPOs, see Advisory Council on Historic Preservation, State Historic Preservation Officers, http://www.achp.gov/shpo.html.

137. For a list of THPOs, see Advisory Council on Historic Preservation, Tribal Historic Preservation Officers, http://www.achp.gov/thpo.html.

138. 33 C.F.R. pt. 325, app. C, § 4a.

139. 33 C.F.R. pt. 325, app. C., § 4b.

140. *Id.*

141. 33 C.F.R. pt. 325, app. C, §§ 5, 6.

142. 33 C.F.R. pt. 325, app. C, §§ 7–9.

143. *Id.*

144. Under the NHPA, as long as the Corps consults with the ACHP and considers the impact of a project on historic properties, the Corps can issue a permit for the project even though it will adversely affect historic properties. 36 C.F.R. § 800.6(c)(2).

145. 33 C.F.R. pt. 325, app. C, § 10a.

146. 33 C.F.R. pt. 325, app. C, § 10b.

147. 33 C.F.R. § 320.4(j)(1).

148. 33 C.F.R. §§ 320.4(j)(5); 325.2(e)(3).

149. RGL 92-01, *supra* note 19. *See also* 33 C.F.R. § 320.4(c) (comments on fish and wildlife); Slagle v. U.S. By and Through Baldwin, 809 F. Supp. 704, 712 (D. Minn. 1992) (Corps must consider the comments of local agencies); Sierra Club v. Alexander, 484 F. Supp. 455 (N.D. N.Y. 1980), *aff'd*, 633 F.2d 206 (2d Cir. 1980).

If the Corps receives conflicting comments from various state agencies in the same state, and the state has not designated a single responsible coordinating agency for the permit, the Corps will ask the governor to express his or her views or to designate a responsible agency to represent the state. 33 C.F.R. § 320.4(j)(3).

The Corps must accept the decisions of state and local governments on zoning and land use matters unless there are significant issues of overriding national importance. 33 C.F.R. § 320.4(j). If the Corps makes a decision contrary to state or local zoning or land use decisions, it must identify the significant issues of overriding national importance in the statement of findings or record of decision that it issues with the final decision. *Id.* § 325.2(a)(6).

Pursuant to Section 404(q) of the Clean Water Act, 33 U.S.C. § 1344(q), the Corps has entered into Memoranda of Agreement with EPA, the FWS, and the NMFS to clarify their relationship in the decision-making process. Pursuant to the memoranda, the agencies can elevate disputes regarding permit decisions from the local Corps district level to higher-level decision makers within the Corps. The Corps-EPA MOA is available at http://www.usace.army.mil/inet/functions/cw/cecwo/reg/epa404q.htm.

150. RGL 92-01, *supra* note 19.

151. *Id.*

152. *See* Chapter 9 of this book.

153. 33 C.F.R. §§ 320.4(j)(1); 325.2(d)(4).

154. 33 C.F.R. § 323.6(b). EPA's veto authority, and the veto procedures, are described in Chapter 9.

155. 33 C.F.R. § 325.2(d)(4).

156. 33 C.F.R. § 320.4(j)(1). When the Corps denies a permit without prejudice, the applicant may reinstate processing of the permit application if the applicant subsequently receives the federal, state, or local approval or authorization that was denied. *Id.*

A Corps Regulatory Guidance Letter states that the agency should terminate permit review as soon as a state denies 401 certification or informs the Corps that a project does not comply with its coastal zone management program, or as soon as it becomes clear that the project would violate the Endangered Species Act, the MPRSA, the NHPA, or the 404(b)(1) guidelines, among other requirements. RGL 88-12, Processing Time; Regulatory Thresholds (Sept. 9, 1988), *available at* http://www.usace.army.mil/inet/functions/cw/cecwo/reg/rgls/rgl8812.htm.

157. *Id.*

158. *Id.*

159. 33 C.F.R. § 325.2(d)(3). For a summary of the percentage of permits issued in less than sixty days during 1998–2002, see U.S. Army Corps of Engineers Regulatory Program, *Percent of All Actions Completed > 60 Days Fiscal Year 2003 Performance, available on page 9 of the document at* http://www.usace.army.mil/inet/functions/cw/cecwo/reg/2003webcharts.pdf.

160. The Corps does not have to make a decision within sixty days if (1) it is precluded by law or by procedures required by law from making the decision within that time frame; (2) the case must be referred to a higher authority; (3) the comment period on the application is extended; (4) a timely submittal of information or comments is not received by the applicant; (5) the processing of the application is suspended at the request of the applicant; or (6) information needed by the district engineer for a decision on the application cannot reasonably be obtained within the sixty days. 33 C.F.R. § 325.2(d)(3).

161. 33 C.F.R. §§ 325.2(a)(6); 325.8. However, district engineers will refer permit applications to the division engineer for decision when (1) a referral is required by a memorandum of agreement with other federal agencies; (2) the recommended decision is contrary to the written position of the Governor of the state in which the permitted activity will take place; (3) there is substantial doubt as to authority, law, regulations, or policies applicable to the proposed activity; (4) a higher authority requests that the application be forwarded for decision; or (5) the district engineer is precluded by law or procedures from taking final action on the application. 33 C.F.R. § 325.8(b). The division engineer may refer the application to the Chief of Engineers in similar situations. *Id.* § 325.8(c).

162. 33 C.F.R. § 325.2(a)(6). If an EIS was prepared for the decision, the Corps must prepare a record of decision for the decision instead of a statement of findings. *Id.*

163. 33 C.F.R. § 325.2(a)(7).

164. 33 C.F.R. §§ 325.2(a)(7); 325.4.

165. 33 C.F.R. § 325.2(a)(7).

166. *Id.*

167. 33 C.F.R. § 320.4(g).
168. 33 C.F.R. § 325.2(a)(8).
169. *Id.*
170. 33 C.F.R. § 325.6(b). "Permits for the existence of a structure or other activity of a permanent nature are usually for an indefinite duration with no expiration date cited." *Id.* However, where the permit authorizes temporary fills, it will include a definite expiration date. *Id.*
171. 33 C.F.R. § 325.6(c).
172. 33 C.F.R. § 325.6(d).
173. *Id.*
174. RGL 91-01, Extensions of Time for Individual Permit Authorizations (Nov. 6, 1991), *available at* http://www.usace.army.mil/inet/functions/cw/cecwo/reg/rgls/rgl91-01.htm.
175. 33 C.F.R. § 325.7(a).
176. *Id.*
177. *Id.*
178. 33 C.F.R. § 325.7(b).
179. 33 C.F.R. § 325.7(a). Those changes must be made through the normal permit application and review procedures. *Id.*
180. 33 C.F.R. § 325.7(b).
181. *Id.*
182. *Id.*
183. 33 C.F.R. § 325.7(c).
184. *Id.*
185. *Id.*
186. *Id.*
187. *Id.*
188. 33 C.F.R. § 325.7(d).
189. *Id.*
190. 33 C.F.R. § 320.1(a)(2).
191. *Id.*
192. 33 C.F.R. § 331.4.
193. 33 C.F.R. § 331.6.
194. 33 C.F.R. § 331.7.
195. 64 Fed. Reg. 11,707, 11,711 (Mar. 9, 1999).
196. Chapter 12 of this book describes judicial review of the Corps's decisions.

CHAPTER 7

The Section 404(b)(1) Guidelines and Practicable Alternatives Analysis

MARK T. PIFHER

I. Introduction/Scope

The Environmental Protection Agency (EPA) and the United States Army Corps of Engineers (Corps) are co-regulators under Section 404 of the Clean Water Act. The Corps is responsible for issuing permits, including individual permits,[1] the conditions of which are governed by the Corps's regulations and guidelines promulgated by EPA (in consultation with the Corps) pursuant to Section 404(b)(1).[2] Notwithstanding the title of "guidelines," EPA's Section 404(b)(1) Guidelines are binding, substantive rules applied by the Corps in considering applications for individual permits to discharge dredged or fill material in wetlands.[3] A Section 404 permit cannot be issued unless the Guidelines are satisfied.[4]

The Guidelines establish four separate restrictions on dredged and fill discharges. These restrictions are set forth in 40 C.F.R. § 230.10(a)–(d). The restrictions imposed by the Guidelines are as follows: (1) a prohibition against the discharge of dredged or fill material if a practicable alternative with less adverse impact is available;[5] (2) prohibitions against discharges of dredged or fill material that cause or contribute to violations of applicable water quality standards, violate toxic effluent standards or prohibitions, jeopardize endangered or threatened species, or violate the requirements of the Marine Protection, Research, and Sanctuaries Act of 1972;[6] (3) prohibitions against discharges of dredged or fill material that "cause or contribute to significant degradation of the waters of the United States;"[7] and (4) prohibitions against discharges of dredged or fill material "unless appropriate and practicable steps have been taken which will minimize potential adverse impacts of the discharge on the aquatic ecosystem."[8] This chapter focuses primarily on the Guidelines's prohibition against the discharge of dredged or fill material if there exists a "practicable alternative" to such a discharge.[9] Section II of this chapter describes the regulations governing the practicable alternatives requirement. Section III discusses issues that may arise in its application, including problems in defining project purpose and the factors considered in identifying practicable alternatives.

II. Overview of Regulatory Requirements

The practicable alternatives requirement has been described as "the cornerstone of the Section 404 program since its earliest iteration."[10] The pertinent EPA regulation provides:

> No discharge of dredge or fill material will be permitted if there is a practicable alternative to the proposed discharge which would have less adverse impact on the aquatic ecosystem, so long as the alternative does not have other significant adverse environmental consequences.[11]

Corps regulations also contain an alternatives requirement, which provides that "[w]here there are unresolved conflicts as to resource use," the Corps is required to consider "the practicability of using reasonable alternative locations and methods to accomplish the objective of the proposed structure or work."[12] Because this regulation treats the availability of alternatives as just one factor among others that the Corps must consider in the "general balancing process" of the agency's public interest review,[13] it is considerably less demanding than the "practicable alternatives" requirement of the Guidelines. The Guidelines' practicable alternatives requirement generally may not be weighed against other factors; if a practicable alternative is available, a permit may not be issued.

The Guidelines' practicable alternatives requirement is best understood when considered in light of the fundamental precept of the Guidelines: "[D]redged or fill material should not be discharged into the aquatic ecosystem, unless it can be demonstrated that such a discharge will not have an unacceptable adverse impact."[14] For purposes of the Guidelines, wetlands are "special aquatic sites."[15] Discharges that destroy or degrade special aquatic sites are "considered to be among the most severe environmental impacts covered by [the] Guidelines."[16] Such impacts are to be avoided if either the purposes sought to be accomplished by discharging dredged or fill material into wetlands can be realized by practicable alternative means or the discharge will cause significant degradation of the aquatic ecosystem.[17] The regulations provide general descriptions of practicable alternatives, including but not limited to

- Activities that do not involve a discharge of dredged or fill material into the waters of the United States or ocean waters
- Discharges of dredged or fill material at other locations in waters of the United States or ocean waters[18]

An alternative will be considered "practicable" if it is "available and capable of being done taking into consideration cost, existing technology, and logistics in light of overall project purpose."[19] Hence, the permitting authority's evaluation and definition of project purposes will significantly affect the identification of practicable alternatives. Sites not owned by the applicant may be considered available and practicable. The Guidelines provide that "an area not presently owned by the applicant which could reasonably be obtained, utilized, expanded or managed in order to fulfill the basic purpose of the proposed activity may be considered."[20] Practicable alternatives that have "less adverse impact on the aquatic ecosystem" than the proposed discharge and do not have other "significant adverse environmental consequences" will preclude the issuance of a permit for the proposed discharge.[21]

The Guidelines establish two presumptions for proposed discharges into wetlands and other special aquatic sites. First is the "water dependency" test, which presumes that a practicable alternative is available "[w]here the activity associated with a discharge which is proposed for a special aquatic site . . . does not require access or proximity to or siting within the special aquatic site in question to fulfill its basic purpose."[22] The second presumption provides that "where a discharge is proposed for a special aquatic site, all practicable alternatives to the proposed discharge which do not involve a discharge into a special aquatic site are presumed to have less adverse impact on the aquatic ecosystem."[23] These presumptions are rebuttable, but the applicant bears the burden of presenting evidence that clearly demonstrates that the presumed facts will not obtain if the proposed activity is authorized.[24]

The general procedures for determining whether a proposed discharge complies with the Guidelines stress the importance of the practicable alternatives requirement. After ascertaining the general requirements of the Guidelines and determining whether the discharge may fall within the terms of a general permit (and assuming here that it does not), the permitting authority—i.e., the district engineer—is required to "[e]xamine practicable alternatives to the proposed discharge," including the alternatives of not discharging into jurisdictional waters or choosing a site with "less damaging consequences."[25] If such alternatives are determined to be available, the proposal is deemed to be out of compliance with the Guidelines and, hence, impermissible. No further regulatory scrutiny is deemed appropriate. It is only upon determining that practicable alternatives are unavailable that the Corps will examine the possibility of permitting the discharge under the general weighing of costs and benefits that informs the Corps's public interest review or considering the Guidelines's other requirements, such as changes in the proposed activity that minimize damage to the wetland site or compensatory mitigation.[26] This general approach—avoidance, minimization, and compensatory mitigation of adverse environmental impacts—is known as "sequencing" and is discussed briefly below and in more detail in Chapter 8.

III. Implementation of the Guidelines: The Practicable Alternatives Requirement

A. Flexibility in Application

All wetlands are regarded by Corps regulations as special aquatic sites, and their protection is subject to "heightened solicitude," particularly in applying the practicable alternatives requirement.[27] Nonetheless, the Guidelines as well as guidance issued jointly by EPA and the Corps in 1993 (1993 Guidance) permit some flexibility in application.[28] The agencies recognize that impacts from discharges of dredged or fill material vary widely in terms of severity, extent, and duration, depending on both the proposed activity and the wetland functions and values that may be affected by the activity.[29] Accordingly, the demanding regulatory scrutiny generally required for wetland fills may be relaxed to some degree in appropriate circumstances. The 1993 Guidance concludes that, for the purpose of determining the availability of practicable alternatives, the Section 404(b)(1) Guidelines "do not contemplate that the same intensity of analysis will be required for all types of projects but instead envision a correlation between the scope of the evaluation and the potential extent of adverse impacts on the aquatic environment."[30]

The Guidelines also contemplate a flexible approach to their application: "[T]he compliance evaluation procedures will vary to reflect the seriousness of the potential for adverse impacts on the aquatic ecosystems posed by specific dredged or fill material discharge activities."[31] Likewise, the Guidelines state that "[i]t generally is not intended or expected that extensive testing, evaluation or analysis will be needed to make findings of compliance" with the Guidelines for "routine cases" that "have little, if any, potential for significant degradation of the aquatic environment."[32] Accordingly, regulatory scrutiny and its associated documentation "should reflect the significance and complexity of the discharge activity."[33] The 1993 Guidance applies this general principle specifically to the implementation of the practicable alternatives requirement of the Guidelines: "[T]he amount of information needed to make [an alternatives] determination and the level of scrutiny required by the [Section 404(b)(1) Guidelines] is commensurate with the severity of the environmental impact . . . and the scope/cost of the project."[34]

As would be expected, there is less stringent review—i.e., less concern about comprehensively identifying all practicable alternatives—for those projects with only minor impacts, while the level of scrutiny increases for broader and more environmentally costly undertakings. In *Town of Norfolk v. U.S. Army Corps of Engineers*,[35] for example, the court concluded that "[c]learly, the guidelines contemplate an analysis which varies in magnitude depending on the impact of the proposed discharge."[36] When the proposed discharge's "direct impact on the aquatic ecosystem . . . is negligible," the Corps need not apply "dogmatic scrutiny," and in appropriate cases, the agency may rely on analyses performed by state or other federal agencies in applying the practicable alternatives requirement.[37]

According to the 1993 Guidance, a project will be considered to have minor impacts if there is little potential for degradation of the aquatic environment and the proposed discharge (1) is to be placed in aquatic resources of limited natural function, (2) is small in size with little direct impact, (3) possesses little potential for secondary or cumulative impacts, or (4) will cause only temporary impacts.[38] Moreover, under a Memorandum of Agreement between the Corps and EPA, if EPA and the Corps agree that a proposed discharge will cause only "insignificant environmental losses," the Corps is authorized to deviate from the analytical sequence of avoidance, minimization, and compensatory mitigation that otherwise requires the Corps to deny a permit if practicable alternatives are available.[39] Furthermore, if there is "no identifiable or discernible difference in adverse impact on the environment between the applicant's proposed alternative and all other practicable alternatives," the applicant's proposal is considered to have met the guidelines.[40]

While courts often cite the flexible nature of the alternatives analysis when they uphold the Corps's permits for development proposals that have minimal or negligible environmental impacts, the United States Court of Appeals for the Tenth Circuit recently relied on the flexibility of the Guidelines to uphold the Corps's issuance of a permit for a housing and golf course development that would have more than minimal or negligible impacts.[41] In *Greater Yellowstone Coalition v. Flowers*, environmental groups argued that the Corps acted arbitrarily and capriciously in conducting the alternatives analysis for the project when the agency failed to consider whether the applicant could purchase additional property adjacent to the proposed development and relocate certain features of the development to avoid impacts to the wetlands.[42] Although the court determined that the Corps failed to examine "whether any commitment of [adjacent] property" would meet the purpose of the applicant's development proposal, the court concluded that the agency's analysis was not arbitrary and capricious.[43] The court stressed that the level of documentation for the agency's decision should "reflect the significance and complexity of the discharge activity,"[44] and it concluded that the Corps's analysis was sufficiently detailed "to reflect the seriousness of the potential for adverse impacts on the aquatic ecosystem posed by [the] discharge activities."[45]

B. Determining Project Purpose

To identify alternatives to a proposed discharge that are practicable and available, it is essential to define the "basic" or "overall" purpose of the project associated with the proposed discharge.[46] It is only "in light of overall project purposes" that alternatives to proposed discharges can be evaluated for their practicability.[47] Defining purpose can heavily influence, and in some cases be determinative of, pertinent regulatory issues. A statement of a project's purpose effectively sets the scope of what may considered to be potential, practicable alternatives and may determine whether the presumption against projects that are not "water dependent" is applicable to a proposed discharge.

If the project's purpose is defined very narrowly, the range of alternatives may be severely limited, increasing the chances of permitting the proposed activity. By contrast, a more general description of a project's purpose may open for consideration a wide range of alternatives, precluding a conclusion that the proposed discharge complies with the Guidelines.[48] Consider, for example, a proposal to develop a residential community that includes access to Lake X for boating and other recreation in or on the waters of the lake. A narrow definition of the proposal's purpose may be to "provide a residential community with access to Lake X for boating and other water-related recreation."[49] A more general description of the purpose may simply be "housing."[50] Obviously, if the more general description of the project's purpose were deemed appropriate, the range of alternative sites is much broader than would be the case if the narrow definition were accepted. In many cases, therefore, project purpose is defined by the applicant in a very restrictive manner, limiting the availability of practicable alternatives.[51] As a result, the Corps's approach to defining project purposes and the extent to which it must defer to an applicant's statement of the basic purpose of a proposal become issues of considerable controversy.

1. The Corps's Role in Defining Project Purpose

In the past, the Corps often extended substantial deference to the applicant's statement of project purpose.[52] In *Louisiana Wildlife Federation v. York*,[53] the court rejected the notion that the Guidelines required the Corps to consider only environmental impacts in assessing practicable alternatives, with no consideration due the applicant's purpose in seeking a Section 404 permit. To the contrary, the court concluded that

> "[u]nder the[] Guidelines, . . . not only is it permissible for the Corps to consider the applicant's objective; the Corps has a duty to take into account the objectives of the applicant's project. Indeed, it would be bizarre if the Corps were to ignore the purpose for which the applicant seeks a permit and to substitute a purpose it deems more suitable."[54]

The court accordingly affirmed the Corps's decision to issue permits to convert 5,000 acres of bottomland hardwood wetlands to agricultural use and the agency's finding of no practicable alternatives. In doing so, the court agreed with the Corps that it was proper to accept the applicant's description of the project's purpose, namely "to increase soybean production or to increase net return on assets owned by the company."[55]

The court's decision in *Louisiana Wildlife Federation* initially was received by the Corps as an invitation—indeed, a requirement—to accept without much scrutiny an applicant's view of a proposed project's purpose. In guidance issued in 1986, the decision was said to "require[ ] that alternatives be practicable to the applicant and that the purpose and need for the project must be the applicant's purpose and need."[56] Some districts interpreted the case even more stringently, concluding that "whatever information [an applicant offers] should be accepted as his basic purpose."[57]

EPA, by contrast, consistently advocated that the Guidelines required the Corps to make an independent determination concerning the "basic purpose" of proposed activities rather than deferring to the applicant's stated purpose.[58] The Corps has since acquiesced in EPA's position. The Corps clarified its approach to defining project purpose in a series of four cases that were elevated over a two-year period for purposes of considering the Corps's implementation of the Guidelines. The first case involved the proposed Plantation Landing resort in Louisiana.[59] In reviewing the New Orleans District's decision to issue a permit for this development, the Department of the Army's Director of Civil Works described the manner in which the purpose of a proposed project should be evaluated and the error made by the New Orleans District

> The effect of [the New Orleans District's] deferring to and accepting the applicant's definition of the basic purpose . . . was to ensure that no practicable alternative could exist. . . . That is not an acceptable approach to interpret and implement the 404(b)(1) Guidelines. *Only* if the *Corps, independently* of the applicant, were to determine that the *basic* purposes of the project cannot practicably be accomplished unless the project is [permitted as proposed] would . . . conditions [stated by the applicant] be relevant to the 404(b)(1) Guidelines' alternative review. The fact that those conditions may be part of the proposal as presented by the applicant is by no means determinative of that point. Once again, the Corps, not the applicant, must define the *basic* purpose underlying the applicant's proposed activity.[60]

The decision goes on to reinterpret the court's ruling in *Louisiana Wildlife Federation v. York* and previous Corps guidance. It concludes that "the Court [in *Louisiana Wildlife Federation*] clearly indicated that the *Corps* was in charge of defining project purpose and determining whether practicable alternatives exist," and that prior "guidance was *not* intended to allow the applicant to control those two or any other aspect of the 404(b)(1) Guidelines review."[61] The decision makes clear that, in the Corps's view, nothing in *Louisiana Wildlife Federation v. York* nor the Guidelines "require[s] the Corps to accept or use the applicant's preferred definition of project purpose or to adopt without question the applicant's conclusion regarding the availability of practicable alternatives."[62]

These conclusions were forcefully reiterated in elevated decisions involving permits for the Hartz Mountain Development Corporation's proposal to fill wetlands for a housing development in the New Jersey Meadowlands,[63] Old Cutler Bay Associates's proposal for a golf course community in south Florida,[64] and Twisted Oaks Joint Venture's proposal for residential development in South Carolina.[65]

More recently, the Corps's approach to defining project purpose has received explicit judicial approval. In its decision concerning Denver's proposed Two Forks water project,[66] the Corps specifically rejected the applicant's description of the basic purpose of the proposed development, choosing instead to characterize the basic purpose of the proposal in more general terms. In reviewing that decision, the court noted that "EPA and the Corps were both required independently to review and define the project's overall purpose. They were not restricted to the definition contained in the application."[67]

Corps regulations integrating the National Environmental Policy Act (NEPA) into the Section 404 program currently require an independent determination of project purpose. The pertinent regulation provides:

> [W]hile generally focusing on the applicant's statement, the Corps will, in all cases, exercise independent judgment in defining the purpose and need for the project from the applicant's and the public's perspective.[68]

The same approach to defining project purpose apparently now controls the Corps's implementation of the Guidelines's practicable alternatives requirement.

2. *Multi-Component Projects and Project Purpose*

The Corps's responsibility to independently evaluate and determine the basic purpose of proposed discharges does not necessarily mean that the Corps will opt for more general, rather than narrow, descriptions of project purposes. In some circumstances, the Corps has accepted very narrow descriptions of a project's purpose. The primary examples of such circumstances involve projects that include several components, some of which do not involve the discharge of dredged or fill material and, accordingly, are not subject to Corps jurisdiction under Section 404. These projects have typically involved some combination of upland development coupled with an application for a permit to develop contiguous wetlands for purposes related to the upland development.

In *Sylvester v. U.S. Army Corps of Engineers*,[69] for example, the Corps acquiesced in the applicant's statement of project purpose in issuing a permit to fill eleven acres of wetlands for a golf course. The golf course was part of a larger resort development, major portions of which were to be constructed on uplands not subject to Corps jurisdiction. In these circumstances, the Corps limited its consideration of the proposal's purpose to the proposed golf course, with this resulting narrow definition of the project's purpose

> To construct an 18-hole, links style, championship golf course and other recreational amenities in conjunction with the development of the proposed Resort at Squaw Creek. Research conducted for the applicant has indicated that a quality 18-hole golf course is an essential element for a successful alpine destination resort.[70]

This definition of project purpose was upheld by the court over vigorous objection that it "impermissibly skewed the 'practicable alternatives' analysis in favor of" the project.[71] The Corps found it unnecessary to consider off-site alternatives for the proposed golf course because such alternatives would not "meet [the developer's] basic purpose and need."[72] In approving the Corps's issuance of the permit, the court held that while the Corps may regard as practicable alternatives such sites as cannot "accommodate components of a project that are merely incidental to the applicant's basic purpose," it was reasonable to conclude that the relationship between the proposed golf course and other components of the project was more than incidental.[73] The court concluded that the Corps reasonably viewed an on-site golf course as an integral part of the applicant's overall project, thus making consideration of off-site alternatives unnecessary. Such alternatives were inconsistent with the basic purpose of the proposal.[74]

A similar conclusion was reached in *National Wildlife Federation v. Whistler.*[75] The Corps issued a permit to construct a boat dock and launching facilities in conjunction with a housing development, defining the project's purpose as "to provide boat access to the Missouri River from [the] planned development." Alternative sites were rejected as not practicable because they would not serve the defined purpose.[76] In upholding the Corps's decision, the court held that the housing development and the boat facilities could reasonably be viewed as two separate projects, given that the housing was to be located on uplands and was not subject to Corps scrutiny.[77] Again, the Corps's conclusion on practicable alternatives turned on its consideration of the relationship between the regulated activity and the larger project.[78]

In neither *Sylvester* nor *National Wildlife Federation* did the courts provide much guidance concerning the kind of relationship to nonjurisdictional activities that will permit the Corps to regard one component of a project as merely "incidental"—and thus not sufficiently integral to the project to be regarded as part of the project's "basic purpose." The Corps's own decisions are likewise so fact-specific that firm conclusions on this issue are elusive. The cases discussed above suggest that if a permit is sought only for the wetland component of a project involving both upland and wetland development, that component's basic purpose will be segregated from the overall project and separately evaluated by the Corps. In such circumstances, a narrow definition of project purpose is likely to be accepted.

As with the definition of a project's purpose, the Corps need not defer to an applicant's insistence that, for the proposed project to be economically viable, components of the project involving wetland development must be integrated with nonwetland components. Arguments of this sort must be supported by evidence. In *National Audubon Society v. Hartz Mountain Development Corporation,* for example, the Corps issued a permit to fill 127 acres of wetlands in the New Jersey meadowlands for a complex of office buildings, warehouses, and shopping facilities.[79] While the Corps ultimately concluded that no practicable alternatives to the proposed project were available, it regarded as unpersuasive the applicant's contention that "the shopping center–office park–warehouse distribution center was an inextricably related project which required development on a single interconnected site."[80] Instead, the Corps considered the proposal as three separate developments, each of which was subject to a separate alternatives analysis. Accordingly, the Corps considered alternative sites that could accommodate each of the activities either in combination or individually.[81] The basis for this conclusion appears to be the Corps's rejection of the applicant's claims that disaggregating the project into three distinct components, each of which could be located at different sites, would not be cost effective and that "[a] successful project requires a large scale development, offering all these things . . . which is of sufficient size to be self-sustaining as a magnet to attract business."[82]

Similarly, in *Plantation Landing Elevation,* the Corps made clear that, absent supporting evidence, it will not simply accept an applicant's suggestion that several components of a large project must be "fully-integrated" to realize the purpose of the project.[83] The agency concluded that "[t]he concepts of 'integration,' 'contiguity,' and 'waterfront' must not be used . . . to preclude the existence of practicable alternatives."[84] Only if the applicant can demonstrate that the success of the project turns on the integration of the components into a contiguous waterfront location would such a narrow approach to defining project purposes be deemed appropriate.[85]

3. *Project Purpose and Water Dependency*

Defining a project's basic purpose also plays an important, sometimes determinative, role in evaluating whether the proposed project is "water dependent." A project's characterization as non–water dependent raises a presumption that practicable alternatives not involving discharges into special aquatic sites are available.[86] That presumption has been described as "very strong,"[87] thus "creating an incentive for developers to avoid choosing wetlands when they could choose an alternative upland site."[88] Applicants will often describe the purpose of their proposed project as water dependent.

The presumption does not preclude a permit for non–water dependent projects to be located in aquatic sites, but it "should necessitate a more persuasive showing than otherwise concerning the lack of alternatives."[89] Similarly, a finding that a proposal is water dependent does not guarantee that a permit will be issued. The Corps of Engineers elucidated its position on the water dependency question in a 1992 Regulatory Guidance Letter

> Based on [40 C.F.R. § 230.10(a)(3)] an evaluation is required in every case for use of non-aquatic areas and other aquatic sites that would result in less adverse impact to the aquatic ecosystem, irrespective of whether the discharge site is a special aquatic site or that the activity associated with the discharge is water dependent. A permit cannot be used, therefore, in circumstances where an environmentally preferable practicable alternative for the proposed discharge exists (except as provided for under Section 404(b)(2)).[90]

Hence, even applicants who propose water dependent projects must demonstrate that the proposal is the least environmentally damaging.[91] These presumptions are oftentimes difficult to overcome, because the alternatives analysis is based on qualitative factors involving the exercise of best professional judgment as compared to more concrete quantitative determinations.[92]

In cases other than those involving commercial or residential development, such as water supply projects, water dependency is often not very controversial. Because the basic purpose of such projects necessitates "access or proximity to or siting within" an aquatic resource, [93] the practicable alternatives analysis will not involve issues of choosing alternative upland sites.[94] Similarly, some projects, like ordinary commercial or residential development, are clearly not water dependent.[95]

Water dependency and project purpose issues are intertwined and more complex when, as in the cases considered above, the project purpose turns on the relationship between component parts of a proposed project involving both upland and wetland development. In *Shoreline Associates v. Marsh*,[96] the court upheld the Corps's denial of a permit to develop a townhouse community in wetlands. The court, like the Corps, found unpersuasive the applicant's contention that the project was dependent upon a boat storage facility and a launching area, thus making the project water dependent. The court concluded that "[t]he primary aspect of the proposed project is the construction of a townhouse community, not the construction of a boat storage facility and launch which are incidental to it."[97] Hence, the court accepted the Corps's determination that certain upland property owned by the developer constituted a suitable alternative site for the proposed project: "Shoreline has failed to show, in compliance with the regulations, why it is necessary for the townhouses to be located on the wetlands rather than the uplands, except for its preference to build on the wetlands."[98]

A similar conclusion was reached in *Korteweg v. United States Army Corps of Engineers,*[99] in which the court also upheld the Corps's denial of a permit for a waterfront residential development. Both the court and the Corps concluded that the project was not water dependent simply because a part of the project included a proposed adjacent dock. The purpose of the project was "housing" and "the docks are neither essential to the [lots] nor are they integral to their residential use."[100] The same conclusion was reached concerning the Deltona Corporation's proposal to fill 2,152 acres of wetlands to create a housing development with "finger canals" in Marco Island, Florida.[101]

By contrast, in *National Wildlife Federation v. Whistler,*[102] noted above, the Corps accepted as water dependent a proposal to provide boat access to a planned residential community by reopening an old river channel. This conclusion was driven by the Corps's acceptance of the applicant's description of the basic purpose of the proposal—i.e., "to provide boat access to the Missouri River from [the applicant's] planned development."[103] *Shoreline Associates* and *Korteweg* were distinguishable; unlike the proposal in *National Wildlife Federation,* neither of these cases involved proposals in which the housing portion of the project was to be located entirely on uplands not subject to the Corps's Section 404 jurisdiction. And unlike the applicant in *National Wildlife Federation,* the applicants in *Shoreline Associates* and *Korteweg* could not successfully characterize "the overall project as encompassing two severable projects," one of which fell within Corps jurisdiction and was properly considered water dependent and another that was not subject to the Corps's regulatory scrutiny.[104] The applicants in *Shoreline Associates* and *Korteweg* "could have presumably relocated the entire developments to other locations."[105]

In *Friends of the Earth v. Hintz,*[106] the nature of the relationship between component parts of a project also resulted in a determination that a component was water dependent. The proposed project was a log storage facility to be used for both domestic and export purposes by an existing "sawmill/sorting yard/log export complex."[107] The Corps concluded that "log storage is not a water dependent use unless the storage is tied to an exporting facility."[108] Characterizing the applicant's facility as "an integrated complex," the court concluded that the relationship between the proposed storage facility and the applicant's existing operations provided a sufficient basis to uphold the Corps's finding that the "applicant's log and lumber export operations require immediate proximity to navigable waters," making the proposed facility water dependent.[109]

The Corps's willingness to separately consider the wetland-impacting components of a project involving related upland development, as in *National Wildlife Federation,* can sometimes work to the applicant's advantage in securing a permit to fill or otherwise develop wetlands. But such an approach can also work to the applicant's disadvantage. For example, in the *Plantation Landing Elevation* case, also noted above, the Corps rejected the applicant's description of the project's basic purpose as a "fully-integrated, contiguous, waterfront resort complex," concluding that by aggregating all parts of the project, the applicant improperly gained the benefits of proposing a "water dependent" project. The appropriate approach was instead to identify "the 'basic purpose' of each component of the proposed Plantation Landing Resort . . . in terms of its actual, non-water-dependent function."[110] The Corps insisted that the project be disaggregated to ensure that the purpose of the water dependency and practicable alternatives requirements of the Guidelines were not defeated.[111]

C. Identifying Practicable Alternatives

To be considered practicable, an alternative must be "available and capable of being done taking into consideration costs, existing technology, and logistics in light of overall project purposes."[112] The information necessary to conduct an appropriate alternatives analysis may be produced by the Corps, which in some cases may rely on an alternatives analysis prepared pursuant to NEPA or a state-administered program.[113] Often, the applicant is best advised to prepare an alternatives analysis that can be presented with the application for a permit.[114] The Guidelines specify that a permit application will fail to comply with the Guidelines when "[t]here does not exist sufficient information to make a reasonable judgment as to whether the proposed discharge will comply with these Guidelines."[115] The Corps considers it the applicant's burden to demonstrate compliance with the Guidelines.[116] Accordingly, applicants should supply the Corps with an alternatives analysis that contains sufficient information to enable the agency to make a reasoned judgment of compliance with the practicable alternatives requirement. For cases in which more information is needed, the Corps may request the applicant to supply an alternatives analysis or supplement information previously submitted to the agency.[117] The failure to supply such information may result in permit denial.[118]

Some of the factors considered in identifying available practicable alternatives are considered in the following subsections.

1. *Ownership and Availability*

According to the Guidelines, an alternative is available even if the property is not presently owned by the applicant so long as it "could reasonably be obtained, utilized, expanded or managed" in order to meet the basic project purpose.[119] In *Slagle v. United States,* the court applied this regulation in upholding the Corps's conclusion that practicable alternatives were available to an applicant seeking to fill over five acres of wetlands for residential development.[120] The court concluded that the applicant "has not come forward with any specific facts . . . as to the availability of alternative sites, and has failed his burden under the statute."[121]

Subsequent guidance limits the application of the foregoing rule, stating that for the construction or expansion of a home, farm building, or a small business facility that affects no more than two acres of wetlands, alternatives located on property not owned by the applicant are presumed to be not practicable.[122] The guidance cautions that the presumption may be rebutted; "a more thorough review of practicable alternatives would be warranted for individual sites comprising a subdivision of homes, if following issuance of this policy statement, a real estate developer subdivided a large, contiguous wetlands parcel into numerous parcels."[123]

2. *Timing of Availability: The "Market Entry" Test*

Availability was a pivotal issue in *Bersani v. Robichaud.*[124] When the developer applied for a Section 404 permit to build a shopping mall on a site containing 49.5 acres of wetlands, a competitor had already purchased a nearby alternative site. The Corps, having examined the mitigation package, granted the permit. EPA stopped the project by exercising its Section 404(c) veto authority, concluding that the competing site was "available" when the applicant "entered" the market for a shopping center site, and hence permit denial was appropriate. In EPA's view, the date on which the applicant entered the market for a suitable development site, as compared to the time of permit application, controlled the scope of the practicable alternatives requirement. The court found EPA's preferred analysis to pass the "arbitrary and capricious" test of review, and upheld the veto. This analysis is not, however, a codified statutory regulatory mandate, and since the *Bersani* decision, further application has not been tested in court.[125]

3. *Geographic Scope*

Because the availability of alternative sites must be considered in light of overall project purposes, it often becomes important to determine the geographic scope within which available alternative sites may be deemed practicable. As noted above, in both *Sylvester* and *National Wildlife Federation,* the Corps deemed it unnecessary to consider off-site locations for the proposed projects in light of accepted project purposes. Likewise, in *Stewart v. Potts*[126] the Corps limited its consideration of alternatives to sites within the applicant city when reviewing a proposal to fill wetlands for a municipal golf course. This limitation on the geographic scope of considered alternatives was deemed appropriate, given that the purpose of the proposal was "to build a golf course within the city of Lake Jackson."[127]

In *Citizens Alliance v. Wynn,*[128] the applicant defined its project purpose as "to construct and operate a thoroughbred horse racing tract in Auburn, Washington, to replace the former Longacres Park in Renton, Washington." Ignoring this tightly drawn geographic description, the Corps redefined the project purpose:

> To develop and operate an economically viable thoroughbred horse racing facility in Western Washington to meet the long-terms needs of Washington's thoroughbred horse racing industry.

Nevertheless, despite this rather significant modification in the description of the geographic scope of the project, no more-favorable alternatives were discovered.

An overly restrictive view of the geographic scope of a proper alternatives analysis resulted in a remand of a Corps-issued permit in *Hough v. Marsh.*[129] The court found that the Corps had not explained why its consideration of alternatives to a wetland site for residential construction was limited to sites within a specified "prime residential" area.[130]

More recently, in *Alliance for Legal Action v. United States Army Corps of Engineers,* a federal district court upheld the Corps's decision to eliminate off-site locations from its analysis of alternatives for a permit to develop an overnight express air cargo hub.[131] The challengers urged the Corps to consider off-site alternatives for the development that would be available to Federal Express, since it would be the lessee of the facility.[132] However, the court concluded that the Corps did not act arbitrarily and capriciously when it limited its focus to alternatives that were available to the permit applicant, the Piedmont Triad Airport Authority (PTAA).[133] As the court noted, the PTAA "could not reasonably obtain, expand or manage any of the rejected airports. . . . Off-site alternatives . . . are neither available to PTAA nor prudent for PTAA to pursue in terms of costs or logistics."[134]

4. *Availability and Other Legal Obstacles to Alternatives*

In a few instances, sites otherwise identified as practicable alternatives may encounter obstacles based on federal, state, or local law. In *James City County v. EPA*,[135] for example, EPA exercised its veto authority, claiming that practicable alternatives existed to a proposed municipal water supply project. The Fourth Circuit rejected EPA's position on this point, finding that alternatives located in another county were not practicable because the county government unequivocally opposed the project.[136] Nor was groundwater a practicable alternative when further withdrawals of groundwater were prohibited by state law.[137] The Corps and the courts have also held that zoning restrictions may render some alternatives impracticable.[138] Similarly, legal restrictions on a government entity's authority to spend money may render some alternatives impracticable.[139] Finally, a suitable, alternative upland site was considered unavailable in *Sierra Club v. U.S. Army Corps of Engineers*, because the owner of this site refused to sell it.[140]

By contrast, in *Alameda Water and Sanitation District v. Reilly*,[141] the court upheld an EPA veto of a Corps-issued permit, even in the face of "very substantial regulatory and legal obstacles" to the construction of the alternative water supply projects in question.[142] These obstacles included the necessity of court consent for the transfer of water rights, a presidential exemption to build under a wilderness area, and agency approval to move an entire town. While the court found it "doubtful that the necessary permits could be obtained,"[143] it upheld EPA's determination under 404(c) to override the Corps's decision to issue a Section 404 permit.

5. *Cost and Economic Viability of Alternatives*

Under a given set of facts, an alternative may not be considered practicable if it is more costly to utilize than the proposed project. The preamble to the Guidelines makes clear, however, that "[t]he mere fact that an alternative may cost somewhat more does not necessarily mean it is not practicable."[144] Cost will render an alternative impracticable when the "alleged alternative is unreasonably expensive to the applicant."[145]

If an alternative "does not provide economically viable opportunities relative to the basic project purpose(s)," it will not be considered by the Corps to be practicable.[146] The costs of an alternative can, of course, render it economically not viable, but viability is a function of other factors as well. To be considered economically viable by the Corps, an alternative must "provide similar logistical opportunities, provide that the project can realistically be operated and/or constructed and result in the applicant's incurring no more than reasonable, additional costs."[147] In making determinations of viability, the Corps generally considers the position of a "typical" applicant, rather than the particular financial circumstances of the applicant.[148] Under this approach, a project's viability is not determined by reference to the applicant's expected profits from the development of wetlands; a project purpose such as "to allow the applicant to realize a profit on its investment" will be rejected as "inappropriate . . . because it suggests that judgments of practicability will incorporate requirements of profitability in circumstances too specific to the particular applicant."[149] Similarly, in the *Plantation Landing Permit Elevation,* the Corps concluded that care must be exercised in defining project purposes by reference to the applicant's desire to minimize costs:

> While the applicant's wish to minimize his costs is obviously a factor which the Corps can consider, that factor alone must not be allowed to control or unduly influence the Corps' definition of project purpose or "practicable alternative," or any other part of the [Section] 404(b)(1) evaluation. . . . This is an important point, because often wetland property may be less expensive to a developer than comparably situated upland property. The Guidelines obviously are not designed to facilitate a shift of development activities from uplands to wetlands, so the fact that an applicant can sometimes reduce his costs by developing wetland property is not a factor which can be used to justify permit issuance under the Guidelines.[150]

There are several cases in which the additional costs of alternatives were deemed sufficiently unreasonable to render them impracticable. In *James City County v. U.S. Environmental Protection Agency,* for example, the court held that an alternative failed the practicability test, in part, because its cost would be more than 50 percent higher than the proposed project.[151]

Cost was also a factor in *Hough v. Marsh.*[152] In this case, applicant wanted to construct two residences and a tennis court on a three-acre parcel abutting a harbor. Based on correspondence from a local real estate agent indicating that the only other available lot in the area was valued at $90,000, the Corps division engineer determined that, because of the cost, there was no practicable alternative. The court rejected this conclusion, stating that the Corps should have considered sites not owned by the applicants, including sites located outside the prime residential area and those that were very highly priced, so long as that price was not unreasonable. It also noted that "[t]he 'exorbitant cost' of [the other residential] parcel, furthermore, by itself carries little weight; although cost is relevant to an assessment of an alternative's 'practicability,' the Corps conducted no examination of whether the price was unreasonably high, whether the defendants could afford it, and whether the wetlands parcel could be sold for a comparable or greater amount."[153]

In *Friends of the Earth v. Hall,* the court found that although "additional cost can constitute a bona fide reason for classifying an alternative as not practicable, . . . significant additional cost can prove determinative, in and of itself, only if the competing alternatives can reasonably be viewed as equivalent with respect to other factors," such as "technological feasibility, potential for environmental harm, ability to be monitored, and potential for remedial action."[154] Cost was considered determinative in *Friends of the Earth v. Hintz,* where the alternative sites would have increased handling costs by over one million dollars per year—a considerable sum in view of overall operating margins.[155]

The court in *Sierra Club v. U.S. Army Corps of Engineers*[156] similarly found that the Corps had engaged in a reasonable analysis in reaching the conclusion that a baseball stadium parking lot could be constructed in a wetlands area. In the eyes of the court, the Corps had adequately examined the possibility of obtaining additional "uplands" for the project from private landowners and appropriately considered that such an alternative would have more than doubled construction costs. This increase in cost rendered upland alternatives impracticable.[157]

6. *Logistics and Technological Feasibility*

Under the Guidelines, the Corps, in addition to considering costs of alternatives, must consider whether proffered alternatives present any logistical problems or are technologically infeasible so as to make such alternatives impracticable.[158] A variety of logistical problems may be considered by the Corps in the course of its alternatives evaluation. For example, in *Sierra Club v. U.S. Army Corps of Engineers,* the court upheld as reasonable the Corps's conclusion that minimizing wetland losses by constructing a multi-level parking deck as an alternative to a proposed surface parking lot was logistically infeasible.[159] Such an alternative would require relocating a pond and access road, and might not be suitable for the site from an engineering point of view.[160] Logistical problems were also cited as a basis for upholding the Corps's conclusion in *Friends of the Earth v. Hintz,* that alternative upland sites for a log sorting facility were impracticable because of the sites' distance from the applicant's primary facility.[161] Another example of logistical problems making an alternative impracticable is provided in *Conservation Law Foundation v. FHA.*[162] There, the court concluded that the Corps had properly ruled out alternatives to a proposed highway project because they "could lead to traffic congestion and safety problems."[163]

Technological infeasibility has rarely been considered in reported Corps permit decisions as a basis for ruling out alternatives to wetland development. Technological problems were invoked in *James City County v. U.S. Environmental Protection Agency*[164] as one basis for overturning an EPA veto of a Corps-issued permit. EPA's veto of the permit was based, in part, on the agency's determination that practicable alternatives to the proposed discharge were available. One such alternative to the applicant's proposed water supply project involved desalinization, which the court rejected as impracticable because the technology needed to implement it was "still experimental."[165]

7. *Comparison of Environmental Impacts*

The alternatives analysis also includes an assessment of the environmental effects of choosing different sites. To be considered practicable, these alternatives must "have less adverse impact on the aquatic ecosystem" and must "not have other significant adverse environmental consequences."[166] This determination is obviously fact specific, and there is very little judicial or regulatory guidance thereon.

a. Scope of Analysis

In comparing the environmental effects of proffered alternatives with those of an applicant's proposal, the Corps may consider a wide range of environmental matters. In *Conservation Law Foundation v. Federal Highway Administration,*[167] the court specifically noted that the Corps could consider all environmental impacts associated with the highway project in deciding whether there was a practicable alternative. Similarly, in *Greater Yellowstone Coalition v. Flowers*[168] and *Fund for Animals, Inc. v. Rice,*[169] courts upheld the Corps's determinations that alternative sites would have resulted in either potentially greater wetland loss or harm to federally or state listed endangered species.

b. The Role of Mitigation

Historically, several Corps districts considered an applicant's mitigation proposals in conducting practicable alternatives analyses, enabling the applicant to "buy down" some or all of the adverse impacts associated with the proposed project and thus making the proposal more likely to be considered the least environmentally damaging practicable alternative.[170] Corps regulations arguably support using mitigation to achieve compliance with the Guidelines.[171] In *Town of Norfolk and Town of Walpole v. U.S. Army Corps of Engineers*,[172] the court upheld this approach, specifically rejecting the proposition that "mitigation measures may not be used to meet the practicable alternatives analysis."[173] It held that "it is reasonable for the Corps to consider, under the practicable alternatives analysis, the functional value of the wetland to be impacted and the mitigation measures proposed to avoid secondary impacts."[174]

The Corps has since rejected this "buy down" approach.[175] In its Memorandum of Agreement (MOA) with EPA on mitigation, the Corps agreed that avoiding wetland impacts through the application of the practicable alternatives requirement "does not include compensatory mitigation."[176] The MOA established the "sequencing" approach to permit evaluation that was noted above. Permit applicants must initially demonstrate that there are no practicable alternatives to the proposed activity that would avoid the adverse environmental effects of filling wetlands. If there is no such alternative, the applicant must minimize the project's adverse impacts on wetland functions and values. Finally, compensatory mitigation is required for any unavoidable loss of aquatic resources. The court in *Alameda Water and Sanitation District v. Reilly*[177] found this sequencing approach to be a "reasonable" exercise of the agency's discretion.

IV. Conclusion

The practicable alternatives analysis is indeed a linchpin of the wetlands permitting process. There is little doubt that if a project is not water dependent, every effort must be made to locate a viable alternative outside the aquatic ecosystem. Indeed, even if the activity is water dependent, such as a water delivery or storage project, minimization of the wetland disturbance is a must.

It is best to involve the local Corps office early and often in the analysis process. This is especially true if the project is significant in scope. This will allow for a dialogue on the concept of "project purpose" and the identification of a universe of possible alternatives that could meet that purpose while avoiding other significant environmental impacts.

Before embarking upon the alternatives analysis portion of the permitting effort, a thoughtful consideration of the following questions may serve as a "reality check."

- What is the purpose of this project?
- Is it truly a water-dependent project?
- What will be the extent of wetland impacts under the project purpose as currently defined?
- Are there any available practicable alternatives?
- Is an alternative site available?
- What costs are associated with the alternative site?
- Are there significant technical or logistical constraints associated with the alternative site?
- What are the "other environmental impacts" associated with the alternative site?

Notes

1. 33 U.S.C. § 1344(a) (2000). EPA may, however, "veto" a permit issued by the Corps. *Id.* § 1344(c). This authority is discussed in Chapter 9 of this book.

2. *See* 33 U.S.C. § 1344(b).

3. *See* Bersani v. Robichaud, 850 F.2d 36, 39–40 (2d Cir. 1988), *cert. denied,* 489 U.S. 1089 (1989).

4. *See* 33 C.F.R. § 323.6 (2004). Early case law suggested that the "no practicable alternatives" requirement of the Guidelines was simply one factor to be considered in a general balancing of costs and benefits under the Corps's public interest review. *See* 1902 Atlantic Ltd. v. Hudson, 574 F. Supp. 1381, 1389 (E.D. Va. 1983). Later cases have made clear that the requirement must be satisfied before the Corps may issue a permit. *See, e.g., Bersani v. Robichaud, supra.*

5. 40 C.F.R. § 230.10(a).

6. 40 C.F.R. § 230.10(b).

7. 40 C.F.R. § 230.10(c).

8. 40 C.F.R. § 230.10(d).

9. 40 C.F.R. § 230.10(a) (1996).

10. *See* Oliver A. Houck, *Hard Choices: The Analysis of Alternatives under Section 404 of the Clean Water Act and Similar Environmental Laws,* 60 U. COLO. L. REV. 773, 777 (1989).

11. 40 C.F.R. § 230.10(a).

12. 33 C.F.R. § 320.4(a)(2)(ii); *see also* 33 C.F.R. pt. 325, App. B, § 9.b(5) (National Environmental Policy Act's alternatives analysis for Corps activities).

13. 33 C.F.R. § 320.4(a)(1).

14. 40 C.F.R. § 230.1(c); *see* Army Corps of Engineers, Regulatory Guidance Letter 93-02, Guidance on Flexibility of the 404(b)(1) Guidelines and Mitigation Banking (Aug. 23, 1993), *reprinted in* 62 Fed. Reg. 31,497 (June 9, 1997) [here-

inafter RGL 93-02], *available at* http://www.usace.army.mil/inet/functions/cw/cecwo/reg/rgls/rgl93-02.htm. Although RGL 93-02 expired in 1998, the Corps maintains that "unless superseded by specific provisions of subsequently issued regulations or RGLs, the guidance provided in RGLs generally remains valid after its expiration date." 65 Fed. Reg. 12,518 (Mar. 9, 2000).

15. 40 C.F.R. § 230.3(q–l) (1996); *see* Louisiana Wildlife Federation v. York, 761 F.2d 1044, 1046 (5th Cir. 1985).

16. 40 C.F.R. § 230.1(d).

17. *Louisiana Wildlife Federation,* 761 F.2d at 1046–47.

18. 40 C.F.R. § 230.10(a)(1).

19. 40 C.F.R. §§ 230.3(q) and 230.10(a)(2).

20. 40 C.F.R. § 230.10(a)(2).

21. 40 C.F.R. § 230.10(a).

22. 40 C.F.R. § 230.10(a)(3).

23. *Id.*

24. *Id.; see* Utahns for Better Transportation v. U.S. Dept. of Transportation, 305 F.3d 1152, 1163, 1187 (10th Cir. 2002).

25. 40 C.F.R. § 230.5(c).

26. This sequencing of the Guidelines' requirement was clarified in a Memorandum of Agreement between the Environmental Protection Agency and the Department of the Army concerning the Determination of Mitigation under the Clean Water Act Section 404(b)(1) Guidelines 3 (Feb. 6, 1990) [hereinafter Mitigation MOA], *available at* http://www.usace.army.mil/inet/functions/cw/cecwo/reg/moafe90.htm; *see also* Regulatory Guidance Letter 95-01, Guidance on Individual Permit Flexibility for Small Landowners, 65 Fed. Reg. 12,518, 12,518–19 (Mar. 9, 2000), *available at* http://www.usace.army.mil/inet/functions/cw/cecwo/reg/rgls/rgl95-01.htm. The Corps application of this approach in a particular case is approved and discussed in Fund for Animals, Inc. v. Rice, 85 F.3d 535, 542–44 (11th Cir. 1996).

27. Hough v. Marsh, 557 F. Supp. 74, 82 (D. Mass. 1982).

28. RGL 93-02, *supra* note 14.

29. *Id.*

30. *Id.*

31. 40 C.F.R. § 230.10.

32. 40 C.F.R. § 230.6(a).

33. 40 C.F.R. § 230.6(b); *see* Greater Yellowstone Coalition v. Flowers, 359 F.3d 1257, 1270 (10th Cir. 2004).

34. *Id.*

35. 968 F.2d 1438 (1st Cir. 1992).

36. *Id.* at 1447; *see also Greater Yellowstone Coalition,* 359 F.3d at 1270; Stewart v. Potts, 996 F. Supp. 668, 678 (S.D. Tex. 1998) ("the degree of documentation required to support a section 404 permitting decision must correspond to the degree of risk the proposed project poses to the aquatic environment"); Northwest Environmental Defense Center v. Wood, 947 F. Supp. 1371, 1376–77 (D. Ore. 1996), *affd.* 97 F.3d 1460 (9th Cir. 1996) ("The regulations contemplate a certain

degree of flexibility in an agency's application of the practicable alternatives test under certain circumstances.").

37. *Town of Norfolk,* 968 F.2d at 1447–48. *See also infra* note 113 (discussing reliance on NEPA documents). While the Corps *may* rely on analyses performed by other agencies in applying the practicable alternatives analysis, the Corps is entitled to rely on its own experts in conducting the analysis "even when their opinions conflict with those of other federal agencies, as long as [the Corps's] decisions are not arbitrary and capricious." *See Greater Yellowstone Coalition,* 359 F.3d at 1271, n.14.

38. RGL 93-02, *supra* note 14; *see Town of Norfolk,* 968 F.2d at 1447 (upholding Corps conclusion that impacts of discharge on 600-square-foot artificial wetland were "negligible").

39. Mitigation MOA, *supra* note 26, at 3.

40. RGL 93-02, *supra* note 14.

41. *See Greater Yellowstone Coalition,* 359 F.3d at 1271.

42. *Id.* at 1269–70.

43. *Id.* at 1271.

44. *Id.*

45. *Id.*

46. Memorandum from Patrick J. Kelly, Director of Civil Works, to Commander, U.S. Army Corps of Engineers, New Orleans District, Permit Elevation, Plantation Landing Resort, Inc. 3 (Apr. 21, 1989) [hereinafter Plantation Landing Elevation]. In the past, the Corps distinguished "basic project purpose" from "overall project purpose." The former is defined as the fundamental, essential purpose of the proposal, and can be used to determine if the project is water dependent. The latter, which is the focus of the analysis under the guidelines, is determined through a further refinement of the basic purpose so as to describe the applicant's specific project purpose.

47. 40 C.F.R. § 230.10(a)(2).

48. "The cumulative destruction of our nation's wetlands that would result if developers were permitted to artificially constrain the Corps' alternatives analysis by defining the projects' purpose in an overly narrow manner would frustrate the statute and its accompanying regulatory scheme." National Wildlife Federation v. Whistler, 27 F.3d 1341, 1346 (8th Cir. 1994).

49. *See, e.g., id.* at 1345 ("the project's purpose is to provide boat access to the Missouri River from lots [the applicant] proposes to develop adjacent to the project area").

50. *See* Shoreline Associates v. Marsh, 555 F. Supp. 169, 179 (D. Md. 1983) ("The primary aspect of the proposed project is the construction of a townhouse community, not the construction of a boat storage facility and launch which are incidental to it.").

51. *See, e.g.,* Plantation Landing Elevation, *supra* note 46, at 4 (describing applicant's proposal for a "fully-integrated, waterfront, contiguous water-oriented recreational complex" as a asserting a "project purpose in such a way as to preclude the existence of practicable alternatives").

52. *See* William L. Want, The Law of Wetlands Regulation, § 6.21 (2004).

53. 603 F. Supp. 518 (W.D. La. 1984), *aff'd in part, vacated in part, and remanded,* 761 F.2d 1044 (5th Cir. 1985).

54. *Id.* at 1048 (footnote omitted); *see* City of Angoon v. Hodel, 803 F.2d 1016, 1021 (9th Cir. 1986) ("[W]hen the purpose is to accomplish one thing, it makes no sense to consider the alternative ways by which another thing might be achieved"; court rejected district court definition of purpose as too much of a "broad social interest" rather than an "exclusive 'purpose and need'"). *But see* Korteweg v. United States Army Corps of Engineers, 650 F. Supp. 603, 605 (D. Conn. 1986) (court afforded little deference to the applicant's asserted need for waterfront houses, finding that there is little social redemption gained by building such housing for the affluent); Deltona Corp. v. Alexander, 504 F. Supp. 1280, 1283 (M.D. Fla. 1981) (court rejected applicant's claim that desire to build a waterfront resort project was water dependent as the basic purpose was "housing," which need not be located near water or in a wetland area).

55. *Louisiana Wildlife Federation,* 761 F.2d at 1047. The Corps's position was, at least in part, undoubtedly a reaction to the Reagan-era drive to ease regulatory burdens. This philosophical bent is described in GAO/RCED-88-110, U.S. General Accounting Office, The Corps of Engineers' Administration of the Section 404 Program 26 (1988). For a discussion of the political history of the alternatives analysis, see Houck, *supra* note 10, at 780–84; Note (William K. McGreevey), *A Public Availability Approach to Section 404(b)(1) Alternatives Analysis: A Practical Definition for Practicable Alternatives,* 59 Geo. Wash. L. Rev. 379, 403 (1991).

56. Memorandum from H. J. Hatch, Director of Civil Works, to Division Commanders, "Application of 404(b)(1) Guidelines—Louisiana Wildlife Federation v. York, Civ. No. 84-4699 (May 31, 1985)"(Apr. 22, 1986).

57. Houck, *supra* note 10, at 782 (quoting Memorandum from W. Jack Hill, Jr., Chief of Construction—Operations Division, Lower Mississippi Valley District, U.S. Army Corps of Engineers, to Commander, New Orleans District (Mar. 26, 1986)).

58. *See* Van Abbema v. Fornell, 807 F.2d 633, 638 (7th Cir. 1986) (court found that the Corps did not sufficiently evaluate overall public interests as compared to interests of the applicant).

59. Plantation Landing Elevation, *supra* note 46.

60. *Id.* at 5–6 (emphasis in original).

61. Plantation Landing Elevation, *supra* note 46, at 8 (emphasis in original). The decision goes on to provide specific guidance to the New Orleans District in determining what the "basic purpose" of the project should be for purposes of implementing the practicable alternatives requirement of the Guidelines. *See id.* at 10–12.

62. *Id.* at 8. *See also* National Wildlife Fed'n. v. Whistler, 27 F.3d 1341, 1346 (8th Cir. 1994) (noting that the Corps should not permit developers to "artificially constrain the Corps' alternatives analysis by defining the projects' purposes in an overly narrow manner.")

63. Memorandum of Patrick J. Kelly, Director of Civil Works, to Commander, U.S. Army Corps of Engineers, New York District, Permit Elevation, Hartz Mountain Development Corporation 3–6 (Aug. 17, 1989) [hereinafter Hartz Mountain Elevation].

64. Memorandum from Patrick J. Kelly, Director of Civil Works, to Commander, U.S. Army Corps of Engineers, Jacksonville District, Permit Elevation, Old Cutler Bay Associates 6–8 (Sept. 13, 1990) [hereinafter Old Cutler Bay Elevation].

65. Memorandum from Patrick J. Kelly, Director of Civil Works to Commander, U.S. Army Corps of Engineers, Charleston District, Permit Elevation, Twisted Oaks Joint Venture 4–9 (March 15, 1991) [hereinafter Twisted Oaks Elevation].

66. Alameda Water and Sanitation District v. Reilly, 930 F. Supp. 486, 992 (D. Colo. 1996).

67. *Id.; see* Bersani v. U.S. Environmental Protection Agency, 674 F. Supp. 405, 415 (N.D.N.Y. 1987), *aff'd sub nom.* Robichaud v. U.S. Environmental Protection Agency, 850 F.2d 36 (2d Cir. 1988) ("Since an applicant presumably usually selects the site which is best from his perspective, alternatives are almost by definition 'second best'; to eliminate non-wetland sites on that basis would be inappropriate."). *Cf.* Alliance for Legal Action v. United States Army Corps of Engineers, 314 F. Supp. 2d 534, 549 (M.D. N.C. 2004) ("If the applicant's purpose is legitimate, then the Corps is not entitled to reject the purpose and substitute for it one it deems more appropriate") (citing Sylvester v. U.S. Army Corps of Engineers, 882 F.2d 407, 409 (9th Cir. 1989)); Stewart v. Potts, 996 F. Supp. 668, 675–76 (S.D. Tex. 1988) (in considering practicable alternatives, "the Corps has an affirmative duty to accord weight to the objectives of the applicant") (citing *Louisiana Wildlife Federation*, 761 F.2d at 1048).

68. 53 Fed. Reg. 3136 (Feb. 3, 1988), *incorporated at* 33 C.F.R. 325, app. B(9)(c)(4). *See also* RGL 88-13, National Environmental Policy Act (NEPA) Scope of Analysis and Alternatives (Nov. 3, 1988) ("while the Corps should recognize the applicant's purpose and need, and evaluate those alternatives available to the applicant that meet his purpose and need, it is sometimes necessary, under NEPA, to analyze alternatives beyond the applicant's capability in order to make an informed public interest decision"), *available at* http://www.usace.army.mil/inet/functions/cw/cecwo/reg/rgls/rgl88-13.htm; Department of the Army, Memorandum for Commander, South Pacific Division (Oct. 21, 1992) (practicable alternative must be reasonable and available to the applicant or from the applicant's perspective as determined by the Corps).

69. 882 F.2d 407 (9th Cir. 1989).

70. *Id.* at 408.

71. *Id.* at 409.

72. *Id.; see Stewart*, 996 F. Supp. at 675–76 (S.D. Tex. 1988) (upholding Corps decision to restrict alternatives analysis to sites within applicant City of Lake Jackson, because "the permittee's purpose was to build a golf course within the City of Lake Jackson").

73. *Sylvester*, 882 F.2d at 409.

74. *Id.* at 409–10.

75. 27 F.3d 1341 (8th Cir. 1994).

76. *Id.* at 1343.

77. *Id.* at 1345–46.

78. *Id.* at 1345 (quoting *Sylvester,* 882 F.2d at 410).

79. 14 ENVTL. L. REP. 20,724 (D.N.J. 1983).

80. *Id.* at 20,731.

81. *Id.*

82. *Id.*

83. Plantation Landing Elevation, *supra* note 46, at 11–12.

84. *Id.* at 12.

85. *See id.* The Corps's failure to disaggregate a proposed project into smaller component parts resulted in a remand in Hough v. Marsh, 557 F. Supp. 74 (D. Mass. 1982). In that case, the Corps granted a permit to fill wetlands for the purpose of constructing two residences and a tennis court, concluding that no practicable alternatives were available. In remanding, the court found that alternatives had not been sufficiently considered, in part because neither the Corps nor the applicants "explained the need to construct their respective dwellings side-by-side." *Id.*

86. 40 C.F.R. § 230.10(a)(3).

87. *See Whistler,* 27 F.3d at 1344 (quoting Buttrey v. United States, 690 F.2d 1170, 1180 (5th Cir. 1982)).

88. *Id.* (quoting Bersani v. Robichaud, 850 F.2d 36, 44 (2d Cir. 1988), *cert. denied,* 489 U.S. 1089 (1989)).

89. *Hough,* 557 F. Supp. at 83; *see* Conservation Law Foundation v. Federal Highway Admin., 827 F. Supp. 871, 886 (D. R.I. 1993) (quoting *Louisiana Wildlife Federation,* 603 F. Supp. 518, 527, *aff'd in part and vacated in part,* 761 F.2d 1044 (5th Cir. 1985)). Examples of cases in which the Corps has issued permits for non–water dependent projects include Greater Yellowstone Coalition v. Flowers, 359 F.3d 1257 (10th Cir. 2004) (golf course); Fund for Animals v. Rice, 85 F.3d 535 (11th Cir. 1996) (municipal landfill); *Conservation Law Foundation* (highway); Sylvester v. U.S. Army Corps of Engineers, 882 F.2d 407 (9th Cir. 1989) (golf course); Alliance for Legal Action v. United States Army Corps of Engineers, 314 F. Supp. 2d 534 (M.D. N.C. 2004) (overnight express air cargo hub); Northwest Environmental Defense Center v. Wood, 947 F. Supp. 1371 (D. Ore. 1996) (fabrication plant); Sierra Club v. U.S. Army Corps of Engineers, 935 F. Supp. 1556 (S.D. Ala. 1996) (stadium); Citizens Alliance to Protect Our Wetlands v. Wynn, 908 F. Supp. 825 (W.D. Wash. 1995) (horse racing facility).

90. RGL 92-02, Water Dependency and Cranberry Production, 57 Fed. Reg. 32,523 (1992).

91. *See* Alameda Water & Sanitation District v. Reilly, 930 F. Supp. 486 (D. Colo. 1996) (EPA veto of water-dependent project due in part to less damaging alternatives).

92. EPA previously considered but rejected the establishment of a "irrebuttable presumption" against discharges to wetlands or other special aquatic sites. 45 Fed. Reg. 85,338–39 (1980).

93. 40 C.F.R. § 230.10(a)(3).

94. *See, e.g.*, The City of Shoreacres v. Waterworth, 2004 U.S. Dist. LEXIS 13354 (S.D. Tex. 2004) (marine terminal); Alameda Water & Sanitation District v. Browner, 9 F.3d 88 (10th Cir. 1993) (water supply); James City County v. EPA, 955 F.2d 54 (4th Cir. 1992) (water supply); The Water Works & Sewer Board of the City of Birmingham v. U.S. Army Corps of Engineers, 983 F. Supp. 1052 (N.D. Ala. 1997) (water supply); Fox Bay Partners v. U.S. Army Corps of Engineers, 831 F. Supp. 605 (N.D. Ill. 1993) (commercial marina).

95. *See, e.g.*, Smereka v. Glass, 34 Envtl. Rep. Cas. (BNA) 1353 (6th Cir. 1991) (housing); Sylvester v. U.S. Army Corps of Engineers, 882 F.2d 407 (9th Cir. 1989) (golf course); Bersani v. Robichaud, 850 F.2d 36 (2d Cir. 1988) (shopping mall); Citizens to Protect Our Wetlands v. Wynn, 908 F. Supp. 825 (W.D. Wash. 1995) (horse racing facility); Northwest Environmental Defense Center v. Wood, 947 F. Supp. 1371 (D. Ore. 1996) (manufacturing plant).

96. 555 F. Supp. 169 (D. Md. 1983) *aff'd*, 725 F.2d 677 (4th Cir. 1984).

97. *Id.* at 179.

98. *Id.*

99. 650 F. Supp. 603, 606 (D. Conn. 1986).

100. *Id.* at 605.

101. *See* Deltona Corp. v. Alexander, 504 F. Supp. 1280, 1283 (M.D. Fla. 1981).

102. 27 F.3d 1341 (8th Cir. 1994).

103. *Id.* at 1343.

104. *Id.* at 1346.

105. *Id.*

106. 800 F.2d 822 (9th Cir. 1986).

107. *Id.* at 824.

108. *Id.* at 832.

109. *Id.*

110. Plantation Landing Elevation, *supra* note 46, at 11.

111. *Id.* at 12.

112. 40 C.F.R. § 230.10(a)(2).

113. 40 C.F.R. § 230.10(a)(4) provides:

> For actions subject to NEPA, where the Corps of Engineers is the permitting agency, the analysis of alternatives required for NEPA environmental documents, including supplemental Corps NEPA documents, will in most cases provide the information for the evaluation of alternatives under these Guidelines. On occasion, these NEPA documents may address a broader range of alternatives than required to be considered under this paragraph or may not have considered the alternatives in sufficient detail to respond to the requirements of these Guidelines. In the latter case, it may be necessary to supplement these NEPA documents with this additional information.

See Utahns for Better Transportation, 305 F.3d at 1163; *Alliance for Legal Action*, 314 F. Supp. 2d 534.

In addition, 40 C.F.R. § 230.10(a)(5) provides:

> To the extent that practicable alternatives have been identified and evaluated under a Coastal Zone Management program, a Section 208 program, or other planning process, such evaluation shall be considered by the permitting authority as part of the consideration of alternatives under the Guidelines. Where such evaluation is less complete than that contemplated under this subsection, it must be supplemented accordingly.

In Town of Norfolk v. U.S. Army Corps of Engineers, 968 F.2d 1438, 1447–48 (1st Cir. 1992), the court concluded that the Corps, in conducting its practicable alternatives analysis, could reasonably rely on alternative analyses prepared by EPA and a state agency. *See* Sierra Club v. U.S. Army Corps of Engineers, 935 F. Supp. 1556, 1572–73 (S.D. Ala. 1996) (discussing relationship between NEPA's and Guidelines' alternatives requirements).

Although the Corps may rely on analyses provided by other agencies, it has a duty to verify the accuracy of the information supplied by an applicant. *See Utahns for Better Transportation,* 305 F.3d at 1165.

114. *See Northwest Environmental Defense Center,* 947 F. Supp. at 1377–79 (discussing applicant's submission of alternatives analysis).

115. 40 C.F.R. § 230.12(a)(3)(iv); *see Utahns for Better Transportation,* 305 F.3d at 1187:

> The burden of proof to demonstrate compliance with the § 404(b) permit Guidelines rests with the applicant; where insufficient information is provided to determine compliance, the Guidelines require that no permit be issued. . . . Issuance of the permit with insufficient information concerning [alternatives] was arbitrary and capricious.

116. *See* RGL 93-02, *supra* note 14.

117. *See, e.g.,* Hartz Mountain Elevation, *supra* note 63, at 4, 6.

118. *See* Carabell v. U.S. Army Corps of Engineers, 257 F. Supp. 2d 917, 934 (E.D. Mich. 2003) (upholding permit denial for a non–water dependent project where applicant failed to address practicable alternatives).

119. 40 C.F.R. § 230.10(a)(2).

120. 809 F. Supp. 704, 713 (D. Minn. 1992).

121. *Id.*

122. RGL 95-01, 65 Fed. Reg. at 12,518–19.

123. *Id.*

124. 850 F.2d 36 (2nd Cir. 1988), *cert denied,* 489 U.S. 1089 (1989).

125. The government advanced the market entry theory in Smereka v. Glass, 34 Envtl. Rep. Cas. (BNA) 1353 (6th Cir. 1991), but the court found it unnecessary to address the issue, concluding that Corps could properly deny the permit "based on practicable alternatives which existed at the time of . . . application."

126. 996 F. Supp. 668 (S.D. Tex. 1998).

127. *Id.* at 675.

128. 908 F. Supp. 825 (W.D. Wash. 1995).

129. 557 F. Supp. 74 (D. Mass. 1982).
130. *Id.* at 84.
131. 314 F. Supp. 2d 534 (M.D. N.C. 2004).
132. *Id.* at 544.
133. *Id.* at 546.
134. *Id.*
135. 955 F.2d 54 (4th Cir. 1992).
136. *Id.* at 259–60.
137. *Id.* at 260.
138. *See* Borough of Ridgefield v. U.S. Army Corps of Engineers, 20 ENVTL. L. REP. 21,387 (D.N.J. 1990); National Audubon Society v. Hartz Mountain Development Corp., 14 ENVTL. L. REP. 20,724 (D.N.J. 1983).
139. *See* The City of Shoreacres v. Waterworth, 2004 U.S. Dist. LEXIS 13354 (S.D. Tex. 2004) (off-site property was not an available alternative for the Port of Houston Authority's proposed marine terminal, since the Port could not use its eminent domain power to condemn the property and could not spend the proceeds of bond revenues to purchase the property).
140. 935 F. Supp. 1556, 1577–78 (S.D. Ala. 1996).
141. 930 F. Supp. 486 (D. Colo. 1996).
142. *Id.* at 492.
143. *Id.* at 492.
144. 45 Fed. Reg. 85,336, 85,339 (Dec. 24, 1980). *See also* Bahia Park, S.E. v. United States of America, 286 F. Supp. 2d 201, 207 (D. P.R. 2003).
145. 45 Fed. Reg. at 85,343.
146. Old Cutler Bay Elevation, *supra* note 64, at 8.
147. *Id.* at 8–9.
148. *Id.*
149. Twisted Oaks Elevation, *supra* note 65, at 6.
150. Plantation Landing Elevation, *supra* note 46, at 8–9.
151. 955 F.2d 254, 259–60 (4th Cir. 1992).
152. 557 F. Supp. 14 (D. Mass. 1982).
153. *Id.* at 84.
154. 693 F. Supp. 904, 946–47 (W.D. Wash. 1988).
155. 800 F.2d 822, 833–34 (9th Cir. 1986).
156. 935 F. Supp. 1556 (S.D. Ala. 1996).
157. *Id.* at 1575–76.
158. 40 C.F.R. § 230.10(a)(2).
159. 935 F. Supp. 1556, 1575 (S.D. Ala. 1996).
160. *Id.*
161. Friends of the Earth v. Hintz, 800 F.2d 822, 833–34 (9th Cir. 1986).
162. 24 F.3d 1465 (1st Cir. 1994).
163. *Id.* at 1476.
164. 955 F.2d 254 (4th Cir. 1991).
165. *Id.* at 260.
166. 40 C.F.R. § 230.10(a).

167. 827 F. Supp. 871 (D. R.I. 1993), *aff'd* 24 F.3d 1465 (1st Cir. 1994).

168. 359 F.3d 1257 (10th Cir. 2004).

169. 85 F.3d 535, 543–44 (11th Cir. 1996).

170. *See, e.g.,* Twisted Oaks Elevation, *supra* note 65, at 4 (describing the Charleston District's "acceptance of mitigation to 'buy down' the Guidelines' requirement . . . that, generally speaking, the Corps can only permit the least environmentally damaging practicable alternative"); *see generally* Royal C. Gardner, *The Army-EPA Mitigation Agreement: No Retreat from Wetlands Protection,* 20 ENVTL. L. REP. 10,337(Aug. 1990).

171. *See* 33 C.F.R. §§ 320.4(r), 325.4(a); *see also* 51 Fed. Reg. 41,206, 41,208 (Nov. 13, 1986) ("Mitigation considerations occur throughout the permit application review process.").

172. 968 F.2d 1438 (1st Cir. 1992).

173. *Id.* at 1449.

174. *Id.*

175. Twisted Oaks Elevation, *supra* note 65, at 5.

176. Mitigation MOA, *supra* note 26, at 3 n.4. *Cf.* 33 C.F.R. § 330, app. A, subsec. C.13(d) (for some nationwide permits, "the District Engineer will consider any optional mitigation the applicant has included in the proposal in determining whether the net adverse environmental effect of the proposed work are minimal"); 56 Fed. Reg. 59,145 (1991); EPA Guidance on 404(b)(1) Alternative Analysis, EPA Region IX (Apr. 11, 1986) (mitigation buy-down concept is still a part of the NWP program).

177. *Alameda Water & Sanitation District,* 930 F. Supp. at 492.

CHAPTER 8

Mitigation

ROYAL C. GARDNER

I. Introduction/Scope

The Oxford English Dictionary defines mitigation as the "alleviation of anything painful, oppressive, or calamitous."[1] In the context of the federal regulation of wetlands, mitigation is required to alleviate harm to the aquatic environment by activities subject to the Section 404 program and is regarded as "a central premise of Federal wetland regulatory programs."[2] Mitigation is usually reduced to three core elements: avoidance, minimization, and compensation. Avoidance refers to the requirement that a Section 404 permit applicant search for less environmentally damaging practicable alternatives, a topic described briefly below and in greater detail in Chapter 7. Having satisfied this requirement, the applicant must then agree to minimize unavoidable adverse impacts to wetlands. Finally, the permit applicant must compensate for any remaining wetland impacts by restoring a former wetland area, enhancing degraded wetlands, creating new wetlands, or preserving existing wetlands.

This chapter will explain the sources of the mitigation requirements (statute, regulations, and guidance documents) and examine agency roles and responsibilities. It will review the concepts of avoidance, minimization, and compensation and discuss the relationship of these three core elements to one another and how they are generally applied in a sequential fashion. The chapter will then consider the importance of mitigation to the goal of no net loss of wetland functions and values, the use of mitigation in the nationwide permit program, the role of mitigation banking and in-lieu-fee arrangements, and the enforcement of mitigation conditions. The chapter concludes with a discussion of the relationship between wetland mitigation and the National Environmental Policy Act (NEPA).

II. Sources of Mitigation Requirements

A. Statutory Provisions

Section 404 of the Clean Water Act (CWA) does not expressly impose mitigation requirements on permit applicants. Section 404(b)(1) does, however, provide authority for the U.S. Environmental Protection Agency (EPA) to promulgate guidelines, in conjunction with the United States Army Corps of Engineers (Corps), to regulate the discharge of dredged or fill material into waters of the United States, including wetlands.[3]

The Section 404(b)(1) Guidelines (which are binding regulations) must "be based on criteria comparable to the criteria applicable" to ocean dumping permits and listed in Section 403(c) of the Clean Water Act.[4] The Section 403(c) criteria mandate that permits for marine discharges be issued only after consideration of "other possible locations and methods of disposal . . . including land-based alternatives"[5] and "the effect of the disposal at varying rates, of particular volumes and concentrations of pollutants."[6] Thus, by reference to the Section 403(c) ocean dumping criteria, Section 404(b)(1) implicitly requires that permits be issued only after the practicability of avoiding and minimizing wetland impacts is considered.

B. Regulatory Provisions

Each of the two agencies responsible for administering the Section 404 program has regulations pertaining to mitigation. The Section 404(b)(1) Guidelines, promulgated by EPA, include the more significant mitigation requirements and are at 40 C.F.R. Part 230. The Corps has a separate mitigation regulation, a remnant of its older permit program under the Rivers and Harbors Act.[7] This regulation is at 33 C.F.R. § 320.4(r).

1. Section 404(b)(1) Guidelines

The Section 404(b)(1) Guidelines are binding regulations having the force of law. Although the Guidelines do not employ the term "mitigation," they provide a regulatory basis for requiring permit applicants to avoid and minimize the adverse wetland impacts of their proposed activities and, where appropriate, to provide compensation for any remaining impacts. The Guidelines discuss avoidance and the alternatives analysis in 40 C.F.R. § 230.10(a), and minimization of potential impacts is required by 40 C.F.R. § 230.10(d). Subpart H of the Guidelines (40 C.F.R. §§ 230.70–.77) further explains measures that can minimize impacts. In the Guidelines, compensatory mitigation is alluded to within the framework of minimization at 40 C.F.R. § 230.75(d), which provides that applicants may be required to develop or restore habitat to compensate for damage that their proposed activities will cause to plants and animals.

2. *Corps Regulations*

The Corps regulates a number of activities in the waters of the United States, and in addition to its Clean Water Act responsibilities, the Corps issues permits under the Rivers and Harbors Act and the Marine Protection, Research, and Sanctuaries Act.[8] The Corps regulation governing mitigation, which is applicable to all these permit programs, neither substitutes for nor trumps the Section 404(b)(1) Guidelines' mitigation requirements for Section 404 permits.[9] Instead, the Corps regulation provides authority to impose mitigation conditions beyond those mandated by the Guidelines, although it is rarely invoked for that purpose.

C. Guidance Documents

The clearest explanation of mitigation requirements is found in guidance documents. These documents can appear in various forms, such as regulatory guidance letters (issued by the Corps), memoranda of agreement (signed by the Corps, EPA, and occasionally other agencies), and joint memoranda to the field (issued by the Corps and EPA). The purpose of the guidance documents is to provide instruction to field personnel who make case-by-case mitigation determinations in the process of considering applications for permits.

The guidance documents do not modify regulatory mitigation requirements; they are designed to interpret the requirements or to fill in the interstices of the regulations. Because the Corps and EPA characterize their guidance documents as interpretive rules or general statements of policy, rather than legislative rules, guidance documents are not published in the Code of Federal Regulations. The Corps makes compilations of current guidance available on its Regulatory Program home page.[10]

III. Agency Roles and Responsibilities

The Corps is responsible for making final Section 404 permit decisions, including the decision to impose mitigation conditions.[11] In making mitigation determinations, the Corps views itself as an objective project manager. It is neither an opponent nor an advocate for the proposed project. Before reaching a decision, the Corps must consider information regarding mitigation that is provided by the permit applicant, federal resource agencies—principally, EPA, U.S. Fish and Wildlife Service (FWS), and National Marine Fisheries Service (NMFS)—state and local resource agencies, and the interested public, including environmental organizations.

Ordinarily, any decision concerning mitigation is made at the Corps district level. Under a series of memoranda of agreement (MOAs), EPA, FWS, or NMFS may seek to "elevate" review of the permit application to higher-level Corps officials when the agency believes that a permit will result in unacceptable impacts to an aquatic resource of national importance.[12] These MOAs allow the resource agencies to request Corps headquarters or the Office of the Assistant Secretary of the Army (Civil Works) to render a final permit decision. The final decision may include greater mitigation requirements, as was the case in the Old Cutler Bay elevation, which involved a Jack Nicklaus signature golf course.[13]

If EPA is unsatisfied with a Corps decision to issue a permit and concludes that the discharge will result in unacceptable adverse impacts to the aquatic ecosystem, EPA has the authority under Section 404(c) of the Clean Water Act to veto the Corps decision.[14] In practice, however, EPA rarely exercises its Section 404(c) authority. EPA's veto authority is discussed in Chapter 9.

IV. Avoidance

Initially, it seems counterintuitive to classify avoidance as a form of mitigation. If one avoids wetland impacts altogether, no harm is caused and, hence, mitigation (either minimization or compensation) is not required. Nevertheless, the Corps and EPA consider avoidance an integral part of wetland mitigation requirements.[15]

The principal thrust of avoidance is the search for the least environmentally damaging practicable alternative. The Section 404(b)(1) Guidelines require the permit applicant to demonstrate that there is no "practicable alternative to the proposed discharge which would have less adverse impact on the aquatic ecosystem."[16] This requirement is discussed in Chapter 7.

V. Minimization

If wetland impacts are unavoidable, a permit applicant must take appropriate and practicable steps to minimize them.[17] Subpart H of the Section 404(b)(1) Guidelines provides an illustrative list of possible actions to minimize adverse wetland effects:

- Actions concerning the discharge's location (e.g., confining the discharge to minimize the smothering of organisms or selecting a site that has been previously used as a dredged material discharge area);[18]
- Actions concerning the discharged material itself;[19]
- Actions controlling the material after discharge (e.g., using cover vegetation to prevent erosion or using lined containment areas to prevent leaching);[20]
- Actions affecting the method of dispersion (e.g., using silt screens to confine turbidity and suspended particulates);[21]
- Actions related to technology (e.g., using mats under heavy equipment to reduce wetland surface compaction and rutting);[22]
- Actions affecting plant and animal populations (e.g., timing discharges to avoid spawning, migration, or nesting seasons)[23]

In most mitigation determinations, the Corps (after discussion with the permit applicant, resource agencies, and other interested parties) decides whether such actions are appropriate in light of impacts to wetland functions and values and are practicable considering the project's overall purpose.

VI. Compensatory Mitigation

If wetland impacts remain after avoidance and minimization, the permit applicant will be called upon to provide appropriate and practicable compensatory mitigation.[24] Compensatory mitigation consists primarily of activities designed to restore, enhance, create, or preserve wetland functions. Recently, however, the Corps has issued guidance that adopts a watershed approach, which focuses on entire water systems and their constituent parts.[25] As part of this more holistic approach, the Corps has indicated that, in certain limited circumstances, mitigation credits may be available for establishing and maintaining vegetated buffers and including upland areas within mitigation projects.[26] Significant compensatory mitigation issues include agency preferences regarding types of compensation (e.g., restoration versus creation), mitigation location (on-site or off-site), wetland functions (in-kind or out-of-kind), and the use of in-lieu payments (cash donations as mitigation).

A. Restoration, Enhancement, Creation, and Preservation

Restoration of historic wetland areas is the preferred compensatory mitigation alternative. In a 1990 MOA, the Corps and EPA identified restoration as "the first option" to be considered because the likelihood of success in such projects is greater than in other forms of compensatory mitigation.[27] Moreover, restoration activities in a former wetland site reduce the likelihood that environmentally significant uplands will be affected.[28]

Restoration may include re-establishment of former wetlands or rehabilitation of degraded wetlands or both.[29] A common restoration project targets for improvement an area in agricultural use where the hydrology has been significantly altered. Removing drains and filling in drainage ditches promote a return to the natural hydrological conditions of the area. Ceasing crop production and replanting native aquatic vegetation are also necessary components to a successful restoration effort. The completed project should be a self-sufficient wetland (such as a prairie pothole in the Midwest or bottomland hardwood in the Southeast) that provides ecological functions that were lost when the natural conditions of the area were altered.

Enhancement involves improving the functional value of a degraded wetland.[30] Enhancement projects could include replanting native vegetation or removing invasive exotic species. In Florida, for example, nonindigenous species such as Brazilian pepper and maleleuka interfere with wetland functions by displacing native plants. Other enhancement projects involve removing fill from a degraded wetland and returning it to its original contours. The distinction between restoration and enhancement is that restoration applies to an area that no longer functions as a wetland, while enhancement applies to a site that remains a wetland and still provides some associated, albeit diminished, wetland functions.

Creation is the construction of a wetland in an upland area; a wetland is placed in an area where one did not previously exist. Even more than other types of compensatory mitigation, a creation project requires technical expertise. It will typically require excavating, berm building, and extensive diking. The Corps and EPA have recognized the "continued uncertainty regarding the success of wetland creation,"[31] and several studies have raised serious questions regarding the suitability of using creation projects as mitigation.[32] Accordingly, the agencies prefer restoration and enhancement over creation.[33] Moreover, because of the uncertainties associated with creation efforts, the permit applicant may be required to provide higher mitigation ratios—i.e., produce more net acres of wetlands than would be required if restoration or enhancement were selected for purposes of mitigation.[34]

Preservation is accomplished by placing conservation easements or land-use restrictions on a wetland site or transferring title to a governmental agency or private conservation entity that is dedicated to protecting the area. As with creation, the Corps and EPA do not readily accept preservation of existing wetlands as an appropriate form of compensatory mitigation. Its use is reserved for "exceptional circumstances."[35] Preservation is disfavored because it yields a net loss of wetland functions, unless it is used in conjunction with other forms of compensatory mitigation. Preserving twenty acres of wetlands in exchange for permission to fill ten acres of wetlands results in a net loss of ten acres. The agencies, however, do accept preservation as a component of larger mitigation packages, especially where the preserved area is a highly functional or rare wetland type that is threatened with development.[36]

Buffers are vegetated areas that separate wetlands or other aquatic resources from uplands that are developed or used for agricultural purposes. The Corps may require a permittee to establish and maintain vegetated buffers as part of mitigation project to ensure that the project achieves functional objectives. The use of buffers as mitigation has been controversial and the Corps has promised further guidance on this issue.[37]

B. Location: On-Site versus Off-Site

Corps and EPA guidance expresses a preference for on-site, rather than off-site, compensatory mitigation.[38] On-site mitigation involves a project in an area "adjacent or contiguous to the discharge site."[39] The permit applicant may provide off-site mitigation if on-site mitigation is impracticable or off-site mitigation "provides more watershed benefit than on-site mitigation, e.g., is of greater ecological importance to the region of impact."[40] If it is necessary to resort to off-site mitigation, the agencies prefer that it take place "in close physical proximity" to the discharge and, "to the extent possible, [within] the same watershed" as the discharge.[41] In considering off-site or on-site mitigation, the Corps takes account of a project's likelihood of success, its ecological sustainability, practicability of long-term monitoring and maintenance, and relative costs of mitigation alternatives.[42]

In a February 1990 MOA, the Corps and EPA (and other agencies) stated that the preference for on-site mitigation "should not preclude the use of a mitigation bank" to provide required compensatory mitigation.[43] The MOA noted that reliance on a mitigation bank may be more environmentally beneficial than on-site mitigation, especially for projects with minor wetland impacts.[44] Mitigation banks are discussed in more detail in Section X of this chapter.

C. Wetland Functions: In-Kind versus Out-of-Kind

As discussed in Chapter 2, wetlands provide many important functions: They filter pollutants, recharge aquifers, offer flood control protection, and provide habitat for flora and fauna. Of course, not every wetland provides all of these functions or performs them at the same level. In the compensatory mitigation context, the in-kind versus out-of-kind debate centers upon whether a permit applicant must compensate for the particular wetland functions affected by the proposed project or whether a permit applicant may provide mitigation that relates to other wetland functions. "In-kind" compensation for a wetland loss involves replacement of a wetland with a wetland of the same physical and functional type.[45] "Out-of-kind" compensation involves replacement of a wetland with a wetland of different physical or functional type.[46]

Corps and EPA guidance states that in-kind mitigation is generally preferred,[47] but consider out-of-kind compensation "appropriate when it is practicable and provides more environmental or watershed benefit than in-kind compensation (e.g., of greater ecological importance to the region of impact)."[48] Accordingly, if a proposed golf course destroys a freshwater marsh that provided habitat for migratory waterfowl, the agencies' initial inclination will be to require mitigation that increases such habitat elsewhere. Although decisions on in-kind or out-of-kind mitigation are made on a case-by-case basis, the agencies have emphasized that "non-tidal wetlands should typically not be used to compensate for the loss or degradation of tidal wetlands."[49]

VII. Sequencing

The general rule is that avoidance, minimization, and compensation must be applied in a sequential fashion when individual permit applications are considered.[50] An applicant must first avoid wetlands where practicable, then minimize unavoidable impacts, and finally provide compensatory mitigation for any remaining impacts.[51] Sequencing precludes a permit applicant from offering a compensatory mitigation package up front in an effort to "buy down" impacts and lessen the avoidance requirement.

Prior to 1990, some Corps districts permitted applicants to use the buy-down approach. Applicants could promise to restore, enhance, or create more wetlands than the permitted activity would destroy, and could thereby contend that the overall project would not result in a net loss of wetlands (or that it would even result in a net gain). If the overall project did not result in a net loss, the applicant could forgo avoidance and minimization. Of course, the environmental utility of the buy-down approach is contingent on the successful completion of the promised compensatory mitigation. If the compensatory mitigation fails, a net loss occurs, even though less environmentally damaging alternatives may have been practicable.

A 1990 EPA–Corps MOA rejected buy-downs, enshrining sequencing as the preferred mitigation process.[52] The MOA clarifies that the term *avoidance* "does not include compensatory mitigation"[53] and that "[c]ompensatory mitigation may not be used as a method to reduce environmental impacts in the evaluation of the least environmentally damaging practicable alternatives[.]"[54] Thus, the 1990 MOA generally precludes the use of the buy-down approach and imposes an "avoid first" requirement.

The 1990 MOA and sequencing proved to be controversial. More recently, the agencies have issued guidance that lessens the "avoid first" requirement in certain contexts. In particular, the avoidance requirement is relaxed where the proposed project will affect wetlands of limited ecological value or where the project involves the construction or expansion of a home or farm building or the expansion of a small business.[55] Although the guidance documents that allow flexibility in the alternatives analysis do not expressly authorize a deviation from strict sequencing, the effect is the same. These permit applicants, in effect, may skip the avoidance step.

VIII. Mitigation and the Goal of No Net Loss

A. No Net Loss

Recognizing the ecological importance of wetlands, the federal government has adopted a short-term goal of no net loss of wetland functions and values and a long-term goal of net gain.[56] Notwithstanding these goals, thousands of acres of wetlands will continue to be lost each year through permitted activities. In fiscal year 2003, for example, the Corps issued 4,035 individual permits, while denying only 299.[57] It is unrealistic to prohibit all property owners from filling their wetlands, especially when doing so would result in significant loss of economic value. Nor is it possible to stop all the illegal filling and natural processes that contribute to wetland losses. Accordingly, compensatory mitigation plays a critical role in achieving the no net loss and net gain goals.

Although no net loss is an overall goal of the Section 404 program, it is not a required outcome in each permit decision. The Corps and EPA agree that compensatory mitigation may not be practicable and appropriate in every permit action.[58] In their 1990 MOA, the agencies concluded "that no net loss of wetlands functions and values may not be achieved in each and every permit action."[59] In recent guidance, the Corps reiterated this point, but added that "all Districts will strive to achieve [the no net loss] goal on a cumulative basis, and the Corps will achieve the goal programmatically."[60]

The programmatic goals of no net loss and even net gain have significantly affected the Corps's permit decisions. In fiscal year 2003, the Corps authorized, through individual permits, verified general permits, and letters of permission, activities affecting approximately 21,000 acres of waters of the United States. To offset these impacts, the Corps required over 43,000 acres of compensatory mitigation.[61] The figures thus suggest a net gain of wetland acres.

Of course, the actual net gain may be lower (or may actually yield a net loss). It is almost certain that the 21,000 acres permitted to be filled will, in fact, be filled. It is not so certain that the 43,000 acres of required mitigation will be completed successfully. The 43,000-acre figure simply represents a promise that the permittees will perform the mitigation in the future. Unfortunately, permittees are often unable or unwilling to comply with compensatory mitigation requirements.[62]

Accordingly, it is much too early to declare that the no net loss goal has been attained. Indeed, the National Research Council's report, *Compensating for Wetland Losses Under the Clean Water Act,* concluded that the Corps's regulatory program was falling short of that goal.[63] The Corps has stated that it will endeavor to report success and failure rates of mitigation projects to provide a more accurate picture of wetland losses and gains. In addition, in response to the National Research Council's report, which identified a number of problems with compensatory mitigation under the Section 404 program, the Corps and EPA have devised a National Wetlands Mitigation Action Plan to "ensure effective restoration and protection of the functions and values of our Nation's wetlands."[64] The Corps's recent guidance on compensatory mitigation is also a direct response to the problems identified by the National

Research Council and includes operational guidelines recommended by the council.[65] Continued attention to the actual functioning of compensatory mitigation projects may improve progress toward achieving the no net loss goal.

B. Compensatory Mitigation Ratios

To achieve the overall program goal of no net loss, the Corps and EPA have concluded that, where appropriate and practicable, compensatory mitigation "should provide, at a minimum, one for one functional replacement (i.e., no net loss of values), with an adequate margin of safety to reflect the expected degree of success associated with the mitigation plan."[66] Where site-specific data are lacking, the Corps may use acreage "as a reasonable surrogate for no net loss of functions and values."[67] For example, ten acres of restored wetlands may be used to offset the adverse impacts of filling ten acres. The Corps may require more than 1:1 mitigation in two general circumstances: (1) The functional value of the wetlands to be filled is high and the functional value of the replacement wetlands is low[68] and (2) the success of the mitigation project is questionable (as in creation projects).[69] Conversely, if the functional value of the replacement wetlands is higher than that of the filled wetlands and the success of the mitigation efforts is probable, then the Corps may require mitigation at a ratio below 1:1.[70] Some Corps districts have issued guidance relating to mitigation ratios. For example, the Chicago District has announced that it will typically require a minimum of 1.5 acres for every acre of impacted wetland.[71]

C. Evaluation Methodologies

When determining an appropriate compensatory mitigation ratio, the Corps must assess the environmental damage that will result from a proposed project and the environmental gain that will flow from proposed restoration, enhancement, creation, or preservation. Although acreage or best professional judgment may be employed, the Corps also relies on more refined methodologies that focus on particular wetland functions. The most widely used methodologies are the Habitat Evaluation Procedures (HEP),[72] the Wetland Evaluation Technique (WET),[73] and the hydrogeomorphic (HGM) approach to functional assessment.

HEP, developed by the Fish and Wildlife Service, provides information regarding the amount of habitat support a site provides. A regulator assigns a site a numerical ranking (from 0 to 1.0) based on the site's suitability for certain indicator species. The numerical value is then multiplied by the relevant number of acres to quantify the site's habitat units (HUs)—the site's value in providing habitat. For example, if a 10-acre freshwater marsh had an index value of 0.6, this area contains six HUs. If a permit applicant sought to fill the ten acres, the Corps may require mitigation that provides six replacement HUs, such as the enhancement of a twenty-acre wetland site from an index value of 0.2 to 0.5 ($20 \times (0.5 - 0.2) = 6$ HUs).

For sites where multiple functions must be considered, the Corps may rely on WET. WET enables a regulator to assess eleven different wetland functions in a qualitative fashion (low, moderate, or high). WET does not, however, offer a more detailed evaluation of these functions and accordingly has been described as a "'broad-brush screening tool.'"[74]

The HGM approach provides a means to assess multiple functions on a more quantitative basis. The first phase of this methodology involves classifying the wetland into one of seven major categories: riverine, estuarine fringe, lacustrine fringe, slope, depressional, mineral soil flats, and organic soil flats. The assessment phase relies on a set of regional reference wetlands; based on its functions, each reference wetland is assigned an index number from 0 to 1.0. The proposed project site or mitigation site is then compared to the reference site to determine their respective adverse impacts or environmental benefits. In accordance with a National Action Plan, the Corps and other agencies will develop national guidebooks for each major class of wetlands.[75] The national guidelines will then "provide a template for developing [approximately twenty-five to thirty] regional guidebooks for regional wetland subclasses."[76] The National Action Plan contemplates that the Corps will rely on the HGM approach for 80 percent of its Section 404 assessment responsibilities.[77]

D. Timing of Mitigation

In general, the Corps prefers that the construction of mitigation projects proceed concurrently with authorized impacts to wetlands. In this way, temporal functional losses can be minimized and compliance with mitigation conditions can better be monitored.[78] The Corps will permit impacts to wetlands before mitigation projects are constructed in some circumstances—for example, where authorized activities would harm on-site compensatory mitigation or where a simple restoration project is contemplated.[79]

If compensatory mitigation is to be achieved after the completion of authorized impacts to wetlands, Corps districts will require (1) a Corps-approved mitigation plan, (2) a secured mitigation site, (3) financial assurances from the permittee, and (4) legally protected water rights, if necessary.[80] In general, the initial physical and biological improvements of a mitigation plan must be completed no later than the first full growing season after the authorized impacts. If a longer period is necessary, the amount of mitigation to be completed may be adjusted to account for the increased temporal loss of wetland functions.[81]

IX. Mitigation and Nationwide Permits

As discussed in Chapter 5, Section 404(e) authorizes the Corps to issue general permits on a state, regional, or nationwide basis, so long as the authorized activity causes only minimal adverse environmental impacts.[82] By its own terms, the 1990 EPA–Army MOA that established sequencing as the preferred mitigation process applies only to standard permits, not to general permits.[83] Thus, until recently, an individual proceeding with a project authorized by a nationwide permit (NWP) need not necessarily avoid, minimize, and compensate, in that order. Indeed, NWPs traditionally did not require compensatory mitigation at all.

Although the 1990 MOA technically does not apply to NWPs, its spirit is evident in recent modifications to the NWP program. In March 2000, the Corps amended the NWP general condition regarding mitigation to require that any project authorized by an NWP "must be designed and constructed to avoid and minimize adverse effects" to wetlands to the maximum extent practicable.[84] Of course, while the Corps can evaluate whether a prospective permittee has avoided and minimized impacts when the proposed project triggers a preconstruction notification (PCN), most NWPs do not require a PCN.[85] Accordingly, there is no agency oversight of these activities, and the "avoid and minimize" requirement may simply be aspirational in these cases.

For NWPs that call on prospective permittees to file a PCN, however, the Corps may also require compensatory mitigation at a minimum of a 1:1 ratio.[86] As with individual permits, the Corps district engineer is responsible for determining whether, to what extent, and in what form mitigation will be required for a given project. The district engineer must consider whether mitigation is appropriate (in light of the permitted activity's impacts on wetland functional values) and practicable (considering mitigation costs, technology, and logistics in light of the permitted activity's purpose).[87] Examples of appropriate and practicable mitigation for impacts associated with activities authorized by NWPs include "reducing the size of the project; establishing and maintaining wetland or upland vegetated buffers to protect open waters such as streams; and replacing losses of aquatic resource functions and values by creating, restoring, enhancing or pressuring similar functions and values, preferably in the same watershed."[88] The Corps has expressed a preference that NWP compensatory mitigation requirements be satisfied by consolidated mitigation, where an applicant procures credits from a mitigation bank or contributes "in-lieu fees" to organizations such as The Nature Conservancy or state or county natural resource management agencies.[89] The Corps has emphasized, however, that the district engineer retains the discretion to determine that "activity-specific compensatory mitigation is more appropriate" than consolidated mitigation.[90]

The Corps has made clear that compensatory mitigation may not be used to buy down impacts so that a project satisfies the acreage limitations governing certain NWPs.[91] For example, NWP 39 authorizes the filling of wetlands for residential, commercial, and institutional development, so long as no more than a half-acre of nontidal waters is lost. A prospective permittee may not offer a half-acre of created wetlands to attempt to convert a one-acre development project into a half-acre project that may qualify under NWP 39. Thus, the Corps has emphasized that the acreage limits for particular NWPs are "absolute" and "cannot be increased by any mitigation plan offered by the applicant or required by the District Engineer."[92]

X. *Mitigation Banking*[93]

Mitigation banking, a relatively recent resource management tool, offers advantages over traditional compensatory mitigation. The popularity of mitigation banks has increased. In 1993, forty-four banks were in operation, while sixty-eight others were planned. By December 1997, more than one hundred banks were in operation with another 110 in the planning stages.[94] By January 2000, the Corps estimated that more than 230 banks had been established.[95] Through a series of guidance documents, the Corps and EPA have provided guidelines for establishing and operating mitigation banks. In 1998, in the Transportation Equity Act for the 21st Century, Congress expressed its preference that mitigation banks authorized in accordance with agency guidance provide compensatory mitigation to offset wetland impacts caused by federally funded highway projects.[96]

A. Definitions

A November 1995 federal guidance document defines a mitigation bank as "a site where wetlands and/or other aquatic resources are restored, created, enhanced, or in exceptional circumstances, preserved expressly for the purpose of providing compensatory mitigation in advance of authorized impacts to similar resources."[97] The operator of the mitigation bank, known as the bank sponsor, may be a public or private entity.[98] A bank sponsor may implement mitigation activities to offset wetland impacts caused by its own development projects or may sell mitigation credits to others.[99] The former is an example of single-client bank; the latter is an entrepreneurial bank.

B. Benefits of Mitigation Banking

A well-run mitigation banking system can provide benefits to the environment, to the permit applicant, and to the regulatory agencies.

1. *Benefits to the Aquatic Environment*

Traditionally, the Corps has allowed permittees to fill wetlands based on a promise of future compensatory mitigation. Unfortunately, that compensatory mitigation has often failed. Mitigation banking, which is premised on advance compensation, offers a remedy for this problem. A mitigation bank "is typically implemented and functioning in advance of project impacts,"[100] so that credits obtained from the bank reduce the temporal loss of wetland functions associated with requirements for future mitigation. Additionally, mitigation from a bank is more likely to be successful in the long term. The agencies recognize that a mitigation bank provides an opportunity to consolidate "financial resources, planning and scientific expertise not practicable to many project-specific compensatory mitigation proposals."[101] More expertise and more money translate into greater mitigation success.

Mitigation banking can also benefit the environment by compensating for the cumulative impact of small projects. Mitigation banks generally involve large sites that are in most cases functionally more valuable than isolated mitigation produced by small landowners.[102] An additional advantage of mitigation banking is that it fosters private investment in wetland restoration, enhancement, and creation, especially if the Corps and EPA authorize and encourage the use of entrepreneurial banks.

2. *Benefits to Permit Applicants*

Mitigation banking effectively offers the regulated community two highly valued items: time and money. By relying on mitigation banks that offer functioning wetlands, permit applicants may reduce the time that the Corps and resource agencies devote to reviewing proposed (and speculative) compensatory mitigation proposals.[103] With a mitigation bank, much of that review has already been done and the permit processing time should be reduced. In addition to more timely permit decisions, mitigation banking should offer permit applicants more cost-effective mitigation options.[104] The economies of scale resulting from a mitigation bank project should provide mitigation that is less expensive on a per acre basis than most on-site mitigation. Furthermore, as will be discussed in Section XII, by procuring mitigation bank credits, a permittee shifts the legal responsibility for the ecological success of the mitigation project to the bank sponsor.

3. *Benefits to the Regulatory Agencies*

Wetland mitigation banking simplifies the task of enforcing permit conditions relating to mitigation.[105] Because a mitigation bank consolidates compensatory mitigation into a large parcel or contiguous parcels, a regulator need not visit dozens of separate sites to evaluate permit compliance. Instead, the regulator can monitor a particular site. With the time saved on site visits, the agencies should be able to focus additional resources to investigate unpermitted activities and to review pending permit applications.

A hidden, but potentially significant, benefit that wetland mitigation banking offers to regulatory agencies is protection from regulatory takings claims,[106] which are discussed in Chapter 13. If mitigation banks provide additional options for compensatory mitigation, the Corps may deny fewer permits. Fewer permit denials would lead to fewer ripe takings claims. Furthermore, even if the Corps denies a permit to fill wetlands, the permit denial may not destroy all economically beneficial use of the property when a mitigation banking system is in place. The wetland that is the subject of the denial may have value as part of a mitigation bank, and this value may defeat a takings claims. For example, where a wetland has economic value as a wetland, the categorical rule of *Lucas v. South Carolina Coastal Council*[107] would be inapplicable. Much of this protection, however, is dependent on the Corps's willingness to credit the preservation of high-quality wetlands, which are most likely to be the subject of a regulatory takings case.

C. Establishing a Mitigation Bank

1. *Planning Considerations*

a. Site Selection

Site selection is the most important factor for bank sponsors to consider when establishing a mitigation bank. The site must support the goals and objectives of the bank, providing the particular resource needs of the watershed. It should offer reliable hydrologic sources (to ensure that the site will be self-sufficient) and be compatible with adjacent land uses. Use of a site for a mitigation bank should not adversely affect other environmentally significant resources, such as mature forests, cultural sites, and habitat for protected species. Although banks may be located on private or public lands, the amount of mitigation credit generated by a bank on public land will be based solely on those values that supplement existing or planned public programs.[108]

b. Technical Feasibility

Noting that mitigation banks should be designed to be self-sustaining, the November 1995 guidance emphasizes that "restoration should be the first option considered when siting a bank."[109] Restoration in this sense includes reviving areas that no longer qualify as wetlands and enhancing the functions of substantially degraded wetlands. The agencies view creation projects with some skepticism, because of the technical uncertainty associated with such activities. Similarly, certain enhancement projects are discouraged. For example, the conversion of a wetland to open water may increase its value as duck habitat, but degrade its ability to perform other functions. The agencies will consider the utility of the bank in light of its overall environmental benefits.[110]

c. Credit for Preservation

Preservation of existing wetlands may generate mitigation credit when done in conjunction with other restoration, enhancement, or creation activities.[111] Banks that rely solely on preservation will be approved only "in exceptional circumstances."[112] Bank sponsors may also receive limited credit for certain upland areas contained in the bank site, such as buffer zones, if these areas "increase the overall ecological functioning of the bank."[113]

2. Prospectus and Mitigation Banking Instruments

To initiate formal agency review, the bank sponsor must submit a prospectus to the Corps. The prospectus should contain information regarding the bank's objectives, how it will be established, and how it will be administered. The information contained in the prospectus will serve as the basis for a more formal document—the mitigation banking instrument.[114]

The bank sponsor and the Mitigation Bank Review Team, consisting of the Corps and concurring federal, state, and local resource agencies, will sign the banking instrument. If the proposed mitigation involves discharges of fill or dredged material into wetlands (as is likely in the case of many restoration and enhancement projects), the Corps will incorporate the banking instrument into any permit issued for the discharge. The banking instrument should discuss, *inter alia*, the following subjects: bank goals and objectives; site plans and specifications; the bank site's baseline conditions; its geographic service area; classes of impacts for which the bank may provide compensation; credit and debit methodology; performance standards; reporting requirements and monitoring plans; financial assurances; compensation ratios; and long-term management and maintenance plans.[115] The Corps's Institute for Water Resources has developed a model mitigation banking agreement.

3. The Role of the Mitigation Bank Review Team (MBRT)

The primary purpose of the MBRT is to negotiate and conclude mitigation banking instruments that will provide effective compensatory mitigation.[116] The MBRT may be made up of representatives from the Corps, EPA, FWS, NMFS, the National Resources Conservation Service, and state, tribal, and local regulatory and resource agencies. Generally, the Corps representative will serve as MBRT chair. Although the Corps representative is the final decision maker regarding the banking instrument's terms and conditions, the November 1995 guidance states that "the MBRT will strive to obtain consensus on its actions."[117] Accordingly, and depending on how forcefully the Corps representative exercises his or her authority, each MBRT representative has, at a minimum, the ability to delay the development of banking instruments.

D. Operation of Wetland Mitigation Banks

1. Relationship to Other Mitigation Requirements

The availability of mitigation credits from a bank does not alter sequencing requirements.[118] Permit applicants must still avoid and minimize impacts to the extent appropriate and practicable. Mitigation banks are intended to provide another option for compensatory mitigation and may not be used to buy down impacts to sidestep the avoid-first principle.

The November 1995 guidance emphasizes that the preference for on-site mitigation does not preclude the use of mitigation banks. The agencies recognize that there are circumstances in which on-site mitigation is not practicable or does not provide the environmental benefits offered by an off-site mitigation bank. For example, the guidance concludes that, as a general rule, "use of a mitigation bank to compensate for minor aquatic resource impacts (e.g., numerous, small impacts associated with linear projects; impacts authorized under NWPs) is preferable to on-site mitigation."[119]

There are, however, geographic limits to the use of mitigation banks. A mitigation bank may not be used to offset the impacts of a project several states away; instead, the bank's service area is restricted to an area that "can reasonably be expected to provide appropriate compensation" for wetland impacts.[120] Examples of such areas include watersheds and counties.[121]

2. Timing of Credit Withdrawal

The use or sale of mitigation credits is generally precluded until the planned mitigation project is functioning.[122] The November 1995 guidance does, however, allow for a limited withdrawal of credits in the bank's early stages. For example, in some cases it may be appropriate to withdraw fifteen percent of the total anticipated credits prior to the completion of restoration, enhancement, or creation projects.[123]

Early withdrawal of mitigation credits is heavily conditioned. No early credits may be used unless (1) the MBRT has approved the banking instrument and mitigation plan; (2) the bank sponsor has obtained the mitigation site; and (3) the banking instrument contains "appropriate financial assurances."[124] Furthermore, these early credits will be subject to higher mitigation ratios.[125] In those "exceptional circumstances" in which preserved wetlands are part of the bank, the guidance states that these credits may be withdrawn as soon as the wetlands have adequate legal protection.[126]

3. Long-Term Management and Maintenance

The federal guidance emphasizes that the bank sponsor is responsible for the management of mitigation sites during the bank's operational life and thereafter.[127] The banking instrument must specify how the mitigation site will remain protected from future development. In most cases, this can be secured by conservation easements and restrictive deeds.[128] The banking instrument must also identify the entity that will oversee the mitigation site once the bank's credits are exhausted.[129] The bank sponsor may provide long-term maintenance, or a conservation organization or governmental agency might assume the duties. In either case, the bank sponsor will remain financially responsible for maintenance.[130] Additionally, the MBRT will require performance bonds or other formal financial assurances to guarantee that funds will be available for long-term maintenance and remedial actions.

XI. In-Lieu-Fee Mitigation

A permittee may perform compensatory mitigation itself or it may purchase credits from a mitigation bank. Additionally, a permittee may have the option to satisfy compensatory mitigation requirements through the use of in-lieu fees. "In-lieu fee" mitigation occurs in circumstances where the Corps authorizes the permittee to provide funds to a third party that is implementing a mitigation project.[131]

Corps headquarters has encouraged the use of in-lieu fees as one method to offset wetland impacts from activities authorized by NWPs,[132] and Corps districts have authorized fee mitigation for both individual and general permits.[133] While some approvals were on an ad hoc basis, some Corps districts have entered in MOAs with groups such as The Nature Conservancy, to establish guidelines for the use of in-lieu fees.[134] For example, the Norfolk District and The Nature Conservancy agreed to create the Virginia Wetlands Restoration Trust Fund.[135] Permittees proceeding under NWPs (and "in other cases if accepted by all involved parties") may satisfy compensatory mitigation obligations by contributing money to the fund. The Nature Conservancy committed to use the fund to conduct wetland mitigation projects approved by the Norfolk District.

A recent survey found that at least thirty-one of thirty-eight Corps districts had approved, at least on one occasion, the use of in-lieu fees.[136] In October 2000, the Corps, EPA, FWS, and the National Oceanic and Atmospheric Administration issued comprehensive guidance on in-lieu-fee mitigation.[137]

A. Definitions

The agencies define an in-lieu fee as a payment of funds to a natural resource entity, which then uses the funds to undertake wetland mitigation projects.[138] The entities receiving the funds may be public agencies or private conservation organizations. A significant difference between mitigation banks and in-lieu-fee arrangements is the timing of the mitigation actions. Mitigation banks should provide mitigation in advance of project impacts, while in-lieu-fee arrangements, by definition, pool funds for use in future mitigation projects. Moreover, at least prior to the October 2000 guidance, in-lieu-fee arrangements were not subjected to the MBRT process.

B. Benefits of and Concerns with In-Lieu-Fee Mitigation

In-lieu fees can benefit the aquatic environment by compensating for the cumulative impacts of small projects. In the past, the Corps generally did not require compensatory mitigation to offset the impacts of activities authorized by NWPs. The existence of in-lieu fees makes it easier for the Corps to require some mitigation for small projects.

From a permit applicant's perspective, an in-lieu fee provides certainty. Under such an arrangement, compensatory mitigation costs are fixed and the legal responsibility for mitigation success is shifted to the natural resource entity. Such certainty is generally lacking when the applicant must perform (or oversee) wetland restoration, enhancement, or creation efforts.

Some environmental groups, such as those receiving the in-lieu fees, also favor such arrangements. To others, however, an in-lieu fee looks suspiciously like permit buying: An applicant with enough money could, in effect, purchase a permit and avoid the sequencing requirement. Because many in-lieu-fee arrangements specify that the Corps districts retain control of the funds, fee mitigation may also raise conflict of interest and fiscal law issues for the Corps.[139] A General Accounting Office report was critical of the Corps's in-lieu-fee arrangements, questioning whether they properly offset wetland impacts and noting that the Corps lacked the data to track and assess the effectiveness of in-lieu-fee arrangements.[140] Furthermore, concerns have been expressed about the timing of mitigation from in-lieu fees, the purposes for which the funds are actually used, and the legal responsibility of the in-lieu-fee recipients.[141] These concerns and the increased use of in-lieu fees led to the issuance of the October 2000 guidance.

C. October 2000 In-Lieu-Fee Guidance

The new guidance may have the effect of limiting the use of in-lieu fees. For example, in-lieu fees may now be used to compensate for impacts authorized by individual permit only if the in-lieu-fee organization enters into a formal agreement through the MBRT process.[142] The guidance states that such agreements are to be "consistent with the Banking Guidance," which suggests that the in-lieu-fee arrangement should produce advance mitigation, as mitigation banks are required to do.

With respect to mitigating impacts associated with general permits, the in-lieu-fee guidance reaffirms the traditional agency preference for on-site over off-site mitigation. When off-site mitigation is more appropriate, however, the agencies conclude that the "use of a mitigation bank is preferable to in-lieu-fee mitigation where permitted impacts are within the service area of a mitigation bank approved to sell mitigation credits, and those credits are available."[143] The agencies justify the preference for mitigation banks because banks typically provide mitigation in advance of impacts, while in-lieu-fee arrangements often do not "provide a clear timetable for the initiation of mitigation efforts."[144] Still, the mitigation bank preference is not absolute; an in-lieu-fee arrangement that would provide in-kind restoration trumps a mitigation bank that provides only out-of-kind mitigation or preservation credits.[145] The guidance requires the Corps and the in-lieu-fee recipient to enter into a formal agreement that is very similar to mitigation bank agreements.

XII. Enforcement Issues

A permittee that fails to perform mitigation that is a condition of a Section 404 permit may be subject to an enforcement action. Under Section 404(s), the Corps may issue a compliance order or institute a civil action for a violation of permit conditions.[146] Although EPA has enforcement authority as well, a Corps–EPA Memorandum of Agreement designates the Corps as the lead enforcement agency for permit condition violations.[147]

Section 404(s) establishes a maximum civil penalty of $25,000 per day for violations,[148] but monetary penalties are rarely assessed for failure to provide compensatory mitigation. Instead, if the permittee fails to comply with a Corps order demanding corrective action, the Corps may employ its authority to suspend or revoke the permit.[149] The ability to revoke or suspend a permit is powerful leverage to encourage permittees to provide required mitigation without having to resort to judicial actions.

A final enforcement issue concerns mitigation banks and in-lieu-fee arrangements. When a permittee pays money to a bank sponsor or in-lieu-fee administrator, the permittee has typically satisfied its compensatory mitigation obligations; the legal responsibility for the ecological success of the mitigation site is transferred to the recipient of the money. For example, the November 1995 guidance states that the "bank sponsor is responsible for assuring the success of the debited restoration, creation, enhancement and preservation activities at the mitigation bank."[150] The banking instrument and any required Section 404 permit must clearly express the extent of the bank sponsor's responsibility.[151] Once incorporated in a federal permit, those responsibilities are federally enforceable. Accordingly, the bank sponsor may be subject to enforcement actions for failing to provide or maintain mitigation. Similarly, the federal guidance calls upon the Corps to enter into formal agreements with entities operating in-lieu-fee funds to ensure that the mitigation will be implemented.[152]

XIII. Wetland Mitigation and the National Environmental Policy Act (NEPA)

The Corps's decision to grant or deny a Section 404 permit is a federal action that implicates NEPA. For most permit decisions, the Corps will prepare an environmental assessment.[153] For projects that will result in significant environmental impacts, the Corps must prepare a more comprehensive environmental impact statement (EIS). An interesting issue is whether a mitigation plan may be used to reduce impacts and obviate the need for an EIS in cases where, absent the mitigation, an EIS would be required.

In *Preserve Endangered Areas of Cobb's History, Inc. v. United States Army Corps of Engineers*,[154] the Corps granted a Section 404 permit to fill

3.8 acres of wetlands for a highway project.[155] The mitigation plan included preserving 19.7 acres of wetlands and restoring 7.8 acres.[156] The Eleventh Circuit concluded that the Corps's finding of no significant impact, in light of the proposed mitigation, was not arbitrary or capricious.[157] Similarly, in *Friends of the Earth v. Hintz*,[158] the Ninth Circuit stated that a Section 404 permit condition requiring off-site mitigation served "to relieve the Corps of the obligation of preparing an EIS."[159] Thus, although the Corps is generally precluded from using mitigation to buy down impacts when applying the Section 404(b)(1) Guidelines, the Corps may use mitigation to buy down impacts when considering NEPA requirements.

XIV. Conclusion

Mitigation—avoid, minimize, and compensate—is a central premise of the Section 404 program and is a critical component to achieving the goals of no net loss and net gain of wetlands. In particular, effective compensatory mitigation (restoration, enhancement, creation, and preservation) is necessary to offset the impacts of permitted activities, including activities authorized by general permits. Although the Corps and EPA generally prefer on-site compensatory mitigation, the agencies recognize that consolidated off-site mitigation, such as mitigation banks or in-lieu-fee arrangements, may offer greater environmental benefits. Accordingly, the agencies have offered permit applicants more flexibility with respect to mitigation. In addition to providing traditional on-site compensatory mitigation, many permit applicants may also have the option of purchasing credits from a mitigation bank or contributing money to a conservation organization.

It is important to note that federal wetland mitigation policy is constantly evolving. Indeed, Congress has called upon the Corps to promulgate new regulations by November 2005 that "maximize available credits and opportunities for mitigation" and "apply equivalent standards and criteria to each type of compensatory mitigation."[160] A challenge for the agencies will be to ensure that the new regulations and the ongoing work of the National Wetlands Mitigation Action Plan complement each other. If the outcome is more options and clearer guidelines, permit applicants may not find the imposition of mitigation requirements itself to be something "painful, oppressive, or calamitous."

Notes

1. The Compact Oxford English Dictionary 909 (2nd ed. 1991).

2. White House Office on Environmental Policy, *Protecting America's Wetlands: A Fair, Flexible, and Effective Approach* (Aug. 24, 1993), *available at* http://

www.usace.army.mil/inet/functions/cw/cecwo/reg/aug93wet.htm (last visited June 30, 2004).

3. 33 U.S.C. § 1344(b)(1) (2000).

4. 33 U.S.C. § 1343(c).

5. *Id.* § 1343(c)(1)(F).

6. *Id.* § 1343(c)(1)(E).

7. *See* 33 U.S.C. §§ 401, 403, 404, 407 & 408.

8. 33 U.S.C. § 1413.

9. 33 C.F.R. § 320.4(r) (2004).

10. *See* U.S. Army Corps of Engineers, Regulatory Program, http://www.usace.army.mil/inet/functions/cw/cecwo/reg/ (last visited June 30, 2004).

11. 33 U.S.C. § 404(a).

12. Memorandum of Agreement between the Department of the Interior and the Department of the Army (Section 404(q) Elevation) (Dec. 1992); Memorandum of Agreement between the Department of Commerce and the Department of the Army (Section 404(q) Elevation) (Aug. 1992); Memorandum of Agreement between the Environmental Protection Agency and the Department of the Army (Section 404(q) Elevation) (Aug. 1992).

13. HQUSACE Review and Findings: Old Cutler Bay Permit 404(q) Elevation (Sept. 13, 1990).

14. 33 U.S.C. § 404(c).

15. Memorandum of Agreement between the Environmental Protection Agency and the Department of the Army concerning the Determination of Mitigation under the Clean Water Act Section 404(b)(1) Guidelines, 55 Fed. Reg. 9210, 9211 (1990) [hereinafter Mitigation MOA], *available at* http://www.usace.army.mil/inet/functions/cw/cecwo/reg/moafe90.htm (last visited June 30, 2004).

16. 40 C.F.R. § 230.10(a).

17. 40 C.F.R. § 230.10(d).

18. *Id.* § 230.70.

19. *Id.* § 230.71.

20. *Id.* § 230.72.

21. *Id.* § 230.73.

22. *Id.* § 230.74.

23. *Id.* § 230.75.

24. Mitigation MOA, *supra* note 15, at 9212.

25. RGL 02-02, Guidance on Compensatory Mitigation Projects for Aquatic Resource Impacts under the Corps Regulatory Program Pursuant to Section 404 of the Clean Water Act and Section 10 of the Rivers and Harbors Act of 1899 (Dec. 24, 2002), at 1, *available at* http://www.usace.army.mil/inet/functions/cw/cecwo/reg/RGL2-02.pdf (last visited June 30, 2004).

26. *Id.* at 5–6.

27. Mitigation MOA, *supra* note 15, at 9212.

28. *Id.*

29. RGL 02-02, *supra* note 25, at 4.

30. Federal Guidance for the Establishment, Use and Operation of Mitigation Banks, 60 Fed. Reg. 58,605, 58,613 (1995) [hereinafter Mitigation Banking Guidance].

31. Mitigation MOA, *supra* note 15, at 9212.

32. *E.g.*, NATIONAL RESEARCH COUNCIL, COMPENSATING FOR WETLAND LOSSES UNDER THE CLEAN WATER ACT (2001), http://www.nap.edu/books/0309074320/html/ (last visited June 30, 2004); U.S. EPA and U.S. Fish and Wildlife Serv., *Interagency Follow-Through Investigation of Compensatory Wetland Mitigation Sites* (May 1994); *see also* Florida Dep't. of Envtl. Reg., *Report on the Effectiveness of Permitted Mitigation Sites* (Mar. 1991).

33. Mitigation MOA, *supra* note 15, at 9212.

34. *Id.*

35. *Id.*

36. RGL 02-02, supra note 25, at 4–5.

37. *Id.* at 5.

38. *Id.*

39. *Id.*

40. RGL 02-02, *supra* note 25, at 5.

41. Mitigation MOA, *supra* note 15, at 9212.

42. RGL 02-02, *supra* note 25, at 5. In 2004, as part of a National Wetlands Mitigation Action Plan, EPA issued draft guidance to clarify when it is environmentally preferable to use off-site mitigation. *See* U.S. Environmental Protection Agency, Draft Federal Guidance on the Use of Off-Site and Out-of-Kind Compensatory Mitigation under Section 404 of the Clean Water Act, 69 Fed. Reg. 22,028 (April 23, 2004) (hereinafter Draft Site/Kind Guidance). The guidance, available online at http://www.mitigationactionplan.gov/040407SiteKindGuidance.html, is designed to "move the program to a more watershed-based approach to mitigation site selection and planning and improve the success of required mitigation." *See* U.S. Environmental Protection Agency, Draft Qs and As for Federal Guidance on the Use of Off-Site and Out-of-Kind Compensatory Mitigation, http://www.mitigationactionplan.gov/040420SiteKindQsAsfinaldraft1.html (last visited June 30, 2004).

43. Mitigation Banking Guidance, *supra* note 30, at 58,611.

44. *Id.*

45. RGL 02-02, *supra* note 25, at 5.

46. *Id.*

47. Mitigation MOA, *supra* note 15, at 9212.

48. RGL 02-02, *supra* note 25, at 5. EPA's Draft Site/Kind Guidance attempts to clarify when it is environmentally preferable to use out-of-kind mitigation. *See* U.S. Environmental Protection Agency, Draft Federal Guidance on the Use of Off-Site and Out-of-Kind Compensatory Mitigation under Section 404 of the Clean Water Act, 69 Fed. Reg. 22,028 (April 23, 2004).

49. Mitigation Banking Guidance, *supra* note 30, at 58,611. Although this statement was made in the context of mitigation banks, one can assume it applies with equal force to traditional compensatory mitigation.

50. Mitigation MOA, *supra* note 15, at 9211–12.

51. *Id.*

52. Mitigation MOA, *supra* note 15, at 9211–12.

53. *Id.* at 9212.

54. *Id.*

55. RGL 95-01, Guidance on Individual Permit Flexibility for Small Landowners (March 31, 1995), *available at* http://www.usace.army.mil/inet/functions/cw/cecwo/reg/rgls/rgl95-01.htm (last visited June 30, 2004).

56. U.S. Environmental Protection Agency & U.S. Army Corps of Engineers, National Wetlands Mitigation Action Plan, at 1 (Dec. 24, 2002), *available at* http://www.epa.gov/OWOW/wetlands/guidance/ (last visited June 30, 2004).

57. U.S. Army Corps of Engineers, Regulatory Statistics—FY 2003, *available at* http://www.usace.army.mil/inet/functions/cw/cecwo/reg/2003webcharts.pdf.

58. Mitigation MOA, *supra* note 15, at 9212.

59. *Id.*

60. RGL 02-02, *supra* note 25, at 2.

61. *See* Regulatory Statistics—FY 2003, *supra* note 57.

62. National Research Council, Compensating for Wetland Losses under the Clean Water Act 101–03 (2001), http://www.nap.edu/books/0309074320/html/ (last visited June 30, 2004).

63. *Id.* at 2–3.

64. National Wetlands Mitigation Action Plan, *supra* note 56, at 1.

65. RGL 02-02, *supra* note 25, at Appendix B.

66. Mitigation MOA, *supra* note 15, at 9212; *see* RGL 02-02, at 3.

67. Mitigation MOA, *supra* note 15, at 9212.

68. *Id.*

69. *Id.*

70. *Id.*

71. U.S. Army Corps of Engineers, Chicago District, Chicago District Mitigation Requirements, at http://www.lrc.usace.army.mil/co-r/mitgr.htm.

72. U.S. Fish and Wildlife Serv., Ecological Services Manual, Standards for the Development of Habitat Suitability Index Models 103-ESM (1981).

73. 2 Paul R. Adams et. al, Wetland Evaluation Technique Methodology (1987).

74. Environmental Law Institute, Wetland Mitigation Banking 85 (1993) (quoting Adams and Clairan 1988)).

75. The National Action Plan to Implement the Hydrogeomorphic Approach to Assessing Wetland Functions, 62 Fed. Reg. 33,607, 33,609 (1997).

76. *Id.*

77. *Id.*

78. RGL 02-02, *supra* note 25, at 7.

79. *Id.*

80. *Id.*

81. *Id.*

82. 33 U.S.C. § 1344(e).

83. Mitigation MOA, *supra* note 15, at 9211 n.1.

84. 65 Fed. Reg. 12,817, 12,896 (March 9, 2000).

85. If a nationwide permit includes a PCN condition, the permittee must submit a preconstruction notification to the Corps of Engineers, and may not begin the activity authorized by the nationwide permit until the Corps provides

notice that the activity may proceed under the nationwide permit or a specified time period for the Corps to review the notice has expired. *See* 33 C.F.R. § 330.6(a)(1).

86. *Id.* Tens of thousands of minor projects are authorized each year under NWPs. To ensure that activities authorized by NWPs do not result in more than "minimal adverse environmental impacts," either individually or cumulatively, the Corps has specified mitigation requirements for particular NWPs. In particular, for those NWPs that have a PCN condition—such as NWP 14 (Linear Transportation Crossings), NWP 21 (Surface Coal Mining Activities), NWP 29 (Single-Family Housing), NWP 39 (Residential, Commercial, and Institutional Developments), NWP 40 (Agricultural Activities), NWP 42 (Recreational Facilities), and NWP 44 (Mining Activities)—the project proponent must provide the Corps a compensatory mitigation plan. *Id.* at 12,894–95.

87. 40 C.F.R. § 230.10.

88. 65 Fed. Reg. at 12,896.

89. *Id.*

90. *Id.*

91. *Id.* at 12,882.

92. 61 Fed. Reg. at 65,917.

93. Portions of this section have been adapted from Royal C. Gardner, *Banking on Entrepreneurs: Wetlands, Mitigation Banking, and Takings*, 81 Iowa L. Rev. 527 (1996).

94. Complete Joint Statement of Michael L. Davis, Deputy Assistant Secretary of the Army for Civil Works and Robert H. Wayland III, Director, Office of Wetlands, Oceans and Watersheds, Environmental Protection Agency, before the Transportation and Infrastructure Committee, Subcommittee on Water Resources and Environment, United States House of Representatives, Wetlands Protection and Mitigation Banking 7 (December 9, 1997), *available at* http://www.usace.army.mil/civilworks/cecwp/pdf/davis120997.pdf.

95. *See* Institute for Water Resources, U.S. Army Corps of Engineers, *Existing Wetland Mitigation Bank Inventory, Spring 2000* (Jan. 2000), *available at* http://www.iwr.usace.army.mil/iwr/regulatory/banks.pdf (last visited June 30, 2004).

96. Pub. L. No. 105-178, 112 Stat. 107,139 (1998). The Department of Transportation, EPA, and the Corps issued *Guidance on the Use of the TEA-21 Preference for Mitigation Banking to Fulfill Mitigation Requirements under Section 404 of the Clean Water Act* in July 2003, and it is available at http://www.usace.army.mil/civilworks/cecwo/reg/TEA-21Guidance.pdf (last visited June 30, 2004).

97. Mitigation Banking Guidance, *supra* note 30, at 58,614.

98. *Id.* at 58,613.

99. *Id.* at 58,607.

100. *Id.*

101. *Id.* Organizations such as the Society of Wetlands Scientists have also recognized the benefits of mitigation banking and endorsed the concept. *See Society of Wetlands Scientists, Wetland Mitigation Banking Position Statement*, available at http://www.sws.org/wetlandconcerns/banking.html.

102. Mitigation Banking Guidance, *supra* note 30, at 58,607.
103. *Id.*
104. *Id.*
105. *Id.*
106. *See* Gardner, *supra* note 93, at 560–61.
107. 505 U.S. 1003 (1992).
108. Mitigation Banking Guidance, *supra* note 30, at 58,608.
109. *Id.*
110. *Id.*
111. *Id.* at 58,608–09.
112. *Id.* at 58,608.
113. *Id.* at 58,609.
114. *Id.* The Institute for Water Resources developed a model banking instrument as part of its 1997 National Wetland Mitigation Banking Study, *see* Institute for Water Resources, U.S. Army Corps of Engineers, *National Wetland Mitigation Banking Study, Model Banking Instrument,* IWR Technical Paper WMBTP-1 (May 1996), *available at* http://www.iwr.usace.army.mil/iwr/pdf/wmb_tp1_May96.pdf (last visited June 30, 2004).
115. Mitigation Banking Guidance, *supra* note 30, at 58,609.
116. *Id.* at 58,610.
117. *Id.*
118. *Id.* at 58,611.
119. *Id.*
120. *Id.*
121. *Id.*
122. *Id.* at 58,612.
123. The proposed guidance that was put out for notice and comment contained this example. 60 Fed. Reg. 12,286, 12,291 (1995). Because some commentators viewed this level as a floor and others considered it a ceiling, the agencies omitted it from the final guidance. Thus, the decision regarding the exact percentage of withdrawals will be made on a case-by-case basis.
124. Mitigation Banking Guidance, *supra* note 30, at 58,612.
125. *Id.*
126. *Id.*
127. *Id.* at 58,613.
128. *Id.* at 58,612.
129. *Id.*
130. *Id.* at 58,613.
131. Federal Guidance on the Use of In-Lieu-Fee Arrangements for Compensatory Mitigation under Section 404 of the Clean Water Act and Section 10 of the Rivers and Harbors Act, 65 Fed. Reg. 66,914 (2000) [hereinafter In-Lieu-Fee Guidance].
132. *See, e.g.,* 61 Fed. Reg. 65,874, 65,922 (1996).
133. *See* Royal C. Gardner, *Money for Nothing? The Rise of Fee Mitigation,* 19 VA. ENVTL. L.J. 1, 18–33 (2000).
134. *Id.* at 23–30.

135. Memorandum of Understanding between the Nature Conservancy and the U.S. Army Corps of Engineers (1995).

136. *See* Gardner, *supra* note 133, at 18.

137. *See* In-Lieu-Fee Guidance, *supra* note 131.

138. *Id.* at 66,915; Mitigation Banking Guidance, *supra* note 30, at 58,613.

139. *See* Gardner, *supra* note 133, at 45–51.

140. U.S. General Accounting Office, Wetlands Protection, Assessments Needed to Determine Effectiveness of In-Lieu-Fee Mitigation, GAO-01-325 (May 2001).

141. E.g., Gardner, *supra* note 133, at 39–45. *See also* Environmental Law Institute, Banks and Fees: The Status of Off-Site Wetland Mitigation in the United States 124–25 (2002).

142. In-Lieu-Fee Guidance, *supra* note 131, at 66,915.

143. *Id.*

144. *Id.*

145. *Id.* at 66,915–16.

146. 33 U.S.C. § 1344(s).

147. Memorandum of Agreement between the Department of the Army and the Environmental Protection Agency concerning Federal Enforcement for the Section 404 Program of the Clean Water Act 4 (Jan. 19, 1989), *available at* http://www.usace.army.mil/inet/functions/cw/cecwo/reg/enfmoa.htm (last visited June 30, 2004).

148. 33 U.S.C. § 1344(s).

149. 33 C.F.R. § 325.7.

150. Mitigation Banking Guidance, *supra* note 30, at 58,612.

151. *Id.*

152. *Id.* at 58,613.

153. 33 C.F.R. pt. 325, app. B.

154. 87 F.3d 1242 (11th Cir. 1996).

155. *Id.* at 1245.

156. *Id.*

157. *Id.* at 1248.

158. 800 F.2d 822 (9th Cir. 1986).

159. *Id.* at 838.

160. National Defense Authorization Act for Fiscal Year 2004, Pub. L. No. 108–136 (Nov. 24, 2003), 117 Stat. 1392, 1431.

CHAPTER 9

The EPA Veto and Related Matters

WILLIAM B. ELLIS

I. Introduction/Scope

When Congress created the modern program for water pollution control in 1972, it created a distinct permit program, separate from the U.S. Environmental Protection Agency (EPA)'s National Pollutant Discharge Elimination System (NPDES) program, to govern a subset of point source discharges consisting of "dredged or fill material."[1] Congress divided authority over the resulting Section 404 program between the United States Army Corps of Engineers (Corps) and EPA.

The differing histories, outlooks, and missions of the Corps and EPA precipitated conflict between them in administering the Section 404 program. Particularly during the second decade of implementing the Clean Water Act (CWA), the Corps and EPA were often at odds both with respect to policy and to its application in particular cases. Such disagreements made it necessary for the agencies themselves, and in some instances the federal courts, to clarify the division of regulatory responsibilities between these agencies. Advocates and opponents of controversial projects are well advised to understand the roles of both agencies in this complex regulatory structure.

The most important statutory provisions with respect to the division of responsibility for this permit program are (1) Section 404(a), granting the Corps authority to issue permits for the discharge of dredged or fill material; (2) Section 404(b)(1), granting EPA authority ("in conjunction with" the Corps) to develop "guidelines" to be applied by the Corps in making permit decisions; (3) Section 404(q), requiring the Corps to reach agreements with various federal agencies (including EPA) regarding efficient processing of permit applications; and (4) Section 404(c), granting EPA the ability to proscribe discharges of dredged or fill material in a defined area.

This chapter examines EPA's implementation of Section 404(c) and how it has affected the division of responsibilities between the Corps and EPA.[2] Section II provides background and traces EPA's implementation of its Section 404(c) "veto" authority. Section III analyzes pertinent caselaw, and Section IV describes the impact of EPA's veto authority on the administration of the Section 404 program. Each of the cases in which EPA has chosen to veto Corps-approved projects pursuant to Section 404(c) is described in an Appendix to this chapter.

II. Background and Implementation of Section 404(c)

A. EPA's Role in the Section 404 Permitting Process

Although Congress gave the Corps of Engineers the authority to issue Section 404 permits, it gave EPA several important responsibilities in the process. First, Congress gave EPA, in conjunction with the Corps, the power to develop the Section 404(b)(1) Guidelines that are used by the Corps to determine whether to issue a Section 404 permit.[3] Second, Congress gave EPA the power to review Section 404 permit applications and to provide comments to the Corps on the applications.[4] Finally, through Section 404(c), Congress gave EPA the authority to "prohibit discharges of dredged or fill material if the [EPA] Administrator determines that the discharge will have an unacceptable adverse effect on municipal water supplies, shellfish beds and fishery areas . . . , wildlife, or recreational areas."[5] Through Section 404(c), EPA can effectively veto a permit that the Corps of Engineers issued or planned to issue. As discussed below, since EPA reviews and provides comments on many Section 404 permit applications, the agency's veto power can influence the Corps's decision to issue a permit, and the conditions to include in a permit, even when EPA does not exercise or threaten to exercise the veto power.

B. The Legislative History of Section 404(c)

1. The Senate Bill

As originally introduced by Senator Edmund Muskie on October 28, 1971, Senate Bill 2770, which later became the CWA, did not include a separate program for permitting discharges of dredged or fill material. It would have regulated such discharges in precisely the same manner as waste discharges subject to the bill's NPDES program.[6] EPA would exercise regulatory authority over all discharges of "pollutants"—a term that expressly included "dredged spoil" (but not clean fill)—and require mandatory technology-based controls to reduce or eliminate them.

Although the bill was strongly supported by Senator Muskie and backed by EPA officials, it ran into political trouble on the Senate floor. Senator Allen Ellender introduced an amendment designed to separate discharges of "dredged materials" from other polluting discharges and to vest sole permitting authority over the former in the Corps.[7] Senator Ellender stressed that such a change was necessary to avoid the "catastrophical" effects that could accompany EPA and technology-based regulation of navigation projects.[8] Senator Muskie responded with a proposed Section 402(m) as a substitute for Senator Ellender's amendment. This proposal would keep discharges of dredged spoil within EPA's NPDES program, but would have *required* EPA to issue a permit if the Corps certified that "the area chosen for disposal is the only reasonably available alternative."[9] Even upon such a Corps determination, Senator Muskie's amendment would permit EPA to deny a permit if it found that "the matter to be disposed of will adversely affect municipal water supplies, shellfish beds, wildlife, fisheries . . . or recreation areas."[10]

Senator Muskie's substitute amendment was accepted and Senate Bill 2770 passed the Senate on November 2, 1971. Significantly, neither Senator Muskie nor Senator Ellender focused specifically on discharges of fill material, which ordinarily are not undertaken for "disposal" purposes, but instead are part of a process to convert wetlands and other aquatic environments into uplands capable of supporting a wide variety of development projects.

2. *The House Bill*

House Bill 11896 was introduced by Representative John Blatnik on November 19, 1971. From the outset it provided for a separate program governing the discharge of "dredged or fill material," and this program was to be administered by the Corps.[11] It required the Corps, when considering applications for permits, to apply guidelines developed by EPA and to give "due consideration" to the views of EPA in making permit decisions.[12] EPA would be permitted to designate "sites where certain material may not be discharged" when this was "found necessary to protect critical areas."[13] The Corps was authorized to override such a designation upon finding "that there is no economically feasible alternative reasonably available."[14] House Bill 11896 was passed by the House without amendment to this section on March 27, 1972.

Thus, going into conference both the Senate and the House agreed that the Corps would have the final say regarding whether alternative sites are feasible. Both also agreed that EPA should have authority to restrict discharges when the material to be discharged would pollute certain critical areas. Differences centered on whether permits would be issued by EPA under the mandates of the NPDES program or by the Corps under its more traditional balancing approach. The Senate and the House also disagreed on whether an EPA "environmental" designation should trump, or be trumped by, a Corps certification on site feasibility.[15]

3. The Conference Committee Compromise: Section 404(c)

The Conference Committee, and finally the Congress, agreed to allow the Corps to administer the dredge and fill permit program, choosing as a basic structure the provisions of Section 404 as set forth in House Bill 11896. In deciding whether to issue a permit, the Corps was to apply "guidelines developed by [EPA], in conjunction with the [Corps] . . . and . . . in any case where such guidelines . . . alone would prohibit the specification of a site, through the application additionally of the economic impact of the site on navigation and anchorage."[16] This authority was, however, made "subject to" Section 404(c), which as enacted provides:

> The Administrator [of EPA] is authorized to prohibit the specification (including the withdrawal of specification) of any defined area as a disposal site, and he is authorized to deny or restrict the use of any defined area for specification (including the withdrawal of specification) as a disposal site, whenever he determines, after notice and opportunity for public hearings, that the discharge of such materials into such area will have an unacceptable adverse effect on municipal water supplies, shellfish beds and fishery areas (including spawning and breeding areas), wildlife, or recreational areas. Before making such determination, the Administrator shall consult with the [Corps]. The Administrator shall set forth in writing and make public his findings and his reasons for making any determination under this subsection.[17]

The Conference Report simply repeats the compromise language and affords no further insight as to the meaning of the compromise bill.

Debate on the conference committee report revealed very different viewpoints on what the compromise accomplished, particularly with respect to EPA's authority under Section 404(c). Senator Muskie prepared a written exhibit to his remarks on the compromise bill, and requested and received permission to insert it into the Congressional Record just before the final vote on the bill.[18] Thus, it was not read or considered by his fellow Senators prior to their vote. In Senator Muskie's opinion, Section 404(c) provided EPA with broad authority to veto Corps-issued permits to ensure that environmental values were carefully protected.[19]

In the House, Representative Walter Jones said Section 404(c) conferred a much more limited role upon EPA owing to "the importance of navigation and waterborne commerce to the economic well-being of the United States."[20] This difference in views about EPA's new authority under Section 404(c) has yielded considerable controversy in the agency's implementation of this statutory provision.

C. Procedures Governing EPA's Section 404(c) Authority

1. Timing

EPA has interpreted Section 404(c) to authorize the agency to take two types of actions. First, "EPA may exercise a veto over the specification by the [Corps] or a state of a site for the discharge of dredged or fill material."[21] Second, EPA "may also prohibit the specification of a site . . . with regard to any existing or potential discharge site before a permit application has been submitted to or approved by the Corps or a state."[22] Thus, EPA may exercise its Section 404(c) authority "before a permit is applied for, while an application is pending, or after a permit has been issued."[23] In *Russo Development Corp. v. Reilly,* the court held that Section 404(c) even authorizes EPA to veto an after-the-fact permit issued by the Corps.[24] The court rejected plaintiff's contention "that the use of the future tense 'will have' in § 404(c) limits EPA's authority to act once land is filled, and the avoidance of future adverse impact is no longer possible."[25]

In promulgating its Section 404(c) regulations, EPA expressed a clear preference for exercising its veto authority prior to Corps decisions on particular permit applications,[26] but in practice, EPA has exercised its Section 404(c) authority only after a Corps decision, or expression of intent, to issue a permit for particular discharges.[27] When a state has taken over the authority to issue Section 404 permits, in lieu of the Corps, EPA retains the authority to veto the permits.[28]

2. Section 404(q) Elevation

If EPA and the Corps disagree about whether a Section 404 permit should be issued, or what conditions should be included in a permit, EPA will normally try to resolve the agencies' disagreement through the

Section 404(q) "elevation" process before it institutes Section 404(c) veto proceedings. The Section 404(q) process starts when EPA requests "elevation" of a Corps permit decision from the Corps's district engineer to the Assistant Secretary of the Army for Civil Works. Section 404(q) provides that the Corps shall enter into agreements with various federal resource agencies, including EPA, "to minimize, to the maximum extent practicable, duplication, needless paperwork, and delays in the issuance of permits under this section." Congress's stated purpose was to assure that "a decision with respect to an application for a permit . . . will be made not later than the ninetieth day after the date the notice for such application is published."[29]

Over the years, the Corps has entered into several such Memoranda of Agreement (MOAs) with various federal agencies, including EPA. The present MOA between the Corps and EPA establishes the following procedures to be followed when an EPA regional office is concerned that a particular proposed permit may warrant higher-level scrutiny.

First, EPA must provide project-specific comments on the proposal within the public comment period, which may be extended at EPA's request to a maximum of sixty days (or longer if the applicant requests). During the comment period, the EPA regional administrator (or designee) must notify the district engineer "that in the opinion of EPA the project *may* result in substantial and unacceptable impacts to aquatic resources of national importance."[30] Second, within twenty-five days after the close of the comment period, the regional administrator must notify the district engineer that EPA has determined "the discharge *will* have a substantial and unacceptable impact on aquatic resources of national importance."[31]

The district engineer may respond by proposing to issue the permit notwithstanding EPA's objection or by proposing to issue a permit modified in an effort to resolve EPA's objection (in which cases the district engineer must provide a draft permit and decision document to EPA within five days of this decision). Alternatively, without having determined to issue a permit, the district engineer may notify EPA that the project has been modified or conditioned so that there no longer are "substantial and unacceptable impacts to aquatic resources of national importance." No time limit is prescribed in the MOA for the district engineer to perform this step, which is governed by the Corps's permit processing regulations.[32]

If EPA remains dissatisfied, its regional administrator must, within fifteen days, recommend that the Assistant Administrator, Office of Wetlands, Oceans and Watersheds, request elevation of the permit decision from the Assistant Secretary of the Army for Civil Works. The assistant administrator then has twenty days to make such a request to the assistant secretary. According to the MOA, the district engineer is to hold permit issuance in abeyance pending review of such a request at Corps headquarters.[33]

Finally, the assistant secretary has thirty days to (1) direct the district engineer to continue processing of the permit notwithstanding EPA's objections, or (2) instruct the district engineer to proceed in a prescribed way, or (3) make the final permit decision.[34]

If EPA remains displeased with the Corps's final resolution of the permit application following this Section 404(q) elevation process, it may move to veto the permit under Section 404(c). The MOA provides:

> The EPA reserves the right to proceed with Section 404(c). To assist the EPA in reaching a decision on whether to exercise its Section 404(c) authority, the District Engineer will provide EPA a copy of the Statement of Findings / Record of Decision prepared in support of a permit decision after the ASA(CW) review. The permit shall not be issued during a period of 10 calendar days after such notice unless it contains a condition that no activity may take place pursuant to the permit until such 10th day, or if the EPA has initiated a Section 404(c) proceeding during such 10 day period, until the Section 404(c) proceeding is concluded and subject to the final determination in such proceeding.[35]

3. *The Veto Process*

EPA's actions under Section 404(c) must follow regulatory procedures adopted by the agency.[36] Section 404(c) proceedings are initiated by EPA's regional administrators, each of whom may do so when he or she has "reason to believe after reviewing the information available . . . that an 'unacceptable adverse effect' could result from the specification or use for specification of a defined area for the disposal of dredged or fill material."[37] The process consists of three steps: issuance of a proposed determination by the regional administrator, issuance of a recommended determination by the regional administrator, and issuance of a final determination by the administrator.[38]

The first step begins when the regional administrator notifies the applicant and the district engineer of the regional administrator's intent to issue public notice of a proposed determination to prohibit or restrict the discharge.[39] If, within fifteen days after such notice, the regional administrator has not been satisfied that no "unacceptable adverse effects" will occur, the regional administrator is to proceed with publication of public notice of the proposed determination[40] and shall receive public comment for between thirty and sixty days.[41]

Within fifteen days after the close of the public comment period, or thirty days after the conclusion of a public hearing, the regional administrator must either prepare a recommended determination or decide to withdraw the proposed determination.[42] If a recommended determination is prepared, the regional administrator must "promptly" forward it, along with the administrative record (including "where possible a copy of the record of the Corps or the state pertaining to the site in question") to the EPA administrator in Washington, D.C.[43]

Upon receiving the recommended determination and the administrative record, the EPA administrator has thirty days to initiate consultation between "the Chief of Engineers, the owner of record, and, where applicable, the State and the applicant, if any."[44] They then have fifteen days "to notify the Administrator of their intent to take corrective action to prevent an unacceptable adverse effect(s)."[45] Within sixty days after receiving the recommended determination and administrative record, the administrator must make a final determination affirming, modifying, or rescinding the recommended determination.[46]

Although the time deadlines provided in EPA's regulations appear to establish a reasonably expeditious schedule, "[t]he Administrator or the Regional Administrator may, upon a showing of good cause, extend the time requirements in these regulations" simply by publishing notice in the Federal Register.[47]

D. The Substantive Standard: "Unacceptable Adverse Effects"

EPA may exercise its authority under Section 404(c) if the agency determines that the proposed discharge will have an "unacceptable adverse effect" on specified resources. EPA's regulations define an "unacceptable adverse effect" broadly to include an

> impact on an aquatic or wetland ecosystem which is likely to result in significant degradation of municipal water supplies (including surface or groundwater) or significant loss of or damage to fisheries, shellfishing, or wildlife habitat or recreation areas. In evaluating the unacceptability of such impacts, consideration should be given to the relevant portions of the section 404(b)(1) guidelines.[48]

This rule was first published on October 9, 1979—some seven years after the original passage of Section 404.[49] The reference in the definition of "unacceptable adverse effect" to the "relevant portions" of the Section 404(b)(1) Guidelines[50] has proven to be a catalyst for controversy in the administration of the Section 404 program, as EPA has interpreted the "relevant portions" language broadly.

The regulation's language does not strongly suggest that EPA viewed Section 404(c) as an appellate process through which the agency could correct any misapplication by the Corps of the Guidelines. Nonetheless, in the preamble to its Section 404(c) regulations, EPA concluded that the Section 404(b)(1) Guidelines establish not only the criteria for permit issuance by the Corps but also "the substantive criteria by which the acceptability of a proposed discharge is to be judged" for purposes of Section 404(c).[51] Under this view, EPA may veto a Corps decision if, in its judgment, the Corps misapplied the Guidelines with respect to the permit application.[52] As discussed in the next section, the courts that have considered the issue thus far have deferred to this interpretation of Section 404(c).

EPA has reviewed compliance with several provisions of the 404(b)(1) Guidelines as "relevant" to the determination of whether a discharge will have an "unacceptable adverse effect" on an aquatic ecosystem. First, the agency has focused on provisions in the Guidelines governing the determination of whether a discharge may cause significant degradation of an aquatic ecosystem.[53] For wetlands, the Guidelines provide a listing of the possible losses in wetland values and functions that may be associated with discharges of dredged or fill material.[54]

In addition, EPA has used Section 404(c) to review the Corps's application of the Guidelines' requirement that no permit shall be issued if practicable alternatives to the proposed discharge are available.[55]

EPA has also used Section 404(c) to review the Corps's application of the Guidelines' requirement that no permit be issued unless "appropriate and practicable steps have been taken which will minimize potential adverse impacts . . . on the aquatic ecosystem."[56]

In practice, EPA has preferred to adopt a case-by-case approach involving a wide range of discretionary factors, rather than firm rules, in exercising its Section 404(c) authority. Of course, in the vast majority of applications for Section 404 permits, EPA involvement will be minimal and applicants can expect a Corps decision on the application to be final. For more significant projects, it is difficult to ascertain in advance whether EPA may choose to become involved and on what basis it might do so.

III. *Judicial Interpretation of Section 404(c)*

EPA's exercise of its veto authority under Section 404(c) has almost always spawned litigation. Similarly, the agency's failure to exercise its veto authority has spawned litigation.

In *City of Olmstead Falls v. United States Environmental Protection Agency*, a federal district court held that EPA's exercise of its veto authority is discretionary, so federal courts lack jurisdiction to review the agency's failure to veto a Section 404 permit.[57] EPA's *initiation* of the Section 404(c) process is also not reviewable in court, as it is not a final agency action.[58] Plaintiffs must wait until the agency has vetoed a permit before they can sue.

When EPA exercises its Section 404(c) authority and challengers successfully invoke federal jurisdiction, courts review EPA's action under the arbitrary and capricious standard.[59] As the United States Court of Appeals for the Fourth Circuit explained in *James City County v. Environmental Protection Agency*, "[t]he scope of review under the 'arbitrary and capricious' standard is narrow and a court is not to substitute its judgment for that of the agency."[60]

In light of that deferential standard, courts have shown little inclination to limit EPA's discretion to determine what kinds of impacts from discharges may be considered "unacceptable adverse effects" for purposes of Section 404(c). In *Bersani v. EPA*,[61] for example, a New York District Court made three important conclusions that endorse a wide-ranging review by EPA under Section 404(c). First, the court held that EPA's review for unacceptable adverse effects may properly include review of the Corps's application of the Section 404(b)(1) Guidelines. The court determined that the Guidelines "provide a means to evaluate the desirability of discharges into the aquatic environment" and that "[a]pplying these standards to a proposed discharge in a particular context does no violence to the policy underlying the Act."[62] In the court's view, the Guidelines provide EPA with "a useful tool for evaluating discharges into the aquatic environment."[63]

Second, the court concluded that "EPA's interpretation that the avoidability of a loss may be considered in conjunction with its magnitude in determining whether it is 'unacceptable' within the meaning of Section 404(c) and 'significant' within the meaning of the implementing regulation is reasonable."[64] The court thus rejected the argument that even if EPA's regulatory definition of "unacceptable adverse effect" does not preclude consideration of the Guidelines, the only "relevant portions" for purposes of Section 404(c) are those pertaining to "the degree or magnitude of an effect"—i.e., those portions of the Guidelines that govern the determination of whether a discharge will cause "significant degradation" of an aquatic ecosystem.[65] More specifically, the court held that EPA may veto a permit if it concludes that the Corps erred in finding that no practicable alternatives to the proposed discharge site were available.[66]

Finally, the court refused to preclude EPA from engaging in de novo review of the Corps's application of the Guidelines.[67] The court thus dismissed the notion that such review would "allow the EPA unbridled authority to second guess every application by the Corps of the 404(b)(1) guidelines and will effectively vitiate the scheme of review envisioned by Congress."[68] After reviewing the text and legislative history of Section 404(c), the court concluded that nothing therein "indicates Congress' desire to limit the EPA's role in assessing the environmental acceptability of a site."[69] The Second Circuit upheld this interpretation.[70]

The *Bersani* court's deferential interpretation of EPA's authority under Section 404(c) was echoed by the Fourth Circuit in *James City County v. EPA*.[71] There, the court held that it was proper for EPA to consider whether alternatives are available to the applicant under the Section 404(b)(1) Guidelines when it vetoed a permit issued by the Corps. However, the Fourth Circuit found that the record did not support EPA's conclusion that practicable alternatives were available to the proposed water supply project, and EPA's veto was set aside.[72] Nonetheless, the court remanded the matter to the agency, concluding that EPA should be given the opportunity to determine whether "considerations of environmental effects would alone justify a veto."[73]

On remand, EPA concluded that the water supply project would have unacceptable adverse environmental effects. On review of that decision, the Fourth Circuit rejected the argument that EPA was required to consider the absence of alternatives, just as it had previously considered the claimed existence of alternatives, in deciding whether the environmental effects of the proposed reservoir were "unacceptable."[74] According to the court, EPA *may* consider, but cannot be *required* to consider, "non-environmental" factors such as a city's need for a dependable supply of water.[75] While acknowledging that Congress intended the Corps "in the initial permitting process to consider the total range of factors bearing on the necessity or desirability of [a proposed project], including whether the project was in the public interest,"[76] the court broadly concluded that "[EPA's] authority to veto to protect the environment is practically unadorned."[77] Accordingly, the court accepted EPA's argument that although the agency has the discretion to consider non-environmental factors, such as the need for water, "the only requirement placed on it by Congress is to consider the project's adverse impacts on the environment."[78]

The same conclusion was reached in *Alameda Water & Sanitation District v. Reilly,*[79] another case in which EPA chose to veto a Corps decision to issue a permit for a proposed water supply project. In upholding EPA's veto, the court stated:

> The plaintiffs have presented a very powerful argument that EPA has frustrated the will and efforts of local government in resolving a local problem by erecting a bureaucratic barrier to the project. They have not, however, proved that EPA acted in excess of its statutory authority or made an arbitrary and capricious decision.[80]

The court also upheld EPA's use of mitigation sequencing in application of the 404(b)(1) Guidelines to determine that there was a practicable alternative to the activity authorized by the Corps's permit.[81]

Other attempts to define limits to EPA's authority under Section 404(c) have also been rejected by the courts. In *Creppel v. Army Corps of Engineers,* for example, the plaintiff argued that in requiring a finding of an unacceptable adverse effect, Section 404(c) mandates that EPA employ "a balancing process . . . in 'which significant adverse environmental effects must be weighed and balanced along with all other considerations of public interest to determine whether such effects are "acceptable" under the circumstances.'"[82] The court rejected this argument, and concluded that "[S]ection 404(c) does not require a balancing of environmental concerns against 'the public interest.'"[83] Likewise, in *City of Alma v. United States,* the court quickly dismissed an argument that EPA had improperly vetoed a project by relying on impermissible "'non-wildlife factors,' such as water quality and the loss of wetlands."[84] And in *Alameda Water & Sanitation District v. Reilly,* the court held that EPA's veto authority is not restricted to effects associated with changes in water quality. EPA may properly consider changes in water quantity from inundation resulting from the proposed construction of a dam. The court concluded that such inundation "would have enough impact on [an affected] water resource as to authorize EPA to give careful consideration to the effects on recreational uses and aquatic life under Section 404(c)."[85]

IV. The Influence of EPA's Authority on the Section 404 Program

EPA's interpretation of Section 404(c), coupled with the courts' broad interpretation of the agency's authority under that statutory provision, has yielded two major results, both of which have had significant effects on the overall administration of the Section 404 program. First, EPA's use of Section 404(c) to police the Corps's application of the Section 404(b)(1) Guidelines has produced some dramatic changes in the Corps's administration of the Section 404 permit program. When publishing its regulations of July 16, 1977, the Corps stressed that "[t]he decision whether to issue a permit will be based on an evaluation of the probable impact of the proposed activity and its intended use on the public interest," including "a careful weighing of all those factors which become relevant in each particular case."[86] According to the Corps, "[t]he benefit which reasonably may be expected to accrue from the proposal must be balanced against its reasonably foreseeable detriments" to determine if a permit should issue.[87] Regarding the Section 404(b)(1) Guidelines, the rules said:

> If the EPA guidelines alone prohibit the designation of a proposed disposal site, the economic impact on navigation and anchorage of the failure to authorize the use of the proposed disposal site will also be considered in evaluating whether or not the proposed discharge is in the public interest.[88]

This interpretation treats compliance with the Guidelines as one factor to be considered by the Corps in its broader "public interest" balancing of costs and benefits.

When the Corps next revised its rules on July 22, 1982—after publication of EPA's veto rules and the current Guidelines—it again addressed the relationship between its public interest review and the Guidelines.[89] This time, the Corps placed the Guidelines at the center of the permitting process, concluding that "[t]he guidelines and the public interest review go hand-in-hand. Once all aspects of the public interest have been considered, if a project does not conform to the guidelines, the permit would be denied."[90] In practice today, the Corps's public interest review is usually easier to satisfy than the Guidelines.

In addition to this general shift in the relative importance of the Corps's public interest review and the Guidelines, EPA's veto authority has likely influenced the Corps to accede to EPA's views on important matters of interpretation involving the Guidelines. For example, the Corps has now accepted EPA's views on how the "practicable alternatives" analysis is to be conducted, including the role of mitigation and the applicant's statement of project purposes. The current views on these important aspects of the Guidelines represent significant departures from prior Corp decisions.[91]

The second effect of EPA's interpretation of its Section 404(c) authority and role in the permitting process is that compliance with the Guidelines, and a showing that a proposal is favorable under the Corps's public interest review, cannot necessarily be relied upon by applicants as sufficient for obtaining a Section 404 permit. Applicants and Corps regulators must additionally consider whether the proposed project is likely to instigate EPA opposition because of the proposal's environmental effects, notwithstanding any public benefits that may be realized by the project's completion.

This effect carries with it two additional consequences. First, it requires applicants to prepare for, and be able to withstand, the possibility of protracted regulatory proceedings before different decision makers who may, at times, disagree over fundamental policy issues as well as the merits of particular permit applications.[92] Second, it forces attention to what may be considered an "unacceptable adverse effect" by EPA, requiring applicants to make careful decisions when pursuing a Section 404 permit. As discussed above, this may be quite difficult given the open-ended nature of EPA's definition of "unacceptable adverse effect" and the courts' endorsement of such a definition.

In addition to these considerations, EPA's Section 404(c) authority has been quite influential in encouraging permit applicants to revise proposed projects, sometimes very substantially, to avoid adverse environmental effects. In fact, the threat or proposal of an EPA veto has undoubtedly induced many applicants simply to abandon proposed projects.

These same effects may result from EPA requests, pursuant to Section 404(q), to elevate to Corps headquarters decisions by district engineers to issue permits. For example, in response to EPA's consultation with the jurisdictions of the metropolitan Denver area pursuant to 40 C.F.R. § 231.6, those jurisdictions proposed reducing the scope of the proposed Two Forks Dam and Reservoir from a 1.1 million acre-feet project to a 0.45 million acre-feet project—a revised proposal that EPA nevertheless vetoed.[93] ARCO Alaska, Inc., fared better with revised plans for a well production pad and access road that reduced wetland impacts from the 21.5 acres that would have been affected by the original proposal to 17.9 acres.[94]

As these considerations reveal, the cumulative effect of EPA's implementation of its Section 404(c) authority and its expanding interpretation of its role in the Section 404 permitting process, particularly on the allocation of power between the Corps and EPA, extends far beyond the specific permits EPA has chosen to veto. EPA has most often used its formal authority under Section 404(c) to block construction of significant public infrastructure projects. This proved unpopular with many state and local officials, and a significant political movement developed in the 1990s to reduce EPA's authority in the Section 404 program. Beginning in 1991, a number of bills were introduced in Congress that would eliminate EPA's veto authority.[95]

It was in this context of impending legislative action that EPA entered into its new MOA with the Corps regarding Section 404(q) elevation on August 11, 1991, discussed above.[96] That MOA strongly implies that EPA will limit its Section 404(c) power in the future to cases involving "unacceptable adverse effects to aquatic resources of national importance."[97] While the agency has threatened to exercise its 404(c) power since that time, EPA last completed a Section 404(c) veto on March 27, 1992.

V. Conclusion

In 1972, Congress vested in the Corps the authority to administer a flexible permit program governed by a weighing and balancing of all relevant social values. It also authorized EPA to prohibit discharges of particular dredged or fill materials at particular sites where discharges of such materials would have an "unacceptable adverse effect." Congress did not, however, provide clear lines of authority between these agencies. Nor did Congress provide unambiguous guidance on how conflicts between the agencies were to be resolved. With acquiescence from the federal courts, EPA used its veto authority during the mid-1980s to the early 1990s to overrule Corps permit decisions and to establish and enforce controlling policy interpretations of the statute and the Guidelines. EPA continues to view its role in the permitting process as central to the Section 404 program, and in certain instances will use the various tools available to it to influence permit decisions and policy interpretations.

Notes

1. 42 U.S.C. § 1344 (2000).

2. For a discussion of this authority from the point of view of the regulating agencies, *see* U.S. Environmental Protection Agency, EPA's Clean Water Act Section 404(c): Veto Authority, http://www.epa.gov/owow/wetlands/facts/fact14.html (last accessed August 2004); U.S. Army Corps of Engineers, Regulatory Decision Safeguards, http://www.usace.army.mil/civilworks/cecwo/reg/press/safeguards.pdf (last accessed August 2004).

3. 33 U.S.C. § 1344(b).

4. 33 U.S.C. § 1344(q).

5. 33 U.S.C. § 1344(c).

6. Cong. Research Service, 93d Cong., A Legislative History of the Water Pollution Control Act Amendments of 1972 (Comm. Print 1973) [hereinafter Legis. Hist.] at 1534.

7. *Id.* at 1386. The Corps had been regulating such matters in waters that are truly "navigable" since passage of the Rivers and Harbors Act of 1890, a responsibility the Corps continues to hold under the Rivers and Harbors Act of 1899. 33 U.S.C. §§ 401, 403.

8. Senator Ellender explained the purpose and effect of his amendment as follows:

> One of the main deficiencies of [Senate Bill 2770] is that it treats dredged materials the same as industrial waste, sewage, sludge, or refuse introduced into a river system, lake estuary or ocean. . . .
>
> * * *
>
> The principal difference [between the offered amendment and the original bill] is that [under the amendment] the permit authority remains with the Secretary of the Army. . . . [Senate Bill 2770] as reported would in effect give the Environmental Protection Agency a veto power over the spoil disposal areas required for construction and maintenance of all navigation projects. [Under the amendment t]he Secretary of the Army will not be obligated to require strict compliance with the effluent requirements established by the Environmental Protection Agency in issuing permits. The strict adherence to the published standards would result in 90 percent of the ports and harbors of the United States being closed, until such time as land disposal areas are provided. This would create a catastrophical situation with respect to our foreign and domestic commerce.

Legis. Hist., *supra* note 6, at 1386–87.

9. Legis. Hist., *supra* note 6, at 1392.

10. *Id.* Senator Muskie explained this substitute amendment as follows:

> Let me state what I think the language means. First, it retains the permit issuing authority in the EPA. . . . That is the principal point. Second, it specifies the particular environmental risks that we conceived of as being incurred by the disposal of spoil. So in a sense, by being more specific rather than general it should expedite the process. Finally, it retains authority for the Secretary of the Army to make the judgments he should as to the economic feasibility or other feasibility in selecting the site.

Id.

11. Legis. Hist., *supra* note 6, at 1063–64.

12. *Id.*

13. *Id.* at 1064.

14. *Id.* at 1063–64. In reporting to the House on H.R. 11896 on March 11, 1972, the Committee on Public Works stated:

> In referring to "critical areas," the types of areas the Committee has in mind are shellfish beds, breeding or spawning areas, highly susceptible

> resort beaches, and similar areas. . . . [T]his action to create in effect, "prohibited areas" for discharging certain materials is to be used with circumspection. . . . In establishing criteria for dumping, the Administrator is required to consider economic factors and these in turn would be taken into account in the designation of . . . prohibited sites or times for discharging.
>
> * * *
>
> The Committee further notes that under Section 404 the Secretary of the Army shall have final decision-making responsibility and he shall not abdicate this responsibility to any other agency. For example, the Secretary can override the Administrator's designation if he determines that it is not economically feasible to use the designated site.

H.R. REP. NO. 92-911, 92nd Cong., 2d Sess. 130, *reprinted in* LEGIS. HIST. at 753, 817.

15. The legislative history provides no suggestion that Congress focused on the apparent difference in coverage between the Senate bill (which applied to "dredged spoil") and the House bill (which applied to both dredged and fill material).

16. LEGIS. HIST., *supra* note 6, at 71; 33 U.S.C. § 1344(b).

17. 33 U.S.C. § 1344(c).

18. LEGIS. HIST., *supra* note 6, at 161–84.

19. *Id.* at 177. According to Senator Muskie:

> The Conferees were uniquely aware of the process by which the dredge and fill permits are presently handled and did not wish to create a burdensome bureaucracy in light of the fact that a system to issue permits already existed. At the same time, the Committee did not believe there could be any justification for permitting the Secretary of the Army to make determination as to the environmental implications of either the site to be selected or the specific spoil to be disposed of in a site. Thus, the Conferees agreed that the Administrator of the Environmental Protection Agency should have the veto over the selection of the site for dredged spoil disposal and over any specific spoil to be disposal of in any selected site.

20. *House Debate on the Conference Report,* LEGIS. HIST. at 236. According to Rep. Jones:

> [I]t is the position of the House Conferees that any restriction or prohibition of any defined area as a disposal site must be made with circumspection in view of the importance of navigation and waterborne commerce to the economic well-being of the United States. Thus, it is expected that disposal site restrictions or prohibitions shall be limited to narrowly defined areas where it can be clearly demonstrated that the discharge of dredged material at such specified location will have an unacceptable adverse effect on critical areas intended to be protected.

21. 40 C.F.R. § 231.1(a) (2004).

22. *Id.*

23. City of Alma v. United States, 744 F. Supp. 1546, 1558 (S.D. Ga. 1990) (citations omitted).

24. 20 Envtl. L. Rep. 20,938, 20,939 (D.N.J. 1990).

25. *Id.*

26. In the preamble to the regulations, EPA explained that it "feels an important distinction should be drawn between the Agency's right to use 404(c) after issuance [of a permit] and its choice to do so. The statute on its face clearly allows EPA to act after the Corps has issued a permit; it refers twice to the "withdrawal of specification," which clearly refers to action by EPA after the Corps has specified a site. . . . On the other hand, EPA recognizes that where possible it is much preferable to exercise this authority before the Corps . . . has issued a permit, and before the permit holder has begun operations." 44 Fed. Reg. 58,077 (1979), *quoted in* City of Alma, 744 F. Supp. at 1558–59.

27. In rare instances, EPA has attempted to use an advanced identification of disposal sites procedure, which is included as part of the Section 404(b)(1) Guidelines. *See* 40 C.F.R. § 230.80. The regulation governing this procedure provides:

> Consistent with [the Section 404(b)(1)] Guidelines, EPA and the permitting authority, on their own initiative or at the request of any other party and after consultation with any affected State that is not the permitting authority, may identify sites which will be considered as:
>
> (1) Possible future disposal sites, including existing disposal sites and non-sensitive areas; or
>
> (2) Areas generally unsuitable for disposal site specification[.]

Id. at § 230.80(a)(1)–(2). The avowed purpose of this procedure is "to aid applicants [for Section 404 permits] by giving advance notice that they would have a relatively easy or difficult time qualifying for a permit to use particular areas. Such advance notice should facilitate applicant planning and shorten permit processing time." Environmental Protection Agency, Guidelines for Specification of Disposal Sites for Dredged or Fill Material, Final Rule, 45 Fed. Reg. 85,336, 85,342 (Dec. 24, 1980); *see also* 40 C.F.R. § 230.80(b). However, the effect of advanced identification under this procedure is not binding. Withdrawal of a site under Section 404(c) has the effect of denying the Corps any authority to issue a permit for the discharge of dredged or fill material at that site. By contrast, regulations governing the advanced identification procedure included in EPA's Section 404(b)(1) Guidelines provide:

> The identification of any area as a possible future disposal site should not be deemed to constitute a permit for the discharge of dredged or fill material within such area or a specification of a disposal site. The identification of areas that generally will not be available for disposal site specification should not be deemed as prohibiting applicants for permits to discharge dredged or fill material in such areas. Either type of

identification constitutes information to facilitate individual or General permit application and processing.

40 C.F.R. § 230.80(b). EPA has rarely used the advanced identification procedure. For such a rare example, see EPA, Identification of Disposal Areas (AIDA): Faulkner Lake Area Wetland Complex, Arkansas, 51 Fed. Reg. 35,688 (Oct. 7, 1986).

28. 40 C.F.R. § 230.80.

29. 33 U.S.C. § 1344(q).

30. Memorandum of Agreement between the Environmental Protection Agency and the Department of the Army (Aug. 11, 1992) at 7 (emphasis in original), *available at* http://www.usace.army.mil/inet/functions/cw/cecwo/reg/epa404q.htm (last accessed August 2004).

31. *Id.* (emphasis in original).

32. *See* 33 C.F.R. pt. 325.

33. Memorandum of Agreement between the Environmental Protection Agency and the Department of the Army (Aug. 11, 1992), *supra* note 30, at 8.

34. *Id.*

35. *Id.* at 9–10.

36. *See* 40 C.F.R. pt. 231.

37. 40 C.F.R. § 231.3(a).

38. 40 C.F.R. § 231.1(b).

39. 40 C.F.R. § 231.3(a)(1).

40. 40 C.F.R. § 231.3(a)(2).

41. A public hearing may be held on the proposed determination if the regional administrator determines that the public interest warrants one, and must be held if an affected landowner or the permit applicant requests one. 40 C.F.R. § 231.4(b). Any public hearing must occur at least twenty-one days after the public notice, and fifteen days prior to the close of the public comment period. 40 C.F.R. § 231.4.

42. 40 C.F.R. § 231.5(a).

43. 40 C.F.R. § 231.5(b).

44. 40 C.F.R. § 231.6.

45. *Id.*

46. *Id.*

47. 40 C.F.R. § 231.8.

48. 40 C.F.R. § 231.2(e).

49. 44 Fed. Reg. 58,076 (Oct. 9, 1979).

50. 40 Fed. Reg. 41,292 (Sept. 5, 1975).

51. 44 Fed. Reg. 58,076 (Oct. 9, 1979).

52. For example, in its preamble to the new Section 404(b)(1) Guidelines, EPA said that "if the Guidelines are properly applied [by the Corps], EPA will rarely have to use its 404(c) veto." 45 Fed. Reg. 85,337 (Dec. 24, 1980).

53. *See* 40 C.F.R. §§ 230.10(c), 230.22 & subparts C–G.

54. *See* 40 C.F.R. § 230.41(b). Nonetheless, none of these provisions describes what kinds of losses will be considered "unacceptable" for purposes of Section 404(c).

55. *See, e.g.*, James City County v. EPA, 955 F.2d 254 (4th Cir. 1992); Bersani v. EPA, 674 F. Supp. 405 (N.D.N.Y. 1987), *aff'd sub nom.* Bersani v. Robichaud, 850 F.2d 36 (2d Cir. 1988).

56. *See* James City County, 955 F.2d 254.

57. 266 F. Supp. 718, 723 (N.D. Ohio 2003). The court also rejected the plaintiff's claim that the 404(b)(1) Guidelines create a nondiscretionary duty on EPA. *Id.* at 723–24. The court held that the Guidelines impose a duty on the Corps of Engineers, but not on EPA. *Id.*

58. Newport Galleria Group v. Deland, 618 F. Supp. 1179, 1185 (D.D.C. 1985).

59. *See* James City County v. EPA, 12 F.3d 1330, 1338 (4th Cir. 1993); Bersani v. EPA, 674 F. Supp. 405, 412–13 (N.D.N.Y. 1987), *aff'd*, 850 F.2d 36 (2d Cir. 1988), *cert. denied*, 489 U.S. 1089 (1989); Alameda Water & Sanitation District v. Reilly, 930 F. Supp. 486, 491 (D. Colo. 1996); Russo Development Corp. v. Thomas, 735 F. Supp. 631, 635 (D.N.J. 1989).

60. 12 F.3d 1330, 1338 (4th Cir. 1993), citing Motor Vehicle Mfrs. Ass'n of the United States, Inc. v. State Farm Mut. Auto. Ins. Co., 463 U.S. 29 (1983).

61. 674 F. Supp. 405 (N.D.N.Y. 1987), *aff'd sub nom.* Bersani v. Robichaud, 850 F.2d 36 (2d Cir. 1988).

62. *Id.* at 414; *see also City of Alma*, 744 F. Supp. at 1567.

63. *Bersani*, 674 F. Supp. at 414.

64. *Id.* at 415.

65. *Id.* at 414–15. The "significant degradation" portion of the Section 404(b)(1) Guidelines is set forth at 40 C.F.R. § 230.10(c).

66. *Bersani*, 674 F. Supp. at 415.

67. *Id.* at 415.

68. *Id.*

69. *Id.* at 417; *see also* Newport Galleria Group v. Deland, 618 F. Supp. 1179, 1182 n.2 (D.D.C. 1985) (noting in *dicta* that "it would be extraordinary if Congress granted the EPA veto power over the Corps's permit decision, but precluded it from reconsidering those issues the Corps considered in granting the permit in the first place").

70. Bersani v. Robichaud, 850 F.2d 36 (2d Cir. 1988).

71. 955 F.2d 254 (4th Cir. 1992), *later proceeding after remand*, 12 F.3d 1330 (4th Cir. 1993).

72. *Id.* at 259.

73. *Id.* at 260.

74. In requesting the remand following judicial invalidation of its first veto of the Ware Creek Reservoir in James City County, Virginia, EPA argued:

> The statutory term "unacceptable" must certainly authorize the Agency to consider and balance a wide variety of pertinent factors, including the scope and severity of a project's environmental effects in light of the benefits to be obtained from it.

Reply Brief For Appellants EPA and Corps of Engineers (May 16, 1991), filed in James City County v. EPA, 955 F.2d 254 (4th Cir. 1992).

75. *James City County,* 12 F.3d at 1335–36.
76. *Id.* at 1335.
77. *Id.* at 1336.
78. *Id.* at 1335.
79. 930 F. Supp. 486, 491 (D. Col. 1996).
80. *Id.* at 493.
81. *Id.* at 492.
82. 19 Envtl. L. Rep. 20,134, 20,136 (E.D. La. 1988).
83. *Id.*
84. 744 F. Supp. 1546, 1567 (S.D. Ga. 1990).
85. 930 F. Supp. at 491.
86. 42 Fed. Reg. 37,122, 37,136 (July 19, 1977); 33 C.F.R. 320.4(a) (1978).
87. *Id.*
88. 42 Fed. Reg. 37,122, 37,147 (July 19, 1977); 33 C.F.R. 323.5(a) (1978).
89. 47 Fed. Reg. 31,794 (July 22, 1982).
90. *Id.*

91. For a detailed discussion of these shifts in the Corps's view of the Section 404(b)(1) Guidelines, particularly with respect to the practicable alternatives analysis, see Chapter 7 of this book. The shift in Corps policy respecting the practicable alternatives analysis is evident in Army Corps of Engineers, Permit Elevation, Plantation Landing Resort, Inc. (Apr. 21, 1989). The shift in the Corps view of the role of mitigation may be seen in *Alameda Water & Sanitation District,* 930 F. Supp. at 492.

92. For an extreme example, see *City of Alma,* 744 F. Supp. at 1550–54 (describing history of City's efforts, over a period extending longer than a decade, to secure a Section 404 permit to construct a recreational lake).

93. *See* Water Pollution Control; Final Determination of the Assistant Administrator for Water Pursuant to Section 404(c) of the Clean Water Act concerning the Two Forks Water Supply Impoundments in Jefferson and Douglas Counties, CO, 56 Fed. Reg. 76 (1991).

94. *See* 56 Fed. Reg. 58,247 (1991).

95. On January 8, 1991, Rep. John Paul Hammerschmidt introduced the Wetlands Protection and Regulatory Reform Act of 1991, which among other things would have repealed Section 404(c). *See* H.R. 404, 102d Cong. (1991). It was followed on March 7, 1991, by introduction of the Comprehensive Wetlands Conservation and Management Act of 1991, by Rep. Jimmy Hayes of Louisiana and fifty-three other Congressmen. *See* H.R. 1330, 102d Cong. (1991). It, too, would have eliminated EPA's authority to veto Corps permit decisions.

The movement developed more slowly in the Senate, where Environment and Public Works Committee Chairman Senator John Chafee attempted to block any weakening of EPA's authority in the Section 404 program. On March 15, 1991, Senator Max Baucus introduced a Clean Water Act "reauthorization" bill (the Water Pollution Prevention and Control Act of 1991) that proposed no changes to Section 404. *See* S. 1083, 102d Cong. (1991).

Later, in 1995, Senators J. Bennett Johnston and Lauch Faircloth introduced a bill that bore much in common with the original House bill, H.R. 1330, including its consolidation of Section 404 authority in the Corps and elimination of EPA's "veto" power. *See* S. 851, 104th Cong. (1995). However, neither that bill, nor a similar bill in the House, H.R. 961, were enacted.

96. *See* Section II.C.2 of this chapter.

97. Memorandum of Agreement between the Environmental Protection Agency and the Department of the Army (Aug. 11, 1992), *supra* note 30, at 6–7.

APPENDIX

EPA's Veto Decisions

Following publication of its regulations in late 1979, the U.S. Environmental Protection Agency (EPA) proposed its first veto on August 1, 1980.[1] It then issued a total of twelve final vetoes from 1981 through March 27, 1992. Each of EPA's final veto actions is described below. These decisions illustrate the variety of environmental effects and regulatory rationales that may underlie an EPA veto decision.

I. City of North Miami Beach, Florida

In 1976, the Corps's Jacksonville District issued a permit to the City of North Miami Beach, Florida, to fill 103 acres of wetlands on a 291-acre site near Biscayne Bay.[2] Neither the Corps's public notice nor its permit disclosed that the 1.5 million cubic yards of fill to be used would be municipal solid waste. The project was begun and resulted in leachate from the solid waste collecting in waters on the site, including ammonia in concentrations as high as 500 parts per million.[3] The contamination threatened to extend to Biscayne Bay, which supports recreational and commercial fisheries and two endangered species (the Eastern brown pelican and the West Indian manatee).

The Corps issued public notice of a proposed permit amendment on March 25, 1977, to dispose of several more million cubic yards of waste and to excavate both a mangrove preserve and three shallow tidal ponds as borrow areas.[4] EPA Region IV Administrator Rebecca Hanmer responded with a written objection on July 1, 1977.[5] She was not successful in resolving matters to her satisfaction with the Corps's Jacksonville district engineer or with its South Atlantic division engineer. EPA then elevated the matter to EPA's deputy administrator and the Assistant Secretary of the Army for Civil Works pursuant to Section 404(q) of the Clean Water Act. When this step also failed to produce a suspension of the Corps permit, Hanmer initiated the first Section 404(c) action, publishing notice of her proposed determination on August 1, 1980.[6] A public hearing was held October 2, 1980, followed by the regional administrator's recommended determination on November 28, 1980. The record was forwarded to Washington, and EPA Administrator Douglas Costle signed a final determination restricting all future discharges at the site to clean fill only on January 19, 1981.[7]

II. The M.A. Norden Site, Mobile, Alabama

In 1980, M.A. Norden applied to the Mobile District for a permit to fill fifty-five acres of tidal wetlands within the Three Mile Creek floodplain near Mobile, Alabama.[8] Public notice of this proposal elicited numerous objections from several agencies including EPA, U.S. Fish and Wildlife Service (FWS), and National Marine Fisheries Service (NMFS).[9] In a January 1981 letter to the Corps, EPA recommended denial of the permit application based on noncompliance with the 404(b)(1) Guidelines.[10] Pursuant to these objections, Norden modified his permit application on April 21, 1982, by reducing the proposed fill area to twenty-five acres. He also indicated that he had considered upland alternatives but determined that the alternatives were cost prohibitive.[11]

EPA responded that the revised proposal still did not comply with the Guidelines and that no ecological justification was found to alter the previously stated EPA position.[12] On August 3, 1983, the acting division engineer for the South Atlantic Division of the Corps wrote to EPA indicating the Division's decision to issue the permit for the revised project. EPA responded by invoking the provisions of Section 404(q), requesting review by the Assistant Secretary of the Army for Civil Works. On September 22, 1983, the Assistant Secretary found that the issue was a technical disagreement and declined to refer the matter to a higher authority. He instead indicated that the provisions of Section 404(c) were more appropriate for addressing technical disagreements between the agencies.[13]

On September 30, 1983, EPA initiated veto procedures. In its November 10, 1983, proposed determination, EPA reiterated its position that the Guidelines were not being followed. Specifically, EPA said there had been no demonstration that other practicable, less environmentally damaging alternatives were unavailable. In addition, EPA cited several negative environmental impacts of the proposed project including loss of wetland filtering capacity, loss of flood prevention capacity, and damage to recreational and commercial fisheries.[14]

EPA issued its final determination on July 18, 1984.[15] The final determination recited numerous environmental values of the site that would be impacted by the proposed action and asserted that practicable, cost-effective alternatives to the site were available.[16]

III. Jack Maybank Site, Charleston County, South Carolina

In December 1982, Jack Maybank applied for a permit to impound approximately 2,000 acres of wetlands adjacent to the South Edisto River in Charleston County, South Carolina, primarily for duck hunting.[17] Pursuant to state permit requirements, Maybank modified this proposal in October 1983, reducing the acreage to approximately 900 acres. EPA, FWS, and NMFS objected to the project. The FWS notified the Corps that the most significant impacts could be mitigated by limiting the impoundment to a single, 160-acre site on the highest part of Jehossee Island. Maybank rejected this proposal on the basis that it would not satisfy project needs.[18]

The Corps notified EPA on April 11, 1984, that it intended to issue the permit.[19] EPA then initiated the Section 404(q) elevation process and notified the Corps of its intent to invoke Section 404(c) procedures.[20] The Acting Assistant Secretary of the Army for Civil Works declined referral of the application.[21]

On July 26, 1984, EPA published a proposed determination.[22] It asserted that the wetlands in question provided ecological services to the downstream estuary and served as valuable feeding, nursery, and spawning habitat for various finfish, shellfish, and other wildlife.[23] In addition, EPA said the proposed impoundments would eliminate public access to much of the area. EPA said impounding the areas would attract and concentrate waterfowl, which in turn would result in the addition of nutrients to the ecosystem and possibly cause algal blooms.[24] Finally, EPA stated that impounding the wetlands would eliminate the natural tidal influence, thus further diminishing the ecological value of the area.[25]

On May 15, 1985, EPA issued a final determination.[26] It reiterated the above objections and commented on the negative cumulative effects of removing wetlands from the area of the Maybank site.[27]

IV. Sweedens Swamp Site, Attleboro, Massachusetts

In 1983, the Pyramid Companies (Pyramid) chose a parcel of land in and around Sweedens Swamp (near South Attleboro, Massachusetts) as a site upon which to build a 700,000-square-foot shopping mall. The proposal required a discharge of 850,000 cubic yards of fill into thirty-two acres of wetlands and the alteration of an additional thirteen acres of forested wetlands. Pyramid proposed detailed mitigation plans, including onsite mitigation as well as the creation of thirty-six acres of artificial wetlands roughly two miles away. By 1984, Pyramid was in negotiations with EPA and the Corps regarding the necessary permits and approvals.[28]

Pyramid hoped to take advantage of nationwide permits for its proposal, but at the request of EPA, the Corps refused to verify a nationwide permit. Instead, the Corps required Pyramid to apply for an individual Section 404 permit.[29] Pyramid applied for this permit in July 1984.[30] In October 1984, EPA commented that the permit should be denied because the proposal did not comply with the Guidelines. Specifically, EPA said that non-water-dependent activities (such as building a mall) must be presumed to have less environmentally damaging, practicable alternatives and that Pyramid had failed to demonstrate that no practicable alternative to filling wetlands existed.[31] Further, EPA asserted that Pyramid's mitigation plan was immaterial because mitigation may be used only to compensate for unavoidable wetlands impacts, and not to "buy down" impacts in the alternatives analysis.[32]

On May 2, 1985, after further studies and public hearings, the Corps's division engineer recommended that Pyramid's permit application be denied. He found that (1) the proposal did not comply with the Guidelines because there was a practicable, environmentally preferable site; and (2) the proposal was not in the overall public interest.[33] On May 31, 1985, in a highly unusual move, the Director of Civil Works in the Office of the Chief of Engineers overruled the division engineer and ordered preparation of a notice of intent to issue a permit.[34] On June 28, 1985, the Corps informed EPA and FWS of its intent to issue a permit.[35]

On July 23, 1985, EPA Region I initiated Section 404(c) proceedings, and the FWS supported EPA's 404(c) action. On August 21, 1985, EPA published its proposed determination,[36] and a public hearing was held with over 1,000 in attendance. A majority supported construction of the mall.[37] Pyramid submitted a new mitigation plan to the Corps and negotiated with EPA, agreeing to complete off-site mitigation prior to disturbing Sweedens Swamp and to post a $1 million performance bond on the wetland construction.[38]

When it appeared these efforts would not appease EPA, Pyramid sued the agency on August 27, 1985, seeking to enjoin the 404(c) process and to compel immediate issuance of the 404 permit by the Corps.[39] The court dismissed Pyramid's complaint, noting that Section 404(c) gives the EPA administrator wide discretion and sets no threshold requirements for the initiation of such proceedings.[40] The court also concluded that initiation of Section 404(c) proceedings is not final agency action.[41]

In June 1986, EPA issued a final determination prohibiting the proposed discharge.[42] It rested largely on a finding that there was a practicable, less environmentally damaging alternative to the proposed site; therefore, the Guidelines required denying the application.[43] EPA recognized that the alternative site became unavailable during the course of the permitting process (it was bought by a competitor), but found that that fact was not relevant. At the time of market entry, the alternative site was available to Pyramid.[44] Pyramid challenged this determination in court, where the Second Circuit ultimately upheld EPA's decision to evaluate alternatives as of the time the permit applicant "entered the marketplace."[45]

V. Bayou Aux Carpes Site, Jefferson Parish, Louisiana

EPA initiated Section 404(c) proceedings in response to litigation surrounding a Corps flood control project that originated in the 1960s. Over the years, EPA and other agencies objected to the Corps's proposed flood control project because of the "significant adverse effects" that would be caused by the draining of wetlands. In 1975, EPA recommended a modified design, replacing dams with flood control gates in order to maintain the integrity of the wetlands. Landowners interested in the project filed suit in state court and won a judgment that enjoined Jefferson Parish from any activity other than completion of the original plan.[46]

The landowners also sued in federal court in the eastern district of Louisiana. This court upheld the modification of the plan.[47] The decision was appealed to the Fifth Circuit, which remanded the case for consideration of whether Section 404 of the Clean Water Act might prevent completion of the original project.[48] The district court ruled that the original project should go forward. EPA filed a Motion to Reconsider, arguing that the ruling deprived the agency of the opportunity to invoke Section 404(c). The district court judge issued an order that allowed EPA a window of time in which to begin Section 404(c) proceedings.[49]

EPA did so, claiming the original project would have unacceptable adverse impacts to "shellfish beds and fishery areas (including spawning and breeding areas), wildlife, and recreational areas."[50] Its final determination broadened this finding, asserting that the proposed original project would have unacceptable adverse impacts to every factor enumerated in Section 404(c) with the exception of municipal water supplies.[51] EPA's final determination prohibited the original flood control plan, but allowed the modified plan to be implemented. Landowners challenged the final determination, asserting that EPA failed to balance the environmental effects against the public interest in the project as originally conceived. The U.S. District Court for the Eastern District of Louisiana upheld EPA's final determination, holding that Section 404(c) does not require EPA to balance environmental effects against "the public interest."[52]

VI. Russo Development Corp., Carlstadt, New Jersey

Russo Development Co. purchased forty-four acres of land in Carlstadt, New Jersey, in 1979. By 1982, Russo had filled all of the tract, which was in the Hackensack Meadowlands Development District, for construction of warehouses. This was consistent with the Hackensack Meadowlands development scheme.[53] In 1985, Russo had developed six warehouses on the property and had plans to build a seventh, and it purchased an adjoining 13.5-acre parcel and began filling 8.5 acres of wetlands there in preparation for construction of additional warehouses. The Corps discovered the activity pursuant to an anonymous phone call, asserted jurisdiction over the 13.5-acre parcel, and orally ordered Russo to cease and desist. The Corps then notified Russo that it asserted jurisdiction over some or all of the forty-four-acre tract and ordered Russo to stop construction of the seventh warehouse on that site.

The Corps informed Russo that it needed a permit to fill the 13.5-acre parcel, but that this permit would not be issued unless Russo also obtained an after-the-fact permit for the forty-four-acre parcel. In March 1987, the Corps issued a notice of intent to issue a Section 404(b) permit to Russo. The Corps considered the two parcels together for this permit and its associated mitigation. The mitigation proposal entailed enhancement of existing wetlands within the Hackensack Meadowlands for a 0.5:1 (enhance:loss) compensation for the wetlands lost, and a deed restriction securing permanent preservation of twenty-three acres of wetlands outside the Hackensack river basin.[54] EPA objected and requested Section 404(q) elevation. Its request was denied and it commenced Section 404(c) proceedings.[55]

On May 9, 1988, EPA published its final determination.[56] According to EPA, the filling, both past and proposed, resulted in unacceptable adverse impact to various resources, including wildlife. The decision was based largely on the cumulative effects of wetland losses in the

Hackensack Meadowlands and the relative rarity of the type of wetland that was affected.[57]

Russo filed suit in the U.S. District Court for the District of New Jersey.[58] The court severed all consideration of the forty-four-acre parcel from the litigation, holding that the two parcels should never have been permitted together.[59] Russo then moved for summary judgment asserting that EPA may not veto after-the-fact permits. The court held otherwise.[60] In a final motion for summary judgment, the court held that EPA's veto action as to the 13.5-acre parcel was arbitrary and capricious because the initial linking of the two parcels tainted the entire permit process.[61]

VII. Three East Everglades Properties (Rem Estate), Dade County, Florida

Landowners proposed to use an agricultural technique known as "rockplowing" to create farmland out of wetlands. The technique uses a bulldozer to drag a multitoothed plowlike implement, which breaks up the limestone substrate and redistributes it to fill wet pockets. The Corps announced its plans to issue permits for rockplowing on the Rem site, was in the process of considering an application to permit rockplowing on a second site, and had suggested that it would allow rockplowing on a third site, if requested. EPA initiated Section 404(c) procedures for all three sites.[62]

EPA concluded that rockplowing these sites would result in unacceptable adverse impacts to fish and wildlife habitat, food-chain production, recreation, and groundwater and surface water quality. EPA also cited adverse cumulative impacts on habitat diversity in its decision. EPA did not engage in any analysis of alternatives in determining that the proposed activity would result in unacceptable adverse impacts.[63]

VIII. Lake Alma, Bacon County, Georgia

Beginning in 1971, the city of Alma, Georgia, began assessing the possibility of creating a recreational lake by damming Hurricane Creek.[64] From the very beginning, the project was controversial, as the flooding of wetlands would have negative consequences for numerous wildlife species. To mitigate some of these consequences, FWS recommended creating fourteen Greentree Reservoirs (GTRs), small impoundments to be managed for wildlife and drawn down annually.

Two permits were at issue in this project, one for the dam across Hurricane Creek and one for the fourteen GTRs. In November 1981, the Corps issued a Section 404 permit for discharges associated with the construction of the dam across Hurricane Creek. Environmental organizations and landowners sued, challenging the Corps's actions under the National Environmental Policy Act and the CWA.[65] Eventually, the Eleventh Circuit held that a supplemental environmental impact statement (SEIS) needed to be prepared for the mitigation plan and that a Section 404 permit was required for the GTRs.[66]

EPA advised the Corps to expand the SEIS to include the impacts of the overall lake project. Commenting on the draft SEIS, EPA renewed its opposition to the project.[67] In 1988, the Corps notified EPA of its intention to issue a Section 404 permit for the project. EPA subsequently initiated Section 404(c) proceedings and ultimately determined that the proposed project would result in unacceptable adverse effects on wildlife.[68] These effects included direct negative effects as well as secondary and cumulative effects. On February 14, 1989, EPA published its final determination.[69] The City of Alma and Bacon County, Georgia, filed suit in the U.S. District Court for the Southern District of Georgia alleging that EPA's Section 404(c) veto was arbitrary and capricious and contrary to law.[70] The district court disagreed, holding that EPA's decision was supported by the record.[71]

IX. Ware Creek Reservoir, James City County, Virginia

In 1981, representatives of James City County, Virginia, their consultants, and relevant federal and state agencies met to discuss proposals to impound Ware Creek in order to create a municipal water supply reservoir. The parties recognized that issuing a Section 404 permit for this proposed activity would constitute a "major federal action" and began preparing an environmental impact statement (EIS).[72]

EPA assessed the draft EIS in 1985 and concluded it was unsatisfactory.[73] The major flaw, according to EPA, was a failure to address the full range of feasible alternatives. The Corps and the applicant performed substantial additional investigations of alternatives, and in September 1987 the Corps issued a final EIS. It concluded that impounding Ware Creek was the only practicable alternative for the water supply project.[74] The final EIS also expanded the proposed mitigation measures, including acquiring and enhancing off-site wetlands and breaching an existing dam on nearby Yarmouth Creek.[75] EPA commented on the final EIS, again stating that the full range of alternatives had not been addressed. EPA indicated it was considering a Section 404(c) action on any permit issued by the Corps.[76]

In July 1988, the Corps issued a notice of intent to issue a permit for the impounding of Ware Creek.[77] In August, EPA Region III informed the Corps that it was initiating Section 404(c) proceedings. First, EPA said that the environmental resource values of the Ware Creek site were very high and probably irreplaceable. Second, EPA claimed there were feasible, less environmentally damaging alternatives.[78] The recommended determination, issued by the regional administrator, cited various alternatives including a pipeline from the James River, conservation, use of groundwater, desalinization of brackish groundwater, and the construction of three smaller dams on Ware Creek.[79]

EPA issued a final determination to veto the permit in July, 1989. Once again, EPA claimed that alternatives existed.[80] The final determination explicitly stated that the three-dam project was a viable alternative, but rejected the pipeline.[81] It also claimed that groundwater, groundwater desalinization, and conservation were practicable alternatives.[82]

James City County sued EPA in the U.S. District Court for the Eastern District of Virginia. The district court granted summary judgment to the county, finding that the record established that no practicable alternatives existed. Accordingly, it set aside EPA's Section 404(c) action.[83] The district court ordered the Corps to issue the permit and rejected EPA's request for a remand.[84] EPA appealed this decision.

On appeal, the Fourth Circuit upheld the district court's conclusion that the record established that no practicable alternatives were available.[85] EPA suggested the three-dam project as the primary alternative. However, this project would require the cooperation of a neighboring county, one that categorically opposed the damming of Ware Creek within its jurisdiction. The court rejected EPA's use of "market entry analysis" and concluded that this proposed alternative did not satisfy the regulatory definition of a practicable alternative.[86] The appeals court further held that the remaining alternatives suggested by EPA were also impracticable.[87] On the issue of remand, however, the Fourth Circuit overturned the district court, concluding that EPA was entitled to consider whether the environmental effects of the project were "unacceptable" given the absence of a practicable alternative.[88] For EPA's action on remand, see Two Forks Dam and Reservoir, below.

X. Big River Reservoir, Kent County, Rhode Island

The proposed Big River Reservoir project entailed building a dam and creating a 3,400-acre reservoir to be used for a municipal water supply.[89] In the 1960s, Rhode Island acquired approximately 8,000 acres of land surrounding the Big River in anticipation of the project. At times the project has been both a state project and a proposal by the Corps itself.

In 1981, the Corps completed an EIS for the proposed reservoir as part of a federal flood control project. By 1982, EPA had informed the Corps that, in its opinion, the project did not comply with the 404(b)(1) Guidelines.[90] In 1986, Rhode Island informed the Corps that it wished to pursue the reservoir as a state project and applied for a Section 404 permit.

The Corps informed Rhode Island that a supplemental EIS would be required to correct oversights and changes since the original EIS. For example, the original EIS indicated that approximately 570 acres of wetlands would be lost. However, new information led the Corps to believe that the true acreage was closer to 1,000.[91] During 1986 and 1987, EPA voiced concerns about the project, stating that it could not comply with the Guidelines. In a 1988 letter, EPA urged the Corps to deny the permit because the project would cause significant degradation of the aquatic environment and could not be adequately mitigated.[92] In July 1988, the Corps wrote to Rhode Island's governor, informing him that the project, as proposed, would not conform to the Guidelines and probably could not receive a Section 404 permit.[93] In an odd turn of events, however, the Corps indicated to the governor that the reservoir might again become a federal project.[94]

In August 1988, EPA informed the Rhode Island Water Resources Board, the governor, and the Corps of its intent to begin Section 404(c) procedures.[95] In response, Rhode Island withdrew its Section 404 permit application and asked the Corps to build the dam instead. EPA published its proposal to prohibit the project in February 1989, and indicated that the Section 404(c) action applied to both the state's proposal and to the Corp's flood control project.[96]

EPA grounded its objection on negative environmental effects and a failure by the parties to explore all alternatives.[97] EPA said that an alternative, or combination of alternatives, could be used to satisfy the state's water needs. In addition, EPA asserted that building the dam would destroy valuable wetlands and habitat, and would cause several of the state's rivers to not meet state water quality standards.[98] In March of 1990, EPA issued its final determination.[99] It was based on negative environmental consequences and the availability of alternatives.[100]

XI. *Two Forks Dam and Reservoir, Jefferson County, Colorado*

Denver, Colorado, its surrounding counties, and forty-one municipal and quasi-municipal entities entered into two agreements, in 1982 and 1984 respectively, creating a regionwide water supply plan. The heart of the plan was the construction of a dam and a reservoir.[101] In 1982, Denver signed a contract with the Corps to conduct a systemwide EIS for the project. After evaluating numerous alternatives, the Two Forks site was selected as the site for the dam and reservoir. This site lies just downstream of the confluence of the North Fork of the South Platte River and the South Platte River. It is two miles upstream from Denver's Strontia Springs Dam.

An application for a Section 404 permit was submitted to the Corps in March 1986. In 1988, the Corps issued the final EIS for the project. EPA commented on the final EIS, stating that Two Forks was the most environmentally damaging of the alternatives considered.[102] In March 1989, the Corps filed a formal notice of its intent to issue the Section 404 permit.[103] EPA informed the Corps that it intended to initiate Section 404(c) proceedings. On March 26, 1990, EPA Region VIII issued a recommended determination that the proposed Two Forks site be prohibited.[104] The recommended determination included a finding that the proposed project would have unacceptable environmental impacts on fisheries, wildlife, and recreation. Additionally, it stated that there were practicable, less damaging alternatives.[105]

In response, the applicants crafted a corrective action proposal that reduced the size of the proposed reservoir and imposed additional mitigation. In addition, the proposal required that mitigation be successful before project construction could begin.[106] In spite of the proposal, EPA issued its final determination prohibiting use of the Two Forks site. The final determination based the prohibition on unacceptable adverse impacts to fisheries, wildlife, and recreation as well as on the presence of less damaging, feasible alternatives.[107]

Eight of the forty-one municipal and quasi-municipal entities that were a part of the regional agreement filed suit in the U.S. District Court for the District of Colorado.[108] The court granted summary judgment for EPA based on the plaintiff's lack of standing.[109] The court decided, however, to analyze the merits of the case. The plaintiffs took issue with EPA's "sequencing" approach to analyzing alternatives. In this method of analysis, the alternatives are compared before mitigation is taken into account. The court held that this approach was acceptable.[110]

The plaintiffs also took issue with EPA's finding that practicable alternatives existed. In one of EPA's suggested alternatives, a presidential exemption would have been required to build a tunnel in a dedicated wilderness area. Another of the alternatives would have required moving a town and its 200 residents. Recognizing that EPA knew of and considered these obstacles, the court determined that it was obliged to defer to EPA's expertise in determining whether these alternatives were practicable. The court concluded that EPA had neither acted outside the scope of its authority nor acted arbitrarily or capriciously.[111]

XII. Ware Creek II

In 1992, the Fourth Circuit set aside EPA's veto of the Ware Creek Reservoir, finding that the administrative record established that no practicable alternative existed. However, it remanded the matter to the agency for further consideration.[112] On remand, EPA again determined to wield its Section 404(c) powers a second time. This time, EPA based its decision entirely on environmental considerations, and did not acknowledge the established lack of alternatives.[113] Once again, James City County filed suit in district court and was granted summary judgment. The district court ruled that EPA was required to consider the absence of any practicable alternative and the County's need for an expanded water supply in deciding if the effects of the proposal were "unacceptable."[114] EPA appealed.

The Fourth Circuit characterized the issue before it as whether the phrase "unacceptable adverse impacts" imposed an obligation on EPA to consider a wide range of factors, including the county's needs and the unavailability of alternatives, or whether EPA need only consider the environmental effects of the proposed project.[115] James City County argued that if EPA can consider the availability of alternatives in deciding whether environmental effects are "unacceptable," then it must also be required to consider the unavailability of alternatives in making the same determination. EPA argued that it could, in its sole discretion, consider the need for water, but that Section 404(c) imposed no obligation to do so. The Fourth Circuit concluded that EPA could base its Section 404(c) action solely on environmental effects and ignore the county's water needs and the unavailability of alternatives.[116]

Notes

1. 45 Fed. Reg. 51,275 (Aug. 1, 1980).
2. *Id.* at 51,276.
3. *Id.*
4. *Id.*
5. *Id.*
6. 45 Fed. Reg. 51,275 (Aug. 1, 1980).
7. 46 Fed. Reg. 10,203 (Feb. 2, 1981).
8. *See* Proposed Determination to Prohibit, Deny, or Restrict the Specification, or the Use for Specification, of an Area as a Disposal Site; Public Hearing, 48 Fed. Reg. 51,732 (1983).
9. *Id.* at 51,732.
10. *Id.* at 51,733.

11. *Id.* at 51,732.

12. *Id.* at 51,733.

13. *Id.*

14. *Id.*

15. Final Determination of the Administrator concerning the M.A. Norden Site Pursuant to Section 404(c) of the Clean Water Act, 49 Fed. Reg. 29,142 (1984).

16. *Id.*

17. *See* Notice of Public Hearing and Proposed Determination to Prohibit Specification of Area as a Disposal Site, 49 Fed. Reg. 30,112, 30,113 (1984) [hereinafter Maybank Proposed Determination].

18. *Id.* at 30,113–14.

19. *See* Final Determination of the Assistant Administrator for External Affairs concerning the Jack Maybank Site on Jehossee Island, South Carolina, Pursuant to Section 404(c) of the Clean Water Act, 50 Fed. Reg. 20,291 (1985) [hereinafter Maybank Final Determination].

20. *Id.*

21. *Id.*

22. *See* Maybank Proposed Determination, *supra* note 114.

23. *Id.* at 30,113.

24. *Id.*

25. *Id.*

26. *See* Maybank Final Determination, *supra* note 116.

27. *Id.*

28. *See* Proposed Determination to Prohibit or Restrict the Specification of an Area for Use as a Disposal Site; Notice of Public Hearing, 50 Fed. Reg. 33,835, 33,836 (1985) [hereinafter Sweedens Swamp Proposed Determination].

29. *See* Final Determination of the Assistant Administrator for External Affairs concerning the Sweedens Swamp Site in Attleboro, Massachusetts, Pursuant to Section 404(c) of the Clean Water Act, at 5 (availability announced in 51 Fed. Reg. 22,977 (1986)) [hereinafter Sweedens Swamp Final Determination].

30. *Id.*

31. *Id.* at 15.

32. *See* Sweedens Swamp Proposed Determination, *supra* note 125, at 33,837.

33. *Id.* at 33,836.

34. *Id.*

35. *Id.*

36. *Id.*

37. *See* Sweedens Swamp Final Determination, *supra* note 126, at 6.

38. *See* Recommendation of the Regional Administrator (Region 1) concerning the Sweedens Swamp Site in Attleboro, Massachusetts Pursuant to Section 404(c) of the Clean Water Act, at 7–8 (March 4, 1982) (unpublished).

39. *See* Newport Galleria Group v. Deland, 618 F. Supp. 1179 (D.D.C. 1985).

40. *Id.* at 1182.

41. *Id.* at 1185–86.

42. *See* Sweedens Swamp Final Determination, *supra* note 126.

43. *Id.* at 31.

44. *Id.* at 23–24.

45. *See* Bersani v. Robichaud, 850 F.2d 36, 44 (2nd Cir. 1988).

46. *See* Creppel v. Parish of Jefferson, 384 So.2d 853 (La. App. 4th Cir. 1980).

47. *See* Creppel v. U.S. Army Corps of Engineers, 500 F. Supp. 1108, 1119 (E.D. La. 1980).

48. *See* Creppel v. U.S. Army Corps of Engineers, 670 F.2d 564, 574–75 (5th Cir. 1982).

49. For a discussion of the procedural history of this complicated litigation, *see* Creppel v. U.S. Army Corps of Engineers, 19 ENVTL. L. REP. 20,134, 20,134–35 (E.D. La. 1988).

50. *See* Proposed Determination to Prohibit, Deny, or Restrict the Specification, or the Use for Specification, of an Area as a Disposal Site; Notice and Public Hearing, 50 Fed. Reg. 20,602 (1985).

51. *See* Final Determination of the U.S. Environmental Protection Agency's Assistant Administrator for External Affairs, concerning the Bayou Aux Carpes Site in Jefferson Parish, Louisiana, Pursuant to Section 404(c) of the Clean Water Act (availability announced in 50 Fed. Reg. 47,267 (1985)).

52. *See Creppel*, 19 ENVTL. L. REP. at 20,138–39.

53. For an excellent narration of the facts of this agency action, *see* Russo Development Corp. v. Reilly, 21 ENVTL. L. REP. 21,345 (D.N.J. 1991).

54. *See* Proposed Determination to Prohibit or Restrict the Specification of an Area for Use as a Disposal Site, 52 Fed. Reg. 29,431, 29,432 (1987).

55. *Id.*

56. *See* Water Pollution Control; Final Determination of the Assistant Administrator for Water concerning the Russo Development Corporation Site; Carlstadt, NJ, 53 Fed. Reg. 16,469 (1988).

57. *Id.* at 16,470.

58. *See* Russo Development Corp. v. Reilly, 20 ENVTL. L. REP. 20,938, 20,939 (D.N.J. 1990).

59. *See* Russo Development Corp. v. Thomas, 20 ENVTL. L. REP. 20,290, 20,292 (D.N.J. 1989).

60. *See* Russo Development Corp. v. Reilly, 20 ENVTL. L. REP. at 20,939.

61. *See* Russo Development Corp. v. Reilly, 21 ENVTL. L. REP. 21,345, 21,349 (D.N.J. 1991).

62. *See* Proposed 404(c) Determination to Prohibit, Deny, or Restrict the Specification of Use of Three East Everglades Areas as Disposal Sites; Notice and Public Hearing Announcement, 52 Fed. Reg. 38,519 (1987).

63. *See* Final Determination of the U.S. Environmental Protection Agency's Assistant Administrator for Water, concerning Three Wetland Properties for Which Rockplowing Is Proposed in East Everglades, Dade County, Florida (availability announced in 53 Fed. Reg. 30,093 (1988)).

64. For a discussion of the history of this case, *see* City of Alma v. United States, 744 F. Supp. 1546, 21 ENVTL. L. REP. 20,266 (S.D. Ga. 1990).

65. National Wildlife Federation v. Marsh, CV No. 582–98 (S.D. Ga. 1982).

66. National Wildlife Federation v. Marsh, 721 F.2d 767, 782–86 (11th Cir. 1983).

67. *See City of Alma,* 744 F. Supp. at 1553.

68. *See* Final Determination of the U.S. Environmental Protection Agency's Assistant Administrator for Water Pursuant to Section 404(c) of the Clean Water Act concerning the Proposed Lake Alma Impoundment and Proposed Mitigation of Associated Environmental Impacts, Alma, Bacon County, Georgia (availability announced in 54 Fed. Reg. 6749 (1989)).

69. *Id.*

70. *See City of Alma,* 744 F. Supp. at 1554.

71. *Id.* at 1567.

72. *See* Proposed Determination to Prohibit, or Deny the Specification, or the Use for Specification, of an Area as a Disposal Site: Ware Creek, James City County, VA, 53 Fed. Reg. 46,656, 46,657–58 (1988).

73. *Id.* at 46,658.

74. *Id.*

75. *Id.*

76. *Id.*

77. *Id.*

78. *Id.* at 46,658–59.

79. *Id.* at 46,659.

80. *See* Water Pollution Control; Final Determination of the Assistant Administrator for Water Pursuant to Section 404(c) of the Clean Water Act concerning the Proposed Ware Creek Water Supply Impoundment in James City County, VA, 54 Fed. Reg. 33,608 (1989).

81. *See* James City County v. EPA, 955 F.2d 254, 258 (4th Cir. 1992).

82. *Id.*

83. *See* James City County v. EPA, 758 F. Supp. 348 (E.D. Va. 1990).

84. *Id.*

85. *See James City County v. EPA,* 955 F.2d at 259.

86. *Id.* at 259–60.

87. *Id.* at 260.

88. *Id.* at 260–61.

89. *See* Proposed Determination to Prohibit the Use of Big River, Mishnock River, Their Tributaries and Adjacent Wetlands as Disposal Sites, RI, 54 Fed. Reg. 5133, 5134 (1989).

90. *Id.* at 5134.

91. *Id.*

92. *Id.*

93. *Id.*

94. *Id.*

95. *Id.*

96. *Id.*

97. *Id.* at 5135–36.

98. *Id.*

99. *See* Final Determination of the U.S. Environmental Protection Agency's Assistant Administrator for Water Pursuant to Section 404(c) of the Clean Water Act concerning the Proposed Big River Water Supply Impoundment, Kent County, Rhode Island (availability announced in 55 Fed. Reg. 10,666 (1990)).

100. *Id.*

101. For a discussion of the history of this project, *see generally* Alameda Water & Sanitation District v. EPA, 930 F. Supp. 486 (D. Colo. 1996).

102. *Id.* at 489.

103. *Id.*

104. *See* Proposed Determination to Prohibit, Restrict, or Deny the Specification, or the Use for Specification, of an Area as a Disposal Site; South Platte River, 54 Fed. Reg. 36,862 (1989).

105. *Id.* at 36,865–66.

106. *See Alameda Water & Sanitation District*, 930 F. Supp. at 489.

107. *See* Water Pollution Control; Final Determination of the Assistant Administrator for Water Pursuant to Section 404(c) of the Clean Water Act concerning the Two Forks Water Supply Impoundments in Jefferson and Douglas Counties, CO, 56 Fed. Reg. 76 (1991).

108. *See Alameda Water & Sanitation District*, 930 F. Supp. at 488.

109. *Id.* at 490–91.

110. *Id.* at 492.

111. *Id.* at 493.

112. *See* James City County v. EPA, 955 F.2d 254 (4th Cir. 1992).

113. *See* James City County v. EPA, No. 89 156-NN (E.D. Va. 1992).

114. *Id.*

115. *See* James City County v. EPA, 12 F.3d 1330, 1335 (4th Cir. 1993).

116. *Id.* at 1336.

CHAPTER 10

State Roles in the Implementation of the Section 404 Program

ROLF R. VON OPPENFELD

I. Introduction/Scope

The relationship between state and federal agencies in wetland protection is complex and dynamic. Congress, in enacting the Clean Water Act (CWA), deemed it important "to recognize, preserve, and protect the primary responsibilities and rights of States to prevent, reduce, and eliminate pollution, to plan the development and use (including restoration, preservation, and enhancement) of land and water resources, and to consult with [EPA] in the exercise of [its] authority under [the CWA]."[1] At the same time, Congress gave the U.S. Environmental Protection Agency (EPA) and the United States Army Corps of Engineers (Corps) primary responsibility to jointly administer the most significant federal wetlands regulatory program, the CWA's Section 404 program.[2] Despite the prominence of federal law and federal agencies in this program, state participation in federal wetlands regulation may be substantial.[3] Congress's policy of cooperative federalism is most noticeably reflected in the broad non-preemption clauses of the CWA, which generally permit the states to adopt standards and/or to enforce common law restrictions regarding the use of water resources (including wetlands) that are more stringent than those mandated by federal law.[4] The specifics of individual state wetland programs that supplement the Section 404 program are beyond the scope of this chapter.[5] But even in the absence of such additional state programs and/or standards—and most states do not have specific wetland programs—the states play important roles in the implementation of the Section 404 program. This chapter describes those roles.

The CWA authorizes states to become involved in the Section 404 program in a variety of ways, and with differing degrees of responsibility. The most substantial role that states may assume in the Section 404 program is provided for in Section 404(g) of the CWA. Under this statutory authority, states may, subject to EPA approval, assume administration of a program for individual and general permits for the discharge of dredged or fill material into state waters.[6] The requirements that a state must meet to assume such authority are discussed in Section II of this chapter.

For those states that choose not to assume such an extensive role in the implementation of federal policy, Congress has in Section 404(e) authorized the Corps to issue state programmatic general permits (SPGPs). SPGPs are a form of general permit pursuant to which states may assume significant regulatory authority over some categories and classes of activities affecting wetlands, but without incurring the significant fiscal and administrative expense of assuming full authority pursuant to Section 404(g). SPGPs are described in Section III of this chapter.

Finally, permits issued by the Corps are subject to two significant certifying requirements, through which states may deny or condition such permits. Section 401 of the CWA grants states authority to certify, condition, or deny licenses and permits issued by federal agencies, including Section 404 permits, depending on the effects that the licensed or permitted activity may have on state water resources and water quality.[7] Likewise, the Coastal Zone Management Act (CZMA) ensures that states retain authority to regulate the use of coastal wetlands by conditioning the issuance of federal permits on state determinations that the authorized activity is consistent with the state's coastal zone management programs.[8] Where applicable, certifications from state authorities pursuant to Section 401 and the CZMA are prerequisites to the Corps's issuance of a Section 404 permit. Sections IV and V of this chapter discuss these certification requirements.

II. State Assumption of Permitting Authority Pursuant to Section 404(g)

Section 404(g) of the CWA authorizes states to administer their own individual and general permit programs for the discharge of dredged or fill material into the navigable waters within the state's jurisdiction.[9] To assume administrative responsibility for the Section 404 permit program, a state must regulate all discharges of dredged or fill material that are not specifically excluded from state jurisdiction. A partial program cannot be approved by EPA.[10] States may adopt more stringent requirements or adopt a program with broader scope than the federal program.[11] More stringent requirements or broader programs are not part of the federally approved program and are not subject to federal oversight or enforcement. A state may not authorize activities on the basis of standards that are less stringent than those applicable to the federally administered program.[12]

Congress excluded certain waters from state jurisdiction under the Section 404 permit program. Thus, states may assume permitting authority over only waters of the state

> other than those waters which are presently used, or are susceptible to use in their natural condition or by reasonable improvement as a means to transport interstate or foreign commerce shoreward to their ordinary high water mark, including all waters which are subject to the ebb and flow of the tide shoreward to their mean high water mark, or mean higher high water mark on the west coast, including wetlands adjacent thereto.[13]

Where a state has adopted a program with broader scope than the federal program or has adopted more stringent requirements, the state may simultaneously regulate waters over which the Corps retains primary jurisdiction, but regulation of waters outside of the scope of the assumed authority is not part of the federally approved program. State requirements governing waters outside the scope of the assumed authority are not subject to federal enforcement or oversight.[14] Additionally, for activities in these waters, a Corps permit may be required.[15]

States seeking permitting authority pursuant to Section 404(g) must develop and submit for EPA approval a full and complete program that meets the requirements of Sections 404(g) and (h) and EPA's implementing regulations.[16] The Corps is generally not involved in such an approval process.

Once a state program has been approved, EPA retains some limited oversight responsibilities. Under Section 404(j) of the CWA, each administering state must provide to the appropriate regional administrator of EPA notice and an opportunity to comment on each proposed individual or general permit considered by the state.[17] The regional administrator will, in turn, solicit comments from the Corps and the U.S. Fish and Wildlife Service or the National Marine Fisheries Services as appropriate. After considering any comments of the resource agencies, the regional administrator will make the final decision on whether to submit comments to the permitting state.[18] If EPA objects to the proposed permit, the state or any other interested party may request a hearing,[19] but until EPA's concerns have been adequately addressed, the state may not issue the proposed permit.[20] If the state does not revise the permit to meet EPA's concerns, the permit is transferred to the Corps for processing under its ordinary rules and standards.[21] In *Friends of the Crystal River v. EPA*, the Sixth Circuit held that once the permit has been transferred from a state program to the Corps, EPA lacks authority to return the permit to the state by withdrawing objections that were not addressed by the state within prescribed time limits.[22] In that case, the court reasoned that once the state failed to take action within the statutory time limits, Congress intended "to completely divest the original agency of jurisdiction, and vest authority in the Army Corps following expiration of the deadline."[23]

Subject to certain exceptions,[24] EPA may waive its Section 404(j) oversight powers for categories of discharges within the state submitting the program.[25] For any such waiver, EPA must promulgate regulations establishing the categories of discharges that will not be subject to federal oversight.[26] EPA may terminate a waiver at any time upon providing written notice to the state.[27]

If EPA determines that a state is not administering an approved program in accordance with federal requirements, EPA may withdraw approval of the program. To initiate a withdrawal, EPA must first notify the state that it is not properly administering its permit program. The state must then take appropriate corrective action within a reasonable amount of time but no more than ninety days after the state has been notified of its noncompliance. If corrective action is not taken by the state, EPA may withdraw approval of the program until the corrective action is taken and notify the Corps that it must resume the Section 404 permit program for those activities for which the state was issuing permits. The Corps will retain authority until EPA determines that corrective action has been taken and the state assumes authority over the program once again.[28] States that have assumed authority may also voluntarily transfer program responsibilities required by federal law to the Corps, thus terminating state authority.[29]

To date, only two states—Michigan and New Jersey[30]—have assumed full permitting authority pursuant to Section 404(g). No other states have evidenced interest in full-scale assumption in recent years. States may be reluctant to administer such an extensive permitting program for a variety of reasons, including inadequate funding and administrative resources, potential liability for "takings" under the Fourteenth Amendment to the Constitution of the United States, and perceived resistance by the Corps to cede its authority over the Section 404 program.[31] In the face of such obstacles, the trend is toward greater state involvement in the implementation of the Section 404 program pursuant to other authorities in the CWA—particularly state programmatic general permits and Section 401 certification—and in the CZMA.

III. State Programmatic General Permits

A. Description and General Requirements

In addition to authorizing nationwide and regional permits, CWA Section 404(e) authorizes the Corps to issue general permits on a state level.[32] These permits have become known as state programmatic general permits (SPGPs).[33] Corps regulations state that programmatic permits are "a type of general permit founded on an existing state, local or other federal agency program and designed to avoid duplication with that program."[34] Programmatic general permits, like all general permits, can be issued only for activities that are "similar in nature, will cause only minimal adverse environmental effects when performed separately, and will have only minimal cumulative adverse effect on the environment."[35] The CWA limits the duration of such permits to five years,[36] during which time the Corps may revoke or modify the SPGP if the Corps "determines that the activities authorized by such general permit have an adverse effect on the environment or such activities are more appropriately authorized by individual permits."[37]

SPGPs are developed in recognition of existing or planned state regulatory programs that, while not federally approved for full assumption pursuant to Section 404(g), are as protective or more protective of some or all of the waters regulated by the Corps pursuant to Section 404. In the absence of an SPGP, a person seeking authority to fill wetlands might be required to obtain separate state and federal individual permits, invoking duplicative regulatory measures. An SPGP provides one way of avoiding such duplication. It does not completely eliminate Corps involvement over such activities, but may substantially reduce requirements and procedures for permit applicants. Thus, in developing SPGPs, the Corps seeks to simplify the regulatory process, reduce duplicative project evaluations, and promote more effective and efficient use of Corps regulatory resources while providing environmental protection for aquatic resources at least equivalent to (and sometimes more protective than) the protection provided by the Corps's 404 permitting program.[38] An SPGP "is the written vehicle identifying the terms, limitations, and conditions under which specific projects regulated by [an existing state, local, or federal authority] may be authorized under the Corps Regulatory Program with a much more efficient and abbreviated review by the Corps."[39]

The most recent general guidance on the subject, a 1996 proposed Corps regulatory guidance letter, states that an SPGP must meet five minimum criteria:

1. Every project authorized under [an SPGP] can cause no more than minimal adverse environmental effects, individually or cumulatively, based on compliance with the terms and conditions of the [SPGP];
2. [SPGP] implementation *must* simplify the evaluation process for applicants (preferably through one-stop shopping) and reduce duplication between the Corps and [state authorities], and must not increase the number of standard Corps permits [emphasis in original];
3. [An SPGP] must provide protection for aquatic resources at least equivalent to the overall Corps Regulatory Program (and sometimes will enhance environmental protection);
4. [SPGP] implementation must not increase the Corps overall workload; and
5. Every project authorized under [an SPGP] must comply with all Federal environmental laws and must ensure that all relevant Federal interests will be protected (e.g., national defense, navigation, endangered species).[40]

The guidance advances a variable approach to Corps review of activities subject to an SPGP, with the level of review tied to the impact the activities may have on aquatic resources.[41] SPGPs that authorize activities that are limited in nature or are developed for narrow state programs generally will not require case-by-case review by the Corps. For these SPGPs, the Corps need only engage in periodic oversight of the functioning of the SPGP. By contrast, SPGPs authorizing a broad spectrum of projects will generally include categories of activities, some of which will be reviewed and screened on a case-by-case basis according to procedures developed jointly by the Corps and the state.

The proposed guidance offers a model consisting of four categories of activities, the first three of which apply to these broader SPGPs.[42] Category 1 includes those projects that do not require notification to the Corps. These are projects that clearly will result in no more than minimal adverse environmental effects, individually or cumulatively. As an example of Category 1 activities, the guidance suggests projects involving less than 5,000 square feet of fill within inland waterways or wetlands, including secondary impacts from drainage, flooding, or clearing.[43]

Category 2 likewise involves projects that will clearly not cause more than minimal adverse environmental effects, but may have impacts of particular concern to the Corps—e.g., projects involving impacts near a federal navigation project.[44] Projects in this category require a preconstruction notification (PCN) to the Corps and/or joint review of applications by the Corps and the state. This review is intended to ensure that the Corps's interests or concerns, including those related to Corps Civil Works responsibilities (e.g. real estate and navigational projects), are satisfied. It does not, however, involve coordination with the other federal resource agencies, such as the U.S. Fish and Wildlife Service.

Category 3 involves activities that require a PCN to the Corps with federal resource agency coordination to ensure that the project results in no more than minimal adverse environmental effects, individually or cumulatively.[45] This category covers projects having larger adverse impacts on the aquatic environment—e.g., projects causing losses of 5,000 square feet to one acre of wetlands or other jurisdictional waters. The PCN in this category will trigger a process through which federal resource agency comments are solicited and considered fully during a specified comment period. Furthermore, SPGPs should include a provision to allow the federal resource agencies to request that review of a specific project be conducted by the Corps pursuant to standard permit procedures. The guidance suggests that when a federal resource agency requests such a "kickout" for a project otherwise authorized by an SPGP, the resource agency must provide a written statement of its concerns, along with recommended measures that, if undertaken, would obviate those concerns.[46]

Category 4 involves projects that are subject to state regulation, but exceed established project and/or acreage thresholds of the SPGP—e.g., projects causing wetland losses of more than 1 acre. Such projects require standard—i.e., individual—permit evaluation by the Corps.[47]

In addition to or in conjunction with the evaluation accompanying the reissuance required every five years for all permits under Section 404(e),[48] the guidance calls upon the Corps Regulatory Program to conduct periodic reviews of SPGPs to ensure that the state program is continuing to provide environmental protection at least equivalent to that which would otherwise be provided by the overall Corps Section 404 program.[49]

One advantage of SPGPs as opposed to state assumption of the Section 404 permit program is that SPGP programs can be implemented gradually. A state may, for example, assume an SPGP program for a single watershed. The Corps has emphasized that "[o]ne of the key benefits of [SPGPs] is the flexibility they afford [states] in terms of the projects regulated and the geographic scope of regulation."[50] For instance, SPGPs can apply to waters that would be excluded from assumption authority under Section 404(g), and they can be flexibly tailored for a particular activity. Furthermore, federal oversight is limited because SPGPs apply only to *de minimis* activities, and the state can more easily monitor *de minimis* activities within its borders. Though the flexibility of the SPGPs may result in some inconsistency in enforcement between states, SPGPs ultimately may be better at protecting wetlands because a state is likely to have a more thorough understanding of local issues and wetland areas than the federal government does. Among the primary benefits for the regulated community, SPGPs offer a process that is more streamlined with fewer levels of agency involvement than would otherwise be applicable.

Currently, eight states have SPGPs that apply to all waters of the state, two have SPGPs for limited areas, and two are in the process of developing an SPGP.[51] Maine, Vermont, New Hampshire, Massachusetts, Rhode Island, Connecticut, Pennsylvania, and Maryland have SPGPs that apply to all waters of the state. Florida has an SPGP for specific waters, and North Carolina has an SPGP for the coastal zone. Oregon and California are in the process of developing SPGPs.

B. Example: The Massachusetts SPGP

The Massachusetts programmatic general permit (MAPGP) has been used as a model for other states.[52] It "expedites review of minimal impact work in coastal and inland waters and wetlands within the Commonwealth of Massachusetts."[53] The MAPGP suspends the Corps's nationwide permit program in Massachusetts.

The MAPGP provides that where state approvals are required, they must be obtained prior to authorization under the MAPGP. These state approvals include water quality certifications, coastal zone management consistency determinations, final orders of conditions under the state Wetlands Protection Act, and waterways licenses or permits.[54] The MAPGP imposes thirty specific conditions that apply to all activities authorized under the permit.

Project eligibility under the MAPGP is divided into three categories: Category 1 (Nonreporting) activities, which may proceed without application or notification to the Corps; Category 2 (Reporting—Requiring Screening) activities, which are screened by the Corps and other federal agencies; and an Individual Permit Category, which requires individual Corps permits.

For Category 2 activities, an application must be submitted to the Corps and proposed projects may not proceed until written notification is received from the Corps and the applicable certifications or waivers concerning water quality and coastal zone management are completed. Applicants are required to file directly to the appropriate local Conservation Commission and/or Massachusetts Department of Environmental Protection (DEP) and submit copies of the DEP Environmental Notification Form in certain cases.[55] Category 2 applications must submit a significant amount of information with the application, including project purpose, delineations, drawings, and impact descriptions, as well as other relevant information.[56]

After an application is received, the Corps reviews the submission and determines if the project (1) requires additional information, (2) is appropriate for screening with the Federal Resource Agencies, (3) is ineligible under the terms and/or conditions of the MAPGP, or (4) will require Individual Permit review, regardless of whether the terms and conditions of the MAPGP are met, based on concerns for the aquatic environment or any other factor of the public interest.

Projects subject to interagency coordination are screened by the federal resource agencies at meetings held every three weeks. Applicants can expect an oral response on their application within ten working days of this meeting and a written response within twenty working days. The federal resource agencies may recommend special conditions for projects to avoid or minimize adverse environmental effects and to ensure that the terms and conditions of the general permit are met. The Corps will determine, however, that a project is ineligible under the MAPGP and will begin its individual permit review "if any one of the federal agencies . . . expresses a concern within their area of expertise, states the resource or species that could be impacted by the project, and describes the impacts that, either individually or cumulatively, will be more than minimal."[57]

As shown in Tables 1 and 2, the three categories are distinguished primarily by the size of the project.

TABLE 1. Inland Waters and Wetlands (Waters of the United States)*

Activity	Category I: Nonreporting	Category II: Screened	Category III: Individual Permit Required
Fill	Less than 5,000 square feet inland waterway and/or wetland fill and secondary impacts (e.g., areas drained, flooded, or cleared). Fill includes temporary and permanent fill except for incidental fallback. This category includes dams, dikes, water diversions, and water withdrawals.	5,000 square feet to 1 acre inland waterway and/or wetland fill and secondary impacts (e.g., areas drained, flooded, or cleared). Fill includes temporary and permanent fill, except incidental fallback. Any dam, dike, water diversion, or water withdrawal.	Greater than 1 acre inland waterway and/or wetland fill and secondary impacts (e.g., areas drained, flooded, or cleared). Fill includes temporary and permanent fill, except incidental fallback.
Bank stabilization projects	Inland bank stabilization less than 500 linear feet and less than 1 cubic yard fill per linear foot below ordinary high water mark, provided no fill is placed in wetlands and various other conditions are met	Projects that do not meet the terms under Category I	
Repair/ maintenance of previously authorized fill	For currently serviceable fills with no expansion or change in use.	Replacement of nonserviceable fill, or repair/maintenance of currently serviceable fills with expansion of any amount up to 1 acre, and/or change in use.	Replacement or repair/maintenance with expansion of greater than 1-acre fill.

*"Inland waters" are inland rivers, lakes, streams, and wetlands.
Source: MAPGP Appendix A.

IV. Section 401 Certification

Section 401(a) of the CWA provides:

> Any applicant for a Federal license or permit to conduct any activity including, but not limited to the construction or operation of facilities, which may result in any discharge into the navigable waters, shall provide the licensing or permitting agency a certification from the State in which the discharge originates or will

TABLE 2. Coastal and Navigable Waters of the United States*

Activity	Category I: Nonreporting	Category II: Screened	Category III: Individual Permit Required
Fill	Only those authorized under Massachusetts Ch. 91 Amnesty Program (e.g., seawalls or bulkheads).	Up to 1 acre waterway fill and/or secondary waterway or wetland impacts (e.g., areas drained or flooded). Fill includes temporary and permanent waterway fill.	Greater than 1 acre waterway fill and/or secondary waterway or wetland impacts (e.g., areas drained or flooded). Fill includes temporary or permanent waterway fill.
		Up to 1 acre temporary fill or excavation in special aquatic sites except where associated with a proactive restoration project.	Temporary fill or excavation greater than 1 acre and all permanent fill or excavation in special aquatic areas.
Repair and maintenance work	For currently serviceable authorized structures or fill with no expansion or change in use, rebuilt in same footprint.	Replacement of nonserviceable structures and fills or repair/maintenance of serviceable structures or fill, with fill replacement or expansion up to 1 acre.	Replacement or repair/maintenance of structure or fill greater than 1 acre.
Dredging	Maintenance dredging less than 1,000 c.y. with upland disposal, provided proper siltation controls are used; limited to dredging and disposal operations conducted between Nov. 1 and Jan. 15 in any season and other limitations, including no impacts to special aquatic sites.	Maintenance dredging greater than 1,000 c.y. or new dredging up to 25,000 c.y. or projects that that do not meet the terms in Category 1; upland, beach renourishment or approved open water disposal required.	Maintenance dredging (any amount) in or affecting a special aquatic site,† or with open water disposal. New dredging greater than 25,000 c.y. or of any amount in or affecting a special aquatic site.†
Moorings	Private, noncommercial, nonrental, single boat moorings not associated with any boating facility and subject to other limitations.‡	Moorings associated with a boating facility or that do not meet the terms in Category 1 or located within the buffer zone.	Moorings within the horizontal limits, or with moored vessels that extend within the limits, of Corps Federal Navigation Projects.

(continued)

TABLE 2. *(continued)*

Activity	Category I: Nonreporting	Category II: Screened	Category III: Individual Permit Required
Pile-supported structures and floats	Private, bottom-anchored floats not associated with any boating facility,‡ up to 400 square feet in size; or private, pile-supported structures for navigational access less than or equal to 400 square feet in size, with attached floats totaling less than or equal to 400 square feet. Any of the above must be supported off the substrate at low tide; and not positioned over vegetated shallows§ or special aquatic areas and meeting certain other limitations. Certain piers and structures licensed by Chapter 91, so long as not positioned over vegetated shallows§ or salt marsh.	Private piers and floats that do not meet the terms in Category I; pile-supported structures or floats that are within the buffer zone of the horizontal limits of a Corps Federal Navigation Project; expansion to existing boating facilities.‡	Pile-supported structures or floats associated with a new or previously unauthorized boating facility;‡ pile-supported structures or floats within the horizontal limits of a Corps Federal Navigation Project; certain work in the area of the Cape Cod Canal.
Miscellaneous	Temporary buoys, markers, floats, and similar structures for recreational use during specific events, provided they are removed within 30 days after use is discontinued; Coast Guard–approved aids to navigation; oil spill clean-up temporary structures and fill; fish and wildlife harvesting structures and fill; and scientific measurement devices and survey activities such as exploratory drilling, surveying, and sampling activities. Does not include oil and gas exploration and fill for roads or construction pads.	Structures or work in or affecting tidal or navigable waters that are not defined under any of the previous headings listed above, including but not limited to utility lines, aerial transmission lines, pipelines, outfalls, boat ramps, and bridges. Also includes certain shellfish aquaculture facilities in compliance with the Aquaculture Guidelines.	Environmental impact statement (EIS) required by the Corps; certain shellfish aquaculture facilities, including those not in compliance with the Aquaculture Guidelines, including those facilities within 25 feet of eelgrass beds.

*"Navigable waters" are waters that are subject to the ebb and flow of the tide, and federally designated navigable rivers (in Massachusetts, the Merrimack River, the Connecticut River, and the Charles River to the Watertown Dam).

† "Special aquatic sites" include wetlands (salt marsh), mudflats, riffles and pools, and vegetated shallows.

‡ "Boating facilities" are facilities that provide, rent, or sell mooring space, such as marinas, yacht clubs, boat clubs, boat yards, town facilities, and dockominiums.

§ "Vegetated shallows" are subtidal areas that support rooted aquatic vegetation such as eelgrass.

Source: MAPGP Appendix B

> originate, or, if appropriate, from the interstate water pollution control agency having jurisdiction over the navigable waters at the point where the discharge originates or will originate, that any such discharge will comply with [various provisions of the CWA dealing with effluent limitations and water quality standards]. . . . No license or permit shall be granted until the certification required by this section has been obtained or has been waived. . . . No license or permit shall be granted if certification has been denied by the State. . . .[58]

This section of the CWA thus authorizes states[59] to review proposed federal permits, including CWA Section 404 permits, and to determine whether the activities authorized by such permits will violate applicable state law. A state may exercise its Section 401 power by certifying a Section 404 permit, attaching comments or conditions to a permit, waiving its certification authority, or denying certification. This certification is sometimes referred to as a "water quality" certification.[60] If a state denies certification, no Section 404 permit may be issued. If a state attaches conditions, a federal permit cannot be issued unless those conditions are incorporated in that permit.[61]

Certification authority—and the associated power to deny certification or impose conditions—is conferred only on the state in which a "discharge" from a permitted activity "originates or will originate."[62] Certifications are not required from downstream states whose waters may be affected by discharges originating in another state, though, as discussed below, Section 401(a)(2) provides procedures through which the water quality interests of downstream states may be considered.

A. 401 Certification Procedure and Requirements

1. Corps Procedures

The Corps has promulgated regulations relating to state certification of discharges subject to Section 404. The basic procedures governing certifications for individual permits are found in 33 C.F.R § 325.2(b). Procedures governing certification of nationwide permits are found at 33 C.F.R. § 330.4(c).

For individual permits, if the district engineer determines that Section 401 certification is required, the district engineer must notify the applicant. District engineers may issue provisional permits, the validity of which is contingent upon the Corps's receipt of state certifications or of waivers.[63] The district engineer may then obtain a copy of the state certification from the applicant or the certifying agency.[64] State certification is a powerful tool for states to protect water quality because "[n]o permit will be granted until required certification has been obtained or has been waived."[65] If a state denies certification, the Corps will generally dismiss a permit application without prejudice.

2. *Certifying State Procedures*

Section 401(a) requires certifying states to "establish procedures for public notice in the case of all applications for certification by it and, to the extent it seems appropriate, procedures for public hearings in connection with specific applications."[66] State courts interpreting Section 401(a) have concluded that certifying agencies are not required, as a matter of federal law, to conduct hearings on certification requests.[67] Those same courts have concluded that, as a matter of state law, neither the applicant nor other interested parties is necessarily entitled to a hearing on a certification request.[68] Attorneys are advised to consult state law to determine what hearing procedures, if any, may be available or required in obtaining certification from the appropriate state agency.

B. Waiver of Certification

A state may waive certification. A waiver may occur in either of two ways: (1) The state provides a formal notice of waiver, or (2) the state fails or refuses to act on a request for certification within a reasonable period of time. The statute limits the "reasonable" period of time to one year after receipt of a request for certification.[69] Corps regulations further limit the waiver period, stating that a waiver

> will be deemed to occur if the certifying agency fails or refuses to act on a request within sixty days after receipt of such a request unless the district engineer determines a shorter or longer period is reasonable for the state to act. . . . In determining whether a waiver period has commenced or a waiver has occurred, the district engineer will verify that the certifying agency has received a valid request for certification.[70]

The waiver period begins to run only after a valid request for certification has been received by the state water quality agency.[71] Accordingly, it is generally advisable to seek a return receipt on the certification request. The "validity" of any request for certification is most likely to be determined by state law governing such requests—including, for example, filing requirements—although the case law is mixed on whether a federal agency may disregard state filing procedures for purposes of determining whether or when the waiver period has commenced.[72] The Corps regulations simply state that "[i]n determining whether or not a waiver period has commenced or waiver has occurred, the district engineer will verify that the certifying agency has received a valid request for certification."[73] It is, accordingly, advisable to consult state procedural requirements governing requests for certification.

C. Denial of Certification

In exercising their certification authority, states may determine that some effects of a federally permitted activity may violate applicable effluent limitations, water quality standards, or other appropriate requirements of state law. In such circumstances, the certifying agency may deny certification.[74] As noted above, if a state denies certification, the Corps will generally dismiss a permit application without prejudice.

D. Conditional Certification

A state agency's authority to impose conditions related to the state's water quality laws is found in Section 401(d) of the CWA, which provides:

> Any certification provided under this section shall set forth any effluent limitations and other limitations, and monitoring requirements necessary to assure that any applicant for a federal license or permit will comply with any applicable effluent limitations and other limitations, under section 1311 or 1312 of this title, standard of performance under section 1316 of this title, or prohibition, effluent standard, or pretreatment standard under section 1317 of this title, and with any other appropriate requirement of state law set forth in such certification, and shall become a condition on any federal license or permit subject to the provisions of this section.[75]

EPA and Corps regulations provide minimal guidance on the sorts of conditions a state may appropriately require of federally permitted activities pursuant to Section 401(d).[76] As a general matter, the Corps relies on state certifications to identify and consider any adverse effects that the proposed activity may have on water quality.[77]

In determining whether to certify, condition, or deny a request for certification, a state may consider effects beyond those caused by the discharge(s) that confers jurisdiction on the Corps and provides a basis for certification. Corps regulations provide that "[a] certification obtained for the construction of a facility must also pertain to the subsequent operation of the facility."[78] Likewise, EPA regulations provide that any certification must include a statement by the certifying agency that there is "a reasonable assurance that the activity will be conducted in a manner which will not violate applicable water quality standards" and must contain a statement of "any conditions which the certifying agency deems necessary or desirable with respect to the discharge *or the activity*" (emphasis added).[79] These interpretations of the scope of state scrutiny under Section 401 were confirmed by the Supreme Court in *PUD No. 1 of Jefferson County v. Washington Dept. of Environmental Quality*.[80] The Court held that Section 401(d) "is most reasonably read as authorizing additional conditions and limitations on the activity as a whole once the threshold condition, the existence of a discharge, is satisfied."[81] Accordingly, state authorities may consider any expected effects on water quality resulting from the continuing operation of the permitted activity and deny certification on the basis of such effects or impose conditions to minimize or eliminate them.

1. *Conditions Based on State Water Quality Standards*

The principal concern of the Section 401 certification process relates to the federally permitted activity's effects on the quality of waters within the certifying state. Thus, a state may impose conditions on the activity to ensure that water quality is protected. Water quality standards promulgated pursuant to the CWA provide the most prominent source of law upon which such conditions may be based.

a. Water Quality Standards

Water quality standards are established pursuant to Section 303 of the CWA.[82] States are given primary authority for promulgating such standards, subject to EPA review and approval.[83] EPA has adopted comprehensive regulations that require states to adopt water quality standards reflecting three key components: (1) use designations, (2) criteria to protect those uses, and (3) an antidegradation policy.[84] While states are generally required to meet minimum federal standards, they may also choose to adopt standards that are more stringent than the federally required baseline.[85]

Use Designations. States may designate uses for water resources that cover a wide spectrum, ranging from recreation and public water sources to waste disposal.[86] In general, however, the goal established by the CWA is to ensure water quality sufficient for the protection and propagation of fish, shellfish, and wildlife as well as for recreation in and on the waters.[87] This federally mandated baseline is commonly referred to as the "fishable/swimmable" designation.

Criteria. State-designated uses for water resources may be regarded as the goals to which state and federal regulatory efforts are directed. Water quality criteria are the specific targets for achieving such goals; they "can be defined as ambient water standards, or legal expressions of permissible amounts of pollutants allowed in a defined water segment."[88] Criteria are of two types: pollutant-specific numeric criteria and narrative criteria. A numeric criterion is an allowable concentration limit for a particular pollutant that has been set to achieve a certain water quality goal.[89] A narrative standard generally states the conditions necessary to achieve designated uses, but does not state precise numerical limits on the concentration of any specific pollutant.[90]

Antidegradation. EPA has adopted a rule that requires each state to establish an antidegradation policy as part of its water quality standards. At a minimum, the antidegradation policy must (1) protect and maintain existing instream water uses; (2) protect and maintain water quality that exceeds the federal fishable/swimmable goals, except in limited circumstances; and (3) protect and maintain high-quality waters constituting an outstanding national resource.[91]

b. Water Quality Standards for Wetlands

Many of the original water quality criteria that were adopted by states were not developed with wetlands, the Section 404 program, or related Section 401 certifications in mind. In 1990, EPA published and disseminated a guidance document to assist state water quality agencies in developing water quality standards for wetlands that would provide more effective protection in the Section 401 certification process.[92] According to that EPA guidance, the requirements necessary for effectively using state water quality standards to protect wetlands should include (1) incorporating wetlands into the definitions of "state waters," (2) designating uses for all wetlands, (3) adopting aesthetic narrative criteria and appropriate numeric criteria for wetlands, (4) adopting narrative biological criteria for wetlands, and (5) applying the state's antidegradation policy and implementation methods to wetlands.[93] While many states have included wetlands in their definition of state waters, fewer have adopted standards specifically for wetlands.

The antidegradation policy is applied differently for wetlands than for other waters. Congress anticipated and authorized some degradation of wetlands and other waters by providing for Section 404 permits. Correspondingly, EPA's Section 404 Guidelines provide that, except in the case of outstanding resource waters, the "existing use" requirements of the antidegradation policy are met if the wetland fill does not cause or contribute to "significant degradation" of the aquatic environment as defined by EPA regulations.[94]

A significant degradation determination is based on the following factors, considered individually or collectively: (1) effects on human health or welfare, including effects on municipal water supplies, plankton, fish, shellfish, wildlife, and special aquatic sites (e.g., wetlands); (2) effects on life stages of aquatic life and other wildlife dependent on aquatic ecosystems, including the transfer, concentration, or spread of pollutants or their byproducts beyond the site through biological, physical, or chemical process; (3) effects on aquatic ecosystem diversity, productivity, and stability, including loss of fish and wildlife habitat or loss of the capacity of a wetland to assimilate nutrients, purify water, or reduce wave energy; and (4) effects on recreational, aesthetic, and economic values.[95] EPA guidance indicates that significant degradation should be considered by states as a minimum antidegradation policy for wetland fills: "States are free to adopt stricter requirements for wetland fills in their own antidegradation policies, just as they may adopt more stringent requirements than federal law requires for their water quality standards in general."[96]

The antidegradation provisions in state standards, when applied in the Section 401 certification process, may prevent the Corps from issuing a Section 404 permit for any project that would eliminate an existing use of the affected wetland. Specifically, EPA has taken the position that "no activity is allowable . . . which could partially or completely eliminate any existing use."[97] Accordingly, states must implement an antidegradation policy that, at a minimum, ensures that "[e]xisting instream water uses and the level of water quality necessary to protect the existing uses shall be maintained and protected."[98]

Despite the 1990 EPA guidance document,[99] few states monitor wetland health or have fully incorporated wetlands into water quality programs. To take further steps to remedy these shortfalls, in 2001 EPA began to design modules to give states and tribes "state of the science" information to assist in developing biological assessment methods to evaluate both the overall ecological condition of wetlands and nutrient enrichment (one of the primary stressors on many wetlands).[100]

c. Conditions Based on Water Quality Standards

In *PUD No. 1 of Jefferson County v. Washington Dept. of Environmental Quality*,[101] the United States Supreme Court held that, pursuant to Section 401(d), states may impose conditions based on each of the components of the states' water quality standards—use designations, criteria, and antidegradation standards. Specifically, the Court held that Section 401(d) authorized the state of Washington to require maintenance of minimum stream flow in the Dosewallips River as a condition of certification for a hydroelectric facility.[102]

The minimum stream flow condition imposed by the state of Washington was based on the state water quality use designations governing the Dosewallips River, which identified "salmonid migration, rearing, spawning, and harvesting" as protected uses.[103] The state determined that its minimum stream flow condition was necessary to ensure that the Dosewallips River would continue to provide for these uses. Rejecting the contention that Section 401(d) authorized only conditions based on duly enacted state water quality criteria, the Court held that the state's determination of impairment based on the applicable use designation, as well as the state's resulting condition, were properly imposed pursuant to Section 401(d).[104] The Court noted that the distinction between use designations and water quality criteria can sometimes be difficult to discern, particularly when a state has chosen to protect designated uses through broad narrative criteria. In *PUD No. 1*, the Court suggested that "broad, narrative criteria based on, for example, 'aesthetics'" may support state certification conditions.[105]

PUD No. 1 also affirms that state antidegradation policies may provide a basis for imposing conditions on federally permitted activities. In addition to its reliance on use designations, the state of Washington justified its minimum stream flow condition as necessary to implement its antidegradation policy. That policy provided that "existing beneficial uses shall be maintained and protected and no further degradation which would interfere with or become injurious to existing beneficial uses will be allowed."[106] The Court concluded that "the State's minimum stream flow condition is a proper application of the state and federal antidegradation regulations" and that a state may enforce those regulations through conditions imposed pursuant to Section 401(d).[107]

2. Conditions Based on "Other Appropriate Requirements of State Law"

The Court's decision in *PUD No. 1* firmly establishes that "limitations imposed pursuant to state water quality standards adopted pursuant to § 303 [of the CWA] are 'appropriate' requirements of state law" for purposes of Section 401(d).[108] The Court refused, however, to "speculate on what additional state laws, if any, might be incorporated by" Section 401(d)'s reference to conditions based on "any other appropriate requirement of State law."[109]

State courts have reached different conclusions on that question. In *Arnold Irrigation District v. Dep't of Envt'l Quality*,[110] the Oregon Department of Environmental Quality (ODEQ) determined that a project to divert water for hydroelectric generation was incompatible with land use ordinances and a county land management plan. It denied the applicant's request for certification. EPA nevertheless issued the necessary permits. On appeal, the Oregon court held that the ODEQ had exceeded its authority under Section 401(a) of the CWA by denying certification based on a failure to comply with land use regulations. The court further held that, while the state's power to impose conditions on a permit is not limited to the sections specified in Section 401(a) of the CWA, the conditions must nevertheless relate to water quality. The court remanded the case to ODEQ because the agency had not found that its conditions were related to water quality considerations. Significantly, however, the court concluded that, even though the management plan and ordinances are not expressly provided for in Section 401(a), the state could still consider them "appropriate requirement[s] of State law" under Section 401(d), should the agency conclude that noncompliance with such requirements may affect water quality.[111]

In a more limited interpretation of state authority, the New York Court of Appeals held in *Niagara Mohawk Power Corp. v. New York State Department of Environmental Conservation* that only water quality standards adopted by the state and approved by EPA pursuant to Section 303 of the CWA may be considered in the Section 401 certification process.[112] It rejected the certifying agency's claim that Section 401(d)'s reference to "any other appropriate requirement of State law" permitted the agency to consider state laws that may bear upon water quality, but that were not promulgated pursuant to Section 303. In the Court of Appeals's view, such an interpretation of Section 401 "would enable [the certifying agency] to impose onerous conditions that could contradict or undermine Federal licensing by superimposing unrelated conditions not within the EPA mandates and specifications."[113]

In 2002, the Washington State Supreme Court held in *Public Util. Dist. No. 1 v. Dep't of Ecology* that the state Department of Ecology had the authority to condition a Section 401 water quality certification on maintenance of minimum instream flows, even where such conditions affected existing water rights protected under a state surface-water statute.[114] This holding specified that the authority to impose instream flow conditions in a state water quality certification existed "regardless of whether the applicant for the federal license has existing water rights."[115]

E. Failure to Obtain Certification

Failure to obtain Section 401 certification or a waiver can result in an illegal fill, requiring the payment of penalties, restoration of the wetland, or even criminal prosecution. Indeed, even purchasers of property may potentially be held liable for violations caused by prior owners or operators if such violations should have been discovered in a due diligence prepurchase inquiry.[116] In short, a Section 404 permit cannot be granted for a proposed project until the Section 401 certification, from the appropriate state water quality agency, is either received or waived.[117]

F. Certification of Nationwide Permits

The Corps regulatory program provides authorization for the vast majority of jurisdictional activities under nationwide permits (NWPs), as opposed to individual permits.[118] NWPs are discussed in detail in Chapter 5. The Section 401 certification requirement is applicable to all permit applications, including those for projects seeking authorization pursuant to an NWP.[119]

Once a specific NWP has been certified by a state (or a waiver has occurred with respect to such nationwide permit), it is not necessary to obtain any additional certification for individual projects authorized by that particular NWP. Several states have refused to certify or waive state certification on some nationwide permits. In these states, applicants seeking to use NWPs must obtain certification from the appropriate state agency on a project-by-project basis.[120] It is best to check with the district engineer or with the appropriate state agency to determine which activities authorized by an NWP require an individual state water quality certification.[121]

G. Section 401(a)(2) and Other Affected States

A state that lacks certification authority over particular discharges (because the discharges originate in another state)[122] may seek to protect water quality within its jurisdiction under the procedures specified in Section 401(a)(2) of the CWA and in Corps regulations.[123] Upon receiving a certification, the Corps must notify EPA of the permit application and the certification. If EPA determines that the proposed activity may affect water quality in any noncertifying state, EPA will notify the potentially affected state. That state may then request a public hearing. The Corps will then determine whether conditions should be imposed on the permit, based on the recommendations of the affected state and EPA. If the district engineer determines that a permit cannot be conditioned in a manner that ensures that its authorized activity will comply with applicable water quality standards, the Corps must deny the permit.[124]

H. Review of State Certification Decisions

Corps regulations require that all applications for permits be evaluated for compliance with applicable effluent limitations and water quality standards.[125] As a matter of practice, state certification of a proposed activity is generally presumed to be conclusive of water quality issues.[126] Corps regulations provide an exception to this general rule in circumstances where EPA advises the Corps of "other water quality aspects" that should be examined, but were not addressed in the state certification.[127] In a regulatory guidance letter clarifying this regulation, the Corps stated: "Other water quality aspects . . . include water quality concerns outside the scope of the state's § 401 certification review, indirect impacts on water quality aspects that the state certification does not address, and matters addressed in the state certification with which the EPA has a different viewpoint."[128] Where EPA raises such "other water quality aspects," state certification is not deemed conclusive of water quality considerations, and the Corps district engineer will exercise his or her own independent judgment concerning water quality impacts.[129] Nonetheless, if a state continues to deny certification on water quality grounds, a Section 404 permit may not be issued.[130]

Neither the Corps nor EPA enjoys express statutory authority to review conditions contained in a state certification. The courts have also held that federal permitting agencies lack authority to review conditions imposed by state certifying agencies pursuant to Section 401(d). These cases hold that the permitting agency lacks discretion to alter or to refuse to include such conditions in a permit. In *Roosevelt Campobello International Park Comm. v. EPA,*[131] the First Circuit reviewed EPA's decision to issue a discharge permit pursuant to Section 402 of the CWA without including conditions imposed by a state agency. The court held this to be error, concluding that "federal courts and agencies are without authority to review the validity of a requirement proposed under state law or in a state's certification."[132]

Likewise, in *American Rivers, Inc. v. Federal Energy Regulatory Commission,*[133] the court found unlawful the Federal Energy Regulatory Commission's (FERC) refusal to include state certification conditions in hydropower licenses. FERC contended that the conditions were beyond the scope of authority conferred upon the state by Section 401. The court held that FERC "does not possess a roving mandate to decide that substantive aspects of state-imposed conditions are inconsistent with the terms of § 401."[134] In the court's view, agency review of state-imposed conditions was inconsistent with the plain language of Section 401. The court also rejected FERC's contention that review of state conditions by federal agencies was necessary to prevent the states from holding federal agencies "hostage through the § 401 process."[135] The court identified safeguards against the inclusion of unlawful, state-imposed conditions in federally issued permits. First, such conditions could be reviewed by "courts of appropriate jurisdiction"—i.e., state courts. Second, in the event that no party challenged such conditions in an appropriate court, FERC could "protect its mandate by refusing to issue a license which, as conditioned, conflicts with" governing federal law.

Corps regulations[136] and guidance authorize district engineers to review certification conditions, but do not authorize district engineers to issue permits that omit or alter such conditions. In Regulatory Guidance Letter 92-4, the Corps noted that there may be cases in which state certifications of nationwide permits include "unacceptable conditions."[137] In such cases, the guidance letter concludes that the certifications "shall be considered administratively denied," and "authorization for an activity which meets [otherwise applicable requirements] is denied without prejudice."[138] Likewise, an EPA General Counsel opinion states that the agency possesses only limited authority to review a state certification,[139] concluding that "beyond determining that a certification . . . 'sets forth the appropriate requirement of state law' upon which it is based, EPA is without authority to review the substance of a facially valid State Certification."[140] As a result, EPA generally will not challenge a particular condition in a state water quality agency's Section 401 certification.[141]

In general, the only avenue for review of state certification conditions is that provided by applicable state law.[142] Under certain narrow exceptions, a federal court may exercise jurisdiction to review certification issues. These include a state agency's attempt to revoke a certification once it has been issued,[143] a case in which the United States is the applicant for certification and challenges the state's decision,[144] and a case in which a citizen suit is brought to determine whether or not state certification is required for a particular federal permit.[145] Additionally, to the extent that a state court bases a certification decision on interpretations of federal law, that decision is subject to review by the Supreme Court of the United States, as illustrated by *PUD No. 1*.[146]

V. Coastal Zone Management Act Consistency Determinations

In 1972, Congress passed the Coastal Zone Management Act (CZMA) to further "a national interest in the effective management, beneficial use, protection and development of the Coastal Zone."[147] In order to achieve its goals,[148] the CZMA requires states to develop management programs for its coastal waters and wetlands.[149] Each program must be approved by the Secretary of Commerce to ensure consistency with federal guidelines and standards.[150] Once a program is approved, the federal government has limited oversight authority but continues to provide funding through grant programs.[151]

If any nonfederal activity requiring a federal permit or license will be conducted in a manner that will affect "any land or water use or natural resource of a coastal zone" of a state with an approved management program, the applicant "shall provide in the application to the licensing or permitting agency a certification that the proposed activity complies with the enforceable policies of the state's approved program and that such activity will be conducted in a manner consistent with the program."[152] If such a CZMA certification is not submitted, the Corps generally will not issue a 404 permit.[153]

Corps procedures governing CZMA certification are found at 33 C.F.R. § 325.2(b)(2). Upon receipt of an applicant's certification, the Corps will forward a copy of the public notice of the application to the appropriate state agency, seeking its concurrence or objection. If the state agency objects or requests further review, the Corps will not issue a Section 404 permit.[154] As in the Section 401 process, it is presumed that a state has approved a project if it fails to respond to the Corps's request for approval within a reasonable period of time, not to exceed six months.[155]

The CZMA has been successful in coordinating state and federal agencies by giving state agencies broad authority and requiring that states certify that a federally permitted activity is consistent with its CZMA. One reason the CZMA has been successful is that the federal government provides continuous funding for states to develop CZMA programs. In addition, states have a great deal of flexibility and can define their own jurisdiction. Moreover, the Secretary of Commerce exercises minimal oversight.[156] If a state is "failing to adhere to" an approved program, however, the Secretary of Commerce may withdraw funding.[157] Finally, the CZMA provides no federal cause of action against states, local governments, or private parties in violation of the act.[158] In sum, the CZMA is implemented differently in each state. States have primary authority under the CZMA, but federal agencies provide limited oversight, minimum standards, and funding.

VI. Conclusion

Federal and state agencies coordinate in the protection of wetlands under many different authorities and in many different ways. State certification of Section 404 permits is currently the most extensively used mechanism for federal and state coordination in wetland protection. States have implemented SPGP permit programs and regulate coastal wetlands through the CZMA as well. The federal government has oversight authority in all of these programs. While the federal government exercises limited oversight in the SPGP and CZMA programs, the federal government is actively involved in and has primary authority over the issuance of Section 404 permits through the Corps and EPA, except in the two states where authority has been delegated.

Before the CWA, states were primarily responsible for the protection of wetlands. Because many states were ineffective at protecting wetlands in the past, Congress passed the CWA and gave EPA and the Corps authority over the protection of our nation's wetlands. Presently, the pendulum appears to be shifting again, giving greater and greater authority and responsibility back to the states. Most likely, this intricate dynamic of federal and state cooperation will continue to evolve in a way that ensures states have primary authority over the regulation of wetlands, while the federal government provides the underlying framework to ensure the states do their job, and ultimately to ensure that the nation's wetlands are protected. Ideally, the system will reflect the dynamic balance of federalism, achieving a streamlined permitting system that effectively protects wetlands, allows for appropriate development and resource use, and remains responsive to regional and local concerns, while also being applied relatively uniformly across the states.

Notes

1. 33 U.S.C. § 1251(b) (2000).
2. 33 U.S.C. § 1344.
3. *See generally* U.S. Environmental Protection Agency, State, Tribal, Local, and Regional Roles in Wetlands Protection, *available at* http://www.epa.gov/OWOW/wetlands/facts/fact21.html.

4. *See* 33 U.S.C. §§ 1365(e), 1370. Readers are advised to consult sources of state law to determine whether activities affecting wetlands may be regulated or restricted in ways that exceed the requirements of federal law.

5. For general information about state programs, one good starting place is the Association of State Wetland Managers, State Wetland Protection Statutes, *available at* http://www.aswm.org/swp/states.htm.

6. *See* 33 U.S.C. § 404(g)–(h).

7. 33 U.S.C. § 1341.

8. 16 U.S.C. § 1451–1464.

9. 33 U.S.C. § 1344(g).

10. 40 C.F.R. § 233.1(b) (2004).

11. 40 C.F.R. § 233.1(c).

12. 40 C.F.R. § 233.1(d).

13. 33 U.S.C. § 1344(g).

14. 40 C.F.R. § 233.1(c).

15. Chapters 5 and 6 of this book provide information about activities that require federal permits.

16. 33 U.S.C. § 1344(g); 40 C.F.R. § 233.10(a), (b), and (c). The basic components of an approvable program include sufficient state authority

a. To issue permits that apply, and assure compliance with, any applicable requirements of Section 404, are for fixed terms not exceeding five years, and can be terminated or modified for cause;

b. To issue permits that apply to, and assure compliance with all applicable requirements for, inspection, monitoring, entering property, and requiring reports under the CWA;

c. To ensure that the public, and any other state the waters of which may be affected, receives notice of each application for a permit and an opportunity for public hearing before a ruling on each application;

d. To ensure that EPA receives notice of each application for a permit;

e. To ensure that any other state whose waters may be affected by the issuance of a permit may submit written recommendations to the permitting state and the EPA with respect to any permit application and that the permitting state will timely respond to the recommendations if rejected;

f. To ensure that no permit will be issued if anchorage and navigation of any of the navigable waters would be substantially impaired thereby;

g. To abate violations of the permit or the permit program, including civil and criminal penalties and other ways and means of enforcement;

h. To ensure continued coordination with federal and federal-state water related planning and review processes.

33 U.S.C. § 1344(h)(1). EPA's regulations governing program submissions and approval are set forth at 40 C.F.R. pt. 233, subpt. B. Along with a full and complete description of the program it intends to administer, the state must submit a statement from an appropriate state legal officer—e.g., attorney general or independent legal counsel for state agency—"that the laws of such State . . . provide adequate authority to carry out the described program." 33 U.S.C. § 1344(g).

EPA regulations additionally require the state to submit a Memorandum of Agreement with the Regional Administrator of EPA and a Memorandum of Agreement with the Secretary of the Army as well as copies of all applicable state statutes and regulations. 40 C.F.R. § 233.10(d), (e), and (f). The Memorandum of Agreement between the regional administrator and the directors of any state agencies must set out the state and federal responsibilities for program administration and enforcement. 40 C.F.R. § 233.13. The Memorandum of Agreement between the Army Corps of Engineers and the directors of any state agencies in charge of administering the permit program must describe the waters over which the Corps retains jurisdiction, provide procedures for transferring existing permit applications to the state, and identify all general permits over which the state intends to assume authority. 40 C.F.R. § 233.14. Additionally, the U.S. Fish and Wildlife Service and the Army Corps of Engineers may submit comments to EPA on the proposed program and statement. *Id.*

17. 33 U.S.C. § 1344(j); 40 C.F.R. § 233.50(a).

18. 40 C.F.R. § 233.50(b).

19. 40 C.F.R. § 233.50(g).

20. 40 C.F.R. § 233.50(f).

21. 33 U.S.C. § 1344(j); 40 C.F.R. § 233.50(j).

22. 35 F.3d 1073, 1080 (6th Cir. 1994). The time limits within which a state must act to address EPA objections are set forth in 33 U.S.C. § 1344(j). If a public hearing is conducted, the state must address remaining EPA objections within thirty days after completion of the hearing. If no hearing is conducted, the state must address EPA's objections within ninety days of receiving them.

23. *Friends of the Crystal River*, 35 F.3d at 1080.

24. The following discharges are not eligible for a waiver from the Section 404(j) federal oversight provisions:

a. Draft general permits,

b. Discharges with reasonable potential for affecting endangered or threatened species as determined by the Fish and Wildlife Service,

c. Discharges with reasonable potential for adverse impacts on waters of another state,

d. Discharges known or suspected to contain toxic pollutants in toxic amounts or hazardous substances in reportable quantities,

e. Discharges located in proximity of a public water supply intake,

f. Discharges within critical areas established under state or federal law, including but not limited to national and state parks, fish and wildlife sanctuaries and refuges, national and historical monuments, wilderness areas and preserves, sites identified or proposed under the National Historic Preservation Act, and components of the National Wild and Scenic Rivers System.

40 C.F.R. § 233.51(b).

25. 33 U.S.C. § 1344(k).

26. 33 U.S.C. § 1344(l).

27. 40 C.F.R. § 233.51(c).

28. 33 U.S.C. § 1344(i).

29. 40 C.F.R. § 233.53.

30. *See* 40 C.F.R. § 233.70 (Michigan); 40 C.F.R. § 233.71 (New Jersey).

31. *See* Oliver A. Houck & Michael Rolland, *Federalism in Wetlands Regulation: A Consideration of Delegation of Clean Water Act Section 404 and Related Programs to the States*, 54 Md. L. Rev. 1242 (1995).

32. Programmatic general permits need not be based on an existing or proposed statewide program. PGPs may be developed in response to existing or proposed regulatory programs under the jurisdiction of what the Corps describes as "other regulatory authorities," including federal, state, tribal, and local authorities. The Corps has indicated that the statutory requirements for issuing a PGP are, however, the same, regardless of whether the "other regulatory authority" is a state, federal agency, local authority, or tribal authority. *See* 61 Fed. Reg. 18,575 (1996), *available at* http://www.epa.gov/owow/wetlands/pdf/spgp.pdf. Regardless of the geographic scope of a PGP, it is regarded as an SPGP if it is based on a state program. *See* Houck & Rolland, *supra* note 31, at 1283 n.293.

33. Examples of six different state programmatic general permits can be found on the Corps New England District Web site, *available at* http://www.nae.usace.army.mil/reg/index.htm. The state programmatic general permit for the State of Florida is available at http://www.dep.state.fl.us/water/wetlands/erp/spgp.htm. The Pennsylvania state programmatic general permit is available at http://www.nap.usace.army.mil/cenap-op/regulatory/spgp.html#paspgp2.

34. 33 C.F.R. § 325.5(c)(3).

35. 33 U.S.C. § 1344(e)(1).

36. *Id.* at § 1344(e)(2).

37. *Id.*

38. 61 Fed. Reg. at 18,575.

39. *Id.*

40. *Id.* at 18,577.

41. *Id.* at 18,577–78.

42. *Id.*

43. *Id.* at 18,577.

44. *Id.*

45. *Id.* at 18,577–78.

46. *Id.* at 18,578.

47. *Id.* at 18,578.

48. 33 U.S.C. § 1344(e).

49. 61 Fed. Reg. at 18,578. The frequency of review is discretionary ("[t]he Corps may conduct an annual review of the [SPGP], may require annual reporting by the [State] . . . or may conduct an overall review prior to expiration of the [SPGP] for consideration in the reevaluation of the [SPGP] for reissuance."). *Id.*

50. *Id.* at 18,576. For an example of a limited SPGP, see Department of the Army General Permit New Jersey-SPGP-17, *available at* http://www.nap.usace.army.mil/cenap-op/regulatory/spgp17.pdf. (This general permit authorizes the construction of structures, performance of work, and discharge of dredged and

fill material in substantially developed artificial tidal lagoons and their access channel.)

51. Based upon a telephone conversation with John Meagher, Director of the Wetlands Division of EPA's Office of Wetlands, Oceans, and Watersheds.

52. Based upon a telephone conversation with John Meagher, Director of the Wetlands Division of EPA's Office of Wetlands, Oceans, and Watersheds.

53. Department of the Army, Programmatic General Permit, Commonwealth of Massachusetts, U.S. Army Corps of Engineers, New England District, Application No. 200300120 (Jan 11, 2000, as modified June 30, 2003), 1 [hereinafter Programmatic General Permit], *available at* http://www.nae.usace.army.mil/reg/mapgp.pdf.

54. *Id.* at 1–2.

55. *Id.* at 3–4.

56. The additional information required to be submitted may include

a. purpose of the project;
b. $8^1/_2'' \times 11''$ locus map, $8^1/_2'' \times 11''$ plan views of the entire property, and project limits with existing and proposed conditions (legible, reproducible plans required);
c. wetland delineation for site, Corps wetland delineation data sheets (see Web site), and calculations of waterway and wetland impact areas (see Condition 2);
d. typical cross-section views of all wetland and waterway fill areas and wetland replication areas;
e. delineation of submerged aquatic vegetation, e.g., eelgrass beds, in tidal waters;
f. volume, type, and source of fill material to be discharged into waters and wetlands, including the areas (in square feet or acres) of fill in wetlands, below the ordinary high water in inland waters and below the high tide line in coastal waters;
g. mean low water, mean high water, and high tide elevations in navigable waters;
h. limits of any Federal Navigation Project in the vicinity of the project area and State Plane Coordinates for the limits of the proposed work closest to the Federal Navigation Project;
i. alternatives analysis submitted to the DEP for WQC review, and/or additional information compiled on alternatives;
j. identification and description of potential impacts to essential fish habitat (see Condition 10);
k. photographs of wetland/waterway to be impacted.

Programmatic General Permit, *supra* note 53, at 4.

If the project involves dredging, applicants may be required to conduct sediment testing, including physical, chemical, and biological testing. *Id.*

Furthermore, applicants are requested to submit a copy of their application materials to the State Historic Preservation Officer of the Massachusetts Historical Commission and various Tribal Preservation Officers. *Id.* at 3–4. Projects that extend the coastline or baseline from which the territorial sea is measured must be coordinated with the Minerals Management Service (MMS) and Outer Continental Shelf Survey Group. The Corps forwards project information to the MMS for review and the review is coordinated with the Department of the Interior. *Id.* at 6.

57. Programmatic General Permit, *supra* note 53, at 5.

58. 33 U.S.C. § 1341(a)(1). *See* 33 C.F.R. § 320.4 (d).

59. States are authorized to require discharges associated with federally licensed or permitted activities to meet applicable effluent limitations pursuant to the state's administration of the permit program established under Section 402 of the CWA. In states having no authority to give such a certification, EPA certification is required. *See* 33 U.S.C. sec. 1341(a)(1).

60. U.S. Environmental Protection Agency, Section 401 Certification and Wetlands, *available at* http://www.epa.gov/owow/wetlands/facts/fact24.html.

61. *See* 33 U.S.C. § 1341(d).

62. 33 U.S.C. § 1341(a)(1); *see* North Carolina v. FERC, 112 F.3d 1175, 1187 (D.C. Cir. 1997).

63. *See* RGL 93-01, Provisional Permits (April 20, 1993), *reprinted at* 61 Fed. Reg. 30,994 (June 8, 1996), *available at* http://www.usace.army.mil/inet/functions/cw/cecwo/reg/rgls/rgl93-01.htm.

64. 33 C.F.R. § 325.2(b)(i).

65. 33 C.F.R. § 325.2(b)(ii).

66. 33 U.S.C. § 1341(a).

67. *See* Summit Hydropower Partnership v. Commissioner of Environmental Protection, 226 Conn. 792, 804–07, 629 A.2d 367, 372–75 (Conn. 1993); Triska v. Department of Health & Environmental Control, 292 S.C. 190, 196–97, 355 S.E.2d 531 (1987).

68. *See Summit Hydropower,* 226 Conn. at 811–12, 629 A.2d at 376; *see also* Flax v. Ash, 142 Misc. 2d 828, 832, 538 N.Y.S.2d 891, 894 (Sup. Ct. 1988).

69. 33 U.S.C. § 1341(a)(1); 40 C.F.R. § 121.16(b).

70. 33 C.F.R. § 325.2 (b)(l)(ii). *See also* RGL No. 87-03, Section 401 Water Quality Certification (Apr. 14, 1987), *available at* http://www.usace.army.mil/inet/functions/cw/cecwo/reg/rgls/rgl87-03.htm.

71. *North Carolina v. FERC,* 112 F.3d at 1184; City of Fredericksburg v. FERC, 876 F.2d 1109, 1111–12 (4th Cir. 1989).

72. *Compare City of Fredericksburg v. FERC,* 876 F.2d 1109 at 1111–12 (concluding that under FERC regulations "a valid request for certification occurs only if the prospective licensee complies with the state agency's filing procedures"), *with* California v. FERC, 966 F.2d 1541, 1552–54 (9th Cir. 1992) (deferring to FERC determination of when waiver period commenced over objection by state certifying agency).

73. 33 C.F.R. § 325.2(b)(ii).

74. For example, see Connecticut Department of Environmental Protection, 401 Water Quality Certification Fact Sheet, *available at* http://dep.state.ct.us/pao/IWRDfact/401wqc.htm.

75. 33 U.S.C. § 1341(d).

76. 44 Fed. Reg. 32,854, 32,888 n.l (1979).

77. 33 C.F.R. § 320.4(d).

78. 33 C.F.R. § 320.3(a). The regulation may reflect the provisions of § 401(a)(3) of the CWA, which provides:

> The certification obtained pursuant to [Section 401(a)(1)] with respect to the construction of any facility shall fulfill the requirements of this section with respect to certification in connection with any other Federal license or permit required for the operation of such facility unless, after notice to the certifying State, . . . the State . . . notifies [the permitting or licensing] agency within sixty days after receipt of such notice that there is no longer reasonable assurance that there will be compliance with [various provisions of the CWA] because of changes since the construction license or permit certification was issued in (A) the construction or operation of the facility, (B) the characteristics of the waters into which the discharge is made, (C) the water quality criteria applicable to such waters or (D) applicable effluent limitations or other requirements.

33 U.S.C. § 1341(a)(3).

79. *See* 40 C.F.R. § 121.2(a)(3) and (4).

80. 511 U.S. 700 (1994).

81. *Id.* at 712.

82. 33 U.S.C. § 1313. For general background information on water quality standards, see U.S. Environmental Protection Agency, Water Quality Standards, available at http://www.epa.gov/waterscience/standards/.

83. 33 U.S.C. § 1313(c). Whenever states adopt new or revised standards, they must be approved by EPA. If EPA does not approve the standards, it must notify the state of changes required to secure EPA approval. If those changes are not made, EPA has the authority to promulgate standards applicable to the state. States can adopt standards that are more stringent than the federal floor. 33 U.S.C. § 1311(b)(1)(C); 40 C.F.R. § 131.4(a). In setting standards, each state must comply with the following broad requirements:

> Such standards shall be such as to protect the public health or welfare, enhance the quality of water and serve the purposes of this chapter. Such standards shall be established taking into consideration their use and value for public water supplies, propagation of fish and wildlife, recreational [and other purposes].

33 U.S.C. § 1313(c). Additionally, Section 303(c)(1) provides that states "shall from time to time (but at least once every three year period . . .) hold public hearings for the purpose of reviewing applicable water quality standards and, as appropriate, modifying and adopting standards." 33 U.S.C. § 1313 (c) (1); *see also* 40 C.F.R. § 131.1–.22.

84. 40 C.F.R. § 131.1–.22.

85. *See* 33 U.S.C. § 1370.

86. A library of policy and guidance documents dealing with water quality standards is available online. U.S. Environmental Protection Agency, Water Quality Policy and Guidance, *available at* http://www.epa.gov/waterscience/standards/policy.htm. For an older but extensive discussion of water quality standards, see ABA, SECTION ON NATURAL RESOURCES, ENERGY, AND ENVIRONMENTAL LAW, THE CLEAN WATER ACT HANDBOOK (Parthenia Evans, ed., 1994).

87. 33 U.S.C. § 1251(a)(2).

88. WILLIAM H. RODGERS, JR., ENVIRONMENTAL LAW 343 (2d ed. 1994).

89. The Water Quality Act of 1987 required states to adopt numeric criteria for more than 100 toxic pollutants. 33 U.S.C. § 1317.

90. The most common narrative criteria are the so-called "four free-froms" or "four freedoms," which require that a state's waters shall be free from:

a. Substances that will cause the formation of putrescent or otherwise objectionable bottom deposits;
b. Oil, scum, and floating debris in amounts that are unsightly or deleterious;
c. Materials that cause odor, color or other conditions in such degree as to cause a nuisance;
d. Substances in concentrations or combinations harmful or toxic to humans or aquatic life.

RODGERS, *supra* note 88, at 344 n.8 (quoting U.S. EPA, Criteria and Standards Division, Standards Branch, State Water Quality Standards for Toxics, Oct. 1984, p.2).

91. 40 C.F.R. § 131.12. "Outstanding resource waters" are high-quality waters that constitute an "outstanding National resource, such as waters of National and State parks and wildlife refuges and waters of exceptional recreational or ecological significance." 40 C.F.R. § 131.12(3). The water quality of outstanding resource waters must be "maintained and protected."

92. *See Water Quality Standards for Wetlands: National Guidance,* U.S. EPA Office of Water Publication, EPA 440/S-90-011 (July 1990).

93. *Id.* at vii.

94. 40 C.F.R. § 230.10(c); *Wetlands and 401 Certification: Opportunities and Guidelines for States and Eligible Indian Tribes,* EPA Office of Water Publication at 14 (April 1989); EPA, *Questions and Answers on Antidegradation* 3 (August 1985), in EPA, WATER QUALITY STANDARDS HANDBOOK at App. G (1993).

95. 40 C.F.R. § 230.10(c).

96. *Wetlands and 401 Certification, supra* note 94, at 14.

97. *Questions and Answers on Antidegradation, supra* note 94, at 3.

98. 40 C.F.R. § 131.12(1).

99. *Water Quality Standards for Wetlands: National Guidance, supra* note 92.

100. *See* U.S. Environmental Protection Agency, Nutrients: Methods for Evaluating Wetland Condition, *available at* http://www.epa.gov/waterscience/criteria/wetlands/.

101. *PUD No. 1 of Jefferson County,* 511 U.S. at 718 (quoting 40 C.F.R. § 131.12 (1992)).

102. *Id.* at 719. The state of Washington's antidegradation policy provides that "existing beneficial uses shall be maintained and protected and no further degradation which would interfere with or become injurious to existing beneficial uses will be allowed." *Id.* (quoting WAC 173-201-035(8)(a)).

103. Wash. Admin. Code 173-201-045(1)(b)(iii) (1990). This section of the Code has now been repealed.

104. State courts have also held that a state may deny certification on the grounds that the proposed activity will violate state water quality use designations. *See* Bangor Hydro-Electric Co. v. Board of Environmental Protection, 595 A.2d 438, 442–43 (Me. 1991).

105. 511 U.S. at 731; *see id.* at 713 ("state water quality standards . . . are among the 'other limitations' with which a State may ensure compliance through the [Section] 401 certification process" and water quality standards may also be regarded as "any other appropriate requirement of State law") (quoting 33 U.S.C. § 1341(d)).

106. Wash. Admin. Code 173-201-035(8)(a) (1990).

107. 511 U.S. at 719.

108. *Id.* at 729.

109. *Id.* at 714.

110. Arnold Irrigation District v. Dept. of Envtl. Quality, 717 P.2d 1274 (Or. App. 1986).

111. *Id.* at 1279.

112. Niagara Mohawk Power Corp. v. New York State Department of Environmental Conservation, 82 N.Y.2d 191, 197–201, 624 N.E.2d 146, 149–51 (Ct. App. 1993).

113. 82 N.Y.2d at 199, 624 N.E.2d at 150.

114. 146 Wn.2d 778; 51 P.3d 744 (2002).

115. Id. at 766.

116. *See* Note, *Purchaser Liability for Restoration of Illegally Filled Wetlands Under Section 404 of the Clean Water Act,* 18 B.C. Envtl. Aff. L. Rev. 320 (1991).

117. 33 C.F.R. § 325.2 (b)(1)(ii).

118. In fiscal year 2003 (the most recent year for which complete information is available), the Corps processed 4,035 individual permits, and a total of 81,843 nationwide permits, regional permits, and letters of permission. U.S. Army Corps of Engineers, All Permit Decisions FY2003, *available at* http://www.usace.army.mil/inet/functions/cw/cecwo/reg/2003webcharts.pdf.

119. United States v. Marathon Dev. Corp., 867 F.2d 96, 100 (1st Cir. 1989).

120. 33 C.F.R. §§ 330.4(c)(3), (6).

121. Such information can often be found on a Corps's district Web site. A list of Corps district offices and links to most Corps district Web sites is available at http://www.usace.army.mil/inet/functions/cw/cecwo/reg/ district.htm.

122. *See supra* note 52 and accompanying text.

123. 33 U.S.C. § 1341(a)(2); 33 C.F.R. § 325.2(b)(i).

124. 33 U.S.C. § 1341(a)(2); 33 C.F.R. § 325.2(b)(i).

125. 33 C.F.R. 320.4(d).

126. *Id.* ("Certification of compliance with applicable effluent limitations and water quality standards required under provisions of section 401 of the Clean Water Act will be considered conclusive with respect to water quality considerations unless the Regional Administrator, Environmental Protection Agency (EPA), advises of other water quality aspects to be taken into consideration.") *See* Friends of the Earth v. Hintz, 800 F.2d 822, 834 (1986).

127. *See* 33 C.F.R. § 320.4(d).

128. *See* RGL No. 90-04, Water Quality Considerations (March 13, 1990), 56 Fed. Reg. 2410–11 (January 22, 1991), *available at* http://www.usace.army.mil/inet/functions/cw/cecwo/reg/rgls/rgl90-04.htm.

129. *Id.*

130. 33 C.F.R. § 325.2(b)(1)(ii).

131. 684 F.2d 1041 (1st Cir. 1982).

132. *Id.* at 1056.

133. 129 F.3d 99 (2d Cir. 1997).

134. *Id.* at 110–11.

135. *Id.* at 112.

136. 33 C.F.R. §§ 325.4, 330.4(c).

137. RGL No. 92-04, Section 401 Water Quality Certification and Coastal Zone Management Act Conditions for Nationwide Permits, 61 Fed. Reg. 30,992, 30,993 (June 18, 1996), *available at* http://www.usace.army.mil/inet/functions/cw/cecwo/reg/rgls/rgl92-04.htm.

138. *Id.*

139. EPA, Decision of the General Counsel No. 44, *In re Texaco. Inc.* (June 22, 1976).

140. *Id.*

141. EPA, Decision of the General Counsel No. 58, *In re Bethlehem Steel Corp.* (March 29, 1977).

142. The availability of judicial review of a state agency's decision on a certification request is a matter of state administrative law. In some states, such judicial review may not be available. *See Summit Hydropower, supra* note 67.

143. Keeting v. FERC, 927 F.2d 616, 623–24 (D.C. Cir 1991).

144. United States v. Puerto Rico, 551 F. Supp. 864, 865 (D.P.R. 1982), *aff'd,* 721 F.2d 832 (1st Cir. 1983).

145. Oregon Natural Desert Ass'n v. Thomas, 940 F. Supp. 1534, 1538 (D. Or. 1996).

146. 511 U.S. 700 (1994).

147. 16 U.S.C. § 1451(a).

148. *See* 16 U.S.C. § 1452.

149. 16 U.S.C. § 1452. To access state-specific information regarding coastal zone management, including state and territory coastal management program summaries and links to program home pages, see National Oceanic and Atmospheric Administration, State and Territory Coastal Management Program Summaries, *available at* http://coastalmanagement.noaa.gov/czm/czmsitelist.html.

150. 16 U.S.C. § 1455(d).

151. For general information about the federal Coastal Zone Management program, see http://coastalmanagement.noaa.gov/czm/national.html.

152. 16 U.S.C. § 1456(c)(3)(A). *See also* 33 C.F.R. §§ 320.3 (b) and 320.4 (h). Activities conducted by federal agencies that may affect coastal zone resources are subject to different procedures. *See* 16 U.S.C. § 1456(c)(1)–(2).

153. 33 C.F.R. § 325.2 (b)(2)(ii).

154. 33 C.F.R. § 325.2(b)(2)(ii). The Secretary of Commerce may, upon request of the applicant or on the secretary's own initiative, override the state's objections upon finding that "the activity is consistent with the objectives of [the CZMA] or is otherwise necessary in the interest of national security." 16 U.S.C. § 1456(c)(3)(A); 33 C.F.R. § 325.2(b)(2)(ii).

155. *Id.*

156. *See* Houck & Rolland, *supra* note 31, at 1294–99.

157. 16 U.S.C. § 1458(e)(1) (Supp. V 1993).

158. *See* Houck & Rolland, *supra* note 31, at 1296.

CHAPTER 11

The Corps Administrative Appeal Process

KIM DIANA CONNOLLY

I. Introduction/Scope

A recent addition to the United States Army Corps of Engineers (Corps) regulatory process is an internal appeal for permit applicants. The Corps implemented this administrative appeal process over a two-year period, in 1999 and 2000.[1] The relatively new process lets a Section 404 permit applicant bring an appeal[2] to one of eight regional offices if that applicant disagrees with a Corps district office decision on a permit application or a jurisdictional determination.[3] The stated intent of the program is to "promote and maintain a [process] that is independent, fair, prompt and efficient."[4] An administrative appeal may be required to exhaust administrative remedies before a permit applicant can institute legal action in a federal court for certain permitting and other Corps regulatory decisions.[5]

This chapter focuses exclusively on the history, mechanics, and application of the administrative appeal process. Related topics are discussed in previous chapters, including the standards for individual permits (Chapters 4 and 6) and standards for jurisdictional determinations (Chapter 3). Section II of this chapter summarizes the history and development of the program. Section III discusses the process for appeals of denied or declined permits as well as the process for appeals of jurisdictional determinations. Section IV provides an overview of various administrative appeals from a number of Corps divisions.

II. History and Development of the Administrative Appeal Process

The Corps Regulatory Program[6] regulates a variety of activities, including the discharge of dredged or fill material into the waters of the United States under Section 404 of the Clean Water Act.[7] The structure and design of Corps regulatory activities are deliberately decentralized.[8] In fact, the primary work on each permit application is performed by one project manager, and usually approved by the leadership of one of the local district offices.[9] While it has its advantages,[10] one obvious disadvantage of such a system is that it can lead to inconsistent decision making.[11] Prior to the implementation of an administrative appeal process, dissatisfied permit applicants were forced to seek initial redress for decisions with which they disagreed through the judicial process.[12]

In part as a response to that perceived complexity, the Corps's administrative appeal process was proposed as a component of a forty-point plan developed by the 1993 White House Wetlands Working Group entitled *Protecting America's Wetlands: A Fair, Flexible, and Effective Approach.*[13] Proposed in the Federal Register in 1995,[14] it took a number of years and several congressional directives to get the administrative appeal regulations in place.[15]

The 1995 proposal involved a two-step process for appeals of a decision by the Corps that a particular area was subject to its jurisdiction, and a one-step process for appeals of denied permits or permits proffered with conditions to which an applicant objects.[16] The initial proposed rule specifically noted that "[a]n ideal administrative appeal regulation for some people would be one that allows all third parties to request an administrative appeal of jurisdictional determinations and permit decisions."[17] However, citing expense and administrative complication, third-party-initiated appeals were not promulgated as part of the final rule.[18] Furthermore, the final rule limited all appeals to a single-step process.[19]

As will be discussed further in a later section of this chapter, the anticipated flood of Corps administrative appeals never materialized. Nevertheless, there is a steady stream of appeals that can help inform how applicants should approach the permitting process.[20]

III. Undertaking an Administrative Appeal: The Process

Permit applicants can use the process set forth in 33 C.F.R. Part 331 to "pursue an administrative appeal of certain Corps of Engineers decisions with which they disagree."[21] The decisions that can be appealed include "approved jurisdictional determinations (JDs), permit applications denied with prejudice, and declined permits."[22] Declined permits are permits offered to an applicant, but which the applicant refuses to accept.[23]

Appeals are available only to an "affected party,"[24] defined as "a permit applicant, landowner, a lease, easement or option holder (i.e., an individual who has an identifiable and substantial legal interest in the property) who has received an approved JD, permit denial, or has declined a proffered individual permit."[25] Affected parties may proceed pro se or through an attorney or agent.[26]

As set forth in the regulations, ultimate responsibility for deciding appeals rests with the division engineer, the senior employee at each of the Corps's nine divisions.[27] The main players in the process, however, are the review officers (ROs)[28] designated for each division.[29] In a number of divisions, more than one person has served as RO since the inception of the appeals process.[30] Note that this regionalized process involving different divisions departs from the centralized approach to internal appeals common in most other agencies, such as the Environmental Appeals Board (EAB) of the U.S. Environmental Protection Agency (EPA).[31]

The actual appeal process unfolds when an eligible decision is rendered by the Corps.[32] The Corps is required to provide notification of the available appeal process when rendering an eligible decision, including a Notice of Appeal (NAP) fact sheet[33] and a Request for Appeal (RFA) form,[34] as well as the relevant decision document.[35] In cases where an individual permit is proffered for the first time to a permit applicant, the Corps must also provide a Notification of Applicant Options (NAO) fact sheet.[36] This initial proffer does not become an appealable action until the actual proffer is made.[37] A flow chart explaining the process with respect to initial proffered permits is available on the Corps Web site.[38]

Applicants wishing to appeal must submit an RFA within sixty days of receipt of an approved JD, permit denial, or declined permit.[39] When submitting an RFA, the appellant must grant a right of entry for the Corps to the project site, to allow the RO to clarify the record, or to conduct field tests/sampling directly related to the appeal.[40] A submitted RFA is reviewed by an RO, and a determination of acceptability (meaning completeness and meeting the criteria for appeal) must be issued within thirty days.[41] An RFA found to be incomplete or not meeting the criteria may be resubmitted within thirty days and reevaluated by the division office.[42] A decision will typically be issued within ninety days of receipt of an acceptable appeal, though site visits may delay a decision.[43]

An RFA must state the reasons for appeal.[44] Examples of reasons provided in the Corps administrative appeal regulations include procedural error; incorrect application of law, regulation, or officially promulgated policy; material fact omission; incorrect application of current regulatory criteria and associated guidance for identifying, delineating, and permitting activities in jurisdictional waters; and use of incorrect data.[45] Jurisdictional errors may be included in the appeal of a declined or denied permit, even if the original jurisdictional determination was not appealed.[46]

For appeals challenging a JD, the RO has the option to schedule an appeal meeting or a conference call, both of which are meant to be informal.[47] The appellant can have an agent (such as a lawyer or engineer) present at the meeting.[48] The appellant must bear his or her own costs to participate.[49] The meeting must be scheduled at a location convenient to the appellant and near the site where the JD was conducted.[50]

For appeals of permit denials and declined permits, informal conferences to "to provide a forum that allows the participants to discuss freely all relevant issues and material facts associated with the appeal"[51] are normally scheduled within sixty days of filing of an RFA.[52] Such conferences should be at a location reasonably convenient for the appellant, and should include the RO, the appellant, the appellant's agent(s) as appropriate, and Corps district staff.[53] Such a conference is intended to be informal,[54] and should focus on "relevant issues needed to address the reasons for appeal contained in the RFA."[55]

Not all actions are subject to appeal.[56] Situations where appeals are not available include those where a permit applicant signs a permit; a court has issued a decision on a site-specific matter; a controlling factor is outside of Corps control; an application has been modified; the sixty-day deadline for filing an RFA has been missed; or decision documents are preliminary.[57]

The regulations require the RO to approve the district office's decision unless there is a finding that "the decision on some relevant matter was arbitrary, capricious, an abuse of discretion, not supported by substantial evidence in the administrative record, or plainly contrary to a requirement of law, regulation, an Executive Order, or officially promulgated Corps policy guidance."[58] The RO is to review the record using a substantial evidence standard.[59] District office decisions are reviewed for errors in both procedure and substantive analysis.[60] All RO decisions must be documented in writing.[61]

In certain situations, appeals may be filed for after-the-fact permit applications issued for unauthorized activities.[62] Initial corrective measures may be required before such an appeal can be heard,[63] and administrative penalties will still apply if the appeal is found to be without merit.[64] For appeals of decisions related to unauthorized activities, a signed tolling agreement must be included with the RFA unless one has previously been furnished to the Corps district office.[65]

As of spring 2004, there have not been any challenges to the administrative appeal process that have resulted in published court opinions. The 1995 proposed rule projected that significant resources would have to be directed at the Corps administrative appeal program, due to the anticipated volume of appeals.[66] The most recent figures available, for fiscal years 2002–2003, demonstrate that the Corps evaluates close to 90,000 permit applications annually, of which approximately 4,000, or nearly 4 percent, are standard, individual permits.[67] In the same fiscal years, the Corps made almost 75,000 jurisdictional determinations.[68] Based on this volume of decisions, initial projections were that the Corps would be receiving thousands of appeal requests annually.[69] As it turns out, however, the volume of appeals is rather light. In the first three years of the full program, no division exceeded sixty appeals.[70] The highest total number of appeals requested in all Corps divisions in one month was ten, and most months see significantly fewer.[71] Accordingly, less than one percent of individual permits and jurisdictional determinations are appealed. A few examples of those appeals are discussed in the next section.

IV. Learning from Examples of Administrative Appeals

The Corps administrative appeal regulations explicitly state that individual administrative appeal decisions have no precedential value.[72] The regulations direct that appeal decisions are not to be cited in other administrative appeals.[73] Nevertheless, copies of appeals are to be sent to Corps headquarters, to be reviewed periodically for consistency.[74]

Furthermore, at this point, all final appeal decisions for the various divisions can be reviewed at their division Web sites. The eight divisions are as follows: Great Lakes & Ohio River Division,[75] Mississippi Valley Division,[76] North Atlantic Division,[77] Northwestern Division,[78] Pacific Ocean Division,[79] South Atlantic Division,[80] South Pacific Division,[81] and Southwestern Division.[82] While administrative appeal decisions may not be precedential, they are certainly informative. Accordingly, this section presents a brief discussion of a few representative samples for informational purposes.

Insight into the appeal process for permit decisions can be gleaned from examining two decisions on appeals of denied permits in the Pacific Ocean Division,[83] one found to have merit and one found not to have merit. The first was issued in July 2003 regarding certain property in Alaska, where the Pacific Ocean Division RO issued a finding of "no merit."[84] In that appeal, an owner of property near Ketchikan, Alaska, wanted to construct a commercial and recreational haul-out facility and associated services that would involve dredging of 22,600 cubic yards of substrate and depositing it in such a way as to disturb certain sensitive ecosystems.[85] The Corps denied the permit, finding that less damaging practicable alternatives[86] were available.[87] The RO assessed each ground for appeal in turn,[88] and concluded that the record reflected the district's decision was "reasonable and a sufficient basis to deny the Appellant's permit."[89] Despite the finding of no merit, the RO also directed that the district remain open to a review of new information regarding practicable alternatives for the application at issue.[90]

A subsequent 2004 decision by the Pacific Ocean Division issued a finding of "partial merit" on multiple "reasons for appeal."[91] In that decision, the applicant applied for a permit to fill a small pond and associated wetlands and mudflats in a business center in downtown Anchorage[92] in order to increase storage and handling space for marine cargo.[93] The RO concluded that the first six main reasons for appeal all had partial merit, and that the seventh main reason for appeal was beyond the scope of the pending administrative procedure.[94] Accordingly, the decision was remanded to the Alaska District office.[95] It is worth noting that the appeal in that case took almost a year to process.[96] The RO attributed the delay to both "the cumbersome way in which the RFA [was] organized, its lack of sequential pagination or section numbering, and its inordinant [*sic*] length"[97] as well as an administrative record "compiled and submitted in alternating forward and reverse chronological order and with no discernable separation between documents, attachments to documents, and attachments to attachments."[98] It is also worth noting that both of the Pacific Ocean Division appeals discussed here involved the RO reviewing both substantive and procedural compliance with Corps regulations.

Likewise, a review of two appeal decisions with respect to jurisdictional determinations in the South Atlantic Division also provides insight into the appeal process for those types of decisions. The first is a decision issued in May of 2004 finding "merit" in that particular appeal and remanding to the Jacksonville District for further consideration.[99] The property owner, Barry Allen, appealed a finding of jurisdictional wetlands on property in Santa Rosa County, Florida,[100] claiming that the wetlands were isolated and thus no longer regulated under the *Solid Waste Agency of Northern Cook County v. Corps of Engineers* (*SWANCC*) decision.[101] The RO found a failure to comply with certain guidance documents and criteria specific to the Florida area.[102] The remand directed "reconsideration of the jurisdictional determination decision consistent with the instructions in this administrative appeal decision."[103]

Later that year, however, the South Atlantic Division found that an appeal did "not have merit" in a jurisdictional determination in which the appellant also raised a challenge to the jurisdictional determination in light of the *SWANCC* decision.[104] In that case, the company, Environmental Services, Inc., challenged a finding that a wetland on a 47-acre tract in Effingham County, Georgia, was not isolated.[105] Noting that site inspections had "resulted in the determination that this wetland is connected via a system of surface ditches, concrete pipe, and unmanned [sic] and named (i.e., Black Creek) tributaries to the Savannah River," a navigable water of the United States,[106] the RO found that the Savannah District had "evaluated and documented their approved jurisdictional determination . . . according to applicable laws, regulations and policy guidance."[107] It thus upheld the district's decision.

Appeal decisions such as the ones discussed above do, as the regulations indicate, depend "on the facts, circumstances, and physical conditions particular to the specific project and/or site being evaluated."[108] The low numbers of appeals since the inception of the program make meaningful comparisons among divisions difficult. Nevertheless, potential appellants and their representatives would probably be well served to review appeal decisions in their particular division before completing a Request for Appeal.[109]

V. Conclusion

Fully deployed in 2000, the Corps administrative appeal process remains a relatively new program. Most permit applicants, practitioners, and Corps employees have learned the basics of the process, but the realities of implementation will continue to evolve. One thing can be said for certain: The initial volume of administrative appeals has been significantly lower than expected in the original proposal.[110] Whether this continues to be true is something that environmental permitting professionals and other stakeholders will be watching.

Notes

1. Administrative Appeal Process Establishment for the Regulatory Program of the Corps of Engineers, Final Rule, 64 Fed. Reg. 11,708 (Mar. 9, 1999); Final Rule Establishing an Administrative Appeal Process for the Regulatory Program of the Corps of Engineers, 65 Fed. Reg. 16,486 (Mar. 28, 2000), amending 33 C.F.R. pts. 320, 326 and 331 (2004).

2. The regulations define "appealable action" as "an approved [jurisdictional determination], a permit denial, or a declined permit." 33 C.F.R. § 331.1.

3. 33 C.F.R. pt. 331, *available at* http://www.usace.army.mil/inet/functions/cw/cecwo/reg/33cfr331.htm. For a list of the Corps district offices, *see* United States Army Corps of Engineers, Where We Are, http://www.usace.army.mil/where.html#Divisions.

4. 33 C.F.R. § 331.1(a).

5. 33 C.F.R. §§ 331.10. That regulation states that "[t]he final Corps decision on a permit application is the initial decision to issue or deny a permit, unless the applicant submits an RFA, and the division engineer accepts the RFA, pursuant to this Part." *Id.* If an action is appealed, the final Corps decision depends on the merit of the appeal

> (a) If the division engineer determines that the appeal is without merit, the final Corps decision is the district engineer's letter advising the applicant that the division engineer has decided that the appeal is without merit, confirming the district engineer's initial decision, and sending the permit denial or the proffered permit for signature to the appellant; or (b) If the division engineer determines that the appeal has merit, the final Corps decision is the district engineer's decision made pursuant to the division engineer's remand of the appealed action. These regulations provide that the Corps' initial decision to issue or deny a permit is the final decision on a permit application. For an appealed action, where the division engineer determines that the appeal has merit, the final Corps permit decision is the district engineer's decision pursuant to the division engineer's remand.

Id. See Ozark Soc'y v. Melcher, 229 F. Supp. 2d 896 (E.D. Ark. 2002); Bay-Houston Towing Co. v. United States, 58 Fed. Cl. 462, 471 (2003).

6. The Corps Regulatory Program, "[w]orking to provide strong protection of the Nation's aquatic environment, efficient administration of the Corps' regulatory program, and fair and reasonable decision-making for the regulated public," has its home page at http://www.usace.army.mil/inet/functions/cw/cecwo/reg/.

7. 33 U.S.C. § 1344 (2000). The Corps also issues permits for the obstruction of navigation under Section 10 of the Rivers and Harbors Act of 1899, 33 U.S.C. § 403, and permits for dumping of dredged material into the ocean pursuant to Section 103 of the Ocean Dumping Act. Marine Protection Research and Sanctuaries Act of 1972, 33 U.S.C. § 1413.

8. As stated on one Corps district site, "[t]he Regulatory geographic responsibilities of the Corps of Engineer Districts are generally based upon water basins. The district office that will process your activity will not necessarily fall within state boundaries of the project; field units are numerous, however, and you may be further directed to a closer field office." *See* http://www.sac.usace .army.mil/permits/offices.html. To locate the Corps district office nearest a particular location, use the U.S. Army Corps of Engineers "What Districts Are in My State" Web page, http://www.usace.army.mil/where.html#State.

9. U.S. Army Corps of Engineers, Regulatory Program Overview, *available at* http://www.usace.army.mil/inet/functions/cw/cecwo/reg/oceover.htm ("Corps districts operate under what is called a project manager system, where one individual is responsible for handling an application from receipt to final decision. The project manager prepares a public notice, evaluates the impacts of the project and all comments received, negotiates necessary modifications of the project if required, and drafts or oversees drafting of appropriate documentation to support a recommended permit decision.").

10. As one recent National Academy of Sciences report put it, "[o]ne advantage of this structure is that district offices may have greater flexibility to pursue innovative efforts and novel actions tailored to local conditions and preferences." National Research Council, Adaptive Management for Water Resources Project Planning (2004), *available at* http://www.nap.edu/openbook/0309091918/html/37.html.

11. *See, e.g.*, United States General Accounting Office, Waters and Wetlands: Corps of Engineers Needs to Evaluate Its District Office Practices in Determining Jurisdiction (GAO-04-297, Feb. 2004), *available at* http://www.gao.gov/new.items/d04297.pdf ("Corps districts differ in how they interpret and apply the federal regulations when determining which waters and wetlands are subject to federal jurisdiction." *Id.* at 3.).

12. Proposal to Establish an Administrative Appeal Process for the Regulatory Programs of the Corps of Engineers, 60 Fed. Reg. 37,280 (July 19, 1995).

13. White House Office on Environmental Policy, *Protecting America's Wetlands: A Fair, Flexible, and Effective Approach, available at* http://www.wetlands.com/fed/aug93wet.htm. An administrative appeal proposal was identified among the four proposals in that report to address landowner concerns, specifically designed to "allow for administrative appeals of the Corps' determination that it has regulatory jurisdiction over a particular parcel of property, permit denials, and administrative penalties."

14. Proposal to Establish an Administrative Appeal Process for the Regulatory Programs of the Corps of Engineers, 60 Fed. Reg. 37,280 (July 19, 1995).

15. *See* H.R. 2605 (introduced July 26, 1999), making appropriations for energy and water development for the fiscal year ending September 30, 2000, and for other purposes. This bill appropriated a total of $117 million dollars for the Corps Regulatory budget, "Provided, That the Secretary of the Army, acting through the Chief of Engineers, is directed to use $5,000,000 of funds appropriated herein to fully implement an administrative appeals process for the Corps of Engineers Regulatory Program, which administrative appeals process shall provide for a single-level appeal of jurisdictional determinations." *See also* House Conference Report No. 106-336 (Sept. 27, 1999). In this accompanying report, the Conference Committee noted that "[t]he conferees have provided $5,000,000 to fully implement an administrative appeals process for the Regulatory Program of the Corps of Engineers. This process shall provide for a single-level appeal of jurisdictional determinations, the results of which shall be considered final agency action under the Administrative Procedures Act. This language is not intended to create a new cause of action or legal mechanism that would result in

additional litigation. The conference agreement deletes language proposed by the House providing that the results of a single-level appeal of jurisdictional determinations shall be considered final agency action under the Administrative Procedures Act."

16. Proposal to Establish an Administrative Appeal Process for the Regulatory Programs of the Corps of Engineers, 60 Fed. Reg. 37,280 (July 19, 1995). The Corps explained its proposal as follows:

> The appeal process is designed to allow administrative appeals to the Corps regarding two distinct decisions: (1) That a geographic area, including a particular parcel of property that is determined to be a wetland as defined in 33 CFR 328.3(b) and delineated in accordance with the Federal manual for delineating and identifying wetlands, is subject to Corps regulatory jurisdiction pursuant to Section 404 of the Clean Water Act and/or Section 10 of the Rivers and Harbors Act of 1899; and (2) denial with prejudice by the District Engineer of a Department of the Army permit, which includes cases where a proffered permit is refused by the applicant because the applicant objects to the terms or special conditions of the proffered permit and the permit is subsequently denied with prejudice by the District Engineer. *Id.*

17. *Id.* at 37,284.

18. *Id.* at 37,284–85.

19. 65 Fed. Reg. at 16,486.

20. For links to administrative appeal decisions, *see* U.S. Army Corps of Engineers, Administrative Appeals Information, *at* http://www.usace.army.mil/inet/functions/cw/cecwo/reg/appeals.htm.

21. 33 C.F.R. § 331.1(a).

22. *Id.*

23. 33 C.F.R. § 331.2 ("Declined permit means a proffered individual permit, including a letter of permission, that an applicant has refused to accept, because he has objections to the terms and special conditions therein. A declined permit can also be an individual permit that the applicant originally accepted, but where such permit was subsequently modified . . . in such a manner that the resulting permit contains terms and special conditions that lead the applicant to decline the modified permit, provided that the applicant has not started work in waters of the United States authorized by such permit. Where an applicant declines a permit (either initial or modified), the applicant does not have a valid permit to conduct regulated activities in waters of the United States, and must not begin construction of the work requiring a Corps permit unless and until the applicant receives and accepts a valid Corps permit." *Id.*).

24. *Id.*

25. *Id.*

26. 33 C.F.R. § 331.7(e)(3).

27. 33 C.F.R. § 331.7 and § 331.3 ("The division engineer may act as the review officer (RO), or may delegate, either generically or on a case-by-case basis, any authority or responsibility described in this part as that of the RO. With the exception of JDs, as described in this paragraph (a)(1), the division

engineer may not delegate any authority or responsibility described in this part as that of the division engineer. For approved JDs only, the division engineer may delegate any authority or responsibility described in this part as that of the division engineer, including the final appeal decision. In such cases, any delegated authority must be granted to an official that is at the same or higher grade level than the grade level of the official that signed the approved JD. Regardless of any delegation of authority or responsibility for ROs or for final appeal decisions for approved JDs, the division engineer retains overall responsibility for the administrative appeal process." *Id.*).

28. 33 C.F.R. § 331.3.

29. *Id.*

30. Review officers contact information can be found on the division Web sites, accessible through the U.S. Army Corps of Engineers, Administrative Appeals Information, *at* http://www.usace.army.mil/inet/functions/cw/cecwo/reg/appeals.htm.

31. The home page of the EAB is http://www.epa.gov/eab/ ("The Appeals Board is the final Agency decisionmaker on administrative appeals under all major environmental statutes that the Agency administers. It is an impartial four-member body that is independent of all Agency components outside the immediate Office of the Administrator. The Appeals Board sits in panels of three judges and makes decisions by majority vote. Currently, nine experienced attorneys serve as counsel to the Board." *Id.*).

32. 33 C.F.R. § 331.4.

33. 33 C.F.R. § 331.2 ("Notification of Appeal Process (NAP) means a fact sheet that explains the criteria and procedures of the administrative appeal process. Every approved JD, permit denial, and every proffered individual permit returned for reconsideration after review by the district engineer in accordance with Sec. 331.6(b) will have an NAP form attached." *Id.*).

34. *Id.* ("Request for appeal (RFA) means the affected party's official request to initiate the appeal process. The RFA must include the name of the affected party, the Corps file number of the approved JD, denied permit, or declined permit, the reason(s) for the appeal, and any supporting data and information. No new information may be submitted. . . . The affected party initiates the administrative appeal process by providing an acceptable RFA to the appropriate Corps of Engineers division office. An acceptable RFA contains all the required information and provides reasons for appeal that meets the criteria identified in Sec. 331.5." *Id.*).

35. 33 C.F.R. § 331.4.

36. 33 C.F.R. § 331.4. "Notification of Applicant Options (NAO) means a fact sheet explaining an applicant's options with a proffered individual permit under the administrative appeal process." *Id.* at § 331.2.

37. The regulations define a proffered permit as

> a permit that is sent to an applicant that is in the proper format for the applicant to sign (for a standard permit) or accept (for a letter of permission). The term "initial proffered permit" as used in this part refers to the first time a permit is sent to the applicant. The initial proffered

> permit is not an appealable action. However, the applicant may object to the terms or conditions of the initial proffered permit and, if so, a second reconsidered permit will be sent to the applicant. The term 'proffered permit' as used in this part refers to the second permit that is sent to the applicant. Such proffered permit is an appealable action.

Id.

38. Available through a link at 33 C.F.R. pt. 331, Administrative Appeals Process, *at* http://www.usace.army.mil/inet/functions/cw/cecwo/reg/33cfr331.htm.

39. 33 C.F.R. § 331.6(a).

40. 33 C.F.R. § 331.2. *See also* 33 C.F.R. § 331.7(c), discussing specifics with respect to site investigations.

41. 33 C.F.R. § 331.7(a) ("If the RFA is acceptable, the RO will so notify the appellant in writing within 30 days of the receipt of the acceptable RFA. If the RO determines that the RFA is not complete the RO will so notify the appellant in writing within 30 days of the receipt of the RFA detailing the reason(s) why the RFA is not complete. If the RO believes that the RFA does not meet the criteria for appeal (see Sec. 331.5), the RO will make a recommendation on the RFA to the division engineer. If the division engineer determines that the RFA is not acceptable, the division engineer will notify the appellant of this determination by a certified letter detailing the reason(s) why the appeal failed to meet the criteria for appeal. No further administrative appeal is available, unless the appellant revises the RFA to correct the deficiencies noted in the division engineer's letter or the RO's letter." *Id.*).

42. *Id.* ("The revised RFA must be received by the division engineer within 30 days of the date of the Corps letter indicating that the initial RFA is not acceptable. If the RO determines that the revised RFA is still not complete, the RO will again so notify the appellant in writing within 30 days of the receipt of the RFA detailing the reason(s) why the RFA is not complete. If the division engineer determines that the revised RFA is still not acceptable, the division engineer will notify the appellant of this determination by a certified letter within 30 days of the date of the receipt of the revised RFA, and will advise the appellant that the matter is not eligible for appeal. No further RFAs will be accepted after this point.").

43. 33 C.F.R. § 331.8.

44. 33 C.F.R. § 331.5(a).

45. *Id.*

46. *Id.*

47. 33 C.F.R. § 331.7(d).

48. *Id.*

49. *Id.*

50. *Id.*

51. 33 C.F.R. § 331.7(e).

52. *Id.* A delay beyond this sixty-day window may be appropriate if "the RO determines that unforeseen or unusual circumstances require scheduling the conference for a later date." *Id.*

53. *Id.* at § 331.7(e)(1–3).

54. *Id.* at § 331.7(e)(7).

55. *Id.* at § 331.7(e)(6). "Any material in the administrative record may be discussed during the conference . . . [but i]ssues not identified in the administrative record by the date of the NAP for the application may not be raised or discussed, because substantive new information or project modifications would be treated as a new permit application." *Id.*

56. 33 C.F.R. § 331.5(b).

57. *Id.* The entire list of nonappealable actions is as follows:

> 1. An individual permit decision (including a letter of permission or a standard permit with special conditions), where the permit has been accepted and signed by the permittee. By signing the permit, the applicant waives all rights to appeal the terms and conditions of the permit, unless the authorized work has not started in waters of the United States and that issued permit is subsequently modified by the district engineer pursuant to 33 CFR 325.7;
>
> 2. Any site-specific matter that has been the subject of a final decision of the Federal courts;
>
> 3. A final Corps decision that has resulted from additional analysis and evaluation, as directed by a final appeal decision;
>
> 4. A permit denial without prejudice or a declined permit, where the controlling factor cannot be changed by the Corps decision maker (e.g., the requirements of a binding statute, regulation, state Section 401 water quality certification, state coastal zone management disapproval, etc. (See 33 CFR 320.4(j));
>
> 5. A permit denial case where the applicant has subsequently modified the proposed project, because this would constitute an amended application that would require a new public interest review, rather than an appeal of the existing record and decision;
>
> 6. Any request for the appeal of an approved JD, a denied permit, or a declined permit where the RFA has not been received by the division engineer within 60 days of the date of the NAP;
>
> 7. A previously approved JD that has been superceded by another approved JD based on new information or data submitted by the applicant. The new approved JD is an appealable action;
>
> 8. An approved JD associated with an individual permit where the permit has been accepted and signed by the permittee;
>
> 9. A preliminary JD; or
>
> 10. A JD associated with unauthorized activities except as provided in Sec. 331.11.

58. 33 C.F.R. § 331.8(b).

59. *Id.*

60. *Id.*

61. *Id.* Links to these appeal decisions may be found on the Corps Headquarters Regulatory Program Web page, *at* http://www.usace.army.mil/inet/functions/cw/cecwo/reg/appeals.htm.

62. 33 C.F.R. § 331.11.

63. *Id.* at § 331.11(a).

64. *Id.* at § 331.11(b).

65. *Id.* at § 331.11(c).

66. 60 Fed. Reg. at 37,283 ("[b]ecause of the variable scope of wetlands among Corps districts and developmental pressures on those wetlands, limited data is available to assess the potential cost of the administrative appeal program for wetland delineations and jurisdictional determinations. However, assuming that 10% of the approximately 35,000 jurisdictional determinations conducted annually by Corps districts are appealed, and that the average costs associated with each appeal is $1200–1500 (Salary/travel/data collection), the annual cost of the program could range from $4.2–$ 5.25 million.") and 37,284 ("Based on past regulatory program experience, it is reasonable to estimate that annually 250 permit denials may be appealed under the proposed rule. To accommodate this increased work effort, it would be necessary to establish one to two RO positions in each of the ten Corps divisions to implement the administrative appeal process. It is estimated that the resulting annual expense would be $ 2.5 million.").

67. U.S. Army Corps of Engineers, U.S. Army Corps of Engineers Regulatory Program—All Permit Decisions FY 2003, available through the News and Information: Regulatory Statistics link at http://www.usace.army.mil/inet/functions/cw/cecwo/reg/index.htm.

68. *Id.*

69. *See supra* note 66.

70. These numbers are compiled from the various district office Web sites, which can be accessed through the Corps Headquarters Web site *at* http://www.usace.army.mil/inet/functions/cw/cecwo/reg/appeals.htm.

71. *Id.*

72. 33 C.F.R. § 331.7(g) ("Because a decision to determine geographic jurisdiction, deny a permit, or condition a permit depends on the facts, circumstances, and physical conditions particular to the specific project and/or site being evaluated, appeal decisions would be of little or no precedential utility. Therefore, an appeal decision of the division engineer is applicable only to the instant appeal, and has no other precedential effect. Such a decision may not be cited in any other administrative appeal, and may not be used as precedent for the evaluation of any other jurisdictional determination or permit application." *Id.*).

73. *Id.*

74. "While administrative appeal decisions lack precedential value and may not be cited by an appellant or a district engineer in any other appeal proceeding, the Corps goal is to have the Corps regulatory program operate as consistently as possible, particularly with respect to interpretations of law, regulation, an Executive Order, and officially-promulgated policy. Therefore, a copy of each

appeal decision will be forwarded to Corps Headquarters; those decisions will be periodically reviewed at the headquarters level for consistency with law, Executive Orders, and policy." *Id.*

75. U.S. Army Corps of Engineers Great Lakes & Ohio River Division, Table of Appeals, *at* http://www.lrd.usace.army.mil/regulatory/tableappeals/.

76. U.S. Army Corps of Engineers Mississippi Valley Division Administrative Appeals, Table of Appeals, *at* http://www.mvd.usace.army.mil/Nwsinfo/MVD_Appeals/table_of_appeals.htm.

77. U.S. Army Corps of Engineers North Atlantic Division, Administrative Appeals Received—North Atlantic Division Regulatory Program, *at* http://www.nad.usace.army.mil/appeals.htm.

78. U.S. Army Corps of Engineers Northwestern Division Regulatory Appeals Program, Current Appeals Status, *at* http://www.nwd.usace.army.mil/et/reg/appeals_status.asp.

79. U.S. Army Corps of Engineers Pacific Ocean Division, Regulatory Appeals, *at* http://www.pod.usace.army.mil/Regulatory/Regulatory.htm.

80. U.S. Army Corps of Engineers South Atlantic Division, South Atlantic Division Appeals Received, *at* http://www.sad.usace.army.mil/regulatory/regulatory.htm.

81. U.S. Army Corps of Engineers South Pacific Division, South Pacific Division Administrative Appeal Process, *at* http://www.spd.usace.army.mil/cwpm/public/ops/regulatory/adminAppeals/index.htm.

82. U.S. Army Corps of Engineers Southwestern Division, Table of Appeals, *at* http://www.swd.usace.army.mil/regulatoryappeals/table_of_appeals.htm.

83. As of November 2004, the Pacific Ocean had processed only a total of six administrative appeals since the program was implemented. *See* http://www.pod.usace.army.mil/Regulatory/Regulatory.htm.

84. Administrative Appeal Decision for Permit Denial for the Head Property, Craig, Alaska, Army Corps of Engineers File 2-2001-0477 (July 14, 2003), *available at* http://www.pod.usace.army.mil/Regulatory/Regulatory.htm.

85. *Id.*

86. See Chapter 7 for a discussion of the requirements associated with the practicable alternatives analysis.

87. Administrative Appeal Decision for Permit Denial for the Head Property, Craig, Alaska, Army Corps of Engineers File 2-2001-0477 (July 14, 2003), *available at* http://www.pod.usace.army.mil/Regulatory/Regulatory.htm.

88. The applicant argued that he had provided sufficient evidence that his proposal was the least damaging practicable alternative, *id.* at 2, that he was being subjected to a different evaluation standard than three nearby projects, *id.* at 6, that the district incorrectly determined that the project would adversely affect navigation, *id.* at 7, that the project was a water-dependent use, *id.* at 8–9, that conclusions with respect to the impact to eelgrass were incorrect, *id.* at 9, that the district's conclusion with respect to significant degradation of the aquatic environment was flawed, *id.* at 10, and that a variety of faulty conclusions in the district's decision document lead to an incorrect decision, *id.* at 11. Each of these reasons for appeal was found not to have merit.

89. *Id.* at 13. The RO went on to note, however, that "I identified flaws in the District's analysis of several other factors supporting its conclusion to deny this permit. If the Appellant should submit new information and/or project modifications regarding whether practicable alternatives to his proposed project are available, the District should review that material . . . as well as reconsider its conclusions in those areas where I identified flaws in the District's analysis." *Id.* at 13–14.

90. *Id.*

91. Final Appeal Decision concerning Permit Modification Denial, Swan Bay Holdings, Inc. File No. Z-1984-0184, Ship Creek 7 (Oct. 5, 2004), *available at* http://www.pod.usace.army.mil/Regulatory/Regulatory.htm (hereinafter Swan Bay Administrative Appeal). The RO identified seven discrete "reasons for appeal" and then added many unnumbered sections containing "no less than 152 separate additional" reasons for appeal. *Id.* at 12. The RO identified these additional reasons for appeal as seemingly related, though not directly, to the original seven. *Id.* The appeal decision limited its analysis to the seven major reasons. *Id.* at 25.

92. *Id.* at 2.

93. *Id.* at 4.

94. *Id.* at 25.

95. Cover letter, *available at* http://www.pod.usace.army.mil/Regulatory/Regulatory.htm.

96. *Id.*

97. Swan Bay Administrative Appeal at 12.

98. *Id.*

99. Administrative Appeal Decision, Barry Allen, File Number 200206120 (Jf-Eps), Jacksonville District, (May 21, 2004), *available at* http://www.sad.usace.army.mil/regulatory/appeals/appeals%202003.xls.

100. *Id.* at 1.

101. 531 U.S. 159 (2001). For a discussion of issues related to determining whether a wetland is "jurisdictional," or regulated by Section 404 of the Clean Water Act, see Chapter 3 of this book.

102. *Id.* at 2.

103. *Id.*

104. Administrative Appeal Decision, File No. 200106610, Savannah District (Sept. 15, 2004), *at* http://www.sad.usace.army.mil/regulatory/appeals/appeals%202003.xls.

105. *Id.* at 1.

106. *Id.*

107. *Id.*

108. 33 C.F.R. § 331.7(g).

109. *See supra* notes 75–82 and accompanying text for direct links to administrative appeal decisions for all eight Corps divisions.

110. *See supra* note 66.

CHAPTER 12

Enforcement and Judicial Review

JAMES G. O'CONNOR AND DOUGLAS R. WILLIAMS

I. Introduction/Scope

The judicial system has played a major role in the development of federal wetlands policy. Courts become involved with wetlands regulation when agencies or citizens sue to enforce the Clean Water Act Section 404 program requirements or when permit applicants or other stakeholders seek judicial review of agency decisions. Section II of this chapter discusses issues related to enforcement and Section III discusses issues related to judicial review. Because many of the concepts related to enforcement and judicial review overlap, there are frequent cross-references between the sections.

II. Enforcement

The Clean Water Act (CWA) provides the government an extensive array of measures to enforce the requirements of the Section 404 program. Citizens are also authorized to enforce these requirements, but citizens do not enjoy the broad range of remedies available to the government. The government may seek criminal, civil, and administrative remedies for violations. Citizens may seek civil remedies. This section of the chapter describes the framework for enforcement of the Section 404 program requirements. Enforcement of State wetlands programs is beyond the scope of this book.

Under the CWA, government enforcement of wetlands regulations is a shared responsibility of the U.S. Environmental Protection Agency (EPA), the United States Army Corps of Engineers (Corps), and the Department of Justice. EPA has civil and administrative enforcement power pursuant to Section 309 of the CWA.[1] The Corps's enforcement authority is provided in Section 309 and Section 404.[2] The Department of Justice, including its U.S. attorneys, represents the government in civil proceedings and is responsible for prosecuting persons who engage in activities made criminal by Section 309(c).[3]

The government has several enforcement options. EPA and the Corps may issue administrative orders and cease and desist letters, respectively, requiring compliance with Section 404 program requirements.[4] Both may assess administrative penalties.[5] The government is authorized to commence civil actions for injunctive relief, including restoration of damaged wetlands, and/or civil penalties.[6] The CWA authorizes the Corps[7] and EPA[8] to commence civil actions to enforce the requirements of the Section 404 program in certain circumstances, but such actions are in practice referred by these agencies to the Department of Justice and its U.S. attorneys across the country.[9] Additionally, EPA and the Corps may refer particular violations to the Department of Justice for possible criminal prosecution.

This section of the chapter will discuss basis of liability; administrative enforcement (including orders, penalties and procedures, public participation, judicial review, and after-the-fact permits); civil enforcement (including jurisdictional issues and available remedies); criminal enforcement (including knowledge requirements, factors that might trigger criminal liability, corporate/officer liability, and sentencing guidelines); and citizen enforcement (including standing, who can be sued and when, notice requirements, and suits against the agencies).

A. Basis of Liability

1. *Overview of the Elements of a Violation*

Violations of the wetland protection measures of the Section 404 program generally fall into two categories: (1) discharges of dredged or fill material into wetlands without a Section 404 permit,[10] and (2) actions that are inconsistent with the terms and conditions of a permit issued pursuant to Section 404. Failure to comply with an EPA or Corps order may also constitute a violation subject to substantial civil penalties.[11]

CWA Section 404 requires permits "for the discharge of dredged or fill material into the navigable waters at specified disposal sites."[12] CWA Section 301 makes unpermitted discharges into jurisdictional wetlands unlawful.[13] The elements of a prima facie case for violations of Section 404 and related sections of the CWA include (1) the defendant is a "person" (as defined by the CWA) who (2) discharged a pollutant (3) from a point source (4) into "waters of the United States" (5) without a permit, or not in accordance with the terms and conditions of a permit.[14]

These elements are sufficient to support administrative and civil liability. Because the CWA adopts a standard of strict liability, a violator's good faith or state of mind does not provide a defense to civil enforcement actions.[15] Good faith on the part of the violator may, however, affect the amount of any penalty that may be imposed.[16] In civil enforcement actions, the government has the burden of proving each element by a preponderance of the evidence.[17]

There are various exemptions to the general prohibition against discharging dredged or fill material into wetlands without a Section 404 permit. These exemptions are discussed in detail in Chapter 4 of this book. If an alleged violator seeks to defend his or her conduct as falling into one or more of these exemptions, the violator has the burden of demonstrating the exemption's applicability, assuming the government has otherwise presented a prima facie case of liability.[18]

2. *Persons Subject to Liability*

The definition of persons subject to liability for wetland violations is broad. The CWA's general definition of a "person" is "an individual, corporation, partnership, association, State, municipality, commission, or political subdivision, or any interstate body."[19] For purposes of criminal liability, the term "person" also includes any "responsible corporate officer."[20]

The scope of persons who may be held liable is not limited to those with specific intent to violate the act or even direct knowledge of a violation. For instance, in *U.S. v. Board of Trustees of Florida Keys Community College*,[21] a Florida district court found that a contractor who performed work without a federal permit was liable even though his agreement with the owner specifically required the owner to obtain the necessary state and federal permits. The court noted that the contractor easily could have confirmed whether the permit had been obtained.[22]

By contrast, in *United States v. Sargent County Water Resource Dist.*,[23] the North Dakota District Court concluded that a consultant's involvement in an unauthorized dredging operation was "too attenuated for liability to attach."[24] The consultant's involvement was limited to providing drawings of the work area and placing stakes on the site. The consultant was not retained for the purpose of obtaining necessary permits, did not prepare specifications, was not involved in the bidding process, and did not supervise any work performed at the site.

Moreover, the consultant did not provide instructions about where material was to be placed.[25]

B. Administrative Enforcement

1. *Responsibilities of the Corps and EPA and Decisions to Enforce*

Either EPA or the Corps will initially investigate suspected violations of Section 404 and related sections. The majority of investigations are conducted by the Corps, which has greater field resources than EPA.[26] If the investigation uncovers violations that require immediate intervention, a notification letter or a cease and desist order is issued to the alleged violator.[27] Following discovery of a violation and any necessary initial response, the agencies determine which one will deal with the violation and thus serve as the "lead agency."

A 1989 Memorandum of Agreement (MOA) between EPA and the Corps divided enforcement responsibilities between both agencies.[28] The Corps is generally the lead agency for permit violations, while EPA is often the lead agency for violations involving discharges without a Section 404 permit. In particular cases, EPA can also request to be lead agency, or the Corps may recommend that EPA pursue an administrative penalty.[29] This is likely in cases that involve either damage to valuable wetlands, such as those providing habitat for a threatened species, or a violator of special interest, such as a person previously convicted of environmental crimes or one who engages in flagrant violations.[30] The 1989 MOA's allocation of enforcement authority does not create any enforceable rights; courts will not block an enforcement action simply because it departs from the norms of the MOA.[31]

The Corps and EPA consider a number of factors in determining whether to bring an enforcement action. Among these are the severity of the harm, the nature and value of the affected wetlands, any history of prior violations, and regulatory contact regarding the affected site.[32] When enforcement action is deemed appropriate, the first enforcement step by the Corps or EPA is likely to be the issuance of an administrative order.[33]

2. *Administrative Orders*

Under Section 309(a) of the CWA, EPA is empowered to issue administrative orders in response to violations of the Section 404 program requirements.[34] The Corps has similar authority pursuant to Section 404(s)(1).[35] Administrative orders are one of the most frequently used enforcement mechanisms.

EPA administrative orders will typically include a statement of statutory authority, a summary of the agency's findings, and the specific actions that must be undertaken by the alleged violator to bring the violator into compliance with regulatory requirements.[36] By statute, these orders must "state with reasonable specificity the nature of the violation, and shall specify a time for compliance not to exceed thirty days," though EPA may specify a longer period for compliance in some circumstances.[37] For violations of Section 404 program requirements, administrative orders will generally require that all continuing violations cease and damaged wetlands be restored.[38] Restoration projects may require continued monitoring and maintenance and, thus, can be very costly.

The Corps's administrative enforcement follows somewhat more detailed procedures, which are outlined in 33 C.F.R. Part 326.[39] These procedures focus primarily on responses to violations of permit conditions or other matters pertaining to the permitting process. Under the Corps's regulations, district engineers are authorized to conduct surveillance and investigations of suspected wetland violations.[40] Upon discovery of a violation, the district engineers will notify affected parties. The form of notice may vary, depending on the nature of the violation. If the violation is a continuing one, a cease and desist order will issue. If the violation involves completed work, the Corps will generally not issue a cease and desist order, but will instead issue a notice of the violation and, if deemed appropriate by the district engineer, a demand for remedial action. In limited circumstances involving emergencies, the district engineer may determine that it is appropriate to allow violations to continue, "subject to appropriate limitations and conditions as he may prescribe" pending resolution of the violation.[41] Regardless of which form of notification is used, the district engineer will identify the statutory basis for the notice, describe potential consequences for violations, and "direct the responsible parties to submit any additional information that the district engineer may need at that time to determine what course of action he should pursue in resolving the violation."[42] By statute, Corps orders must be personally served, must identify the violation with "reasonable specificity," and must "specify a time for compliance, not to exceed thirty days."[43]

The district engineer may, after consultation with EPA and other agencies with wetland expertise, determine that remedial measures are appropriate and order the suspected violator to undertake such measures. Orders requiring corrective measures are based on considerations of whether "serious jeopardy to life, property, or important public resources . . . may be reasonably anticipated to occur" pending resolution of the violation.[44] Destruction of wetlands is likely to be considered a case in which serious jeopardy to important public resources is present.[45] The Corps may also conduct follow-up inspections and issue compliance orders as needed.[46]

To facilitate quick responses to environmental problems, courts uniformly hold that EPA and Corps compliance orders are not subject to judicial review until civil proceedings to enforce such orders are commenced.[47] In extreme cases, where the agency "completely overextends its authority," courts may intervene in pre-enforcement activity.[48]

Administrative orders cannot be enforced by the agencies themselves through the exercise of contempt powers or other means; instead, the agencies must proceed in a civil action in federal court to enforce such orders. Nonetheless, ignoring or otherwise failing to comply with a compliance order is a risky course of action; unexcused failures to comply with administrative orders may result in civil penalties of up to $27,500 per day.[49] Additionally, these orders may later be used by the government to establish "knowing" violations for purposes of criminal liability or as a basis for severe civil penalties.

3. *Administrative Penalties*

a. Statutory Authority

In addition to issuing administrative compliance orders, EPA and the Corps may impose administrative penalties in response to wetland violations.[50] Section 309(g) of the CWA authorizes the assessment of two classes of penalties in administrative enforcement actions.[51] Class I penalties may be assessed after an informal hearing. Class II penalties require a formal hearing that meets the requirements of the Administrative Procedure Act (APA) governing on-the-record adjudications.[52] Class I penalties may not exceed $11,000 per violation or a total of $27,500 for all violations. Class II penalties may not exceed $11,000 per day, but the maximum penalty may reach $137,500.[53] Since the agencies can only impose penalties pursuant to Section 309(g), restoration and other compliance measures must be sought under a Section 309(a) order or an appropriate civil action.[54]

b. EPA Penalty Policy

In 2001, EPA issued a Revised CWA Section 404 Settlement Penalty Policy.[55] EPA identified a number of goals in the CWA Settlement Policy. Primarily, EPA's enforcement actions require alleged violators to promptly correct their violations and to remedy any harm caused by those violations.[56] As part of an enforcement action, EPA also seeks monetary penalties that recover the economic benefit of the violations plus an appropriate gravity amount that will deter future violations by the same violator and by other members of the regulated community.[57] EPA also uses penalties to level the playing field within the regulated community by ensuring that violators do not obtain an unfair economic advantage over competitors who have complied with the Act.[58] To that end, the Policy incorporates the following formula: Penalty = Economic Benefit + (Preliminary Gravity Amount +/– Gravity Adjustment Factors) – Litigation Considerations – Ability to Pay – Mitigation Credits for Supplemental Environmental Projects.[59] Under this policy, the benefit derived and severity of the violation are combined with the several adjustment factors raising or lowering the penalty amount. The Section 404 penalty policy encourages the use of a computer model to calculate the economic benefit gained from the violation in question.[60] The guidance includes detailed criteria for assessing the gravity of the violation, including environmental significance, compliance significance, and adjustments for recalcitrance or quick settlement. These factors, along with others, are to be assigned values and plotted in a settlement penalty calculation worksheet to arrive at a "bottom-line cash settlement penalty."[61]

In theory, EPA's penalty policy allows violators to reach a penalty settlement that reflects the economic benefit and/or environmental harm attributable to their noncompliance. The policy pursues a goal of relatively evenly applied penalties across the country. In fact, however, penalties vary widely with the facts of each case and are not as predictable as EPA might hope.

EPA's settlement and penalty policies also encourage violators to undertake supplemental environmental projects (SEPs), which the 2001 policy defines as "environmentally beneficial projects that a violator agrees to undertake as part of a settlement, but is not otherwise legally obligated to perform."[62] Examples of such projects include purchase and dedicated use of buffers around wetlands and deeding over conservation easements in wetlands. Mitigation to remedy violations is not considered a SEP.[63] A violator who agrees to undertake a supplemental environmental project can expect "[f]avorable penalty consideration . . . because the SEP provides environmental benefit above and beyond what is required to remedy the violation(s) at issue in the enforcement action."[64]

c. Administrative Procedure

i. Class I Penalty Procedure

The Corps's regulations governing Class I penalty proceedings[65] authorize district engineers to propose and prepare penalty orders upon finding that "a recipient of a Department of the Army permit . . . has violated any permit condition or limitation contained in that permit."[66]

Notice is provided to the alleged violator, to the public, and to the state agency for the state in which the violation occurred.[67] Upon request of the violator, a hearing will be conducted before a presiding officer, who is selected from the Corps's counsel staff or is an "other qualified person."[68] The right to a hearing will be deemed waived if the violator does not request a hearing in writing within thirty days of receiving notice of the proposed order.[69]

Hearings on proposed penalties are informal and by statute are not subject to the requirements governing on-the-record adjudications in Sections 554 and 556 of the APA.[70] Nonetheless, the Corps's regulations require that its Class I penalty proceedings observe certain formal procedural protections, including separation of adjudicative and prosecutorial functions,[71] prohibitions on ex parte communications,[72] and a decision based on evidence of record.[73]

The presiding officer will recommend a decision, which, with supporting reasons, is submitted to the district engineer.[74] The district engineer may, in turn, request additional information from parties, "giving all participants a fair opportunity to be heard on such additional matters."[75] The district engineer may withdraw, modify, or issue the recommended decision based on the evidence of record.[76] The district engineer's decision becomes effective thirty days following its issuance,[77] and constitutes final agency action for purposes of judicial review.[78] The Corps makes no provision for administrative appeals of district engineers' penalty orders.

EPA procedures governing Class I penalties are included in the agency's general consolidated rules of practice, which are codified at 40 C.F.R. Part 22. The Class I procedures are substantially similar to the procedures EPA employs in assessing Class II penalties, which are discussed in the next subsection. The primary difference between Class I and Class II procedures is that in Class I proceedings the presiding officer need not be an administrative law judge, as is required in Class II proceedings. Instead, the presiding officer at Class I hearings may be a regional judicial officer, who is an EPA lawyer.[79] Additionally, Class I proceedings are subject to greater limitations on discovery.[80] Interlocutory appeals in Class I proceedings are prohibited.[81]

ii. Class II Penalty Procedures

EPA regulations governing Class II penalty proceedings and hearings are found at 40 C.F.R. Part 22. The Corps has not promulgated Class II penalty procedures. EPA regulations generally incorporate and expand upon the procedural requirements governing on-the-record adjudications under the APA.[82] Hearings are conducted before administrative law judges[83] who are authorized to perform a variety of adjudicative matters, including rule on motions, order discovery, issue subpoenas, and generally "[d]o all . . . acts and take all measures necessary for the maintenance of order and for the efficient, fair and impartial adjudication of issues."[84] The presiding administrative law judge will issue an initial decision containing findings of fact and conclusions of law, along with a recommended penalty and a proposed final order.[85] If the recommended penalty differs from the penalty recommended in the complaint, the administrative law judge must set forth specific reasons for departing from the recommended penalty.[86] An administrative law judge may not impose on a defaulting party a penalty greater than that recommended in the complaint.[87]

Initial decisions may be appealed to EPA's Environmental Appeals Board.[88] Absent such an appeal, initial decisions are deemed to be final forty-five days after its service upon the parties.[89] Payment of assessed penalties is due within thirty days after receipt of a final order of the Environmental Appeals Board.[90]

iii. Public Participation

The Clean Water Act and EPA and Corps regulations mandate opportunities for public participation in administrative processes leading to the assessment of penalties. The CWA does not distinguish between Class I and Class II penalties with respect to such requirements.

The agency that proposes to assess a penalty must provide notice to the public, and interested parties must be given an opportunity to comment on the proposed order.[91] Moreover, if a hearing is conducted, interested parties who have submitted comments must be given notice of the hearing and "a reasonable opportunity to be heard and to present evidence."[92] If no hearing is conducted, commenting parties may file a petition with EPA or the Corps seeking to set aside the order and to provide a hearing on the penalty.[93] Section 309 directs EPA and the Corps to grant such a petition if the evidence presented by the petitioner in support of the petition is material and was not considered in the issuance of the order.[94] If such a petition is denied, the agency must "provide to the petitioner, and publish in the Federal Register, notice of and the reasons for such denial."[95]

d. Judicial Review

Any party against whom a Class II administrative penalty has been assessed, or any party who commented on a proposed penalty, may seek judicial review of a final order within thirty days in the United States Court of Appeals for the District of Columbia Circuit or in the court of appeals for the circuit in which that person resides or transacts business.[96] Review of Class I penalty orders lies in the United States District Court for the District of Columbia or the district in which the violation occurred and also must be filed within thirty days from the issuance of the civil penalty order.[97] The courts, when reviewing either Class I and Class II penalties, will not conduct de novo review of assessed penalties. Review is generally confined to the administrative record, and the court must uphold the assessed penalty if there is substantial evidence in the administrative record to support it and no abuse of discretion on the agency's part.[98]

Before seeking judicial review, parties are required to exhaust administrative remedies. EPA's rules provide:

> Where a respondent fails to appeal an initial decision to the Environmental Appeals Board pursuant to § 22.30 and that initial decision becomes a final order pursuant to paragraph (c) of this section, respondent waives its rights to judicial review. An initial decision that is appealed to the Environmental Appeals Board shall not be final or operative pending the Environmental Appeals Board's issuance of a final order.[99]

e. Civil Enforcement of Penalty Orders

Failure to pay an administrative penalty after an order has become final or after the appropriate court has entered a final judgment upholding the order may result in a civil action in federal district court by the government to enforce the order. In any such proceeding, "the validity, amount, and appropriateness of such penalty shall not be subject to review."[100] Thus, unlike judicial review of administrative compliance orders, the failure to seek pre-enforcement judicial review of an assessed penalty may severely limit an alleged violator's ability to challenge the agency's action.

4. *After-the-Fact Permits*

The Corps may issue an "after the fact" permit, which authorizes a previous fill as if it had been permitted at the outset, thereby releasing the landowner from further enforcement liability.[101] In order to receive an after-the-fact permit, the applicant must complete a permit application similar to the application for an initial wetland permit.[102] The regulations specify that the Corps is to process the after-the-fact permit application in accordance with the same procedures as are applicable to the processing of initial permits under 33 C.F.R. Parts 320–325.[103] The regulations list situations where the after-the-fact permit must be either denied or deferred. For example, "no permit application will be processed when restoration of the waters of the United States has been completed that eliminates current and future detrimental impacts to the satisfaction of the district engineer."[104] No application may be accepted where the district engineer determines that legal action is appropriate, or where litigation has already been initiated against the applicant by the federal, state, or local regulatory agencies.[105] Additionally, the district engineer "must determine that the work involved is not contrary to the public interest."[106] Furthermore, EPA has authority to veto after-the-fact permits.[107]

Critics charge that after-the-fact permits are issued too frequently by the Corps, providing an end run around permitting regulations.[108] Cases dealing with these permits confirm that the Corps has substantial discretion in determining whether to take this approach.[109]

C. Civil Enforcement

Sections 309(b) and (d) of the CWA provide for civil judicial actions to enforce the requirements of the Section 404 program. The Corps and EPA coordinate enforcement actions with the local U.S. attorney's office when the agencies believe judicial action is warranted. A district engineer will typically recommend civil or criminal actions for violations that are "willful, repeated, flagrant, or of substantial impact."[110] The government may seek temporary restraining orders and injunctions to prevent further damage, orders to require remediation of affected wetlands,[111] and civil penalties.[112] The maximum civil penalty is $27,500 per day for each violation.[113]

1. Jurisdiction, Venue, and Jury Trials

EPA or the Corps may bring a civil action in federal district court to enjoin or seek other relief for any violation for which a compliance order could be issued.[114] The defendant's location, residence, or place of business establishes the appropriate venue.[115] Defendants are entitled to a jury trial on liability issues, but not on penalties.[116] Accordingly, the case may be tried before a jury or may be split into jury and bench trial phases such as on liability and damages.[117]

2. Remedies

With the exception of a few statutory and regulatory guidelines, EPA has broad discretion with respect to how, when, where, and against whom to pursue enforcement actions. For example, EPA may seek administrative orders[118] and penalties,[119] both temporary and permanent injunctions,[120] and both criminal and civil penalties.[121] Further, EPA takes the position that under the CWA, there is no right to an immediate hearing on its administrative orders. Courts have upheld this position, notwithstanding that failure to comply with such an order is an independent basis for a civil penalty of up to $27,500 per day per violation.[122]

a. Injunctive Relief

The courts enjoy broad discretion in fashioning appropriate injunctive relief upon proof of violations of Section 404 program requirements.[123] While injunctions requiring defendants to cease unlawful activities are common, the courts have also ordered a variety of other injunctive remedies. For example, in *United States v. Van Leuzen*,[124] the court ordered the defendant to remove an illegal fill and septic system, restore the wetlands, and pay $350 per month for eight to twelve years to fund the restoration work. In addition, the court ordered the defendant to

> have erected at his own cost, a ten foot by twenty foot billboard, six feet off the ground, on the Site facing Highway 87, or utilize an existing billboard across the street from the Site, facing Highway 87, and post [a] message . . . to alert passersby that illegal fill, placed without a permit, is being removed from the Site by the filler, at his own expense, that the filler is also paying a fine, and that the filler is also committed to continue Site restoration when he has additional funding. The billboard shall remain clearly visible to passersby until the work Ordered in this Section of the Order is complete, and for 30 days thereafter.[125]

As *Van Leuzen* illustrates, an order requiring removal of illegal fill material and restoration of wetlands is a key feature of the injunctive relief typically sought by the government for violations of the Section 404 program requirements. In considering requests for such remedies, the courts will typically "conduct a hearing in which the merits, demerits, and alternatives to the restoration plan [proposed by the government] are fully developed."[126] The court then will fashion an appropriate restoration plan that (1) confers maximum environmental benefits, (2) is technically feasible and practicable, and (3) bears an equitable relationship to the violation for which it is intended as a remedy.[127]

b. Civil Penalties

In addition to injunctive relief, the government will generally seek imposition of civil penalties. The penalties that may be assessed pursuant to Section 309(d) can be quite substantial. The statute as amended by the Federal Civil Penalties Inflation Adjustment Act authorizes penalties up to $27,500 per day for each violation.[128] Under the "continuing violation" theory, the original act constituting the violation and each day that the initial violation remains uncorrected are regarded as separate violations for purposes of calculating appropriate penalties.[129] Thus, when dredged or fill material is illegally discharged, the courts may impose the maximum daily penalty for each day that the illegal fill material remains. A finding of a "continuing violation," as opposed to a discrete one-day violation, may subject a defendant to millions, rather than thousands, of dollars in penalties.[130]

While the "continuing violation" theory creates potentially onerous liability for defendants, courts are instructed to consider mitigating factors. Section 309 provides:

> In determining the amount of a civil penalty the court shall consider the seriousness of the violation or violations, the economic benefit (if any) resulting from the violation, any history of such violations, any good-faith efforts to comply with the applicable requirements, the economic impact of the penalty on the violator, and such other matters as justice may require.[131]

Courts may employ a two-step process in fashioning appropriate penalties. First, the court should determine the maximum penalty that could be assessed against the violator. Then, using the maximum penalty as a guideline, the court may reduce the fine in accordance with the factors listed in Section 309(d).[132]

D. Criminal Enforcement

Most wetland enforcement activities fall within the civil sphere, but criminal enforcement has become increasingly common.[133] Potential criminal penalties under the CWA are substantial.[134] For negligent violations, fines of up to $25,000 per day of violation and imprisonment for up to one year are possible.[135] For knowing violations, fines may range up to $50,000 per day of violation and imprisonment for three years.[136] For knowing endangerment violations, fines of up to $250,000 per day of violation and imprisonment for up to fifteen years are authorized.[137] In all cases, repeat offenders are subject to a doubling of maximum fines and prison terms.[138]

The same course of conduct may give rise to both negligent and knowing violations. For example, in *United States v. Ellen*,[139] a contractor who supervised the work and assumed responsibility for all environmental permits was convicted of knowing violations for his direct involvement in an illegal fill operation. The property owner pled guilty to a negligent violation for his indirect involvement in the illegal fill activity.[140]

1. *Knowledge Requirement*

Courts have struggled with the distinction between the mental element required for negligent versus knowing violations, although the courts of appeals have uniformly rejected the argument that to establish a "knowing" violation, the government must prove that the defendant knew that his conduct was illegal.[141] Although the law typically frowns on holding individuals criminally liable for negligent behavior, courts have noted that the Clean Water Act explicitly provides for negligent violations and rejected constitutional arguments against criminal liability without proof of specific intent.[142]

In *United States v. Wilson,*[143] the Fourth Circuit considered arguments regarding the level of deliberateness required and the practical meaning of a "knowing" violation. The court concluded that the government would meet its burden by proving the defendant's knowledge of the essential facts required for each element of the substantive offense and did not need to prove that defendant knew that his conduct was illegal. Thus, the defendant "knowingly violates" the CWA if the government proves

> (1) that the defendant knew that he was discharging a substance, eliminating a prosecution for accidental discharges; (2) that the defendant correctly identified the substance he was discharging, not mistaking it for a different, unprohibited substance; (3) that the defendant knew the method or instrumentality used to discharge the pollutants; (4) that the defendant knew the physical characteristics of the property into which the pollutant was discharged that identify it as a wetland, such as the presence of water and water-loving vegetation; (5) that the defendant was aware of the facts establishing the required link between the wetland and waters of the United States; . . . and (6) that the defendant knew he did not have a permit. This last requirement does not require the government to show that the defendant knew that permits were available or required. Rather, it, like the other requirements, preserves the availability of a mistake of fact offense if the defendant has something he mistakenly believed to be a permit to make the discharges for which he is being prosecuted.[144]

Because the district court's jury instructions "did not adequately impose on the government the burden of proving knowledge with regard to each statutory element," the Fourth Circuit concluded that a new trial was necessary.[145]

Similarly, in *United States v. Ahmad,* the court of appeals reversed a conviction for "knowingly violating" the CWA because the district court's jury instructions did not clearly inform the jury that the government was required to prove that the defendant knew that the material he discharged was a "pollutant."[146] Absent such proof, the court noted, "one who honestly and reasonably believes he is discharging water may find himself guilty of a felony if the substance turns out to be something else."[147]

2. *Knowing Endangerment*

Knowing endangerment cases involve conduct that knowingly causes acute health hazards, "plac[ing] another person in imminent danger of death or serious bodily injury."[148] The statute imposes severe criminal sanctions for such conduct, including imprisonment for as much as fifteen years.[149] Such conduct, while unusual, could occur with a discharge of hazardous materials to wetlands.[150] Although there has not been a reported prosecution for knowing endangerment involving a discharge to wetlands, in *United States. v. Plaza Health Laboratories, Inc.,*[151] a lab director was convicted of two counts of knowing endangerment for placing used blood sample vials in openings in a seawall near his home.[152] The district court set aside these convictions on the basis of improper jury instructions. The court concluded that

> "imminent danger" must connote something more than the mere possibility or risk that death or serious bodily injury is a foreseeable consequence of a discharge. Thus, at the very least, "imminent danger" must mean danger that is a highly probable consequence of a discharge. . . . It is this particular level of danger that the defendant must have known existed when he discharged the blood vials into the Hudson River.[153]

Other convictions obtained by the government against the director were reversed on grounds that the discharges did not involve "point sources" and, accordingly, were not subject to criminal prosecution under the Clean Water Act.[154] Nonetheless, the case illustrates that in matters involving highly toxic materials, the government may seek severe criminal sanctions. If toxic waste or some other material presenting an imminent danger was placed into a coastal wetland where it could easily move to a public beach, a prosecution for illegally filling the wetland could include a knowing endangerment count for the added risk to people on neighboring properties.

3. *Factors That May Trigger Criminal Actions*

While one needs to know the maximum penalties, the more pressing question is when will the government seek criminal sanctions. Some indication of who will be prosecuted can be gleaned from guidance documents issued by the relevant agencies. The Justice Department's widely discussed memorandum on internal audits and voluntary disclosure is one such source.[155] This memorandum suggests that a party who comes forward after discovering a violation through an audit or other self-review is less likely to be charged than one who waits for the government to ferret out the violation. Additional favorable consideration is given to violators who have established compliance programs and seek to improve compliance after discovering the violation.[156]

The referral criteria identified in a June 14, 1990, Corps memorandum on criminal actions include the following: ongoing unauthorized activity; violators who knew they were in violation through written or oral notice from enforcement agencies or prior enforcement actions; danger to valuable aquatic resources; the threat of wider environmental impact; and the potential for significant economic benefit from a continuing violation.[157] The government favors prosecuting cases likely to receive public attention and thus have the maximum deterrent effect. The operator of a bulldozer who fills wetlands or the construction supervisor on site may avoid prosecution, but the owner who knowingly proceeds with improper work may well be the subject of a criminal investigation.

4. *Corporate and Officer Liability*

Another important consideration is that the Justice Department and EPA will seek to indict a person as far up the corporate ladder as possible when charging environmental crimes. As noted above, CWA Section 309(c)(6) defines "person" to mean "any responsible corporate officer."[158] Under the responsible corporate officer doctrine, an officer may be convicted even though he or she was not directly involved in or had direct knowledge of the violation. Managers have been held culpable based on the position they occupy in the organization, their access to information on the violation, and their ability to control the harmful activity.[159]

In *United States v. MacDonald & Watson Waste Oil Co.*, however, the court rejected responsible officer liability, requiring proof of actual knowledge in a prosecution involving alleged violations under the Resource Conservation and Recovery Act of 1976.[160] More recently, a federal district court in West Virginia held that liability under the CWA is based on either the performance of unauthorized work, or responsibility for or control over the performance of unauthorized work.[161] By contrast, in *United States v. Lambert,* the defendant was held liable for an independent contractor's work because the defendant owned the property on which the work was performed, paid for the raw materials and necessary equipment, and paid the contractor a substantial sum to perform the work. The court suggested that, regardless of the extent of the defendant's knowledge, he could be held liable based on his position.[162] The decision in *U.S. v. Wilson,* discussed above, while not directly addressing the responsible corporate officer issue, certainly supports the proposition that direct knowledge of the relevant facts must be proven.

In *U.S. v. Mango,* a case dealing with construction in 1991 and 1992 of the 370-mile Iroquois pipeline project from Ontario, Canada, to Long Island, New York, criminal charges were brought against a vice president and director of engineering and construction for a partnership and its agent as well as the president and principal owner of a company providing environmental inspections for the partnership.[163] Although the charges were dismissed in part and the case remanded for other reasons, the fact remains that high-level officers were potentially liable for serious criminal liabilities under CWA Section 404.

Corporations are also subject to criminal prosecution for wetland violations. In *United States v. Marathon Dev. Corp.,* defendant Marathon was indicted for wetland violations arising from the preparation of a site for commercial development.[164] Marathon ultimately pled guilty and paid a fine. One Marathon officer was sentenced to a suspended prison term, probation, and a fine.

5. *Consequences of Ignoring Agency Warnings*

One famous criminal case involving wetlands is *United States v. Pozsgai.*[165] This case illustrates the slippery slope from warnings to civil enforcement to criminal charges to imposition of a prison term. Pozsgai was characterized in the press as everything from an innocent landowner filling in his backyard to the archenemy of wetlands everywhere. However one portrays his conduct, it is clear he was notified that the government considered his fill activity unlawful, and that he continued the operation nonetheless. Despite repeated warnings by the Corps and a civil action that included a temporary restraining order, Pozsgai continued the fill activity, which ultimately led to criminal charges.

Pozsgai was convicted of forty-one felony CWA violations and was sentenced to three years' imprisonment, followed by five years' probation with one year of supervised release and a fine of $200,000. This fine was reduced to $5,000 based on his ability to pay. Probation was imposed in part to ensure implementation of the restoration plan for the site. The court focused on the repeated warnings that Pozsgai received from government officials, in person and in writing, which he consistently ignored.[166] This is the type of case that will almost invariably result in criminal prosecution.[167]

The widely publicized case of James J. Wilson is another example of the severe penalties that can befall a developer who fills wetlands despite repeated warnings from the Corps. Wilson, the chairman of Interstate General Co., a real estate development company, was found guilty of illegally destroying seventy acres of federally protected wetlands in Maryland, in violation of Section 404 of the Clean Water Act.[168] On June 17, 1996, a federal district court sentenced Wilson to twenty-one months in prison and fined him $1 million.[169] In addition, the judge levied a record $3 million in fines against Interstate General and its subsidiary, St. Charles Associates, and ordered the defendants to restore approximately fifty acres of wetlands.[170]

The Fourth Circuit reversed Wilson's conviction on a variety of grounds, including the applicable definition of waters of the United States and the proof standard applicable to the mental element for the offenses. In ordering a new trial, the circuit court concluded that the trial court had failed to instruct the jurors properly on the requisite mental elements. The court focused on the history of the property development that led to the charges. The court appeared to be particularly impressed with the uncertainty within the Corps as to the classification of the wetlands at issue. The court focused on facts indicating that the developer may have acted in good faith in some of the fill and drain activities at issue. The key holding, however, was the court's explicit statement of the level of knowledge required for defendant to be held liable. It clearly turns away from the case law interpreting the Clean Water Act as equivalent to the strict liability of public health acts.[171]

6. *Impact of Federal Sentencing Guidelines*

The Comprehensive Crime Control Act of 1984 established the U.S. Sentencing Commission, which promulgated the Sentencing Guidelines for United States Courts.[172] Implementation of the sentencing guidelines has resulted in a sometimes mechanistic approach to punishment imposed in environmental cases, including the imposition of prison terms in wetland cases.[173] While the crimes involved are of a type that traditionally might not have led to imprisonment, the guidelines leave judges with little discretion but to impose jail terms.[174] In *United States v. Ellen*, discussed above, for example, defendant was sentenced to imprisonment, even though the conviction was his first and the crime did not involve violence. The imposition of imprisonment in such circumstances is generally inappropriate, unless the offense is considered a "serious" one under the guidelines. Unfortunately for Ellen, the guidelines classified the offense for which he was convicted as a serious one, mandating the imposition of jail time.[175] In early 2005, the U.S. Supreme Court ruled that federal judges are no longer bound by mandatory sentencing guidelines but need only consult them when they punish federal criminals.[176]

E. Citizen Enforcement

Section 505 of the CWA provides for citizen suits[177] as a means to supplement government enforcement of the CWA.[178] Citizen suits are of two general types: They may be brought by "any citizen," subject to the limitations discussed below, (1) against "any person . . . who is alleged to be in violation of . . . an effluent standard or limitation under [the CWA]";[179] and (2) against EPA or the Corps alleging that the agency has failed to perform a nondiscretionary act or duty.[180] In appropriate cases, the district courts are authorized "to enforce such an effluent standard or limitation . . . or to order [EPA] to perform such act or duty, as the case may be, and to apply any appropriate civil penalties under [Section 309(d) of the CWA]."[181] This section describes the basic requirements governing citizen suits.[182]

1. *Standing*

For purposes of the statute's citizen suits, the CWA defines the term "citizen" as "a person or persons having an interest which is or may be adversely affected."[183] The chief limitation on who may prosecute a citizen suit does not derive primarily from this restriction. Rather, Article III standing requirements provide significant limits on the class of persons who may commence such actions.

To establish Article III standing to sue,[184] persons[185] must show (1) that they have suffered "an injury in fact—a harm suffered by the plaintiff that is concrete and actual or imminent, not conjectural or hypothetical"; (2) "causation—a fairly traceable connection between the plaintiff's injury and the complained-of conduct of the defendant"; and (3) "redressability—a likelihood that the requested relief will redress the alleged injury."[186] Decisions by the Supreme Court in recent years show that these elements of standing may in certain cases limit third-party challenges to agency decisions.[187]

For those actions reviewed under the APA, parties must additionally show that they have "suffer[ed] legal wrong because of agency action, or [been] adversely affected or aggrieved within the meaning of a relevant statute."[188] The federal courts have interpreted this language to impose "prudential" standing requirements in addition to those associated with Article III.[189] In particular, the courts require persons to demonstrate that "the interest sought to be protected [is] . . . arguably within the zone of interests to be protected or regulated by the statute . . . in question."[190] This prudential standing requirement denies review to persons whose interests are "marginally related to or inconsistent with the purposes implicit in the statute" under which the challenged agency action was taken.[191] It does not apply to citizen suits initiated pursuant to Section 505, in which Congress overrode prudential standing limitations by authorizing suit by "any citizen."[192]

2. *Suits against "Any Person Alleged to Be in Violation"*

Once the statutory definition of a "citizen" and constitutional requirements governing standing have been satisfied, there are several additional requirements that must be met to maintain a citizen suit under Section 505(a)(1). These requirements are (1) that the defendant is "alleged to be in violation"[193] of (2) an "effluent standard or limitation"; (3) that the plaintiff has complied with the notice requirements of Section 505(b),[194] and (4) that neither EPA nor a State "has commenced and is diligently prosecuting a civil or criminal action in a court of the United States or a State to require compliance with the standard, limitation, or order."[195]

a. "Any Person"

Section 505(a)(1) permits a citizen suit "against any person (including (i) the United States, and (ii) any other governmental instrumentality or agency to the extent permitted by the eleventh amendment to the Constitution) . . . ." [196] While the scope of the term "person" is discussed earlier in this chapter, it is important to note in particular here that the CWA defines the term "person" to include a "State."[197] The Supreme Court's decision in *Seminole Tribe of Florida v. Florida*,[198] however, almost certainly bars a citizen suit against a state under Section 505(a)(1). In *Seminole Tribe*, the Court held that Congress's power under the Indian Commerce Clause did not include authority to override a state's immunity from suit under the Eleventh Amendment.[199] The same conclusion applies to Congress's power under the Commerce Clause, the constitutional grant of authority upon which Congress's enactment of the Clean Water Act rests.[200] Nevertheless, the Ninth Circuit held that citizens may bring suit seeking injunctive relief—though not civil penalties—against state officials under Section 505(a)(1), utilizing the *Ex Parte Young*[201] exception to a state's Eleventh Amendment's immunity.[202]

b. "Alleged to Be in Violation of an Effluent Standard or Limitation"

Section 505(a)(1) requires that the suit be maintained against a person "alleged to be in violation of an effluent standard or limitation." Section 505(f) defines an "effluent standard or limitation" to include "an unlawful act under [Section 301(a) of the CWA]."[203] Section 301(a), in turn, prohibits the discharge of any pollutant into waters of the United States except in conformity with a permit issued by an authorized agency pursuant to the CWA, which includes the unpermitted placement of dredged or fill material into wetlands.[204] The courts have uniformly held that such prohibited activities constitute a violation of an "effluent standard or limitation" that may be the subject of a citizen suit under Section 505(a)(1).[205]

In addition to authorizing particular discharges, Section 404 permits typically include conditions, such as mitigation measures. The definition of "effluent limitation" includes conditions included in permits issued under Section 402's National Pollutant Discharge Elimination System program, but does not similarly include conditions included in permits issued under Section 404. In *Northwest Envtl. Defense Ctr. v. U. S. Army Corps of Engineers,*[206] the court held that such conditions may not be enforced through citizen suits under Section 505(a)(1) because the conditions were not "effluent limitations."[207]

The courts disagree, however, on the circumstances that will satisfy Section 505(a)(1)'s requirement that the defendant be "alleged to be in violation" of such an effluent standard or limitation. After the Supreme Court's decision in *Gwaltney of Smithfield, Ltd. v. Chesapeake Bay Foundation,*[208] this requirement clearly is not satisfied when the suit involves "wholly past violations."[209] In *Gwaltney,* the Court concluded that Section 505(a)(1) only "confers jurisdiction over citizen suits when the citizen-plaintiffs make a good-faith allegation of continuous or intermittent violation" of an effluent standard or limitation.[210] As a result, citizen suits may be maintained only for violations that are continuing or reasonably likely to recur beyond the date the complaint is filed.[211] As with statute of limitations issues, however, the courts have parted company on the question of whether the continued and unauthorized presence in wetlands of previously discharged dredged or fill material constitutes an ongoing violation.

In *North Carolina Wildlife Federation v. Woodbury,* the court held that in the absence of appropriate remedial work, the presence in wetlands of illegally discharged material constitutes an ongoing violation for purposes of Section 505(a)(1).[212] The court concluded that illegal wetland fills "having persistent effects that are amenable to correction . . . constitute continuing violations, until remedied, under Gwaltney."[213] In contrast, the court in *Bettis v. Town of Ontario* did not address the continuing violation theory, concluding that past discharges of dredged or fill material into wetlands were not properly the subject of a citizen suit under Section 505(a)(1).[214]

c. Notice

Section 505(b)(1) provides that no citizen suit may be commenced unless sixty days' notice of the alleged violation has been given to EPA, to the state in which the alleged violation occurs, and to the alleged violator.[215] The notice requirements are jurisdictional in nature, and failure to comply with them is a basis for dismissal.[216]

EPA regulations governing notice for purposes of citizen suits are found at 40 C.F.R. §§ 135.1–.3. The regulations specify to whom notice must be given, the form of service required, and the content of such notice. If the alleged violator is an individual or corporation, service of notice must be made by certified mail or by personal service upon "the owner or managing agent of the building, plant, installation, vessel, facility or activity alleged to be in violation."[217] Copies of the notice must be mailed to the Administrator of EPA, the Regional Administrator of EPA for the region in which the alleged violation occurred, and the chief administrator of the relevant state water pollution control agency. If the alleged violator is a corporation, notice must also be mailed to the corporation's registered agent, if any, in the state where the violation allegedly occurred.[218] If the alleged violator is a state or local agency, service of notice must be made by registered mail or personal service upon the head of the agency. Copies must be mailed to the EPA Administrator and Regional Administrator, and to the state water pollution control agency administrator.[219] The notice must "include sufficient information to permit the recipient to identify the specific standard, limitation, or order alleged to have been violated, the activity alleged to constitute a violation, the person or persons responsible for the alleged violation, the location of the alleged violation, the date or dates of such violation, and the full name, address, and telephone number of the person giving notice."[220] The notice must also identify the legal counsel, if any, representing the person giving the notice.[221]

Compliance with EPA's regulations will almost certainly be regarded by the courts as adequate for purposes of maintaining a suit under Section 505(a)(1). The courts have come to different conclusions about what constitutes adequate notice when the regulations are not met. Courts have rejected citizen suits where the notice provided to the alleged violator failed to identify the time frame during which the violations occurred.[222] While courts may not require that the notice give specific dates of violations, some indication of the time frame of the violations must be provided. Similarly, a court excluded one of the citizen groups in an action because that group had failed to give the notice required under the statute.[223] Although an allied citizen group had provided adequate notice, the court declined to accept notice by one group as being adequate for all. The effect was to reduce the attorney's fees recovered by the common counsel for the two citizen groups. Other courts have allowed multiple citizen suit plaintiffs to rely upon the notice provided by one group as effective notice for all.[224]

d. Diligent Prosecution by EPA or a State

Section 505(b)(1)(B) bars a citizen suit "if [EPA] or State has commenced and is diligently prosecuting a civil or criminal action in a court of the United States, or a State to require compliance with the standard, limitation, or order."[225] It also provides that where such diligent prosecution is under way, "any citizen may intervene as a matter of right."[226]

The courts give wide deference to agencies in determining the best approach to enforcement. Thus, the burden on citizen suit plaintiffs in proving that the state or federal government has failed to diligently prosecute an action against a violator is a heavy one.[227] The courts will not require that an agency achieve the particular goal of the citizen suit plaintiff so long as the agency is clearly trying to enforce the statute.[228] While some courts will look for application of a state statute that is closely aligned with the federal counterpart, such as a requirement that a penalty provision apply,[229] judicial deference to state authorities' decisions on how to address a violation is the norm. For example, in *Williams Pipe Line Co. v. Bayer Corp.*,[230] the court found that the citizen suit was barred because of diligent prosecution by the state agency even though the nature of that state action was limited to imposing a permit and negotiating changes in the operation without imposing any penalties or having any other enforcement action pending. There are nonetheless limits to such deference. In *Friends of the Earth v. Laidlaw Environmental Services*,[231] the Supreme Court agreed with a federal district court's conclusion that a citizen suit was not barred due to "diligent prosecution" by an agency, where the agency's prosecution was essentially dictated by the violator. After receiving the citizen-plaintiff's notice of intent to sue for violations of the CWA, the defendant asked a state agency to file a lawsuit against it; the defendant's lawyer drafted the state's complaint and the defendant paid the filing fees; and on the last day before the expiration of the statutory notice period, the defendant and the state agency settled the matter with a small penalty and the defendant's agreement to make "every effort" to comply with permit obligations.[232]

Importantly, the issuance of a compliance order by EPA or the Corps does not preclude a citizen suit. Such compliance orders are not federal court proceedings, and thus do not constitute "a civil or criminal action in a court of the United States."[233]

e. Citizen Remedies

When a citizen brings a civil action against an alleged violator, the citizen basically takes the place of EPA or the Corps.[234] Section 505 of the CWA provides that any citizen can file a suit in federal district court, without regard to the amount in controversy, against anyone "who is alleged to be in violation" of any CWA effluent standard or limitation, or any federal or state order with respect to such standard or limitation.[235] However, as indicated above, Section 505 imposes certain limitations on the "citizen-plaintiff," including notice requirements and a bar against suits where the federal or state government has commenced and is diligently prosecuting a civil or criminal action.[236] Also, Section 505(c)(2) expressly allows the Administrator of EPA to intervene as a matter of right in any citizen suit action.[237]

Section 505 also limits the remedies that are available to citizens. Like the government, citizens may seek both injunctive relief and civil penalties. However, because there is no private right of action under the CWA, the citizen-plaintiff cannot recover damages.[238] As noted above, citizens cannot seek remedies, including civil penalties, for wholly past violations.[239]

In some cases, courts may be called upon to consider the terms of settlement in citizen suit litigation. Section 505(d) does grant the court the discretion to award litigation costs to a prevailing or substantially prevailing party when the court determines that such an award would be appropriate.[240]

3. *Suits to Enforce Nondiscretionary Duties*

a. Actions against EPA or the Corps

Section 505(a)(2) permits citizens to bring suit against "the Administrator" of EPA "where there is alleged a failure of the Administrator to perform any act or duty under [the CWA] which is not discretionary with the Administrator."[241] With respect to administration of the Section 404 program, this citizen suit provision may be employed against EPA, but its use to force the Corps to perform nondiscretionary duties is less well established.

In *National Wildlife Federation v. Hanson,* the Court of Appeals for the Fourth Circuit held that in certain circumstances the Corps may be sued under Section 505(a)(2).[242] The court reasoned that "Congress cannot have intended to allow citizens to challenge erroneous wetlands determinations when the [EPA] Administrator makes them but to prohibit such challenges when the Corps makes the determination and the [EPA] fails to exert its authority over the Corps's determination. Section [505(a)(2)] should be interpreted in conjunction with Rule 20 (joinder) to allow citizens to sue the Administrator and join the Corps when the Corps abdicates its responsibility to make reasoned wetlands determinations and the Administrator fails to exercise the duty of oversight imposed by [Section 404(c)]."[243] More recent cases have held that a suit against the Corps cannot properly be maintained under Section 505(a)(2). Applying the principle that waivers of sovereign immunity must be strictly construed, these courts have held that Section 505(a)(2) "does not clearly and ambiguously waive sovereign immunity in regard to the Army Corps of Engineers. . . . We must conclude that Congress did not intend to waive sovereign immunity in regard to suits against the Army Corps of Engineers under the Clean Water Act."[244] However, suits have been successfully brought against the Corps under the APA[245] and the general federal question statute[246] rather than the Clean Water Act.[247]

b. Nondiscretionary Duties

The types of duties that courts have found to be nondiscretionary and thus a proper basis for an action under 505(a)(2) vary.[248] Attempts to force the Corps or EPA to take enforcement action against a particular person are likely to be seen as discretionary duties and thus may not be subject to citizen suit. A determination by EPA whether to veto a Corps decision on a wetland permit is a discretionary function and therefore is not the proper subject of a citizen suit action.[249] Similarly, where EPA had no duty to oppose a state's plan to deal with non–point source runoff, any EPA action was necessarily discretionary and not subject to citizen suit enforcement.[250] A federal district court rejected the citizen suit argument that EPA's failure to review and/or reverse a Corps decision on an individual wetland permit was subject to citizen suit action. The court concluded that EPA does not have a nondiscretionary duty to perform such functions as to individual wetland permits.[251] This contradicted a holding in an earlier case that EPA was required to review such individual Corps determinations as a nondiscretionary duty based on EPA's ultimate responsibility for the protection of wetlands.[252] Thus, courts may disagree as to the scope of EPA's discretionary or nondiscretionary duties that are subject to citizen suit enforcement.

c. Notice Requirements

The Clean Water Act requires that persons intending to commence a citizen suit for violations of the Act must first provide sixty days' notice of the alleged violation to EPA, the state where the violation occurs, and the alleged violator.[253] Interpreting virtually identical language under the Resource Conservation and Recovery Act, the Supreme Court held that compliance with the sixty-day notice provision is a "mandatory, not optional, condition precedent" for a citizen suit.[254] Where a plaintiff fails to meet the sixty-day notice requirement, the district court is required to dismiss the action.[255] In addition to providing the sixty days' notice, the notice letter must provide adequate notice of the nature of the alleged violations. Where the notice fails to provide adequate information to advise the alleged violator of the nature of the violation, the citizen suit will not be allowed to proceed as to any violation for which there was not clear notice.[256]

4. Recovery of Litigation Costs

Section 505(d) provides that the court "may award costs of litigation (including reasonable attorney and expert witness fees) to any prevailing or substantially prevailing party, whenever the court determines such award is appropriate."[257] In order to be awarded litigation costs, the court must first determine that the party seeking costs is a prevailing party, i.e., that they have succeeded on some significant issue in the litigation.[258] Even where the bringing of the citizen suit is a factor in achieving the environmental goal at issue, unless the court is satisfied that the citizen suit directly achieved that goal, it may not award costs.[259] For many years, where a citizen suit plaintiff had not obtained a judgment on the merits, but had successfully forced action by the violator, and thus had acted as a "catalyst" in achieving outcomes sought by the litigation, most courts awarded litigation costs.[260] However, in 2001 the Supreme Court held that the "catalyst theory" was not a permissible basis for awarding attorney's fees, and that a "material alteration of the legal relationship of the parties" is required before attorney's fees may be awarded.[261] A subsequent Eighth Circuit decision construed the 2001 Supreme Court ruling narrowly in the Clean Water Act context.[262]

F. Conclusion on Enforcement

Enforcement of Section 404's protection of wetlands is complicated by the division of authority between EPA and the Corps. Responding effectively to an enforcement action requires a careful balancing of the client's interest in minimizing any civil or criminal penalties and proceeding with a project involving wetlands. Trying to achieve that balance, the advocate must also manage the interplay of the two enforcement agencies. The case law in the wetland enforcement area is predictably muddled. With fact-intensive issues at play, it is not surprising that there are few bright lines when assessing a potential wetland enforcement matter. One theme that does stand out from reported decisions is the likelihood that penalties increase with the severity of the impact to wetlands or the obstinacy of the alleged violator. The difficulty of precisely identifying wetlands and the unclear lines of authority between the agencies guarantee that litigation over wetland enforcement will continue to be active.

III. Judicial Review

Federal agency actions concerning wetlands are generally subject to judicial review, although requirements governing the timing and scope of review impose limitations on judicial scrutiny of agency action. In general, principles of federal administrative law govern review of these agency actions. Accordingly, questions concerning jurisdiction, timing, and scope of review are generally resolved by reference to the body of law established to govern judicial review of administrative action.

This section of the chapter describes the basic legal framework governing judicial review of decisions of EPA and the Corps in implementing the Clean Water Act's Section 404 program. The agency decisions considered here include rules, wetland determinations, permit decisions, EPA vetoes, and enforcement orders. Judicial consideration of claims alleging that EPA or the Corps action has effected a taking of property in violation of the Fifth Amendment to the Constitution of the United States is discussed in Chapter 13.

A. Basis for Federal Court Jurisdiction

1. Nonstatutory Review under the Administrative Procedure Act (APA)

With a few exceptions, discussed below, the Clean Water Act does not specifically provide for judicial review of EPA or Corps rules, jurisdictional determinations concerning particular activities or areas, determinations involving exemptions and general or nationwide permits, permit decisions, or cease and desist orders. Accordingly, judicial review of these actions will typically be governed by the APA,[263] which provides a limited waiver of the government's sovereign immunity.[264] This form of review is commonly referred to as "nonstatutory review" because it is not premised on the provisions of the CWA or any other substantive statute from which EPA and the Corps obtain authority to act. Because the APA provides a cause of action but does not itself provide a jurisdictional basis for judicial review,[265] jurisdiction in federal court over most Section 404 administrative actions is premised on general federal question jurisdiction pursuant to 28 U.S.C. § 1331 or other general jurisdictional statutes.[266]

2. *Statutory Review under the CWA*

a. Jurisdiction to Review Administrative Penalties

Section 309(g)(8) of the CWA authorizes federal courts to exercise jurisdiction to review EPA or Corps orders imposing administrative penalties.[267] The appropriate court in which such review may be sought depends on whether the penalty imposed is a Class I or Class II penalty. For Class I penalties, which may not exceed $11,000 per violation with a maximum penalty of $27,500,[268] jurisdiction is vested "in the United States District Court for the District of Columbia or in the district court in which the violation is alleged to have occurred."[269] Review of Class II penalties, which may not exceed $11,000 per day for each violation with a maximum penalty of $137,500,[270] is "in the United States Court of Appeals for the District of Columbia Circuit or for any other circuit in which [the person seeking review] resides or transacts business."[271] Review of administrative penalty orders may be had by the party against whom the penalty is assessed or other interested persons, although the category of interested third parties who may seek such review is limited to those "who commented on the [agency's] proposed assessment of such penalty in accordance with" the requirements set forth in 33 U.S.C. § 1319(g)(4).[272]

b. Review through Citizen Suits

Pursuant to Section 505(a)(1) of the CWA, "any citizen may commence a civil action on his own behalf . . . against any person[273] . . . who is alleged to be in violation of (A) an effluent standard or limitation . . . or (B) an order issued by the [EPA] . . . with respect to such a standard or limitation."[274] Section 505(a)(2) further authorizes suits "against the Administrator [of EPA] where there is alleged a failure of [EPA] to perform any act or duty under [the Clean Water Act] which is not discretionary."[275] Jurisdiction over citizen suits is in the federal district courts. Citizen suits are discussed in greater detail in the first section of this chapter.[276]

B. Barriers to Judicial Review

1. *Standing to Seek Review*

Persons challenging EPA and Corps actions, as well as citizen suits against private parties under Section 505(a)(1), must satisfy the standing requirements associated with the "case or controversy" limitation on federal jurisdiction imposed by Article III of the Constitution of the United States.[277] Ordinarily, these requirements will be met without difficulty by persons against whom the agency action is directed—e.g., persons who have applied for and been denied a Section 404 permit. Third parties—such as citizens or environmental advocacy groups challenging a Corps decision to issue a Section 404 permit—may have more difficulty demonstrating their standing to sue.[278] Issues related to standing are discussed in greater detail in Section II of this chapter.[279]

2. *Timing of Review*

The timing of judicial review of EPA or Corps action is affected by statutory filing requirements, statutes of limitations, judicially crafted doctrines of ripeness, exhaustion of administrative remedies, and bars on pre-enforcement review of agency action.

a. Statutory Filing Deadlines and Notice Requirements

i. Administrative Penalty Orders

In suits seeking review of administrative penalty orders issued by the Corps or EPA, the CWA requires that a notice of appeal be filed in the appropriate court within thirty days of the date on which the civil penalty order is issued. A copy of the notice of appeal must simultaneously be sent by certified mail to the agency that issued the penalty order.[280]

ii. Citizen Suits

Citizen suits pursuant to Section 505 of the CWA may not be commenced prior to sixty days after notice of an intent to sue has been given to EPA. If the suit is seeking to enforce an effluent standard or limitation or EPA order, sixty days' notice must additionally be given to the state in which the violation is alleged to have occurred and to the alleged violator.[281] EPA regulations specify the manner in which notice must be given and the content required of such notice.[282]

Cases challenging EPA or Corps action pursuant to the judicial review provisions of the APA are not subject to any specific filing deadlines apart from general statutes of limitations, although such actions may be subject to common law equitable defenses such as laches.[283]

iii. Statutes of Limitation

Neither the CWA nor the APA includes a statute of limitations governing review of EPA or Corps action pursuant to Section 404.[284] Several circuits have held that the six-year statute of limitations governing "every civil action commenced against the United States" and set forth in 28

U.S.C. § 2401(a) applies to actions under the APA,[285] including actions against the Corps relating to its implementation of Section 404.[286] Although not widely considered or followed, one court has held that citizen suits against EPA pursuant to Section 505(a)(2) are not subject to any statute of limitations.[287]

Suits seeking civil penalties against persons alleged to be in violation of the Clean Water Act are generally governed by the five-year statute of limitations set forth in 28 U.S.C. § 2462. Most courts have held that citizen suits seeking injunctive relief against private parties are not subject to any specific limitation period, but may be barred by the equitable doctrine of laches.[288]

b. Exhaustion of Administrative Remedies

Rules requiring the exhaustion of administrative remedies are fully applicable to review of Corps actions under Section 404. The general rule is that persons must "exhaust prescribed administrative remedies before seeking relief from the federal courts."[289] The rule "serves the twin purposes of protecting administrative agency authority and promoting judicial efficiency."[290]

Section 10(c) of the APA provides that "agency action otherwise final" will be deemed final for purposes of judicial review even where an administrative appeal is available, "unless the agency otherwise requires by rule and provides that the action meanwhile is inoperative," pending "appeal to superior agency authority."[291] In *Darby v. Cisneros*,[292] the Supreme Court, interpreting Section 10(c),[293] held that persons seeking review of final administrative action pursuant to the APA need exhaust available administrative remedies only if a relevant statute or administrative rule imposes such a requirement. The Court reasoned that because Section 10(c) "explicitly requires exhaustion [only] of all intra-agency appeals mandated either by statute or by agency rule[,] it would be inconsistent with the plain language of § 10(c) for the courts to require litigants to exhaust optional appeals as well."[294]

Administrative appeals of Corps actions are governed by 33 C.F.R. Part 331.[295] In general, the rules provide an opportunity for an administrative appeal of jurisdictional determinations, permit denials, or permits that are issued by the agency but are declined by the permit applicant.[296] Appeals may be taken only by an "affected party"—i.e., "a permit applicant, landowner, a lease, easement or option holder . . . who has received an approved [jurisdictional determination], permit denial, or who has declined a proffered individual permit."[297] Third parties may not seek administrative appeals, nor may they participate in such appeals.[298] Corps rules provide that "[n]o affected party may file a legal action in the Federal courts based on a permit denial or declined individual permit until after a final Corps decision has been made and the appellant has exhausted all applicable administrative remedies."[299] The rules also identify Corps actions deemed to be a "final Corps decision."[300] In explaining its rules, the Corps noted that "[i]n response to *Darby v. Cisneros*, the Corps is including [the exhaustion rule] to make it explicit that persons dissatisfied with permit decisions must avail themselves of the administrative appeal process established in this rule, and have received a final Corps decision on the merits of the appeal, prior to seeking redress in the Federal courts."[301] The Corps administrative appeal process is covered in depth in Chapter 11.

For Corps actions other than jurisdictional determinations, permit denials, or declined permits, immediate resort to judicial review is available, subject to otherwise applicable jurisdictional and timing issues. For these actions, the only possibility for higher administrative review may be EPA review pursuant to Section 404(c). The CWA, EPA rules, and Corps rules do not require that EPA review be sought prior to seeking judicial review of these Corps decisions.[302] Accordingly, under *Darby* and Section 10(c) of the APA, persons seeking judicial review of such decisions need not exhaust any further administrative remedies.

For those decisions that may be appealed administratively and for which subsequent judicial review is sought, exhaustion rules generally limit the issues that may be considered on judicial review to those that are raised in the administrative appeal.[303]

c. Finality, Ripeness, and Pre-Enforcement Review of Corps and EPA Exercises of Section 404 Jurisdiction

The Corps and EPA make a variety of decisions in implementing the Section 404 program that may have adverse effects on private parties, ranging from positive jurisdictional determinations to issuance of cease and desist orders to denials of permit applications. In general, judicial review of agency actions other than final decisions on permit applications will be withheld on a variety of timing grounds. For example, the APA provisions for judicial review are generally applicable only to "final agency action."[304] While Corps regulations provide that determinations by district engineers "concerning the applicability of the Clean Water Act . . . to activities or tracts of land and the applicability of general permits or statutory exemptions to proposed activities" are "Corps final agency action,"[305] the courts have held that these types of decisions are not "final" within the meaning of the APA for purposes of judicial review.

For example, in *Route 26 Land Dev. v. United States*,[306] the court noted that the Corps's assertion of jurisdiction over certain activities lacked finality because the dispute between the parties could be resolved in a number of different ways, each depending on what further actions the Corps might choose to take. Possible Corps actions include acting favorably on a permit application, resolving the matter through informal discussions, or initiating a civil enforcement action. Neither a jurisdictional determination nor a cease and desist order could be considered "final," because neither action by itself or in combination "carries [any] legal consequences for the Plaintiff and . . . does not determine the rights and obligations of the Plaintiff or the Corps."[307] The court rejected the notion that the costs of pursuing a permit, even if substantial, warranted a conclusion of finality.[308]

Other courts have concluded that decisions other than final permit decisions are not subject to immediate review, but have offered different reasons for this conclusion, including doctrines of primary jurisdiction and ripeness.[309] Moreover, in *Hoffman Group, Inc. v. EPA*,[310] the court, relying on CWA Section 309,[311] broadly held that Congress in the CWA impliedly precluded such review:

> In drafting the Clean Water Act, Congress chose to make assessed administrative penalties subject to review while at the same time it chose not to make a compliance order judicially reviewable unless the EPA decides to bring a civil suit to enforce it. . . . And, since the enforcement proceeding is the only forum for enjoining violations of the Act, Hoffman cannot be compelled to comply with the Compliance Order without an opportunity to challenge the Order's validity in court. Therefore Hoffman has been unable to persuade us that a potential defendant in an enforcement suit is entitled to a pre-enforcement suit judicial declaration that it has not violated the Act. Having provided a detailed mechanism for judicial consideration of a compliance order via an enforcement proceeding, Congress has impliedly precluded judicial review of a compliance order except in an enforcement proceeding.[312]

A few courts have permitted immediate judicial review of cease and desist orders and positive jurisdictional determinations,[313] but these cases appear not to command the respect of the courts that have more recently considered the issue.[314] The clear trend in the cases is that review of jurisdictional determinations and cease and desist orders may be had only after the Corps has denied an application for a permit or the government has commenced an action to enforce its orders.

Like the treatment of jurisdictional determinations and cease and desist orders, the courts have generally held that a Corps decision that a particular activity does not qualify for a nationwide or general permit, and thus must be reviewed in an individual permit proceeding, is not subject to immediate judicial review.[315] A contrary result was reached by the Tenth Circuit in *Riverside Irrigation Dist. v. Stipo*.[316] More recently, that court has distanced itself from the holding in that case, concluding that "it was written before the 1987 amendments to the CWA providing for judicial review of civil penalties; and . . . addressed the issue of finality, not reviewability."[317] The court therefore followed the Fourth[318] and Seventh Circuits,[319] holding that compliance orders issued by the Corps are not subject to immediate judicial review.[320]

There may be circumstances in which a party seeking review will have submitted to the Corps permitting procedures, been denied a permit, and then face an EPA or Corps cease and desist order. *Salt Pond Associates v. U.S. Army Corps of Engineers*[321] involved such circumstances. Plaintiff sought declaratory and injunctive relief, including an order enjoining any further enforcement actions on the government's part. The government successfully maintained that the court lacked jurisdiction to enjoin any future enforcement action. The court concluded, however, that review of the Corps's permit decision was appropriate: "Unlike the Plaintiff's express request for an injunction preventing the Government from bringing an enforcement action in the future for Plaintiff's alleged environmental violations, judicial review of issues relating to the completed permitting process does not constitute judicially proscribed, pre-enforcement review of agency enforcement matters."[322]

d. Review of Agency Failure to Assert Jurisdiction

In contrast to the cases considered above, in which the Corps has determined that an area and/or activity is within the Corps's Section 404 jurisdiction and made decisions short of a final permit decision, courts have permitted immediate judicial review of Corps decisions not to assert jurisdiction over particular areas and activities.[323] Likewise, courts have permitted immediate review of Corps decisions allowing activities to proceed under nationwide permits, eliminating the need for individual permit proceedings.[324] In such cases, problems of finality and ripeness are not present; no further administrative proceedings are available. At least one case suggests, however, that a suit to compel EPA or the Corps to exercise jurisdiction under the CWA may be dismissed if the plaintiff has made no attempt to exhaust administrative remedies, such as a petition to the relevant agency requesting action.[325]

An agency's decision not to enforce the terms of a permit at the request of third parties should be distinguished from an agency decision finding that jurisdiction is lacking. In the former cases, courts have held that the decision whether or not to take enforcement actions is "committed to agency discretion" within the meaning of APA Section 706(a)(2) and is, therefore, not subject to judicial review.[326]

EPA has occasionally resisted judicial review of its decision not to exercise jurisdiction. In *Friends of the Crystal River v. EPA*,[327] the agency resisted review of its decision to withdraw objections to a proposed permit, arguing broadly that the CWA "precludes judicial review of interlocutory determinations made prior to ultimate issuance of the permit."[328] The agency appears also to have asserted that judicial review pursuant to the APA is precluded because the agency decision is "committed to agency discretion by law" within the meaning of APA Section 701(a)(2). The case is somewhat complex, involving an about-face by EPA on review of a permit proposed to be issued by the Michigan Department of Natural Resources pursuant to the state's approved Section 404(h) program. EPA objected to the proposed permit, with the result that the Corps assumed jurisdiction over the permit application pursuant to Section 404(j). EPA then attempted to withdraw its objection and return the permit to the state agency for approval. In considering EPA's objections to judicial review, the Sixth Circuit in dicta stated that "an EPA decision to object does not constitute final agency action, while a decision not to object is within the sole discretion of the agency. Accordingly, neither action may be subjected to judicial review."[329] As pertinent to the case before it, however, the court concluded that EPA's attempt to transfer permitting authority back to the state constituted a "non-discretionary act" and that the agency's "withdrawal of its objections is a final decision that, if unreviewed, will terminate the federal government's role in this case."[330] The court, thus "faced with a final, non-discretionary agency act," concluded that "review is appropriate."[331] By contrast, in a somewhat related case, a federal district court concluded that EPA's refusal to initiate proceedings to withdraw Michigan's authority to operate its Section 404(h) permitting program was not subject to review.[332]

C. Scope of Review

1. *Review Limited to the Administrative Record*

In general, federal courts will not conduct evidentiary hearings in reviewing decisions of the Corps and EPA. The rule is that judicial review under the APA is limited to the record that was before the agency at the time the decision was rendered.[333] While there are exceptional circumstances in which a court might conduct an evidentiary hearing,[334] the vast majority of cases involving challenges to Corps or EPA decisions are resolved by reference to the administrative record alone.[335]

The same rule applies to review of EPA or Corps administrative penalty orders. Section 308(g)(8) provides that review is limited to determining whether the order is supported by "substantial evidence in the record, taken as a whole."[336]

2. *Standard of Review*

Review pursuant to the APA is generally deferential to agency decisions. Under APA Section 706, courts are empowered to set aside agency decisions only to the extent that the decisions are "arbitrary, capricious, an abuse of discretion, or otherwise not in accordance with law."[337] Following general principles of administrative law, the Fifth Circuit in *Avoyelles Sportsmen's League v. Marsh*[338] explained this standard of review in the following terms:

> This standard of review is highly deferential. A final agency decision is "entitled to a presumption of regularity." *Citizens to Preserve Overton Park, Inc. v. Volpe,* 401 U.S. 402, 415, 91 S. Ct. 814, 823, 28 L. Ed. 2d 136 (1971). While the court "must consider whether the decision was based on a consideration of the relevant factors and whether there has been a clear error of judgment," and while "this inquiry into the facts is to be searching and careful, the ultimate standard of review is a narrow one." *Id.* at 416. . . . In *Overton Park,* the Supreme Court stated unequivocally that the "court is not empowered to substitute its judgment for that of the agency." *Id.*[339]

The court further emphasized that the Corps's technical decisions, such as wetland delineations, are "normally accorded significant deference by the courts."[340] Other courts have agreed.[341] The arbitrary and capricious standard applies to cases involving Corps permit decisions,[342] EPA vetoes,[343] and rulemakings, including promulgation of nationwide permits.[344]

When agency decisions turn on whether the agency has properly interpreted its statutory authority, the courts have generally applied the standard of review set forth by the Supreme Court in *Chevron, U.S.A. v. Natural Resources Defense Council,*[345] in which the Court held:

> When a court reviews an agency's construction of the statute which it administers, it is confronted with two questions. First, always, is the question whether Congress has directly spoken to

> the precise question at issue. If the intent of Congress is clear, that is the end of the matter; for the court, as well as the agency, must give effect to the unambiguously expressed intent of Congress. . . . If, however, the court determines Congress has not directly addressed the precise question at issue, the court does not simply impose its own construction on the statute, . . . as would be necessary in the absence of an administrative interpretation. Rather, if the statute is silent or ambiguous with respect to the specific issue, the question for the court is whether the agency's answer is based on a permissible construction of the statute.[346]

While the *Chevron* standard can be applied quite deferentially, it has not blocked the court's efforts to turn aside agency interpretations of law that the court believes impermissibly stretch the reach of the Corps's jurisdiction.[347]

3. *Remedies*

The remedies available to parties challenging Corps or EPA decisions pursuant to the APA are limited. In general, the courts are authorized by the APA to "set aside" agency action found to be arbitrary and capricious or not in accordance with law.[348] In most circumstances, a court ruling in favor of a challenger will issue declaratory relief and reverse and remand the matter to the agency for reconsideration. On remand, the agency is free either to change its decision or stick to its original outcome while developing a new record to support it. Thus, federal agencies may get an opportunity for two (or more) bites at the apple. For example, in *James City County v. EPA*[349] the court upheld a challenge to an EPA veto of a water supply project, finding that EPA's conclusion that there were practicable alternatives to the proposal advanced by the permit applicant was arbitrary and capricious. Despite strenuous arguments against a remand, the court returned the matter to EPA for reconsideration.[350] On remand, EPA concluded that the adverse environmental impacts of the proposal alone justified a veto, and on further review, the court agreed.[351] For a discussion of the remedies available in citizen suits, see Section II of this chapter.

4. *Review in Enforcement Proceedings*

Judicial review of agency attempts to enforce orders or impose civil penalties is vastly different from judicial review in cases initiated by private parties seeking to overturn agency action. First, in actions by the government seeking civil penalties, the Supreme Court has held that the defendant is entitled to a jury trial on the issue of liability.[352] Jury trials are inconsistent with deferential review of an administrative record, and accordingly the jury's fact-finding is effectively de novo. Second, in enforcement actions, several courts have expressly rejected the government's contention that issues concerning Corps jurisdiction over particular areas or activities and violations should be resolved under APA standards of review. Instead, and because enforcement proceedings are not challenges to agency decision making, the courts have required the government to adduce evidence sufficient to support its claims by a preponderance of the evidence. For example, in *Stoeco Development, Ltd. v. Army Corps of Engineers,*[353] the court held that in cross-moving to enforce its orders, the Corps was required to prove the existence of a wetland by a preponderance of the evidence adduced before the court. The court reasoned that, unlike private party challenges to agency action, in enforcement actions the Corps itself "seeks to invoke the power of the court in order to impose penalties and injunctive relief, including the removal of intrusive construction."[354] The court concluded that applying the arbitrary and capricious standard in such actions "would turn the normal burden of proof at trial on its head."[355]

D. Conclusion on Judicial Review

Judicial review of most Corps decisions follows general principles of administrative law. Specifically, review is ordinarily governed by the terms and standards of review set forth in the APA. Likewise, administrative law doctrines of exhaustion of administrative remedies, finality, ripeness, and preclusion, along with constitutional standing requirements, can pose significant barriers to review of Corps decisions, particularly decisions other than final action on permit applications.

Notes

1. 33 U.S.C. § 1319 (2000). EPA also has authority under Section 504 of the CWA to seek equitable judicial remedies "upon receipt of evidence that a pollution source or combination of sources is presenting an imminent and substantial endangerment to the health of persons or to the welfare of persons where such endangerment is to the livelihood of such persons, such as inability to market shellfish." 33 U.S.C. § 1364(a). This authority has, however, rarely been invoked.
2. 33 U.S.C. § 1344(s).
3. 33 U.S.C. § 1319(c).
4. 33 U.S.C. § 1319(a) (EPA); 33 U.S.C. § 1344(s)(1) (Corps).
5. 33 U.S.C. § 1319(g).

6. 33 U.S.C. § 1319(b), (d) (EPA); 33 U.S.C. § 1344(s)(3)–(4) (Corps).
7. 33 U.S.C. § 1344(s)(1).
8. 33 U.S.C. § 1319(b).
9. Section 506 of the CWA provides:

> The Administrator [of EPA] shall request the Attorney General to appear and represent the United States in any civil or criminal action instituted under [the CWA] to which the Administrator is a party. Unless the Attorney General notifies the Administrator within a reasonable time, that he will appear in a civil action, attorneys who are officers or employees of the Environmental Protection Agency shall appear and represent the United States in such action.

33 U.S.C. § 1366.

10. Such discharges violate the prohibition of Section 301(a) of the CWA, which provides, in relevant part: "Except as in compliance with . . . [Section 404], the discharge of any pollutant by any person shall be unlawful." 33 U.S.C. § 1311(a).
11. 33 U.S.C. §§ 1319(d), 1344(s)(4).
12. 33 U.S.C. § 1344.
13. 33 U.S.C. § 1311.
14. *See, e.g.*, United States v. Brace, 41 F.3d 117, 120 (3d Cir. 1994); *see* Smith v. Hankinson, No. 98-0451-P-S, 1999 U.S. Dist. LEXIS 5151, at 21 (S.D. Ala. Mar. 31, 1999).
15. Kelly v. United States, 203 F.3d 519, 522 (7th Cir. 2000); Stoddard v. Western Carolina Regional Sewer Authority, 784 F.2d 1200, 1208 (4th Cir. 1986); Piney Run Preservation Ass'n v. County Comm'rs, 82 F. Supp. 2d 464, 471–72 (D. Md. 2000), *vacated and remanded on other grounds*, 268 F.3d 255 (4th Cir. 2001); PIRG v. U.S. Metals Refining Co., 681 F. Supp. 237, 240 (D.N.J. 1987).
16. The state of mind requirements associated with criminal liability are discussed in Section II.D of this chapter.
17. *See* Stoeco Dev., Ltd. v. Corps of Eng'rs, 792 F. Supp. 339 (D.N.J. 1992).
18. *See* United States v. Larkins, 657 F. Supp. 76, 85 & n.22 (W.D. Ky. 1987), *aff'd*, 852 F.2d 189 (6th Cir. 1988).
19. 33 U.S.C. § 1362(5). EPA regulations similarly define the term "person" broadly to include "an individual, association, partnership, corporation, municipality, State or Federal agency, or an agent or employee thereof." 40 C.F.R. § 232.2 (2004).
20. 33 U.S.C. § 1319(c)(6).
21. 531 F. Supp. 267 (S. Dist. Fla. 1981).
22. *Id.* at 273–74.
23. 876 F. Supp. 1081 (D. N.D. 1992).
24. *Id.* at 1089.
25. *Id.*
26. *See* Memorandum of Agreement between the Department of the Army and the Environmental Protection Agency concerning Federal Enforcement for

the Section 404 Program of the Clean Water Act 1 (January 19, 1989) [hereinafter 1989 MOA].

27. *Id.* at 3.

28. *Id.* at 3–4.

29. *Id.*

30. *Id.*

31. *Id.* at 5.

32. U.S. Army Corps of Engineers, Memorandum for All District and Division Engineers, Subject: Commitment to Enforcement of the Clean Water Act and Rivers and Harbors Act (June 14, 1990).

33. *Id.*

34. 33 U.S.C. § 1319(a) (1986).

35. 33 U.S.C. § 1344(s)(1).

36. Environmental Protection Agency, *Guidance and Procedures for Administrative Orders Issued under Section 309 of the Clean Water Act* (September 26, 1986).

37. 33 U.S.C. § 1319(a)(5)(A).

38. *Kelly v. United States*, 203 F.3d at 521.

39. A summary of 33 C.F.R. pt. 326 can be found on the Corps's Web site, *at* http://www.usace.army.mil/civilworks/cecwo/reg/press/enforcement.pdf.

40. 33 C.F.R. § 326.3–4.

41. 33 C.F.R. § 326.3(c).

42. 33 C.F.R. § 326.3(c)(3).

43. 33 U.S.C. § 1344(s)(2).

44. 33 C.F.R. § 326. 3(d).

45. *See* 33 C.F.R. § 320.4(b) (describing most wetlands as "productive" and "valuable").

46. 33 C.F.R. § 326.4.

47. Laguna Gatuna, Inc. v. Browner, 58 F.3d 564 (10th Cir. 1995); Southern Pines v. EPA, 912 F.2d 713, 715–16 (4th Cir. 1990); Hoffman Group Inc., v. EPA, 902 F.2d 567, 569 (7th Cir. 1990). *See* Southern Oil Coal v. Office of Surface Mining, 20 F.3d 1418, 1427 (6th Cir. 1994) (holding also that district courts lack jurisdiction to enjoin pre-enforcement EPA investigatory activities).

48. *See* Routh v. EPA, 13 F.3d 227 (7th Cir. 1993) (acknowledging the possibility for abuse, but rejecting claimant's argument that EPA lacks authority to regulate wetlands).

49. 33 U.S.C. § 1319(d). The figures in the original Act were amended by Federal Civil Penalties Inflation Adjustment Act, 28 U.S.C. § 2461 note, as amended by the Debt Collection Improvement Act, 31 U.S.C. § 3701 note. *See* Civil Monetary Penalty Inflation Adjustment Rule, 62 Fed. Reg. 35,038 (June 27, 1997).

50. *See* 33 C.F.R. § 326.6(a)(2).

51. 33 U.S.C. § 1319(g)(2). The figures in the original Act were amended by Federal Civil Penalties Inflation Adjustment Act, 28 U.S.C. § 2461 note, as amended by the Debt Collection Improvement Act, 31 U.S.C. § 3701 note. *See* Civil Monetary Penalty Inflation Adjustment Rule, 62 Fed. Reg. 35,038 (June 27, 1997).

52. *Id.*

53. *Id.*

54. 33 U.S.C. § 1319(g).

55. EPA, Clean Water Act Section 404 Settlement Penalty Policy, Dec. 21, 2001, *available at* http://www.epa.gov/Compliance/resources/policies/civil/cwa/404pen.pdf. EPA has a separate, more general penalty policy for the Clean Water Act that may inform some decisions related to wetland enforcement actions. EPA, *Interim Clean Water Act Settlement Penalty Policy* (Mar. 1, 1995) *available at* http://www.epa.gov/Compliance/resources/policies/civil/cwa/cwapol.pdf. Other related enforcement policies including the *Interim Guidance on Administrative and Civil Judicial Enforcement Following Recent Amendments to the Equal Access to Justice Act (SBREFA Policy)* (May 28, 1996); *Incentives for Self-Policing: Discovery, Disclosure, Correction and Prevention of Violations* (EPA Audit Policy) (Apr. 11, 2000); and the *EPA Supplemental Environmental Projects Policy* (SEP Policy) (May 1, 1998) can be found on the EPA Clean Water Act (CWA) Enforcement Policy and Guidance Web site *at* http://cfpub.epa.gov/compliance/resources/policies/civil/index.html.

56. *Id.* at 2.

57. *Id.*

58. *Id.* at 2–3.

59. *Id.* at 8.

60. *Id.* at 9. This model, known as the BEN model, and user's manual are available at http://www.epa.gov/Compliance/civil/econmodels/index.html, along with other enforcement modeling systems.

61. Clean Water Act Section 404 Settlement Penalty Policy, *supra* note 55, at 8. The worksheet can be found in the policy as Attachment 1.

62. *Id.* at 20.

63. *Id.*

64. *Id.*

65. 33 C.F.R. pt. 326.

66. 33 C.F.R. § 326.6(b)(1).

67. *Id.* § 326.6(b)(2)–(4).

68. *Id.* § 326.6(g), (h)(3).

69. *Id.* § 326.6(g)(2).

70. *See* 33 U.S.C. § 1319(g)(2)(A); 33 C.F.R. § 326.6(h)(1).

71. *See* 33 C.F.R. §§ 326.6(h)(4), (h)(5)(ii), (j)(3).

72. *Id.* § 326.6(h)(5).

73. *Id.* § 326.6(j)(1).

74. *Id.*

75. *Id.* § 326.6(j)(4).

76. *Id.* § 326.6(j)(5).

77. *Id.* § 326.69(k)(1).

78. *Id.* § 326.6(j)(5).

79. *See* 40 C.F.R. § 22.51.

80. 40 C.F.R. § 22.52.

81. 40 C.F.R. § 22.50(b).
82. *See* 5 U.S.C. §§ 554, 556–57.
83. *See* 40 C.F.R. § 22.21(a).
84. 40 C.F.R. § 22.04(c).
85. 40 C.F.R. § 22.27(a).
86. 40 C.F.R. § 22.27(b).
87. *Id.*
88. 40 C.F.R. § 22.27(c); *see* 40 C.F.R. §§ 22.29, 22.30. Decisions of the Environmental Appeals Board can be found at http://www.epa.gov/eab.
89. 40 C.F.R. § 22.27(d).
90. 40 C.F.R. § 22.31(c).
91. 33 U.S.C. § 1319(g)(4)(A); 33 C.F.R. § 326.6(c); 40 C.F.R. § 22.38(d).
92. 33 U.S.C. § 1319(g)(4)(B); 33 C.F.R. § 326.6(c)(2); 40 C.F.R. § 22.38(d).
93. 33 U.S.C. § 1319(g)(4)(C); 33 C.F.R. § 326.6(c)(3); 40 C.F.R. § 22.38(f).
94. 33 U.S.C. § 1319(g)(4)(B); *see* 33 C.F.R. § 326.6(c)(3); 40 C.F.R. § 22.38(f).
95. 33 U.S.C. § 1319(g)(4)(B); 33 C.F.R. § 326.6(c)(3); 40 C.F.R. § 22.38(f).
96. 33 U.S.C. § 1319(g)(8)(B).
97. 33 U.S.C. § 1319(g)(8)(A).
98. 33 U.S.C. § 1319(g)(8).
99. 40 C.F.R. § 22.27(d).
100. 33 U.S.C. § 1319(g)(9). In addition to the assessed penalty, the violator may be liable for attorney fees and costs for collection proceedings, as well as a nonpayment penalty. *See* 33 U.S.C. § 1319(g)(10).
101. 33 C.F.R. § 326.3(e).
102. William W. Sapp, *Improving Wetlands Enforcement Through Field Citation*, 1 ENVTL. LAW 747, 772 (1995).
103. 33 C.F.R. § 326.3(e)(1).
104. 33 C.F.R. § 326.3(e)(1)(i).
105. 33 C.F.R. § 326.3(e)(1)(ii), (iv).
106. 33 C.F.R. § 326.3(e)(2).
107. Russo Dev. Corp. v. Reilly, 20 ENVTL L. REP. 20,938, 20,939 (D.N.J. Mar. 16, 1990).
108. *See, e.g.*, Mark C. Rouvalis, *Restoration of Wetlands under Section 404 of the Clean Water Act: An Analytical Synthesis of Statutory and Case Law Principles*, 15 B.C. ENVTL. AFF. L. REV. 295 (1988).
109. For example, in Bayou Des Familles Dev. Corp. v. U.S. Corps of Engineers, 541 F. Supp. 1025 (E.D. La. 1982), the Corps denied the plaintiff's after-the-fact permit application. The court held that the Corps has broad discretion in evaluating such applications, and that the Corps's decision should not be overturned unless the decision was arbitrary or capricious, or an abuse of discretion. Since the court found that the Corps evaluated all relevant factors, and that the decision to deny the application was based on ecological grounds, there was no violation of the arbitrary or capricious standard. *Id.* at 1038.
110. 33 C.F.R. § 326.5(a).
111. 33 U.S.C. § 1319(b).

112. 33 U.S.C. § 1319(d).

113. *Id.* The figures in the original Act were amended by Federal Civil Penalties Inflation Adjustment Act, 28 U.S.C. § 2461 note, as amended by the Debt Collection Improvement Act, 31 U.S.C. § 3701 note. *See* Civil Monetary Penalty Inflation Adjustment Rule, 62 Fed. Reg. 35,038 (June 27, 1997).

114. 33 U.S.C. § 1319(b).

115. 33 U.S.C. § 1319(b).

116. Tull v. United States, 481 U.S. 412 (1987).

117. *See, e.g.,* United States v. Hobbs, 736 F. Supp. 1406, 1409–10 (E.D. Va. 1990).

118. 33 U.S.C. § 1319(a).

119. 33 U.S.C. § 1319(g).

120. 33 U.S.C. § 1319(b).

121. 33 U.S.C. § 1319(c), (d).

122. *See e.g.,* City of Baton Rouge v. U.S. EPA, 620 F.2d 478 (5th Cir. 1980).

123. *See generally* Weinberger v. Romero-Barcello, 456 U.S. 305 (1982).

124. United States v. Van Leuzen, 816 F. Supp. 1171 (S.D. Tex. 1993).

125. *Id.* at 1182.

126. United States v. Weisman, 489 F. Supp. 1331 (M.D. Fla. 1980).

127. *Id.; see* United States v. Sexton Cove Estates, Inc., 526 F.2d 1293, 1301 (5th Cir. 1976).

128. 33 U.S.C. § 1319(d). The figures in the original Act were amended by Federal Civil Penalties Inflation Adjustment Act, 28 U.S.C. § 2461 note, as amended by the Debt Collection Improvement Act, 31 U.S.C. § 3701 note. *See* Civil Monetary Penalty Inflation Adjustment Rule, 62 Fed. Reg. 35,038 (June 27, 1997).

129. Sasser v. Administrator, U.S. E.P.A., 990 F.2d 127, 129 (4th Cir. 1993); *see* United States v. Cumberland Farms, 647 F. Supp. 1166, 1183–84 (D. Mass. 1986), *aff'd*, 826 F.2d 1151 (1st Cir. 1987); United States v. Ciampitti, 669 F. Supp. 684, 700 (D.N.J. 1987).

130. Albert C. Lin, *Application of the Continuing Violations Doctrine to Environmental Law*, 23 Ecology L. Q. 723, 730 (1996).

131. 33 U.S.C. § 1319(d).

132. *See, e.g.,* Weber v. Trinity Meadows Raceway, Inc., 42 Envtl. Rep. Cas. (BNA) 2063 (N.D. Tex. June 20, 1996). *Trinity Raceway* concerned a racetrack that had been discharging pollutants into a river. Even though the raceway had committed twenty-three violations, the court imposed a significantly reduced penalty to reflect the fact that the discharges were mainly of natural materials, such as wood shavings, and posed no harm to human health.

133. *See generally* William L. Want, The Law of Wetlands Regulation, § 12:12.

134. For example, in 2004, the Eleventh Circuit Court of Appeals affirmed the conviction and sentencing of a Florida man to three years in jail, three years of supervised release, and payment of restitution and a $25,000 fine for illegally filling wetlands to make a ramp to transport his jet skis to nearby Lake Okeechobee. U.S. v. Perez, 366 F.3d 1178 (11th Cir. 2004).

135. 33 U.S.C. § 1319(c).

136. *Id.*

137. *Id.*

138. *Id.*

139. 961 F.2d 462 (4th Cir. 1992).

140. *Id.* at 464 n.1.

141. *See* United States v. Weitzenhoff, 35 F.3d 1275, 1283–86 (9th Cir. 1993) (discussing "knowing" requirement and concluding that government need not prove that defendants knew that their conduct was illegal); United States v. Ahmad, 101 F.3d 386, 390–91 (5th Cir. 1996) (same); United States v. Hopkins, 53 F.3d 533, 539 (2d Cir. 1995) (same); United States v. Sinskey, 119 F.3d 712, 715–16 (8th Cir. 1997) (same).

142. *See, e.g.*, U.S. v. Baytank (Houston), Inc., 934 F.2d 599 (5th Cir. 1991).

143. 133 F.3d 251 (4th Cir. 1997), *post-conviction relief denied,* United States v. Interstate Gen. Co., 152 F. Supp. 2d 843 (D. Md. 2001), *aff'd,* United States v. Interstate Gen. Co., L.P., 32 Envtl. L. Rep. 20,781 (2002).

144. *Id.* at 264; *see* United States v. Ellis, 48 Envtl. Rep. Cas. (BNA) 1168, 1178 (4th Cir. 1999).

145. *Wilson,* 133 F.3d at 265.

146. *Ahmad,* 101 F.3d at 391.

147. *Id.*

148. 33 U.S.C. § 1319(c)(3)(A).

149. *Id.*

150. In United States v. Borowski, 977 F.2d 27 (1st Cir. 1992), the government sought to convict corporate managers for a knowing endangerment violation based on unlawful practices that placed employees in imminent danger before hazardous pollutants were discharged into publicly owned sewers and treatment works. The court reversed a conviction, holding that "a knowing endangerment prosecution cannot be premised upon danger that occurs before the pollutant reaches a publicly-owned sewer or treatment works." *Id.* at 32.

151. United States v. Plaza Health Laboratories, Inc., 3 F.3d 643 (2d Cir. 1993).

152. The knowing endangerment counts were dismissed postverdict by the trial court because there was no showing of a high probability of imminent danger. United States v. Villegas, 784 F. Supp. 6, 13–14 (E.D.N.Y. 1991). The remaining knowing violation counts were reversed based on the Court of Appeals' conclusion that the statute did not envision a person disposing of waste in this manner as a point source. *Plaza Health,* 3 F.3d at 648–50.

153. *Villegas,* 784 F. Supp. at 20.

154. *Plaza Health,* 3 F.3d at 649.

155. *See* United States Dep't of Justice, *Factors in Decisions on Criminal Prosecutions for Environmental Violations in the Context of Significant Voluntary Compliance or Disclosure Efforts by the Violator* (1991), *available at* http://www.usdoj.gov/enrd/factors.htm.

156. EPA and the Corps postponed indefinitely a wetlands enforcement initiative planned for early 1991, apparently as a result of the controversy over

changes in the delineation manual, which is discussed in Chapter 3 of this book. The intent of the proposed initiative was to identify and to prosecute high-visibility, high-impact violators, using those cases to encourage compliance. *See, e.g.*, United States Army Corps of Engineers, Subject: Commitment to Enforcement of the Clean Water Act and Rivers and Harbors Act (June 14, 1990).

157. *Id.*

158. 33 U.S.C. § 1319(c)(6).

159. *See* United States v. Dotterweich, 320 U.S. 277, 284–85 (1943) (shipment of adulterated and misbranded drugs in interstate commerce in violation of Food, Drug, and Cosmetic Act); United States v. Park, 421 U.S. 658, 670–73 (1975) (same); United States v. Dee, 912 F.2d 741, 747 (4th Cir. 1990), *cert. denied,* 111 S. Ct. 1307 (1991) (criminal violations of the Resource Conservation and Recovery Act).

160. United States v. MacDonald & Watson Waste Oil Co., 933 F.2d 35, 55 (1st Cir. 1991).

161. United States v. Lambert, 915 F. Supp. 797, 802 (D.W. Va. 1996).

162. *Id.; see also* United States v. Brittain, 931 F.2d 1413 (10th Cir. 1991).

163. United States v. Mango, 199 F.3d 85 (2d Cir. 1999).

164. United States v. Marathon Dev. Corp., 867 F.2d 96 (1st Cir. 1989).

165. 757 F. Supp. 21 (E.D. Pa. 1991).

166. *Id.* at 21.

167. *See* United States v. Ellen, 961 F.2d 462 (4th Cir. 1992), *cert. denied,* 506 U.S. 875 (1992); *Marathon Dev. Corp.*, 867 F.2d 96.

168. Piper & Marbury, L.L.P., *Severe Penalties for Wetlands Violations Assessed,* 5 MD. ENVTL. L. LETTER 2 (1996).

169. Wetlands Convictions in Maryland Bring Fines and a Prison Term; Interstate General Co. to Appeal, 5951 WL 339386 (1996).

170. Wilson reportedly spent $5.7 million in legal fees, not including the fines. His company posted a $3 million loss in 1995. Maryann Haggerty, *Md Developer Struggles to Escape Legal and Debt Swamps,* THE WASH. POST, Apr. 22, 1997, at C1.

171. After the Fourth Circuit's reversal, the government entered into a plea agreement that imposed substantial fines on Interstate General, but dropped all charges against Wilson. *See* United States v. Interstate Gen. Co., 152 F. Supp. 2d 843, 845 (D. Md. 2001), *aff'd,* 2002 U.S. App. LEXIS 13232 (4th Cir. July 2, 2002).

172. 28 U.S.C. §§ 991–98; 52 Fed. Reg. 18,046 (1987).

173. *See e.g.,* United States v. Suarez, 1994 U.S. App. LEXIS 913 (9th Cir. 1994); United States v. Mills, No. 88-03100 (N.D. Fla. Apr. 21, 1989) and United States v. Pozsgai, 897 F.2d 524 (3d Cir.), *cert. denied,* 498 U.S. 812 (1990).

174. *See* United States v. Eidson, 108 F.3d 1336 (11th Cir. 1997).

175. *United States v. Ellen,* 961 F.2d at 467–68.

176. United States v. Booker and United States v. Fanfan, 543 U.S. 125 S. Ct. 738 (2005), 2005 U.S. LEXIS 628, *available at* http://www.ussc.gov/Blakely/04-104.pdf.

177. *See generally* James R. May, *Now More Than Ever: Trends in Environmental Citizen Suits at 30,* 10 WID. L. SYMP. J. 1 (2003).

178. 33 U.S.C. § 1365.

179. 33 U.S.C. § 1365(a)(1). *See* Northwest Envtl. Advocates v. Portland, 56 F.3d 979 (9th Cir. 1995) (listing types of permit conditions that citizens may enforce); Committee to Save Mokelumne River v. East Bay Mun. Util. Dist., 13 F.3d 305 (9th Cir. 1993), *cert. denied,* 115 S. Ct. 198 (1994) (citizen suit may compel an alleged violator to obtain a permit).

180. 33 U.S.C. § 1365(a)(2).

181. 33 U.S.C. § 1365(a).

182. *See generally* WILLIAM L. WANT, THE LAW OF WETLANDS REGULATION, § 8:11–24.

183. 33 U.S.C. § 1365(g).

184. The circuits have split on the question of whether Article III standing to sue must be demonstrated to intervene in an ongoing action. Cases holding that standing must be demonstrated include Rio Grande Pipeline Co. v. FERC, 178 F.3d 533, 538 (D.C. Cir. 1999); Mausolf v. Babbitt, 85 F.3d 1295, 1300 (8th Cir. 1996); Solid Waste Agency v. United States Army Corps of Eng'rs, 101 F.3d 503, 507 (7th Cir. 1996), *reversed in later proceeding on other grounds,* 531 U.S. 159 (2001). Cases reaching the opposite conclusion include Ruiz v. Estelle, 161 F.3d 814, 830 (5th Cir. 1998); Associated Builders & Contractors v. Perry, 16 F.3d 688, 690 (6th Cir. 1994) (same), Yniguez v. Arizona, 939 F.2d 727, 731 (9th Cir. 1991); Chiles v. Thornburgh, 865 F.2d 1197, 1213 (11th Cir. 1989); United States Postal Serv. v. Brennan, 579 F.2d 188, 190 (2d Cir. 1978).

185. "[An] association has standing to bring suit on behalf of its members when: (a) its members would otherwise have standing to sue in their own right; (b) the interests it seeks to protect are germane to the organization's purpose; and (c) neither the claim asserted nor the relief requested requires the participation of individual members in the lawsuit." International Union, UAW v. Brock, 477 U.S. 274, 282 (1986) (quoting Hunt v. Washington State Apple Advertising Comm'n, 432 U.S. 333, 343 (1977)).

186. Steel Co. v. Citizens for a Better Environment, 118 S. Ct. 1003, 1016–17 (1998) (citations and internal quotation marks omitted).

187. *See, e.g., id.;* Lujan v. Defenders of Wildlife, 504 U.S. 555 (1992); Lujan v. National Wildlife Federation, 497 U.S. 871 (1990). The Court took a more liberal approach to standing in Friends of the Earth v. Laidlaw Envtl. Servs., 528 U.S. 167 (2000).

188. 5 U.S.C. § 702.

189. *See* National Credit Union Administration v. First National Bank & Trust Co., 522 U.S. 479, 488 (1998).

190. *Id.* (citations and internal quotations omitted).

191. Clarke v. Securities Industry Association, 479 U.S. 388, 399 (1987).

192. *See* Bennett v. Spear, 117 S. Ct. 1154, 1162–63 (1997) (holding that suits brought pursuant to the citizen suit provision of the Endangered Species Act—which, similarly to Section 505's authorization of suits by "any citizen," authorizes review at the behest of "any person"—are not subject to the zone-of-interests test for standing).

193. For a discussion of the class of "persons" who may be subject to suit under Section 505(a)(1), see *infra*.

194. 33 U.S.C. § 1365(b).

195. 33 U.S.C. § 1365(b)(1)(B).

196. 33 U.S.C. § 1365(a)(1).

197. 33 U.S.C. § 1362(5).

198. 517 U.S. 44 (1996).

199. *Id.* at 21.

200. *See* Natural Resources Defense Council v. California Department of Transportation, 96 F.3d 420, 423–24 (9th Cir. 1996).

201. 209 U.S. 123, 28 S. Ct. 441 (1908).

202. *Natural Resources Defense Council*, 96 F.3d at 424.

203. 33 U.S.C. § 1365(f).

204. *See* 33 U.S.C. § 1311(a).

205. *See, e.g.*, National Wildlife Federation v. Hanson, 859 F.2d 313 (4th Cir. 1988); Environmental Defense Fund v. Tidwell, 837 F. Supp. 1344, 1349–50 (E.D.N.C. 1992); Save Our Community v. EPA, 741 F. Supp. 605 (N.D. Tex. 1990), *rev'd on other grounds*, 971 F.2d 1155 (1992); Avoyelles Sportsmen's League v. Alexander, 511 F. Supp. 278 (W.D. La. 1981), *aff'd in part and rev'd in part*, 715 F.2d 897 (5th Cir. 1983).

206. 118 F. Supp. 2d 1115 (D. Ore. 2000).

207. *Id.* at 1118–19.

208. 484 U.S. 49 (1987).

209. *Id.* at 64.

210. *Id.*

211. *Id.; see* Orange Environment, Inc. v. County of Orange, 811 F. Supp. 926 (S.D.N.Y. 1993) (violation no longer "continuing" if there is an agency-approved mitigation).

212. North Carolina Wildlife Federation v. Woodbury, 29 Envtl. Rep. Cas. (BNA) 1941, 1989 U.S. Dist. LEXIS 13915 (E.D. N.C. 1989).

213. *Id.; see* Sasser v. EPA, 990 F.2d 127, 129 (4th Cir. 1993) ("Each day the pollutant remains in the wetlands without a permit constitutes an additional day of violation."); Atlantic States Legal Found., Inc. v. Hamelin, 182 F. Supp. 2d 235, 248 n.20 (N.D. N.Y. 2001); Informed Citizens United, Inc. v. USX Corp., 36 F. Supp. 2d 375, 377–78 (S.D. Tex. 1999); United States v. Reaves, 923 F. Supp. 1530, 1534 (M.D. Fla. 1996). Although not expressly agreeing with this holding, the court in *Orange Environment, Inc. v. County of Orange* dismissed as moot a citizen suit against a defendant who had completed an EPA-ordered mitigation project. Orange Environment, Inc. v. County of Orange, 923 F. Supp. 529, 540 (S.D.N.Y. 1996). The court concluded that the completed mitigation put the defendant "in compliance with the CWA." *Id.* Presumably, until the work was completed, the defendant remained "in violation" of the CWA. In such cases, the defendant might properly be subject to a citizen suit if all other prerequisites are satisfied. Similarly, one court held that when the terms of a settlement are such that CWA violations are likely to continue, the "continuing violation" requirement will be

met for purposes of a citizen suit. Atlantic States Legal Foundation, Inc. v. Eastman Kodak Co., 933 F.2d 124, 128 (2d Cir. 1991).

214. Bettis v. Town of Ontario, 800 F. Supp. 1113, 1119 (W.D.N.Y. 1992).

215. 33 U.S.C. § 1365(b)(1).

216. *See* Hallstrom v. Tillamoock County, 493 U.S. 20, 25–32 (1989) (interpreting a parallel notice requirement in 42 U.S.C. § 6972(b)(1) under the Resource Conservation and Recovery Act); National Environmental Found. v. ABC Rail Corp., 926 F.2d 1096, 1097–98 (11th Cir. 1991); Proffitt v. Rohm & Haas, 850 F.2d 1007 (3d Cir. 1988).

217. 40 C.F.R. § 135.2(a)(1).

218. *Id.*

219. 40 C.F.R. § 135.2(a)(2).

220. 40 C.F.R. § 135.3(a).

221. 40 C.F.R. § 135.3(c).

222. Hudson River Keeper Fund Inc. v. Putnam Hospital Center, 891 F. Supp. 152 (S.D.N.Y. 1995).

223. New Mexico Citizens for Clean Air and Water v. Espanola Mercantile Co., 72 F.3d 830 (10th Cir. 1996). *Accord,* Washington Trout v. McCain Foods, Inc., 45 F.3d 1351 (9th Cir. 1995).

224. *See, e.g.,* Klickitat County v. Columbia River Gorge Commission, 770 F. Supp. 1419 (E.D. Wash. 1991); Environmental Defense Fund v. Tidwell, 837 F. Supp. 1344 (E.D.N.C. 1992).

225. 33 U.S.C. § 1365(b)(1)(B).

226. *Id.*

227. Arkansas v. The ICI Americas, Inc., 842 F. Supp. 1140 (E.D. of Arkansas 1993), *aff'd,* 29 F.3d 376 (8th Cir. 1994).

228. Supporters to Oppose Pollution, Inc. v. Heritage Group, 973 F.2d 1320 (7th Cir. 1992).

229. North & South Rivers Watershed Association v. Scituate, 949 F.2d 552 (1st Cir. 1991).

230. 964 F. Supp. 1300 (S.D. Iowa 1997).

231. 528 U.S. 167 (2000).

232. *Id.* at 176–77.

233. *Orange Environment,* 811 F. Supp. at 932.

234. Phillip M. Bender, Comment, *Slowing the Net Loss of Wetlands: Citizen Suit Enforcement of Clean Water Act 404 Permit Violations,* 27 Envtl. L. 245 (1997); *See generally* Lori A. Terry, *Clean Water Act Citizens Suits: Key Elements and Defenses,* 4 J. Envtl. L. & Pract. 1 (1996).

235. 33 U.S.C. § 1365(a)(1).

236. *See supra* notes 216–233 and accompanying text.

237. 33 U.S.C. § 1365(c)(2).

238. Walls v. Waste Resource Corp., 761 F.2d 311 (6th Cir. 1985), *rev'd and remanded on other grounds by* Dedham Water Co. v. Cumberland Farms Dairy, 889 F.2d 1146 (1st Cir. Mass. 1989).

239. *See supra* notes 208–211 and accompanying text.

240. 33 U.S.C. § 1365(d).

241. 33 U.S.C. § 1365(a)(2).

242. 859 F.2d 313, 316 (4th Cir. 1988).

243. *Id.; see* Environmental Defense Fund v. Tidwell, 837 F. Supp. 1344, 1354 (E.D.N.C. 1992) (Corps may be joined with EPA as a defendant in a Section 505(a)(2) suit where it "possesses but abdicates authority under" Section 404, even when EPA has assumed the authority to make the disputed determination).

244. Preserve Endangered Areas of Cobb's History, Inc. v. Corps of Engineers, 87 F.3d 1242, 1249–50 (11th Cir. 1996); *see* Cascade Conservation League v. M.A. Segale, Inc., 921 F. Supp. 692, 696–97 (W.D. Wash. 1996) (concluding that "the Court may not extend the [Section 505(a)(2)'s] waiver [of sovereign immunity] beyond the statute's express terms to include the Corps").

245. 5 U.S.C. §§ 551 *et seq.*

246. 28 U.S.C. § 1331.

247. Golden Gate Audubon Soc'y v. United States Army Corps of Engineers, 717 F. Supp. 1417 (N.D. Cal. 1988).

248. 33 U.S.C. § 1365(a)(2).

249. *Preserve Endangered Areas of Cobb's History,* 87 F.3d at 1249.

250. Cross Timbers Concerned Citizens v. Saginaw, 991 F. Supp. 563, 570 (N.D. Tex. 1997).

251. Cascade Conservation League v. M.A. Segale, Inc., 921 F. Supp. 692, 696–99 (W.D. Wash. 1996).

252. Environmental Defense Fund v. Tidwell, 837 F. Supp. 1344, 1354 (E.D.N.C. 1992).

253. 33 U.S.C. § 1365(b)(1)(a). *See also supra* notes. 215–224 and accompanying text.

254. Hallstrom v. Tillamook County, 493 U.S. 20, 26 (1989).

255. *Id.* at 33.

256. *See, e.g.,* Upper Chattahoochee Riverkeeper Fund v. Atlanta, 986 F. Supp. 1406, 1421 (N.D. Ga. 1997).

257. 33 U.S.C. § 1365(d).

258. Public Interest Research Group of New Jersey, Inc. v. Windall, 51 F.3d 1179, 1185 (3d Cir. 1995). *See also* Idaho Conservation League, Inc. v. Russell, 946 F.2d 717 (9th Cir. 1991).

259. Northwest Environmental Defense Center v. Army Corps of Engineers, 806 F. Supp. 891, 895–96 (D. Or. 1992).

260. *See, e.g.,* Dague v. City of Burlington, 732 F. Supp. 458, 471–72 (D. Vt. 1989). The Fourth Circuit has, in a series of cases, concluded that, to recover fees, plaintiffs must actually obtain some relief on the merits, rejecting the "catalyst" theory for awarding fees. *See* Friends of the Earth v. Laidlaw Environmental Services, 149 F.3d 303, 307 n.5 (4th Cir. 1998), *rev'd on other grounds,* 528 U.S. 167 (2000).

261. Buckhannon Bd. & Care Home, Inc. v. W. Va. Dept. of Health & Human Resources, 532 U.S. 598, 604 (2001).

262. *See, e.g.,* Sierra Club v. City of Little Rock, 351 F.3d 840 (8th Cir. 2003).

263. 5 U.S.C. §§ 551 *et seq.* For cases reaching this conclusion, *see, e.g.*, Friends of the Earth v. Hintz, 800 F.2d 822, 830–31 (9th Cir. 1986); Sierra Club v. United States Army Corps of Engineers, 772 F.2d 1043, 1050 (2d Cir. 1985).

264. *See* 5 U.S.C. § 702; Industrial Highway Corporation v. Danielson, 796 F. Supp. 121, 126 (D.N.J. 1992) (quoting Fairview Tp. v. EPA, 773 F.2d 517 n.19 (3d Cir. 1985) ("The APA 'provides a waiver of sovereign immunity by the United States from suits to review agency action.'").

265. *See* Friends of the Crystal River v. EPA, 35 F.3d 1073, 1077 n.10 (6th Cir. 1994).

266. *See, e.g.*, 28 U.S.C § 1361 (mandamus); 28 U.S.C. § 1337 (commerce and antitrust).

267. 33 U.S.C. § 1319(g)(8).

268. 33 U.S.C. § 1319(g)(2)(A). The figures in the original Act were amended by Federal Civil Penalties Inflation Adjustment Act, 28 U.S.C. § 2461 note, as amended by the Debt Collection Improvement Act, 31 U.S.C. § 3701 note. *See* Civil Monetary Penalty Inflation Adjustment Rule, 62 Fed. Reg. 35,038 (June 27, 1997).

269. 33 U.S.C. § 1319(g)(8)(A).

270. 33 U.S.C. § 1319(g)(2)(B). The figures in the original Act were amended by Federal Civil Penalties Inflation Adjustment Act, 28 U.S.C. § 2461 note, as amended by the Debt Collection Improvement Act, 31 U.S.C. § 3701 note. *See* Civil Monetary Penalty Inflation Adjustment Rule, 62 Fed. Reg. 35,038 (June 27, 1997).

271. 33 U.S.C. § 1319(g)(8)(B).

272. 33 U.S.C. §§ 1319(g)(8), 1319(g)(4)(a).

273. Although the CWA defines the term "person" to include a "State," 33 U.S.C. § 1362(5), the citizen suit provision does not expressly abrogate States' Eleventh Amendment immunity from suit in federal court. *See* 33 U.S.C. § 1365(a)(1)(ii); Froebel v. Meyer, 13 F. Supp. 2d 843 (E.D. Wis. 1998). For a discussion of state immunity pursuant to the Eleventh Amendment and more generally as it relates to environmental matters, see Stephen R. McAllister & Robert L. Glicksman, *State Liability for Environmental Violations: The U.S. Supreme Court's "New" Federalism*, 29 ENVTL. L. REP. NEWS & ANALYSIS 10,665 (Nov. 1999).

274. 33 U.S.C. § 1365(a)(1).

275. 33 U.S.C. § 1365(a)(2).

276. *See supra* Section II.E.

277. U.S. Const. Art. III, § 2.

278. *See, e.g.*, Save Ourselves v. U.S. Army Corps of Engineers, 958 F.2d 659, 662 (5th Cir. 1992); Informed Citizens United, Inc. v. USX Corp., 36 F. Supp. 2d 375, 378 (S.D. Tex. 1999). *See generally* Lujan v. Defenders of Wildlife, 504 U.S. 555, 561–62 (1992):

> When the suit is one challenging the legality of government action or inaction, nature and extent of facts that must be averred (at the summary judgment stage) or proved (at the trial stage) in order to establish standing depends considerably upon whether the plaintiff is himself an

> object of the action (or forgone action) at issue. If he is, there is ordinarily little question that the action or inaction has caused him injury, and that a judgment preventing or requiring the action will redress it. When, however, . . . a plaintiff's asserted injury arises from the government's allegedly unlawful regulation (or lack of regulation) of someone else, much more is needed.

279. *See supra* Section II.E.

280. *Id.*

281. 33 U.S.C. § 1365(b).

282. *See* 40 C.F.R. pt. 135 (2004).

283. *See, e.g.*, Save Our Wetlands v. United States Army Corps of Engineers, 549 F.2d 1021, 1026 (5th Cir.), *cert. denied*, 434 U.S. 836 (1977).

284. *See* Village of Elk Grove Village v. Evans, 997 F.2d 328, 331 (7th Cir. 1993).

285. *See, e.g.*, Sierra Club v. Penfold, 857 F.2d 1307, 1315 (9th Cir. 1988); Impro Products, Inc. v. Block, 722 F.2d 845, 850 & n.8 (D.C. Cir. 1983).

286. *See, e.g.*, Sierra Club v. Slater, 120 F.3d 623, 631 (6th Cir. 1997); Florida Keys Citizen Coalition v. West, 996 F. Supp. 1254, 1256 (S.D. Fla. 1998).

287. Natural Resources Defense Council v. Fox, 909 F. Supp. 153, 159 (S.D.N.Y. 1995).

288. *See, e.g.*, North Carolina Wildlife Federation v. Woodbury, 19 ENVTL. L. REP. 21,308 (E.D. N.C. 1989).

289. McCarthy v. Madigan, 503 U.S. 140, 144–45 (1992).

290. *Id.* at 145.

291 U.S.C. § 704.

292. 509 U.S. 137 (1993).

293. 5 U.S.C. § 704 provides, in relevant part:

> Except as otherwise expressly required by statute, agency action otherwise final is final for purposes of [judicial review] whether or not there has been presented or determined an application for a declaratory order, for any form of reconsideration . . ., or, unless the agency otherwise requires by rule and provides that the action meanwhile is inoperative, for an appeal to superior agency authority.

294. *Darby*, 509 U.S. at 147.

295. Prior to *Darby* and the Corps's rules on administrative appeals, several courts have refused review of EPA or Corps decisions involving jurisdictional determinations and/or the issuance of cease and desist orders on grounds that those seeking review have failed to exhaust other, available administrative remedies. For example, in Deltona Corp. v. Alexander, 682 F.2d 888 (11th Cir. 1982), the plaintiff sought a judicial determination of the extent of wetlands on its property. Although the Corps had denied a permit for the activities proposed by plaintiff because of adverse effects on wetlands, it had not definitively determined which portions of the plaintiff's property were subject to regulation pursuant to Section 404. *Id.* at 893. The court concluded:

> The parties all agree that at least some of Deltona's proposed construction involved wetlands, hence the Corps concededly had the authority to deny the requested permit. Whatever controversy exists as to the extent of Corps jurisdiction may well be settled by an administrative determination of how much of Deltona's property constitutes wetlands, thus avoiding unnecessary judicial intervention. The wetlands determination, moreover, is precisely the type of decision that falls within the rest of the policies supporting the exhaustion requirement. Even appellant concedes that the decision will require extensive expert testimony, including a thorough analysis of the vegetation on the property; committing this determination to the Corps in the first instance permits complete development of the factual record, utilizes the agency's expertise in this technical area, and encourages the development of uniform standards to guide future decisions. Nor are any of the exhaustion exceptions applicable. Deltona's administrative remedy is neither inadequate nor futile. . . .

Id. at 893–94; *see also* Howell v. United States, 794 F. Supp. 1072, 1075 (D.N.M. 1992) (dismissing challenge to cease and desist order on exhaustion grounds). The continuing vitality of these cases may be questioned under *Darby,* but the same result is likely to obtain pursuant to the Corps's new rules governing appeals. Moreover, as explained in the text, the exhaustion doctrine is just one of a variety of legal tools that courts invoke to bar judicial review of Corps decisions other than completed and final permit decisions.

296. 33 C.F.R. § 331.2; *see* 33 C.F.R. § 320.1(a)(2).

297. 33 C.F.R. § 331.2.

298. *See* 65 Fed. Reg. 16,486, 16,488 (Mar. 28, 2000).

299. 33 C.F.R. § 331.12.

300. 33 C.F.R. § 331.10.

301. 64 Fed. Reg. 11,708, 11,713 (Mar. 9, 1999).

302. For a detailed discussion of the 404(c) veto authority and its implementation, see Chapter 9.

303. *See* Richard J. Pierce, Jr., et al., Administrative Law and Process 193–94 (3d ed. 1999).

304. 5 U.S.C. § 704.

305. 33 C.F.R. § 320.1(a)(6).

306. 753 F. Supp. 532 (D. Del. 1990), *aff'd without opinion,* 961 F.2d 1568 (3d Cir. 1992).

307. *Id.* at 540.

308. *Id.* (citing FTC v. Standard Oil, 449 U.S. 232, 242–43(1980)). For decisions reaching the same conclusion, see Rueth v. EPA, 13 F.3d 227, 230 (7th Cir. 1993); Child v. United States, 851 F. Supp. 1527, 1535 (D. Utah 1994); Howell v. United States, 794 F. Supp. 1072, 1075 (D.N.M. 1992); Mulberry Hills Dev. Corp. v. United States, 772 F. Supp. 1553, 1558 (D. Md. 1991); Fercom Aquaculture Corp. v. United States, 740 F. Supp. 736 (E.D. Mo. 1990); Lotz Realty Co. v. United States, 757 F. Supp. 692, 693 (E.D. Va. 1990).

309. *See, e.g.*, Howell v. Army Corps of Engineers, 794 F. Supp. 1072 (D.N.M. 1992).

310. 902 F.2d 567 (7th Cir. 1990).

311. 33 U.S.C. § 1319. Specifically, the court noted that while Section 309(g)(8) provides for judicial review of administrative penalties, no similar provision for judicial review was made for cease and desist orders. On the latter point, the court noted that Section 309(a)(3) gives EPA the option of either issuing an administrative order or instituting a civil action. That section provides:

> (3) Whenever on the basis of any information available to him the Administrator finds that any person is in violation of [section 1311, 1312, 1316, 1317, 1318, 1328, or 1345 of this title,] or is in violation of any permit condition or limitation implementing any of such sections in a permit issued under [section 1342] of this title by him or by a State or in a permit issued under [section 1344] of this title by a State, he shall issue an order requiring such person to comply with such section or requirement, or he shall bring a civil action in accordance with subsection (b) of this section.

33 U.S.C. § 1319(a)(3).

312. *Hoffman Group*, 902 F.2d at 569; *see* Rueth v. EPA, 13 F.3d 227, 230 (7th Cir. 1993); Southern Pines Associates v. U.S., 912 F.2d 713, 715 (4th Cir. 1990) ("the statutory structure and history of the CWA provides clear and convincing evidence that Congress intended to exclude this type of action").

313. Swanson v. United States, 600 F. Supp. 802 (D. Idaho 1985), *aff'd* 789 F.2d 1368 (9th Cir. 1986); Bailey v. United States Army Corps of Engineers, 647 F. Supp. 44 (D. Idaho 1986).

314. *See, e.g.*, Child v. United States, 851 F. Supp. 1527, 1534 (D. Utah 1994) (distinguishing *Swanson* and *Bailey*); *Route 26 Land Dev. Ass'n*, 753 F. Supp. at 539 (criticizing *Swanson* and *Bailey*).

315. Avella v. U.S. Army Corps of Engineers, 20 Envtl. L. Rep. 20,920 (S.D. Fla. 1990), *aff'd*, 916 F.2d 721 (11th Cir. 1990); Inn of Daphne v. United States, 1998 U.S. Dist. LEXIS 13,991 (S.D. Ala., Aug. 26, 1998), at 22–23; Industrial Highway Corp. v. Danielson, 796 F. Supp. 121, 129 (D.N.J. 1992); Lotz Realty Co. v. United States, 757 F. Supp. 692 (E.D. Va. 1990).

316. 658 F.2d 762 (10th Cir. 1981).

317. Laguna Gatuna, Inc. v. Browner, 58 F.3d 564, 566 (10th Cir. 1995).

318. Southern Pines Assocs. v. United States, 912 F.2d 713 (4th Cir. 1990).

319. Rueth v. EPA, 13 F.3d 227 (7th Cir. 1993).

320. *Laguna Gatuna*, 58 F.3d at 566.

321. 815 F. Supp. 766 (D. Del. 1993).

322. *Id.* at 771.

323. Environmental Defense Fund v. Tidwell, 837 F. Supp. 1344 (E.D.N.C. 1992); Golden Gate Audubon Society v. United States Army Corps of Engineers, 717 F. Supp. 1417 (N.D. Cal. 1988).

324. *See* Orleans Audubon Society v. Lee, 742 F.2d 901 (5th Cir. 1984).

325. *See* Cross Timbers Concerned Citizens v. Saginaw, 991 F. Supp. 563, 570 (N.D. Tex. 1997).

326. *See, e.g.,* Harmon Cove Condominium Ass'n v. Marsh, 815 F.2d 949, 951–53 (3d Cir. 1987); *see generally* Heckler v. Chaney, 470 U.S. 821, 832 (1985) (holding that an "agency's decision not to take enforcement action should be presumed immune from judicial review under § 701(a)(2)" of the APA).

327. 35 F.3d 1073 (6th Cir. 1994).

328. *Id.* at 1078.

329. *Id.* at 1079.

330. *Id.*

331. *Id.*

332. National Wildlife Federation v. Adamkus, 936 F. Supp. 435, 444 (W.D. Mich. 1996).

333. Camp v. Pitts, 411 U.S. 138, 142 (1973) ("The focal point for judicial review should be the administrative record already in existence, not some new record made initially in the reviewing court.").

335. In *Preserve Endangered Areas of Cobb's History v. U.S. Army Corps of Engineers,* the court noted:

> a court may go beyond the administrative record only where: 1) an agency's failure to explain its action effectively frustrates judicial review; 2) it appears that the agency relied on materials not included in the record; 3) technical terms or complex subjects need to be explained; or 4) there is a strong showing of agency bad faith or improper behavior.

87 F.3d 1242, 1246 n.1 (11th Cir. 1996) (citing Animal Defense Council v. Hodel, 840 F.2d 1432, 1436–37 (9th Cir. 1988)).

In a number of cases, courts have permitted parties to present evidence outside the administrative record, but have not explained the reasons for doing so. For example, in Bayou Des Familles Dev. Corp. v. U.S. Army Corps of Engineers, 541 F. Supp. 1025 (E.D. La. 1982), *aff'd* 709 F.2d 713 (5th Cir. La. 1983), the court first held that "[b]ased on the evidence in the administrative record before the Corps at the time it denied plaintiff's permit application," the Corps decision should be upheld. *Id.* at 1038. Then, however, the court stated, "Nothing in the evidence presented at trial by plaintiffs suggests to the court that the decision to deny the permit was based on less than a full investigation of conditions and application of the relevant statutes to the facts adduced by the Corps." *Id.* at 1039. The court does not explain why it was necessary to conduct an evidentiary hearing.

335. *See, e.g., Preserve Endangered Areas of Cobb's History,* 87 F.3d at 1246–47 (11th Cir. 1996); Friends of the Earth v. Hintz, 800 F.2d 822, 828–29 (9th Cir. 1986); Avoyelles Sportsmen's League v. Marsh, 715 F.2d 897, 907 (5th Cir. 1983); Sierra Club v. U.S. Army Corps of Engineers, 772 F.2d 1043, 1052 (2d Cir. 1985); Stewart v. Potts, 996 F. Supp. 668, 674 (S.D. Tex. 1998); National Wildlife Federation v. Hanson, 623 F. Supp. 1539, 1544–45 (E.D.N.C. 1985).

336. 33 U.S.C. § 1319(g)(8).

337. 5 U.S.C. § 706(2)(a).

338. 715 F.2d 897 (5th Cir. 1983).

339. *Id.* at 904.

340. *Id.* at 906.

341. *See* Alaska Center for the Environment v. West, 157 F.3d 680, 682 (9th Cir. 1998); National Wildlife Federation v. Hanson, 623 F. Supp. 1539, 1545 (E.D.N.C. 1985); O'Connor v. Corps of Engineers, 801 F. Supp. 185, 189–90 (N.D. Ind. 1992).

342. *See, e.g.,* Preserve Endangered Areas of Cobb's History v. U.S. Army Corps of Engineers, 87 F.3d 1242, 1249 (11th Cir. 1996).

343. James City County v. EPA, 12 F.3d 1330, 1338 (4th Cir. 1993).

344. *See Alaska Center for the Environment*, 157 F.3d 680.

345. 467 U.S. 837 (1984).

346. *Id.* at 842–43.

347. *See, e.g.,* American Mining Congress v. United States Army Corps of Engineers, 951 F. Supp. 267 (D.D.C. 1997), *aff'd sub nom.* National Mining Association v. United States Army Corps of Engineers, 145 F.3d 1399 (D.C. Cir. 1998).

348. 5 U.S.C. § 706.

349. 955 F.2d 254 (4th Cir. 1992).

350. *Id.* at 260–61.

351. James City County v. EPA, 12 F.3d 1330, 1339 (4th Cir. 1993).

352. *See* Tull v. United States, 481 U.S. 412 (1987).

353. 792 F. Supp. 339 (D.N.J. 1992).

354. *Id.* at 343.

355. *Id.* The court further noted:

> This court's conclusion is bolstered by the impressive list of cases in which, in an enforcement action, the trial court took evidence and decided the "existence of wetlands" issue de novo without objection from the Corps. [United States v. Ciampitti, 583 F. Supp. 483 (D.N.J. 1984), *aff'd*, 772 F.2d 893 (3rd Cir. 1985)]; United States v. Rivera Torres, 656 F. Supp. 251 (D.P.R. 1987), *aff'd*, 826 F.2d 151 (1st Cir. 1987); United States v. Larkins, 657 F. Supp. 76 (W.D. Ky. 1987), *aff'd*, 852 F.2d 189 (6th Cir. 1988); Leslie Salt [Company v. United States, 700 F. Supp. 476 (N.D. Cal 1988)], *rev'd on other grounds*, 896 F.2d 354 (9th Cir. 1990). *See also* United States v. Riverside Bayview Homes, Inc., 474 U.S. 121 (1985). This observation is not meant to imply that there is some sort of estoppel operating in this case. If the Corps has been given the right to prevail at trial without proving the existence of wetlands by a preponderance of the evidence, its failure to assert that right in previous cases does not destroy that right. It seems inconceivable, however, that so many appellate courts could review so many trial transcripts without someone arguing that a de novo determination of the wetlands issue by the trial court was improper.

Id.

CHAPTER 13

Wetlands and Regulatory Takings

ROBERT MELTZ

I. Introduction/Scope

Wetlands in the contiguous forty-eight states are predominantly in private hands.[1] As a result, federal (and state) efforts to restrict destruction of private wetlands by regulation have been for decades a prime generator of "takings" litigation.[2] The claim is that by restricting the economic use of such wetlands, the United States Army Corps of Engineers (Corps) or the U.S. Environmental Protection Agency (EPA) has "taken" the property within the meaning of the Takings Clause of the Fifth Amendment.[3] In the public relations arena, property rights activists assert that wetlands regulation is a major locus of federal intrusion into property rights, while government agencies and environmental groups sharply dispute their accounts.

This chapter speaks to the takings question solely as it arises under the Section 404 program. It does not consider federal efforts to encourage voluntary preservation efforts by wetland owners through economic incentives and disincentives.[4] By definition, these nonregulatory approaches do not coerce, at least not in the legal sense of the term, and so do not generally become targets of takings litigation.

The Supreme Court typically paints its takings jurisprudence in broad strokes; and it has never ruled on the merits in a federal wetlands taking case. This situation gives added importance to the takings decisions of the lower courts. Under the Tucker Act, the U.S. Court of Federal Claims[5] (CFC) is given exclusive jurisdiction over almost all takings claims against the United States when the compensation sought exceeds

$10,000.[6] Appeals of CFC decisions are exclusively to the U.S. Court of Appeals for the Federal Circuit.[7] It is these two courts, then, that have filled in the details of takings jurisprudence as applied to federal government actions, such as those under Section 404.

Section II of this chapter provides a history of the shifting trends in the takings case law spawned by the Section 404 program. Section III sketches the pertinent Supreme Court takings jurisprudence. Section IV discusses the ripeness question—when, in the unfolding of a dispute between wetland owner and federal government, courts will consider the merits of a taking claim. Section V analyzes the substantive takings criteria articulated by the CFC and Federal Circuit in deciding Section 404 cases. Section VI reviews the special criteria used by those courts when temporary delays are the basis of the taking claim. Section VII addresses the "parcel as a whole" issue. Section VIII analyzes takings issues arising when both federal and state/local governments are involved at the same wetland site. Section IX concludes with general comments concerning wetlands and regulatory takings.

II. The Historic Pendulum

The first takings decision involving federal wetlands regulation came in 1970, in *Zabel v. Tabb*.[8] There, the Fifth Circuit addressed the Corps's denial of a permit to fill in a privately owned bay bottom, summarily spurning the taking claim based on the federal navigation servitude.[9] Following *Zabel* and continuing through the early 1980s, all of the Section 404 takings cases held for the government.[10] These decisions cited the Supreme Court's tendency to uphold land-use restrictions supported by the public interest, even where landowners suffered precipitous loss in value. Also, the challenged permit denials were held not to deny all reasonable uses of the landowner's parcel *as a whole*—either because the property included uplands not affected by the permit denial or because a permit had been granted for the filling in of some of the wetlands on the parcel.[11]

By the mid-1980s, the winds of change were blowing, possibly because the Section 404 program had now taken hold and confronted a more conservative judiciary. In 1983, a Section 404 permit denial was seen by a court to work a taking for the first time.[12] Then followed two important interim rulings favorable to wetland-owner plaintiffs. In 1986, in *Florida Rock Industries v. United States*,[13] the Federal Circuit again weighed the public interest in wetlands preservation against the landowner's loss, as it had in the early 1980s. But this time the court concluded that the balance tipped toward the landowner (though vacating the lower court's finding of a taking on other grounds). Two years later, a key ruling went against the United States in another wetlands taking case, *Loveladies Harbor, Inc. v. United States.*[14] When the U.S. Claims Court reached the merits in *Florida Rock* and *Loveladies Harbor* in 1990, it found takings in both, on the same day.[15]

People started to take notice. *Loveladies, Florida Rock,* and other new CFC rulings took an unmistakably less deferential attitude toward the public interest in wetlands than did earlier federal decisions. *Loveladies* and *Florida Rock* in particular decided key unresolved issues of takings law against the government. In the following round, in 1994, the Federal Circuit affirmed *Loveladies Harbor*[16] and remanded *Florida Rock*[17] with guidance to the CFC that led that court in 1999 to find a taking once again.[18]

Since 1994, this swing of the judicial pendulum toward the property owner has been less clear. Indeed, a review of *final* wetlands takings decisions during this period shows that the United States has won every one except the 1999 *Florida Rock* decision.[19] Moreover, almost all the CFC's wetlands/takings decisions against the government come from one judge.[20] Still, in order to prevail in a wetlands taking case, the government must offer a convincing defense. The current pattern of government wins may stem more from an increased willingness in the U.S. Department of Justice to settle the difficult cases than from any judicial pendulum shift back toward the government side.

III. Supreme Court Takings Precepts Most Relevant to Federal Wetlands Regulation

Takings challenges against wetlands regulation are of the "regulatory taking" variety. Such a claim asserts that the government has effectively taken private property solely by restriction of its use, in the absence of physical invasion or appropriation.[21] The concept of regulatory takings debuted in 1922, with the Supreme Court's decision in *Pennsylvania Coal Co. v. Mahon.*[22] Justice Holmes, writing for the Court, concluded that "while property may be regulated to a certain extent, if regulation goes too far it will be recognized as a taking."[23] It would be several decades, however, before the Court attempted to provide a coherent framework for determining whether a regulation has gone "too far." That effort began in 1978 with its decision in *Penn Central Transportation Co. v. New York City,*[24] and continues to this day. This section briefly sketches that Supreme Court framework. Recall, however, that much fleshing out has been provided by the CFC and Federal Circuit.

Before a wetlands/taking plaintiff may litigate a taking claim on the merits, the plaintiff, like any other takings claimant, generally will need to show that it owned the land in question on the date of the alleged taking.[25] Ordinarily, this initial hurdle will be surmounted with ease by the wetlands/taking plaintiff.

A more formidable preliminary obstacle for takings plaintiffs is the Supreme Court's ripeness doctrine. Ripeness requirements in takings litigation, as elsewhere, serve to avoid involving the federal courts in disputes prematurely, before federal agencies have made "final" decisions that are fit for judicial review.[26] In takings law, a final decision is further necessitated by the very nature of the takings inquiry which, as we shall see, focuses heavily on the economic consequences of the government action for the property owner. As the Court put it: "A court cannot determine whether a regulation has gone 'too far' unless it knows how far the regulation goes."[27]

In *Williamson County Regional Planning Comm'n v. Hamilton Bank*,[28] the Court held that a takings claim is not ripe for adjudication on the merits unless and until the claimant has obtained a "final, definitive position" from the pertinent agency as to the degree of development allowed on the land.[29] As explicated a year later in *MacDonald, Sommer & Frates v. Yolo County*,[30] a final, definitive position may not be established simply by having one's initial development proposal denied, since denial, without more, does not establish that "less ambitious," yet still economically viable, plans will also be denied. This means that the Corps's rejection of the wetland owner's initial permit application does not, in and of itself, ripen a taking claim. Generally, further applications based on reconfigured or scaled-down proposals are necessary.[31]

Ripeness doctrine does not require claimants to suffer through an endless series of agency rulings, however. "[O]nce . . . the permissible uses of the property are known to a reasonable degree of certainty, a takings claim is likely to have ripened."[32] In related fashion, under the "futility exception" the landowner need not submit variant proposals if circumstances indicate that doing so would be pointless.[33] In Section IV, we shall see that the CFC has been quick to discern such futility-establishing circumstances, making the customary subsequent-application requirement of little importance to date in the CFC.

Once these hurdles (and occasionally others) are surmounted, the case proceeds to a determination of whether a regulatory taking has occurred. That determination is governed by either "*per se* rules" or "*Penn Central* balancing."

The so-called per se rules treat certain government actions as automatic takings, irrespective of many (but not all) of the considerations that normally factor into the takings analysis. There are several per se rules, but the one that recurs in wetlands takings claims is the "total taking" rule of *Lucas v. South Carolina Coastal Council*.[34] As subsequently described by the Supreme Court, this rule declares that when government regulation eliminates *all* economically beneficial use and value of a parcel, the regulation effects a taking.[35] The major exception discussed in *Lucas* is that such regulation is not a taking if its restrictions could have been imposed under "background principles of the State's law of property and nuisance" extant at the time the property was acquired.[36] The scope of this "background principles" concept, one that logically cannot be confined to the "total taking" context in which it was born, has long been debated. (See Section V.B.) The *Lucas* rule is also generally inapplicable to restrictions designated at the outset as temporary—chiefly, land use moratoria—notwithstanding any total deprivation of use and value during the restricted period. Such prospectively temporary deprivations must instead be tested under the *Penn Central* balancing test, discussed below.[37]

If, as happens far more frequently, regulation does not work a *Lucas* total taking—i.e., leaves the owner with some economic use or value—the property owner still must be given the opportunity to establish a "partial regulatory taking" under the multifactor balancing test announced by the Supreme Court in *Penn Central Transportation Co. v. New York City*.[38] The governing factors are (1) the economic impact of the government action, (2) the degree to which it interferes with reasonable investment-backed expectations, and (3) the "character" of the government action.[39]

The amorphous nature of these factors means that where the deprivation is less than total, as it almost always is, the takings inquiry is ad hoc, case-by-case, and fact intensive. For guidance, one must plunge into interpretive lower-court decisions. The Supreme Court has, however, indicated that to make a persuasive taking claim on the basis of the "economic impact" factor, the plaintiff must show a very substantial decline in property value or severe curtailment of economic use.[40] But a total economic wipeout of the type involved in *Lucas* is not essential.

The "interference with reasonable investment-backed expectations" factor requires, among other things, a canvassing of the statutory and regulatory landscape at the time the property was acquired.[41] The inquiry is whether, in light of such laws, the plaintiff had a reasonable expectation that he or she would remain free of the challenged government restriction. The fact that the restriction was imposed under a regulatory regime existing when the parcel was acquired does not automatically defeat a taking claim, however, but is merely one ingredient to be considered.[42]

The "character of the government action" factor is often said by the Court to embody the principle that a taking is more likely to be found when the government physically invades property than when it merely restricts the uses to which the property may be put. Beyond this, the Court has given the factor little explicit content, though the expansiveness of the term "character" suggests that the Court views this factor as an elastic clause. One probably could regard it as embracing various elements of takings analysis noted sporadically by the Court without being inserted into the *Penn Central* framework. Among these elements are the balance between the societal interest furthered by the regulation and the burden imposed on the plaintiff,[43] and whether the regulation effects an "average reciprocity of advantage"—that is, whether the plaintiff receives an offsetting benefit from the fact that others are similarly burdened by the same regulatory scheme.[44]

Whether a regulatory taking claim is evaluated under the *Penn Central* factors or the *Lucas* categorical rule, the regulation's impact on the plaintiff's property is assessed in a relative sense, comparing the use or value lost to what is retained. For this reason, a court must define with care the precise extent of the property it will examine in the taking analysis. This is referred to as the "parcel as a whole" or "relevant parcel" or "denominator" issue.[45] The general predilection of the Supreme Court has been against segmenting the parcel: " 'Taking' jurisprudence does not divide a single parcel into discrete segments and attempt to determine whether rights in a particular segment have been entirely abrogated. In deciding whether a particular governmental action has effected a taking, this Court focuses . . . on the nature of the interference with rights in the parcel as a whole."[46] Thus, at the very least, takings law bars the parsing of a property based solely on the regulated versus nonregulated status of different portions, in an effort to show that the regulation's effect on the regulated portion meets the high thresholds of the pertinent takings test. Beyond this, the Court has said that the relevant parcel is defined by its "metes and bounds," arguably suggesting a bias against segmentation of contiguous parcels.[47] But the Court has left for lower-court illumination such issues as how to deal with noncontiguous tracts owned by the plaintiff, or a portion of an original purchase sold off prior to the alleged taking. In addition to its resistance to *spatial* segmentation of property, the Court has disapproved of fractionating plaintiff's *rights* in a parcel,[48] and of fragmenting the *temporal* aspect of the owner's property interest (see Section VI).[49]

IV. Ripeness

This section considers the ripeness question at various stages in the Corps's exercise of authority under Section 404. As will be shown, establishing ripeness, long a bête noire of takings plaintiffs challenging state and local land use restrictions, has stymied takings plaintiffs in the CFC and Federal Circuit only when suit was brought in advance of being denied a permit on the merits. Each subsection should be read in conjunction with the final subsection on futility.

A. Corps's Assertion of Jurisdiction

A landowner may first encounter the Section 404 program on being informed by the Corps that part of his or her property is a jurisdictional wetland and that most uses the owner may wish to make of the property will require a Section 404 permit. A taking claim based only on these facts would be deemed unripe, or would simply fail on the merits. In *United States v. Riverside Bayview Homes, Inc.*, the Supreme Court held that the Corps's mere assertion of Section 404 jurisdiction over private property does not establish a taking.[50] Because it is possible that the permit, if applied for, will be granted, the extent to which regulation has affected the owner's property remains, at best, uncertain.

The same rule applies to those property owners who begin work in a jurisdictional wetland without a permit and then are confronted with a cease and desist order from the government. Under the rationale of *Riverside Bayview*, ripeness (or a taking holding) eludes the landowner where the order makes clear that it terminates once the owner secures a permit.[51] Once again, because the possibility of securing a permit remains, the cease and desist order is not final agency action for purposes of a taking claim.

B. Delay Based on Permit Processing Time

It would make little sense to insist that a wetlands/taking plaintiff present the court with a permit denial to achieve ripeness when the claim is that of a temporary taking based on excessive permit processing time by the Corps. Accordingly, the delay cases, discussed in Section VI, omit discussion of the customary permit-denial prerequisite.

C. Withdrawals and Denials "Without Prejudice" of Permit Applications

The Corps frequently withholds Section 404 permits because the applicant lacks the requisite state and local approvals or has failed to submit complete information. Formally, the application is said to be "withdrawn" or denied "without prejudice"—the latter a reference to the applicant's ability to try again once the missing requirements have been satisfied.[52] A taking claim based on such Corps actions generally is unripe, if the Corps is careful not to indicate that, had a complete application been submitted, the proposed project and all other economic uses would have been disapproved anyway.

The decisions in *Heck v. United States*[53] and *City National Bank v. United States*[54] illustrate this last point. In *Heck,* the Corps denied without prejudice a Section 404 permit application, stating that it would hold the application "in abeyance until such time as [plaintiff has] received the necessary state permits for the work."[55] The CFC found the taking claim unripe, reasoning that the Corps "did not reach a 'final, definitive position' as to how it would apply Section 404(b)(1) of the Clean Water Act to plaintiff's proposed development. Rather, the Corps withdrew plaintiff's application before substantively addressing its merits."[56]

By contrast, in *City National Bank* the Corps's denial without prejudice of an incomplete application was accompanied by clear indications that the proposed project would be denied even if the applicant supplied the requisite information. "A plain reading of the [Corps's denial letter]," said the CFC, "indicates that the Corps made a merits-based determination, based on the record, that plaintiff's proposed project did not satisfy the . . . 404(b)(1) guidelines."[57] Notwithstanding the "without prejudice" designation, therefore, the court found the taking claim ripe. More generally, it rejected the argument that mere delineation of a permit denial as "without prejudice" dictates a finding of unripeness; such a rule, it said, "could lead to agency abuse."[58]

D. Need to Submit Alternative Proposals

The CFC has often invoked the futility doctrine when the United States has argued that, based on *MacDonald,* the Corps's denial of plaintiff's initial Section 404 permit application did not confer ripeness. Recall that under that decision, rejection of a property owner's ideal development scenario does not, by itself, imply that scaled-down, yet still economic, proposals might not be acceptable to the regulator. Thus, the first denial may not confer ripeness. The CFC, however, has always discerned circumstances surrounding the first permit denial indicating to the court that no economic development of whatever intensity would be acceptable on the wetlands.[59]

The Corps has reported instances where a wetland owner, perhaps encouraged by general plaintiff-friendly trends in takings law, has "draw[n] a line in the sand" during permit negotiations.[60] That is, it has refused to negotiate further (or at all) with the Corps over possible alternatives to, or mitigation conditions on, the owners' desired projects. This approach may present difficulties to the potential takings claimant. To surmount the ripeness hurdle, the applicant may need to settle in for good-faith negotiations over a reasonable period; abruptly leaving the table, or submitting inadequate responses to Corps information requests, may not sit well with a court.[61] Indeed, the courts may be inclined to view such recalcitrance as posing the same problem the Supreme Court confronted in *Williamson County* and *MacDonald*: "A court cannot determine whether a regulation has gone 'too far' unless it knows how far the regulation goes."[62]

The Corps may employ a slightly different strategy for permit applicants who resist compromise. The agency may issue a permit for a portion of the project even though the applicant has not sought it. This strategy permits the Corps to avoid the argument that any further proceedings would be futile and defend the case based on residual economic value in the developable portion of the property.[63] This strategy should not be confused with the facts in *Cooley v. United States*,[64] where the Corps issued a highly provisional permit not requested by the applicant three years after the initial permit denial and on the eve of the taking trial.

E. Serial Applications for Segments of a Wetland

Ripeness issues may arise when development of a wetland parcel proceeds piecemeal, with serial permit applications. A wetland owner, upon being denied a permit to develop a portion of the parcel, may assert that denial effectively resulted in a taking of the entirety. Whether such a claim is ripe turns on the facts. In *Florida Rock*, the Federal Circuit limited plaintiff's taking claim to the ninety-eight-acre parcel included in its permit application, rejecting the plaintiff's claim that the effect of the Corps's permit denial was to make clear that any development on the larger, 1,560-acre parcel of which the ninety-eight acres was a part would also be prohibited. As to the remaining acreage, the court concluded that it was uncertain whether the Corps would, in fact, deny a permit, particularly after the agency considered the likelihood that such a denial would increase the government's exposure to a takings remedy.[65] Subsequently, however, the CFC, noting the passage of much time since the earlier decision, certified for immediate appeal the question of whether plaintiff may pursue its claim that the entire 1,560 acres has been taken.[66]

By contrast, in *Formanek v. United States*,[67] the court considered ripe the plaintiff's claim that although the permit application concerned only eleven acres of a larger 112-acre parcel, the entire parcel should be considered taken because the effect of the permit denial was to render the remainder of the parcel unfit for development.

F. Variances and Appeals

Exhaustion of variance possibilities, a perennial takings-ripeness concern for builders denied local approvals, is not a problem for the wetland owner denied a Section 404 permit. The reason is simple enough: Corps procedures do not allow for variances or analogous relief.[68]

Nor, until recently, did they provide for administrative appeals. The Corps now has an administrative appeal process under which applicants for Section 404 permits may appeal within the Corps a denial with prejudice of an individual permit, a declined proffer of an individual permit, or a geographic (but not activity-based) jurisdictional determination.[69] Important here, the new regulations assert that no federal court action based on a permit denial or declined permit may be filed until the applicant "has exhausted all applicable administrative remedies."[70] It remains to be seen, however, whether the CFC, which has not always found pursuit of agency appeals to be necessary for takings ripeness,[71] will acquiesce in this agency requirement.[72]

G. Futility Exception

The principal exception to the foregoing ripeness requirements of good-faith negotiation between applicant and the Corps, permit denial on the merits, and reapplication is the futility doctrine. Recall the CFC cases finding, in light of futility, that no reapplication was necessary following first permit denial.[73]

But while reapplication has not yet been required, the CFC and Federal Circuit have proved extremely resistant to invoking futility in the absence of an initial merits-based permit denial. Thus, the permit applicant cannot plead futility "whenever faced with long odds or demanding procedural requirements."[74] Rather, there must be a definitive indication from the government that the permit cannot be obtained. The permit application must be pursued to the end even when several federal agencies have recommended to the Corps that the permit be denied, since the Corps in the past has not always followed such recommendations.[75] Similarly, the fact that Section 404's presumptions against development that is not water dependent reduce the chance of receiving a permit does not support a futility argument.[76]

Indeed, one Federal Circuit decision appears to categorically reject use of the futility exception to excuse making the initial permit application.[77] As noted, the exception is generally applied to soften the requirement for later, scaled-down proposals. The Federal Circuit rule seems in tension with the CFC pronouncement that an administrative process may be so burdensome as to deprive a property of significant value by its mere existence, and obviate permit application.[78] The CFC, however, has twice rejected efforts to characterize the Section 404 program as overly burdensome and thus invoke this rule.[79]

V. The Regulatory Takings Test in the CFC and Federal Circuit

A. Overview

The takings canon in the CFC and Federal Circuit is the two-tiered one prescribed by the Supreme Court. First, the court asks whether a *Lucas* total taking has occurred. If not, the court proceeds to a partial regulatory taking analysis under *Penn Central.*

The Federal Circuit has admonished the CFC to address all three of the *Penn Central* factors in the latter analysis, including the often-neglected "character of the government action."[80] It remains to be seen whether this directive will result in more than perfunctory consideration of the character factor. Even now, the CFC and Federal Circuit simply repeat the mantra that wetlands preservation is an important goal, and rarely dissect the wetland values at issue in the particular case. Moreover, as discussed later in this section, the Federal Circuit itself has created an exception to its consider-all-factors directive when there is a complete absence of investment-backed expectations.[81]

Almost all the cases in this section stem from Corps permit denials, which generate the large majority of the reported wetlands/takings decisions. Such denials, however, are actually relatively infrequent compared to the number of occasions on which the Corps offers to grant the permit with conditions. Often, these conditions require the permit holder to "mitigate" the environmental impacts of the proposed project, possibly at considerable expense. Given their ubiquity, it is curious that mitigation conditions on wetlands permits have kept such a low profile in the takings cases.[82] Such conditions are not discussed further here, but one should be aware that some Corps-imposed mitigation conditions arguably fall within the scope of the Supreme Court's takings test for exaction conditions on development permits,[83] and may someday be judicially tested against that standard.

We now turn to two threshold substantive issues: whether the taking claim is precluded by the *Lucas* concept of "background principles of the State's law of property and nuisance" or by the "unauthorized acts rule." Following that, we examine the *Penn Central* factors that have played the greatest role in Section 404 takings decisions: economic impact and interference with investment-backed expectations.

B. Threshold Issue: "Background Principles"

The Supreme Court in *Lucas* held that even where regulation removes *all* economic use from a property, the government owes no compensation if the regulation inheres "in the restrictions that background principles of the State's law of property and nuisance already place upon land ownership."[84] The rationale is that where a property owner never acquired a right to use a property in a particular way, a regulation barring that use takes nothing the property owner ever had. No principled reason seems to exist for confining this holding to the *Lucas* total takings context. Thus, where the government successfully invokes the background principles defense, plaintiff never reaches the issue of whether *Lucas*, or *Penn Central*, dictates a taking.

The Corps has often sought to avail itself of the background principles concept, defending Section 404 takings actions by arguing that the activities in wetlands for which permits were denied would constitute a harm, "noxious use," or common law nuisance.[85] This "nuisance defense" actually predates the *Lucas* notion of "background principles of the State's law of property and nuisance," and indeed traces back to some of the earliest Supreme Court takings decisions.[86] For a variety of reasons, the CFC and Federal Circuit have refused so far to characterize any proposed wetlands activity as a nuisance.

One reason for finding no nuisance has been the presence nearby of permitted or otherwise lawful activities similar to the proposed development. Thus, when the Corps rejected a permit for limestone quarrying in a wetland, the nuisance defense was spurned, in part, on the ground that similar operations were proceeding in the area.[87] Parenthetically, the invocation of nearby similar ongoing operations illustrates the difficulty faced by the government where the activities of early arrivers (the existing quarries) have an acceptable level of ecosystem impact, but where a latecomer (the plaintiff) would, if allowed to proceed, push the cumulative impact over the danger threshold.

Other no-nuisance indicia in the cases include the historical absence in state law of any conclusion that the wetland activity constitutes a nuisance;[88] the issuance by state or local authorities of a permit for the plaintiff's or similar activity;[89] the moderate, short-lived, and nontoxic effects of the pollution that would be caused by the prohibited dredging or filling;[90] and (what seems an unjustifiably high threshold) the absence of any "extreme threat to public health, safety, and welfare" associated with the prohibited activity.[91] Citing one or more of these factors, the CFC has declared a seemingly context-independent rule that the building of homes in the wetland lots of a subdivision is not a nuisance.[92] By contrast, *Lucas* itself had no hesitation in concluding that where the filling of a "lakebed" (read "wetland") would flood others' land, there is surely no taking when that filling is prohibited.[93]

Precisely what the background principles concept of *Lucas* includes beyond common law nuisance has been much debated. Does the concept include statutes, not merely common law, existing when the property was acquired? Does it include federal as well as state law? Laws adopted just a few years before the government action alleged to be a taking, or only those of longstanding duration?

Usually, the CFC and Federal Circuit take a narrow view of background principles, restricting the concept to state common law of nuisance, or statutes embodying that common law.[94] The notion embraced by many courts, that background principles include *all* law existing when the property was acquired,[95] made little inroad in the CFC and Federal Circuit, and recently was firmly repudiated by the Supreme Court.[96] At the same time, the Court suggested that background principles are more inclusive than the CFC/Federal Circuit view, including at least some statutes and regulations outside the state's common law tradition.[97]

State decisions such as *Just v. Marinette County*[98] and, more recently, *McQueen v. South Carolina Coastal Council*,[99] have treated the public trust doctrine as a background principle of law that will defeat a takings claim. The Ninth Circuit also has applied the public trust doctrine to defeat a takings claim directed at the city of Seattle.[100] Applying Washington state law, the court held that the public trust doctrine "unquestionably burdens [plaintiff's] property," that the development proposed for the property would be precluded by the public trust doctrine, and that, as a consequence, the city's refusal to permit such development could not be considered a taking.[101]

In contrast, the CFC and Federal Circuit have shown no disposition to include within background principles anything resembling a public trust doctrine, or otherwise to regard wetlands as water resources vested with a unique public character. Wetlands generally have been treated by these courts in much the same way as any other land.

A notable exception to the CFC and Federal Circuit's usual emphasis on state law as the source of background principles is their continued endorsement of the federal navigation servitude. Under the federal navigation servitude, a corollary of the Commerce Clause, the United States may regulate private activity in navigable waters in the interests of navigation or commerce without effecting a taking. Though the Supreme Court rejected a navigation servitude defense to takings claims arising from man-made navigable waters,[102] the defense retains vitality for some wetlands. To apply, the wetland must be within the servitude's shoreward reach, generally held to be the ordinary high-water mark. Recently, in *Palm Beach Isles Assocs. v. United States*,[103] the Federal Circuit anointed the servitude a *Lucas* background principle, though this formal recognition seems only to reaffirm its long-established power as a government defense.[104] *Palm Beach Isles* also affirmed that the federal navigation servitude is available as a takings defense only for Section 404 permit denials having a navigational purpose.[105]

C. Threshold Issue: The "Unauthorized Acts Rule"

It is well settled in the CFC and Federal Circuit that the United States cannot be held liable for a taking based on an unauthorized act of the United States.[106] The principal rationale is that such acts cannot be regarded as acts of the government, hence it is inappropriate to hold the government accountable for them. The unauthorized acts rule is similar to, but distinct from, another CFC/Federal Circuit rule: One pressing a taking action against the United States must concede, at least for purposes of the CFC litigation, that the government action (e.g., the permit denial) was valid. Because the CFC generally possesses authority to award only monetary relief, claims based on an agency's violation of statutory or regulatory authority must be brought in district court.

In 2001, the unauthorized acts rule and the Section 404 program intersected. As covered elsewhere in this book, in that year, the Supreme Court held in *Solid Waste Agency of Northern Cook County v. U.S. Army Corps of Engineers (SWANCC)* that the Corps's assertion of Section 404 jurisdiction over isolated waters by means of its "migratory bird rule" went beyond its statutory authority.[107] The question then arose whether the United States could defend any takings claims arising from the period of mistaken jurisdiction by resort to the unauthorized acts rule. Thus far, there are no reported decisions on this issue under Section 404.[108]

D. Economic Impact

1. *Amount of Loss Required*

The economic impact factor of *Penn Central* largely translates, in the CFC and Federal Circuit, into a percentage calculation of the loss in the parcel's fair market value measured from immediately before to immediately after the permit denial.[109]

Until 1994, the value diminutions in cases where Section 404 permit denials were found to cause takings (together with Supreme Court decisions previously discussed[110]) led many observers to assume that to succeed, a takings plaintiff had to show a value loss of roughly 90 percent or greater.[111] In that year, a Federal Circuit ruling in *Florida Rock*, in discussing the concept of a "partial regulatory taking," plainly assumed that a value diminution amounting to only 62 percent might in proper circumstances be sufficient to take.[112] On remand, this appellate assumption allowed the CFC to find a partial regulatory taking based in part on a 73 percent value loss.[113] Though the courts had never declared any particular level of value loss as necessary for a regulatory taking, these developments in *Florida Rock* were thought to suggest an easing of the degree of economic impact needed. More recently, a different CFC judge declared that a diminution "on the order of 60 percent or less" cannot support a taking, critiquing the CFC decision in Florida Rock as "disharmonious" with Supreme Court precedent.[114]

The *Florida Rock* rulings allowing regulatory takings at lower-than-customary degrees of value loss also create issues of remedy. Previous CFC decisions finding takings on account of Section 404 permit denials, based as they were on near-total value losses, awarded compensation in the form of requiring the United States to buy fee simple title from the plaintiff. With 26.9 percent of the parcel's value remaining, however, the CFC in *Florida Rock* could not require the United States to buy the parcel outright—the government cannot be required to pay for what it has not taken. Rather, the CFC required payment for only the right to use the property—akin to a negative easement.[115]

At the low end of the value-loss spectrum, losing the use of only 15 percent of one's land while still able to turn a profit on the entire parcel plainly is not a taking,[116] nor is a 25 percent loss in value where the remaining value far exceeds plaintiff's cost basis.[117]

2. *Other Aspects of the Economic Impact Factor*

While value loss dominates the economic impact factor, other issues often arise. One, as just noted, is whether a wetland owner, following permit denial, can recoup his or her cost basis in the parcel.[118] Cost basis is not limited to the original purchase price, but may include other capital expenditures on the property.[119] The Federal Circuit has held that cost basis should not be adjusted for inflation.[120]

A second economic-impact component is "average reciprocity of advantage"—an inquiry into whether the burdens imposed on the property owner by the challenged regulatory regime have been offset by benefits accruing to the owner from the very same regime. In finding a taking in *Florida Rock,* for example, the CFC found that plaintiff's "disproportionately heavy burden was not offset by any reciprocity of advantage" conferred on it by the compliance of nearby wetland owners with the Section 404 program.[121]

A third component is the availability of transferable development rights (TDRs) and mitigation-banking value that may offset the economic impact of permit denial. The availability of TDRs to a wetland owner plainly confers something of value to the owner of a development-prohibited wetland that may have little. Whether such TDR value may be used to deflect a taking claim—rather than being confined to the calculation of compensation, where a taking occurs—is a more or less settled question in takings law today. The Supreme Court in 1978 answered yes,[122] and a majority of the current Court seems disposed to do likewise.[123] A wetlands/taking decision by the CFC has explicitly done so.[124]

A wetland tract may retain value as part of a wetlands mitigation banking scheme, whereby the owner may obtain some return on investment by selling mitigation credits to others seeking to satisfy Section 404's compensatory mitigation requirements or, perhaps, selling to entrepreneurs willing to invest in a mitigation bank.[125] Though the Corps of Engineers currently takes the view that it lacks authority to implement mitigation banking, the agency nonetheless encourages permit applicants to use such banks on a voluntary basis.[126] Should the Corps eventually be granted authority to do mitigation banking, the question surely will arise whether the value thereby imparted to a permit-denied wetland can be considered in the takings calculus.[127]

As in land valuation generally, when the government seeks to support its valuation of a permit-denied wetland by alleging remaining economic uses, the offered uses must meet a "showing of reasonable probability that the land is both physically adaptable for such use *and* that there is a demand for such use in the reasonably near future."[128] Also, after-value attributable to a potential use will be rejected by the court where such use is unlikely under deed and zoning restrictions.[129] These tests also apply to property uses offered by plaintiffs in support of pre-permit-denial value.

Even if permit denial robs a wetland of all immediate economic use, it may retain value because some persons are willing to gamble on the prospect that wetlands restrictions may be relaxed in the future. In *Florida Rock,* the court held that the takings inquiry into whether the permit-denied property has remaining economic use must include its desirability to speculators willing to buy it despite current restrictions.[130] The court cautioned, however, that post-permit-denial offers from speculators are adequate to establish residual value only if the speculator can reasonably be assumed to be knowledgeable of all regulatory restrictions. Offers from "suckers"—e.g., victims of fraud or persons unfamiliar with American law—must be discarded. Importantly, this standard does not require the government to undertake a detailed inquiry into the sophistication of each buyer of a comparable parcel. Though clearly discrepant sales may be disregarded, "an assessor may not disregard an *entire* market as aberrational."[131]

E. Investment-Backed Expectations

How the plaintiff's development expectations when the wetland property was acquired should factor into the takings equation has, in the past, often hinged on timing: Was the wetland acquired before or after the enactment of Section 404 (or some related date in the emergence of the Section 404 program)? Recent Supreme Court opinions, however, have spurned the prevailing categorical analysis of this distinction. It is useful nonetheless to review the prior case law, elements of which may still survive.

1. *Property Acquired Before Enactment of Section 404 (or Related Date)*

When the land was acquired before enactment of Section 404 (or related date), the expectations factor may cut for or against a taking, depending on circumstances. According to *Florida Rock,*[132] interference with investment-backed expectations points more strongly toward a taking when the plaintiff's "primary" expectations for the site are thwarted. (Plaintiff bought the wetland solely to mine the underlying limestone; that goal was entirely thwarted.) Also relevant is how much of the parcel has been burdened by the regulation. (The limestone underlay the entire parcel.) And, the expectations factor may include a look at plaintiff's ability to earn a reasonable return on investment—similar to the recoupment of cost basis noted under economic impact.

2. *Property Acquired after Enactment of Section 404 (or Related Date)*

During the 1990s, a strong judicial trend emerged in both state and federal courts rejecting takings claims based on property that the plaintiff acquired after adoption of the regulatory program under which the challenged restriction was imposed.[133] Such courts viewed post-adoption plaintiffs either as lacking a compensable property interest in the blocked development proposal, citing *Lucas,* or as having no reasonable investment-backed expectations of development, per the *Penn Central* test.

The canonical statement of the notice rule in the Federal Circuit arrived in 1994, in *Loveladies Harbor.* The investment-backed expectations factor of *Penn Central,* said the Circuit, limits takings to "owners who . . . bought their property in reliance on a state of affairs that did not include the challenged regulatory regime."[134] Legally, explained the court, such an owner has no reliance interest; he or she assumed the risk of any economic loss. Economically, it said, the market has discounted in theory for the restraint in the claimant's purchase price. Possibly owing to this rationale, the CFC and Federal Circuit have been quick to note when the plaintiff is sophisticated in real estate matters, and thus likely to have had actual as well as constructive notice of the regulatory risks taken when the wetland was bought.[135]

The *Loveladies Harbor* statement was accepted in the CFC and Federal Circuit as a substantial, if not absolute, bar to takings claims based on land purchased after the critical date.[136] In terms of the *Penn Central* test, such a purchase was seen as precluding reasonable development expectations, and that absence of development expectations, by dispensing with the need to consult the other *Penn Central* factors, was fatal to the taking claim.[137]

In 2001, the Supreme Court rejected the absolute version of the notice rule, but made relatively clear the following year that the pre-acquisition existence of the challenged regulatory scheme still plays *some* role in the *Penn Central* analysis, even if not a determinative one, through the investment-backed expectations factor.[138] The Court offered no guidance as to what circumstances might affect the weight accorded the pre-existing regime, suggesting that the factors cited in prior lower-court case law as supporting a categorical analysis may still be at least relevant. An early Federal Circuit reading of the Supreme Court came in *Rith Energy, Inc. v. United States,* asserting in a non-wetland case that the postadoption plaintiff's expectations were particularly relevant because "[t]he likelihood of regulatory restraint is especially high with regard to possible adverse environmental effects."[139]

One question, at present, is whether investment-backed expectations, hence timing issues, are also relevant to a *Lucas* total taking claim. In *Good v. United States,*[140] one Federal Circuit panel squarely held yes, but was criticized by another Federal Circuit panel a year later.[141] Another issue, presumably still relevant after the Supreme Court's downgrade of pre-existing regimes, is what the critical date triggering reduced expectations should be in a given case. Depending on the facts, some candidates for "critical date" in a particular case might be emergence of a "regulatory climate" in the 1960s putting buyers on notice of possible future restrictions (or the mere existence of the Rivers and Harbors Act), enactment of Section 404 in 1972 (the most commonly used date), judicial recognition of Section 404's application to wetlands in *NRDC v. Callaway*[142] in 1975, promulgation of Corps regulations pursuant to *Callaway*'s mandate in 1977,[143] publication of the wetlands delineation manual on which the Corps's assertion of jurisdiction is based, and topographical changes converting nonwetland to wetland. When a plaintiff waits many years following acquisition before filing the Section 404 permit application, the court's analysis of his or her reasonable development expectations may also reflect any additional regulatory demands put into place during those years.[144]

VI. The Regulatory Takings Test in the CFC and Federal Circuit: Special Formulation for Project Delays

Even when development of a privately owned wetland is ultimately allowed by the Corps to proceed, temporary takings claims have been asserted based on project delays. In contrast with the permit denial cases, however, there are no reported court decisions finding takings as the result of Section 404 program-related delays.

One delay scenario, the one most often addressed by the CFC and Federal Circuit, involves the sometimes lengthy period between application for a Section 404 individual permit and its grant or denial. Decisions of these courts make clear that the key factor in the temporary taking analysis of administrative delays is whether the wait was, under the circumstances, unreasonable or "extraordinary." This inquiry may comprise many factors in addition to the length of the delay, such as the complexity of the application, whether the plaintiff failed to take actions that might have shortened the processing time,[145] and especially whether the government acted in bad faith.[146] But extraordinariness, hence a taking, is almost never found, and never as yet in a Section 404 case. To date, the CFC and Federal Circuit have held that waiting periods for individual permits up to two years did not, under the circumstances, work a taking.[147]

Teasing apart the delay attributable to the agency from that caused by the plaintiff can be pivotal to the case. In *Walcek v. United States*,[148] all but one year of an eight-year span between first permit application and permit issuance was laid at the feet of the wetland owners. Their applications, said the court, had lacked the requisite information and state permits, and they had opted for litigation over completing the application or submitting a scaled-down proposal. The one year of government-caused delay, it held, was not "extraordinary," particularly where no bad faith or negligence is shown.

A second delay scenario occurs when an agency's assertion of jurisdiction over a wetland, or its denial of a permit, is withdrawn or invalidated. In *Tabb Lakes, Inc. v. United States*,[149] the Corps issued a cease and desist order requiring a developer to stop subdivision work until it obtained a Section 404 permit, but was judicially informed three years later that its claim of jurisdiction was procedurally defective. No taking, said the Federal Circuit. The cease and desist order had specifically left the door open to development by obtaining a permit. Invoking a powerful principle for government regulators, the court further noted that "mere fluctuations in value during . . . government decisionmaking, absent extraordinary delay, . . . cannot be considered a taking."[150]

A final scenario found in the cases arises when delays are caused by the wetlands delineation or re-delineation process. In one case, a plaintiff claimed a temporary taking where a fully designed subdivision had to be substantially reworked when the Corps enlarged the designated wetlands acreage on a parcel as a result of going from the 1987 to 1989 delineation manuals, allegedly causing a seven-year delay.[151]

A potent source for confusion is the role played in the temporary taking analysis by the presence or absence of economic use *during* the restricted period. In making temporary taking determinations, the CFC has focused on first, whether there has been extraordinary delay, and second, whether the government's actions temporarily deprived the owner of all or substantially all economic use.[152] It is unclear whether this second factor means that even in the delay or cease and desist order case, where the government action by its very nature is likely to be temporary, a deprivation of substantially all economic use during the restricted period can, of itself, support a temporary taking. In *Tabb Lakes*, involving such a Corps cease and desist order, the trial court in the resulting temporary-taking litigation homed in on the existence of tax returns showing profitability during the period when the order was in effect to deny the taking claim.[153]

A recent Supreme Court ruling suggests that as long as there remains a reasonable probability that the delay will end in the foreseeable future, the availability of economic use during the permit-processing period, cease and desist order, or the like, is not determinative. Viewed in its temporal sense, said the Court, the "parcel as a whole" in this circumstance must include the post-delay period when use and value return.[154]

VII. Parcel as a Whole

A plaintiff's tract often consists of wetlands and developable uplands combined, making the "parcel as a whole" determination a ubiquitous one in the wetlands takings cases. The issue can make or break the plaintiff's case.[155] Applying the general rule against segmenting a parcel based on the differing regulatory status of each portion, courts historically have rejected takings claims when the wetland owner could not show that economic use of the unrestricted (nonwetland) portion of the property was infeasible. Conversely, a narrow delineation of the "parcel as a whole," drawn tightly around the restricted wetlands, makes more likely that a taking will be found. The "total taking" rule of *Lucas* buttresses this point. Deeming the wetland portion alone to be the relevant parcel increases the chances that the court will find complete loss of economic use and value—a *Lucas* "total taking"—as a result of the permit denial.[156]

The Supreme Court has shed little light on how to define the relevant parcel in the many complex circumstances that arise with land ownership. As a result, at various times wetland owners have argued that acreage should be excluded from the relevant parcel because, among other things, it was noncontiguous with the regulated tract, subdivided as different lots, owned by a different (though related) entity, owned by plaintiff in different form (e.g., legal title versus equitable title), in a different zoning or tax assessment status, acquired at a different time through a different transaction, or sold off before some relevant date.

The CFC and Federal Circuit have been in the forefront on parcel-as-a-whole issues. An early wetlands decision of a Federal Circuit predecessor court, after asserting that contiguous uplands had to be included in the relevant parcel, reasoned that the relevant parcel also included sections of the original purchase that had been developed and sold off prior to the permit denial.[157] In *Loveladies Harbor,* by contrast, the Claims Court opted for a narrow definition, refusing to factor in three portions of the developer's original 250-acre purchase: the lots it had developed and sold off by the date of the alleged taking (193 acres); acreage that it had agreed to preserve in return for receiving necessary permits (38.5 acres); and developed but not yet sold upland lots that were not contiguous with the land for which the permit was denied (six acres).[158]

On appeal, the Federal Circuit in *Loveladies Harbor* rejected arguments for bright-line rules governing the parcel-as-a-whole issue, concluding that "a flexible approach, designed to account for factual nuances" better served the constitutional inquiry.[159] These nuances, it said, include the timing of property transfers, leading it to affirm the Claims Court's view that in this case, land "developed *or* sold before the regulatory environment existed" should not be included in the "parcel as a whole."[160] The 193 acres had been sold, and the six upland acres at least developed, before the "regulatory environment" of Clean Water Act Section 404 was enacted in 1972. More recently, the Circuit in *Palm Beach Isles Assocs. v. United States*[161] stressed that the fact that land was sold off before a regulatory regime was in place is one, but not the only, factor in determining whether it should be included in the relevant parcel. After acknowledging that the Rivers and Harbors Act that led to the permit denials had been in place when the acreage was sold off, the court found offsetting factors, discussed below, that counseled against inclusion.

How the developer itself treated the acreage in question has proved a key factor in fixing the relevant parcel. In *Ciampitti v. United States*,[162] the CFC lumped a developer's wetland with a nearby—but noncontiguous—upland it owned that was "inextricably linked in terms of purchase and financing" with the wetland.[163] Similarly, in *Forest Properties, Inc. v. United States*,[164] the Federal Circuit found that the developer had treated its combined lake bottom and upland parcel as a single income-producing unit for purposes of financing, planning, and development. It could not now segregate the wetland portion, said the court, for purposes of its taking claim.[165] Conversely, the Circuit in *Palm Beach Isles* was influenced by the fact that even though jointly purchased, the adjacent parcels had never been viewed by the investors as for a single development, and, in fact, the development of one section had been "physically and temporally remote from" development of the other.[166] For this and other reasons, the relevant parcel was deemed to include only the wetlands/submerged lands portion.

Other decisions of these two courts have differed over whether individual subdivision lots in common ownership should be considered together for takings purposes. The more extended analyses, dealing with cases where the lots were purchased together and sought to be developed together under a single permit, have strongly rejected separate consideration.[167]

As a final point, it should be noted that how a court formulates its relevant parcel doctrine may affect whether individuals arrange their land transactions so as to put themselves in the best position for bringing a taking action, should the occasion arise. This is the "strategic behavior" issue. For example, the developer might sell the nonwetland portion of its property before applying to fill in the wetland—then, if a permit is denied, claim a severe percentage loss in value as to the wetland. Several decisions of the CFC and Federal Circuit indicate, implicitly or explicitly, sensitivity to the strategic behavior implications of their relevant parcel analyses.[168]

VIII. Federal–State Issues

It often happens that both the Corps and a state or local agency are regulatorily involved at the same wetland site. The presence of multiple governments raises several issues for the takings analysis.

First, there are issues of liability attribution. Who, for example, should pay for a taking when permission to fill or drain the wetland is denied by *both* authorities? Clearly, courts must be alert to the temptation for each level of government to shift takings liability to another.[169] The courts' task is not made easier by the fact that owing to jurisdictional rules, it is usually not possible to join both federal and state/local takings defendants in the same court.

The federal liability issue is unclear, if the court reaches it at all, when the Corps's denial of a Section 404 permit is based solely on prior state denials.[170] On the one hand, the Corps seemingly must deny the permit under the Clean Water Act demand that the applicant first obtain state water-quality and other certifications[171] and the Coastal Zone Management Act precondition that the state find the project consistent with its federally approved coastal zone plan.[172] (The administrative reality is somewhat different.[173]) On the other hand, the action of the United States in enacting these state-approval prerequisites was plainly a voluntary one. In the only case to address this circumstance on the merits, the court rejected the Corps's argument that the compulsoriness of the permit denial creates a per se defense to federal takings liability.[174] Quite appropriately, a state is held to bear no taking liability for a Corps Section 404 permit denial where the state's denial of water quality certification is not the cause in fact of the Corps action.[175] The implication that state liability might exist otherwise is tantalizing, however.

Could the fact that the state restriction is imposed under a delegated Section 404 program be a sufficient basis to impute taking liability to the Corps? The question remains unanswered.[176] To be sure, a state that assumes delegation of the federal wetlands program does so voluntarily, suggesting that takings liability would not transfer to the United States. Liability transfer may occur notwithstanding if the court finds the delegated state to be acting as an agent of the United States, under federal authority, and with federal assistance.[177]

Finally, there is the issue of sequential regulation—for example, when a county bans development of a wetland under an agricultural zoning ordinance, then the Corps denies a Section 404 permit for the same parcel. Is the Corps liable even though development was previously prohibited? Dictum in one case says no, pointing out that denial of the Section 404 permit "would not appear to have taken anything of value . . . , as no residential development of the property was permissible at the time of the alleged taking."[178]

A second federal–state issue blurs into the attribution question, but focuses on land value. It asks whether a prior restriction imposed by another government can be invoked by the government accused of a taking in an effort to lower the wetland parcel's "before value." In this situation, the CFC has held that where a local development ban was only remotely linked to Clean Water Act requirements, the reduced value of plaintiff's land under that ban is appropriately used in evaluating the taking claim based on the Corps's later permit denial.[179]

IX. Conclusion

Wetlands-takings cases fully reflect the general characterization of takings law as ad hoc, case-by-case, and fact-intensive. In the majority of cases, the need for factual development requires extensive discovery on both sides before arguments based on *Lucas* or the *Penn Central* factors can be crafted.[180] Thus, wetlands-takings litigation, as takings litigation generally, remains time-consuming and expensive to all parties. The CFC and Department of Justice have long been involved in alternative dispute resolution efforts to reduce these burdens.[181] The Corps of Engineers, for its part, claims to administer the Section 404 program so as to minimize burdens on private wetland owners.[182]

Ultimately, one bumps up against the conflicting philosophical strands as to the nature of property rights in an age of heightened environmental awareness. Many commentators have noted the implicit adoption in *Lucas* of the land-as-economic-potential view of property and argued that the inexorable dictates of ecology may compel adjustments in this notion.[183] If the courts are to go down this path, however, they should do so in a way that minimizes disruption of legitimate wetland owner expectations. In the meantime, the significant economic impact of at least some Section 404 permit delays, permit denials, condition proffers, and enforcement actions ensures that takings litigation as a result of federal wetlands regulation will be with us for some time.

Notes

1. Seventy-four percent of the jurisdictional wetlands in the contiguous forty-eight are privately owned. U.S. FISH AND WILDLIFE SERVICE, WETLANDS: MEETING THE PRESIDENT'S CHALLENGE 19 (1990).

2. *See generally* U.S. General Accounting Office, Clean Water Act: Private Property Takings Claims as a Result of the Section 404 Program (RCED-93-176FS 1993).

3. U.S. Const. amend. V: "[N]or shall private property be taken for public use, without just compensation."

4. Examples include the "Swampbuster" program, 16 U.S.C. §§ 3821–3823 (2000); Wetlands Reserve Program, 16 U.S.C. §§ 3837 *et seq.;* and Partners for Wildlife program (authorized only by appropriation acts). These programs are discussed in Chapter 14.

5. The name of the Court of Federal Claims has changed over time. Citations in this chapter refer to the court's name at the time the decision under discussion was rendered. Prior to 1982, the tribunal was named the U.S. Court of Claims (cited as "Ct. Cl."), and combined trial and appellate divisions. In 1982, Congress split these functions, transferring the trial duties to a U.S. Claims Court (cited as "Cl. Ct.") and vesting appellate responsibilities in a U.S. Court of Appeals for the Federal Circuit. Finally, in 1992, Congress changed the name of the Claims Court, this time with no changes in its jurisdiction, to U.S. Court of Federal Claims (cited as "Fed. Cl.").

6. 28 U.S.C. § 1491(a)(1). The district courts have concurrent jurisdiction with the CFC over such claims against the United States for amounts not exceeding $10,000. 28 U.S.C. § 1346(a)(2) ("Little Tucker Act").

7. 28 U.S.C. § 1295(a)(3). The Federal Circuit also has exclusive jurisdiction over appeals from actions heard in the district courts under 28 U.S.C. § 1346(a)(2).

8. 430 F.2d 199 (5th Cir. 1970), *cert. denied,* 401 U.S. 910 (1971). *Zabel* arose from the precursor of the 404 program, Section 10 of the Rivers and Harbors Act of 1899 (33 U.S.C. § 403), which remains in effect.

9. 430 F.2d at 215.

10. The leading decisions of the period are Deltona Corp. v. United States, 657 F.2d 1184 (Ct. Cl. 1981), *cert. denied,* 455 U.S. 1017 (1982), and Jentgen v. United States, 657 F.2d 1210 (Ct. Cl. 1981), *cert. denied,* 455 U.S. 1017 (1982).

11. *See, e.g., Jentgen,* 657 F.2d at 1213 ("the Corps did offer plaintiff the necessary permits to develop over 20 acres of the 80 acres covered by his applications, . . . [and] the tract contains approximately 20 additional acres of developable uplands which can be developed without first obtaining Corps permits").

12. 1902 Atlantic Ltd. v. Hudson, 574 F. Supp. 1381 (E.D. Va. 1983) (dictum).

13. 791 F.2d 893 (Fed. Cir. 1986), *cert. denied,* 479 U.S. 1053 (1987).

14. 15 Cl. Ct. 381 (1988).

15. *Loveladies Harbor,* 21 Cl. Ct. 153 (1990); *Florida Rock,* 21 Cl. Ct. 161 (1990).

16. 28 F.3d 1171 (Fed. Cir. 1994).

17. 18 F.3d 1560 (Fed. Cir. 1994), *cert. denied,* 513 U.S. 1109 (1995).

18. 45 Fed. Cl. 21 (1999).

19. *See, e.g.,* Walcek v. United States, 303 F.3d 1349 (Fed. Cir. 2002); Forest Properties, Inc. v. United States, 177 F.3d 1360 (Fed. Cir.), *cert. denied,* 528 U.S. 951 (1999); Heck v. United States, 134 F.3d 1468 (Fed. Cir. 1998); Bayou des Familles v.

United States, 130 F.3d 1034 (Fed. Cir. 1997); Beekwilder v. United States, 55 Fed. Cl. 54 (2002); Pax Christi Memorial Gardens, Inc. v. United States, 52 Fed. Cl. 318 (2002); City National Bank v. United States, 33 Fed. Cl. 759 (1995).

20. *See* David Coursen, *The Takings Jurisprudence of the Court of Federal Claims and Federal Circuit,* 29 ENVTL. L. 821, 830 (2000).

21. The only recorded effort in the 404 case law to prove a *physical* taking is in Formanek v. United States, 26 Cl. Ct. 332, 334 n.5 (1992). There, the court gave short shrift to a wetland owner's argument that such a taking was effected by repeated unconsented entries by a Corps ecologist to photograph rare plants and take samples. Such minimal invasions, it held, were at most trespass.

22. 260 U.S. 393 (1922).

23. *Id.* at 415.

24. 438 U.S. 104 (1978).

25. United States v. Dow, 357 U.S. 17, 20–21 (1958). The Supreme Court appeared to relax this rule in the regulatory takings context in Palazzolo v. Rhode Island, 533 U.S. 606, 628 (2001).

26. *See* Abbott Laboratories v. Gardner, 387 U.S. 136 (1967).

27. MacDonald, Sommer & Frates v. Yolo County, 477 U.S. 340, 348 (1986).

28. 473 U.S. 172, 191 (1985).

29. Or, as the Court phrased it a year later, "a final and authoritative determination of the type and intensity of development legally permitted on the subject property." *MacDonald,* 477 U.S. at 348.

30. *Id.* at 353 n.9.

31. The Supreme Court's most recent discussion of the "final decision" component of its takings/ripeness test is in Palazzolo v. Rhode Island, 533 U.S. 606 (2001).

32. *Id.* at 620.

33. *MacDonald,* 477 U.S. at 350 n.7.

34. 505 U.S. 1003 (1992). Other per se takings criteria, such as the "permanent physical occupation" and "essential nexus/rough proportionality" rules, have been pivotal in hundreds of cases outside the federal wetlands/takings area.

35. The pertinent description by the Court, indicating that application of the *Lucas* rule requires complete elimination of *value* as well as complete elimination of economic *use,* came in dicta in Tahoe-Sierra Preservation Council, Inc. v. Tahoe Regional Planning Agency, 535 U.S. 302, 320, 330, 332 (2002). The property rights bar had long argued that the *Lucas* rule required only the latter. Notwithstanding the *Tahoe-Sierra* clarification, most lower courts continue to mention only complete elimination of economic use when describing *Lucas.* As a practical matter, of course, loss of use and loss of value tend to go hand in hand, though they are not identical.

36. 505 U.S. at 1029.

37. *Tahoe-Sierra,* 535 U.S. 302.

38. 438 U.S. 104 (1978). Doubts as to the continuing vitality of the *Penn Central* test recently were laid to rest by the Supreme Court. In both *Palazzolo* and

Tahoe-Sierra, the Court rejected per se *Lucas* takings claims in favor of using *Penn Central* balancing.

39. *Id.* at 124.

40. Supreme Court takings decisions continue to cite early Court rulings in which government-caused losses in property value of 92.5 and 75 percent provoked no constitutional objection. *See,* most recently, Concrete Pipe & Products, Inc. v. Construction Laborers Pension Trust, 508 U.S. 602, 645 (1993). *See also Tahoe-Sierra,* 535 U.S. at 322 n.17 (suggesting that regulatory takings occur when restrictions are "so severe that they are tantamount to a condemnation or appropriation.").

41. Ruckelshaus v. Monsanto Co., 467 U.S. 986 (1984).

42. Palazzolo v. Rhode Island, 533 U.S. 606, 626–30 (2001); *Tahoe-Sierra,* 535 U.S. at 336 (dicta quoting Justice O'Connor's concurrence in *Palazzolo*).

43. Agins v. City of Tiburon, 497 U.S. 255, 261 (1980).

44. *See Tahoe-Sierra,* 535 U.S. at 341.

45. *See, e.g.,* Tahoe-Sierra, 535 U.S. at 327, 331–32; Keystone Bituminous Coal Ass'n v. DeBenedictis, 480 U.S. 470, 497 (1987).

46. *Penn Central,* 438 U.S. at 130–31.

47. *Tahoe-Sierra,* 535 U.S. at 331–32.

48. *Keystone,* 480 U.S. at 497 (quoting Andrus v. Allard, 444 U.S. 51, 65–66 (1979)).

49. *Tahoe-Sierra,* 535 U.S. at 331–32.

50. 474 U.S. 121, 126–27 (1985). *See* Robbins v. United States, 40 Fed. Cl. 381, 385, 387 (claim that wetland delineation was itself a taking is ripe without permit application, but under *Riverside Bayview* cannot succeed on merits), *aff'd without opinion,* 178 F.3d 1310 (Fed. Cir. 1998), *cert. denied,* 527 U.S. 1038 (1999).

51. Tabb Lakes, Ltd. v. United States, 10 F.3d 796, 801 (Fed. Cir. 1993).

52. 33 C.F.R. § 320.4(j)(1) (denials without prejudice).

53. 37 Fed. Cl. 245 (1997).

54. 33 Fed. Cl. 224 (1995).

55. 37 Fed. Cl. at 249 (brackets in original). *But see* Marks v. United States, 34 Fed. Cl. 387 (1995) (ripeness exists where denial without prejudice was based on state's refusal to issue water quality certificate, since at the time state did not require certification), *aff'd without opinion,* 116 F.3d 1496 (Fed. Cir. 1997), *cert. denied,* 522 U.S. 1075 (1998).

56. 37 Fed. Cl. at 250. *Accord,* Pax Christi Memorial Gardens, Inc. v. United States, 52 Fed. Cl. 318 (2002) (Corps's withdrawal of permit application, based solely on applicant's failure to submit requested information, did not ripen taking claim).

57. 33 Fed. Cl. at 228.

58. *Id.*

59. Cooley v. United States, 46 Fed. Cl. 538 (2000), *aff'd in relevant part and remanded on other grounds,* 324 F.3d 1297 (Fed. Cir. 2003); Cristina Inv. Corp. v. United States, 40 Fed. Cl. 571 (1998); City Nat'l Bank v. United States, 30 Fed. Cl. 715 (1994); Formanek v. United States, 18 Cl. Ct. 785 (1989); Beure-Co. v. United

States, 16 Cl. Ct. 42 (1988); Loveladies Harbor, Inc. v. United States, 15 Cl. Ct. 381 (1988).

60. *See, e.g.*, Plantation Landing Resort, Inc. v. United States, 30 Fed. Cl. 63, 66 (1993), *aff'd without opinion*, 39 F.3d 197 (Fed. Cir. 1994).

61. In *Plantation Landing Resort*, the court said it could not view a Corps permit denial as a taking when the denial was the result of plaintiff's failure to reach agreement with the Corps on mitigation requirements. 30 Fed. Cl. at 69. Though the decision was not couched in the language of ripeness, it nonetheless highlights the duty of the wetland owner to pursue reasonable negotiations as to permit conditions before claiming a taking. *See also Pax Christi*, 52 Fed. Cl. 318.

62. MacDonald, Sommer & Frates v. Yolo County, 477 U.S. 340, 348 (1986).

63. *See, e.g.*, Walcek v. United States, 49 Fed. Cl. 248 (2001), *aff'd*, 303 F.3d 1349 (Fed. Cir. 2002).

64. 324 F.3d 1297 (Fed. Cir. 2003).

65. *Florida Rock*, 791 F.2d at 905.

66. 2000 WL 331830 (Fed. Cl. Mar. 28, 2000) (unpublished). In 2001, the case was settled, the United States purchasing the entire 1,560-acre parcel in fee simple for $21 million.

67. 18 Cl. Ct. 42 (1988).

68. Cooley v. United States, 46 Fed. Cl. 538, 545 and n.6 (2000), *aff'd in relevant part and remanded on other grounds*, 324 F.3d 1297 (Fed. Cir. 2003).

69. 33 C.F.R. pt. 331 (2004).

70. 33 C.F.R. § 331.12 (2004).

71. *See, e.g.*, Cristina Inv. Corp. v. United States, 40 Fed. Cl. 571 (1998).

72. Once a permit applicant pursues an administrative appeal, however, a takings challenge to the Corps's permit decision will not be ripe until the agency resolves the appeal. *See* Bay-Houston Towing Co. v. United States, 58 Fed. Cl. 462, 471 (2003).

73. *Supra* note 59.

74. Heck v. United States, 37 Fed. Cl. 245, 252 (1997), *aff'd*, 134 F.3d 1468 (Fed. Cir. 1998); *see* Beekwilder v. United States, 55 Fed. Cl. 54 (2002).

75. *Heck*, 37 Fed. Cl. at 252.

76. *Id.*

77. *Heck*, 134 F.3d at 1472. *Accord*, Pax Christi Memorial Gardens, Inc. v. United States, 52 Fed. Cl. 318, 325 (2002).

78. *See, e.g.*, Hage v. United States, 35 Fed. Cl. 147, 164 (1996).

79. Robbins v. United States, 40 Fed. Cl. 381, *aff'd without opinion*, 178 F.3d 1310 (Fed. Cir. 1998), *cert. denied*, 527 U.S. 1038 (1999); Lakewood Assocs. v. United States, 45 Fed. Cl. 320 (1999).

80. Broadwater Farms Joint Venture v. United States, 121 F.3d 727 (Fed. Cir. 1997) (table entry).

81. Good v. United States, 189 F.3d 1355 (Fed. Cir. 1999), *cert. denied*, 529 U.S. 1053 (2000).

82. In Beekwilder v. United States, 55 Fed. Cl. 54, 61–62 (2002), plaintiff argued that his taking claim was ripe, even though he had not applied for a per-

mit, because any permit issued by the Corps would require mitigation that cost more than the plaintiff's property was worth. The CFC rejected this argument, concluding that "Plaintiff's failure to submit a proposal or seek a permit prevents the Corps from determining the amount or type of mitigation necessary . . . [and] makes plaintiff's assertion that the costs of mitigation will substantially exceed the value of the subject property problematic at best." *Id.* at 62.

83. *See* Nollan v. California Coastal Comm'n, 483 U.S. 825 (1987); Dolan v. City of Tigard, 512 U.S. 374 (1994). Guidance as to the scope of the *Dolan* exactions test (and by implication the *Nollan* test as well) was provided in City of Monterey v. Del Monte Dunes, 526 U.S. 687, 702–03 (1999).

84. 505 U.S. at 1029.

85. The burden of proof is on the government. Bowles v. United States, 31 Fed. Cl. 37, 45 (1994).

86. *See, e.g.,* Miller v. Schoene, 276 U.S. 272 (1928); Mugler v. Kansas, 123 U.S. 623 (1887).

87. Florida Rock Indus. v. United States, 21 Cl. Ct. 161, 166–67 (1990), *vacated on other grounds,* 18 F.3d 1560 (Fed. Cir. 1994), *cert. denied,* 513 U.S. 1109 (1995). The text proposition was reiterated on remand. 45 Fed. Cl. 21, 30 (1999). *Accord,* Lucas v. South Carolina Coastal Council, 505 U.S. 1003, 1031 (1992) (lack of common law prohibition ordinarily implied by fact that other landowners, similarly situated, are permitted to continue use denied to claimant).

88. *Florida Rock,* 21 Cl. Ct. at 167. The text proposition was reiterated on remand. 45 Fed. Cl. 21, 29–30 (1999).

89. Loveladies Harbor, Inc. v. United States, 28 F.3d 1171, 1182, 1183 (Fed. Cir. 1994).

90. *Florida Rock,* 21 Cl. Ct. at 166.

91. Formanek v. United States, 26 Cl. Ct. 332, 340 (1992). *Formanek* was decided a month before *Lucas.*

92. Bowles v. United States, 31 Fed. Cl. 37, 51–52 (1994); Loveladies Harbor, Inc. v. United States, 15 Cl. Ct. 381, 389 (1988), *aff'd,* 28 F.3d 1171 (Fed. Cir. 1994) (emphasizing on appeal the wetlands filling, rather than the ultimate use of the filled wetland for housing). The Supreme Court was *slightly* more qualified in its assertion that the building of homes is not a common-law nuisance, saying that such was "unlikely." *Lucas,* 505 U.S. at 1031.

93. 505 U.S. at 1029. *See also id.* at 1030–31 (general discussion of nuisance).

94. The chief articulation of the state common law of nuisance view is in the plurality opinion in Preseault v. United States, 100 F.3d 1525 (Fed. Cir. 1996) (en banc), a rails-to-trails case. A Federal Circuit opinion endorsing this view in a wetlands/taking case is Bayou des Familles Dev. Corp. v. United States, 130 F.3d 1034, 1038 (Fed. Cir. 1997). *But see* M & J Coal Co. v. United States, 47 F.3d 1148, 1153 (Fed. Cir.) (background principles "may also stem from federal law"), *cert. denied,* 516 U.S. 808 (1995).

95. *See, e.g.,* City of Virginia Beach v. Bell, 498 S.E.2d 414, 418 (Va.), *cert. denied,* 525 U.S. 826 (1998).

96. Palazzolo v. Rhode Island, 533 U.S. 606, 626–30 (2001).

97. *Id.* at 629–30.

98. 56 Wis. 2d 7, 201 N.W.2d 761 (1972).

99. 580 S.E.2d 116 (S.C. 2003).

100. Esplanade Properties, LLC v. City of Seattle, 307 F.3d 978 (9th Cir. 2002), *cert. denied,* 539 U.S. 926 (2003).

101. *Id.* at 986, 987.

102. Kaiser Aetna v. United States, 444 U.S. 164 (1979).

103. 208 F.3d 1374, 1384 (Fed. Cir.), *aff'd on rehearing,* 231 F.3d 1354 (2000).

104. The conclusion that the federal navigation servitude is a background principle is compelled by the *Lucas* decision itself, which includes a federal navigation servitude case in its discussion of the background principles concept. 505 U.S. at 1028–29. *See also* United States v. 30.54 Acres of Land, 90 F.3d 790, 795 (3d Cir. 1996).

105. It is irrelevant that nonnavigational purposes are served by the government action as well. *See, e.g.,* United States v. Twin City Power, 350 U.S. 222, 224 (1956), *quoted with approval in Palm Beach Isles,* 208 F.3d at 1385.

106. *See, e.g.,* Del Rio Drilling Programs, Inc. v. United States, 146 F.3d 1358 (Fed. Cir. 1998) (clarifying that not all unlawful government actions constitute "unauthorized acts" for purposes of the rule).

107. 531 U.S. 159 (2001).

108. See, however, Laguna Gatuna, Inc. v. United States, 50 Fed. Cl. 336 (2001), in which owing to *Solid Waste Agency,* EPA abandoned its claim of jurisdiction as to a playa lake under Clean Water Act Section 402 (the National Pollutant Discharge Elimination System permit program). The agency's unauthorized acts defense to the taking claim was rejected. Among other reasons, the court explained that EPA's withdrawal of jurisdiction came too late in that for nine years under EPA's cease and desist order the tract was without economic use.

109. Florida Rock Indus. v. United States, 18 F.3d 1560, 1567 (Fed. Cir. 1994), *cert. denied,* 513 U.S. 1109 (1995); Bowles v. United States, 31 Fed. Cl. 37, 46 (1994).

110. *Supra* note 40.

111. Loveladies Harbor, Inc. v. United States, 28 F.3d 1171 (Fed. Cir. 1994) (99 percent value loss); *Florida Rock,* 21 Cl. Ct. 161 (1990) (95 percent value loss), *vacated and remanded,* 18 F.3d 1560 (Fed. Cir. 1994) (holding that trial court used improperly low "after value," but not disputing that such value warranted finding a taking), *cert. denied,* 513 U.S. 1109 (1995); Bowles v. United States, 31 Fed. Cl. 37 (1994) (finding 100 percent value loss, but holding that even if government estimate of 92 percent value loss was correct, there was taking); and Formanek v. United States, 26 Cl. Ct. 332 (1992) (88 percent value loss).

112. 18 F.3d at 1567.

113. 45 Fed. Cl. 21 (1999).

114. Walcek v. United States, 49 Fed. Cl. 248, 271 and 271 n.37 (2001), *aff'd,* 303 F.3d 1349 (Fed. Cir. 2003).

115. The United States has acquired less-than-fee interests as part of *settlements* in its regulatory takings litigation.

116. Forest Properties, Inc. v. United States, 177 F.3d 1360 (Fed. Cir.), *cert. denied,* 528 U.S. 951 (1999).

117. Ciampitti v. United States, 22 Cl. Ct. 310, 320 n.5 (1991).

118. Florida Rock Indus. v. United States, 791 F.2d 893, 905 (Fed. Cir. 1986), *cert. denied,* 479 U.S. 1053 (1987). The most extended discussion of this factor is in *Walcek,* 49 Fed. Cl. at 266–67. Where, as often happens, many years (or decades) pass between property acquisition and permit denial, allowing for substantial appreciation in property value, this factor obviously will favor the government.

119. *Walcek,* 49 Fed. Cl. at 266. *But see* Good v. United States, 39 Fed. Cl. 81 (1997) (suggesting that postpurchase expenses may not figure into cost basis when made against a backdrop of increasingly stringent regulation), *aff'd,* 189 F.3d 1355 (Fed. Cir. 1999), *cert. denied,* 529 U.S. 1053 (2000).

120. Walcek v. United States, 303 F.3d 1349, 1357 (Fed. Cir. 2002). Thus, Florida Rock Indus. v. United States, 45 Fed. Cl. 21, 38 (1999), holding that cost basis should be adjusted for inflation, is no longer good law.

121. *Florida Rock,* 45 Fed. Cl. at 37.

122. Penn Central Transp. Co. v. New York City, 438 U.S. 104, 137 (1978).

123. Suitum v. Tahoe Regional Planning Agency, 520 U.S. 725 (1997) (appearing to assume relevance of TDRs to takings determination, though expressly declining to reach question).

124. *Good,* 39 Fed. Cl. at 108.

125. Compensatory mitigation requirements and mitigation banking are discussed in detail in Chapter 8.

126. The Corps, EPA, and several other federal agencies have established guidelines for the establishment, use, and operation of mitigation banks. *See* 60 Fed. Reg. 58,605 (Nov. 28, 1995).

127. *See, e.g.,* William J. Haynes II and Royal Gardner, *The Value of Wetlands as Wetlands: The Case for Mitigation Banking,* 23 ENVTL. L. REP. 10,261 (1993).

128. Loveladies Harbor, Inc. v. United States, 21 Cl. Ct. 153, 158 (1990) (emphasis in original), *aff'd,* 28 F.3d 1171 (Fed. Cir. 1994).

129. 21 Cl. Ct. at 159.

130. Florida Rock Indus. v. United States, 791 F.2d 893, 901–03 (Fed. Cir. 1986), *cert. denied,* 479 U.S. 1053 (1987). The development pressure on Florida Rock's tract, located as it was at the outer fringe of greater Miami's expansion, heavily influenced the court to highlight the role of speculators hoping for a less restrictive future.

131. Florida Rock Indus. v. United States, 18 F.3d 1560, 1567 (1994) (emphasis in original), *cert. denied,* 513 U.S. 1109 (1995).

132. 45 Fed. Cl. 21 (1999).

133. See cases collected at Glenn Sugameli, Lucas v. South Carolina Coastal Council: *The Categorical and Other "Exceptions" to Liability for Fifth Amendment Takings of Private Property Far Outweigh the "Rule,"* 29 ENVTL. L. 939, 972–84 (1999).

134. 28 F.3d at 1177. *Accord,* Creppel v. United States, 41 F.3d 627, 632 (Fed. Cir. 1994); Good v. United States, 189 F.3d 1355, 1360 (Fed. Cir. 1999), *cert. denied,* 529 U.S. 1053 (2000).

135. *See, e.g.*, Broadwater Farms Joint Venture v. United States, 45 Fed. Cl. 154, 156 (1999); Forest Properties, Inc. v. United States, 39 Fed. Cl. 56, 77 (1977), *aff'd*, 177 F.3d 1360 (Fed. Cir.), *cert. denied*, 528 U.S. 951 (1999). The takings plaintiff faces a particularly high hurdle when he or she expressly acknowledged at time of acquisition that the necessary permits might be difficult to obtain. *Good*, 189 F.3d at 1357, 1362.

136. *See, e.g.*, *Broadwater Farms*, 45 Fed. Cl. at 156.

137. *Good*, 189 F.3d at 1361 ("Reasonable investment-backed expectations are an element of every regulatory takings case.").

138. *Supra* note 42.

139. 270 F.3d 1347 (Fed. Cir. 2001) (on denial of petition for rehearing), *petition for cert. filed*, 70 U.S.L.W. 3518 (Feb. 4, 2002).

140. 189 F.3d 1355.

141. Palm Beach Isles Assocs. v. United States, 231 F.3d 1354 (Fed. Cir. 2000). CFC decisions after *Palm Beach Isles* generally have adopted the view that expectations have no role in a *Lucas* claim, endorsing *Palm Beach Isles* over *Good*.

142. 392 F. Supp. 685 (D.D.C. 1975).

143. 42 Fed. Reg. 37,122 (1977).

144. *Good*, 189 F.3d at 1362–63.

145. See the extended discussion in Wyatt v. United States, 271 F.3d 1090 (Fed. Cir. 2001), *cert. denied*, 535 U.S. 1077 (2002), involving a delayed federal surface-mining permit.

146. The CFC has held that "courts are unlikely 'to find a taking based on extraordinary delay without a concomitant showing of bad faith.' " Bay-Houston Towing Co. v. United States, 58 Fed. Cl. 462, 476 (2003), citing Cooley v. United States, 324 F.3d 1297, 1307 (Fed. Cir. 2003).

147. 1902 Atlantic Ltd. v. United States, 26 Cl. Ct. 575, 579 (1992) (15 months); Dufau v. United States, 22 Cl. Ct. 156 (1990) (16 months); Lachney v. United States, 22 Envtl. Rep. Cas. 2031 (Fed. Cir. 1985) (2 years).

148. 44 Fed. Cl. 462 (1999), *later proceeding* 49 Fed. Cl. 248 (2001), *aff'd*, 303 F.3d 1349 (Fed. Cir. 2002).

149. 10 F.3d 796 (Fed. Cir. 1993).

150. *Id.* at 801, quoting Agins v. City of Tiburon, 447 U.S. 255, 263 n.9 (1980).

151. Norman v. United States, 38 Fed. Cl. 417, 426–28 (1997). Plaintiff's motion for dismissal of this temporary taking claim was granted May 21, 2002.

152. *See, e.g.*, Walcek v. United States, 44 Fed. Cl. 462, 467 (1999) (collecting cases), *aff'd*, 303 F.3d 1349 (Fed. Cir. 2003).

153. Tabb Lakes, Inc. v. United States, 26 Cl. Ct. 1334, 1345–52 (1992), *aff'd*, 10 F.3d 796 (Fed. Cir. 1993).

154. *Tahoe-Sierra*, 535 U.S. 302.

155. *See generally Walcek*, 49 Fed. Cl. 248, 258–59 (2001), *aff'd*, 303 F.3d 1349 (Fed. Cir. 2003).

156. In Tabb Lakes v. United States, 10 F.3d 796, 802 (Fed. Cir. 1993), the Federal Circuit refused to narrow the parcel as a whole to solely the wetlands portion of a tract, explaining that wetlands permit denials "would [then], *ipso*

facto, constitute a taking in every case." The court was incorrect, however, in asserting that a wetlands-only relevant parcel would *always* yield a taking. Most obviously, development of an economically viable portion of the wetland might be permitted. Also, some wetlands may be developed or put to other use without a discharge of dredged and fill material that triggers 404 jurisdiction. *See, e.g.,* National Mining Ass'n v. Corps of Engineers, 145 F.3d 1399 (D.C. 1998).

157. Deltona Corp. v. United States, 657 F.2d 1184, 1192 (Ct. Cl. 1981), *cert. denied,* 455 U.S. 1017 (1982).

158. 15 Cl. Ct. 381, 391–93 (1988). The six acres of uplands were valued at $2.4 million near the time of the taking, compared with the $300,000 paid by the developer for the entire 250-acre tract. These dollar figures make plain that the court's exclusion of this small fragment of the original tract was essential to its finding of a taking.

159. 28 F.3d at 1181. In *Ciampitti v. United States,* 22 Cl. Ct. 310, 318 (1991), the court stated that courts should consider factors such as "the degree of contiguity, the dates of acquisition, the extent to which the parcel has been treated as a single unit, the extent to which the protected lands enhance the value of remaining lands, and no doubt many others."

160. 28 F.3d at 1181.

161. 208 F.3d 1374 (Fed. Cir.), *aff'd on rehearing,* 231 F.3d 1354 (2000).

162. 22 Cl. Ct. 310 (1991).

163. *Id.* at 319.

164. 177 F.3d 1360, 1365 (Fed. Cir.), *cert. denied,* 528 U.S. 951 (1999).

165. *Accord,* Walcek v. United States, 49 Fed. Cl. 248, 258–61 (2001) (reviewing parcel-as-a-whole decisions of CFC and Federal Circuit), *aff'd,* 303 F.3d 1349 (Fed. Cir. 2003).

166. 208 F.3d at 1381.

167. Broadwater Farms Joint Venture v. United States, 121 F.3d 727 (Fed. Cir. 1997); Tabb Lakes, Inc. v. United States, 10 F.3d 796 (Fed. Cir. 1993). *Cf.* Bowles v. United States, 31 Fed. Cl. 37, 41 n.4 (1994) (evaluating taking claim based on denial of Section 404 permit for one subdivision lot without considering plaintiff's ownership of ten adjacent lots obtained at same time).

168. The United States pressed strategic behavior concerns in *Loveladies Harbor,* 28 F.3d 1171, 1181 (Fed. Cir. 1994). The court may have found merit in them, since the court's adopted view—that the development or sale of land before the regulatory environment existed is a factor cutting against inclusion in the relevant parcel—could act to minimize strategic behavior. Later wetlands/takings decisions noting strategic behavior concerns include Forest Properties, Inc. v. United States, 39 Fed. Cl. 56 (1997), *aff'd,* 177 F.3d 1360 (Fed. Cir.), *cert. denied,* 528 U.S. 951 (1999). *But see* Palm Beach Isles Assocs. v. United States, 208 F.3d 1374 (Fed. Cir.) (excluding sold-off nonwetland portion of property from relevant parcel, even though one of the two governing statutes was in effect when portion was sold), *aff'd on rehearing,* 231 F.3d 1354 (2000).

169. The temptation to shift liability may also prompt a state not to impose the restriction in the first place. This may be the explanation for the facts in

Michigan Peat v. EPA, 175 F.3d 422 (6th Cir. 1999), where a delegated state (Michigan) initially offered the Section 404 permit applicant a very limited permit designed to satisfy federal EPA concerns. When the applicant filed a taking action against the state, it issued a state-only permit with fewer constraints, in effect notifying the wetland owner that any further quarrel it had was with the Corps, not the state.

170. Recall from Section IV.C that the absence of required state approvals also may play out as a threshold ripeness issue.

171. Clean Water Act § 401(a); 33 U.S.C. § 1341(a).

172. Coastal Zone Management Act § 307(c)(3)(A); 16 U.S.C. § 1456(c)(3)(A).

173. An issue of longstanding concern to the states is that if a state denies an approval under these statutes, the Corps does not necessarily consider the state's action sufficient cause to deny the Section 404 permit. *See* Claudia Copeland, *Nationwide Permits for Wetlands Projects,* Cong. Res. Serv. Rept. No. 97-223 ENR, at 13 (1999). This fact could undercut a "we had no choice" defense to a taking action against the Corps.

174. Ciampitti v. United States, 18 Cl. Ct. 548, 555–56 (1989). The court's ruling was despite the fact that Corps permit denials based on nonreceipt of state approvals are without prejudice. Where a required state permit has been denied, it would seem difficult for the taking claim based on a later federal permit denial to meet a "but for" causation test. *See* Bowles v. United States, 31 Fed. Cl. 37, 49 (1994) (burden of takings plaintiff is to show that "but for" the federal government's action, plaintiff would have been able to realize its plans).

175. Ventures Northwest Limited Partnership v. State of Washington, 81 Wash. App. 353, 914 P.2d 1180 (1996).

176. The CFC has indicated awareness of the issue, however. City National Bank of Miami v. United States, 33 Fed. Cl. 759, 763, 763 n.4 (1995).

177. *Compare* Hendler v. United States, 952 F.2d 1364, 1378–79 (Fed. Cir. 1991) (state activities under federal superfund program attributable, for takings purposes, to the United States, since the state acts as an agent of the United States) *with* B&G Enterprises v. United States, 220 F.3d 1318 (Fed. Cir. 2000) (state activities under federal substance-abuse grants program not attributable, for takings purposes, to the United States, since no agency relationship exists).

178. Lakewood Assocs. v. United States, 45 Fed. Cl. 320, 339 n.12 (1999).

179. City Nat'l Bank v. United States, 33 Fed. Cl. 759 (1995).

180. In contrast, petitions for review of federal agency action generally involve "record review," precluding the litigants and the court from going outside the formalized agency record on which the action was based.

181. The CFC instituted alternative dispute resolution (ADR) in 1987, with General Rule No. 13. In 2002, this rule was replaced by Appendix H of the newly revised Rules of the United States Court of Federal Claims (Title 28, U.S.C.).

In addition, the CFC now maintains a pilot ADR program. Second Amended General Order No. 40 (effective March 17, 2004). Under it, almost all the cases (including takings cases) assigned to four specified CFC judges are simultaneously assigned to one of four specified ADR judges. The goal is "to determine whether early meetings with a settlement judge will help parties reach a better understanding of their differences and their prospects for settlement." Notice of ADR Pilot Program and ADR Pilot Procedures. Both order and notice are at http://www.uscfc.uscourts.gov.

182. Federal Wetlands Policy: Protecting the Environment or Breaching Constitutional Rights?: Hearing before the House Comm. on Government Reform, 106th Cong. 164 (2000) (statement of Michael L. Davis, Deputy Ass't Sec'y for Policy and Legislation, Office of Civil Works, Dep't of the Army).

183. *See, e.g.*, Fred Bosselman, *Four Land Ethics: Order, Reform, Responsibility, Opportunity*, 24 ENVTL. L. 1439 (1994); Joseph L. Sax, *Property Rights and the Economy of Nature: Understanding* Lucas v. South Carolina Coastal Council, 45 STAN. L. REV. 1433 (1993).

CHAPTER 14

Agricultural Programs

DOUGLAS R. WILLIAMS

I. Introduction/Scope

The preceding chapters have described the centerpiece of federal wetlands regulation—the Clean Water Act's (CWA) Section 404 program. There are additional federal programs to protect the nation's wetlands. Several of these programs employ financial incentives, rather than prohibitions or permit-centered regulation, and are administered by the U.S. Department of Agriculture (USDA). Included among these programs are those established in Chapter 58 of Title 16 of the U.S. Code, many of which were first enacted in the Food Security Act of 1985. The "Swampbuster" program is perhaps the most prominent of these programs. This chapter describes these agricultural programs. Section II of the chapter describes general provisions governing agricultural programs affecting wetlands. Section III analyzes the Swampbuster program in detail. Section IV briefly describes an umbrella program known as the Comprehensive Conservation Enhancement Program and its component parts—the Wetlands Reserve Program, the Conservation Reserve Program, and the Environmental Quality Incentives Program.

II. General Provisions Governing Agricultural Programs

A. Wetlands Defined

With the Food Security Act of 1985, Congress provided considerably more detail in describing the natural resources it intended to protect than it had in Section 404 of the CWA.[1] The Act defines "wetland" as land that

- Has a predominance of hydric soils;
- Is inundated or saturated by surface or groundwater at a frequency and duration sufficient to support a prevalence of hydrophytic vegetation typically adapted for life in saturated soil conditions; and
- Under normal circumstances does support a prevalence of such vegetation.[2]

This definition is similar to the definition of wetlands that the United States Environmental Protection Agency (EPA) and the United States Army Corps of Engineers (Corps) have adopted under the CWA.[3] Under both sets of programs, the same criteria are employed to make wetland determinations: hydrophytic vegetation, hydric soil, and hydrology.[4] For agricultural programs, Congress provided statutory definitions for two of these criteria: "hydric soils"[5] and "hydrophytic vegetation."[6]

The Act also directs the Secretary of Agriculture to develop (1) criteria for identifying hydric soils and hydrophytic vegetation, and (2) lists of such soils and vegetation.[7] In the wake of amendments in 1996, USDA promulgated implementing regulations,[8] which are now codified at 7 C.F.R. Part 12. The term "hydric soils" is defined by language that tracks the statutory definition, as is the term "hydrophytic vegetation."[9] Lists of hydric soils and hydrophytic vegetation are identified by regulation.[10] Local offices of the Natural Resources Conservation Service (NRCS), an agency of USDA, are required to maintain official hydric soil maps.[11]

Not all wetlands are treated the same under the various agricultural programs. USDA regulations classify wetlands by, *inter alia*, specific hydrologic criteria.[12] The significance of this wetland classification scheme is most prominent in the Swampbuster program, which is discussed below.

B. Wetland Determinations

NRCS is responsible for making wetland determinations[13] and delineations[14] on agricultural lands for purposes of the Swampbuster program.[15] These decisions are to be made in accordance with the National Food Security Act Manual (NFSAM),[16] which provides further details on the statutory criteria for wetlands.[17]

The procedures employed by the NRCS are specified at 7 C.F.R. §§ 12.6(c) and 12.30(c). Persons may obtain a wetland determination from

NRCS by written request.[18] NRCS's determinations may be appealed in accordance with procedures codified at 7 C.F.R. Part 614.[19]

The Act also authorizes NRCS to certify previous wetland determinations.[20] The effect of certification is that the wetland determination "remain[s] valid and in effect as long as the area is devoted to an agricultural use or until such time as the person affected by the certification requests review of the certification by" NRCS.[21] USDA regulations provide that "[a]ll wetland determinations made after July 3, 1996, will be done on a tract basis and will be considered certified wetland determinations."[22]

III. Swampbuster

Subtitle B of the Food Security Act, commonly known as Swampbuster, was designed "to discourage the draining and cultivation of wetland that is unsuitable for agricultural production in its natural state."[23] This program conditions eligibility for certain USDA program benefits—such as price support payments and guaranteed loans—on the observance of wetland conservation measures. The Swampbuster program, unlike the Section 404 program, is not "regulatory." The conservation measures are not enforced through permit requirements or civil or criminal remedies. Instead, Swampbuster deploys financial incentives—i.e., eligibility for USDA program benefits—to encourage agricultural producers to observe wetland conservation practices. In brief, persons otherwise eligible for USDA program benefits may become ineligible by engaging in practices that adversely affect wetland functions and values.

A. Activities for Which Persons May Become Ineligible for USDA Program Benefits

When it was initially enacted in 1985, Swampbuster denied USDA benefits to "any person who in any crop year produces an agricultural commodity on converted wetland."[24] Ineligibility for such benefits was limited to the crop year in which agricultural commodities were produced on converted wetlands.[25] In 1990, Congress concluded that this limited basis for denying USDA benefits did not sufficiently discourage inappropriate agricultural uses of valuable wetlands.[26] Accordingly, Congress extended ineligibility to "any person who in any crop year beginning after [November 28, 1990], converts a wetland by draining, dredging, filling, leveling, or any other means for the purpose, or to have the effect, of making the production of an agricultural commodity possible on such converted wetland."[27] Persons engaging in such activities are ineligible for benefits "for that crop year and all subsequent crop years."[28]

The current version of Swampbuster thus identifies two general activities that may render a person ineligible for USDA benefits: (1) the production of an agricultural commodity on converted wetlands, and (2) the conversion of wetlands for the purpose of producing an agricultural commodity or to have the effect of making such production possible.[29]

The terms "agricultural commodity" and "converted wetland," both of which are used by the statute to describe prohibited activities, are defined in the statute. "Agricultural commodities" include only those commodities that are "planted and produced in a State by annual tilling of the soil, including tilling by one-trip planters" and sugarcane.[30] This definition does not include perennial crops or hay, which do not require annual tilling. Accordingly, these crops may be planted without a loss in program benefits,[31] unless in the process of doing so a person "converts" a wetland.

"Converted wetland" is defined as wetland manipulated "for the purpose or to have the effect of making the production of an agricultural commodity possible if . . . such production would not have been possible but for such action."[32] This definition does not include wetland conversions for purposes other than agricultural production and that do not have the effect of making such production possible. USDA regulations provide the following examples of wetland manipulations that will not be considered conversions under Swampbuster: actions undertaken "for fish production, trees, vineyards, shrubs, cranberries, agricultural waste management structures, livestock ponds, fire control, or building and road construction."[33] Those activities may, of course, disrupt or impair wetland functions and values. If the activities involve discharges of dredged or fill material, a Section 404 permit may be required.[34]

B. Graduated Sanctions

As a result of amendments in 1996,[35] a person who engages in the prohibited activities does not necessarily become ineligible for all specified program benefits. Benefits are reduced in "an amount determined by the Secretary [of Agriculture] to be proportionate to the severity of the violation."[36]

USDA regulations set forth a number of factors to be considered by the Farm Service Agency (FSA) in determining an appropriate reduction in program benefits. These factors include

> the information that was available to the affected person prior to the violation, previous land use patterns, the existence of previous wetland violations under [Swampbuster] or under other federal, State, or local wetland provisions, the wetland functions

> and values affected, the recovery time for full mitigation of the wetland functions and values, and the impact that a reduction in payments [of benefits] would have on the person's ability to repay a USDA farm loan.[37]

C. Duration of Sanctions

As noted above, Congress amended Swampbuster in 1990 to provide that any person who converts a wetland for agricultural use after the date of the amendments is ineligible for certain USDA program benefits during the crop year in which the conversion occurred and for "all subsequent crop years."[38]

However, in the 1996 amendments, Congress expanded the use of mitigation techniques to provide farmers with additional flexibility in meeting Swampbuster's requirements. The Act now provides opportunities for persons to use converted wetlands for agricultural production without loss of benefits, provided they adequately mitigate for the loss of wetland functions and values. To qualify, the mitigation must

- Be in accordance with a plan approved by NRCS;
- Be "in advance of, or concurrent with . . . the production of an agricultural commodity";
- Not be at the expense of the federal government;
- Be on lands in the same general area of the local watershed as the converted wetlands;
- Include the grant of an easement to USDA that meets certain requirements; and
- Provide functions and values equivalent to those that will be lost in the conversion.[39]

The 1996 amendments also provide:

> Any person who is determined to be ineligible for program benefits . . . for any crop year shall not be ineligible for such program benefits . . . for any subsequent crop year if, prior to the beginning of such subsequent crop year, the person has fully restored the characteristics of the converted wetland to its prior wetland state or has otherwise adequately mitigated for the loss of wetland values.[40]

USDA's implementing regulations generally track the statute, providing that a person who converts wetland to agricultural production remains ineligible "until the converted wetland is restored or the loss of wetland functions and values have *[sic]* been mitigated."[41]

USDA regulations also provide a more limited basis for regaining eligibility lost as a result of a wetland conversion occurring after November 28, 1990. A person may regain eligibility if, in addition to undertaking a mitigation plan, USDA "determines that the person has acted in good faith and without the intent to violate" the wetland provisions of the Act.[42] This provision for limiting the duration of sanctions is discussed in greater detail below.

D. Exemptions

Swampbuster's general prohibitions against converting wetlands and producing agricultural commodities on converted wetland are subject to an extensive list of exemptions.[43] USDA's regulations place on the person seeking an exemption the burden of producing evidence showing the claimed exemption is applicable.[44]

1. *General Exemptions*

a. Exemptions Based on Wetland Classification

The original Swampbuster provisions included a general exemption for agricultural production on wetland converted before December 23, 1985, the date on which the Food Security Act was enacted.[45] The exemption did not, however, apply to all wetlands that may have been manipulated and used for agricultural purposes at some time in the past. Under prior USDA regulations, wetlands converted before December 23, 1985, could be maintained and used for agricultural production only if such actions "do not bring additional wetland into the production of an agricultural commodity."[46] "Additional wetland" was defined as "any natural wetland or any converted wetland that has reverted to wetland as the result of abandonment of crop production."[47] Converted wetland was deemed "abandoned" when cropping, management, or maintenance of the acreage ceased, "unless it is shown that there was no intent to abandon."[48] A prior converted wetland was also considered abandoned if there had been no crop production on the wetland for five successive years and the land exhibited specific wetland criteria.[49] The effect of the abandonment policy was to make the general exemption for prior converted wetland dependent upon active and continued management of the converted wetland to ensure that wetland characteristics do not become re-established over long periods of time.

USDA regulations also subjected incompletely converted wetlands to Swampbuster's restrictions. The regulations' basic policy was to ensure that USDA benefits are withheld from those who alter wetlands in ways that adversely affect any wetland functions that may have existed when Swampbuster first became law.[50] Thus, to avoid ineligibility for agricultural production on previously manipulated wetland, a person must either ensure that prior manipulation completely eliminated wetland characteristics (and that such characteristics have not returned for significant periods) or that any agricultural use of the land does not alter existing wetland functions and values.

In *Gunn v. Department of Agriculture,* the Court of Appeals for the Eighth Circuit endorsed this policy.[51] The court upheld the USDA's decision to deny program benefits to a person who, in 1992, installed new drainage tiles and dug a ditch to facilitate drainage of a wetland site that, many years before 1985, had been manipulated to produce agricultural commodities. The effect of the more recent manipulations was to eliminate wetland characteristics that prior manipulations had not disturbed. The court agreed with USDA that the 1992 manipulations constituted a prohibited "conversion" that was commenced after December 23, 1985, and accordingly, held that the landowner was ineligible for USDA program benefits. The court stated:

> [Under agency regulations,] land is either wetland or converted wetland. If significant wetland characteristics remain, the land remains wetland and cannot be converted wetland. If the [pre-1985] drainage or other manipulation has been sufficient to make crops producible, as is the case here, the land is best described as "farmed wetland." . . . "Farmed wetland" can continue to be farmed without the loss of benefits, but only so long as . . . wetland characteristics are [not] further degraded in a significant way. In the present case, . . . the 1992 improvements [to the drainage system] have done exactly that. They were designed to and have in fact further degraded the wetland characteristics of the farm. It follows that part of the farm is "converted wetland," but that it did not become converted wetland until 1992.[52]

The 1996 amendments and USDA's implementing regulations altered this approach. The regulations now include an explicit classification of wetlands and associated exemptions. The wetland types are (1) wetland, (2) artificial wetland, (3) commenced conversion wetland, (4) converted wetland, (5) farmed wetland, (6) farmed-wetland pasture, and (7) prior converted cropland.[53]

Four general exemptions are tied to the wetland classifications. The exemptions are (1) an exemption for prior converted cropland, (2) an exemption for some prior converted cropland that currently exhibits wetland characteristics, (3) a conditional exemption for farmed wetland and farmed-wetland pasture, and (4) a general exemption for artificial wetlands.

Prior Converted Cropland. The 1996 amendments retain the general exemption for wetland converted before December 23, 1985.[54] Under USDA's regulations, this exemption is available for "prior converted cropland"[55] and "commenced conversion wetland."[56] The exemption for commenced conversion wetland is discussed later in this chapter. Prior converted cropland is converted wetland that, as of December 23, 1985, "did not support woody vegetation and met [specified] hydrologic criteria."[57] In general terms, this exemption applies to areas that were once wetlands but no longer exhibit wetland characteristics sufficient to be classified as "wetlands." Activities altering prior converted cropland will not affect eligibility for USDA benefits.

Prior Converted Cropland Exhibiting Wetland Characteristics. The 1996 amendments added an exemption for the production of an agricultural commodity on a converted wetland, or the conversion of wetland,

> if the original conversion of the wetland was commenced before December 23, 1985, and the Secretary determines the wetland characteristics returned after that date as a result of—
> (i) the lack of maintenance of drainage, dikes, levees, or similar structures;
> (ii) a lack of management of the lands containing the wetland; or
> (iii) circumstances beyond the control of the person.[58]

USDA regulations interpret this exemption to be available only for "prior converted cropland."[59] Even so limited, the exemption effectively overrides the prior abandonment policy. As noted, under the abandonment policy, previously converted wetlands could be subject to Swampbuster's restrictions if wetland characteristics returned to the site after December 23, 1985, and the person seeking benefits intentionally abandoned the site or failed to produce crops on the site for five consecutive years. The 1996 amendments, in effect, have made the status of "prior converted cropland" permanent, regardless of what happens at the site in the years after December 23, 1985.[60] The only exception to this general rule involves prior converted cropland that is intentionally allowed to return to wetland status as part of a mitigation plan or for purposes of other wetland protection programs. Thus, as a practical matter, once lands are certified as prior converted cropland, they are always regarded as prior converted cropland and remain exempt from Swampbuster's prohibitions.[61]

Farmed Wetland and Farmed-Wetland Pasture. The 1996 amendments also permit the production of an agricultural commodity on converted wetland or the conversion of wetland, if

- The converted wetland was voluntarily restored to wetland conditions;
- NRCS has adequately documented conditions at the site before and after the restoration;
- NRCS approved the proposed conversion prior to implementation; and
- The conversion is limited so that the post-conversion conditions at the site will retain wetland functions and values that are at least equivalent to those that existed prior to the voluntary restoration.[62]

Under USDA regulations, this exemption is available for "farmed wetland" and "farmed-wetland pasture."[63] These categories of wetland are defined in USDA regulations and are essentially wetlands that have been manipulated prior to December 23, 1985, but not in ways that completely eliminated all wetland functions and values as of that date.[64] Under the exemption, then, limited agricultural activities on these wetlands may be conducted, but only if the activities do not diminish the wetland characteristics that existed on December 23, 1985.[65]

Unlike the exemption for prior converted cropland, a site's classification as either farmed wetland or farmed-wetland pasture is not permanent. The abandonment policy continues to apply to these classes of wetland. Thus, "cessation for five consecutive years of management or maintenance operations related to the use of a farmed wetland or a farmed-wetland pasture" will be considered an abandonment.[66] If, after this period, the site meets the criteria of a wetland, it will be reclassified as a "wetland" and any production of an agricultural commodity on, or a conversion of, such land may result in a determination of ineligibility.[67]

Artificial Wetlands. Artificial wetlands are generally exempt from Swampbuster's protections.[68] USDA regulations define an artificial wetland as "an area that was formerly non-wetland, but now meets wetland criteria due to human activities."[69] Conversion of these wetlands does not affect a person's eligibility for USDA program benefits. Relatedly, the regulations exempt: (1) "A wet area created by a water delivery system, irrigation, irrigation system, or application of water for irrigation"; and (2) "A nontidal drainage or irrigation ditch excavated in non-wetland."[70]

Documenting the human activities that led to the creation of wetland can be very important for purposes of this exemption. Under USDA regulations, persons seeking the protection of the exemption for artificial wetland, or any other exemption, bear the "responsibility . . . to provide evidence, such as receipts, crop-history data, drawings, plans or similar information, for purposes of determining whether the conversion or other action is exempt."[71] In *Downer v. United States,* the Court of Appeals for the Eighth Circuit interpreted this regulation to assign the burden of proof on persons seeking an exemption.[72] The court held that Downer's failure to present any evidence indicating that, prior to conversion, the wetland was artificial, rendered him ineligible for an exemption.[73]

b. Other General Exemptions

Conversions That Do Not Make Agricultural Production Possible. USDA regulations exempt wetland conversions that do not make the production of an agricultural commodity possible.[74] This exemption reemphasizes the limited definition of "converted wetland," which is discussed above.

Exemption for Actions with Minimal Effects. The Act and USDA's regulations provide a general exemption for otherwise prohibited actions if those actions, "individually and in connection with all other similar actions authorized by NRCS in the area, would have only a minimal effect on the wetland functions and values of wetlands in the area."[75] USDA may exempt such actions in three ways. First, USDA is authorized to promulgate regulations that identify "categorical minimal effect exemptions on a regional basis."[76] The responsibility for these categorical minimal effect regulations has been delegated to NRCS,[77] although to date no regulations have been promulgated.[78]

Second, USDA regulations provide a procedure through which state conservationists may recommend to NRCS that particular categories of conversion activities be included on lists of categorical minimal effect exemptions. These lists are to be maintained by NRCS and made available to interested persons upon request.[79]

Finally, USDA may make minimal effects determinations on a case-by-case basis.[80] USDA regulations state that "such determination shall be based on a functional assessment of functions and values of the wetland under consideration and other related wetlands in the area, and will be made through an on-site evaluation."[81]

The agency will consider mitigation plans when determining whether a proposed action qualifies for a minimal effect exemption. Thus, a person seeking to convert a wetland may "buy down" adverse effects through mitigation to obtain an exemption. The applicable regulation states: "In situations where the wetland functions and values are replaced by the restoration, enhancement or creation of a wetland in accordance with a mitigation plan approved by NRCS, the exemption provided by the [minimal effects] determination will be effective after NRCS determines that all practices in a mitigation plan are being implemented."[82]

Exemptions for Mitigation Required by Section 404 Permits. Activities in wetlands authorized by a Section 404 permit that requires adequate mitigation are exempt from Swampbuster.[83] The exemption is available for activities authorized either by individual Section 404 permits[84] or by nationwide or regional general permits.[85] The adequacy of any mitigation undertaken in connection with these permits is to be determined by NRCS and based on whether the mitigation has replaced lost wetland functions and values.[86]

Exemption for Wetlands Converted by Third Persons. The final general exemption in USDA's regulations governs wetlands "converted by actions of persons other than the person applying for USDA program benefits or any of the person's predecessors in interest after December 23, 1985, if such conversion was not the result of a scheme or device to avoid compliance with [USDA regulations.]"[87] The regulations presume that the person applying for benefits is responsible for any converted wetlands. Accordingly, to obtain this exemption, a person must show that the conversion was caused by a third party and that the person seeking an exemption was not associated with the third party through a "scheme or device."[88]

The exemption does not apply to persons who claim that a conversion was due to actions of a water resource district, drainage district, or similar entity, unless the actions of such an entity were beyond the control of the person seeking benefits. Additionally, the person seeking benefits must refrain from producing agricultural commodities or forage crops on the converted wetland, or mitigate the loss in wetland functions and values caused by the conversion.[89] Persons seeking this exemption bear the burden of demonstrating that a drainage district's activities should not be attributed to them.[90]

2. *Exemption for Commenced Conversion Wetlands*

Wetland conversions started before December 23, 1985, or conversions for which funds had been obligated prior to that date are exempt from

Swampbuster.[91] For the most part, this exemption will no longer figure prominently in the administration of Swampbuster. Pursuant to USDA's regulations, the exemption was limited to conversions for which FSA had received a request for an exemption by September 19, 1988.[92] Moreover, conversions that were determined to have commenced prior to December 23, 1985, lost their exempt status if the conversion was not completed on or before January 1, 1995.[93]

3. Exemption for Wetlands Farmed under Natural Conditions

The Act provides an exemption for persons who, on wetlands, "use[] normal cropping or ranching practices to produce an agricultural commodity in a manner that is consistent for the area where the production is possible as a result of a natural condition, such as drought, and is without action by the producer that destroys a natural wetland characteristic."[94] USDA regulations are substantially similar to the statutory text.[95]

4. Mitigation Exemption

The 1996 amendments added to Swampbuster an exemption for wetland conversions or the production of an agricultural commodity on converted wetlands if the person engaging in the otherwise disqualifying activity adequately mitigates the loss of wetland functions and values.[96] This exemption may also be used to regain eligibility by persons who were deemed ineligible for benefits because they plant agricultural commodities on wetland converted between the passage of the original Act in 1985 and the passage of the 1990 amendments.[97] The mitigation must meet several requirements[98] and any restored, enhanced, or created wetland must be made subject to an easement granted to USDA that is recorded in public land records and provides that the owner will maintain restored, created, or enhanced wetland for as long as the converted wetland remains in agricultural use or is not returned to its original wetland state.[99]

5. Good-Faith Exemption

In administering Swampbuster, USDA made provision for a good-faith exemption under the general authority provided by 7 U.S.C. § 1339a and implementing regulations. The regulation provided that "performance rendered in good faith in reliance upon action or advice of" certain authorized representatives "may be accepted . . . as meeting the requirements of the applicable program . . . to the extent it is deemed desirable . . . to provide fair and equitable treatment."[100] The application of this "good faith" exemption to Swampbuster was challenged by conservation organizations in *National Wildlife Federation v. Agricultural Stabilization and Conservation Service.*[101] Although the district court held that the exemption applied, the court of appeals reversed and remanded the matter to USDA for reconsideration in light of legislative amendments.[102] The "good faith reliance" exemption is now explicitly applicable to Swampbuster under USDA regulations.[103]

Related exemptions are provided to persons who "tak[e] an action in reliance on a previous certified wetland determination by NRCS" or "in reliance on an incorrect technical determination by NRCS as to the status of" the land on which the action is taken.[104] In the latter case, the exemption is not available if "the person knew or reasonably should have known that the determination was in error because the characteristics of the site were such that the person should have been aware that a wetland existed on the subject land, or for other reasons."[105]

In addition, the 1990 amendments included a good-faith exemption, which was again amended in 1996.[106] FSA may waive ineligibility if it finds "the person acted in good faith and without intent to violate" the Act and "NRCS determines that the person within an agreed to period, not to exceed 1 year, is implementing all practices in a mitigation plan."[107]

E. Ineligibility Determinations

A determination of whether a person is or is not entitled to program benefits is triggered by that person's submission of an application for benefits.[108] The process of making an ineligibility determination primarily involves two USDA agencies: the NRCS and the Farm Service Agency (FSA).

The NRCS's responsibilities, in general, involve the technical wetland determinations that govern the Swampbuster program.[109] In particular, NRCS is responsible for determining whether any portions of an applicant's land are subject to Swampbuster restrictions. This involves (1) a "wetlands determination,"[110]—that is, determining whether any of the agricultural lands involved in an application for benefits are wetlands, and if so, what type of wetland; and (2) a "wetlands delineation,"[111] that is, determining the specific boundaries of any wetlands that are present.

NRCS is also responsible for, *inter alia,* providing technical information to FSA regarding the seriousness of a Swampbuster violation,[112] determining whether otherwise prohibited activities will have only a minimal effect on wetlands functions and values,[113] and approving mitigation plans and monitoring their implementation.[114]

The FSA's responsibilities include determining whether any exemptions may be applicable in particular cases.[115] Ordinarily, it is the FSA that determines whether applicants are eligible for program benefits or to what extent those benefits should be reduced because of the applicant's activities in wetlands.[116] The 2002 Farm Bill amended Swampbuster to provide that the Secretary of Agriculture may not delegate to any private person or entity the authority to determine whether any person has complied with Swampbuster's provisions.[117] The FSA's county committees are also responsible for hearing appeals from NRCS determinations taken by adversely affected program participants.[118]

F. Relationship between Swampbuster and Section 404

1. *Wetland Determinations*

As noted above, NRCS is responsible for making wetland determinations and delineating the boundaries of wetlands for Swampbuster purposes.[119] By a memorandum of agreement (MOA) among USDA's Soil Conservation Service (now the NRCS), EPA, the Corps, and the Fish and Wildlife Service, NRCS's wetland delineations on "agricultural lands" will be accepted by EPA and the Corps for purposes of Section 404 of the CWA.[120] "Agricultural lands" are defined in the MOA as "those lands intensively used and managed for the production of food or fiber to the extent that the natural vegetation has been removed and cannot be used to determine whether the area meets applicable hydrophytic vegetation criteria in making a wetland determination."[121]

Although the narrow definition of agricultural lands provides limited delineation authority to NRCS, the MOA additionally provides for NRCS wetland delineations on other lands of interest to USDA program participants. Specifically, the MOA states that "EPA and the Corps will accept [NRCS] wetland delineations on non-agricultural lands that are either narrow bands immediately adjacent to, or small pockets interspersed among, agricultural lands."[122] Furthermore, NRCS is given authority to delineate wetlands on lands owned or operated by a USDA program participant who requests a wetland delineation and to delineate "other waters for the purposes of Section 404 . . . , such as lakes, ponds, and streams . . . on lands on which [NRCS] is otherwise engaged in wetland delineations pursuant to [the terms of the MOA.]"[123] In both of these cases, however, the NRCS must consult with the Corps, EPA, and/or the Fish and Wildlife Service, as appropriate.[124]

In the MOA, EPA and the Corps have reserved authority to make wetland delineations in "special cases."[125] These special cases may involve wetland delineations within a discrete political or geographic area in which the relevant resource agencies have been unable to resolve particular issues.[126] The Corps has issued a regulatory guidance letter that requires Corps jurisdictional letters and delineations to include a disclaimer indicating that the delineation of jurisdiction under the CWA may not be valid for the Swampbuster program.[127] Accordingly, USDA program participants are advised to obtain an NRCS delineation to ensure compliance with Swampbuster.

2. *Prior Converted Cropland*

EPA and Corps regulations now exclude prior converted cropland from the regulatory definition of "waters of the United States" and, thus, from Section 404 jurisdiction. The regulation provides: "Waters of the United States do not include prior converted cropland. Notwithstanding the determination of an area's status as prior converted cropland by any other Federal agency, for the purposes of the Clean Water Act, the final authority regarding Clean Water Act jurisdiction remains with EPA."[128]

Subsequent developments may affect the status of prior converted cropland under the CWA in two ways. First, since the regulation was promulgated, USDA, EPA, the Corps, and the Fish and Wildlife Service entered into the MOA, discussed above. Thus, while it remains correct that EPA retains final authority to determine Clean Water jurisdiction, the agencies have agreed that NRCS wetland delineations on agricultural lands will be accepted for CWA purposes.

Second, at the time this regulation was promulgated, USDA regulations contained the "abandonment" policy discussed above. In amending the definition of "waters of the United States" to exclude prior converted cropland, EPA and the Corps expressed their intention to employ USDA's abandonment policy.[129] But, as discussed above, that policy no longer applies to prior converted cropland. Nonetheless, EPA and the Corps likely will continue to regulate discharges of dredged or fill material into "abandoned" prior converted cropland under Section 404, even though such areas are no longer subject to Swampbuster's restrictions. The exclusion of prior converted cropland was based on prior Corps guidance that concluded that prior converted croplands do not, under "normal circumstances," exhibit sufficient wetland characteristics to meet EPA's and the Corps's regulatory definition of wetlands.[130] The Corps and EPA will likely consider "abandoned" prior converted cropland that currently meets wetland criteria to exhibit the requisite characteristics under "normal circumstances." This conclusion mirrors the

Corps's treatment of "farmed wetlands," which may in some circumstances be exempt from Swampbuster. If activities on such wetlands involve discharges of dredged or fill material, the Corps regards those activities as subject to Section 404's requirements.[131]

3. *Regulated Activities*

Many activities that will not render a person ineligible for USDA benefits under Swampbuster may be subject to regulation under Section 404. For example, wetland conversions that may qualify for one or more of Swampbuster's exemptions may nonetheless require a Section 404 permit[132]—e.g., wetland conversions for purposes other than agricultural production.[133] The CWA's exemption for "normal farming" may be invoked in some circumstances where an exemption from Swampbuster is also available.[134] In particular, activities qualifying for Swampbuster's exemption for wetlands farmed under natural conditions will likely be considered "normal farming" for purposes of the CWA exemption.

Some activities that are exempt from Swampbuster and involve discharges of dredged or fill material may qualify for a general or nationwide permit (NWP) under the Corps's Section 404 program.[135] In such circumstances, the activity may proceed without an individual permit from the Corps. The specific activities that are authorized by Corps NWPs are varied; the NWPs and any conditions associated with them should be carefully considered before commencing any activity.

IV. Comprehensive Conservation Enhancement Program

In addition to Swampbuster, the Food Security Act of 1985, as amended, includes three programs that have further protected the nation's wetlands: the Wetlands Reserve Program, the Conservation Reserve Program, and the Environmental Quality Incentives Program. These programs fall under an umbrella program entitled the Comprehensive Conservation Enhancement Program (CCEP).[136] Generally, these programs offer financial incentives to farmers to refrain from or reduce activities that adversely affect environmental values, or to implement measures to protect environmental values.

The CCEP authorizes USDA to employ a variety of financial incentives to the agricultural community to promote conservation practices. In particular, Congress directed USDA to implement CCEP "through contracts and the acquisition of easements to assist owners and operators of farms and ranches to conserve and enhance soil, water, and related natural resources, including grazing land, wetland, and wildlife habitat."[137] In the absence of special circumstances, land enrolled in the

Conservation Reserve Program and the Wetlands Reserve Program may not exceed 25 percent of the cropland in any county, nor may more than 10 percent of such cropland be subject to conservation easements acquired by USDA under these programs.[138]

The specific kinds of contracts, easements, and cost-sharing arrangements available under CCEP are detailed in the specific programs.

A. Wetlands Reserve Program

The Wetlands Reserve Program (WRP) authorizes USDA to purchase conservation easements from and enter into cost-sharing agreements with certain persons to restore and protect wetlands.[139] The WRP is administered by NRCS. USDA regulations provide the following general description of the program:

> Under the WRP, [USDA] will purchase conservation easements from, or enter into restoration cost-share agreements with, eligible landowners who voluntarily cooperate in the restoration and protection of wetlands and associated lands. To participate in WRP, a landowner will agree to the implementation of a Wetlands Reserve Plan of Operations (WRPO), the effect of which is to restore, protect, enhance, maintain, and manage the hydrologic conditions of inundation or saturation of the soil, native vegetation, and natural topography of eligible lands. [USDA] may provide cost-share assistance for the activities that promote the restoration, protection, enhancement, maintenance, and management of wetland functions and values. Specific restoration, protection, enhancement, maintenance, and management functions may be undertaken by the landowner or other [USDA] designee.[140]

1. *Eligible Lands*

To be eligible for enrollment in the WRP, land must meet certain requirements. The WRP primarily targets farmed wetlands that can likely be restored in a cost-effective manner, are capable of providing wildlife benefits and wetland values and functions, and would otherwise continue to be devoted to agricultural production.[141] These lands include

- Wetlands farmed under natural conditions;
- Farmed wetlands;
- Prior converted cropland;
- Farmed wetland pasture;
- Farmland that has become a wetland as a result of flooding;

- Rangeland, pasture, or production forestland where the hydrology has been significantly degraded and can be restored;
- Riparian areas that link protected wetlands;
- Lands adjacent to protected wetlands that contribute significantly to wetland functions and values; and
- Previously restored wetlands.[142]

Ineligible lands include

- Wetlands converted after December 23, 1985;
- Lands containing timber or trees under a Conservation Reserve Program contract (discussed below);
- Lands owned by an agency of the United States;
- Lands subject to an easement or deed restriction prohibiting agricultural production for a duration of thirty or more years; and
- Lands where restoration activities would be futile.[143]

The WRP is subject to a total acreage cap of 2,275,000 acres.[144] Additionally, the Act requires USDA, "to the maximum extent practicable," to enroll 250,000 acres per calendar year.[145] Acreage is to be enrolled "through the use of permanent easements, 30-year easements, restoration cost share agreements, or any combination of those options."[146] As of September 2004, there were 1,470,998 acres enrolled in the WRP.[147]

2. *Eligible Persons*

With certain exceptions, any person who has owned eligible land for at least the twelve months prior to the owner's declaration of intent to participate may enroll land in the WRP.[148] The owner must agree to provide information to USDA that the agency deems necessary to make an eligibility determination and to assure appropriate implementation.[149] The regulations define the term "person" to include "an individual, partnership, association, corporation, cooperative, estate or trust, or other business enterprise or other legal entity and, whenever applicable, a State, a political subdivision of a State, or any agency thereof."[150] Persons who do not comply with regulations implementing Swampbuster may be deemed ineligible for participation in the WRP.[151]

3. *Easements*

Land is enrolled in the WRP by the owner's granting of an easement to the United States. The duration of the easement may be permanent or for a term of thirty years or the maximum duration permitted under state law.[152] The easement must also include specific obligations and prohibitions on the owner granting the easement. Among these obligations, the easement must provide for the implementation of a Wetland Reserve Plan of Operations (WRPO).[153] The WRPO specifies the actions to be taken to restore and protect wetlands within the easement area and is to be developed through the NRCS, in consultation with other agencies.[154]

4. *Payments*

In return for the granting of the easement, owners receive payments reflecting the lesser of (1) a geographic rate established by state conservationists, (2) market value, and (3) the landowner offer.[155] Compensation for nonpermanent (thirty-year) easements may not be less than 50 percent nor more than 75 percent of the value of a permanent easement for the area.[156] Compensation is to be paid in not less than five nor more than thirty annual installments.[157] For nonpermanent easements, annual payments to any person are capped at $50,000.[158]

5. *Cost-Sharing Agreements*

In addition to compensation for granting an easement, landowners may qualify for USDA cost-sharing assistance in implementing the WRPO. The statute directs USDA to provide such cost-sharing assistance "to the extent that the [agency] determines that cost sharing is appropriate and in the public interest."[159] For permanent easements, such cost-share payments by USDA may not be less than 75 percent nor more than 100 percent of the costs; for non-permanent easements, such payments may not be less than 50 percent nor more than 74 percent of implementation costs.[160]

The statute also authorizes USDA to enroll land into the WRP without obtaining an easement through cost-share agreements with landowners who agree to restore wetlands on land.[161] Payments by USDA to landowners under such agreements may not be less than 50 percent nor more than 75 percent of the costs of restoration.[162]

6. *Application and Enrollment Process*

Landowners may apply to enroll land in the WRP by filing an application for participation during an announced enrollment period. By filing the application, the landowner consents to NRCS entering the property for the purposes of assessing wetland functions and values and developing a preliminary WRPO.[163]

NRCS makes enrollment decisions by "placing priority on the enrollment of those lands that will maximize wildlife values (especially related to enhancing habitat for migratory birds and other wildlife); have the least likelihood of re-conversion and loss of these wildlife values at the end of the WRP enrollment period; and that involve State, local, or other partnership matching funds and participation."[164] The general considerations NRCS uses to rank lands are

- Costs of restoration and easement acquisition;
- Availability of matching funds;
- Wetland functions and values;
- Likelihood of successful restoration; and
- Duration of the proposed easement.[165]

Upon notification that USDA has tentatively accepted an owner's land in the WRP, the owner has fifteen days to sign a letter of intent to continue. USDA is bound to enroll lands in the WRP for which it has extended tentative offers only after a contract has been executed by the government and the owner.[166]

7. *Modification, Violations, and Remedies*

Easements may be modified only by mutual agreement between the landowner and NRCS. Any such modification "must result in equal or greater environmental and economic values to the United States," and only so long as the modification does not "adversely affect the wetland functions and values for which the easement was acquired."[167]

A landowner who violates the terms of an easement or contract with USDA is liable for any costs incurred by NRCS in remedying the violation, including all administrative and legal costs. Upon discovery of such a violation, NRCS will notify the landowner and provide the owner thirty days as of the date of the notice to voluntarily correct the violation.[168]

B. Conservation Reserve Program

The Conservation Reserve Program (CRP) seeks to "cost-effectively assist[] producers in conserving and improving soil, water, and wildlife resources by converting highly erodible and other environmentally-sensitive acreage generally devoted to the production of agricultural commodities to a long-term vegetative cover."[169] Acting through the Commodity Credit Corporation (CCC) and FSA, USDA enters into contracts with eligible persons in which such persons agree to convert eligible land to a conserving use in accordance with an approved conservation plan and for a period of ten years, with certain exceptions.[170]

1. *Eligible Lands*

The CRP is aimed primarily at lands that are currently being used or have been used for agricultural purposes and upon which the continuation of such uses poses on-site or off-site environmental problems. Three broad categories are eligible:

- Cropland that is physically and legally capable of being used to produce an agricultural commodity and has been so used in two of the five most recent crop years;
- Marginal pasture land that meets certain criteria; and
- Acreage currently enrolled in the CRP.[171]

In addition, the land must be amenable to management that yields specific sorts of environmental benefits, such as wildlife habitat, reduction in erosion, and enhancement of water quality.[172] The regulations treat land "designated as a cropped wetland and appropriate associated acreage" as meeting the environmental criteria.[173] "Cropped wetlands" are defined as "farmed wetlands and wetlands farmed under natural conditions," as these terms are defined in USDA's Swampbuster regulations.[174]

The following lands are ineligible for enrollment in the CRP:

- Federally owned lands;
- Land on which the production of agricultural commodities is restricted by deed or other restrictions; and
- Land currently enrolled in the CRP unless the current contract will expire prior to the effective date of a new CRP contract.[175]

In addition, within the CRP is a "Farmable Wetlands Program."[176] To be eligible for enrollment under this program, the land must have been planted to an agricultural commodity for at least three of the past ten years and is a wetland, including a converted wetland, and/or buffer acreage that provides protection for and is contiguous to the wetland.[177] The size of eligible wetlands and buffers is limited and total enrollment in this program may not exceed one million acres.[178]

2. *Eligible Persons*

USDA may enter into contracts to enroll land in the CRP with owners, operators, or tenants of eligible land.[179] Absent special circumstances, owners must have owned the land for at least twelve months prior to the close of the signup period during which the land is sought to be enrolled. Likewise, operators must have operated the land for the same twelve-month prior period and additionally demonstrate that they will remain in control of the land for the full term of the CRP contract. Tenants are eligible to participate with an eligible owner or operator.[180]

3. *CRP Contracts and Obligations of Participants*

a. General Requirements

To enroll land in the CRP, participants must enter into a contract with CCC that includes the terms and conditions for participation, a conservation plan, and any other materials or agreements CCC determines to be necessary.[181] The participant is obligated to meet requirements set forth in USDA regulations, which include

- Implementing a conservation plan;
- Complying with Swampbuster requirements; and
- Not allowing grazing, harvesting, or other commercial use of crops from the enrolled land, unless approved by CCC.[182]

In return, CRP participants receive annual rental payments, not to exceed $50,000 per year, and may receive cost-share assistance to establish the practices in the conservation plan, subject to a limitation of 50 percent of the actual or average costs.[183] The regulations also provide for "[a]dditional financial incentives . . . to producers who offer contracts expected to provide especially high environmental benefits."[184]

b. Conservation Plan

Conservation plans are defined as "a record of the participant's decisions, and supporting information, for treatment of a unit of land or water, and includes a schedule of operations, activities, and estimated expenditures needed to solve identified natural resource problems by devoting eligible land to permanent vegetative cover, trees, water, or other comparable measures."[185] These plans are subject to review and approval by NRCS and an appropriate conservation district. In general, the practices in the plan must be cost-effective and achieve environmental benefits.[186]

4. *Enrollment Process*

The enrollment process for most eligible land is conducted in specified sign-up periods, which are announced periodically by USDA.[187] A continuous sign-up is available for special, high-priority conservation practices that produce significant environmental benefits. Qualifying persons may enroll land devoted to these high-priority purposes at any time. Currently, special practices qualifying for continuous sign-up are filter strips; riparian buffers; shelter belts, field windbreaks, and living snow fences; grass waterways; shallow water areas for wildlife; salt-tolerant vegetation; and certain practices in EPA-designated wellhead protection areas.[188] Persons initiate the enrollment process in specified sign-up periods and continuous sign-up by submitting bids to local FSA offices indicating the amount they are willing to accept as rental payments to enroll land in the CRP.[189]

USDA regulations provide that contract offers will be evaluated by employing "different factors, as determined by CCC [that] may be considered from time to time for priority purposes to accomplish the goals of the program."[190] Currently, USDA is employing an Environmental Benefits Index to evaluate, score, and rank contract proposals. The index assigns points to the practices included in a contract proposal based on a number of factors, including wildlife benefits, water quality benefits, erosion benefits, enduring benefits, air quality benefits, benefits to conservation priority areas, and cost.[191] USDA has added points to the index for wetland restoration.[192]

The total acreage that may be enrolled in the CRP is currently capped at 39.2 million acres.[193] As of September 2004, almost 35 million acres were enrolled in the CRP.[194]

5. *Termination and Modification of CRP Contracts*

CRP contracts may be terminated by USDA before their full term under certain conditions, including

- Ownership or control of enrolled land changes, and the new owner does not wish to continue the contract.
- The participant voluntarily requests termination in writing and CCC approves the termination.
- The participant fails to comply with contractual terms.
- The acreage is enrolled in another federal, state, or local conservation program.
- The conservation practices fail and the cost of restoring them exceeds environmental benefits.
- The contract was approved based on erroneous eligibility determinations.
- CCC determines that termination is in the public interest.[195]

In addition, for certain lands enrolled before January 1, 1995, participants may unilaterally terminate CRP contracts.[196] USDA regulations also authorize modifications to CRP contracts by mutual agreement between CCC and a participant, and in other specified circumstances.[197]

For land that is suitable for restoration to wetlands or was restored to wetlands under the terms of thc contract, CRP participants may elect to transfer such land to the Wetlands Reserve Program, subject to CCC approval.[198]

C. The Environmental Quality Incentives Program

The third program included within the Comprehensive Conservation Enhancement Program is the Environmental Quality Incentives Program (EQIP). EQIP consolidates in a single program the functions of a number of conservation programs that were repealed in 1996.[199] The purposes of EQIP are

> to promote agricultural production and environmental quality as compatible goals, and to optimize environmental benefits, by—
>
> (1) assisting producers in complying with local, State, and national regulatory requirements concerning—(A) soil, water, and air quality; (B) wildlife habitat; and (C) surface and groundwater conservation;
>
> (2) avoiding, to the maximum extent practicable, the need for resource and regulatory programs by assisting producers in protecting soil, water, air, and related natural resources and meeting environmental quality criteria established by Federal, State, tribal, and local agencies;
>
> (3) providing flexible assistance to producers to install and maintain conservation practices that enhance soil, water, related natural resources (including grazing land and wetland), and wildlife while sustaining production of food and fiber;
>
> (4) assisting producers to make beneficial, cost effective changes to cropping systems, grazing management, nutrient management associated with livestock, pest or irrigation management, or other practices on agricultural land; and
>
> (5) consolidating and streamlining conservation planning and regulatory compliance processes to reduce administrative burdens on producers and the cost of achieving environmental goals.[200]

Half of the funding for EQIP is targeted to persons who experience livestock-related environmental problems, such as waste management.[201] EQIP is jointly administered by NRCS, FSA, and CCC, with NRCS designated as the lead agency.[202]

EQIP authorizes USDA to enter into contracts with eligible persons in which USDA provides cost-share assistance and incentive payments to farmers and ranchers who agree to implement "land management practices" and "structural practices."[203] Land management practices are defined as "a site-specific nutrient or manure management, integrated pest management, irrigation management, tillage or residue management, grazing management, air quality management, or other land management practice carried out on eligible land that the [USDA] determines is needed to protect from degradation, in the most cost-effective manner, water, soil, or related resources."[204] A structural practice means "the establishment on eligible land of a site-specific animal waste management facility, terrace, grassed waterway, contour grass strip, filterstrip, tailwater pit, permanent wildlife habitat, or other structural practice that [USDA] determines is needed to protect, in the most cost-effective manner, water, soil, or related natural resources from degradation; and . . . the capping of abandoned wells on eligible land."[205] These practices are to be included in a conservation plan that is acceptable to NRCS.[206]

EQIP is currently being administered to support "locally-led conservation" in which state technical committees and local work groups advise NRCS on technical issues.[207] NRCS will allocate funds to state conservationists who will implement EQIP at the state and local level. NRCS allocations to state conservationists are based on national priorities,[208] which include (1) reduction of non–point source pollution and groundwater contamination, and conservation of ground and surface water resources; (2) reduction of emissions of air pollutants; (3) reduction in soil erosion and sedimentation, and (4) promotion of at-risk species habitat conservation.[209]

Applications for participation in EQIP are scored according to a ranking system developed by state conservationists. The criteria for this ranking system are

> (1) The degree of cost-effectiveness of the proposed conservation practices, (2) The magnitude of the environmental benefits resulting from the treatment of National priorities and the priority natural resource concerns reflecting the level of performance of a conservation practice, (3) Treatment of multiple resource concerns, (4) Use of conservation practices that provide environmental enhancements for a longer period of time, (5) Compliance with Federal, state, local or tribal regulatory requirements concerning soil, water and air quality; wildlife habitat; and ground and surface water conservation, and (6) Other locally defined pertinent factors, such as the location of the conservation practice, the extent of natural resource degradation, and the degree of cooperation by local producers to achieve environmental improvements.[210]

EQIP contracts must be for a duration of not less than one year after the completion of the last practice adopted and not more than ten years. The contract incorporates a conservation plan that details the specific management practice(s) that the participant will implement.[211] Participants receive cost-share assistance under these contracts that may not exceed 75 percent of the projected cost of establishing a structural practice unless the participant falls into a special category, in which case funding may be as much as 90 percent.[212] Participants may receive both cost-share assistance and incentive payments, subject to a total limitation of $450,000.[213]

V. Conclusion

The agricultural programs discussed in this chapter have made a significant contribution to the nation's efforts to preserve wetlands. Unlike the CWA Section 404 program, participation in these programs is voluntary and the use of financial incentives has induced significant levels of participation on the part of the agricultural community whose practices might otherwise contribute to the loss of valuable wetlands. The toolbox of financial incentives that these programs make available to USDA enables the agency to respond to and counter incentives that induce the agricultural community to conduct activities that threaten the integrity of wetlands.

Notes

1. Pub. L. No. 99-198, 99 Stat. 1507 (1985). One year later, Congress enacted the Emergency Wetlands Resources Act of 1986, which included congressional findings concerning the value of wetlands. *See* 16 U.S.C. § 3901(a) (2000).

2. 16 U.S.C. § 3801(a)(18). The Act excludes from this definition "lands in Alaska identified as having high potential for agricultural development which have a predominance of permafrost soils." *Id.*

3. EPA and the Corps define "wetlands" as

> areas that are inundated or saturated by surface or ground water at a frequency and duration sufficient to support, and that under normal circumstances do support, a prevalence of vegetation typically adapted for life in saturated soil conditions. Wetlands generally include swamps, marshes, bogs, and similar areas.

40 C.F.R. § 230.3(t) (2004); 33 C.F.R. § 328.3(b).

4. For a discussion of these criteria in the Section 404 program, see Chapter 3.

5. 16 U.S.C. § 3801(a)(10) provides: "The term 'hydric soil' means soil that, in its undrained condition, is saturated, flooded, or ponded long enough during

a growing season to develop an anaerobic condition that supports the growth and regeneration of hydrophytic vegetation."

6. 16 U.S.C. § 3801(a)(11) provides:

> The term "hydrophytic vegetation" means a plant growing in—
>
> (A) water; or
>
> (B) a substrate that is at least periodically deficient in oxygen during a growing season as a result of excessive water content.

7. 16 U.S.C. § 3801(b).

8. 61 Fed. Reg. 47,019 (Sept. 6, 1996).

9. *Id.*

10. 7 C.F.R. § 12.31(a)(3)(i) provides that "hydric soils are those soils which meet criteria set forth in the publication 'Hydric Soils of the United States 1985' which was developed by the National Technical Committee for Hydric Soils and which is incorporated by reference. This publication may be obtained upon request by writing NRCS at U.S. Department of Agriculture, P.O. Box 2890, Washington, DC 20013." 7 C.F.R. § 12.31(b)(1) provides that "[a] plant will be considered to be a plant species that occurs in wetland if such plant is listed in the National List of Plant Species that Occur in Wetlands. The publication may be obtained upon request from the U.S. Fish and Wildlife Service at National Wetland Inventory, Monroe Bldg. Suite 101, 9720 Executive Drive, St. Petersburg, Florida 33702."

11. 7 C.F.R. § 12.31(a)(3)(ii). The contents of these soil maps are specified at *id.*

12. *See id.* § 12.2 (definitions of "farmed wetland," "farmed-wetland pasture," and "prior-converted cropland"). In some agricultural programs, USDA relies on a wetland classification scheme published by the Fish and Wildlife Service in Circular 39, Wetlands in America. These programs include the Conservation Reserve Program and the Water Bank program, both of which are discussed in later sections of this chapter. Circular 39 has generally been updated and is no longer relied upon by the Fish and Wildlife Service, which now has published an updated classification of wetlands.

13. The regulations define "wetland determination" as "a decision regarding whether or not an area is a wetland, including identification of wetland type and size." 7 C.F.R. § 12.2.

14. The regulations define "wetland delineation" to mean "outlining the boundaries of a wetland determination on aerial photography, digital imagery, other graphic representation of the area, or on the land." *Id.*

15. *Id.* §§ 12.6(c), 12.30(a)(3).

16. *See* USDA, Highly Erodible Land and Wetland Conservation, Interim final rule, 61 Fed. Reg. 47,019, 47,022 (Sept. 6, 1996); Interagency Memorandum of Agreement concerning Wetlands Determinations for Purposes of Section 404 of the Clean Water Act and Subtitle B of the Food Security Act, 59 Fed. Reg. 2920, 2921 (Jan. 19, 1994) [hereinafter Interagency MOA], *available at* http://www.epa.gov/OWOW/wetlands/guidance/agmoa.html. The National Food Security

Act Manual is available at http://policy.nrcs.usda.gov/scripts/lpsiis.dll/M/M_180.htm.

17. For example, the NFSAM defines the term "growing season"—a term used in the definitions of hydric soils and hydrophytic vegetation, noted above. Natural Resources Conservation Service, *National Food Security Act Manual* 527–69.

18. 7 C.F.R. § 12.6(c)(4).

19. *Id.* § 12.12.

20. *See* 16 U.S.C. § 3821(a)(3); 7 C.F.R. § 12.30(c).

21. 16 U.S.C. § 3821(a)(4). USDA's implementing regulation provides:

> As long as the affected person is in compliance with the wetland conservation provision of this part, and as long as the area is devoted to the use and management of the land for production of food, fiber, horticultural crops, a certification . . . will remain valid and in effect until such time as the person affected by the certification requests review of the certification by NRCS. A person may request review of a certification only if a natural event alters the topography or hydrology of the subject land to the extent that the final certification is no longer a reliable indication of site conditions, or if NRCS concurs with an affected person that an error exists in the current wetland determination.

7 C.F.R. § 12.30(c)(6).

22. *Id.* § 12.30(c)(1). The regulation further provides: "A not-inventoried designation within a certified wetland is subject to change when the soil, hydrology, and vegetation evaluation is completed and identified as to type of wetland or as non-wetland. This change from a not-inventoried designation to an approved wetland designation will be done at the request of the landowner or during a formal investigation of a potential violation." *Id.*

23. S. Rep. No. 99-145, at 303, *reprinted in* 1985 U.S.C.C.A.N. 1103, 1969.

24. Pub. L. No. 99-198, Title XII, Subtitle C, § 1221, 99 Stat. 1507.

25. *Id.*

26. The legislative history of the 1990 amendments identified the deficiencies of the 1985 Act:

> [Under the 1985 Act] a person may drain a wetland and not be in violation of swampbuster until the person produces an agricultural commodity on that land. Therefore, a person can produce on the converted wetland during a time of high commodity prices and stay out of the production adjustment programs. During a year of low commodity prices, the person can simply not produce on the converted wetland and regain eligibility for farm program benefits. The functional value of the wetland, however, is lost as long as it is converted.

S. Rep. No. 101-357, at 236 (1990), *reprinted in* 1990 U.S.S.C.A.N. 4656, 4890.

27. Pub. L. No. 101-624, Title XIV, Subtitle B, § 1421(b), 104 Stat. 3572.

28. *Id.*

29. 16 U.S.C. § 3821(a) provides:

> Except as provided in this subtitle [16 U.S.C.S. §§ 3821 *et seq.*] and notwithstanding any other provision of law, any person who in any crop year produces an agricultural commodity on converted wetland, as determined by the Secretary [of Agriculture], shall be—
>
> (1) in violation of this section; and
>
> (2) ineligible for loans or payments in an amount determined by the Secretary to be proportionate to the severity of the violation.

16 U.S.C. § 3821(c) provides:

> Except as provided in [16 U.S.C. § 3822] and notwithstanding any other provision of law, any person who in any crop year beginning after November 28, 1990, converts a wetland by draining, dredging, filling, leveling, or any other means for the purpose, or to have the effect, of making the production of an agricultural commodity possible on such converted wetland shall be ineligible for [specified program benefits].

USDA regulations governing the basis for ineligibility under Swampbuster are found at 7 C.F.R. § 12.4(a)(1)–(2).

16 U.S.C. § 3821(b) lists the program benefits that may be denied to any person who violates either of these prohibitions.

30. 16 U.S.C. § 3801(a)(1); 7 C.F.R. § 12.2(a).

31. *See* Anthony N. Turrini, *Swampbuster: A Report from the Front*, 24 IND. L. REV. 1507, 1510 (1991).

32. 16 U.S.C. § 3801(a)(5); 7 C.F.R. § 12.2(a).

33. 7 C.F.R. § 12.5(b)(1)(iv).

34. Chapter 4 of this book examines in detail the scope of activities regulated under the CWA.

35. *See* Act April 4, 1996, Pub. L. No. 104-127, Title III, Subtitle C, § 326.

36. 16 U.S.C. § 3821(a)(2). Additionally, the 1996 amendments permit the Secretary of Agriculture to determine which, if any, of the various benefits may be withheld in response to restricted activities. *See* 16 U.S.C. § 3821(b). Prior to the 1996 amendments, graduated sanctions based on the severity of the violation were available only if the violation was found to have been committed inadvertently by a person acting in good faith and only if that person was actively restoring the wetland functions and values that were lost as a result of the violation. *See* Act of Nov. 28, 1990, Pub. L. No. 101-624, Title XIV, Subtitle B, § 1422, 104 Stat. 3573.

37. 7 C.F.R. § 12.4(c).

38. 16 U.S.C. § 3821(c).

39. 7 C.F.R. § 12.5(b)(4).

40. 16 U.S.C. § 3822(i).

41. 7 C.F.R. § 12.4(c).

42. 16 U.S.C. § 3822(h); *see* 7 C.F.R. § 12.5(b)(5).

43. USDA regulations governing these exemptions are found at 7 C.F.R. § 12.5(b).

44. 7 C.F.R. § 12.5(b)(7).

45. Pub. L. No. 99-198, Title XII, Subtitle C, § 1222, 99 Stat. 1508.

46. 7 C.F.R. § 12.33(b) (1987).

47. *Id.*

48. *Id.*

49. *Id.*

50. 7 C.F.R. § 12.33(a) (1987) states that the regulations were "intended to protect remaining functional values of the wetlands described [in the regulation]. Persons may continue to farm such wetlands under natural conditions or as they did prior to December 23, 1985. However, no action can be taken to increase effects on the water regime beyond that which existed on such lands on or before December 23, 1985 unless . . . the effect on remaining wetland values would be minimal."

51. 118 F.3d 1233 (8th Cir. 1997).

52. *Id.* at 1238.

53. 7 C.F.R. § 12.2(a).

54. 16 U.S.C. § 3822(b)(1)(A).

55. 7 C.F.R. § 12.5(b)(1)(i).

56. *Id.* § 12.5(b)(2).

57. The "hydrologic criteria" for prior converted cropland are as follows:

> (i) Inundation was less than 15 consecutive days during the growing season or 10 percent of the growing season, whichever is less, in most years (50 percent chance or more); and
>
> (ii) If a pothole, playa or pocosin, ponding was less than 7 consecutive days during the growing season in most years (50 percent chance or more) and saturation was less than 14 consecutive days during the growing season most years (50 percent chance or more).

58. 16 U.S.C. § 3822(b)(1)(G) (emphasis added). This section is an exemption for planting an agricultural commodity on converted wetland that meets the criteria listed in the text. The exemption for converting wetland is worded a little differently, but does not appear to be substantively different. *See* 16 U.S.C. § 3822(b)(2)(D).

59. 7 C.F.R. § 12.5(b)(1)(ii).

60. *See* 61 Fed. Reg. 47,019, 47,023 (Sept. 6, 1996); Daryn McBeth, *Wetlands Conservation and Federal Regulation: Analysis of the Food Security Act's "Swampbuster" Provisions as Amended by the Federal Agriculture Improvement and Reform Act of 1996*, 21 Harv. Envtl. L. Rev. 201, 255–56 (1997).

61. *See id.* at 256 (1996 amendments "'perfects' the PC [i.e., prior converted cropland] label for a landowner: once a PC, always a PC.").

62. 16 U.S.C. § 3822(b)(1)(H), (b)(2)(E).

63. *See* 7 U.S.C. § 12.5(b)(1)(iii).

64. Farmed wetland is defined as

> wetland that prior to December 23, 1985, was manipulated and used to produce an agricultural commodity, and on December 23, 1985, did not support woody vegetation and met the following hydrologic criteria:
>
> (i) Is inundated for 15 consecutive days or more during the growing season or 10 percent of the growing season, whichever is less, in most years (50 percent chance or more), or
>
> (ii) If a pothole, playa, or pocosin, is ponded for 7 or more consecutive days during a growing season in most years (50 percent chance or more) or is saturated for 14 or more consecutive days during the growing season in most years (59 percent chance or more).

7 C.F.R. § 12.2.

Farmed-wetland pasture is defined as

> Wetland that was manipulated and managed for pasture or hayland prior to December 23, 1985, and on December 23, 1985, met the following hydrologic criteria:
>
> (i) Inundated or ponded for 7 or more consecutive days during the growing season in most years (50 percent chance or more), or
>
> (ii) Saturated for 14 or more consecutive days during the growing season in most years (50 percent chance or more).

Id.

65. *See* 7 C.F.R. § 12.33(a).

66. 7 C.F.R. § 12.33(c).

67. The exception to this general rule is provided in 7 C.F.R. § 12.33(c), which provides that "participation in a USDA approved wetland restoration, set-aside, diverted acres, or similar programs shall not be deemed to constitute abandonment."

68. 7 C.F.R. § 12.5(b)(vii)(A).

69. 7 C.F.R. § 12.2(a). The regulation provides examples of artificial wetlands, such as

> An artificial lake or pond created by excavating or diking land that is not a wetland to collect and retain water that is used primarily for livestock, fish production, irrigation, wildlife, fire control, flood control, cranberry growing, or rice production, or as a settling pond; or
>
> [] A wetland that is temporarily or incidentally created as a result of adjacent development activity. . . .

70. 7 C.F.R. § 12.5(b)(vii)(B), (C).

71. 7 C.F.R. § 12.5(b)(7).

72. Downer v. United States, 97 F.3d 999, 1005 (8th Cir. 1996).

73. *Id.; see* Von Eye v. United States, 887 F. Supp. 1287, 1292 (D.S.D. 1995), *aff'd* 92 F.3d 681 (8th Cir. 1996).

74. 7 C.F.R. § 12.5(b)(1)(iv).

75. 7 C.F.R. § 12.5(b)(1)(v); *see* 16 U.S.C. § 3822(f)(1).

76. 16 U.S.C. § 3822(d).
77. 7 C.F.R. § 12.30(a)(3).
78. *See* USDA, Highly Erodible Land and Wetland Conservation, Interim final rule with request for comments, 61 Fed. Reg. 47,019, 47,025 (Sept. 6, 1996).
79. 7 C.F.R. § 12.31(e).
80. 7 C.F.R. § 12.31(d).
81. *Id.*
82. *Id.*
83. 7 C.F.R. § 12.5(b)(vi).
84. 7 C.F.R. § 12.5(b)(vi)(A).
85. 7 C.F.R. § 12.5(b)(vi)(B).
86. 7 C.F.R. § 12.5(b)(vi)(A)–(B).
87. 7 C.F.R. § 12.5(b)(vii)(D).
88. *Id.* A scheme or device includes such acts as concealing relevant information from, or submitting false information to, USDA; "creating entities for the purpose of concealing the interest of a person in a farming operation or to otherwise avoid compliance with" USDA regulations; and "acquiescence in, approval of, or assistance to acts which have the effect of, or the purpose of, circumventing" USDA regulations. 7 C.F.R. § 12.10.
89. 7 C.F.R. § 12.5(b)(vii)(D).
90. *See* Gunn v. USDA, 118 F.3d 1233, 1238–39 (8th Cir. 1997).
91. Pub. L. No. 99-198, Title XVIII, § 1801, 99 Stat. 1660.
92. 7 C.F.R. § 12.5(b)(2)(ii).
93. 7 C.F.R. § 12.5(b)(2)(iii).
94. 16 U.S.C. § 3821(b)(1)(D).
95. 7 C.F.R. § 12.5(b)(3).
96. 16 U.S.C. § 3822(f)(2).
97. 16 U.S.C. § 3822(f)(3).
98. The statutory requirements are that any mitigating restoration, enhancement, or creation of wetlands be

> (A) in accordance with a wetland conservation plan;
>
> (B) in advance of, or concurrent with, the action;
>
> (C) not at the expense of the Federal Government;
>
> (D) in the case of enhancement or restoration of wetlands, on not greater than a 1-for-1 acreage basis unless more acreage is needed to provide equivalent functions and values that will be lost as a result of the wetland conversion that is mitigated;
>
> (E) in the case of creation of wetlands, on greater than a 1-for-1 acreage basis if more acreage is needed to provide equivalent functions and values that will be lost as a result of the wetland conversion that is mitigated;
>
> (F) on lands in the same general area of the local watershed as the converted wetland.

16 U.S.C. § 3822(f)(2)(A)–(F). The regulations are substantially similar, but define a mitigation plan as "a record of decisions that document the actions necessary to compensate for the loss of wetland functions and values that result from converting a wetland. The mitigation plan may be part of a larger natural resources conservation plan." 7 C.F.R. § 12.5(b)(4)(ii). The NRCS is responsible for evaluating and approving mitigation plans. *See* 7 C.F.R. §§ 12.6(c)(2)(xii), 12.30(a)(3).

99. 7 C.F.R. § 12.5(b)(4)(i)(E); *see* 16 U.S.C. § 3822(f)(2)(G).

100. 7 C.F.R. § 790.2(a) (1994). This regulation has been amended and recodified at 7 C.F.R. § 718.8(a).

101. 955 F.2d 1199 (8th Cir. 1992).

102. *Id.* at 1206.

103. *See* 7 C.F.R. § 12.11.

104. 7 C.F.R. § 12.5(b)(6).

105. 7 C.F.R. § 12.5(b)(6)(ii).

106. *See* 16 U.S.C. § 3822(h).

107. 7 C.F.R. § 12.5(b)(5)(i).

108. *See* 7 C.F.R. § 12.7(a)(2).

109. *See* 7 C.F.R. § 12.6(c).

110. "Wetland determination means a decision regarding whether or not an area is a wetland, including identification of wetland type and size." 7 C.F.R. § 12.2(a).

111. "Wetland delineation means outlining the boundaries of a wetland determination on aerial photography, digital imagery, other graphic representation of the area, or on the land." *Id.*

112. 7 C.F.R. § 12.6(c)(xiii).

113. *Id.* § 12.6(c)(v).

114. *Id.* § 12.6(c)(xii).

115. *See, e.g.*, 7 C.F.R. § 12.6 (b)(3)(vi), (vii), (viii).

116. *See* 61 Fed. Reg. 47,019, 47,024 (Sept. 6, 1996).

117. 16 U.S.C. § 3821(e).

118. 7 C.F.R. § 614.104(b).

119. 7 C.F.R. §§ 12.6(c)(2)(i); 12.30(a)(3).

120. Interagency MOA, 59 Fed. Reg. at 2921.

121. *Id.* The MOA goes on to state:

> Areas that meet the . . . definition may include intensively used and managed cropland, hayland, pasture land, orchards, vineyards, and areas which support wetland crops (e.g., cranberries, taro, watercress, rice). For example, lands intensively used and managed for pasture or hayland where the natural vegetation has been removed and replaced with planted grasses or legumes such as ryegrass, bluegrass, or alfalfa, are considered agricultural lands for the purposes of this MOA.

Id. Excluded from this definition were range lands, forest lands, wood lots, tree farms, and "lands where the natural vegetation has not been removed, even though that vegetation may be regularly grazed or mowed and collected as forage or fodder." *Id.* In the Federal Agriculture Improvement and Reform Act of 1996, Congress specified that, for purposes of the MOA, "agricultural lands" were also to include "native pasture, rangelands, and other lands used to produce or support the production of livestock" and "tree farms." Federal Agriculture Improvement and Reform Act of 1996, § 325(a), Pub. L. No. 104-127, 323, 100 Stat. 888, 992 (1996).

122. MOA, 59 Fed. Reg. at 2921.

123. *Id.*

124. *Id.*

125. *Id.* at 2922–23.

126. *Id.* at 2923.

127. RGL 02-01, Inclusion of Disclaimer Statements in Jurisdictional Letters Indicating that the Clean Water Act (CWA) Jurisdictional Determinations/Delineations May Not Meet the Requirements of the Food Security Act (FSA) of 1985 (Mar. 2002), *available at* http://www.usace.army.mil/inet/functions/cw/cecwo/reg/rgl_0201.pdf.

128. 33 C.F.R. § 328.3(a)(8); 40 C.F.R. § 232.2.

129. 58 Fed. Reg. 45,008, 45,034 (August 25, 1993).

130. See *id.* at 45,032. The preamble to the regulation excluding prior converted cropland from the definition of waters of the United States indicated that the change was "to codify existing policy, as reflected in RGL-90-7." *Id.* at 45,031. RGL 90-07 concluded:

> "[P]rior converted croplands" generally have been subject to such extensive and relatively permanent physical hydrological modifications and alteration of hydrophytic vegetation that the resultant cropland constitutes the "normal circumstances" for purposes of section 404 jurisdiction. Consequently, the "normal circumstances" of prior converted croplands generally do not support a "prevalence of hydrophytic vegetation" and as such are not subject to regulation under section 404. In addition, our experience and professional judgment lead us to conclude that because of the magnitude of hydrological alterations that have most often occurred on prior converted cropland, such cropland meets, minimally if at all, the . . . hydrology criteria.

Army Corps of Engineers, RGL 90-07, Clarification of the Phrase "Normal Circumstances" as It Pertains to Cropped Wetlands (September 26, 1990), *reprinted at* 58 Fed. Reg. 17,210, 17,211 (Apr. 1, 1993), *available at* http://www.usace.army.mil/inet/functions/cw/cecwo/reg/rgls/rgl90-07.htm.

131. *See* 58 Fed. Reg. at 45,031; RGL 90-7, 58 Fed. Reg. at 17,210.

132. *See* United States v. Brace, 41 F.3d 117, 227 (3d Cir. 1994) (determination by USDA that conversion is exempt, as a "commenced conversion" does not affect need for CWA Section 404 permit).

133. As discussed above, these conversions are exempt under Swampbuster pursuant to 7 C.F.R. § 12.5(b)(1)(iv).

134. The "normal farming" exemption is found at 33 C.F.R. § 1344(f)(1)(A) and 33 C.F.R. § 323.4(a)(1), and is discussed in detail in Chapter 5.

135. General and nationwide permits are explained in detail in Chapter 5 of this book.

136. 16 U.S.C. § 3830(a)(3).

137. 16 U.S.C. § 3830(a)(1).

138. 16 U.S.C. § 3843(b)(1). The special circumstances in which these acreage limitations may be disregarded are set forth in 16 U.S.C. § 3843(b)(2)–(3).

139. *See* 16 U.S.C. §§ 3837 *et seq.* USDA regulations governing the program are found at 7 C.F.R. pt. 1467.

140. 7 C.F.R. § 1467.4(a).

141. *See* 16 U.S.C. § 3837(c); 7 C.F.R. § 1467.4(d). The statute also authorizes USDA to enroll the following lands in the WRP: (1) "farmed wetland and adjoining lands, enrolled in the conservation reserve, with the highest wetland functions and values, and that are likely to return to production after they leave the conservation reserve"; (2) otherwise ineligible wetland that "would significantly add to the functional value" of an easement; (3) "riparian areas that link wetlands that are protected by easements or some other device or circumstance that achieves the same purpose as an easement." 16 U.S.C. § 3837(d).

142. *See* USDA, Natural Resources Conservation Service, *2002 Farm Bill: Fact Sheet, Wetlands Reserve Program,* at 2 (Sept. 2004), *available at* http://www.nrcs.usda.gov/programs/farmbill/2002/pdf/WRPFct.pdf.

143. 7 C.F.R. § 1467.4(e).

144. 16 U.S.C. § 3837(b)(1).

145. *Id.*

146. 16 U.S.C. § 3837(b)(2).

147. USDA, Natural Resources Conservation Service, *2002 Farm Bill: Key Points, Wetlands Reserve Program,* at 1 (March 2003), *available at* http://www.nrcs.usda.gov/programs/farmbill/2002/pdf/WRPKyPts.pdf.

148. 7 C.F.R. § 1467.4(c). The twelve-month ownership requirement may be waived if the state conservationist determines "that the land was acquired by will or succession as a result of the death of the previous landowner, or that adequate assurances have been presented to the State Conservationist that the new landowner of [eligible] land did not acquire such land for the purpose of placing it in the WRP." *Id.* § 1467.4(c)(2).

149. 7 C.F.R. § 1467.4(c)(3).

150. 7 C.F.R. § 1467.3.

151. 7 C.F.R. § 1467.4(c).

152. 16 U.S.C. § 3837a(e)(2).

153. 7 C.F.R. § 1467.10(b); *see* 16 U.S.C. § 3837a(b).

154. 7 C.F.R. § 1467.11.

155. 7 C.F.R. § 1467.8(b).

156. 7 C.F.R. § 1467.8(b)(3).

157. 16 U.S.C. § 3837a(f).

158. 7 C.F.R. § 1467.8(h).

159. 16 U.S.C. § 3837c(a)(1). USDA is also directed to "provide necessary technical assistance to assist owners in complying with the terms and conditions of the easement and the [WRPO]." *Id.* § 3837c(a)(2).

160. 7 C.F.R. § 1467.9.

161. 16 U.S.C. § 3837a(h).

162. 16 U.S.C. § 3837c(b)(2).

163. 7 C.F.R. § 1467.5.

164. 7 C.F.R. § 1467.6(a).

165. 7 C.F.R. § 1467.6(b).

166. 7 C.F.R. § 1467.7.

167. 7 C.F.R. § 1467.12.

168. 7 C.F.R. § 1467.14.

169. 68 Fed. Reg. 24,830 (May 8, 2003); *see* 7 C.F.R. § 1410.3(c). USDA regulations implementing the CRP are found at 7 C.F.R. pt. 1410.

170. 7 C.F.R. § 1410.7.

171. 7 C.F.R. § 1410.6(a).

172. 7 C.F.R. § 1410.6(b).

173. 7 C.F.R. § 1410.6(b)(11).

174. 7 C.F.R. § 1410.2. The Swampbuster definitions of "farmed wetlands" and "wetlands farmed under natural conditions" are found at 7 C.F.R. §§ 12.2, and 12.5(b)(3), respectively.

175. 7 C.F.R. § 1410.6(c).

176. 7 C.F.R. § 1410.10.

177. 7 C.F.R. § 1410.10(b).

178. 7 C.F.R. § 1410.10(d)–(f).

179. 7 C.F.R. § 1410.5(a). The term "operator" is defined at 7 C.F.R. § 1410.2.

180. 7 C.F.R. § 1410.5(a).

181. 7 C.F.R. § 1410.32.

182. 7 C.F.R. § 1410. 20.

183. 7 C.F.R. §§ 1410.21, 1410.41(a), 1410.42(d). The "average cost" is an amount "determined by CCC based on recommendations of a State Technical Committee" and may be "the average cost in a State, a county, or part of a State or county." 7 C.F.R. § 1410.41(b).

184. 7 C.F.R. § 1410.42(g).

185. 7 C.F.R. § 1410.2.

186. 7 C.F.R. § 1410.22.

187. A good source for obtaining information about sign-up periods and general information about the CRP is the FSA's Web page at http://www.fsa.usda.gov/dafp/cepd/crp.htm.

188. Descriptions of these special practices are available at USDA, Farm Service Agency, Conservation Reserve Program Fact Sheet, http://www.fsa.usda.gov/pas/publications/facts/html/crpebi03.htm.

189. *Id.*

190. 7 C.F.R. § 1410.31(b). The regulations list the following factors that may be considered:

- Soil erosion
- Water quality
- Wildlife benefits
- Conservation priority area designations
- Likelihood that enrolled land will remain in conserving uses
- Air quality
- Cost of enrolling acreage in the CRP

191. A description of the Environmental Benefits Index can be found at http://www.fsa.usda.gov/pas/publications/facts/ebiold.pdf.

192. *See id.* at 2.

193. 16 U.S.C. § 3831(d).

194. FSA, Conservation Reserve Program, Monthly Summary: September 2004, *available at* http://www.fsa.usda.gov/dafp/cepd/stats/Sept2004.pdf.

195. 7 C.F.R. § 1410.32(f).

196. 7 C.F.R. § 1410.32(g).

197. 7 C.F.R. § 1410.33.

198. 7 C.F.R. § 1410.10(a).

199. *See* 16 U.S.C. § 3839aa(1). General information regarding EQIP can be obtained at http://www.nrcs.usda.gov/programs/eqip/.

200. 16 U.S.C. § 3839aa(2).

201. 7 C.F.R. § 1466.4(e).

202. 7 C.F.R. § 1466.2. Regulations implementing EQIP may be found at 7 C.F.R. pt. 1466.

203. 16 U.S.C. § 3839aa-2.

204. 16 U.S.C. § 3839aa-1(2).

205. 16 U.S.C. § 3839aa-1(5).

206. 7 C.F.R. § 1466.8(b)(4).

207. 7 C.F.R. § 1466.2(c). The definitions of state technical committees and local work groups are provided at 7 C.F.R. § 1466.3.

208. 7 C.F.R. § 1466.5.

209. 7 C.F.R. § 1466.4(a).

210. 7 C.F.R. § 1466.20(b).

211. 7 C.F.R. § 1466.21(b).

212. 7 C.F.R. § 1466.23(a)(1).

213. 7 C.F.R. §§ 1466.24(a).

TABLE OF CASES

1902 Atlantic Ltd. v. Hudson, 574 F. Supp. 1381 (E.D. Va. 1983), 242 n.4, 451 n.12

1902 Atlantic Ltd. v. United States, 26 Cl. Ct. 575 (1992), 458 n.147

Abbott Labs. v. Gardner, 387 U.S. 136 (1967), 452 n.26

Abenaki Nation of Mississquoi v. Hughes, 805 F. Supp. 234 (D. Vt. 1992), *aff'd,* 990 F.2d 729 (2d Cir. 1993), 212 n.91

Agins v. City of Tiburon, 497 U.S. 255 (1980), 453 n.43, 458 n.150

Alameda Water and Sanitation Dist. v. Reilly, 930 F. Supp. 486 (D. Colo. 1996), 237, 241, 246 nn.66–67, 247 n.91, 250 nn.141–43, 251 n.177, 294, 302 n.59, 303 nn.79–81, 85 & 91, 320 nn.101–03, 106 & 108–11

Alameda Water & Sanitation Dist. v. Browner, 9 F.3d 88 (10th Cir. 1993), 248 n.94

Alaska Ctr. for the Env't v. West, 157 F.3d 680 (9th Cir. 1998), 155, 156, 167, 185 nn.20 & 24–26, 186 nn.27 & 32–33, 426 nn.341 & 344

Alaska Ctr. for the Env't v. West, 31 F. Supp. 2d 714 (D. Alaska 1998), 167, 186 nn.48 & 50, 187 n.82

Alliance for Legal Action v. U.S. Army Corps of Engineers, 314 F. Supp. 2d 534 (M.D. N.C. 2004), 236–37, 246 n.66, 247 n.89, 248 n.113, 250 nn.131–34

Am. Mining Congress v. U.S. Army Corps of Engineers, 120 F. Supp. 2d 23 (D.D.C. 2000), 144 nn.151–52

Am. Mining Congress v. U.S. Army Corps of Engineers, 951 F. Supp. 267 (D.D.C. 1997), *aff'd,* 145 F.3d 1399 (D.C. Cir. 1998), 97 n.76, *aff'd sub nom.,* 23 n.89, 117–18, 141 n.57, 142 nn.89–91, 426 n.347

Am. Rivers, Inc. v. Fed. Energy Regulatory Comm'n, 129 F.3d 99 (2d Cir. 1997), 342–43, 354 nn.133–35

Andrus v. Allard, 444 U.S. 51 (1979), 453 n.48

Animal Defense Council v. Hodel, 840 F.2d 1432 (9th Cir. 1988), 425 n.333

INDEX

S

T

U

V

W